AMERICA MOVES
WEST

AMERICA MOVES

Fourth Edition WEST

Robert E. Riegel

Dartmouth College

Robert G. Athearn

University of Colorado

HOLT, RINEHART AND WINSTON, INC.

New York, Chicago, San Francisco, Toronto, London

To

M. C. R.

PREFACE

The uniqueness of the United States is due to both geographical and cultural factors. Its people have come from various nations and races, and through most of their history they have been influenced by the proximity of vast areas of land occupied only by a scattering of native Indians. The results of these factors are still apparent. This book tells the story of the advance of the American population during approximately three centuries (1600–1900), from the Atlantic to the Pacific. Emphasis is on the nature of the expansion and development—a process and its results.

Interest in the westward expansion of the United States has been growing in recent years. The increasing involvement of the United States in world affairs has been accompanied by a greater concern with unique American characteristics, which in many cases can be traced to the influence of the frontier. Many able young scholars are working in the field. Less troubled than a previous generation by theoretical preconceptions, they are exploiting new material and new points of view. Because of such work the characteristics and significance of American population expansion to the West are becoming clearer year by year.

The fourth edition of *America Moves West* is considerably different from its predecessors. The material has been reorganized, and much of it rewritten. Some has been eliminated and some added, particularly for the colonial period. The readings have been brought up to date and brief critical comments included. Illustrations and a number of new maps have been added. Usually the maps show modern state boundaries to help in locating places.

We are deeply grateful to colleagues and students for many helpful suggestions. Obviously a general account such as this one depends heavily on the researches of many scholars in the field. Particular gratitude goes to Professor Robert Feer of Northeastern University and Professor Carl Ubbelohde of the University of Colorado. We hope that readers will find the book interesting and informative.

Hanover, New Hampshire   Robert E. Riegel
Boulder, Colorado   Robert G. Athearn
April 1964

CONTENTS

MAPS

ILLUSTRATIONS

CHAPTER 1

THE FIRST FRONTIER

For approximately three hundred years after the first English settlement at Jamestown the irresistible attraction of land somewhere "beyond" pulled Americans westward. As they conquered the frontier, plowed their fields, and built their cities, they wrote the American story.

That these people should use the word "frontier" so frequently was only natural, for during most of their history a large area of undeveloped country stretching out toward the Pacific Ocean beckoned, and in answering the challenge many of them lived constantly in that forward population wave described by the term. As it does today, when applied to such fields as science, industry, education, or religion, "frontier" meant something new, relatively unknown, but always promising and exciting. To the pioneers the word inevitably suggested the West, but beyond that it had no specific geographic definition. One cannot pinpoint the frontier on a map. Unlike The European concept of the frontier as a national boundary, it was vague and ever-moving, a shadowy thing that combined physical characteristics with mental attitudes. That great exponent of the American frontier, Frederick Jackson Turner, could come no closer than explaining it as a place "between civilization and savagery."

The American frontier movement was part of a much larger development, one that was launched from western Europe and fanned out across the entire Western Hemisphere. Just as the European impact influenced hemispheric development and was in turn affected by the flood of resources discovered in the new lands, so the vast and seemingly illimitable domain that lay before the English colonists along the Atlantic seaboard molded the kind of nation that was to grow in the latitudes between the Rio Grande and the 49th parallel.

Other peoples had pressed forward at other times and in far-flung reaches of the globe, but no other has ever been as successful as the invasion begun on Virginia beaches in the early seventeenth century. That this particular frontier developed differently from the others was due to climate, geography, the reaction of the natives, the mixture of European bloods, and the elements of chance. Within a relatively short time this population surge welded itself into a nation that would have a powerful role in global affairs.

EUROPE MOVES WEST

In many ways the dawn of the sixteenth century was not a time of optimism for Europe. The rise of the national states threatened to fragment the Continent as their jealous monarchs fought one another for ascendancy. Society's stratification, born of medieval times, was beginning to crumble as the young nations passed through a transitional stage whose outcome was in question. The situation did not offer much promise to the common man. With a minimum of precious metals available and a limited supply of raw materials at hand, his opportunities were limited. As if this were not disturbing enough, his church was in the throes of a reformation that would cause division among men and warfare among nations. What the average European needed most at this time was an economic miracle.

The miracle that happened was the discovery of the western hemisphere and the opening of a whole new world. Almost overnight a people who had developed a number of skills and techniques, but who were sorely in need of a wide variety of cheap raw materials, were handed the key to the treasure house. What they did with their new-found riches was an important part of European history for several hundred years after the discovery. In turn, the coming of the European made an enormous change in the new, unexploited land. Spain, in particular, saw her entire course altered, as countries that traded with or fought against the Spanish soon discovered. France, Holland, and Sweden experimented with New World colonization in more northerly regions, but of these only the French became very deeply involved, and their effort proved generally unprofitable.

Of all the people interested in North American real estate the British, who entered the race belatedly, were the most successful. On the face of it this is surprising, especially when one considers that in 1607 these people established that very weak toe hold, Jamestown, well over a century after Columbus made his first voyage. Tardiness, however, did not prove to be a major drawback, for during the sixteenth century England's rapid and widespread commercial development provided valuable schooling in international trade. In those years the Muscovy Company was founded to secure a profitable Russian trade, after which the Cathay Company, the Levant Company, and the East India Company were formed to tap Middle and Far East sources. In each of these ventures hardy British seamen delved more deeply into maritime mysteries, seeking out new routes, learning advanced methods of navigation, and increasing their geographical knowledge. By the time the British entered the business of colonizing in North America they were eminently prepared.

While perfecting their system of international trade Englishmen developed an efficient commercial structure at home. The coincidence of the Reformation and the rise of capitalism blended fortuitously with the age of discovery and colonization, for the ambitious English businessmen much preferred the Puritan doctrine "work and save" to an older, Catholic attitude that found excessive profits sinful. The growing middle class, freed from the strictures of the Catholic Church and in an independent political mood, became well knit and powerful. Joint-stock companies multiplied rapidly on a broad background of highly speculative enterprises as their projectors, the rugged individualists of the day, undertook increasingly complex commercial operations. The application of these commercial techniques to the American frontier at a later date would be a relatively simple operation.

ENGLISH PIONEERS

The English appeared to be in no hurry to enter the business of colonizing. The Elizabethan seadogs, those nautical frontiersmen who ranged the seven seas, had only a passing interest in the new lands along North Atlantic shores. They much preferred to attack Spanish shipping and colonies, an activity that at once satisfied their monarch's commercial and anti-Catholic urges. In an era when British maritime development was in full bloom there was much more emphasis on exploration than on settlement. By the 1570s Sir Martin Frobisher was probing North Atlantic waters for a passage to the Pacific Ocean and made three unsuccessful attempts to find one. In a similar try John Davis found only a strait— Davis strait between Greenland and Baffin Island. Sir Humphrey Gilbert agreed with those who believed in the existence of a sea passage and in 1583 set out to establish a colony in Newfoundland as a staging area for further exploration.

Hunting for new routes of commerce was only one of the motives that sent the English to America. As warfare with the Spanish heightened, it became obvious that the enemy's great economic resources were coming from the western hemisphere and in order to cut into that preserve a foothold along American shores seemed desirable. John Cabot's transatlantic claims for England, which had gathered dust for nearly a century after his voyage in 1497, were now put into play as a strategic weapon against Spain. Gilbert's appearance at St. John's, at this late date, and his elaborate ceremonial rite of discovery—the formal excavation of a piece of turf, accompanied by an announcement that he was taking possession in the Queen's name—signified his nation's intent to establish its earlier claim. Onlooking fishermen, who had worked those waters for decades, must have thought his performance quaint.

Despite their unquestioned abilities in overseas operations, the first English efforts in America were uncertain and fumbling. Gilbert was lost at sea on his return trip and his half brother, Sir Walter Raleigh, took his place in the colonial effort. In 1584 the Queen granted Raleigh a charter to found a colony south of Newfoundland. He called the place Virginia, in honor of the Virgin Queen, and during the following year a small settlement was established on Roanoke Island at the mouth of Albemarle Sound. After spending one winter there the colonists wanted to go home. When Sir Francis Drake, returning from one of his raiding trips, stopped off to see them they clambered aboard, glad to leave their new western homes. Raleigh sent out another group, in 1587, but he was unable to look after it because of the events at home (the Spanish Armada) and by the time a relief ship arrived in 1591 not a settler was to be found. As the seventeenth century neared, the British westward movement appeared to be stalled.

The emptiness of the effort was illusory. Even in failure Raleigh's efforts were sufficiently publicized to arouse interest among those who saw possibilities abroad. Moreover, his charter contained a significant provision: all those who left home for America would carry with them their traditional rights, the legacy of common law, and the liberties thus far accumulated. The inclusion was to have a far-reaching effect, not only on English colonial settlement in America, but on the continued westward movement of that nucleus. Attracted by the Raleigh venture, others followed. In 1605 Captain George Weymouth examined the coast of Maine and returned home with five Indians, whom he had carefully taught enough English to be able to praise the climate and the economic potential of their homeland. Such testimonials, coupled with the fact that the Frenchman Champlain was exploring the country close to Maine, further stimulated the interest of government and private circles in the British Isles. Consequently, the Virginia Company of London found it surprisingly easy to finance a three-ship expedition, under the command of Captain Christopher Newport, which sailed for Virginia in the spring of 1607.

In many ways the tidewater frontiersmen who laid out the little community of Jamestown were typical of millions who followed them. Captain Newport went home to report that the place was so very rich in gold and copper that his passengers had remained to extract the precious resources as quickly and as painlessly as possible. These adventurers, who thought in terms of a quick return and were interested in agriculture only as a means of subsistence, resembled the army of miners on later frontiers. Characteristically, they showed their extreme individualism when John Smith attempted to weld the group into something resembling a civil society. Only under protest did they go forth to hack down trees with which to erect buildings, instead of digging for the gold they so desired, and when their oaths became too obvious Smith declared that any offender would receive a can of cold water poured down a sleeve to cool his temper. Even under such rigorous leadership the colony barely survived the first years in the wilderness and many disillusioned colonists longed to return home. However, the arrival of more ships and supplies from time to time helped to ameliorate their hardships.

In the year that Jamestown was settled, Englishmen established a temporary beachhead farther north. This expedition, headed by George Popham (a brother of one of the promoters) and Raleigh Gilbert (son of Sir Humphrey), landed 120 settlers on the coast of Maine. After spending a winter at these latitudes the colonists decided they had overlooked some opportunities at home and Gilbert agreed to take them back in the summer of 1608. Several other small efforts were made during the next few years— little establishments chiefly engaged in fishing these northerly waters—but there was no solid colonial effort until the "Mayflower" brought approximately a hundred Pilgrims to Cape Cod late in 1620.

In addition to the fact that the settlement of Pilgrims at Plymouth was a permanent one, from whose roots grew an important part of British America, the group made a significant contribution to what later came to be called the American heritage. Finding themselves beyond the jurisdiction of their homeland, or of Virginia, they drew up the famed Mayflower Compact, a declaration intended to provide self-government until English legal machinery could be imported. In this act they established a frontier custom that would be seen again and again in the West: in mining camps, in wagon trains traversing the seas of grass on the prairies, and in any other isolated group that found itself temporarily in a political vacuum.

The movement of peoples from the British Isles, and later from other European countries, to the seaboard of North America and from the low-lying Tidewater area up to the line of falls that barred navigation, beyond to the Piedmont, then finally, across the Appalachian barrier, furnishes a great part of what we call our colonial history. The growth of American political, social, and economic institutions during these years was shaped by frontier conditions found in a raw and undeveloped America. Out of this experience came the refinement of old knowledge and the origination of native-born ideas employed in continuing a westward movement that had commenced in Great Britain. The westward projection of this force over nearly three centuries produced a new and powerful nation.

EARLY FRONTIER CHARACTERISTICS

The westward advance, in any of its many stages, was not something that "just happened." The first seaboard settlers had to be furnished transportation, supplied with enough food until they could raise their own, and reinforced with more men and necessities from the main base before the operation could be termed successful. To accomplish these aims businessmen were required to perfect extensive plans and to raise relatively large sums of money. These entrepreneurs were necessary to those who wanted to emigrate, whether they were families able to cover their own expenses or poor workers with little to offer but their labor. Even the wealthier who wanted to take advantage of the frontier boom economy tended to approach the organizers of frontier projects. To a degree this would be true on later American frontiers although by that time the average American farmer moving west accumulated his own capital and undertook his own moves.

As a rule European emigration to the Americas was sponsored and closely controlled by home governments. Spain and France furnish good examples. The English were unique in the use of private enterprise, the chartered companies that founded early Virginia and Massachusetts settlements being typical, and the aim was economic gain for the investors who put up the risk money. In the proprietary colonies an investor supplied passenger fare to help settlers make the journey, after which they paid him back in rent or in services. Much later, railroad companies would be selling immigrants their lands on time payments under much the same conditions. Whatever frontier one considers, whether it was exploited by the miner or the cattleman or the farmer, land was the dominant factor. Generally speaking, the principal goal was to get labor onto the limitless western acres. This process, begun on Virginia shores, was repeated with variations all the way to the Pacific Ocean. Even the Pilgrims of Massachusetts, whose prime motive for moving was religious, bought out the merchants who had financed their venture so that they might have title to their own lands.

Economic conditions in seventeenth-century England plus an almost limitless area of available American land provided the circumstances for a great migration. As a result of the enclosures, thousands of acres of land in the British Isles were turned into sheep runs, setting adrift a large population of laborers to whom a seven-year indenture service in the colonies looked better than a debtor's prison. After 1665 the imbalance in the supply of and demand for labor was somewhat corrected; a plague reduced the population, and gradually England's infant industrial structure assimilated English laborers. American colonial proprietors and entrepreneurs responded to the consequent decline in immigration by making more attractive the terms under which men might move. Indentured servants were promised bonuses in land on the completion of their obligations, freedom of worship was assured, and there was a general political liberalization characterized by promises of representative government empowered to pass upon taxation. The newer and less developed colonies vied with older ones by offering more generous inducements, particularly in land, and here the "pull" of the frontier movement, as opposed to the "push" from Great Britain, came into play. This economic pendulum, once set in operation, did not lose its momentum until the frontier movement was completed.

TIDEWATER FRONTIERSMEN

Modern Americans visualize the frontiersman as a man who lived off the land, cleverly utilizing nature's resources to provide food and shelter, prospering where less ingenious souls perished. This was a trait that developed slowly, for the first residents along the Atlantic seaboard found great difficulty in making an adjustment to their new environment. Englishmen to the core, they found themselves shackled by tradition, by the habits of their municipal way of life, and by the strictures of a rigid class society. It is quite understandable that they moved inland, away from a sea connection with the old country, slowly and cautiously. In this new, strange, forbidding country they tried to plant a European society, to shape rough logs into clapboards for the construction of traditional housing, to raise crops as before, and to carry on the only kind of life they knew. They went hungry while food abounded all around them; their clothes wore out and they patched the patches; they were cold when they might have been warm.

It was the grandson and the great-grandson of the early settler who moved on, learning how to build a snug log cabin and how to make pole furniture, fences, and clay-lined log fireplaces, and who became the prototype for later pioneers. The trout-filled streams, the wild life of the forests, and the native plants fed and clothed the practical pioneers. They discovered the utility of deerskins, the medicinal value of roots and herbs, and the wonderful versatility of the long rifle. As the Englishmen "went native," a new breed began to emerge, one that would call itself "American," and take pride in its citizenship in the state of nature.

The first colonists also had to cut away some of the political traditions that entwined them if they were going to enjoy any kind of equality in their new country. Despite a surprising liberality on the part of the mother country, these people were a long way from achieving anything like a political democracy. Officials still wore gold braid to denote their rank; the governor's council was exempt from taxation, and in the royal colonies most of the important appointments were made subject to the approval of the home government. The custom of primogeniture kept estates together by allowing only the eldest son to inherit property if his father died without a will; to prevent him from subdividing his inheritance, another custom, entail, was adhered to. These laws and customs tended to perpetuate class distinctions and to make it difficult for anyone to rise above the circumstance of his birth. The main abrasive that finally wore away such traditional strictures was the existence of limitless cheap land. Its extent, and its availability, lessened the need of men to seek security from time-encrusted tradition and privilege; there was sufficient security in the promise of the soil.

Officers of the Virginia Company were not long in learning that they must liberalize their land restrictions. As early as 1613 Governor Thomas Dale decreed that each of the older settlers should have three acres for his own use, a privilege that was extended three years later when those purchasing £12 10s. worth of stock in the company were given fifty acres. By 1618 anyone who emigrated to Virginia received fifty acres for himself and a like amount for each member of his family, servants included. As the better lands were claimed, newcomers were obliged to move deeper inland, or farther back from the navigable rivers.

The first American frontier, that which succeeded the original English settlement, tended to bulge in a balloon-shaped movement pressing first against the fall line and then against the Appalachian mountains. As long as they could these people clung to the rivers that connected them with the sea, regarding these threadlike waterways as a type of umbilical cord that kept alive economic embryos still tied to the mother country. When they moved onto the Piedmont the land-seekers found themselves west of the fall line and closer to a subsistence kind of economy. Once the Appalachians were crossed they had, in effect, passed the point of no return. This was the step they resisted so long.

Nearly a hundred years passed before differences between the prosperous governing classes along the coast and the small farmers who had moved farther inland began to show themselves. The ordinary farmer recognized the fact that the wealthier Tidewater residents ran things, that they dominated not only the economic and political scene but the religious and cultural aspects of society. Cities were separated by great distances and the family unit tended to concentrate on affairs in its own neighborhood, making it very difficult for anyone with notions of reform to get an audience. Those who were dissatisfied with conditions were so ingrained with the notion of "the classes" that they seldom did more than grumble. Besides, most of the offices were held by the aristocrats and to defy them would be to break the law. Those in power correctly judged this attitude and there was little trouble. From time to time they flattered the lower classes with some small attention, enough to give the aggrieved a sense of some importance. Moreover, the increasing numbers of Negro slaves appearing on plantations tended to throw the white classes together. Society continued to be stratified, but it was a condition that everyone recognized, something that had prevailed for a long time, and there was little disposition to upset the established order. Until men went farther west, by choice or by necessity, and until that western balance became more important politically, gentlemen along the seacoast could assure themselves that the *status quo* was not in danger.

A MILD CASE OF INSURRECTION

Before the seventeenth century ended some fissures began to show in the political and social strata that the early colonial leaders had maintained from the outset. By this time the shortage of good farm sites near the coast had forced late-comers farther back into the hinterland. Some of these were indentured servants who had moved on after working off their obligations and now took back seats, so to speak, on farms in the fringe area, where they made unkind remarks about those farther east who held the reins of political power.

Discontent commonly smolders until some precipitating event, not necessarily directly related, sets off an explosion. In Virginia the uproar centered around a young man named Nathaniel Bacon, a relative newcomer, who was a member of Governor Berkeley's Council. The "rebellion" that occurred was not staged by frontiersmen and was aimed at the governor rather than at London's officialdom, but it is of interest here because its origin sprang from frontier conditions. In the spring of 1676 Indians living along the edges of settlement in Virginia and Maryland killed a number of settlers with muskets and ammunition purchased from traders who were sponsored by the governor. Berkeley seemed undisturbed by these events and refused to call out the militia because, as the rumor went, he did not want to disturb the fur trade in which he was financially interested. Without consulting the governor, young Bacon gathered together some volunteers and drove off the Indians, much to the pleasure of the frontiersmen, who were angry over eastern disinterest in their welfare. Hard times, induced by low tobacco prices, and the levying of a poll tax added to the discontent of western farmers. The rest of the story, which did not concern the frontiersmen particularly, involved Bacon's demands for further reform, resultant warfare that sent Governor Berkeley fleeing, and the anticlimactic illness and death of Bacon that ended the insurgency.

Rebellion in Virginia stirred insurrectionary sentiments in neighboring Maryland. Josias Fendall and John Coode, whom Lord Baltimore called "Rank Baconists," were strongly opposed to the proprietor and to the extent of his power. In their feud with Baltimore, which flared up periodically all during the 1680s, to oppose the Catholic management the two men leaned heavily upon frontiersmen, who were largely Protestant. Although there was not the violence that occurred in Virginia, and nothing that might be termed a revolt, the simmering discontent reflected the rise of a western attitude and a growing ideological "apartness" from the East.

SETTLEMENT ADVANCES

As the Virginia frontiersmen moved toward the Appalachian mountains it was natural for them to veer either north or south rather than to continue westward. By moving in a southerly direction, along the mountain front, they were able to keep in touch with the coastal areas by means of the many streams that emptied into the ocean. The land known vaguely as Carolina was thought of as a part of the Virginia claim whereas the Spanish regarded it as theirs. The British government, therefore, was not displeased to see the settlers advance in that direction, and in this instance the area was a frontier in both the European and the American senses.

Although the eight lords proprietors were not awarded their grants in Carolina until 1663, emigration from Virginia commenced a decade earlier with the establishment of a settlement on Albemarle Sound. In 1664 Governor Berkeley (one of the eight lords proprietors) severed the little colony from Virginia and appointed William Drummond as its governor. Albemarle is particularly interesting to students of the American frontier because of its extremely liberal legislation, enacted to attract settlers, and the subsequent history of that practice. For example, in 1669 a law provided that after five years of residence no man could be sued for any cause that originated outside the colony, a provision that must have proved interesting to many a man on the move. Attractive also was the exemption from taxes accorded to new settlers during their first year, as well as the outlawing of all debt contracted elsewhere. A further incentive was provided businessmen by guaranteeing the Indian trade to residents and denying it to transients. That the liberal legislation tended to attract quantity rather than quality is seen in the sobriquet given it by Virginians: "Rogues' Harbour." But then there was very little blue blood anywhere on the frontier.

Into this backwoods country around Albemarle Sound and beyond, across what was to become North Carolina, pushed a group of hardy individuals who either could not adjust to Virginia society or did not find there the land they desired. As on later frontiers, the initial attempts to establish a civil society were rough around the edges and these people were regarded by members of more settled areas as rather lawless. Frontier justice, often dispensed across a tavern table and frequently without any kind of written record, was sufficiently unsophisticated to give the impression of lawlessness when, actually, these people were attending their legal needs as best they could under rather crude circumstances. Similarly, the absence of much religious machinery made the Carolina frontiersmen appear to be godless (a situation repeated many times over in the Far West) but time would bring churches and organized worship.

This spread of population to unsettled areas, this dilution of its density, tended to break down the traditional class structure and bring out the individual's importance in society. It was, for the moment, a rampaging democracy that made the more conservative talk about anarchy, irreligion, and the "wild West." These people were not necessarily the dregs of Virginia society, but were often hard-working, thrifty small farmers who opposed the large plantation owners and the power they represented. Typically, the group appeared to be poor, but it was not poverty-stricken. Although there was as yet no great wealth, there was no real suffering, and in the economic leveling there lay the elements of an egalitarian society, one whose members found equality in their common situation. In their very "sameness" they stood apart from others huddled along the coastal areas; America's first real sectionalism began to take shape. Two hundred years later their descendants in another and more remote West would say critical things about easterners and a New England senator would contemptuously refer to latter-day frontiersmen as "sons of wild jackasses."

NEW ENGLAND'S "WEST"

As the southern frontier bulged against the Appalachian barrier, swelling north and south before bursting through the mountain gaps to flood out into the Mississippi Valley, the Puritan pioneers also felt a westward pull. As always, the nature of the land shaped the ways of men. On the relatively thin soil of New England there sprang up a trading and commercial community unlike the planter society in the South. The commercial or shipbuilding towns tended to preserve the English village system. Even the purely agricultural communities of the New England back country were inclined to keep the village type of life they knew in old England, which permitted the church and community fathers to keep track of their flocks and to develop a more tightly knit kind of settlement. Although this had its restrictive qualities it also permitted the growth of a democratic type of government. Proximity meant the feasibility of the town meeting— that nursery of popular government—out of which grew representative government. On its westward march this small political and economic unit—the town—made a considerable impact upon American development.

As early as 1629 a number of little settlements lay sprinkled along the New England coast and in that year began the "great migration" from England, pouring forth more home seekers, many of whom were obliged to move inland to find suitable sites. Settlement along the coast was attractive to newcomers for about the first fifteen years after the 1620 landing at Plymouth Rock; then they began to look elsewhere. In 1635 the authorities of Massachusetts Bay Colony made a grant of land to a small group of men to found the town of Concord. Recognizing the hardships of this first New England frontier community, the founding fathers exempted the pioneers from taxes for three years. In the next few years others undertook new settlements inland, particularly along the rich Connecticut River Valley, and again, as in the Virginia area, the frontier movement veered off in a southerly direction before heading west.

By 1660 there was an irregular frontier line in New England. Generally it ran from the Penobscot River of Maine down to Manhattan Island, hugging the coast fairly closely except for the occasional bulges westward into little valleys or along rivers that were attractive to the more adventurous frontiersmen. In addition to the advanced settlements that identified the frontier line there was also something of a legal frontier. For example, in 1645 the General Court of Massachusetts officially designated such villages as Concord, Dedham, and Sudbury as frontier towns and prohibited their residents from moving without permission. During the 1670s, particularly in times of Indian troubles, the word "frontier" was used as a term of law and into the American language came a word that meant "edge of settlement" rather than the designation of a line separating two nations. The military line of defense and the frontier of settlement were already coinciding, a condition that would exist in many parts of the West in later times.

After 1660, development proceeded much more rapidly. Although dates are often used rather arbitrarily to designate a general time of change this one has a special significance, for in that year the Stuarts were restored to the English throne in the person of Charles II. When the new monarch began to enact arbitrary policies that harked back to an earlier day of oppression a number of those who disagreed with him were inclined to emigrate. A more positive factor, one that attracted emigrants to America, was the stimulus lent by the King's efforts to pay off old obligations in the form of huge grants in the colonies. New York, Pennsylvania, and the Carolinas are good examples of the results. Not to be overlooked is the benefit gained by all the American colonies in the renewal of British commercial efforts under the Restoration. Trade warfare with the Dutch and the institution of the Navigation Acts had their restrictive aspects, but the boom that resulted was highly beneficial to the economy of the colonies. As land seekers migrated to take up these new opportunities, pressure against the Appalachians increased until it became so great that not even mountains, distances, or Indians could hold back the westward push.

READINGS

INTRODUCTORY. Walter P. Webb's *The Great Frontier* (1952) concerns the projection westward from Europe of the American frontier. It is filled with challenging ideas. Edward P. Cheyney's older work, *European Background of American History 1300–1600* (1904), is still widely used. For an understanding of geographical considerations the first four chapters of Ralph H. Brown's *Historical Geography of the United States* (1948) should be read.

THE COLONIES. Max Savelle, *History of Colonial America* (rev., 1964) and Curtis P. Nettels, *The Roots of American Civilization* (1938) are comprehensive, one-volume colonial histories that touch on the frontier movement. For more detail see Charles M. Andrews, *The Colonial Period of American History* (4 vols., 1934–1938). Wallace Notestein, *The English People on the Eve of Colonization, 1603–1630* (1954) is valuable.

NORTHERN FRONTIERS. E. Douglas Branch, *Westward: The Romance of the American Frontier* (1930) is extremely interesting and easy reading. See Chapter 1, "When Massachusetts Was West." For more detail about the New England frontier the reader will find Lois K. Mathews, *The Expansion of New England* (1909) an old work that has not been superseded. Another excellent and more recent work is Louis B. Wright, *The Atlantic Frontier* (1947). See Chapter 2. Alternative reading is Roy V. Coleman, *The First Frontier* (1948). See also William Bradford, *History of Plymouth Plantation* (1856); the 1952 edition contains notes and introduction by Samuel Eliot Morison.

SOUTHERN FRONTIERS. Thomas P. Abernethy, *Three Virginia Frontiers* (1940), Part I, provides reading of prime importance. It should be supplemented with selections from Thomas J. Wertenbaker, *The Old South: The Founding of American Civilization* (1942), which gives attention to the Tidewater frontiersmen, or Wesley F. Craven, *The Southern Colonies in the Seventeenth Century, 1607–1689* (1949). Harold R. Shurtleff, *The Log Cabin Myth: A Study of the Early Dwellings of the English Colonists in North America* (1939) provides an interesting background of frontier living conditions.

BACON'S REBELLION. Wilcomb E. Washburn, *The Governor and the Rebel* (1958) is the most satisfactory account. Mary Johnston, *Pioneers of the Old South* (1918), Chapters 1, 2 and 13, and Thomas J. Wertenbaker, *Torchbearer of the Revolution* (1940) are also concernd with the young revolutionary.

CHAPTER 2

WESTERN BARRIERS

While the New Englanders edged their way inland, cautiously probing unsettled lands and attempting to maintain a more traditional kind of frontier, those who lived along the southern seaboard roamed the back country in a more adventurous spirit. The Virginians and Carolinians were particularly curious about "the other side of the mountain," a trait that was to send many a man west for more than two centuries.

Almost from the first, the colonists heard interesting tales about strange and mysterious things out west, stories that titillated the imagination and stirred ambitions. In 1649, for example, Governor Berkeley was said to have learned from the Indians that only a few days' travel into the interior lay a great mountain whose watershed drained into a large sea, and from across that body of water came shiploads of quaintly garbed men who brought with them animals that resembled horses. During the next summer Captain Abraham Wood was sent forth to investigate these stories and although he found nothing resembling the description, or, for that matter, anything that was not already known to fur traders, the urge to explore was stimulated. Within a decade most of the western area of Virginia and the Carolinas was fairly well known. In 1670, twenty years after his first efforts, Wood was still examining the back country of Virginia while the German adventurer, John Lederer, was trying to find a pass across the Blue Ridge Mountains.

None of the early Virginia explorers found the great river of the West, the South Sea, or acres of gold nuggets, but they did learn about the wilderness and how best to penetrate it. Lederer advised others to notch trees on their westward travels to avoid becoming lost on the return trip. He pointed out that small groups could move in greater safety because the

Indians were not afraid of them and were inclined to do battle only with larger and more threatening expeditions. Of economic interest was his report that the Indians wanted to trade furs for guns, knives, hatchets, and other articles. "Sometimes you may with brandy or strong liquor dispose them to an humour of giving you ten times the value of your commodoty," he wrote, thus laying down a principle upon which many a subsequent transaction was made. His admission that the more remote Indians still could be separated from their goods with beads, mirrors, and trinkets, but that the nearer and more knowledgeable natives were demanding hardware, was another indication of the frontier's progress westward.

Undeterred by their relatively fruitless efforts at finding great wealth in the woodlands, the Virginians persisted in their explorations. In the spring of 1673 Abraham Wood sponsored another expedition, this time under the leadership of James Needham, the purpose of which was to establish trade with the Cherokee in the Tennessee River country. The venture was successful in spite of the fact that Needham was killed by the jealous Occaneechi, who wanted to stop any such dealings with the rival Cherokee. The appearance of the white man had already sharpened the Indian's business acumen and he was prepared to deal with interlopers in a manner both sides understood.

Proprietors of the Carolina grant showed an interest similar to that of Governor Berkeley in the economic possibilities of the western lands. Anxious for a financial return from the Carolina venture, Lord Ashley and his associates did not overlook the rich fur trade deep in the new land. Within a few years over 50,000 deerskins a year were being sent to London from a country that was described as "one continued park." One of Ashley's friends posed the central question when he asked: "If the Porch be so beautifull, what must the Temple be?" The search for the Temple, sought by so many men in later years, began at once. In 1671 the Carolina proprietors voted a sum of £100 to Henry Woodward to explore the interior of their holdings. So curious were men about the land beyond that some of the more conservative colonists began to worry about draining off the population to a danger point. Their concern must have had some basis for Ashley instructed the governor to "bind the peoples mindes wholy to planting and trade" and to discount rumors about gold in the back country. But, being a man of many parts, Ashley overlooked no possibilities and agreed upon a secret code with Woodward whereby the explorer could send back any word of gold discoveries or other information that would profit the proprietor without disturbing the settlers.

INDIANS

The American frontier did not have to move very far inland before the white and red races came into close contact. In New England that contact began almost at once, and within fifteen years there was trouble. By 1637 the Pequot Indians rose up and tried to hurl out the white newcomers. Thanks to joint action by several villages, and the fact that Roger Williams persuaded the Narragansett to keep the peace, the disturbance was quelled. So effective was the chastisement that the Pequot posed no threat to Massachusetts and Connecticut villages for nearly forty years. That well-known religious thinker must have been dismayed at the enthusiasm with which his fellow Christians went about the business of putting down the native insurrection. The Indians, regarded as children of the Devil, were shown no mercy, as William Bradford later described the slaughter: "Those that escaped the fire were slain with the sword: some hewed to pieces, others run through with their rapiers, so as they were quickly dispatched, and very few escaped. It was conceived they thus destroyed about 400 at this time. It was a fearful sight to see them thus frying in the fire, and the streams of blood quenching the same, and horrible was the stink and scent thereof." But, as Bradford said, the soldiers were grateful for the victory and "gave the praise thereof to God who had wrought so wonderfully for them."

A much more serious Indian war broke out in 1675, one that kept the frontier from Maine to Connecticut in a state of turmoil for two years. The story of its causes, to be told many times over in the years to come, was that of white encroachment, of "purchases" of Indian lands under terms the natives did not understand, and of the rise of a capable leader who organized his forces and fought them well. "King" Philip persuaded most of the New England Indians, including the peaceful Narragansett, that the oncoming frontier must be rolled back and in the effort that followed scalps were lifted and blood flowed in the outlying white settlements. By this time there were about 120,000 white residents in New England, of which some 16,000 were fighting men, but it took all the strength they could muster to put down a threat that really did not end even after Philip's death in 1676.

Such periods of strife tended to dramatize the existence of a frontier in that the line of demarcation between civilization and savagery stood out with greater clarity. The recognition of this condition is seen in an order by the General Court of Massachusetts, set forth in 1703 for 500 pairs of snowshoes and moccasins to be used in counties "lying Frontier next to the Wilderness," to use the court's words. Also, there were numerous demands made by outlying villages for soldiers to "scout the towne while wee get in our hay," demands that would be echoed in Colorado and in Montana in the 1860s.

Pressure against the southern frontier resulted in trouble with the Indians of that region. Despite Lord Ashley's expressed desire to proceed slowly and in an orderly manner, neither he nor his followers could resist the lure of the back country. During the 1670s explorers probed deeper while traders negotiated a treaty of alliance and friendship with the Westo Indians. The agreement was commercial and military in that the Westo agreed to help make war on Indians living farther south under Spanish control. Aside from an occasional white murder the Indians kept their agreement until 1680, when the alliance gave way to open warfare with the settlers. The Carolinians enlisted the help of the Savannah Indians, who campaigned with such vigor that by 1683 the proprietors were informed that only fifty Westo remained.

So anxious were the Carolinians to trade in the back country, and so assiduous were they in capturing natives for sale as slaves, that the need for some kind of governmental intervention came early to this part of the land. The small landholders who moved out to the frontier paid a heavy penalty for the recklessness with which traders dealt with the Indians, and to alleviate their difficulties the colonial government was obliged to formulate an Indian policy. In 1707 the South Carolina legislators set up a board of nine commissioners empowered to issue annual trading licenses. The key figure in this new regulatory structure was the Indian agent, who was paid £250 a year and was to live for at least ten months of that period among the Indians. In addition to being the principal adviser to the local government with regard to Indian matters, he was endowed with a considerable power over those who wanted to trade among the natives. As a contemporary remarked, the enterprising drummers had made it a practice to meet with the natives and "by giving rum and making them Drunk get their Slaves or Skinns for little or nothing, to the great dissatisfaction of the Indians when they are Sober. . . ." It was the agent's duty to eliminate such unsavory commercial methods and, if possible, to prevent the Indians from being swindled.

EARLY WESTERN SETTLEMENTS

Typical of later frontiers, the acceptance of this early West by small farmers was relatively slow to develop. By the turn of the eighteenth century, explorers and traders were generally familiar with the area east of the Appalachians but the average householder was reluctant to move away from the coastal areas any farther than necessary. The colonial population of 1690 is estimated at about 213,000; within twenty years it had jumped to around 357,000. But despite that rapid growth the line of frontier settlement remained almost fixed. Such events as King Philip's War discouraged the movement westward and in some cases drove in the frontier line, so that considerable population pressures had to build before the movement was resumed.

Distances, isolation, Indians, and other dangers were not a sufficient deterrent to the more adventurous. Many a small farmer might hang back, unwilling to risk his possessions and perhaps his life, but there had developed as early as 1675 a class of men in Virginia that came to represent the prototype of the "frontiersman" in later American history. Some of these were men like Abraham Wood, who examined the land and kept a close account of his findings, but most of the vanguard lacked either the ability or the desire to set down much of what they saw. Some years before 1700 the traders, large and small, were familiar with the land beyond the mountains, that country of the "beautiful river" (Ohio) so familiar to the early French trappers. They searched for furs, and even for gold; and even though they were sometimes disappointed in the material aspects of their search they contributed to a growing store of information about the West.

The pattern of the past—and of the future—was followed in that the quest of riches, so often frustrated, led to an interest in the soil itself. The returning explorers, literate or illiterate, tended to talk about the land and its possibilities. These men came largely from a planter class and recognized a crop potential when they saw one. Out of their various sojourns in the West came the desire to speculate in land, particularly in view of the pressures being exerted by land-hungry Germans and Scotch-Irish immigrants who crowded along the seacoast.

By 1730 the frontier line was again on the move and such places as the Shenandoah Valley began to fill up. It was said that Governor Gooch of Virginia was handing out land grants so generously that one Jacob Stover became a man of much property by giving human names to his cattle and using them to take land titles. In another instance a young woman, adept at disguise, presented herself in several variations of male attire and laid claim to an immoderately large acreage. A century and a half later, when Nebraska and Colorado stockmen engaged in similar subterfuges, the practice was called fraudulent.

After New Englanders had recovered from the effects of King Philip's War, their frontier once more edged forward. Francis Parkman, in describing that frontier of two or three hundred miles in length, said it was largely agricultural and its settlements were widely scattered. When the villagers could, they fortified themselves with some kind of a palisade, and in the larger communities much more secure fortifications, replete with blockhouses, afforded protection in times of extreme danger.

In the second quarter of the eighteenth century these settlements crept along river valleys into the Berkshires and other mountains, little clusters of people carrying their Puritan ideals and moral codes, as well as their notions about education, deeper into the new land. Now Huguenots and Scotch-Irish immigrants began to join them. Instead of offering large grants of land to individuals, as was common on the southern frontier, the New Englanders continued their system of group allotments, after which town proprietors might make individual assignments of acreages, and thereby control the nature of the expansion.

By this time the social and religious ideas characteristic of Puritan society were beginning to be set aside in favor of economic and political considerations. Massachusetts illustrated the change when, to protect its boundary claims, it began to locate towns in advance of settlement. In 1736, for example, it laid off five towns on the New Hampshire border; in the years that followed more grants were made in what is now Vermont. These were cash deals, and the rush of speculators who bought up favorable sites for future subdivision indicated a modification of the older religious ideal. As the economic aspects of town-building grew in importance the grasp that community leaders once exercised over their flocks diminished and the "moral police," as Turner called them, began to lose their grip. The result was in increased individualism, one that operated within the framework of the town settlement system, but did not necessarily erode its many virtues.

By the middle of the eighteenth century the emergence of two New Englands was apparent: one a coastal area wedded to the commercial ideal, and the other a more primitive hinterland dominated by agriculture and peopled by men with democratic ideals unafraid of change. Although the development was north and south, running up little valleys, the fact that it was not moving west in no way meant that it lacked the qualities of a frontier movement.

In nearby New York, the spread of settlement up the Hudson River Valley provided another example of the "northward movement." From a very early date Albany was an important fur-trading post and despite the restrictiveness of the Dutch land system a group of small farmers worked its way to the back country. After the British took custody of New York and cultivated friendly relationships with the Iroquois Indians, there was much more inducement for the farmers to take up lands on the fringes of settlement.

Refugees from the strife-torn continent of Europe were welcomed in England and often were sent on to the American colonies. In 1709 Protestant Germans fleeing the troubled Palatinate were given shelter by Queen Anne. Some of them were sent on to North Carolina, where an unsuccessful attempt was made to form a colony, but a much larger group —some 3000—were settled along the Hudson River. The British government, which anticipated the policies of private societies at a later date, advanced the necessary funds for travel, tools, and provisions. It was hoped that these people would produce naval stores for "Mother England," but the immigrants became dissatisfied with the project and turned to farming, with which they were much more familiar. The availability of large amounts of unclaimed land on the frontier made it difficult to discipline the newcomers, who drifted off, many into Pennsylvania, to take up individual farmsteads.

The movement into Pennsylvania's back country was westward. Into the great valleys poured thousands of Germans and Scotch-Irish. The movement picked up speed in the late 1720s and by the time of the American Revolution perhaps a third of the Pennsylvania population was German, or "Pennsylvania Dutch" as they were mistakenly called. Some 200,000 of these people were strung out along the frontier line of the thirteen colonies at the time independence was declared, about half of them living in Pennsylvania. Too poor to buy better lands, they headed for the fringe of settlement, north into New York's Mohawk Valley, south into the Georgia mountains, and westward along a line between these regions. They were good farmers, men who knew how to produce the most from the soil, wedded to the land, and little interested in politics or warfare.

The Scotch-Irish were equally attracted to the new country. Pennsylvania, founded by William Penn in 1681, appealed to them because of its agricultural possibilities and because its proprietor was more interested in economic development than in religious hair splitting. These were rough-minded people, willing to put up with the hardships of frontier life but unwilling to be interfered with. James Logan, one of Penn's agents, characterized them well when he used the term "bold and indigent strangers." He remarked that when questions arose over land titles—a frequent occurrence—the Scotch-Irish stood by their claims, holding that it was against the laws of God and Nature that Christians who wanted to work should be denied the use of idle acres. Stubbornly squatting on their claims, they refused to move or to pay quitrents.

When it came to dealing with the Indians the Scotch-Irish took up the challenge much more quickly than the peace-loving Germans. As Logan wrote, "The Indians themselves are alarmed at the swarms of strangers, and we are afraid of a breach between them—the Irish are very rough to them." The Indians, or anyone else blocking their westward push, found these independent, militant frontiersmen ready to settle matters by a test of arms. Along with other dissident factions, such as the Irish Quakers and the French Huguenots, the Scotch-Irish presented a hard-fighting, individualistic and frequently quick-tempered people ever ready to take up any challenge to their assertion of individual rights. Perhaps more than any other group they came to epitomize the typical frontiersman in the minds of their contemporaries and of later generations.

THE OLD WEST

These early western settlements furnish excellent examples of initial frontier influences. Virginia was not very old before the settlements in the Shenandoah Valley began to have a pronounced effect on the coastal area. At the outset the colony was primarily English, Episcopal, and aristocratic, but before long Scotch Presbyterianism and German Lutheranism, small farms, and democratic tendencies began to reduce the influences of the privileged class. In the House of Burgesses the representatives of these upcountry folk ran head on into eastern ideologies and the result was then, and much later, conflict. Privilege managed to keep its grip for some time, but when the changes came in revolutionary days, when church and state were separated and such feudal vestiges as primogeniture and entail were erased, the changes were the result of back-country pressures. As one historian has remarked, Jefferson has been called the father of democracy, but there is some validity to the notion that the Shenandoah Valley was one of its cradles.

All along the frontier, from the Carolinas northward to New England, old customs and distinctions gradually wore away under the pressures of emphasis upon social equality. Westerners from Massachusetts and Connecticut traded among the New York Dutch and frequently their children intermarried. The same mingling took place on other parts of the frontier, and as time passed a new generation grew up, one that had moved several times, had associated with other religions and languages so much that these were no longer distinctions among people, and from it had come a people simply known as Westerners. These pioneering families enjoyed the open, unfettered life they lived far away from the strictures of society and custom that shackled the business communities along the coast. When these western notions filtered eastward they appealed to people of ordinary means, and men of substance who had ruled so long with so little opposition, were concerned. Ideas of social and political equality gradually spread to the eastern parts of the colonies and to a degree that cannot be measured they affected later thinking.

It is possible, however, to examine some of the more concrete results of the population movement into what Turner called "the Old West." Along the outer edge of colonial settlement, from New England to Georgia, there lay a picket line of men who carried their rifles with their axes, ready to exchange one instrument for the other on a moment's notice as the day's work proceeded. This fighting frontier was tangible and unmistakable, and its residents stood out in sharp contrast to the Tidewater folk. Out on the "front" lived men and women who knew adversity, who frequently had experienced hardships in the old country, and whose environment molded them into a hard-headed people, highly individualistic, ever jealous of their rights. Into this first "melting pot" came immigrants from various European trouble spots, tired of religious persecution, political suppression, and economic inequalities. In their common situation they found a new fellowship, new allegiances, a new unity, and for these they shed old loyalties. When this occurred a new kind of man was bred and the name "American" became more meaningful.

Not all frontier communities intermixed freely. Those that tended to cluster together in linguistic groups were easy to identify. The Dutch, for example, tended to stay together; perhaps to a lesser extent, so did the Germans. This tendency persisted, and much later Russians, German Mennonites, Swedes, Norwegians, and other nationalities clustered in their own settlements out on the high plains. In nearly all cases, however, time and the pressures of frontier movement would break down these religious or national groupings, and parents would lament the fact that their children had lost their pride in the native tongue. Intermarriage, economic opportunities elsewhere, and in some cases an overweening pride in the new national allegiance eroded older attachments.

As new settlements were made farther away from the Atlantic seaboard, there was a tendency for local industry to develop and an internal trade to spring up. Thus the dependence on European products lessened in favor of local or American seaboard markets. Rising eastern commercial firms recognized the importance of these embryonic frontier business communities and rivalries for their attentions soon became apparent. However, the chronic indebtedness of the Westerners tended to set them apart, and animosities between the sections became so permanent that they are today regarded as traditional.

With economic sectionalism came a demand for political and religious independence. This thinly peopled land resented the power wielded by those from the more heavily populated portions of the country, whether the resentment emanated from the back country of the Carolinas or Virginia and was directed toward legislatures, or from a later West that felt neglected in national legislative concerns. As Turner pointed out, these dissatisfactions as well as the shift in political centers of gravity due to the movement westward resulted in the relocation of capital cities in Virginia, South Carolina, North Carolina, New York, and Pennsylvania. Similarly, political and economic demands of the Westerners were revealed in their constitution-making where mortgage stay laws or paper money came under consideration, and in their state-making, where a continual splitting off of territories occurred as a result of growing population needs. The religious splintering that accompanied this political development assured Westerners that their society would be religiously tolerant as well as secular. Continual fragmentation prevented any church from becoming powerful enough to dominate the others.

It was this "Old West" that furnished the manpower for later and distant frontiers. These men, with their notions about individual enterprise, landownership, social, religious, and political independence, were the shock troops that led the westward attack; after them came their sons and grandsons. Time bred a frontiering group, and as they moved across the land, bound for new and more promising places, these peculiarly American people left their mark on the institutions of every community through which they passed.

FRONTIERS IN COLLISION

As the British colonial frontier edged forward a competitor flanked it and pre-empted much of the desirable land that lay between the claimants. In 1605 the French made their first permanent settlement in North America, at Port Royal (now Annapolis Royal) in Nova Scotia, and in 1608 founded Quebec. Although their colonial attempts in America also came relatively late, the French moved much more rapidly than the English. Theirs was a fur-trading endeavor, a fluid movement that flowed freely across the lakes region and along promising river valleys. Yet before many decades had elapsed they were feeling English and Dutch rivalries and had to choose between abandoning or fighting for their lucrative fur trade.

In 1687 the Marquis de Denonville, Governor of New France, directed an attack against the English-sponsored Iroquois Indians. Two years later that visit was repaid when approximately 1500 of those Indians swept into the village of Lachine, a few miles from Montreal. The Comte de Frontenac quickly organized a force that included the friendly Huron and directed a triple-headed invasion of the English colonies. This was in 1690, and by now the French and English were at war in Europe over the French failure to recognize England's new monarch, William of Orange. Frontenac's war parties struck hard at New York, New Hampshire, and Maine frontier settlements, leaving a trail of blood and terror behind them. Sir William Phips, Governor of Massachusetts, countered with a strike against Port Royal and won an easy victory. The victorious Governor celebrated his victory by "liberating" everything he could get his hands on, including silver, the French Governor's shirts, nightcaps, garters, and even his wigs. It was a clean sweep. In the following year the English invaded Canada by way of Lake Champlain and almost reached

The French in North America

Montreal before turning back. In 1696 Frontenac, now so old he had to be carried, directed a counterattack against New York in which the Iroquois allies of the English lost their main village by fire. The Peace of Ryswick, signed the next year, ended the phase of French-English colonial warfare known as King William's War.

The uneasy peace was broken by French refusal to approve Queen Anne's succession to the English throne (1702) and the stand taken by Louis XIV over succession to the Spanish throne. In the general war that resulted in Europe—the War of the Spanish Succession (1702–1714)—fighting again broke out along the American frontier. During 1703 and 1704 the French raided outlying villages in Massachusetts, the famous Deerfield massacre of February 1704 being the bloodiest of several attacks. The killing of some 40 or 50 settlers in this affair so enraged the people of Massachusetts that their authorities offered a bounty for every Indian scalp brought in.

An invasion of Canada in 1710 that led to the capture of Port Royal so encouraged the English that the next year they gathered a large military and naval force designed to take Quebec. Wind, fog, and bad luck in the Gulf of St. Lawrence so disrupted the expeditionary force that the whole scheme was abandoned and no more attacks were tried upon the city before the conclusion of Queen Anne's War in 1713. By the settlement, called the Peace of Utrecht, the British gained from France in America the Hudson's Bay region, Newfoundland and Acadia, and a recognition of the special relationship existing between the English and the Iroquois Indians. The principal problem left unsettled was the disposition of the vast interior, particularly the Ohio Valley, and it was the jockeying for position there that helped to spark the next conflict.

An indication of England's expansive mood is seen in a 1721 Board of Trade statement to the effect that although the Appalachians served as a "very good frontier," there should be no thought of limiting the western boundary to them. On the contrary, said the board, settlements might well be founded west of the mountains and a few forts should be established along the Great Lakes "in proper places." If such posts should be established where they would interrupt French communications between Quebec and the Mississippi, so much the better. Thus, in 1726, Fort Oswego was built near Lake Ontario on land claimed by the French; there would be others. By the end of the 1730s the British frontier bristled with outposts, pinpoints of irritation thrust at the French from the Alabama River to Crown Point on Lake Champlain. The French countered these moves with sporadic raids against outlying settlements, particularly in Massachusetts, and for two decades after about 1720 the harassment continued. Formal war was carried on after 1744 when France and England were once again locked in a conflict known in America as King George's War. After a naval-military struggle in which the English captured the great French fortress of Louisbourg in Nova Scotia, peace was once again restored in 1748. New Englanders, who had contributed much to the expedition against Louisbourg, were astonished and angry when the Treaty of Aix-la-Chapelle handed back that prize at the end of the war.

The indecisiveness of the war was demonstrated by an immediate renewal of French activity in the West. Led by Celeron de Blainville, who moved through the disputed Ohio country burying lead plates to establish a claim to the land, the French once again were on the march. But later, aggressive traders such as Irish George Croghan extended operations into Ohio, trading with the Indians as far west as the Miami Indian country. Croghan paid for his audacity in 1752 when the French struck the little British trading post of Pickawillany, killing its defenders and hauling off a large store of goods. Encouraged by the victory, and the subsequent desertion of part of the Indians under British sponsorship, the French stepped up their endeavors to secure the fur-trading country that lay within their grasp.

Governor Robert Dinwiddie of Virginia, a tough-minded Scot who saw his colony's western claims threatened, not to mention his own trading interests, ordered young George Washington to go out and warn off the intruders. The officer did as he was told, but the Frenchmen flatly refused to move. Returning home, Washington reported that the French were well entrenched, particularly at Fort Venango on the Allegheny River, and that in his opinion it would take more than words to move them. Dinwiddie agreed and sent Washington back to build a fort at the forks of the Ohio in the vicinity of modern Pittsburgh; but again there was disappointment when Washington found that the French had anticipated him by erecting Fort Duquesne at the desired location. Instead of abandoning his mission Washington engaged the French, defending himself behind hastily built fortification dubbed "Fort Necessity," only to be defeated and driven out of the western country.

By now France and England were again at war on the Continent and the sparring that had taken place in America turned into full-scale combat. British strategists, anxious to tighten their American defenses, held a conference at Albany in the summer of 1754, the purpose of which was to consolidate colonial efforts and to reassure the Indians—the Iroquois in particular—of British friendship. (The fact that the struggle was called the French and Indian War in America indicates the importance of participation by the natives.) The Iroquois contended that, although their friendship for the British had not diminished, they were worried by the continual white advance westward and by the French-English struggle for land that they regarded as belonging to the tribes. They asked that their friend Sir William Johnson be made their representative and empowered to represent the northern Indians in dealings with the British government. The request was granted. Similarly, Edmund Atkin was put in charge of the Indians to the south and the first real semblance of a comprehensive Indian policy in America began to emerge.

To integrate defenses in the forthcoming war the home government suggested that intercolonial cooperation be increased. Benjamin Franklin submitted his well-known Albany Plan of Union in which he foresaw a single general government for the American colonies presided over by a president-general and operated by a representative council. Into this organization's hands would go the disposition of all Indian matters affecting the American colonies. The proposal was enthusiastically endorsed by the delegates and just as vigorously rejected by the individual colonies who were asked to approve it.

The first serious challenge to France's military establishment across the mountains came in the spring of 1755 with the arrival of General Edward Braddock in Virginia. With more than 1500 regulars, militiamen, and Indian scouts he marched on Fort Duquesne, only to be severely repulsed (July 9) by a much smaller French and Indian force using ambush tactics. The English reeled back upon Virginia demoralized and disorganized, their commander mortally wounded, while the French retained complete control of the Ohio River country. About the same time another expedition, aimed at Crown Point and headed by Sir William Johnson, succeeded in establishing two forts in the Lake George area, thus checking the French on the north. For more than two years the holding operation continued. By 1758, under William Pitt's political leadership, the English had moved ahead on all fronts. In America the principal strategy involved a two-pronged attack upon the French: one against the great Canadian fortress at Louisbourg and a second up the Hudson River Valley past Lakes George and Champlain into St. Lawrence River country.

One element of the grand assault proposed was a return to the headwaters of the Ohio where the British had been so consistently defeated at the outset of the hostilities. The legislatures of both Virginia and Pennsylvania were anxious to eradicate this stubborn French barrier to their plans for expansion and to repair their tarnished military reputation in that region. This time there was to be no chance of falling into an ambush; the preparations were extensive and complete. A force of more than 6000 men under the command of General John Forbes, marched resolutely upon Fort Duquesne, only to find that its pitifully weak garrison of some 200 men had decided to burn the place rather than surrender it. Taking over the smoldering ruins, Forbes, who had been ill during most of the campaign, notified the home government that the French had departed and the place was renamed "Pittsbourgh" after the great war minister.

The loss of such western outposts as Duquesne was followed by a general contraction of French holdings, particularly during 1759. In September of "the wonderful year," as the British called it, the mighty fortress of Quebec fell. At the battle fought on the Plains of Abraham, General Montcalm, the French commander, and General Wolfe, who headed the invading force, both fell mortally wounded. Within a year the American aspect of the war was over.

In 1763, when the European phase was concluded and the diplomats sat down to write the Treaty of Paris, the formalities of the French demise in America were carried out. That document, signed February 10, had world-wide repercussions. At the stroke of a pen France surrendered all of Canada to the British, with the exception of some small islands in the Gulf of St. Lawrence, and everything east of the Mississippi except the immediate vicinity of New Orleans. The remainder of the terms involved a division of claims around the globe, ranging from Caribbean islands to the Philippines, Africa, and India. For the Americans, by far the most interesting stipulation was that which lowered the French ensign beyond the Appalachians and cleared the way for uninterrupted expansion westward.

READINGS

THE OLD WEST. John A. Caruso, *The Appalachian Frontier: America's First Surge Westward* (1959) treats the history of early trans-Appalachian settlements. So does Frederick Jackson Turner, *The Frontier in American History* (1920), also in paperback with foreword by Ray A. Billington (1962). Thomas P. Abernethy, *Three Virginia Frontiers* (1940), in a section called "Piedmont and the Valley," discusses the preparation for the transmontane move, as does John Fiske, *Old Virginia and Her Neighbors* (2 vols., 1897) in Chapter 2, "From Tidewater to the Mountains." Recommended also is Herbert L. Osgood, *The American Colonies in the 18th Century* (4 vols., 1924), Volume I, Chapter 14, "Development of the Western Frontier." Westward movement by the Southerners is fully described in Verner W. Crane, *The Southern Frontier, 1670–1732* (1928) and John R. Alden, *John Stuart and the Southern Colonial Frontier . . . 1754–1775* (1944). Works previously mentioned, such as Max Savelle, *History of Colonial America;* Lois Mathews, *The Expansion of New England;* E. Douglas Branch, *Westward;* and Louis Wright, *The Atlantic Frontier* all contain pertinent sections. Oliver P. Chitwood, *A History of Colonial America* (3d ed., 1960) has a good chapter (17) entitled "The Old West."

STRUGGLES WITH THE FRENCH. George M. Wrong, *The Rise and Fall of New France* (2 vols., 1928) remains the classic in this field. See also his *The Conquest of New France* (1918). Another standard work is Francis Parkman, *Works* (12 vols., 1901). See Volumes V through XI. Much more recent is L. H. Gipson, *The British Empire before the American Revolution* (9 vols., 1936–1956), Volumes V and VI. The French encirclement is also discussed in Harold A. Innis, *The Fur Trade in Canada* (1930), Part II, sections 3 and 4. See also Louise P. Kellogg, *The French Regime in Wisconsin and the Northwest* (1925). A recent work, written for the general reader, is Dale Van Every, *Forth to the Wilderness:*

The First American Frontier, 1754–1774 (1961), the first of a four-volume study of the early frontier.

Indian troubles along Pennsylvania's frontier are well covered in Robert L. D. Davidson, *War Comes to Quaker Pennsylvania, 1682–1756* (1957). A briefer treatment is George Arthur Cribbs, *The Frontier Policy of Pennsylvania* (1919). John W. Harpster (ed.), *Pen Pictures of Early Western Pennsylvania* (1938) is a collection of contemporary journals and is very informative.

CHAPTER 3

BEYOND THE MOUNTAINS

T he peace that came after 1763 presented problems not uncommon in a postwar era. As always, each of those who participated had his own ideas about the rewards of victory and about new economic directions. To the Americans the coming of peace meant the departure of the French from North America; this thought naturally led to the conclusion that those lands so recently left vacant would be occupied by colonials, who were already indulging in western real-estate speculation. But empire planners, viewing the situation from remote London, saw it otherwise. In the new order of things there must be exercised a greater measure of control. Now the British flag flew over more of the earth's surface than ever before, and to manage properly such far-flung possessions stricter regulations were called into being. In America, for example, there were not only the upstart colonials who had plunged ahead pretty much on their own for years past; there were also some 60,000 residents of New France to be governed—people of a different language, different customs, and different religious faith. In the preceding turbulent decades the English, French, and Indians had become accustomed to warfare against each other and now, if British North America were to prosper, this would have to cease. One of the simplest ways to deal with the matter of quarreling children seemed to be to separate them. This the British tried to do by the Proclamation of 1763.

THE PROCLAMATION OF 1763

Despite the fact that their traders had been buying furs in the Ohio Valley for about seventy-five years, the British knew very little about the land beyond the mountains. The war had aroused considerable interest in the region, but such knowledge as had been gained from the western campaigns was limited to the upper reaches of the rivers flowing into the great valley. Although that part of the country was well known for its furs there was little reason to suppose that it had any agricultural promise. Dr. Samuel Johnson, who knew no more about it than the next man, wrote that large tracts of land acquired as a result of the war were "only the barren parts of the continent, the refuse of the earlier adventurers, which the French, who came last, had taken only as better than nothing." The doctor may be forgiven for his ignorance. Even William Knox, a long-time under-secretary for the colonies and a man who might be expected to know something about them, wrote as late as 1789 that the Americans would not settle western areas for years and that it would be best to assign such lands to the savages. It was a notion that would be current for nearly a hundred years, about other Wests, farther "beyond."

Undoubtedly the average American knew little more about the west beyond the mountains than did Johnson or Knox, but he exhibited a great deal more enthusiasm over the presumed potentialities of the new country. The eighteenth century was one of bold speculation, and land fever was rampant in America. Of the many promotional ventures undertaken, the Ohio Company, formed in 1748, was the best known. A group of wealthy English and Virginia investors was granted 200,000 acres of land along the upper Ohio River, provided a hundred families were located there within seven years. The promoters hoped to profit from the sale of lands and from the Indian trade; the home government saw it as an opportunity to shove back the French. Virginia's interest in the transmontane area was shared by other colonies, particularly Pennsylvania, whose people were concerned about the aggressiveness of the Virginians. Benjamin Franklin openly interested himself in various settlement schemes. Governor Thomas Pownall, of Massachusetts, was another whose advocacy of western development by means of such grants was well known in America. The coming of the French and Indian War temporarily quieted such activities but did not kill the keen speculative interest that had been generated.

The return of peace brought an immediate renewal of interest in the great western country. The Virginians, always alert to the possibilities of westward expansion, promised to reward veterans with transmontane homesites; and Colonel George Washington, who had an interest in some real estate in that area, was a strong advocate of this policy. Early in 1763 land claims were being made, individually and collectively. In June some prominent men of Maryland and Virginia (including Washington) founded the Mississippi Company and asked the Crown for 2,500,000 acres in the valley of that name. Benjamin Franklin reaffirmed his interest in such investments and a group of New Yorkers talked of founding "New Wales" along the Ohio River.

The Appalachian Frontier, 1763

In the spring of 1763 governmental officials in London began to ask each other a number of questions about the American trans-Appalachian West. Turning to the Board of the Trade, the British ministry asked for recommendations. How should the Indians of this unsettled land be governed? How fast and how far ought the whites be allowed to proceed? Should the older colonies govern these new settlements or would it be better to found new colonies? To what juridiction should the Ohio Valley belong—seaboard British America or Quebec?

During the months that answers to such questions were being sought, developments in America suggested the need for an early decision. The British government's concern over the westward press of white settlers was shared by the Indians, who not only resented the intruders but who were considerably annoyed at the London policy makers for their lack of interest in making gifts to the natives now that the war was over. In May the Indians in the Northwest, led by an Ottawa named Pontiac, joined the Six Nations in an all-out effort to evict the white squatters. The rapidity with which the Indians succeeded and the thoroughness with which the frontier line was rolled back dramatized long-standing difficulties between the races. Clearly some kind of boundary was needed, one that would be recognized by both parties, and one that would be practical. Since there were few settlements beyond the mountains and since most of the claims in that area were held by speculators, the obvious answer appeared to be the crest of the Alleghenies.

By a proclamation, signed October 7, 1763, the Crown attempted to set at rest several western problems. As an immediate answer to Indian complaints, a line was drawn along the crest of the mountains, west of which was to be the domain of the natives. Equally important as the segregation of races was the establishment of a new policy that took Indian affairs from the hands of the colonies and gave them to imperial agents. Henceforth, trading was to be carried on only by those licensed for such purposes and their relations with the Indians were carefully controlled. The idea anticipated later efforts made by the American government. The Indian reserve was flanked to the south and north by the new colonies of East and West Florida and Quebec, comprising a vast domain lying between the 45th and 31st parallels. Colonial governors were prohibited from issuing any more land grants, and individuals were warned against making individual purchases from the Indians.

The pressure under which the proclamation was formulated resulted in some important errors of omission. A glaring oversight was the lack of any provision for civil government for the French, many of whom had settled along the lakes and in the Ohio Valley. Not until 1774, by the Quebec Act, was this omission corrected. Again, provision was made to arrest and punish anyone fleeing into unorganized Indian country but there was nothing to cover crimes committed in that part of the land. More serious was the replacement of French law with English law in Quebec, a move that not only aroused the American French but was, in fact, a direct violation of the Treaty of Paris (1763). So great was the uproar over the document that no one was willing to identify himself as its writer, and there were loud outcries from the speculators. Calmer investors, such as George Washington, took a view that such a restriction was only temporary, a gesture toward the irate Indians, and that the westward march would not be delayed for very long.

Washington's assumption was correct. During 1764 the Indian confederation was crushed by British troops and the press of settlement beyond the mountains was renewed. By 1766 loud complaints by settlers and speculators were heard on both sides of the Atlantic. The new Indian trade policies were not working as well as had been expected. Benjamin Franklin was a personal friend of the Earl of Shelburne, who had drawn up the original plan, and it was to Shelburne, now Secretary of State for the Southern Department in charge of American affairs, that the prominent Pennsylvanian turned for help. American arguments must have been powerful, for Shelburne recommended that trade in the Indian country be turned over to the individual colonies and that troops be withdrawn. Before any orders to this effect could be given, Lord Hillsborough took over such American affairs and a compromise measure was enacted. The Treaty of Fort Stanwix, formulated by the shrewd Sir William Johnson in 1768, stretched the line drawn by the Proclamation of 1763 to such an extent that the northern Indians gave up claims to all the country south and east of the Ohio River, while the Treaty of Hard Labor (also 1768) similarly extended the southern portion of the line. Thus the notion of Indian country, open only to licensed settlers, was preserved but at the same time another area of fresh land was opened to the clamorous settlers.

OBJECTIONS TO IMPERIAL POLICY

The westering tendencies of American real-estate promoters were more powerful than British politicians imagined. Although the speculators, particularly those of Virginia, were deeply disappointed by the home government's restrictive policies, as enunciated in the Proclamation of 1763, they found some hope in their remoteness and in the traditional lethargy of London administrators. As later Westerners were to discover, there was some virtue in a convenient breakdown in communications and a general misunderstanding of orders. For those who were of this mind, the appointment of Lord Dunmore as Governor of Virginia, in 1771, was indeed a happy circumstance.

Dunmore, who had been Governor of New York, soon displayed a surprising interest in the West. Earlier he had opposed the Vandalia Company and its projected settlement across the Alleghenies. In 1770 that organization's sponsors had gained permission from the Crown to purchase 2,500,000 acres of western land. Dunmore argued that the location was so far from the coast that it would complicate the matter of defense and, he added, its settlement might help to depopulate the East. These fears were dispelled by Virginia land speculators, who must have convinced the

Governor that there was nothing wrong with joining them and getting rich in America. In any event he became one of the most reckless plungers in the colony.

A group of Virginians, organized by Colonel George Washington, maintained that in 1754 veterans of the recent war had been promised lands by Governor Robert Dinwiddie and that the promise should be kept. The colonel who foresaw great profits in such development, wrote to Dunmore in the autumn of 1773 and urged him to recognize veterans of both the regular and the provincial branches of the service. When the request was granted there ensued a considerable land rush across the mountains, with Washington among those advertising lands in the new country. Several new little towns sprang up in 1774, the most important of which was Harrod's Town (later Harrodsburg). The site of present Louisville, plotted during the previous year, soon would contain a thriving community. The West was beginning to find its place on the map.

The Vandalia Company, upon whose lands the Virginians had encroached, registered such a protest that the British government ordered Dunmore to cease and desist. It was here that the Governor showed his real abilities. He not only denied any knowledge of the boundaries of the Vandalia Company but blandly asserted that he had no notion that the Proclamation Line of 1763 was in force. He cited the Treaty of Lochaber (1770) with the Cherokee as his authority and held that under its terms the expanded boundaries of Virginia put him quite within his rights. While making such bold assertions to British officials he sent one of his agents to take possession of Pittsburgh on the assumption it also was within his realm. Pennsylvania officials reacted by throwing the agent into jail and registering a strong complaint to the home government.

About the time the Virginia-Pennsylvania uproar reached its height matters were further complicated by the outbreak of another Indian war. The Shawnee, unhappy with the Treaty of Fort Stanwix and resultant frontier pressures, launched attacks upon white settlements during 1774. The home government was dismayed at such a turn of events, but Lord Dunmore looked upon the development as the answer to his problems. What he could not take in time of peace he could claim by virtue of conquest in war. What is known as "Lord Dunmore's War" was staged that autumn and was climaxed by the Battle of Point Pleasant, near the mouth of the great Kanawha River, where the Indians were turned back. To this "one-battle war" are attributed the opening of Kentucky and the quelling of the Shawnee, but the best that can be said is that it removed only temporary obstacles. The Indians would be back. Dunmore's activities and the resultant quarrels over land were stifled by the coming of the Revolutionary War. He did prove, however, that the British government's western land

and the Indian policy had its weaknesses and that the Treaty of Fort Stanwix was a failure. However, the same point was to be demonstrated over and over again in later American history.

THE REGULATORS

Turbulence in the colonial West was not limited to northern areas. Clusters of frontier folk who gathered along North Carolina's outer fringe of settlement demonstrated an increasing independence as their contact with both home and colonial governments lessened. Since they had little influence with the bureaucracy that ran the colony from the coast, their grievances tended to go unanswered. Such officials as county justices, sheriffs, and even militia officers were appointed by the governor and it was to him, rather than to the people, that they owed their loyalty. Most civil appointees were interested primarily in the fees they collected and the percentage that was turned back to them as pay. Settlers in remote areas often complained that civil officials not only exacted excessive fees but withheld a much higher portion of the receipts than was due them. Governor William Tryon of North Carolina asserted in 1767 that his colonial sheriffs were embezzling over half the funds they collected. Westerners further complained that a badly apportioned tax load put the heaviest burden on the poor. Scarcity of money in the region, coupled with such resentment, made the life of the tax collector difficult.

As early as August 1766 some of the settlers in Orange County agreed to meet "at some place where there is no liquor" to discuss their grievances. It was the conclusion of that assemblage that officeholders were responsible to the voters, a point of view that was not entirely shared by the appointed officials. In the spring of 1768 it was announced that sheriffs would collect taxes at specified locations and delinquents could expect to be fined. The challenge was met by the formation of a group of men calling themselves "Regulators," who pledged organized resistance to taxes that they regarded inequitable.

Colonel Edmund Fanning, of the Orange County militia, tried to ignore this informal group, but when they called on him and shot the roof of his house full of holes he appealed to the Governor for aid. Governor Tryon played a double game, telling the dissidents to submit a petition containing their grievances, while at the same time ordering Fanning to arrest two leading Regulators named Hermon Husband and William Butler. When the angry mob frightened the officers into giving up the two men, the Governor's secretary persuaded the group to ask Tryon for redress, and again he revealed his double-dealing by disavowing the secretary. However, the petitioners received assurances that there would be no more illegal fees and with this they were temporarily satisfied. Only when these promises were broken did the Regulators again defy the law; Tryon then resolved to use force.

Toward the end of September the Governor, with about 1500 men, appeared before Hillsboro where Husband and Butler, who had not yet cleared themselves in the eyes of the law, were about to be tried. After an inconclusive parley between the two forces the Regulators quietly returned to their homes. That both sides wanted peace was indicated by the result of the trials that followed: Husband was acquitted and Butler received a sentence of only six months. Fanning was tried, found guilty on five counts, and fined one penny on each.

The Regulators, far from satisfied, pressed for the election of their friends to the legislative assembly, only to see the Governor dissolve that excessively liberal body in November 1769. This was too much for the Regulators, who told themselves that every peaceful avenue had been explored in vain. When the superior court met at Hillsboro in the autumn of 1770 they presented it with one last petition, determined to use force if their demands were not answered. Judge Richard Henderson, who shortly would be involved in western land speculation, attempted to put off the petitioners. A mob scene took place in which Henderson was threatened, his law partner was driven into hiding, and Colonel Fanning was beaten. Henderson appeased the mob with promises, but his own duplicity was revealed when he fled, leaving Fanning to fend for himself. After threatening the colonel with death, the angry farmers ran him out of town and burned his house to the ground.

That autumn the assembly charged Hermon Husband with "false and seditious libel" and ordered that he be imprisoned. Only the rumor that the Regulators would march on his jail moved the Governor to release the prisoner, after which he gathered up another army, this time numbering around a thousand men, and once more headed for Hillsboro. About 2000 Regulators waited for him in the vicinity of the Alamance River where, on May 16, 1771, the two forces met. During a two-hour battle in which each side lost 9 killed, the rebels were defeated. Those who took Tryon's proffered oath of allegiance—some 6000 did—were pardoned, and the remainder fled westward beyond the pale of the Governor's law.

Those who moved on, about 1500 of them, had registered a strong protest against arbitrary government and had put their demands for reform into action. They offered no resistance to the home government and were in no way disloyal to the Crown; in fact, some of them later became Loyalists during the Revolution. In this instance, however, they fought for their traditional rights as freemen. Their resistance had nothing to do with the coming Revolution except that it nearly coincided in point of time. The difficulty, however, demonstrated that the colonists were prepared to use armed resistance in the defense of their rights, and from this the mother country might have drawn a lesson it appears to have overlooked.

THE WAY WEST

The blandishments of speculators in western lands, who sang the glories of their new-found agricultural paradise, the diminishing supply of first-rate farmsteads east of the Appalachians, and conditions such as those faced by the Regulators blended into a powerful westering urge among small farmers living along the Piedmont. After more than a century and a half of hesitancy the frontier farmer took his courage in hand and headed for the mountain passes. When he reached the western slope he had, in effect, passed the point of no return, for this big step, one that he had avoided for so many years, put him into a new ideological, economic, social, and political world.

The assault on the western lands was frontal and direct. There was no other way. The French had circled to the north, skirting the British settlements, had moved along the Great Lakes and down the Mississippi Valley. The Spanish made their approach to the West from the South, probing at Florida, the lower Mississippi, and what would one day be the American Southwest. For the British colonials there were several points at which the great Appalachian front might be pierced. In the North, the most desirable route followed the Hudson and Mohawk rivers, and then through central New York from Fort Stanwix beyond Oneida to Lake Erie, whence it was easy to follow the Great Lakes, then to ascend some river flowing into one of the lakes, and eventually to portage to the Ohio-Mississippi system. In general this is the present route of the New York Central Railroad, and an excellent one because of the absence of mountains. Unfortunately for the early traveler, the Iroquois Indians were a more effective barrier than mountains, and before 1800 their friendship was never sufficiently assured to permit safe traveling by the Hudson-Mohawk route.

Farther south there were two routes in Pennsylvania. The first of these, the Kittanning Path, ran along the Susquehanna and Juniata rivers to the mountains, and then crossed the Appalachians to Fort Pitt (Pittsburgh) on the Ohio River; today the Pennsylvania Railroad follows this route. In southern Pennsylvania was the Forbes Road, opened between Philadelphia and Fort Pitt in 1758; the modern Pennsylvania Turnpike follows most of this route.

Along the Potomac River lay another possibility—Braddock's Road, opened in 1755, and later to become the National, or Cumberland, Road. This route followed the Potomac as far as the town of Cumberland, and then cut overland to Fort Pitt. It should be added that when the National Road was built it left the old trail west of Cumberland and had its terminus at Wheeling.

Still farther south was the Cumberland Gap—a beautiful pass through the main range of mountains in the extreme southwestern corner of present Virginia. As a pass through the mountains it was excellent and much used in Revolutionary days. No important settlements arose at either end of the gap, owing largely to the absence of navigable rivers and to the existence of other mountains to the east and west, so that the importance of the Cumberland Gap route tended to decrease with time.

A final important route into the heart of the continent skirted the Appalachians to the south through Georgia. Here the mountains no longer offered a barrier to travel, but in earlier days other handicaps were just as potent. Georgia was still in the earliest stages of her development, and no considerable bodies of people were interested in going farther west. More important, powerful Indian tribes, including the Creeks, lay to the west and they barred travel just as effectively as did the Iroquois in New York.

Most of these routes at one time had been game trails, and all of them were known and used by the Indians. Before the French and Indian War the trails were exceedingly primitive, being only unblazed footpaths. Whenever possible they followed the uplands to avoid the spring floods. A few logs enabled the traveler to pass the worst places. Rivers were crossed on sand bars, which shifted from time to time, so that a crossing could only be made after some experimentation. During the French and Indian War Braddock's Road and the Forbes Road were opened for wagons, but this merely meant that enough trees were felled and brush removed to allow the passage of crude carts. Time and the passage of thousands of families westward would wear away nature's impediments and afford well-marked and widened roadways that, despite considerable improvement, continued for years to be called trails. That they went west fascinated more adventurous Americans.

FIRST SETTLEMENTS

The end of the French and Indian War, and the opening of western lands by the Treaty of Fort Stanwix (1768), attracted settlers to the Fort Pitt region. Aware that at least two passable roads led to the headwaters of the Ohio River and encouraged by the Iroquois land cession, settlers moved west in considerable numbers during the 1769 travel season. They were ordinary farm folk, searching out new homes in a country familiar principally to fur traders and explorers in previous years. It is estimated that by 1770 some 5000 of them had made the mountain crossing to become "men of western waters," as they called themselves. Within the next few years the figure mounted to around 30,000.

Early Pittsburgh was the first permanent British settlement west of the Allegheny front in the present United States, and it immediately assumed a vital importance in business between East and West. At the head of the Ohio River, it was on the natural route of travel for all men and materials moving across the mountains, and it more than earned the appellation "gateway of the West." In its early years it was a commercial rather than a manufacturing center, although it did some manufacturing. Until 1790 all the iron used in Pittsburgh was hauled over the mountains from the East.

The Virginians, many of whom migrated to the headwaters of the Ohio, had an alternate route across the mountains. From the western edge of Virginia or North Carolina, passage into eastern Tennessee by the Cumberland Gap was relatively easy and the headwaters of streams that fed into the Tennessee River were close. One of these, the Watauga, was a branch of the Holston, itself a principal tributary of the Tennessee River. Daniel Boone first saw the attractive Watauga country in 1769 and before long a permanent settlement was located in the area. James Robertson, who came in 1770, also liked the place and returned east to get his family and a group of settlers. He was back in 1771 with sixteen families, some of whom were disgusted Regulators who had lost their bid at the recent Battle at Alamance. They thought they were in Virginia and safe from the North Carolina authorities. Close behind them came Jacob Brown, who marked off a little settlement along the Nolichucky, a branch of the Holston. Another newcomer was Anthony Bledsoe, a surveyor who came up with information that disheartened the migrating Regulators: the place was within the charter limits of North Carolina, not Virginia.

The result of the survey presented a number of disturbing problems. The settlers who had moved in from North Carolina were in no mood to yield to its authority; the settlement was geographically out of touch with both the Virginia and North Carolina seats of government; there was doubt that the little communities were within the area ceded by the Cherokee. In a sense the colonists were in a position similar to that in which the passengers on the Mayflower had found themselves more than a century and a half earlier. The solution to the problem was the same: the formation of a temporary government of their own. In 1772 Robertson, a dour, taciturn Scot, put his talents to work in the formation of the Watauga Association, an organization that included several of the nearby settlements. Here the frontiersmen studied the constitutions of similar groups. In search of a model that would satisfy their own administrative needs, the Association provided authority for making laws, negotiating with the Indians, registering deeds and wills, solemnizing marriages, and performing the other essential functions of government. It was particularly important as the first in a long series of transmontane efforts to set up a governing body when the regularly constituted authorities would not act. As would be true of later experiments, the Watauga Association was temporary, lasting about six years, after which the colony was incorporated into North Carolina as Washington County. So faithfully had the constitution makers followed precedent that no basic changes of law were necessary and, in fact, most of the old officers were retained.

KENTUCKY

The growth of the settlement at Watauga encouraged many people to look farther west and to covet the fertile plains of the Kentucky, the Tennessee, and the Cumberland. One of these visionaries was Judge Richard Henderson of North Carolina, who organized the Transylvania Company (not chartered) to buy land from the Indians and then sell it to white settlers—a procedure that was illegal under the terms of the Proclamation of 1763. In March 1775, he and eight others from North Carolina met the Indians at Sycamore Shoals, on the Watauga, and concluded a treaty with the Cherokee that assigned the promoters about half the modern state of Kentucky. For this they paid about £10,000 worth of goods.

The Transylvania Company at once opened this huge tract of land to purchase on easy terms, and sent Daniel Boone to mark off a trail from the eastern settlements through the mountains and down the Kentucky River to the Ohio. This route, as marked by the famed frontiersman, took the name Wilderness Road. It was the only practical passage through the mountains in that region and it was used extensively by early westbound settlers. In addition, Boone established a small fort (Boonesborough) on the Kentucky River, near the present city of Lexington. As soon as the trail was opened, many settlers began to pour into the Kentucky region, going not only to Boonesborough, but also to nearby places such as Harrod's Town, Boiling Springs, and St. Asaph's. Some of them held Virginia grants, since Virginia did not recognize Henderson's ownership. In consequence, Henderson received but little for his land and his settlement at Boonesborough was not very successful; his company store charged high prices and drove the settlers to other trading centers.

The Transylvania Company's political origins were similar to those of Watauga. Not only was the whole project in direct violation of the Proclamation of 1763, its membership was willing to proceed independently, hopeful that theirs would be accepted as the fourteenth colony. Consequently, elections were held in May 1775, and residents of four small settlements—Boonesborough, Harrod's Town, Floyd's Settlement, and Boiling

Springs—all cast their votes. Judge Henderson announced the existence of local sovereignty in his opening speech before the House of Delegates: "We have the right to make laws for the regulation of our conduct without giving offense to Great Britain or any of the American colonies." This fact established, the delegates proceeded with their endeavors, enacting legislation that established criminal and civil courts, provided for a militia, and—with an eye upon community morals—an "act to prevent profane swearing and Sabbath breaking."

Henderson's promotional schemes caused considerable turmoil in the East. Colonel William Preston warned his friend George Washington that the Transylvania project had its dangers, "for it is certain that a vast number of people are preparing to go out and settle on this Purchase; and if once they get fixed there, it will be next to impossible to remove them or reduce them to Obedience; as they are so far from the Seat of Government." Governor Josiah Martin, of North Carolina, called Henderson a "famous invader" and labeled his followers "an Infamous Company of Land Pyrates." Lord Dunmore, royal Governor of Virginia (who was deeply involved in land speculation himself) demanded that "one Richard Henderson and other disorderly persons, his associates" immediately relinquish their land claims, but "one Richard" ignored the warning. Dunmore, whose thinking appears to have suffered from a lack of logic, complained that Henderson's activities were in violation of the Proclamation of 1763, a document with which he had earlier professed to have only the haziest acquaintance.

With the view of circumventing objections by Virginia and North Carolina, Transylvania's founders approached the recently convened Continental Congress and requested admittance as the fourteenth colony. New England's John Adams quickly pointed out to his colleagues the fact that any solution to differences with the mother country would not be made easier by sanctioning a colony whose very existence violated the King's Proclamation of 1763. Thus, in the autumn of 1775, the colony continued its career as a political orphan and, after bickering between some of the residents and proprietor Henderson, the scheme fell through. In December 1776, the Virginia assembly made Kentucky one of that state's counties.

The failure of Henderson's Transylvania project marked the disappearance of the notion of government under a proprietorship on American soil. Although his promotional efforts were frowned upon by coastal authorities and doomed to failure in the West, the development publicized the existence of rich lands beyond the mountains and brought forth those restless, adventurous souls who would never have accepted the proprietor's authority for any length of time. Their presence beyond the mountains, irritating to future speculators who objected to squatters, was turned to good use before long. The American Revolution was at hand and these stubborn, hard-fighting, independent souls registered a strong objection to British plans for pushing back the frontier as one means of crushing the colonies.

READINGS

LAND SPECULATION. Kenneth P. Bailey, *The Ohio Company of Virginia and the Westward Movement, 1748–1792* (1939) presents a detailed account of one effort. W. S. Lester, *The Transylvania Colony* (1935) describes another effort. See also George E. Lewis, *The Indiana Company, 1763–1798* (1941). More general are A. M. Sakolski, *The Great American Land Bubble* (1932); Shaw Livermore, *Early American Land Companies* (1939); and Everett Dick, *The Dixie Frontier* (1948).

INDIVIDUALS AND THE WESTWARD MOVEMENT. Albert T. Volwiler, *George Croghan and the Westward Movement, 1742–1782* (1926) remains as one of the classic biographies of an early Westerner. An alternative is Nicholas B. Wainwright, *George Croghan: Wilderness Diplomat* (1959). Howard Peckham (ed.) *George Croghan's Journal of His Trip to Detroit in 1767* (1939) provides a firsthand account of an early western trip. Somewhat less satisfactory is Thomas A. Boyd, *Simon Girty, the White Savage* (1928). Development of the Pittsburgh area is seen through the eyes of an individual in Sewell E. Slick, *William Trent and the West* (1947). John Bakeless, *Daniel Boone* (1939) is well written; Carl S. Driver, *John Sevier: Pioneer of the Old Southwest* (1932) is somewhat early transmontane frontiersmen. Louis K. Koontz, *Robert Dinwiddie, His Career in American Colonial Government and Westward Expansion* pedantic; W. H. Masterson, *William Blount* (1954) treats another of the (1941) presents the viewpoint of a colonial governor.

THE WAY WEST. William A. Pusey, *The Wilderness Road* (1921) and Robert L. Kincaid, *The Wilderness Road* (1947) describe a famous westward route. Philip D. Jordan's *The National Road* (1948) provides information about the Cumberland and National roads. Older is C. A. Hanna, *The Wilderness Trail* (1911). Solon J. and Elizabeth H. Buck, *The Planting of Civilization in Western Pennsylvania* (1939) and John E. Wright and Doris S. Corbett, *Pioneer Life in Western Pennsylvania* (1940) adequately treat a segment of the "middle" frontier and a western gateway. Life in the trans-Appalachian West is well described in a number of works. See Temple Bodley, *Our First Great West* (1938); Louis Koontz, *The Virginia Frontier, 1754–1763* (1925); Thomas P. Abernethy, *From Frontier to Plantation in Tennessee* (1932); Charles H. Ambler, *West Virginia: The Mountain State* (1940); Thomas D. Clark, *A History of Kentucky* (1937); and John P. Brown, *Old Frontiers: The Story of the Cherokee Indians . . .* (1938). Also useful is John R. Alden, *The South in the Revolution, 1763–1789* (1957).

The Regulators are discussed in E. Douglas Branch, *Westward: The Romance of the American Frontier* (1930) and Richard M. Brown, *The South Carolina Regulators* (1963).

CHAPTER 4

THE REVOLUTIONARY WEST

T he outbreak of the American Revolution found a relatively small group of colonists nestled along the western slopes of the Appalachians, practically cut off from the eastern settlements, threatened from the west by British-sponsored Indians, unsure of their political status, and, in a sense, a forgotten people. The preoccupation of the new American government with the desperate military situation it faced made it unlikely that any substantial aid could be sent to more remote regions. The frontiersmen had a choice between falling back upon settled regions or making a stand in the new country; most of them chose the latter. The decision meant that for seven years they lived in constant apprehension of attack. Eastern burghers experienced a civilized kind of warfare with formal battles, the taking of prisoners, the occupation of cities, but for those along the fringes of settlement it was a savage conflict in which men, women, and children died at the hands of raiding Indians, a struggle in which no quarter was given and none was expected.

COLONIES AT TIME OF REVOLUTION

The American Revolution was a dramatic indication of the rapidly increasing gap between European and American conditions and points of view. Americans had been conditioned by a century and a half of contact with an untamed wilderness. They had begun to realize their own potentialities—that they could provide their own economic, social, and religious necessities for which they had depended upon Europe for so many years. The Revolution was an indication of a definite cleavage already in existence between the Old and the New World.

Self-confidence and youthful enthusiasm did not necessarily imply strength: when viewed realistically, the English colonies at the time of the

45

Revolution were far from being an awe-inspiring factor in the affairs of the world. Thirteen small colonies straggling along the coast from Maine to Georgia had a population of only some 2,600,000 persons. Virginia was the most populous, and after her followed, in order, Massachusetts, Pennsylvania, North Carolina, and Maryland. Philadelphia was the largest colonial city, her competitors being Boston, Newport, New York, and Charleston. Today none of them would be regarded as a large city. Every important city was either on the seaboard or on some large river that afforded good communication with the sea.

Outside the larger towns, population tended to concentrate along the rivers, so that produce could be shipped to market more easily. The inland limit of civilization was in general the Appalachians, but few people had gone even that far west. To the north and south, settlement became more sparse and finally gave way to the wilderness. In the North a small fraction of Maine was settled; central and northern New Hampshire and Vermount were just being opened; in New York adventurous German immigrants were pushing out along the Mohawk. In the South Georgia was still largely unpopulated.

Agriculture was the predominant pursuit. Everywhere there were small farms, but south of the Potomac were also large plantations using slave labor to grow tobacco, indigo, and rice. Slavery, however, seemed to be an uneconomic and declining institution, and many of the farseeing planters looked forward to the day when slavery would cease to exist. North of the Potomac small farms were almost universal, with the owner, his wife, and his children doing most of the work, with now and then a hired laborer to help with planting and harvesting.

Manufacturing remained largely in the home, since the mother country discouraged any competition with her own new and struggling industries. Here and there iron forges, hat factories, and other small enterprises gave a faint promise of future industrialization.

Shipping was an item of major interest to the northern colonies. The Yankee shipper was a well-known figure on the seas. His business was expanding rapidly, and he was soon to talk of Canton, Singapore, Oregon, the Sandwich Islands (Hawaii), and other far places of the world. South of New England the ports did most of their business in foreign bottoms. The plantation owner tended to deal directly with his European connections, eliminating American middlemen.

Intercolonial business by land was small and unimportant. The first good improved road was not built until after the Revolution. For the most part people depended on the rivers as their best means of communication, most of which flowed from west to east, with the result that trade between the colonies never assumed large proportions. So miserable were the roads that as late as 1803 John Quincy Adams needed twenty days to ride his horse to Washington from his home at Quincy.

The population of the seaboard area of the thirteen colonies was overwhelmingly English, although other racial stocks were represented. A landed Dutch aristocracy dominated the Hudson and Mohawk River valleys; a few Swedes were settled along the Delaware River; some French Huguenots were scattered at various places along the Atlantic Coast. In the main, however, the coast settlements were English in race and heritage.

REDSKINS AND REDCOATS

In 1775, the transmontane West was a very thinly populated area. Its largest town, Pittsburgh, was no more than a collection of some thirty log houses, and Wheeling could barely call itself a village. Scattered along the streams and rivers were widely separated homes whose connection with the western villages was very slight. A majority of the settlers had little interest in British imperial problems, except, of course, for such things as the Proclamation of 1763, which had touched them directly. Commercial restrictions that brought forth loud complaints from seaboard merchants provoked little talk among Westerners. In all probability they were quietly amused at outcries put forth by Easterners who objected to what they called "taxation without representation." The back-country people had for years submitted to a political imbalance in colonial legislative houses, and complaints about inequitable taxation were nothing new to them. The main thing the revolutionary movement meant to these people along the outskirts of colonial settlement was that the Indians would play a prominent part in the coming hostilities and would be allied with the British, who could pay more for their friendship. Frontiersmen also knew that their traditional independence of eastern colonials would be costly and that they could expect little help from that source.

When the American colonists announced their decision to fight, at Lexington and Concord, reverberations were heard in more remote parts of the land. Among other things, the British now had to reverse their old Indian policy and convince the natives that they should fight the colonists. Sir William Johnson had spent a good many patient years weaning away from the French the northern tribes and persuading them to live at peace with the English frontiersmen. John Stuart, working among the southern Indians, had performed a similar task. Now these men, and their associates, had to convince the Indians that they should do the opposite, a shift in policy many of the unsophisticated savages had difficulty in understanding. The Creeks, for example, who had been friendly to the settlers, were mystified by this sudden shift in the attitude of the British administrators.

As word spread across the frontier the tribes made their decisions.

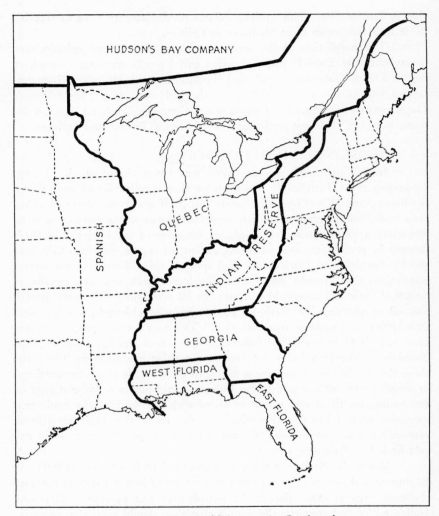

North America in 1774 after the Quebec Act

In 1776, when the Cherokee informed Stuart that they would stay with the British, that agent at once warned such settlements as Watauga of the consequences they invited by deserting the mother country. The response was not long in coming: the settlers strengthened their fortifications and asked Virginia for help. In June and July the blows began to fall: raiding parties struck at scattered settlements, including Watauga, where James Robertson and John Sevier headed a small corps of riflemen that drove off the invaders. Stuart, acting under orders from Lord George Germain, had sent his Indian allies against the colonials at a time when a frontal attack was to be made on Charleston. Not only did the sea invasion fail, when Admiral Peter Parker's forces were repulsed, but so did the diversionary attacks staged by the Indians. The result was so favorable to the colonials that both South Carolina and Georgia were in a position to lend help to the western settlers.

General Charles Lee, in command of American forces at Charleston, invited Virginians to join in an expedition against the Indians. Moved by encouragement from the Continental Congress, and by an enthusiastic response from Thomas Jefferson (who wanted to drive the Indians beyond the Mississippi River), a force of some 2000 colonials was raised in the latter part of 1776. The force, under the command of Colonel William Christian, marched to the Holston River, scattered the Cherokee, and burned the Indian villages and the harvested crops. Not a soldier was lost during the operation. Simultaneously another force, from North Carolina, attacked some of the Cherokee villages, and after suffering a few losses burned more dwellings and crops. The campaign was costly to the Indians, not only in the seriousness of the attacks, but because in 1777 they were obliged to cede additional lands to Georgia, South Carolina, North Carolina, and Virginia. The Cherokee holdings were generally rolled back, some Indians withdrawing as much as a hundred miles.

THE REVOLUTION IN THE NORTHWEST

While the Americans punished the Indians on the southern frontier, the British went ahead with their plans to enlist the natives in the Northwest. This theater of war was one of vast distances and widely separated objects of attack. Except for a few settlements around Pittsburgh, there were few English colonists in the region. From the viewpoint of overall strategy there seemed to be little profit in sending British troops, so hard to provide, across hundreds of barren miles to attack a few scattered white settlements. On the other hand, it was desirable to harass the western fringe of the colonies to force the withdrawal of some colonial troops from the more important operations in the East, or at least to prevent the Westerners from joining the eastern forces.

An effective weapon for the attack on the outlying settlements was available for immediate use—the Indians. Already resenting white encroachments, they needed little urging from the British sponsors to harry the white squatters. Major Henry Hamilton, Lieutenant Governor of New France, directed operations from his headquarters at Detroit. In long councils with the natives, in which lavish gifts were forthcoming, the "Hair Buyer" urged his allies to strike at any and all outlying settlements. He emphasized the psychological value of terror tactics to frighten off the settlers. One British official objected to the slaughter of innocent families by warriors who were reluctant to face armed opponents, but Hamilton persisted, arguing that only these methods would succeed among the tough-minded American frontiersmen. In the warfare that ensued, the Westerners struck back with equal viciousness, scalping and torturing in the Indian fashion, until the war took on an aspect of barbarity rarely witnessed in the New World.

Although the American defense against these raids was bitterly executed, in general it was not very well organized. The states most subject to attack, particularly Pennsylvania, Virginia, North Carolina, and Georgia, made some provision for their own defense, but were usually glad to let the settlers themselves or the central government assume the main burden. The settlers were few and poor, so that providing men and materials for extensive operations proved an almost insurmountable task. The Continental Congress was more than busy in the East and could be persuaded to furnish troops and supplies only when the danger was extremely pressing.

By a law of 1775 three Indian departments were created by the Congress. Commissioners from each of them undertook to win over the Indians with gifts and formal treaties but they were not very successful. An example of the difficulties faced by these men is the murder of a friendly chief named Cornstalk and three of his warriors by some Pennsylvania frontiersmen in the autumn of 1777. The chief's Shawnee followers immediately took to the warpath and engaged in a number of bloody raids on settlements in Kentucky and western Virginia.

The "year of the three sevens," as it has been called, is remembered as the bloodiest and gloomiest of the war in the West. Hostile Indians, particularly the Shawnee and other Ohio tribes, drove back or killed settlers, and even attacked such fortified communities as Boonesborough. The situation was so obviously serious that Congress sent Brigadier General Edward Hand to strengthen Fort Pitt lest this key position fall to the British and Indians. The reinforcements were so weak and their supply problems so great that the Indians were only emboldened by the move. During the following year the fact that Washington sent some of his badly needed troops under General Lachlan McIntosh from Valley Forge, indicates something of the vital urgency of the danger. Both Hand and McIntosh led expeditions against the Indians but neither accomplished more than irritating the tribes.

THE AGGRESSIVE GEORGE ROGERS CLARK

Out of this desperate situation came one of the outstanding exploits of the war—the expedition of George Rogers Clark to the Illinois country. Clark, the son of a Virginia planter, was a surveyor. Moving west in 1772, at the age of twenty, he explored the area, fought the Indians, and helped to organize the militia defense of the Kentucky settlements at the outbreak of the Revolution. In 1776, his dramatic trip to Virginia for powder remains a noteworthy exploit not only for the hardships he endured but also for the hardheaded manner in which he negotiated with Governor Patrick Henry and the Virginia legislators.

In contrast to the majority of Westerners, who thought only in terms of protecting themselves from Indian attacks, George Rogers Clark was bold and enterprising. It was his conviction that the only effective way to protect the scattered settlements from Indian raids was to undertake offensive operations. He realized that security could be obtained only by convincing the Indians of white superiority, and he felt that the English posts, particularly the one at Detroit, should be captured if peace were to come to the frontier. Conditions were at their worst in Kentucky in 1777 —even Boonesborough was attacked twice—but Clark sent his friends Benjamin Linn and Samuel Moore out to investigate British western military strength in the Illinois country. In two months they returned with word that the outposts were virtually unprotected, particularly Kaskaskia, near the junction of the Kaskaskia and Mississippi rivers.

Obviously the West itself could not furnish the men, supplies, and munitions necessary for an extensive expedition into enemy country; hence, late in 1777, Clark again made the long trip back to Virginia to request assistance. Immediately upon his arrival he called upon Governor Patrick Henry and outlined his ambitious plans for the conquest of the Northwest. Governor Henry was reluctant, as well he might be, in view of the situation in the East; on the other hand, such a conquest, if successful, would be of advantage in the prosecution of the war in the East, would greatly enhance Virginia's prestige, and might reinforce her claims to western lands. Henry consulted some of his close friends, including Thomas Jefferson, and after some hesitancy they decided to give Clark as much support as was possible at the moment.

Clark was given two sets of orders. The first, which contained the ostensible reason for his activities, authorized him to raise seven companies (350 men) for the defense of Kentucky, and to purchase arms, ammunition, and supplies on the credit of the state of Virginia. To pay the troops and to keep them loyal he was advanced £1200 in depreciated Virginia paper money and given glowing promises of gifts of land in the West. The second set of orders, which was to remain secret, empowered Clark to undertake offensive operations and to capture "Kaskasky."

Armed with these instructions, Clark made his way to Pittsburgh, the logical gathering place for any expedition planning to descend the Ohio River, where he gathered men and supplies for the campaign. Finding it impossible to recruit the desired 350 men, he set off with only 175. At a time when there were heavy demands upon manpower it was difficult for a soldier, under orders from Virginia, with plans to defend Kentucky, to generate much enthusiasm among Pennsylvanians. The group was hetero- geneous; the men dressed as they pleased, carried a wide assortment of arms, and were unwilling to obey any command they thought unreasonable. Some were frankly homeseekers accompanied by their families in order to take up desirable land at the first favorable opportunity.

The first part of Clark's plan was to descend the Ohio as far as the mouth of the Kentucky and there disembark and drill his men. The topog- raphy of the land led him to change his mind and to camp instead at the falls of the Ohio. Here some of the homeseekers built houses and began farming, thus founding the first white settlement at present-day Louis- ville. Here also Clark divulged his larger plans to his followers. At first there was much grumbling and dissent, but eventually objections were silenced and the expedition was ready to begin its real work.

KASKASKIA AND VINCENNES

On June 24, 1778, the little army shot the rapids at Louisville and started to float down the Ohio River. Nine miles below the mouth of the Tennessee the party left its boats and started overland, partly because of the possibility of being discovered if it continued by water, and partly be- cause of the slow and tedious work involved in working back upstream, once the Mississippi was reached.

After a rigorous march the group arrived at Kaskaskia on July 4, 1778. Sufficient speed and secrecy had been maintained so that the invasion was a complete surprise; Clark and his men met no resistance on entering the town. The residents, largely French, were so thoroughly imbued with the notion that all Americans were barbarians that they prostrated them- selves on the ground, convinced that the end was near. Clark, who was anxious to have their friendship, explained his mission and told his listeners about the Franco-American alliance. Their emotions changed instantly from terror to unrestrained joy and the conquered at once prepared a party for the Americans, decking the streets with flowers and swearing oaths of loyalty to the United States as fast as their sentiments could be recorded.

As Clark established himself at Kaskaskia, Captain Joseph Bowman took over nearby smaller settlements. Cahokia fell without a murmur. Bowman simply rode up to the commanding officer's house and demanded the town's surrender, a request that the surprised officer granted at once. Clark, meanwhile, spread the idea of American military strength in the West by circulating a rumor that the force in Illinois was only a small part of a large army, which even then was encamped at the falls of the Ohio.

Meanwhile, Governor Hamilton at Detroit had begun to hear disturbing reports about American activity in the West. What had been a leisurely plan to attack Pittsburgh was now abandoned in favor of one that would turn back the invading Clark. His new plans were to establish himself at Vincennes, from which point he could recapture the Illinois settlements. After hurried preparations he left Detroit on October 7, 1778, with a force composed of 36 regulars, 45 local volunteers, 79 local militia, and 60 Indians. His army was augmented on the way, mostly by Indians, so that by the time he arrived at Vincennes he had over 500 men. The route was an old familiar Indian pathway—down the St. Clair River, across a part of Lake Erie, up the Maumee, a portage to the Wabash, and then down the Wabash to Vincennes. Here he established himself for the winter, erecting fortifications, drilling his men, planning to move in the spring when the weather permitted. It seemed both to him and to his staff that there was no danger of an attack from Clark at a time when cold weather and flooded rivers made the drainage basin of the Wabash a veritable swamp.

Clark was placed in an exceedingly awkward position by Hamilton's expedition. He was several hundred miles from home and could hope for no reinforcements. His men were on short-term enlistments that would soon expire. The Indians were not friendly and the French had but little interest in the success of their new master. If he stayed at Kaskaskia until spring it seemed evident that Hamilton, aided by the Indians, could defeat him and would then have no difficulty in conquering Kentucky at his leisure. Another than Clark might well have thought the obstacles insuperable, but here was a man whom difficulties did not daunt, and whose idea of fighting was to go, not halfway to meet the enemy, but all the way, and then engage him on his own ground. And so Clark again decided to move forward; the march on Vincennes was to begin at once.

Before the expedition left Kaskaskia, a vessel, the *Willing,* was sent ahead to carry supplies and ammunition for use in the capture of Vincennes. The main body of 170 men was re-enlisted and left Kaskaskia on February 5, 1779, for the march across the wilderness. The project was an exhibition of sheer, reckless courage, rare even on the frontier. In reality it was Clark himself who furnished the greater share of the perseverance and valor that kept the party moving. He spent most of his time trying to keep the men in good spirits by joking, laughing, telling stories, aiding the footsore, and encouraging everyone. At the same time he maintained a wary vigilance for unfriendly Indians, and used all his woodcraft to keep on the right path. In spite of his many duties, he never failed to carry his share of the supplies and to do his part in the necessary manual labor.

Much of the country that Clark and his party traversed was flooded, and for days at a time everyone was soaking wet. For hours they would wade through swamps and creeks, with the water at times to their shoulders, so that the shorter drummer boy had to float on his drum. Food was scarce and many times a tightening of belts took the place of a meal. When fires were impossible because of the wetness of the wood, everyone had to sleep in his wet clothes. As they neared Vincennes conditions became worse. The country was practically one large lake, and both fires and shooting were out of the question because of the danger of making their presence known. All this, too, in the depths of winter, when cold weather intensified all of the other discomforts.

To add the final touch of annoyance and trouble, the *Willing* was not waiting for Clark when he arrived at the Wabash on February 18. Little wonder that the men became discouraged after their two weeks of hardship, cold, and hunger, and that the expedition seemed doomed to failure within the sight of its goal. But Clark's indomitable purpose carried him on. After a wait of two days without food, canoes were finally constructed to ferry the men across the stream. Then the forward movement was resumed. The water was often deep, there was no food, and the rear guard had to be given orders to shoot all deserters. The greatest trial of all was the passage of the Horse-Shoe Plain, then a shallow lake four miles wide. Canoes were used to rescue men whose strength gave out, and to help the shorter men through the deepest places. Eventually all sighed in relief when Vincennes was sighted.

The approach to Vincennes raised new problems. It seemed somewhat doubtful if a small, wet, hungry, poorly armed band of Americans could capture a fortified post garrisoned by upward of 600 fighting men. Again Clark proved himself equal to the emergency. His first effort was to impress the French villagers to keep them neutral. A letter was sent to them offering peace and good treatment if they refrained from participating in the hostilities, but promising severe treatment otherwise. Then Clark marched and countermarched his men as fast as possible to give an impression of a large force. The result was that the French remained neutral.

Upon gaining entrance to the town the Americans at once threatened the fort within it. Clark's ammunition was insufficient for a protracted siege, but, as luck would have it, Hamilton was so impressed by the supposed size of the attacking force that he immediately asked for a truce. Clark audaciously refused the request and insisted upon unconditional surrender. On February 25, 1779, the Americans took complete possession of Vincennes, agreeing to some conditions. The French volunteers in Hamilton's army were permitted to return to Detroit, but Hamilton and some of his officers were sent to Virginia for imprisonment.

Clark's capture of Vincennes was not without its bloody side. Even as he and Hamilton negotiated the terms of surrender, a Frenchman hired by the British marched into town with his Indian followers and unaware of recent developments. Having just returned from raiding the frontier they brought with them two prisoners and a number of fresh scalps. Their hopes for a hearty welcome vanished when it was revealed that the Americans now commanded Vincennes. To teach a lesson to the neighborhood Indians, and to any of the French onlookers whose new-found American loyalties might waver, Clark lined up the Indians of the raiding party and had them tomahawked in full view of the garrison.

The American soldiers were well paid for their recent privations. The goods that Hamilton had so recently brought down from Detroit proved to be a rich haul and even when divided yielded a high share per man. Even better, another consignment of goods came in a few days after the fall of Vincennes, word of the event not yet having reached Detroit. Forty more prisoners were taken along with seven boatloads of goods valued at about $50,000.

With the capture of Vincennes, Clark was apparently in a secure position. The Northwest had been subdued, and Detroit, the center of British influence, lay open to easy conquest. And yet the way was not as clear as it seemed. Clark's men had no stomach for further hardships, and as fast as their enlistments were completed they went home. Despite the small fortunes in booty that the men had acquired, war supplies and ammunition were insufficient for a major campaign. Clark had no option but to settle down at Vincennes with as good grace as he could muster, and wait until spring brought him new men and supplies. When the expected reinforcements did not appear Clark made a trip to Kaskaskia to seek help. By July some 350 men had gathered at Vincennes, but the lack of stores and provisions continued to plague the Americans, making the proposed attack on Detroit too hazardous to risk. Eventually all plans for offensive operations were given up for the year, and Clark moved his headquarters to the falls of the Ohio.

The whole western campaign was characterized by audacity on the part of the Americans, who relied on the element of surprise, and administrative ineptitude on the part of the British, who supplied their outposts with forces and supplies that barely missed being adequate. There were no major battles, and no territory of immediate consequence changed hands. It is impossible to measure the morale value or the extent to which the expedition warded off Indian and British pressures on the northwestern frontier. Another imponderable is the weight the American campaign might have lent to territorial considerations at the peace table in 1783. It can be said, however, that Clark saw an opportunity to strike at a weakly defended region, and did so, with courage and perseverance that must have thrilled a war-weary American public east of the Appalachians.

KING'S MOUNTAIN

By 1780 the British evolved plans of their own for the reconquest of the West. During that year both Charleston and Augusta fell, adding to a list of British-held southern cities that already included Savannah. With the view of making a complete conquest of the southern colonies, London strategists now hoped to capitalize on what they believed to be a western loyalty to the Crown. Since the back-country Scots, in particular, had shown little cooperation with the revolutionary movement, it was mistakenly supposed that they would welcome the Redcoats. Major Patrick Ferguson, known as the best shot in the British army and a man highly regarded by his fellow Scots, was given the new western assignment.

As word spread along the mountain range the Americans began to gather in preparation for the next move. Colonel William Campbell, a Virginia Westerner, joined with the followers of John Sevier, Isaac Shelby, Benjamin Cleveland, and other local leaders to gather an army of frontiersmen who fought as informally as they lived. By common consent, Campbell took command of the group of some 1500 volunteers and marched against Ferguson, who had around 1100 men. Ferguson, with the inferior force, picked his way along the eastern base of the mountains in search of a site that would offer both a satisfactory defensive terrain and one within reach of reinforcements by Lord Cornwallis. He decided upon a wooded area on the southern edge of King's Mountain, just south of the boundary separating North Carolina from South Carolina.

On October 7, in a driving rain, approximately a thousand horsemen from the American group reached the site that Ferguson had chosen to do battle. As the forces readied themselves for the ensuing engagement the sun came out, creating a steamy atmosphere that shrouded the ground and provided a cover for the attackers. In a battle that lasted less than an hour the Americans gave way to bayonet attacks only to spring back, in frontier fighting style, sniping from behind wooded cover, and won their fight. As British men and officers fell, one of Ferguson's subordinates urged him to surrender. "To those damned banditti? Never!" was the resolute answer. Leading his men in one last charge, the leader went down, riddled with bullets. White flags now emerged but the confused fighting could not be halted at once and a great many more casualties occurred.

The surrender lacked the usual formalities of organized warfare. Ferguson's body was stripped of its uniform and thrown into a ditch while the victors divided up his personal belongings. Although a number of the wounded British troops were left to die on the field of battle, the remainder were marched off for further punishment. By the light of pine-knot torches there commenced the systematic program of hanging 38 prisoners summarily adjudged guilty of recent atrocities. After 9 of them were executed the Westerners decided to call off the proceedings and 29 were granted reprieves. In the fray the British had lost 225 killed, the Americans 28; the rest of the Loyalist force, including a large number of wounded, became prisoners of war.

King's Mountain did not mean that the war was over but it had several lessons for the Americans. In a battle where no Indians were involved on either side, Westerners met a British armed force and defeated it completely. The back country, lacking any formal military organization, had gathered men for its own defense and had demonstrated a regional unity that the coastal region lacked. Coupled with Clark's successful campaign in the Northwest, this southern success was enormously heartening not only to Westerners but to the rest of the young nation. It was, as General Washington put it, "proof of the spirit and resources of the country." As is true of Clark's expedition, there has been some tendency to exaggerate the importance of King's Mountain, but most authorities agree that its contributions, somwhat difficult to assess, were directly related to the general movement that now began against Cornwallis and ended with his defeat at Yorktown.

LAST YEARS OF THE REVOLUTION

Individual American victories in the West did not mean the end of British pressure in that region. Sharply stung by their reverses, the King's troopers resolved to renew their attacks upon the Northwest and to drive out the intruder Clark. Plans were also made for attacks on New Orleans and the lower Mississippi Valley now that Spain had elected to join France in its American alliance. So thorough were preparations that General Frederick Haldimand, Governor General of Canada, registered an objection. When the officials at Detroit handed out Indian gifts amounting to more than £84,000 he called the sum "amazing." He was answered with the argument that the pressure of American settlers upon the West was great and that only terror tactics would repel that kind of invasion. It was a simple economic fact that the scalps brought in cost money, and the crop was large. As the Delaware and Shawnee employees of the British continued their work among the American settlers there were loud outcries from the frontier for assistance. Clark, to whom appeals were made, had only a small force and did not want to disperse it to protect scattered settlements. He feared that he might end by giving up the entire Mississippi Valley to the enemy.

The latest British plan called for General Patrick Sinclair to start from Michilimackinac, to capture the Illinois towns of Kaskaskia and Cahokia, and then to take St. Louis. Three smaller forces were to keep

Clark engaged and to punish the Indians: the first was to advance from Detroit toward Vincennes, the second was to watch the plains between the Wabash and the Mississippi, and the third was to move down the Illinois River and chastise the Sauk and Fox Indians. All these plans eventually failed. The British commander in the South never felt he had a sufficient force to move north, and finally was forced to surrender Pensacola to Bernardo de Gálvez, the Spanish commander. The Illinois River expedition burned a few Indian towns and then returned. The Detroit expedition heard rumors of a superior American force and so retreated, leaving Clark free to go westward and defeat Sinclair near St. Louis. In 1781 Spain undertook a retaliatory expedition against England, and succeeded in advancing as far as the present Niles, Michigan.

After the defeat of Sinclair there again seemed to be an excellent opportunity for the conquest of Detroit, and so Clark hurried to Virginia to obtain support for his plans. He found little difficulty in getting encouragement, but unfortunately such aid was almost entirely verbal, and words would not pay troops or feed hungry men. Clark organized a new expedition at Pittsburgh, but when the commander of one division of the little force was defeated overwhelmingly by Indians under Joseph Brant, the entire plan had to be abandoned.

Fortunately for the American cause British campaigns in the West were never particularly successful. During 1781 and 1782 the West hung in the balance: neither side was prepared to put a military force of any size into the area, rationalizing that the outcome in the eastern theater of war would probably govern the fate of the West anyway. The frontier war continued as a fluid campaign in which the Indians played a prominent part. In June 1782, an expedition under Colonel William Crawford fought a sharp engagement at Sandusky in which the colonel and some of his men were made captive. Crawford was burned at the stake. About the same time a body of 300 militiamen captured a group of 90 friendly Delaware Indians who made no effort to escape, and were methodically executed— men, women, and children. It was a vicious, merciless kind of warfare where the torture of prisoners was the general rule and simple death the exception. George Rogers Clark, goaded by constant appeals for help, struck into the Ohio country several times in an effort to relieve the pressure on Kentucky, but as long as the British were paying their Indian allies there could be no cessation of constant isolated attacks upon the frontier. By the end of the war it had become a western way of life.

TREATY OF PEACE

At the conclusion of active fighting the statesmen of the East had the task of confirming the conquests that Clark had made in the West. The commissioners were instructed to make peace only with the concurrence of

The West near the End of the Revolution

our principal ally, France, but they soon discovered that this procedure contained an almost fatal error. France was not primarily interested in the United States; instead, she supported Spain, and Spain was opposed to American expansion. As Vergennes, the French Foreign Minister, admitted: "We have no interest whatever to see America play the part of a power." France and Spain agreed on a plan: Spain would take the Floridas, the Indians would be guaranteed the country between the Appalachians and the Mississippi south of the Ohio under the joint protection of Spain and the United States, and Britain would retain the country north of the Ohio or—better—divide it with the United States.

When the American commissioners heard of these plans of France and Spain they cast their instructions to the winds and independently formulated a treaty with Great Britain. They were favored in this procedure by the British attitude, which preferred American to Spanish expansion. The provisions of the Treaty of Paris as they related to the West were as favorable as the United States had any reason to expect. The entire region south of the Great Lakes went to the United States. The northwestern boundary was to run from Lake Superior to the Lake of the Woods and then directly west to the Mississippi (actually such a line was impossible to run, because a line directly west from the Lake of the Woods would not touch the Mississippi). From this point the boundary was to follow the Mississippi south to 31° north latitude and then along the 31st parallel and the present northern boundary of Florida to the Atlantic coast. A secret agreement provided that if Britain retained West Florida its northern boundary would be the parallel of the mouth of the Yazoo River (32° 28'). These terms were eminently satisfactory to the United States except for the slowness with which Great Britain evacuated the Great Lakes posts that were within the limits of the United States.

But what happened to George Rogers Clark, the chief actor of the drama, and the one man to whom the conquest of the Northwest was due? His principal reward was the gift of some 6000 acres of land in the wilderness of southern Indiana. In addition to the land, he received a letter of thanks from the Governor of Virginia, and an ornamental sword. These gifts of a grateful commonwealth had been won by Clark at the cost of the best years of his life, and the undermining of his health by the privations he had experienced. Both he and his friends were weighted with debts contracted during the Revolution, when they had dug into their own pockets to make up the gap between the appropriations of Virginia and the cost of carrying on the war.

When Virginia removed Clark from his command in 1783 the sad spectacle of a hero without a job led Jefferson to make the suggestion that Congress commission the conqueror to explore the Far West. Congress failed to act (it was Clark's younger brother William who would explore the West), but a renewal of Indian warfare again called the campaigner into the field during the middle 1780s. After his return from fighting the red man, he was drawn into intrigues with the government of Spain, during which he received some funds from the Spanish commander at New Orleans (1787). A little later he was involved in an effort to free Louisiana from Spanish control, but the expedition never materialized. The remainder of his life was a losing struggle to develop his Indiana land, and he died in 1818, poor and discouraged.

The close of the Revolution found an ever-increasing number of settlers pouring into the West, and with the larger population the problem of government immediately became more difficult. The simple local government that had sufficed in an earlier day would not meet the needs of a larger and more intricate social group. Even the county governments established by Virginia and North Carolina did little to alleviate the confusion. Such governments were far from their seaboard sources of power and they lacked authority to solve the very definite and pressing needs of the West.

Peace and order had to be produced from the chaotic conditions created by recent political changes. Marriages, deeds, and wills had to be made legal and made uniform. Land titles had to be more easily obtainable and more exact, for land had been sold in the East upon the vaguest kind of identification, and consequently many of the claims overlapped. Some provision had to be made for the families that came west without land claims. Squabbles among land companies, deferred only by the war, needed solution.

Furthermore, the Indian problem that once perplexed British statesmen now was handed to a new and inexperienced American government whose leaders had no ready answers. For the want of a better solution, Patrick Henry suggested an amalgamation of the two races and recommended a cash bounty for half-breed children. Defense against the Indians remained a problem, for they continued to attack outlying groups and individuals from time to time. The joint action of all the settlers in the region menaced was not a good substitute for effective action by an active government. In warfare against the Indians the best form of defense was always offense, and unorganized settlers found sustained offensive operations difficult. Another menace that required unified action was the possibility of a Spanish advance up the Mississippi Valley. These and many other problems confronted the young and untried government that was soon to feel considerable pressure from a boisterous, growing West.

READINGS

NORTHWEST. For regional and state studies describing the West in the Revolutionary period see Charles H. Ambler, *A History of West Virginia* (1933) and his *West Virginia: The Mountain State* (1940); Beverley W. Bond, Jr., *The Foundations of Ohio* (1941) and *The Civilization of the Old Northwest* (1934); or the brief and factual E. H. Roseboom and F. P. Weisenburger, *A History of Ohio* (1953); Theodore C. Pease, *The Story of Illinois* (rev. ed., 1949); Solon J. and Elizabeth H.

Buck, *The Planting of Civilization in Western Pennsylvania* (1939);
John E. Wright and Doris S. Corbett, *Pioneer Life in Western Pennsyl-
vania* (1940); and Logan Esarey, *A History of Indiana* (2 vols., 1918)
(Vol. I: *From Its Exploration to 1850*). Walter Havighurst, *Land of
Promise* (1946) reads easily. One of the best regional studies is Louise P.
Kellogg, *The British Regime in Wisconsin and the Northwest* (1935).

WESTERN WARFARE. Natalie M. Belting, *Kaskaskia under the
French Regime* (1940) gives a scholarly account of a pivotal point in
Clark's strategy. See also Milo M. Quaife (ed.), *The Capture of Old
Vincennes* (1927) and J. F. McDermott and others (eds.), *Old Cahokia*
(1949). Leland D. Baldwin, *Pittsburgh: The Story of a City* (1937)
contains some pertinent chapters (8 and 9). Randolph C. Downes, *Council
Fires on the Upper Ohio* (1940); see particularly Chapters 8–11 in this
fine work.

PERSONALITIES. Clark's story may be found in Temple Bodley,
George Rogers Clark (1926); John E. Bakeless, *Background to Glory:
The Life of George Rogers Clark* (1957); James A. James, *The Life of
George Rogers Clark* (1928); Theodore C. and Marguerite J. Pease,
George Rogers Clark and the Revolution in Illinois, 1763–1787 (1929);
or F. Palmer, *Clark of the Ohio* (1929). John A. Caruso, *The Great
Lakes Frontier* (1961) also treats Clark. John D. Barnhart, *Henry
Hamilton and George Rogers Clark in the American Revolution* (1950)
includes Hamilton's journal. See also James A. James, *Oliver Pollock*
(1937), a description of a western merchant in the Revolution.

CHAPTER 5

THE WEST
ACQUIRES PATRIOTISM

W esterners of the late eighteenth century did not possess the kind
of patriotism that within a few years led Stephen Decatur to
vow allegiance to "my country right or wrong." They were
risking their lives to advance their personal fortunes and not to promote the
power of a young and relatively unknown central government. Government
to them was meant to serve the interests of the individual, and not to be
a supreme end in itself.

As Westerners considered their situation they found little about
which to be grateful to any eastern government. Problems were numerous
and difficult, while seaboard aid was small or nonexistent. Land titles were
chaotic, the Indians were dangerous, transportation was practically impossible; not only were the refinements of life not provided, but even the
necessities were frequently missing. The eastern states that claimed control
did little more than create county organizations from time to time. The
federal government under the Articles of Confederation was too weak to
be effective. Theoretically it controlled the Indians, but actually such
control was negligible. Land disposition was completely unsatisfactory, as
the states were dilatory in transferring their claims to Congress. The only
effective action of the central government was in providing government, and
even this was long delayed. Little wonder the West felt it must assume
responsibility for its own improvement.

IMPORTANCE OF SPAIN

The West could survive and prosper only if it succeeded economically, and economic progress depended on the Ohio–Mississippi River
system. Since connections between the West and the Atlantic seaboard were

tenuous, with travel slow and expensive, the main western trade outlet was the Mississippi, on which one could float in relative comfort to New Orleans, where he could transship his raw materials to foreign markets. In consequence, the control of the Mississippi, and particularly of its mouth, was vital to the West, and at times seemed more important than cultural and governmental connections with the East.

The end of the Revolution found Spain in control not only of the vital mouth of the Mississippi, but also of the entire border area to the south and west—East Florida, which was present Florida extending as far west as St. Marks on the Gulf; West Florida, roughly from St. Marks to Baton Rouge on the Mississippi, but with the northern boundary in dispute; Louisiana, including not only the present state of that name, but also a vast domain from the Mississippi to the Rockies. Of greatest immediate interest to the West was the Gulf Coast with its control of the outlets of various rivers, particularly the Mississippi.

Spain particularly worried the West during the 1780s because she showed no enthusiasm for the United States, and gave evidence of an increasingly vigorous colonial policy. In 1784 she tried to weaken the American West by closing the Mississippi to all but Spanish traffic. Her negotiations with the southwestern Indians brought some success with the Creeks, who were hostile to the United States. New frontier posts brought Spanish garrisons to the Yazoo River (present-day Vicksburg) in 1791 and Chickasaw Bluffs (near present-day Memphis) in 1795. Farther north was St. Louis, which helped to encircle western settlements. These developments, and particularly the closing of the Mississippi, seemed ominous to all Westerners.

The Spanish show of vigor tended to obscure the essential weakness of the Spanish position. The Floridas and Louisiana were only the extreme outposts of a vast empire, and although Spain desired to halt Anglo-American advance, she had neither men nor money for an effective job. West Florida and Louisiana were under a single governor, who was an army officer; these areas contained almost all the white population, with four fifths in the towns from Mobile to New Orleans. The Governor of Louisiana in 1780 commanded less than 1400 effective troops, of whom about half were at New Orleans and St. Louis; New Orleans was the only fortified southern post. The Governor of East Florida was stationed at St. Augustine, and his realm included few white settlers and fewer troops. Both governors were starved financially, and reinforcements had to be brought from Cuba or Mexico.

SPANISH POLICY

To secure Spain's possessions against aggressive Americans the obvious Spanish policy was to strengthen the military position, to close the river against American trade, and to exclude American settlers. The most immediate drawback of this policy was that closing the river hurt New Orleans as much as or more than it did the American West. Louisiana herself produced primarily tobacco, indigo, furs, and lumber for export; these products had limited markets or cheaper rivals, and hence New Orleans prosperity depended on the American trade. In consequence there was a strong local pressure to reopen the river, which was done in 1788; American goods for export could be sold in New Orleans with a 15 percent tax, which later was reduced.

Another great difficulty with a strong Spanish policy was that Americans had already trickled into the Gulf region in considerable numbers and might revolt successfully if irritated. Moreover, the American settlers of Kentucky and Tennessee vastly outnumbered the Spanish to the south, and there were insufficient Spanish troops to resist a determined advance from the north.

These and other complexities caused Spanish policy to fluctuate. Part of the time the river was closed and American settlers were excluded. More usually the river was open and American settlers were encouraged—provided they would swear loyalty to the Spanish king and embrace the Catholic faith. The unjustified hope existed that they would become good Spanish subjects and strengthen the empire. The policy was a bad mistake, just as later was true of Texas. American always preferred connections with the home folks to loyalty to a remote Catholic king.

Spanish policy, no matter how wisely or foolishly conceived, was badly damaged in its administration. Spanish officials were notoriously corrupt, and the bribe was a recognized institution. The closing of the Mississippi never really stopped trade because enforcement officers frequently winked at violations—for a consideration. The only restriction of trade came from the increased costs of bribery.

THE STATE OF FRANKLIN

Westerners confronted by a menacing Spain and hostile Indians, and with little prospective help from eastern governments, which seemed either uninterested or impotent, fell back on their own resources. Many Westerners favored independence, and then perhaps an alliance, or even union, with Spain. The idea of independence appealed to Spanish governors, who were glad to help potential seceders. The stage was thus set for a plethora of intrigues and plots by Westerners who saw in independence an advantage in terms of power, of payments by Spain, and of land speculation.

That western independence was not merely idle talk became apparent with the formation of the independent state of Franklin. The source of this development in the early 1780s was a strong drive for effective government by the frontiersmen south of the Ohio River. Appeals for statehood were made to Congress, but Congress found difficulty in taking effective action on any subject, and in this case was particularly handicapped because various states were being asked to cede their western land claims. Any Congressional action that violated the presumed rights and powers of such important land-claiming states as Virginia and North Carolina would hardly speed land cessions; hence Congress did nothing.

Western pressure for effective government was strongest in the Holston River region, which was claimed by North Carolina. Long debates in the North Carolina legislature as to what to do with Westerners, who wanted so much and who paid so little taxes, resulted in North Carolina's ceding her western lands to Congress in 1784 by a narrow vote. When Congress dawdled as usual, while western talk of independence grew, North Carolina repealed her act of cession before the end of the same year.

Westerners rapidly grew impatient with the indecision of Congress and North Carolina. Interest in freedom grew, with part of the argument involving two groups of land speculators with different ideas of which government would be the more useful to them. The freedom movement culminated in the Jonesboro convention, which on December 14, 1784, declared the independence of the Holston region by a vote of 28 to 15. The new state was named Franklin in honor of Benjamin Franklin, who might conceivably aid his infant namesake. A temporary constitution provided for a senate and a house of representatives, which jointly were to elect a governor. The first legislature met in March 1785 and passed laws about such matters as land titles, education, militia, county divisions, taxation, and elections. A permanent constitution, based on that of North Carolina, was adopted in November 1785. Especially important for the new state was the attitude of its most influential citizen, John Sevier, who had probably delayed independence by his cautious words of moderation. Sevier's final decision was apparent when he was elected to, and accepted, the office of governor.

Internal affairs of the new nation progressed satisfactorily under the able administration of Sevier, but foreign affairs did not run as smoothly. The Indians were a continual danger, and several successful expeditions by Sevier did little more than keep the trouble under control. Spain was approached for recognition and assistance. Congress was asked for recognition, but as usual was weak and unwilling to meddle, and Benjamin Franklin refused to aid his namesake. The Kentucky area was asked to join the venture, but decided it had more to gain from Congress and from Virginia than from independence. Georgia gave the new nation its greatest success, granting recognition and expressing willingness to cooperate in fighting the Indians. North Carolina naturally objected vigorously to the actions of her ungrateful progeny, but had neither the force nor the desire to conquer the back country. After the failure of efforts at reconciliation, the two states issued manifestoes and countermanifestoes as fast as they could concoct and print them.

The trouble that finally destroyed Franklin was internal rather than external. Sevier's chief rival was John Tipton, and when Tipton failed to win ascendancy in Franklin he obtained recognition and authority from North Carolina. Then followed a comic-opera war between the followers of Sevier and those of Tipton, with Tipton receiving some aid from North Carolina, which outlawed Sevier in 1786. Sevier was finally captured by the Tipton forces in 1788. He was rescued by his friends before he was brought to trial, but the affair resulted in the collapse of Franklin, with North Carolina resuming control. Sevier was pardoned immediately, and participated in the North Carolina convention of 1788, which considered the adoption of the new federal constitution. During the next year North Carolina ceded her western lands to Congress by a decisive vote, but the action was little more than a gesture since most of the land had been sold.

WESTERN INTRIGUES AND WILKINSON

The state of Franklin included only a small part of the area west of the mountains, and elsewhere occurred various plottings, usually with the idea of independence and alliance with Spain, and almost always involving land speculation. Dr. James White was particularly active in present-day Tennessee, having associations with such prominent men as Sevier, Blount, and Robertson. White proposed to the Spanish Minister in 1786 that the West declare its independence and then be taken under the protection of Spain. The Minister was at first interested, but his ardor soon cooled, and he suggested that any Westerner who really liked Spain could move into Spanish territory.

James O'Fallon, a brother-in-law of George Rogers Clark, developed an even more impressive plan in 1790. He talked of a large army under Clark to occupy the lower Yazoo River Valley and create a new state, allied with Spain, and of course offering free land for the adventurers. Those who feared that Spain might be unfriendly were assured that he was on good terms with the Spanish; in fact, O'Fallon had written to the Spanish Governor of Louisiana concerning his "ardent views of promoting the interests of his Catholic majesty." As was true of so many similar plans, those of O'Fallon never materialized.

Most spectacular were the activities of the adventurer William Augustus Bowles, who dreamed of an Indian state in the Spanish territory of Florida. After the rather unusual preparation of obtaining the approval of the British Governor of Nova Scotia, he entered Florida in 1791, but was soon captured by the Spanish. In time he escaped from jail and in 1799 returned to Florida, where he established the state of Muskogee, of which he was Director-General. The new Indian nation had all the white trappings: a capital and a national flag, and even the temerity to declare war on Spain and capture a Spanish fort. Unfortunately for Bowles, the contest was a mismatch, and he died in a Havana prison.

Best known of the plotters of the 1780s and 1790s was James Wilkinson, son of a Maryland planter, who had volunteered in the Revolution and by 1777 had risen to the rank of brevet brigadier general at the age of twenty. After the Revolution Wilkinson settled in Pennsylvania— he had married the daughter of a well-known Philadephia family—and for a time sat in the Pennsylvania legislature. Finding economic success elusive, he moved to Kentucky in 1783 as the representative of several Philadelphia merchants. Immediately he was outstanding in Lexington, where he built a large house and entertained lavishly. As a youthful retired general, as a suave and persuasive man, and as a trader and land speculator, he was soon well known. He was active in several Kentucky statehood conventions even though he preferred independence, as did many of his friends.

In 1784, the year that Spain closed the river, Wilkinson took two flatboats down the Mississippi, stopping at St. Louis en route to tell the Spanish commander that he carried important information concerning an expedition by George Rogers Clark to take Natchez. At New Orleans he talked long and earnestly with the Governor, Esteban Miró, warning him of a potential attack from Kentucky. Moved by his characteristic affinity for the pen, he also addressed a memorial to Spain suggesting that a western revolt be fomented or that American settlers be encouraged to come to Louisiana. In either event he would be willing to accept the appointment of chief Spanish agent.

Spain was soon paying Wilkinson, thanks to his persuasiveness or to Spanish credulity, and by 1791 he was receiving a regular pension. Whether Wilkinson believed his own tales may be doubted, and particularly after they became more complex and contradictory. In Kentucky he worked publicly for independence and an alliance with England if Spain would not open the Mississippi. To Miró he talked of union with Spain, and advocated that the Mississippi be kept closed. To complicate his plans further he also memorialized England, suggesting he be made British agent to work for independence and an attack on New Orleans if Spain did not open the river; to his disappointment the English were not as gullible as the Spanish. The conclusion seems inescapable that toward the end of his association with Spanish officialdom he was milking Spain for everything he could get, and had no idea of carrying out his side of any bargain.

STATEHOOD FOR KENTUCKY AND TENNESSEE

The extension of statehood to Kentucky and Tennessee upset the plans for an independent West during the 1790s. Kentucky had long been dissatisfied with its position as a Virginia county: Richmond was remote and Kentuckians wanted to run their own affairs even at a greater cost. Virginia had no great objection, but mutually agreeable terms were necessary. Kentucky had nine statehood conventions during the years 1784 through 1790, while Virginia passed four enabling acts. Ultimately agreement was reached, and Kentucky was admitted to the Union by Congress in 1792—the first of the trans-Appalachian states.

Tennessee did not attain statehood so promptly. After the North Carolina land cession, Congress created a territorial government corresponding to that of the Northwest. The Governor was William Blount, prince of land speculators, who filled the offices under his control with friends, relatives, and business associates, with special reference to men formerly connected with the state of Franklin. The speculators remained firmly in control until the arrival of statehood in 1796, at which time Sevier became governor and Blount went to the United States Senate.

GENÊT

By the 1790s the opportunities for western intrigue seemed definitely declining. Statehood came to Kentucky and Tennessee. All states but Georgia ceded their western land claims to Congress. The federal government was perceptibly stronger. Wilkinson, with Spanish intrigues less lucrative and with his usual debts, returned to the army with a commission issued by Washington in spite of the rumors of Spanish payments that had reached his ears. Wilkinson was for a time in commond at Fort Washington (Cincinnati), and fought acceptably in the Indian wars of the 1790s while continuing to receive his Spanish pension and to ask for more.

A new complication arose in 1793 with the arrival in the United States of Citizen Edmond Charles Genêt as an emissary of France. The Genêt mission, as it concerned the West, was to raise an American frontier army, pay it with money that the United States still owed France, and capture Florida and Louisiana, where presumably the oppressed inhabitants were panting for an opportunity to accept the ideals of the French Revolution.

Genêt's representative in the West was André Michaux, French scientist and explorer, who commissioned George Rogers Clark as major general of the expedition. Clark, who was so resentful of the smallness of the rewards for his war service that he had smashed a ceremonial sword given to him by Virginia, was particularly interested. Moreover, he was in financial difficulties from his land speculation, and his Spanish intrigues had not proved lucrative. He advertised for men, offering them the princely reward of a dollar a day plus 1000 acres of captured land for each year's service. To the south, an expedition was collected in Georgia under Major General Elijah Clarke, who presumably planned to take St. Augustine and Pensacola.

The promising Genêt plans collapsed in 1794 when President Washington prohibited the enlistments and ordered the Governor of Kentucky to stop Clark. In the South, Elijah Clarke crossed the St. Marys River with some 150 men and established a "Trans-Oconee Republic," but was forced to withdraw when Governor Mathews of Georgia closed the river to needed supplies. Wilkinson took advantage of the excitement by warning Spain of the potential invasion, and by asking to be rewarded for sending the news, but his compensation was seized by bandits on its way to him. Wilkinson remained in the American army, participating in various Indian campaigns, and being second to Anthony Wayne in command at the Battle of Fallen Timbers.

ENGLISH AND SPANISH TREATIES

The federal government was keenly aware of western problems, and Washington worried over the possibility of the independence movements there. A real effort was made in the mid-1790s to improve the situation by expeditions against the Indians and by the negotiation of treaties that would remove at least some of the major western grievances. The Jay Treaty with England in 1794 provided for the transfer of the western post to American control—a transfer that occurred the following year. At this time Anthony Wayne was head of the western army, and when he died in December 1796, Wilkinson succeeded him. By then Wilkinson had received some $30,000 from Spain, and the story had by no means ended.

The treaty with England opened the way for an agreement with Spain, which was no longer allied with England and feared a joint English-American occupation of her North American possessions. By the Treaty of San Lorenzo, negotiated by Thomas Pinckney in 1795, Spain agreed to accept the boundary of 31° north latitude, and to withdraw her troops from north of that line. Even more important, she agreed to the free navigation of the Mississippi and to a three-year right of deposit at New

Orleans: the privilege of landing and storing goods for reshipment without paying duties. This right of deposit was to be continued after the three years elapsed, but not necessarily at New Orleans.

Spanish authorities were slow in carrying out the terms of the Pinckney Treaty, hoping that the West might be detached from the Union; the change of times was evident, however, when Wilkinson jailed Thomas Power, the Spanish agent. Free navigation of the Mississippi went into effect in December 1796, but the right of deposit was not granted for another two years. Transfer of the territory south of 31° north latitude was also delayed, and when Andrew Ellicott, the American representative, arrived to accept and survey the boundaries of the accession, he soon became impatient. Gathering a small armed force, he engineered a "revolution" by American settlers, after which the actual power was exercised by a committee of citizens even though the Spanish commander remained in nominal control. When the Spanish posts were surrendered in 1798, Wilkinson was on hand to extend all possible courtesies to the departing Spaniards.

FURTHER IDEAS OF EXPANSION

With the settling of the Spanish boundary and the statehood of Kentucky and Tennessee, western conditions might theoretically have been presumed to be stabilized. But they were not. William A. Bowles, as described earlier, invaded Florida. Philip Nolan, a Wilkinson protégé and adventurer, tried his luck in Texas. William Blount was involved in a plot in 1796 to gather an army of whites and Indians, and, with the help of a British fleet, to capture the Floridas and Louisiana for Britain; the reward was to be land. The plot was exposed prematurely, and Blount was expelled from the Senate in 1797. An even more impressive plan was concocted by Alexander Hamilton, who had long been disappointed at his failure to obtain military glory in the Revolution. Hamilton envisioned an alliance with England, and war with France and Spain. He himself would lead an army to conquer Florida and Louisiana, and possibly Mexico and Central America, or even more remote areas. Failing to attract support in the West, his expedition never materialized.

Aggressive plans, such as those of Blount and Hamilton, indicated an attitude toward foreign affairs that was typical of the period. The principal motive of the leaders was probably the hope of personal gain in terms of plunder, trade, or land, but patriotism was also stated as a justification. The authors talked of freeing oppressed peoples and of adding territory to the United States. Whatever their real motives, they were developing a procedure that the United States was to use frequently in its expansion of the next half century.

THE LOUISIANA PURCHASE

The United States was not the only nation with an interest in Spanish territory, and it was France that first succeeded in detaching a piece of it. While Americans talked and plotted, France negotiated to obtain Louisiana—partly because revolutionary France felt she had a world mission and partly because of less laudable colonial motives. Spanish diplomats were superficially coy and reluctant, and frequently changed their minds, but had no real objection to selling Louisiana any time after 1795 if the price were right. They saw the immense wilderness of Louisiana, inhabited only by some 50,000 people, as nothing but a drain on the Spanish treasury. The French-Spanish dickering eventually produced in 1800 the Treaty of San Ildefonso, by which France received Louisiana. This treaty was secret, and for the time being the actual transfer of Louisiana was not made.

When Napoleon signed the Peace of Amiens in March 1802 he was freed for a prospective American colonial venture. Immediately he pushed for a quicker transfer, and sent a sizable army to Santo Domingo as a start for operations farther north. French plans envisioned a populous North American colony, which would trade primarily with the homeland and with the French West Indies sugar islands. Rumors of the impending transfer began to circulate in America, to the distress of Americans, who regarded France as a more objectionable neighbor than Spain. These rumors received factual evidence when the French army arrived in Santo Domingo and when, in October 1802, the Intendant of Louisiana stopped the right of deposit at New Orleans. Even though the stoppage was brief and did not prevent American navigation of the Mississippi, it greatly aroused the West, where there was considerable talk of war. Incidentally, although the assumption that Napoleon had ordered the end of the right of deposit was reasonable, it was not true.

President Jefferson found himself in a difficult position. He had long felt that the advance of American settlement would solve the Spanish difficulties, but now this long-run optimism was less easy, and he did not underrate the willingness of the West to act on its own initiative, with independence a possibility. Furthermore, he was sensitive to political factors, and the Federalists were making political capital by urging immediate and forceful action. Finally, and possibly most disturbing, Jefferson had grave constitutional doubts as to the right of the federal government to acquire new territory.

Jefferson at first tried to calm the West while putting pressure on France by suggesting that her American adventure might push the United States into alliance with England. At the same time the American Minister, Robert R. Livingston, was trying unsuccessfully to buy New Orleans, and possibly additional territory. As American sentiment increased in vigor, Jefferson became convinced of the urgency of the matter. He appointed as special emissary James Monroe, who was popular in the West, and provided him with a $2 million fund voted by Congress. Monroe was instructed to buy the Floridas and the Island of Orleans (New Orleans) for not over $10 million; he also had permission to promise favored treatment to French vessels and trade, and even to guarantee French possession of the remainder of Louisiana. Alternate instructions envisioned the purchase of less territory, even the acquisition of a single town on the Mississippi for deposit. Finally, if Napoleon would sell nothing, Monroe and Livingston were authorized to cross the Channel and make an English alliance.

Before Monroe arrived in France, Napoleon had abandoned his American plans. Possibly his difficulties in Santo Domingo played a part in his decision. The heroic resistance of the natives under Toussaint L'Ouverture had supplemented the yellow fever to produce thousands of French graves. But Napoleon as a soldier was not deterred by casualties, and in the fall of 1802 gathered a new army to occupy New Orleans; his armada actually failed to sail because of the cold winter. The decisive factor in pushing the colonial project into obscurity was the prospective renewal of the war with England in the spring of 1803. Napoleon exclaimed pettishly: "Damn sugar, damn coffee, damn colonies," and planned to obtain funds for the English war by selling Louisiana—of course he could reconquer it if he changed his mind.

While Monroe was en route to France, the French offered to sell Livingston all of Louisiana, and Livingston reluctantly exercised the self-restraint necessary to postpone a decision until Monroe arrived. The bargaining was brief, and in 1803 the final treaty transferred all of Louisiana to the United States for approximately $15 million, of which about a quarter was used to settle United States claims on France. The boundaries of the acquisition were stated vaguely, thus opening the way for many future disputes. His constitutional scruples overcome, Jefferson seemed untroubled by the earlier promise of France to Spain never to dispose of the country.

The change of masters occurred late in 1803 at New Orleans, then a dilapidated community of some 8000 inhabitants. On November 30 Louisiana was transferred formally from Spain to France, and on December 20 from France to the United States. The American commissioners who accepted the cession were William C. C. Claiborne, the prospective Governor, and James Wilkinson, head of the western army and future Governor of upper Louisiana Territory. Wilkinson must have regretted the disappearance from New Orleans of his paymaster, but his sorrow was

Territorial Acquisitions, 1803–1819

abated by a Spanish payment of $12,000, in return for which he penned lengthy "Reflections," of which he sent a modified version to Jefferson.

Provision for the government of the new region was made early in 1804. All the portion outside the present Louisiana was first called Louisiana District, with Wilkinson as governor but with the judicial administration attached for the time being to Indiana Territory. The present Louisiana was constituted Orleans Territory, although its eastern boundary fluctuated during the next eight years. Governor Claiborne was received by the French and Spanish with a considerable skepticism that produced serious administrative difficulties in the early years. In 1805 Orleans was given a government like that of the neighboring Mississippi Territory, and with the passage of years the administration came to operate smoothly.

American occupation brought an immediate increase in population, so that in 1812 Louisiana could be admitted to the Union.

BURR

The acquisition of Louisiana seemed on its face to satisfy all current American desires and hence to end American plans to invade Spanish territory, but within the next few years occurred the best advertised of all such expeditions—that under the brilliant, restless, ambitious, dapper, and spendthrift Aaron Burr. The promising political career of Burr appeared to be approaching an end with the completion of his vice-presidency (1801–1805). Jefferson had never forgiven him for failing to withdraw from the presidential voting in 1800, and refused him any important appointment, while the killing of Hamilton in a duel on the fields of Weehawken further hurt his political chances. On the other hand, he was still under fifty, active and vigorous, and in need of money. Like many other men looking for opportunity, Burr turned his eyes to the West, where the killing of Hamilton would be a positive advantage to his reputation.

Burr tried to raise money from both the English and the Spanish ministers on the basis of plans involving the West. To the former he suggested an independent western state, with England providing $500,000 and a fleet at the mouth of the Mississippi. To the latter he outlined a fantastic scheme for capturing both New Orleans and Washington, kidnapping high executives, and taking the contents of an arsenal and a bank. Burr's persuasiveness was demonstrated when he convinced both men, but unfortunately for his bank account their home governments were too far distant to be impressed.

Soon after Burr completed his duties as vice-president he and his beloved daughter Theodosia toured the West, where they were greeted with vast enthusiasm. Inevitably Burr talked to hundreds of men, including Jackson and Clay, but what he said to them is uncertain, since he varied his story to appeal to each listener. Probably he did not advance the wild proposals he had used as bait for the Spanish and English ministers. Possibly he talked of colonization. Later he indicated an interest in becoming emperor of Mexico. Among the men to whom he talked was his old friend James Wilkinson, with whom he had long corresponded in code—not unusual in a day when carriers frequently read the dispatches entrusted to them. Burr and Wilkinson spent four days at Fort Massac in earnest conversation, but what the subjects were remains unknown.

Burr was again in the West in August 1806, collecting men and supplies for a rendezvous late in the year on an island in the upper Ohio River. With the circulation of wild rumors, old plots and intrigues revived. Twice Burr was arrested and tried for treason, and twice he convinced a grand jury that he planned nothing more than colonization. Jefferson heard the rumors of treason, but took no action. Ultimately a disappointingly small party of thirty men started the trip down the river in nine boats. By this time Jefferson had become alarmed and issued a warrant for Burr's arrest, which followed the expedition down the river.

The actions of Wilkinson during 1806 are as difficult to explain as those of Burr. At St. Louis, Wilkinson had been in perpetual trouble as governor, and in June 1806 he had been ordered to move to the vicinity of New Orleans. These orders he obeyed with the greatest of leisure, detouring from Natchez to Natchitoches on the pretext of a slight border incident. At Natchitoches he inquired among his men concerning a possible expedition against Mexico, but could discover no enthusiasm. By September he was back in Natchez, leaving his army to make its own way to New Orleans.

At Natchez, Wilkinson apparently finally made up his mind as to his future course of action. Rather belatedly he sent a note to Jefferson warning him of the Burr expedition, which he said was headed for Vera Cruz. At the same time he warned Spain and Mexico, even sending a man on an unsuccessful mission to Mexico City to collect payment for this information. Then he rushed to New Orleans, and to the surprise of everyone urged martial law and worked frenziedly to prepare the city against an attack. Apparently the pathetic Burr expedition had now become an imposing menace to the United States.

Meantime Burr had been floating leisurely down the river, unaware of either the warrant for his arrest or the actions of Wilkinson. Ultimately he heard of the warrant, became panic-stricken, and fled overland in disguise. He was apprehended by Edmund Gaines of the United States Army on February 19, 1807, and taken to Richmond to stand trial before Chief Justice Marshall for a misdemeanor and treason. He was adjudged not guilty, but many people felt that the verdict was based more on political factors than on the evidence. Burr's public career was ended even though he lived for another thirty years. As for Wilkinson, his testimony in the Burr trial was vague and inconclusive—after all, he had to consider his own vindication. In fact, his conduct was so suspect that he was investigated by congressional and military committees. His explanations of peculiar letters and actions were thin, but the evidence was inconclusive, and he was exonerated in each case.

The Burr episode was only one of many plans made by Americans to invade neighboring lands, but it at least marked a temporary halt to western plans for independence; not until settlement crossed the Rockies were any such ideas again advanced seriously. By the early nineteenth century there was no longer any question that the Mississippi Valley would remain a part of the United States. In fact, the West was in the process of becoming even more blatantly patriotic than the East, with a deep and intense love of the United States, a belief in the superiority of her institutions, and a desire to expand the Union to bring the blessings of its institutions to neighboring peoples.

READINGS

SPANISH INTRIGUES. The standard accounts of relations with Spain are Arthur P. Whitaker, *The Spanish-American Frontier 1783–1795* (1927) and *The Mississippi Question 1795–1803* (1934). The story from 1789 is well told in Thomas P. Abernethy, *The South in the New Nation* (1961). Smaller parts of the situation are covered in Thomas P. Abernethy, *From Frontier to Plantation in Tennessee* (1932); Caroline M. Burson, *The Stewardship of Don Esteban Miró, 1782–1792* (1940); John W. Caughey, *Bernardo de Gálvez in Louisiana, 1776–1783* (1934).

The Louisiana negotiations can be followed in Elijah W. Lyon, *Louisiana in French Diplomacy, 1759–1804* (1934). The previous British occupation is treated carefully in Clinton N. Howard, *The British Development of West Florida, 1763–1769* (1947) and Cecil Johnson, *British West Florida, 1763–1783* (1943).

STATE OF FRANKLIN. Samuel C. Williams, *History of the Lost State of Franklin* (1924) is standard. Shorter and more readable accounts are contained in Archibald Henderson, *The Conquest of the Old Southwest . . . 1740–1790* (1920); Constance L. Skinner, *Pioneers of the Old Southwest* (1919); and John A. Caruso, *The Appalachian Frontier* (1959). Carl S. Driver, *John Sevier* (1932) has much on the subject.

WILKINSON. Best on Wilkinson is James R. Jacobs, *Tarnished Warrior* (1938) and the pertinent parts of the same author's *The Beginning of the United States Army, 1783–1812* (1947); fairly good is Thomas R. Hay and Norris R. Werner, *The Admirable Trumpeter* (1941); Royal O. Shreve, *The Finished Scoundrel* (1933), popular in tone; James Wilkinson, *Wilkinson* (1935) is a justification by a grandson. William Blount is covered clearly in William H. Masterson, *William Blount* (1954). The Kentucky side of the story is told interestingly in Thomas D. Clark, *A History of Kentucky* (1937); Charles G. Talbert, *Benjamin Logan* (1962) also concerns Kentucky.

BURR. An excellent account of the episode is Thomas P. Abernethy, *The Burr Conspiracy* (1954). The best Burr biography is Nathan Schachner, *Aaron Burr* (1937), but also good are Holmes M. Alexander, *Aaron Burr* (1937), which is adverse in tone, and Samuel H. Wandell and Meade Minnigerode, *Aaron Burr* (2 vols., 1925), which is sympathetic. Also pertinent are James A. James, *The Life of George Rogers Clark* (1928) and James W. Silver, *Edmund Pendleton Gaines* (1949).

CHAPTER 6

GOVERNMENTAL PROBLEMS

T he first settlers who crossed the Appalachians were confronted by a virgin wilderness where even the simplest necessities to which they were accustomed did not exist. To fulfill their varied desires, which ranged from the basic needs of survival to complicated cultural ambitions, the new inhabitants had to meet and conquer a strange environment. Quite naturally they tried to retain the customs and ideals that had characterized their life in the East, but these were necessarily modified by western conditions.

CHARACTER OF WESTERN MIGRANTS

Methods of solving western problems depended on the character of the new inhabitants. Although many and diverse elements were present in the West, a few generalizations are still possible. Most obviously, the usual migrant had not been successful in the East. The well-established farmer, businessman, or professional man was more likely to stay in the community of his success. The most important exceptions were slaveowners looking for more fertile land and financiers or land speculators—not infrequently combined in one man—who saw opportunities for gain in a new and expanding community. Of course the land speculator might either lose his money and become like his neighbors, or make large profits and move back to the East.

Unsuccessful Easterners did not for the most part mean completely poverty-stricken Easterners. Most migrants took up farms, and the process was far from costless, particularly if families were involved. Even if a man took up land without immediately paying for it, he still needed sufficient resources to make the trip west, to obtain necessary tools and seed, and to live until he harvested his first crop. If the man were unmarried he might plan to work for wages in the West before starting his own farm, but if he were married he had no such option. Consequently, although Westerners tended to be poor, they were not usually poverty-stricken.

Lack of success in the East did not imply necessarily that Westerners lacked ability. Frequently they came from desirable but unfavored portions of the communities of their origins. Younger members of large New England farming families sought more opportunity than their few relatively infertile acres provided. Slaveowners sought replacements for their worked-out land. Established farmers and artisans sought to improve their conditions of life. Immigrants from Europe were attracted to the West by opportunities for employment or by cheap land. Along with these and other desirable groups came a sprinkling of the less desirable—criminals seeking to escape the law, possibly to start new lives or perhaps to resume the old ways in a new setting; the reckless and the foot-loose, who would probably never become adjusted satisfactorily to any settled society.

Migration to the West implied something of an unusual point of view. The prospective frontiersman must have had a little more intellectual dissatisfaction, a little greater willingness to take a chance than his friends and neighbors. Psychologically he was more restless, perhaps somewhat maladjusted in his relations with family and friends. Normally he said—and believed—that his motives were economic, but behind these very real economic desires may well have been psychological dissatisfactions that were basically noneconomic.

The greatest single group of migrants was composed of young, unmarried farm boys. The usual age was twenty-one, which meant that they had completed their legal obligations to their parents and were free to seek their fortunes. Frequently they worked for a time in the West, returned to marry their childhood sweethearts, and then took farms in the West. When a family migrated, its head might make a preliminary trip to discover a suitable place to settle; otherwise he would depend on reports from friends and neighbors who had gone west earlier. In any case the migrant preferred a fairly definite objective before he moved.

Western migrants tended to travel by the most easily available routes, and as directly west as possible, thus they would expect to find themselves in something like the geographic and climatic conditions to which they were accustomed, and near people from their own part of the country. During the revolutionary years most of the migrants came from the South, passed through the Cumberland Gap, and settled in Kentucky or Tennessee, or went up the Potomac and then overland to the Pittsburgh area. Eventually these streams of settlement overflowed into the region just north of the Ohio River—what is now southern Ohio, Indiana, and Illinois. Later they occupied Missouri and even reached Iowa. Settlers from the Middle Atlantic states went west by way of Pittsburgh and mixed with the southern stream in the Ohio Valley. New England migrants of the eighteenth and early nineteenth centuries flowed largely into New York State, with the farthest advance reaching the Great Lakes; a few New Englanders, however, went into the Ohio Valley, usually by way of Pittsburgh but sometimes through southern New York State.

MAIN WESTERN PROBLEMS

Several of the most serious problems facing these new settlers were of continuing importance throughout the entire history of the West. Of first concern were the Indians. During the period of the Revolution most Indians were hostile; hence the few whites tended to huddle together in fortified settlements, while the isolated settler feared to leave his cabin unprotected and seldom had the temerity to travel at night. The outlook at the end of the war was extremely discouraging because neither the federal government, the states, nor the settlers had the manpower and resources to prosecute successful Indian wars. Almost the only hopeful element was that a few leaders such as Washington saw the importance of the area, and maintained a continuing interest in it.

A second problem of the West was the method by which a settler might obtain land that was good, cheap, and easily available. During and immediately after the Revolution all western lands were claimed by the various states, and conditions were chaotic. Various state claims overlapped, provisions for surveying and marking individual claims were varied, prices fluctuated, and the recording of claims was often difficult. The state claims were eventually released to the federal government, but with considerable reservations that frequently were confusing. Congress then had the problem of devising an adequate plan for the disposition of western lands. Its obvious difficulties were increased by the fact that most of the lands were not actually unoccupied. Should Indian claims be respected and illegally settled whites removed? Such a problem was difficult for a white government.

A third big problem confronting the West was that of money and credit, for the West lacked both. Individual settlers strained their resources in coming West, and needed credit to buy land, machinery, and buildings, to say nothing of meeting current expenses. Communities wanted roads, bridges, schools, jails, churches, and the other trappings of civilization. Large amounts of credit were obviously desirable, and for many years western attitudes were influenced strongly by the fact that the West was a debtor community.

A fourth problem was transportation, which was the very foundation of future prosperity. Western products must be carried to market quickly and cheaply, and news and goods must be brought from the East and from Europe. Each transportational innovation that became popular in the East found a host of ready supporters in the West. The great difficulties were the long and rugged routes between East and West, the lack of available capital, and the paucity of traffic. Various more or less ingenious solutions for these difficulties were tried.

A fifth problem was the development of good and effective government, which was essential to make life and property secure, to defeat the Indians, to record wills, deeds, and marriages, to build roads and bridges. The first efforts to solve the governmental problem were local and spontaneous in origin, but sporadic local efforts proved at best unsatisfactory. A good many troubles, such as Indians, finance, and transportation, were insoluble on the local level. Federal action was essential.

In addition to these five large problems were innumerable others of less pressing urgency. Religion, education, literature, art, medicine, law, and all the other attributes of civilization had to be developed from relatively simple beginnings. As matters turned out, however, the first two problems to be dealt with constructively were land and government.

LANDOWNERSHIP

The ability to acquire land in the West during the years after the Revolution was of vital importance. Most Americans were farmers, and because of the lack of industries, fishing, and shipping in the West they tended to concentrate on farming even more than in the East. The typical farmer owned his own land rather than rented it, and one important reason for western migration was men's hopes of securing farms of their own.

Most of the land of the present United States east of the Mississippi had been granted originally to proprietors or to companies that wanted to exploit or colonize the New World. Because geographical knowledge was inadequate, boundaries specified in charters were often inexact and frequently overlapped, producing colonial disputes over dividing lines. Some charters granted land beyond the mountains. As settlement expanded, the original grantee would sell or give away such land as was needed for the increase of population. The limits of such sales or donations were sometimes so ill-defined that they were impossible to mark, and frequently two or more grants overlapped. In the course of time the Proclamation of 1763 forced the various colonies and proprietors to allow their claims to far western land to lapse for the time being.

The outbreak of the Revolution revived the aspirations of each colony with claims to western territory. Virginia was the most active and fortunate, for it was under her auspices that George Rogers Clark conquered the Northwest. Virginia organized into counties Kentucky and the region north of the Ohio; North Carolina did the same for the Tennessee country, so that all the settled West had at least nominal government. Settlers had not yet moved into the Georgia claim. The situation had some advantages for the states with western counties, but it was not without its drawbacks. Other states also had western claims, and what was to become of them if Virginia and North Carolina monopolized almost the entire West? Furthermore, the West itself was not fully satisfied, for it wanted cheap land and a government that would spend money freely to fight the Indians and to make public improvements; Virginia and North Carolina not only had no money to spend, but were very desirous of increasing their revenues.

Just at the time that the central government needed unusual power to deal with western problems it was at the nadir of its effectiveness. The Continental Congress, from its first meeting in 1774, was a purely voluntary and noncoercive body, with little power and an aversion to arousing enmities by interfering with the West. The new Articles of Confederation finally went into effect with the ratification by Maryland on March 1, 1781, after having been before the states since 1777, but here again was an incredibly weak central authority: no executive, no effective courts, and no power to enforce legislation, made the Articles a frail support on which to lean. But in spite of the serious handicaps surrounding Congress under the Articles of Confederation, it succeeded in putting into force some legislation that was exceedingly important for the West.

STATE CESSIONS

Even before the Articles of Confederation were adopted by Maryland it was proposed by some states (those not having land claims) that all unsold western land be turned over to the central government as a common possession. The states with land claims could see quite obvious objections to such a proposal, but on the other hand they could also see good reasons for making the cessions. Conflicting state claims made problematical the amount of land any one state would be able to hold. The Indians were in the main hostile, and their subjugation would be a long and arduous task. All kinds of public improvements would have to be constructed with eastern money, while the poor Westerners would not be able to pay any considerable taxes for many years. Altogether, it seemed to many persons that the disadvantages of holding western territory far outweighed the possible future benefits that might accrue from land sales.

In view of these various factors the states began to look upon the congressional proposal with favor, and began to cede their western claims to Congress. New York had the honor of being the first (1780)—possibly in part because her claim as heir of the Iroquois pretensions was scarcely tenable. Other states followed, the last being Georgia in 1802. Some of them, such as Virginia and North Carolina, had already sold considerable shares of the lands they theoretically were ceding to Congress. Others made reservations. The unsold land of Kentucky and Tennessee never came under congressional control. The "Connecticut Reserve," including the present city of Cleveland, Ohio, was retained for the benefit of certain sufferers from the Revolution. Virginia withheld large amounts of land, of which the greater share was to go to her revolutionary soldiers. The Georgia cession actually cost the United States more than was received from the lands remaining unsold at the time of the transfer.

LAND DEBATES

As a result of these cessions Congress was endowed with an immense public domain, and a continually increasing influx of population meant that immediate provision must be made for the survey, sale, and government of the regions that had proved attractive to settlers. A considerable number of these settlers had paid no attention to legal ownership, merely occupying and beginning to cultivate whatever land seemed to them good. What should be done with such "squatters"? Furthermore, soldiers of the revolutionary army had been promised land as part payment for their services in the war, and the Newburgh petition of 1783 demonstrated that at least a portion of them had a real desire for the land. What, if anything, should be done for them? Here were two classes that were insistent upon virtually free land—but free land did not sound attractive to a government that was desirous of collecting every possible cent of revenue. Furthermore, both East and West were agreed that some sort of action would have to be undertaken immediately to protect the white man from red depredations. And finally, it was evident to such men as Washington that if the United States did not act immediately and effectively there was a real possibility that the West might either try to settle its own affairs as an independent state or appeal for protection to some foreign power such as Spain.

The debate in Congress on the disposition of the public lands was long and acrimonious. New England practice, in which each township was sold as a unit and then subdivided by its purchasers, was compared with the southern procedure, in which each man picked his land, placed his own boundaries, had his title recorded at the county seat, and then paid a lawyer to fight the cases that rose over disputed boundaries and ownership. The argument over indiscriminate and exact location was won by New England. There were other debates as to whether the new land should be plotted in large or small townships, and whether large or small tracts should be offered for sale. In both these cases compromises were eventually effected. The progress of the discussion can best be understood by reading the reports made to Congress in 1784 and 1785.

6	5	4	3	2	1
7	8	9	10	11	12
18	17	16	15	14	13
19	20	21	22	23	24
30	29	28	27	26	25
31	32	33	34	35	36

HALF SECTION
320 ACRES

QUARTER
SECTION
160 ACRES

HALF QUARTER
SECTION
80 ACRES

QUARTER
QUARTER
SECTION
40 ACRES

System of Land Surveys

THE ORDINANCE OF 1785

Out of the welter of proposals eventually emerged the Ordinance of 1785, which applied to the region north of the Ohio and was designed primarily to obtain revenue from the public domain. The survey system established by the act became universal for all public lands, and continues today to remain the practice in most of the United States. Townships six miles square were to be surveyed prior to sale; each township was to be divided into thirty-six sections, each section thus being one mile square and containing 640 acres. Since the earth is round, these amounts actually varied slightly. The land was to be sold in the eastern states at auction, with a minimum price of one dollar an acre plus the cost of survey. Half of the land was to be sold in townships and the remainder was to be sold in sections. Reservations were made for the revolutionary soldiers and for schools.

Sales of land under the new ordinance were disappointingly slow to a government badly in need of immediate funds. Seven ranges of townships adjacent to the western boundary of Pennsylvania were surveyed in the years 1785–1787 and put on the market. Auctions were held in the city of New York, but only a few speculators attended and little land was sold. Most of the settlers merely squatted and hoped that Congress would some day take pity on their plight; certainly they had no money to go east and buy land at auction.

THE ORDINANCE OF 1784

Efforts to solve the problem of the survey and sale of the public domain were paralleled by discussions about the form of government that should be given to the West; in fact, the first governmental legislation came a year earlier than the land ordinance of 1785. The Ordinance of 1784 was based on a report made by Jefferson to Congress earlier the same year; kind critics have called it a temporary aberration on the part of the usually brilliant Jefferson. The report suggested limited local self-government for the West until its population was sufficiently large to justify the creation of states. To produce areas of sizes appropriate for statehood, the land west of the mountains and north of the Ohio was to be divided in a checkerboard fashion on every other degree of latitude, with a transverse line through the center of the territory. The result would have been ten approximately equal divisions, which were to be given the mellifluous names of Sylvania, Washington, Michigania, Cherronesus, Saratoga, Illinois, Polypotamia, Pelisipia, Metropotamia, and Assenisippia. When any of these regions had a population as large as the smallest state of the United States it was to be admitted to the Union under whatever government it desired. When the report was finally put into law the boundaries were changed, Jefferson's names were abandoned, and provision was made for each region to have a delegate to Congress as soon as it had attained a population of 20,000.

The ordinances of 1784 and 1785 were not final solutions of the land and government problems, but they were important steps in that direction. Most observers agreed that these ordinances were in themselves not quite satisfactory. Land was not being sold and consequently no revenue was being produced. There was still no real provision for government before statehood. In consequence, Congress continued to debate the whole matter, and further action was only a question of time.

THE OHIO COMPANY

While Congress was trying to make up its mind, a movement started that was destined to have an important influence both on Congress and on the settlement of the West. As previously mentioned, the soldiers of the revolutionary army had long been interested in obtaining western land as part of their reward for services in the war, and in 1786 two generals, Israel Putnam and Benjamin Tupper, called a meeting of all interested parties at the Bunch of Grapes Tavern in Boston. At this meeting was formed the Ohio Company, with a nominal capital of $1 million. Each member was to subscribe $1000 in depreciated Continental currency, which was easy to obtain, and $10 in cash, which was more difficult. The $10 subscriptions were to be used for immediate expenses, and it was hoped that Congress would accept the paper money in payment for western lands. General Samuel H. Parsons was delegated to present the proposition to Congress.

When Parsons arrived to talk with Congress he found no Congress in session—a quorum failed to appear from May 12 to July 5, 1787. He finally succeeded in presenting his petition, but any action seemed unlikely since the members of Congress were anything but optimistic. In fact Congress was only marking time, waiting to see what was to happen in the Constitutional Convention, which had begun its meetings May 25.

The gloomy outlook in Congress caused the Ohio Company to take further thought, and finally to send a new representative, Rev. Manasseh Cutler. Cutler had been a chaplain with the revolutionary army and was a man of wide interests and broad culture. He immediately mounted his horse and rode to New York to see what might be done. His first efforts seemed so fruitless that he took a vacation and rode down to Philadelphia to attend some of the meetings of the Constitutional Convention. When he returned to New York he found his prospects more promising, and so embarked on a strenuous program of calling on members of Congress, attending clambakes and receptions, and of cultivating particularly the friendship of the President of Congress, Arthur St. Clair.

The petition of the Ohio Company for land was but one of the matters pressing on Congress for attention. The necessity of affording a better government for the West was a paramount problem, and it was but natural that Cutler, in lobbying for his own pet measure, should become interested in the governmental legislation and have a hand in both affairs. Another modifying factor was the speculative interest of many members of Congress and their friends in western lands. In fact, one of these men, William Duer, was so influential that Cutler felt it necessary to come to an understanding with him. The bargain they made was that Cutler promised to buy extra land for Duer and his associates in return for their support of the proposed Ohio Company purchase. But the congressional committee that was considering Cutler's proposal remained hesitant. Thereupon Cutler grew impatient and threatened to buy his land from the individual states if Congress did not act. According to his statement his threat "appeared to have the effect I wished"; the committee was "mortified," and eventually the grant was made.

The final grant included 6,500,000 acres of Ohio land—1,500,000 acres for the Ohio Company and the remainder for Duer and his associates. The price to the Ohio Company was one dollar an acre, with one third off for bad lands, to be paid in Continental currency, which was then worth twelve and a half cents on the dollar. The actual price was therefore about eight cents an acre, which certainly was not excessive for good Ohio land, even when the state was a wilderness. According to the terms of the contract, $500,000 was to be paid immediately and the remainder when the surveys were completed.

The grant to the Ohio Company immediately stirred that organization to activity. The down payment was made, and plans were evolved for the settlement of at least part of the tract. In 1788 a group of New Englanders made the trip across New York and northern Pennsylvania, and then floated down the Ohio River to the mouth of the Muskingum, where they founded the town of Marietta near Fort Harmar, which had been established three years earlier. Being confirmed New Englanders, they produced a good New England village, including the usual Congregational Church. When the Ohio Company eventually found itself unable to pay the remainder of the purchase price, Congress remitted it and cut the grant in half, so that the company finally received 750,000 acres.

THE SCIOTO COMPANY

Meantime the Duer group (usually known as the Scioto Company, although not organized formally) went ahead with plans to settle its land. Joel Barlow, the well-known author of the *Columbiad,* was sent to France to sell potential American farms. While in France he became associated with William Playfair, an Englishman who took the initiative in organizing a French company to do the actual selling. The wild land of the Scioto Company was advertised as very fertile, well populated, and suited particularly to artisans and mechanics of all kinds; no mention was made of the lack of a final title by the company. Soon the company's office was crowded with hopeful buyers and 3 million acres were sold. In 1790 some 600 of the purchasers started for America. For the most part they were members of the upper middle class, including professional men, artisans, wood carvers, watch- and clockmakers, tailors, wigmakers, and dancing masters. There was something pathetically humorous in the idea of wigmakers and dancing masters migrating to the untamed wilderness of Ohio.

Duer and his friends were both pleased and embarrassed by the success of Barlow and Playfair. They were particularly concerned over their ability to make the necessary payments on their grant, for the cost of 5 million acres was a huge sum, even though the price was only two thirds of a dollar an acre and payments could be made in six installments. When they tried to obtain the proceeds of the French company it was found to be insolvent due to the manipulations of Playfair. The result was the bankruptcy of the Scioto Company, and by the time the French settlers landed in Virginia their prospects were exceedingly gloomy. Eventually the migrants were escorted to the West and there, instead of finding populous towns and plenty of work, they discovered a wilderness containing a few partly completed log cabins. Some drifted away to other parts of the country, while others stayed to form the town of Gallipolis. Actually they were on Ohio Company land, where most of them remained in spite of a congressional donation of land in the present Scioto County.

In addition to the Ohio Company and the Duer group many other individuals and companies applied to Congress for the purchase of large areas in the West. The only other sale was to John Cleves Symmes, a member of Congress from New Jersey. Symmes received in 1788 a grant of 1 million acres east of the Little Miami. The terms were similar to those made to the Ohio Company: he was to pay $82,198 down and the remainder in seven installments. He made the down payment, but defaulted on the remainder, and the grant ultimately was reduced to 300,000 acres along the Ohio River.

THE NORTHWEST ORDINANCE

While these various tracts of land were being granted the matter of government was finally settled. The ordinance that provided for the government of the New West was probably the most remarkable piece of legislation passed by Congress under the Articles of Confederation, particularly in consideration of the fact that the old government was giving its last feeble gasps of life before the new Constitution was completed and put into effect. True it is that the act was mixed with the lobbying efforts of Cutler, Duer, and others, that Cutler himself had a hand in the final outcome, and that Arthur St. Clair aided it partly because he had been promised the governorship of the new territory; and yet the Ordinance of 1787 was a remarkable bit of constructive legislation, of which the principles were to remain in effect during the entire process of frontier advance from the Appalachians to the Pacific. Any act that was used successfully for a century and a half under varying conditions is worthy of respect.

The Ordinance of 1787 applied only to the Old Northwest. This territory was to be divided into three, four, or five states. If three, the dividing lines should run as follows—one along the Wabash River to the meridian of Vincennes and then along that meridian due north to the international boundary; the other was the meridian of the mouth of the Great Miami. These are approximately the present boundaries on the east and west of Indiana. If four or five states were to be created, then an additional line should be drawn directly east and west through the tip of Lake Michigan. This last line was later modified.

Even more important than the division of territory were the provisions for government that remedied the defects of the Ordinance of 1784 by providing an effective administration before statehood. Three stages of government were provided. The first, which was to go into effect immediately, gave control to a governor, a secretary, and three judges, all elected by Congress, which maintained control. When the population of the territory had increased to include 5000 free adult males, the second type of government was to go into effect: all the old officers and provisions remained, but an elective legislature was provided to give the electorate its first taste of self-government. Finally, when the total population reached 60,000 free inhabitants, a constitutional convention could be held and the prospective state could apply for admission to the Union. In addition to these provisions there was also a bill of rights similar to that of the federal Constitution, and a prohibition of slavery, except for those slaves already in the territory.

Immediately following the passage of the Ordinance of 1787 Arthur St. Clair was appointed the first Governor of the Northwest Territory. After a leisurely trip he finally arrived in Marietta on July 9, 1788. He had little to govern, in terms of land or population, and as a man of ambition he was anxious to increase both, which meant that he was particularly desirous of pushing back the Indians who were occupying the larger part of his new domain.

The fact that the Ordinance of 1787 applied only to the Old Northwest is sometimes forgotten. A similar act of 1790 made provision for the territory south of the Ohio. In later years the principles of the Ordinance of 1787 were re-enacted many times to provide for all the new regions west to the Pacific, with the exception of only Texas and California.

FURTHER DEBATES ON LAND

If anyone believed that the idea of making large grants such as that to the Ohio Company would replace the necessity for smaller sales to individuals he was soon disillusioned by the difficulties encountered before the large grants were adjusted. For the most part, existing congressional legislation had no effect whatever: settlers continued to go where they pleased without consideration of the law. Certainly it seemed an imposition to ask a poor land seeker to make the long trip east to have a chance to bid at auction for the land he had already improved. If the prospective settler bought before he moved West, he found himself in equally bad circumstances; either he must buy his land unseen or he must make an expensive and time-consuming trip to the West before he bought. The only logical solution was to establish local land offices reasonably near the land that was to be sold.

The question of price also disturbed Congress. Everyone agreed that the land should produce a revenue to the central government, but there unanimity ceased. What sort of price would produce a maximum return? Too expensive land would mean that the poorer settlers could not afford to buy, and would simply squat; whereupon the government would be faced with the unpleasant necessity of ejecting large numbers of settlers from their homes or giving them the land. Closely allied with this problem was that of deciding the minimum size of a tract that would be sold to one person. Too large a minimum would mean that only the speculator could buy, but a very small one would raise the cost of administration to a prohibitive figure. These and other phases of the land situation were debated continuously by Congress after 1789.

Alexander Hamilton contributed to the discussion in 1790 by a report to Congress in which he suggested a policy designed to increase the stability of the nation. He recommended that preference in land sales be given to large companies, and that the small settler be pacified by making it possible for him to buy tracts of not over 100 acres. The price would be 30 cents an acre and credit would be given for three quarters of the purchase price. Branch land offices would supply local needs. Influenced to some extent by this report, Congress eventually passed the act of 1796, which represented one more step toward the solution of the land problem. There were a few main changes from the Ordinance of 1785: the minimum price was set at $2 an acre, payments could be spread over twelve months, and land offices were to be opened in Pittsburgh and Cincinnati.

THE ACT OF 1800

The most significant legislation of this period came in 1800, when Harrison's frontier bill became law. William Henry Harrison was the first congressional delegate from the territory of Ohio, and his measure represented the western desires of the time—modified to some extent, of course, by the necessities of practical politics. Most of the provisions were not novel, having long been discussed and having been expressed in considerable part in the act of 1796. Local land offices were established at Cincinnati, Chillicothe, Marietta, and Steubenville; each office was to be manned by a registrar (for drawing up the deeds) and a receiver (to control the finances). East of the Muskingum the land was to be sold entirely in tracts of a section apiece (640 acres); west of that river half was to be sold in sections and half in half sections. The auction system was retained, with a minimum price of $2 an acre, the purchaser also paying the cost of survey. Any land remaining unsold after the auction was open to private entry at the minimum price. Only about one twentieth of the purchase price was due at the time of the sale, the remainder of the first quarter being due in forty days, and the other three quarters in three annual payments, the last payment coming due at the end of four years. Interest was charged on the deferred payments, and a discount was given for earlier settlement.

The act of 1800 fulfilled in general the desires of the West. The size of the individual purchase had been reduced, although even 320 acres of uncleared land proved a large amount, and was reduced in 1804 to 160 acres and in 1817 to 80 acres. The price was still high from the standpoint of the

Westerner, but this trouble was alleviated by the credit system; the Westerner might now make the first payment on twice the amount of land that before 1796 he could have bought at $1 an acre; true he was in debt, but few worried when almost everyone expected that within a few years he would be rich.

With the passage of the act of 1800 two of the important western problems had been settled for the time being. No other important land legislation was passed for another twenty years. A scheme of government had been devised that was to last throughout the entire period of the continental expansion of the United States. In view of these accomplishments it becomes possible to consider some of the other problems and conditions of life that surrounded the people of the West in the period immediately after the Revolution.

READINGS

GENERAL. The topics treated in this chapter are covered in various state histories. Useful ones are the scholarly Clarence W. Alvord, *The Illinois Country, 1673–1818* (1920) ; Beverley W. Bond Jr., *The Civilization of the Old Northwest* (1934) ; the readable Walter Havighurst, *Land of Promise* (1946) ; Eugene H. Roseboom and Francis P. Weisenburger, *A History of Ohio* (1953) ; William T. Utter, *The Frontier State 1803–1825* (1943), concerning Ohio. Jay A. Barrett, *Evolution of the Ordinance of 1787* (1891) is old but accurate. Frazer E. Wilson, *Arthur St. Clair* (1944) is highly sympathetic.

LAND LEGISLATION. Roy M. Robbins, *Our Landed Heritage* (1942) is the best history of the public domain; Benjamin H. Hibbard, *A History of the Public Land Policies* (1924) is adequate; Payson J. Treat, *The National Land System, 1785–1820* (1910) is good on the early years. Two good special studies are Thomas P. Abernethy, *Western Lands and the American Revolution* (1937) and Beverley W. Bond Jr., *The Quit Rent System in the American Colonies* (1919).

OHIO AND SCIOTO COMPANIES. Aaron M. Sakolski, *The Great American Land Bubble* (1932) deals generally with land speculation. Joseph S. Davis, *Essays in the Earlier History of American Corporations* (2 vols., 1917) is scholarly and informative. Theodore T. Belote, *The Scioto Speculation* (1907) remains the best on Gallipolis. Alfred P. James, *The Ohio Company* (1959) is best on that subject, and Stewart H. Holbrook, *The Yankee Exodus* (1950) has material on Marietta. Original records are presented in Archer B. Hulbert (ed.), *The Records of the Original Proceedings of the Ohio Company* (2 vols., 1917), and Dwight L. Smith (ed.), *The Western Journals of John May* (1961), concerning an agent of the Ohio Company.

CHAPTER 7

REMOVING THE
INDIAN MENACE

B y no means the least of the dangers facing the western settler was the Indian, who was viewed somewhat contemptuously as "uncivilized" because he was still in the stone age, seminomadic, and with no written language except pictographs. The Indian has been misunderstood by his friends as well as his enemies. His friends have drawn him as an impossibly noble savage, animated always by bravery, generosity, sagacity, and sensitivity; his enemies have painted him as sly, cruel, bloodthirsty, untrustworthy, and depraved. Actually he was a man like other men, by turns generous and selfish, kind and cruel. He was sometimes able and sometimes stupid. Generally he was fun-loving and reasonably garrulous, with strong family devotion. His way of life was different from that of the white, but adapted to his circumstances. His cultural elimination now appears as a tragedy, even though it was inevitable.

Although the original Indian culture was finally almost eliminated, the Indian had numerous effects on his conquerors. Indian names such as Oshkosh, Winnebago, and Arkansas are found throughout the United States. Indian plants of the New World, such as maize, potatoes, tobacco, pumpkin, squash, and tomato, have in time been estimated to constitute over half of all agricultural production. Not only their plants but their methods of cultivation have been adopted and today's methods of preparing such things as hominy, pone, and succotash were originally Indian. Other white adaptations have ranged from lacrosse to scalping. The effect of the Indian has been by no means negligible.

To the north, centering in present New York State, were the ten to twelve thousand of the Iroquois or Six Nations—the Mohawk, Oneida,

Onondaga, Cayuga, Seneca, and Tuscarora—a confederation that represented the highest type of political organization ever developed by the North American Indians. They claimed a nominal overlordship of the tribes as far west as the Mississippi, and now and then enforced part of their claims. During the Revolution the Iroquois were powerful and important, but their power then waned and after 1800 they were no longer significant.

THE OLD NORTHWEST

The second important group of Indians between the Appalachians and the Mississippi was composed of the tribes that occupied the region between the Ohio River and the Great Lakes. Foremost were the Shawnee in present Ohio, the Wyandot near Detroit, the Miami in present Indiana, the Illinois in present Illinois, the Sauk and Foxes north of the Illinois River, and the Potawatomi, Winnebago, Ottawa, and Chippewa in the upper Great Lakes region. Most of them were Algonquian, and in contrast to the Iroquois of the Six Nations, almost always acted independently. Together they totaled possibly fifty thousand persons, but in all probability not over three thousand warriors were on the warpath at any one time.

The Indians north of the Ohio were sufficiently similar to permit a single description. They were normally peaceful, but could on occasion be warlike and cruel. Each tribe, each group, and often each individual acted independently in case of war; each warrior sought whatever shelter he could find, did his fighting, and then went home. Pitched battles were rare. The dead were scalped, since the warrior who could show one or more scalps had proof of his prowess in touching the enemy and of his service to the tribe. Prisoners were sometimes adopted by the tribe, particularly if they were women or children; now and then a captive was tortured, but such incidents were sufficiently unusual to be worthy of particular notice.

Landownership among the Algonquians existed only through use. Whoever planted a crop of corn had possession of that piece of land until the corn was harvested and not longer. Agriculture was limited usually to the raising of corn, with sometimes squash and beans. More important was the fishing and hunting land, for the Indians lived mostly on fish and game. Here also was a rough ownership through use. Each tribe had vague limits to the land over which it could hunt, and invasion by other tribes might mean war. These tribes were not truly nomadic, but a hunting life meant much movement; consequently houses were simple wigwams—usually an oval framework, dome-shaped, and covered with bark. Here and there, at strategic points, permanent towns were constructed.

At the time the whites arrived all the clothing of these Indians was of leather. The man ordinarily wore a breechcloth, moccasins, leggings, and a hunting shirt; on the warpath he limited his attire to a breechcloth and

Indian Tribes, 1800

plenty of bright paint. The woman wore a skirt extending below her knees, and sometimes a jacket. Polygamy was usually permitted, but never was widely practiced, for there was no large surplus of women. Infidelity on the part of the wife was punished by cutting off the end of her nose or by killing her. Such punishment was meted out by the injured husband, since all punishment was a matter of individual vengeance. A woman's life was difficult and arduous. It was she who did the planting and cultivating, gathered herbs and firewood, cooked, dressed the leather, sewed the clothes with sinew, made the utensils, constructed the wigwam, and cared for the children. The men confined their activities mainly to hunting, fishing, and fighting.

Sickness was considered supernatural and due to evil spirits or to the failure to perform the proper ceremonials. The Indian medicine man depended heavily on elaborate rituals designed to drive out the wicked spirits. Incidentally he used simple herbs, which may have had some effect. Frequently the medicine man would suck the part affected, and then spit out of his mouth hair, stones, sticks, or similar material; these articles were supposed to have come from the ailing member and their absence was expected to relieve the patient. Wonderful cures were often made, particularly with wounds, probably because of the sucking, the herbs, and the outdoor life of the patient, but functional disorders and contagious diseases were frequently fatal.

The treatment of sickness was to the Indian but one phase of the continual process of placating the innumerable spirits, both good and bad, that were thought to inhabit the world. There were hundreds of ceremonials to gratify the various Indian desires, such as getting rain, securing good hunting, curing disease, obtaining success against enemies, and producing brave warriors. Each of these ceremonials had complicated ritual, with specified ceremonial actions, decorations, fire, and speeches. Usually it included some kind of instrumental music (drum or whistle), singing, and dancing. Often particular animals, such as the snake and the bear, were mimicked. In addition to the hundreds of small good and bad spirits that had to be placated, most tribes believed in one more important good and one more important bad spirit. Usually they also believed in a future life in which the good Indian would live at his ease, with much fine hunting and fishing, and no accidents or disease.

THE OLD SOUTHWEST

To the south of the Ohio River were the large loose confederations of the Five Civilized Nations—Cherokee, Choctaw, Creeks, Chickasaw, and Seminole—whose destinies in the decade after the Revolution were controlled to some extent by the unusually able Creek half-breed Alexander McGillivray. The Cherokee lived in the mountainous parts of the present states of Tennessee, Alabama, Georgia, and North and South Carolina. They were an industrious and intelligent group, tilling the land, hunting, raising horses, dogs, and poultry, and developing many picturesque dances —ceremonial, erotic, and warlike. One of their amusements was an early form of the present lacrosse. The main differences were that the field was larger, the players were unlimited in number, and the game was even rougher than it is today. The Indian seldom lost his temper, even though he might in a bet lose his entire possessions.

West of the Cherokee, and extending to the Mississippi, were the Chickasaw. The most warlike of the Five Nations, they usually acted together in case of trouble. South of the Chickasaw were the Choctaw, the least important of the groups. They were commonly reported as treacherous, and did not act together. East of them (in present Florida) were the Seminole, who were really a branch of the Creeks.

Strongest of the Five Nations were the Creeks, living south of the Cherokee. Not only were they the strongest; they were probably the most civilized of the Indians within the present boundaries of the United States. Their fields were extensive and sometimes fenced, being worked by communal effort, and producing rice, corn, tobacco, beans, and potatoes. They hunted and fished and also raised horses, hogs, and poultry, and sometimes owned Negro slaves. Their clothing, blankets, and wigwams were well made and beautifully trimmed. Their pottery was of clay, and glazed to give it a hard surface.

The Creeks had permanent towns. In the center of each town was an open square surrounded by four long low buildings in which the warriors were housed according to their rank. The families of the warriors lived in lodges built around the central square and up and down a river or creek; from fifteen to two hundred lodges constituted an ordinary village. For each town there was a head man in addition to the war chiefs, and each town sent representatives to general tribal councils. This rough confederation sometimes resulted in common action.

As was true of all Indians, the Creeks had elaborate rituals and ceremonials. Their principal festival was the green-corn dance, at which the first ear of corn was burned with intricate rites. For three days the men stayed in the square and fasted, while the women bathed frequently. The big ceremony came on the fourth day, when both sexes mingled in the open square. As was usual such ceremonies were connected with the belief in a good and a bad spirit, and in a time of future reward or punishment.

The marital customs of the Creeks had some interesting differences from those of other tribes. Courtship was carried on by a female friend of the male suitor. Both marriage and divorce were easy, either party being permitted to leave his or her mate at any time without warning. The family centered in the woman; the husband moved to his wife's home. Adultery was punished by whipping or by cutting off the hair or ears; such punishment was inflicted either by the husband or by the male relatives of the wife.

ATTITUDE TOWARD THE INDIANS

The first problem of the white settler in regard to the Indian was protection, for from time to time and without announcement the Indian went to war and no settlement was safe. But of almost equal importance was the fact that the Indians possessed land the frontiersmen wished to occupy; moreover, the federal government accepted such claims to ownership. The Westerner himself was not impressed. To the whites land ownership meant small individual holdings with the object of farming. The Indians, from this point of view, were only savages whom God for some inscrutable reason had allowed to hinder the progress of his chosen white people. The Indians had no rights against those of the superior white civilization; killing them was much like killing poisonous snakes. The whites, according to dominant opinion, should eliminate the Indians and enter into their rightful heritage.

The federal government had a different point of view, partly because it was far distant from the scene of the troubles. A whole series of laws made every effort to treat the Indian with the "utmost good faith," as promised in the Northwest Ordinance. Traders in the Indian country were presumably brought under control by a licensing system. Private land purchases were prohibited, and settlers in the Indian country were to be removed—by force if necessary. Agents were sent out and gifts were provided, as in the Intercourse Act of 1793, to try to persuade the natives to adopt settled farming. The enforcement of such legislation, however, was almost impossible. Federal forces were too small to police the Indian country properly. Illegal settlers might be removed from time to time but they soon returned. Persuading the Indian to become a farmer on the white model had little success except among some of the southern tribes. Friction was continual as Indians visited white settlements, whites invaded the Indian country, and frontier cattle roamed freely.

From the standpoint of the federal government the Indians were in fact in an anomalous position. On the one hand they were considered as independent nations exercising the rights of sovereignty; they owned the land they occupied, and land cessions or any other agreements had to be in the form of treaties made by the executive power and ratified by the Senate. On the other hand it was quite evident that, regardless of any polite legal fiction, Indian tribes were not in fact free and independent states. They lived within the territorial limits of the United States, were not recognized by foreign nations, and were subject to controls imposed without their consent, and often without their knowledge.

Both the nation and the Indians suffered from the attempts to maintain an unrealistic theory of Indian independence. The federal government was in a perpetual quandary as to how to treat frontier advance as it impinged on the Indian country. If Indian rights were maintained rigidly there would be no white advance, and a white government could hardly view this prospect with equanimity, particularly when white Westerners could vote and Indians could not. At the same time the federal government had every intention of treating the Indians fairly. The fluctuations and inconsistencies of white policy are at least understandable if not always admirable.

INDIAN TREATIES

The method usually followed in settling a conflict between Indian rights and white desires was to buy the disputed land and open it formally to white settlement. The Indians were summoned to a council at some central spot. Government agents mixed cajolery, threats, food, clothing, and liquor to obtain a treaty of cession. Ordinarily the compensation to the Indians included blankets, cloth, weapons, jewelry, annuities, and frequently aid to settled agriculture. After the signing by Indians and whites, the treaty went to the Senate for approval. In many cases the Senate modified its terms, necessitating an effort, usually futile, to have the modifications accepted by the original signatories.

As soon as the treaty was made and ratified it was considered by the United States as permanently binding on all members of the tribes represented, and on their descendants. Flagrant violations might inspire a punitive expedition to visit justice upon the violators; no clear line of demarcation could be drawn between individual criminals and the tribes of which they were members. As for the ceded land, it was formally surveyed and opened for settlement; usually the original settlers, who had come while the land still technically belonged to the Indians, had their possessions confirmed.

Not only was the treaty policy of the federal government based on an unrealistic theory; it involved all sorts of practical difficulties. The Indians never really understood the white concept of landownership. They had no idea of permanent individual ownership and sale. In a vague way they recognized an ownership by use, but even here their concepts were not clear-cut. They often failed to appreciate that the land they sold was to be closed to them forever. Land was like air and water—plentiful enough for the use of everyone—and it was a perpetual surprise to the Indian that he was prohibited from returning to the land on which he had formerly hunted.

Moreover, the Indians never saw eye to eye with the whites concerning treaties. Both the Indians and the whites agreed in theory that a treaty must be signed by authorized representatives, and then ratified by proper authority—tribe and Senate, respectively. But here agreement ended. Indian signatories frequently had no official status, but were just random braves rounded up by the whites; many times they were befuddled by whiskey when they placed their marks at the bottom of words they could not read. The affected tribe might or might not accept the agreement, and in either case the terms might well not be understood. As for the whites, they assumed that a treaty was binding on the Indians as soon as it was signed, and regardless of technicalities. The possibilities for trouble were obviously unending.

When the Indians violated a treaty, possibly because of lack of understanding, a failure of ratification, or complete unawareness of its existence, further differences between red and white ideology became important. The violation was usually committed by an individual, or by one or more small groups acting independently. The tribe as a whole might have no knowledge of these acts, and feel no responsibility, but the federal government professed to see no difference between the part and the whole. It was difficult to discover and punish the real offenders; hence the punitive expedition waged war on any group of Indians within the district in which the trouble had occurred.

These differences in attitude between white man and red man made conflict inevitable, particularly as white settlers continued to view Indian land with covetous eyes. The clashes should be blamed as much on unavoidable differences of viewpoint as on bad faith on either side. Some of the disastrous results of the conflict might have been avoided if the federal government had abandoned earlier the effort to treat Indian tribes as independent nations, but the central problem of removing the Indians would still have brought untold misery and heartbreak.

THE WEST AT THE END OF THE REVOLUTION

The end of the Revolution found the frontier in turmoil. The fortunes of war had varied, but never had there been a decisive and large-scale defeat of the Indians. For the Indians war still continued, and they harried outlying settlements, killing individuals, capturing families, driving off stock, stealing crops, and destroying improvements. Arguments that the war was over because a few far distant whites had uttered the magic word "peace" carried little conviction. From the Indian standpoint, white intruders were still arriving and the new ones were no less objectionable than their predecessors.

White settlers were on the march, both north and south, and their increasing number made conflict with the reds unavoidable. Indians loved their homes and would not move voluntarily. In the South the expansion was from Georgia and the infant state of Franklin. In the North the occupation of Ohio had begun, with streams of settlement converging from Kentucky and western Pennsylvania. A sprinkling of towns such as Marietta had appeared on the northern bank of the Ohio River.

Also to the north and to the south foreign powers complicated the situation. In the South, Spain was anxious to keep the Indian trade and to provide a buffer against further United States expansion. To accomplish these ends it was cordial toward the Indians and friendly toward Franklin, which it even talked of attaching to itself. In the North, England continued to hold such western posts as Detroit and Mackinac, and to cultivate friendly Indian relations—with the object, of course, of retaining the fur trade. A gesture was made toward restraining the Indians from active war, for American good will was desired, but an Indian confederation was encouraged, and British statements at least implied that assistance would be forthcoming for the Indians in any future trouble with the United States.

Northwest and Southwest were similar in another matter: in each area was an Indian confederation. The southern combination was inspired by Alexander McGillivray and the northern one by the equally able Joseph Brant. Each federation was hostile to any further land cessions to the whites and agreed not to consider such cessions as valid.

INDIAN TREATIES AFTER THE WAR

The federal government under the Articles of Confederation was more optimistic about the Indians than the facts warranted. Flushed with success, Congress held in 1783 that the Indians, as unsuccessful British allies, had lost the war and therefore forfeited all claim to their land—a proposition impossible to maintain in fact. During the same year Congress ordered all white intruders off the Indian lands, even though it had insufficient power to enforce the order, and sent commissioners to obtain treaties of peace and friendship with the various tribes. In 1786 it provided for the administration of Indian affairs through two departments that divided their duties at the Ohio River; both were subject to the Secretary of War.

When the congressional commissioners went west they found their job extremely difficult. Most Indians had little desire to talk and even less to sign treaties—particularly treaties involving land cessions. Ultimately the southern Indians were brought into line with treaties with the Cherokee (1785), Chickasaw and Choctaw (1786), and Creeks (1790). Of these tribes, the Chickasaw and Choctaw were generally friendly to the whites. The Cherokee and Creeks were generally hostile—a hostility not alleviated either by treaties or by various military operations, including those of Georgia and of the state of Franklin.

In the North the congressional commissioners made a parallel series of treaties but with even poorer results—if that were possible. By the Treaty of Fort Stanwix (1784) the Iroquois once more promised to give up their western claims. By the treaties of Fort McIntosh (1786) and Fort Finney (1786) most of the northwestern tribes agreed to accept American sovereignty and to cede their claims to most of Ohio. The trouble with these treaties was that many groups were not represented, and most Indians considered them not binding.

The commissioners tried to show their good faith by ordering Colonel Josiah Harmar in 1785 to eject all unauthorized white settlers who were in the Indian country. Harmar made a few feeble gestures in this direction, and constructed Fort Harmar at the mouth of the Muskingum, but he then decided quite wisely that his force was too small to accomplish the task with which it was charged.

All these treaties made a brave show on the statute books but produced remarkably little change in western conditions. Indian raids continued, to the danger and distress of the West. At this juncture the problem was transferred to the hands of the new government established under the Constitution. Some sort of action was inevitable, especially since President Washington had long been greatly concerned with the West and had watched that section with a keen and active interest.

Arthur St. Clair, as Governor of the Northwest Territory, tried his hand at Indian affairs by concluding a treaty with all available Indians at Fort Harmar in January 1789. Again the Indians bound themselves to keep earlier treaties of peace, but again they showed very little enthusiasm for keeping their agreements. The consequence was that Brigadier General Harmar (his rank had been raised by this time) was sent on a raiding expedition against the hostile tribes. In spite of some minor successes, Harmar's expedition was a failure; instead of pacifying them it made the Indians more hostile.

HARMAR

Harmar's failure necessitated more drastic measures, and in the summer of 1790 Congress empowered President Washington to call out the militia of Kentucky, Virginia, and western Pennsylvania for the defense of the frontier. General Harmar, who was placed in command, was at this time at Fort Washington (Cincinnati) ; hence the new troops were allowed to straggle down the Ohio River on their own initiative and at their own convenience.

The army that finally gathered at Fort Washington was composed of 1453 men, of whom 320 were federal troops with a background of military experience gathered in the Revolution. The others were militiamen mostly from Pennsylvania and Kentucky, and were far from satisfactory fighters. They ranged in age from the very young to the very old. Many were physically incompetent; few had even an elementary idea of how to care for and use a gun. Supplies were poor, clothing was inadequate and shoddy, and food was very bad. These conditions occasioned much grumbling. The militiamen had the usual resentment toward military control; disciplining a western company of militiamen was almost as difficult as enforcing orders on the Ohio River. In addition, the militiamen and the regulars were perpetually jealous of one another. Each group looked on the other with contempt, and came to its assistance only in dire mutual necessity.

Late in September, after the most desultory training, this ill-assorted army left Fort Washington to fight the Indian confederation, of which the most hostile members were the Shawnee, the Miami, and the Kickapoo. Very soon the militia threatened mutiny; some of the volunteers actually started to go home, so that it was necessary to use force to recall them to their duty. A little later, after the army had covered some 170 miles, it accidentally encountered a small group of Indians. Both parties were surprised and alarmed, but the militiamen were more quick-witted than the Indians and started to run first. Again they had to be brought back ignominiously.

The general route of Harmar's slow and badly organized march was up the Little Miami and then north in the region of the present Ohio-Indiana boundary. Supplies were inadequate and the men were discontented, but luckily no considerable body of Indians appeared along the line of march. Finally the army reached one of the more important Indian towns, situated at the present site of Fort Wayne; the Indians fled, and Harmar's men had the satisfaction of destroying the Indian lodges and crops.

This "brilliant victory" was followed by other engagements that were less satisfactory. On September 19 a white detachment was surprised and overwhelmed. Two days later a general engagement was fought. Harmar's army was disorganized, and retreated hurriedly; two hundred whites were killed and thirty-five wounded, the proportion between the two figures showing the thoroughness of the Indian operations. More men would have been killed if the Indians had not been so occupied with taking scalps and loading themselves with plunder. Eventually Harmar's army was restored to partial order, but it was thoroughly disheartened. On November 4 the survivors arrived at Fort Washington.

Harmar's operations were far from successful in subduing the Indians. A court of inquiry examined the affair and exonerated the general. He had probably shown considerable personal bravery and had done the best he could with very poor material, but these factors were of very little importance to a West looking for peace with the Indians. The net result was that a white expedition had been defeated disastrously, and that the Indians continued their depredations with increased self-assurance. Two other small expeditions were sent early in 1791, one of them led by Wilkinson. They succeeded in doing some damage, but not enough to frighten the red man.

ST. CLAIR

In this extremity President Washington ordered Governor St. Clair to take personal command, cautioning him of the many mistakes that had been made in the past and impressing on him the necessity for a successful campaign. St. Clair was a high-minded gentleman of the Federalist school, with noble ideals and great personal courage, but by that time he was elderly and choleric; his strength was waning, his fat was increasing, and he was troubled periodically by gout. He overrated his own military ability. In spite of these handicaps he developed a good plan of campaign, which had as its principal objective the construction of a line of forts from the Ohio River to Lake Erie.

St. Clair's men, like Harmar's, were poor material with which to fight an Indian war. They were gathered for the most part from the cities of the East, often being drawn from the poorhouses and prisons. Most of them were six months' militia, receiving $2.10 a month, lacking military experience, and thriving on dissipation and disorder. This nondescript array came west by way of Pittsburgh, being allowed to follow its own pleasure in descending the Ohio to Fort Washington. Theoretically St. Clair had some 3000 men, but actually his total number of effectives was never larger than 2000. All the bad conditions that had bothered Harmar also harassed St. Clair.

St. Clair's first operation was the dispatch of an advance guard that built Fort Hamilton on the Great Miami about twenty-five miles from Cincinnati. The main army started its advance early in October 1791, but not without much grumbling at leaving the pleasures of garrison life in Cincinnati. The wilderness, however, was made endurable by continued gambling and drinking, as well as by the presence of many women camp followers. On October 12 Fort Jefferson was built six miles south of the present Greenville, Ohio, and here the army rested twelve days before advancing farther north. November 3 saw the expedition encamped on a plateau of the Wabash a hundred miles north of Cincinnati and on the present Ohio-Indiana line.

At daybreak of November 4 the soldiers were startled from their slumbers by Indian war whoops and a shower of arrows coming from the surrounding forest. When the partially clothed whites rushed from their tents they had to fire at an unseen foe. The resulting engagement included many feats of bravery, but no effectively organized resistance. St. Clair was so weak that he had to be lifted to his horse, but once mounted he displayed great valor. Three horses were shot from under him, eight bullets went through his clothes and one clipped his hair. His best efforts, however, failed to produce any semblance of order among his troops. The Indians lurked in the forest, shot down the easily visible whites, and now and then rushed forth to take a scalp. The troops were unaccustomed to Indian fighting, and probably never saw their foes. Soon they began to retreat and shortly their walk turned into a run. As had occurred with Harmar's troops, the Indians were so busy collecting booty that they did not pursue their defeated adversaries.

When St. Clair's army had recovered enough to count its losses it found that 630 had been killed and 283 wounded—in other words, approximately half of the total force had been put out of action. Many of the bodies were left on the field of battle, and these were mutilated by the Indians; a later investigation showed a considerable number of females among the dead. The remnants of the so-called army gradually straggled back to Cincinnati, thoroughly beaten and demoralized. When the news of the defeat reached President Washington, it is related that he had one of his few outbursts of extreme anger. Congress investigated the conduct of the expedition and exonerated St. Clair. His resignation from the army was accepted in April 1792.

WAYNE

Immediately after St. Clair's defeat Washington began to search for a man who would not repeat previous disastrous campaigns. After much cogitation he gave his approval to a former revolutionary hero, Anthony Wayne, even though "Mad Anthony's" daring exploits during the Revolution raised some questions as to his prospective caution in fighting the Indians. A new army was gathered at Pittsburgh, and again it was composed of the kind of men who had "fought" under Harmar and St. Clair. But at this point all similarity with preceding expeditions ended. Wayne joined his command at Pittsburgh and immediately started to drill his 2500 infantry, cavalry, and artillery.

Wayne desired to win the war in a hurry and return to the more pleasant life in the East, but the Secretary of War, backed by the President, vetoed this plan. Accordingly, Wayne moved twenty miles down the river in the fall of 1792 and spent the winter at Legionville doing more drilling. By this time the West was becoming impatient with a "mad" general who spent his time in the barracks while his enemies were laying waste the settlements he was supposed to protect. But Washington insisted that no offensive action be undertaken until after the Indian councils of 1793. In April of that year Wayne moved his camp near Cincinnati, where he devoted the summer and early fall to still more drilling. Discipline was strict and no detail of training was overlooked, the men even being taught how to yell. Undoubtedly this was the best prepared and drilled army that had ever existed in the West. "Mad Anthony" was in a fair way to lose his hard-won nickname, although by no means entirely through his own desire.

While Wayne drilled his men, American commissioners suffered the ignominy of following the Indians to Detroit to try to make peace. The commissioners were authorized to make real concessions, even to the extent of restoring all Indian lands except the Ohio Company and Symmes grants, or to make large additional payments. But the Indians, arrogant and intractable, refused any compromise and insisted on recovering all their land north and west of the Ohio. The humiliated commissioners returned home without an agreement.

Upon the failure of negotiations, Wayne was immediately given the signal to advance. During the fall he moved north slowly, acclimating his men to actual campaigning. At the present Greenville he built Fort Greenville, an imposing stockade, did more drilling, sent out spies, and started road construction. An advance guard was dispatched late in the year to construct Fort Recovery on the scene of St. Clair's defeat.

The Indians gathered some 2000 warriors in the spring of 1794 to oppose the Wayne advance. They made the mistake of attacking Fort Recovery instead of confining themselves to cutting off isolated parties and interfering with supply trains. Discouraged by the failure of their attack on the fort and by the lack of expected British aid, many of them returned home, so that only 1300 remained when Wayne started to move.

Wayne's advance, beginning late in July, was slow and impressive. Due attention was given to communications and to possible surprises. Fort Adams was built on the St. Mary's River and Fort Defiance at the junction of the Maumee and Auglaize. The main body of Indians was encountered August 20 at a place called Fallen Timbers because of the presence of trees overturned by a heavy storm. Amazingly enough, the Indians were willing to fight one of their rare pitched battles. Wayne repulsed the attack but won no clear-cut victory; the Indians lost only some 50 braves and were by no means demoralized. The decisive nature of the battle lay in the Indian realization that they were to receive no active English aid; the silence of the guns at nearby Fort Miamis (British) was more significant than the actual battle.

After Fallen Timbers Wayne returned to Fort Defiance, from which base he destroyed the nearby Miami towns and built Fort Wayne. The winter of 1794–1795 was spent at Greenville. Wayne's objective had been attained. The Indians had come to realize the futility of further immediate resistance, and for the first time in many years the frontier was freed from the menace of Indian attack. Both in the North and in the South the Indians were cowed and peaceful.

Wayne finished his work in the West by putting the results in a

Wayne in the West

treaty. Starting early in 1795 he called the Indian chiefs to a large conference at Fort Greenville. By June there had arrived 1130 Delawares, Potawatomi, Wyandot, Shawnee, Miami, Chippewa, Ottawa, Wea and Piankashaw, Kickapoo, and Kaskaskia. Fifty days were occupied by feasts, speeches, and ceremonies before any action was taken. The resulting Treaty of Greenville settled the status of the Indians of the Old Northwest for the time being—not because it was the first and only treaty of its kind, but because it was the first to be based on a thorough intimidation of the Indians. By its terms a definite line was drawn between red and white territory. The whites received approximately the southeastern two thirds of the present state of Ohio and the southeastern corner of present Indiana, while the rest of the Northwest was left to the Indians. In return for these land cessions the Indians were to receive immediately goods to the value of $20,000 and later about half that amount annually. As soon as the treaty was signed Wayne returned to the East, where he was received as a hero.

THE JAY TREATY

While Wayne was engaged in his victorious campaign in the West, there was in progress another mission of a far different nature, in which the West was also vitally interested. Negotiations concerning the outstanding differences between England and the United States had been in progress for some time, and in June 1794 John Jay was sent on a special mission to England to carry on direct negotiations. The final treaty (November 19, 1794) was a victory for British diplomacy, and intensely unpopular in the United States, where it was accepted by the Senate with the narrowest of possible votes. In so far as it directly affected the West it provided for the surrender of the northwest posts that England had not evacuated at the end of the Revolution. This surrender actually took place in June 1796, and it was only fitting that Anthony Wayne should be the man to accept the most important of them—Detroit.

With the surrender of the northwest posts and the submission of the Indians, the trans-Appalachian region was more available for settlement than it had ever been. The Indians were not again to be ready for any widespread hostilities until the period of the War of 1812. With American possession of the Great Lakes posts the likelihood of English encouragement of the Indians was decreased, and more freedom was possible for American traders, trappers, and settlers.

The result of these developments was an ever-increasing flow of migration to the West. Whereas most of the early settlers had come from the South by way of the Cumberland Gap, now they began to come in large numbers from the central and northern states. The inevitable cycle of Indian relations was soon completed, and almost before the ink of the Greenville treaty was dry new settlers were again pushing into the Indian country. And again the government followed these pioneers, forcing the Indians back still farther. Half a dozen new cessions in the ten years after Greenville emphasized the ephemeral nature of Indian treaty lines and promises.

READINGS

INDIAN DESCRIPTION. Among the more useful works are Flora W. Seymour, *Story of the Red Man* (1929), popular in tone; Alpheus H. Verrill, *The Real Americans* (1954), interesting; Harold E. Driver, *Indians of North America* (1961), anthropological; Clark Wissler, *The American Indian* (3d ed., 1950), and *Indians of the United States* (1946), good anthropology; Ruth M. Underhill, *Red Man's America* (1953); D'Arcy McNickle, *They Came Here First* (1949), early Indian culture; Roy H. Pearce, *The Savages of America* (1953), white ideas about them. Specifically on the northern tribes see Randolph C. Downes, *Council Fires on the Upper Ohio* (1940), excellent; Arthur Pound and Richard E. Day, *Johnson of the Mohawks* (1930), fair; Thomas Boyd, *Simon Girty* (1928), renegade. On the southern tribes see Robert S. Cotterill, *Southern Indians* (1954), good; Angie Debo, *The Rise and Fall of the*

Choctaw Republic (1934) and her *The Road to Disappearance* (1941), very good; Henry T. Malone, *Cherokees of the Old South* (1956); Merritt B. Pound, *Benjamin Hawkins, Indian Agent* (1951). Two useful books on the effect of disease are Percy M. Ashburn, *The Ranks of Death* (1947), mostly before 1700; Esther A. Stearn, *The Effect of Smallpox on the Destiny of the Amerindian* (1945).

INDIAN POLICY. Four monographs, although sometimes not easy to read, cover the subject well: Walter H. Mohr, *Federal Indian Relations, 1774–1788* (1933); Francis P. Prucha, *American Indian Policy in the Formative Years . . . 1790–1834* (1962); George D. Harmon, *Sixty Years of Indian Affairs, 1789–1850* (1941); James R. Jacobs, *The Beginning of the U.S. Army, 1783–1812* (1947).

OHIO WARS. Histories of Ohio always cover the subject, as, for example, Beverley W. Bond, Jr., *The Civilization of the Old Northwest* (1934) and *The Foundations of Ohio* (1941); John A. Caruso, *The Great Lakes Frontier* (1961); Randolph C. Downes, *Frontier Ohio, 1788–1803* (1935); Walter Havighurst, *Land of Promise* (1946), which reads particularly well. Accounts of the military leaders include Thomas Boyd, *Mad Anthony Wayne* (1929), reads well; Harry E. Wildes, *Anthony Wayne* (1941), more detailed; Gayle Thornbrough (ed.), *Outpost on the Wabash, 1787–1791* (1958), including the letters of Harmar; Frazer E. Wilson, *Arthur St. Clair* (1944), overly eulogistic.

CHAPTER 8

ADVANCING SETTLEMENT

T he first really large flow of settlers across the Appalachians came in the twenty years after the Revolution. The number of migrants tended to increase with the years, but there was a slowing down with periods of depression, of war, and of Indian troubles; for example, the Old Northwest could not compete equally with the Old Southwest for new population until after the Treaty of Greenville (1795). Moreover, the new people did not spread equally over the West. Certain areas obviously were more attractive if they had more fertile land and better transportation.

The vast majority of these self-elected Westerners were native-born, and represented a part of the natural increase of population. Throughout the late eighteenth and most of the nineteenth century the United States doubled in population each generation, with little relation to the amount of immigration, which was only of minor importance. These extra people sought economic opportunity either in eastern cities, which grew during the period, or in the farms and towns of the West. Foreign immigrants joined the westward shove, but in relatively small numbers, preferring the work opportunities of the East; a town like Gallipolis was exceptional.

The eastern states viewed the departure of their sons and daughters with mingled pride and alarm. The expansion of the American people increased American power and prestige, demonstrating the virility of a young and ambitious people, and increased trade between East and West to the profit of both sections. On the other hand the departure of many young and vigorous citizens was viewed regretfully by those who had visions of coming local greatness, and particularly by those who wanted labor for expanding eastern stores and mills, or for domestic service, or for the construction and operation of roads and canals. The fact that American labor was comparatively scarce, and hence highly paid, produced difficulties in competing with European production; migration to the West further increased the scarcity of eastern labor.

Westward-bound settlers were of all ages and both sexes but, as already stated, the largest single element consisted of young men who had just attained their majority and were traveling alone or in small groups. Such a man might be sufficiently lucky to be able to buy a farm immediately, after no more than a brief exploratory trip to find the most favorable location. More likely he possessed only a few dollars and planned to do farm work, storekeeping, boating, trapping, surveying,, schoolteaching, or some other work until he acquired the needed capital. Although he might squat on unsurveyed land, he still needed capital to purchase supplies and obtain animals, implements, and seed. Before setting up as an independent farmer he might well return to the East to marry his boyhood sweetheart. A frontier farmer's wife represented a person to love and to cherish, as well as a needed companion and co-worker on the farm.

THE PROCESS OF MIGRATION

When an entire family moved the process was somewhat more complicated, since a family was not as foot-loose as an unmarried man and wanted a more specific idea of where it was going. Possibly relatives or friends had moved earlier and had found a desirable region, or else the father or an older son would make a preliminary tour. In any case a man seldom took his wife and children west of the mountains without some confidence that he could provide for them; there must have been many evenings of earnest conversation before a family decided to leave old friends and surroundings for the newness of the West.

The migrating family sold its eastern possessions before it departed —partly because few articles could be packed into the single farm wagon possible to take, and partly because funds would be required to start farming and to tide them over the first year until crops could be harvested and marketed. Frequently the father enlarged his own small funds by borrowing from family and neighbors, for he realized that even with the greatest frugality moving was costly. Every Westerner advised migrants to bring a good supply of cash, but the eastern family seldom fulfilled the specifications; indeed, if the family had been well-to-do it would have stayed in the East.

Only the bare necessities of life could be given space in the one farm wagon that was the sole means of transportation. Of first importance were implements for erecting a home and for farming—particularly an ax, an auger, an adz, a hammer. Guns and ammunition were necessary. Food consisted primarily of such staples as flour, bacon, sugar, salt, yeast, and vinegar. A spinning wheel was vital, and seeds for the first planting might be taken. Other desirable articles were almost innumerable, and might include clothes, cloth, needles, thread, pots and pans, dishes, and cutlery. Possibly some of the precious space was taken by a clock, a bureau, a bedstead, or other specially prized family possessions.

The westward-bound wagon was usually protected from sun and rain by canvas stretched tightly over curved strips of wood. Sometimes it was drawn by horses, but more frequently by the even more useful and hardy oxen. Mother and the younger children might ride in the wagon, while father plodded beside the team and the older children followed in the rear. A cow or two or an extra horse might be part of the caravan, and it was not unknown to have the children chase chickens along the road to their new home in the West. The speed was that of men and animals walking. At night the family camped by the side of the road and fried its bacon and cooked its biscuits by the heat of an open fire. Rain slowed the trip and made life miserable for the migrants.

SOUTHERN SETTLEMENT

People moving west at the turn of the century, as in every period, moved as directly west as possible. Belts of settlement were being created in which the culture of a particular section of the East was reproduced time after time under new conditions. The bulk of the Virginia and Carolina migration was going to Kentucky and Tennessee, Pennsylvania migration to Ohio, and New England migration to central New York and the region of the Great Lakes.

The most popular mecca for the earliest trans-Appalachian settlers was Kentucky. Its population of 74,000 in 1790 tripled within the next ten years and almost doubled again in the succeeding decade. Although early settlers came almost entirely over the mountains through the Cumberland Gap, later arrivals traveled more frequently by way of Pittsburgh or Wheeling and then down the Ohio River. Louisville was the most important of the river towns of Kentucky; its chief rival was Maysville, lying across the river from the terminus of Zane's Trace, which originated at Wheeling.

Lexington was the great interior metropolis of Kentucky, even though it could claim less than 2000 inhabitants in 1800. It dominated the bluegrass country, overshadowing such rivals as Frankfort, Paris, and May's Lick. Lexington, the trading center for nearby farmers, could boast such varied industries as ropewalks, tanneries, potteries, and powder mills. It was proud of its literary and cultural achievements, being a publishing center of importance and the home of Transylvania, the first western college. Quite naturally it was a political center and capital of the state for the first six months of statehood. Little wonder that an energetic and

Population Density, 1790

45 AND OVER INHABITANTS PER SQUARE MILE

6-44 INHABITANTS PER SQUARE MILE

2-5 INHABITANTS PER SQUARE MILE

LESS THAN 2 INHABITANTS PER SQUARE MILE

ambitious lawyer like Henry Clay decided that Lexington was the proper place to settle during the 1790s.

The population of Tennessee was about half that of Kentucky, although in the generation after 1800 the difference decreased. The earliest settlements were naturally near the Cumberland Gap, in the eastern part of the state, and the road through the gap was improved for wagon traffic in the 1790s. Eastern Tennessee as a region of mountains and valleys was particularly attractive to small farmers practicing a diversified agriculture. The center of population came to be Knoxville, founded in 1789.

Central Tennessee was topographically a continuation of the blue-grass region of Kentucky; it was suitable for cotton culture and the profitable use of slaves, although in fact there were few slaves in the early days. Nashville was the metropolis of the area, and experienced a boom after the opening of a wagon road in 1795. Industries, lawyers, doctors, ministers, churches, and comfortable homes soon appeared, and slavery increased. Cumberland College was organized in 1806. West of the Nashville area, in western Tennessee, little settlement existed before 1810.

South of Tennessee, restless Georgians were pushing into the central and northern parts of the present state, with a roving and avaricious eye cast as far west as the Mississippi, since Georgia claimed land to the river. The state had been exceedingly reluctant to grant this immense empire and possible source of wealth to the federal government, even though powerful Indian groups made immediate settlement impossible. Georgia's policy shortly after the Revolution had been to grant western land as a reward to people who had served the state and to prospective settlers; in fact it early developed a sort of homestead policy. Unfortunately these early grants seldom produced settlement. The grantees tended to sell their claims to speculators, and in some cases a single person amassed a million or more acres. In addition, warrants were issued for several times the amount of land existing in several counties, and these warrants were then resold to unsuspecting buyers in Philadelphia and elsewhere. All such practices meant future trouble.

The Georgia land situation was further confused by several large sales (the Yazoo grants), made ostensibly to help the precarious Georgia finances, but inspired, often by questionable means, by speculators who looked hopefully at the lands near the Mississippi. Particularly attractive was the mouth of the Yazoo River, which had the most promising city site except Natchez; in time it was the location of Vicksburg. Four companies were given grants in 1789, and each made a down payment and tried unsuccessfully to encourage settlement. Three new companies were given additional land in 1795. All told, some 50 million to 70 million acres were granted at prices that were ridiculously low even for wild western

United States, 1790

land, without considering that some of the payments were in worthless Georgia currency. Then in 1796 the state had a change of heart and repealed the grants, holding quite correctly that they had been acquired by fraud and bribery, and that in any case because the lands belonged to the Indians the state had no right to dispose of them.

Confusion became even greater when the companies at one and the same time took back some of their purchase money and brought court action to try to get the act of repeal declared illegal, while those to whom they had sold land sold it to others. Georgia solved her embarrassment by turning over her claims to the federal government in 1802. The federal government ordered all Yazoo claimants to be ejected, and had the land surveyed with the object of sale. This sweeping solution turned out to be impossible, not only because the government was tender of the feelings of settlers, but also because the Supreme Court decided in Fletcher v. Peck (1810) that the first grants were valid contracts and could not be abrogated by the action of one party. Before the affair ended the government bought off the claiming companies for more money than it received from land sales. The only positive accomplishment was the expansion of Mississippi Territory.

Along the Gulf Coast and up the Mississippi as far as Natchez had come colonial settlers after the region was acquired by England at the end of the Seven Years' War. Many of these people obtained grants from the English government. The growth of population was slight, and up to 1810 these small communities continued to cling to the coast and the lower river. Spain reconquered the whole area during the Revolution, and then argued with the United States as to the proper boundary. When Spain withdrew her troops from the disputed area, the United States set up Mississippi Territory (1798), and sent as governor Winthrop Sargent, who had been secretary of the Northwest Territory. In 1804 Mississippi was enlarged to include the Georgia cessions, while other changes came with the acquisition of Louisiana.

NORTHERN SETTLEMENT

North of the Ohio River settlement came very slowly until the Wayne campaign ended the Indian menace. Present Ohio had a negligible population in 1790 and only 45,000 in 1800, but by 1810 the number had jumped to an impressive 231,000—almost as many people as in Tennessee. Early settlements clung closely to the banks of the Ohio, but after 1800 they began to fill the general area of the cessions made at Greenville. A surplus of settlers drifted farther down the Ohio into present southern Indiana and Illinois, but prior to 1810 few men were sufficiently courageous to venture far from a river. Population generally followed the Ohio and the Wabash, particularly in the area of Vincennes.

The earliest migrants of the Old Northwest were predominantly southern in origin, and this southern flow continued into the nineteenth century, coming either by way of the Potomac or through Kentucky. By this later period, however, other population elements were becoming more important. The New England settlement at Marietta, the New Jersey settlement at Cincinnati, and the foreign settlement at Gallipolis were symptomatic of change.

The most important Ohio metropolis was Cincinnati, even though it could boast but 500 residents in 1800. Cincinnati had been founded in 1789 on the Symmes purchase and was a product of land speculation, as were many other Ohio towns, such as Dayton (1795) and Chillicothe (1796). It soon outdistanced its nearest competitiors, but with no great geographic advantage except that it was one of the many towns on the Ohio River. Its position opposite the mouth of the Licking was not particularly important. More significant was the favor of Governor St. Clair, who moved his capital from Marietta to Cincinnati in 1790.

Settlers bound for the Ohio Valley tended increasingly to come by way of Pittsburgh. The population of this thriving potential city was little over 1500 in 1800, but the next few years saw Pittsburgh grow rapidly and outdistance such early competitors as Steubenville, Wheeling, and Marietta. Early Pittsburgh was primarily a commercial rather than a manufacturing center. Its most important early industries were milling and ship building, with ships constructed for ocean as well as for river trade. The coal and iron business was growing, so that within a few years Pittsburgh was to become known as "the Birmingham of America," with products that ranged from nails and other iron articles to leather, paper, glass, hats, and rope.

Another and more northern stream of migration had begun to flow into the region of the Great Lakes by 1800. Settlement had been expanding through central New York State, with the Holland Land Company planning the town of New Amsterdam (Buffalo) in 1799. This young village was to become the northern entry to the West, and thus similar to Pittsburgh, but for the time being growth was small, and the town was burned during the War of 1812. Real expansion came after the war, and particularly after the opening of the Erie Canal.

West of Buffalo a string of hamlets was coming into existence along the southern shore of Lake Erie. Most important of them was Cleaveland, which was a speculation of the Connecticut Land Company. The area of the city was in the "Connecticut Reserve," which had been retained by the state for the benefit of sufferers from the Revolution. The city, whose name was soon modernized, was founded in 1796 by Moses Cleaveland and a group of settlers from Connecticut. At first it had to provide its own government, but in 1800 the administration was assumed by the Northwest Territory. West of Lake Erie the most important town was Detroit, a small trading settlement.

TOWNS AND CITIES

Any description of settlement makes immediately apparent that, although most of the new arrivals were farmers, some of them were interested in town life. Among the migrants were merchants, small manufacturers, lawyers, doctors, millers, shoemakers, and others who gravitated to the urban areas. A number of migrants called themselves artisans, but their definition of the term does not describe the skilled labor of today. The artisan of 1800 had some skill, such as carpentry or ropemaking, but he probably also could farm. His occupation in the West depended on the opportunities offered. Not infrequently a doctor would also farm, or a carpenter would run a livery stable. Occupations tended not to be highly specialized.

The locations of cities depended on both geographical and speculative factors. Certain cities occupied locations that were obviously well suited geographically for their growth. Examples are Pittsburgh at the head of the Ohio River, Louisville at the falls of the Ohio River, and St. Louis just below the junction of the Missouri and Mississippi rivers. Other town had less obvious geographical advantages. Lexington, Kentucky, was merely in the center of a rich farming area. Cincinnati had unfavorable terrain, and its growth can be credited primarily to speculation. With the speculative factor frequently looming large there were bound to be many mistakes, including such towns as New Athens, New Lisbon, Palermo, and others that failed to grow. Most disappointing was Town of America at the junction of the Ohio and Mississippi; the location seemed perfect, but the overflow of the rivers made impossible any considerable settlement.

The new towns of the West had all sorts of obvious troubles. Such problems as street paving and lighting, fire protection, and sanitation were particularly difficult in a new community that lacked adequate wealth. Then too there had to be developed such necessary institutions as newspapers, churches, saloons, libraries, and schools, which were more urban than rural. In general, political, social, and economic innovations came to the cities before they did to the countryside. Also, social distinctions were greater, since almost immediately considerable differences in wealth appeared. The banker's wife and the dock laborer's wife hardly met on a plane of social equality. In other words, the western town reproduced on a smaller scale the conditions of the larger eastern city.

CONDITIONS OF TRAVEL

Roads connecting East and West were in general bad, being improved only enough to permit wagons on the main thoroughfares. In the West, roads were being opened during the 1790s and later to connect the principal towns, such as Lexington and Nashville. Smaller inland towns had to be content with blazed trails, or at most paths that were passable only for pack animals.

Road construction meant cutting the trees, but leaving the stumps, and clearing away most of the brush. Grades were not improved and no roadbed was constructed except for a few specially difficult places; a swampy sector, for example, might receive a few logs over which the wagons could jolt to the comparative safety of higher land. Such roads were bad at any time of the year, but were particularly atrocious during wet weather. Streams were ordinarily forded, but a few of the larger ones could be crossed by private ferries operated at the caprice of their owners, who charged all that the traffic would bear.

Bad roads meant that whenever possible the migrant moved by water, with the current furnishing the motive power, and water transportation meant that the heaviest movement of population was down the Ohio River. The obvious point of embarkation was one of the most easterly towns, which increasingly meant Pittsburgh. Here a westward-moving family acquired a rough and boxlike flatboat. This boat served two functions. First and most obviously it was a means of transportation, carrying the entire possessions of the family. Second, it was an important source of planed lumber and nails for a future home. Both articles were scarce, and hence the flatboat was carefully disassembled so that wood and nails could be used again.

CHOOSING A HOME

Upon arriving in the West, the migrant found nothing as important as his choice of land. Several attributes were considered, and not the least was fertility, which was surprisingly difficult to recognize. One sure test seemed to be whether the land in its native state produced luxurious vegetation. This criterion explains in part why frontiersmen preferred the densely wooded lands near the rivers and why the ring of the woodman's ax was the most characteristic sound of the new settlement. Houses, barns, and fences were ordinarily of wood. The new settler did not, however, find himself attracted by the overflow land of the river bottoms. The other common test for a new settler was to find land that looked similar to that which he had found good in his old home, and here he made many mistakes. The New Englander who looked for oak clearings or the Pennsylvanian who sought reddish soil was starting his western life under a severe handicap.

Practically as important to the settler as good land was the availability of water, both for drinking and for transportation. A spring or a small brook sufficed for drinking, but a navigable stream was necessary for transportation and could also be used for drinking; true it might be dirty, but the dirt would settle, and no one worried about bacteria since no one had heard of them. Here again the settlers tended to build their houses near the larger streams.

Finally, the migrant preferred to be reasonably near a settlement—not only for protection from the Indians, or to be able to buy and sell easily, but also for human companionship and assistance. The transplanted Easterner was no hermit and his family had no desire to be lost in the wilderness. The average settler was a farmer looking for greater opportunity and did not propose to forgo eastern advantages any longer than necessary. If he had sufficient funds he bought land that had been cleared and improved; if not, he sought to reproduce his old surroundings as quickly as possible. The frontiersman who made the original clearings at the very tip of civilization frequently sold out and moved to a newer frontier, which meant that a large share of arrivals took land that had been at least partially cleared and transformed into productive farms.

ACQUIRING LAND

The land selected by the settler might be acquired in any one of several ways. Rather frequently it was bought from the original frontiersman or from a speculator. The speculator was ubiquitous, including not only outstanding men such as Clark, Boone, Sevier, and Blount, but thousands of less known persons down to the poorest frontiersman who acquired unneeded land in the hope that it would inflate in value with the increase of settlement. Eastern speculators were also numerous. The companies obtaining Yazoo grants, the Ohio Company, Symmes, and the rest were merely the outstanding illustrations of eastern land speculation. Although eastern speculators might buy their land in the West, the large companies in the early years were more likely to operate from the East. Some bought directly from the United States or from states with western claims. Others collected land warrants issued by the federal government for revolutionary veterans, or by such states as Connecticut, Virginia, North Carolina, and Georgia. Apparently a large proportion of the land donated to veterans eventually got into the hands of the speculators. The veteran seemed to be more interested in immediate cash than in a prospective farm.

Speculators were interested in good agricultural land, but even more in water power, millsites, and townsites, for here lay the best chance of large profits. An impressive proportion of western towns represented the work of speculators. Marietta, Cincinnati, Chillicothe, Dayton, Boonesborough, and Nashville were but a few of the hundreds that received their original impetus from speculators. But for each such successful settlement there were a dozen that remained entirely in their originators' minds or that eventuated only in a few log cabins. Probably the majority of speculators lost money, with only enough successes to keep the will-o'-the-wisp of huge profits glowing sufficiently to attract other adventuresome souls.

The alternative to buying from an original settler or from a speculator was to purchase from the government. Legally the settler could not occupy land until it had been surveyed and he had bought it at auction, but thousands of settlers started farming without the formality of purchase. They hoped that the government would later confirm their occupancy or that they could buy it at the minimum price when the auction arrived. This feat frequently occurred with the assistance of neighbors similarly situated.

Once a man had picked his land, and sometimes bought it, he started the arduous labor of making it into a real farm. Ordinarily he arrived in the spring to give himself the maximum time to prepare for the winter. For a settler arriving around 1800 the process of starting a farm was similar, regardless of whether he lived in the North or in the South. If in the South he might have a slave or two without thereby changing the picture radically. The movement of large slave coffles, with the establishment of big western plantations, was not common until after the War of 1812.

BUILDING A HOUSE

The first requirement for a family was shelter. A temporary, open, three-sided camp might be constructed from poles and thatched; the front was higher than the back, and the fire was built before the open front of the structure. The labor of erecting such a camp might be avoided if some near neighbor offered his hospitality.

Before a family could consider itself settled it needed a permanent home. Father and the older sons immediately got out their axes and started to chop down the trees on the site of their future home and garden. These trees were transformed into a house, a barn, and rail fences, for the wooden rail fence was practically universal. In the meantime the smaller children collected brush and grubbed out small trees and bushes. Ultimately the whole mass of trash was burned in large bonfires.

The actual construction of the house was a community undertaking, since seldom had a family enough grown sons to perform the necessary backbreaking work. On the day of the house-raising neighbors gathered from miles around. The logs were rolled to the site of the cabin, notched or dovetailed at each end and lifted into place; alternately they were placed on one pair of opposite sides and then on the other pair. Meantime the women had been cooking a feast, which was probably followed by a dance in the new home. A little later the family might aspire to a cabin of squared logs, which excluded more of the weather and permitted better interior and exterior finishes. The ultimate goal was, of course, a house of planed lumber or brick or stone.

The construction of the roof represented a considerable problem as long as nails, sometimes homemade, remained a luxury. The frame of rafters was held in place by wooden pins driven into auger holes. Over the rafters might be placed bark or rude shingles, but more frequently the roof was of clapboard construction, with the boards held in place by saplings fastened with wooden pegs.

After the frame of the house was completed, various openings were cut for doors, windows, and fireplace. All doors were wooden, and swung on leather or wooden hinges. Security could be attained by a heavy wooden bar fitted into brackets on the inside. A simple iron lock or a swinging wooden bar could be opened from the outside by means of a leather thong passed through an auger hole in the door; the latch string hanging outside was an indication of hospitality.

The fireplace was constructed of stone or of logs or sticks covered with clay, depending on the region; the chimney was ordinarily built of logs, and but rarely of stone. The earliest cabins had no windows, but by 1800 most of them had at least small openings, sometimes barred to exclude wild animals, to admit light and air. Window glass was a rarity in the North and somewhat more frequent in the South; a more or less satisfactory substitute was oiled paper. The floor of the log cabin was ordinarily hard-packed earth, but the more particular and industrious frontiersman used puncheons—that is, logs that had been split in the middle and whose more or less flat surfaces were placed uppermost. The finishing touch for the cabin was filling the chinks between the logs with moss or dirt or clay.

The usual log cabin was neither beautiful nor commodious, and certainly could boast but little comfort. It had the one artistic value of being appropriate to its surroundings. Its materials and method of construction made unlikely any great size; in fact the usual cabin was no larger than a moderate-sized modern living room—say fifteen to eighteen feet long and twelve to fourteen feet wide. A partition might create two rooms, but generally there was no such division. A windowless loft could be used as a store room and as sleeping quarters for the children. Now and then two such cabins were built side by side with a common roof. In the South the two-room and even the two-story log cabin soon appeared; the kitchen might be in an ell, and other rooms were added as the family grew.

CLEARING THE LAND

The building of the cabin entailed clearing a portion of the land, but in many cases little more than enough for a garden and chicken yard. Further efforts were necessary before a crop could be planted. The really radical method was to cut down all trees and use oxen to pull the stumps, thus producing completely open fields, but in actual practice this procedure was seldom used: it meant years of labor before reasonably sized fields could be obtained. Most common was the cutting of girdles around the trees, thus killing them; in time they were probably burned. Corn, which was tilled poorly because of the multiplicity of tree roots and which received only the sparse sunlight filtering between dead trees, could hardly be luxuriant, but some corn was better than none.

The process of conquering a wilderness was slow and laborious. Even though the family left the East in the spring as soon as the roads dried and grass was available for the stock, so much time was consumed that first year in making the trip west, in selecting land, in building a cabin, and in clearing the land that nothing more than a small garden could be grown. In fact, with girdled trees, the crops of the first few years might all be very small. This interval between migration and marketable crops emphasized the need for a cash reserve. Even though the father shot game and everyone went on starvation rations, money was still necessary to permit survival. The traditional hospitality of the West was of little advantage since everyone in a particular region was in similar circumstances. Well over a year had to elapse before the family could again be self-supporting.

READINGS

NORTH. Among the general accounts are Beverley W. Bond, Jr., *The Civilization of the Old Northwest* (1934); John A. Caruso, *The Great Lakes Frontier* (1961), which is somewhat episodical; Stewart H. Holbrook, *The Yankee Exodus* (1950), which is more so; Walter Havighurst, *Land of Promise* (1946) is readable, but his *Wilderness for Sale* (1956) is not. Lewis D. Stilwell, *Migration from Vermont 1776–1860* (1937) is an excellent monograph on a subject treated too infrequently. State histories naturally tend to concentrate on their areas, as Beverley W. Bond, Jr., *The Foundations of Ohio* (1941); Randolph C. Downes, *Frontier Ohio* (1935); Eugene H. Roseboom and Francis P. Weisenburger, *A History of Ohio* (1953); William T. Utter, *The Frontier State* (1943); Harlan Hatcher, *The Western Reserve* (1949) reads well; Clarence W. Alvord, *The Illinois Country* (1920) is careful; Milo M. Quaife and Sidney Glazer, *Michigan* (1948). Western Pennsylvania receives interesting treatment in Solon J. and Elizabeth H. Buck, *The Planting of Civilization in Western Pennsylvania* (1939) ; John E. Wright and Doris S. Corbett, *Pioneer Life in Western Pennsylvania* (1940) ; John W. Harpster (ed.), *Pen Pictures of Early Western Pennsylvania* (1935). Paul D. Evans, *The Holland Land Company* (1924) is a fine monograph on the Buffalo region.

SOUTH. Good general accounts are Thomas P. Abernethy, *The South in the New Nation, 1789–1819* (1961) ; Harriette L. S. Arnow, *Seedtime on the Cumberland, 1763–1803* (1960) ; Everett Dick, *The Dixie Frontier* (1948) ; the last two are heavily social, and read well. Kentucky is well covered in Thomas D. Clark, *A History of Kentucky* (1937) and Francis G. Davenport, *Ante-Bellum Kentucky* (1943) ; two good original accounts are Daniel Drake, *Pioneer Life in Kentucky, 1785–1800* (1948) and Harry Toulmin, *The Western Country in 1793* (1948), edited by Thomas D. Clark.

CITIES. Richard C. Wade, *The Urban Frontier* (1959) is a fine study of five western cities between 1780 and 1830. Individual cities are covered in Frederick C. Bald, *Detroit's First American Decade, 1796 to 1805* (1948) ; Leland D. Baldwin, Pittsburgh (1937) is good; Elbert J. Benton, *Cultural Story of an American City: Cleveland* (3 vols., 1943–1946) ; Robert W. Bingham, *The Cradle of the Queen City* (1932) concerns Buffalo. Quite different is Harold R. Shurtleff, *The Log Cabin Myth* (1939), which treats the origin of the log cabin.

CHAPTER 9

LIFE IN THE WEST

The newly established western families were confronted with the problem of building a civilization with simple materials and tools. Most migrants were in no sense revolters from the traditional ways of life desiring a new, different, and simpler environment. They sought only economic opportunity, and were anxious to reproduce the familiar trappings of eastern society as soon as possible. Crude houses and furniture, linsy-woolsey clothes, and bear steaks were only makeshifts until better things could be acquired.

HOUSE FURNISHINGS

While the new civilization was in the making the settler lived in the simplest of home surroundings. The crude, homemade furniture consisted mainly of a rough plank or puncheon table and a few three-legged stools that stood more solidly on the rough floor than did the four-legged variety. The absence of closets was compensated in part by pegs in the wall, with possibly a few shelves. Beds were built against the walls, preferably in the corners; the walls furnished the main supports, but needed the supplement of forked stakes driven into the ground. In lieu of springs was a lattice work of leather thongs, rope, or slats. Mattresses were filled with straw until enough feathers were collected to produce the favored feather beds, which were most comfortable if resting on straw ticks. Covers consisted of bear or buffalo robes or a second feather bed. All reports indicated that in the average cabin these articles were filthy and full of vermin. If cleanliness is next to godliness these people deserved the fears for their spiritual welfare that the East entertained for them.

Privacy in a frontier cabin was practically impossible: the entire family dressed, undressed, and carried on most of its activities in the one room. Here occurred everything from spinning and making bread to child-birth. Some saving of modesty was possible because cold weather deterred one from removing all his clothes at night, while the all-over bath was ordinarily reserved for warm weather and the neighboring stream. Favorite western stories dealt with the embarrassment that resulted when a group of travelers of both sexes spent the night with a large family in a log cabin.

Of the varied activities that made the cabin a busy workshop, none was more important or more frequent than the preparation of food. Cooking was done at the fireplace, and consequently most of the food was either boiled or fried. A crane or iron hook held the pot for boiling, and the three-legged, long-handled frying pan or spider was either held over the coals or allowed to rest on them. Some of the more elaborate fireplaces included ovens, but this was unusual. Roasting could be done on a spit. Frequently the baking was done in a skillet with a tight cover or in a Dutch oven, a large cast-iron pot with a tight lid pushed into the coals and then covered with them. Sometimes the article to be baked was wrapped in cabbage leaves and pushed directly into the coals. The fireplace, in addition to being used for cooking, furnished the only heat for the cabin in winter, and light at night. Tallow candles were made by the women, but the light of the fire was used whenever possible to save labor.

Cooking and eating utensils were of the simplest. The family brought with it from the East a few skillets, pots, and pans, as well as pewter dishes, plates, and spoons. Additional utensils were homemade, and the men spent many a long winter evening carving wooden bowls, trenchers, and noggins (cups). Gourds were used as cups and other containers.

FOOD AND CLOTHES

The food was limited largely to the products the family raised. Wild game was available in the early days, and a deer or some wild ducks or turkeys were welcome additions to the family menu; bears were plentiful, but their meat was coarse and greasy. A staple article of diet was corn, which was used in every conceivable form, including johnnycake, pone, and mush. Mush and milk was a favorite supper; the heavy meal of the day was eaten at noon. Equally universal was pork. Hog and hominy was a better known combination than ham and eggs, for eggs were scarce. The pigs were allowed to run wild in the forest and were shot like wild animals. The meat had to be dried, smoked, or salted for summer use, since there was no ice available. The resulting demand for salt encouraged the development of western salt manufactories at the important saline springs.

Cane sugar was always scarce on the frontier, white sugar being rarer than brown; frequently maple sugar, honey, or molasses were used instead. Milk was also rare, and whenever possible, as on mush, it was replaced by such liquids as gravy or bear's oil. Tea and coffee were luxuries for which the Westerners discovered some substitutes. On the other hand vegetables, including corn, beans, potatoes, peas, squash, and pumpkins, were plentiful. Within a few years supplies of peaches, melons, apples, cherries, plums, and grapes were adequate. All in all, the frontiersman had a plentiful variety of good food—at least in the summer. In the winter his diet was less satisfactory, for then he depended on such staples as corn meal and salt pork. The only methods of preserving fruits and vegetables were covering with sand or pine needles, pickling, or drying, which produced a leathery, tasteless substance that may have been nourishing but certainly was not appetizing.

One of the commonest articles of western diet was corn whiskey, which was drunk by everyone upon any or no pretext. A hospitable home kept a jug of whiskey and a gourd near the door to refresh visitors. Much western corn was made into whiskey because the decreased bulk and increased value were an advantage in transporting it to market. Distilleries were an early and important feature of western life. Tobacco, almost as widely used as whiskey, was raised and consumed in the West at an early date. Tobacco chewing became as universal in the West as it was in the East, and very few travelers could refrain from commenting on the common art of chewing and the lack of delicacy in disposing of the surplus juice.

Frequently shoes or moccasins were made at home by the father with tools he had brought from the East. But the tanning of leather was a difficult operation for the individual family, and so the tanning industry, as carried on by professionals, soon made its appearance in the West. To save shoes members of the family went barefoot whenever possible.

Clothes were nearly all homemade. Flax, hemp, and wool were all produced on the farm; consequently linen cloth was cheaper than cotton. The various processes of home manufacture included combing, carding, spinning, dyeing, weaving, cutting, and sewing the garments. The cloth (usually linsey-woolsey) was heavy and strong, but colors were limited and the finish was not professional: garments were more practical than beautiful. The frontiersman tended to copy his costume from the Indians, even to the extent of leather hunting shirt, leggings, moccasins, and breechcloth, although he might have a cloth shirt and pantaloons. A prosperous Westerner might buy broadcloth to be made into a suit by a tailor, but such a suit was worn only on special occasions, and would last for years. A woman was adequately but not elegantly clothed in a loose, plain dress something like a modern smock; one or more better dresses for churchgoing or other important events followed eastern styles. A small child's wardrobe was usually limited to a simple, loose shirt.

The activities of the interior of the cabin, including preparing the food and making the clothes, were the particular domain of the woman. Her many duties ranged from making soap and candles and caring for small children to acting as family physician. Lest she have any spare moments she usually tended a garden and a flock of chickens; it was not unknown for her to work in the fields. The West could echo with heartfelt fervor the old jingle that "a woman's work is never done." Men worked hard but women, if anything, worked harder; indeed the operation of a farm was almost impossible without the presence of a woman.

FARMING

The main business of farming was the province of the man, and he would have been justified if he had frequently felt discouraged. Not only was he confronted with the prodigious task of clearing and breaking the virgin land; even after he cleared the land he was handicapped by poor tools and methods. Foremost among his tools was a plow, which might be nothing more than a forked stick, and which at the best was a straight wooden implement, sometimes tipped with iron, that needed at least two yoke of oxen in an operation that was man-killing. A harrow was a wooden triangle fitted with wooden or iron teeth to be dragged through the ground.

All grain was planted by hand. Cutting was done with a scythe; the greatest farm improvement of the period was the introduction of the cradle scythe in the late eighteenth century. The grain was separated from the chaff either by driving horses over it or by using a hand flail composed of two sticks connected by a leather thong. Considerable dexterity was necessary if the wielder was to avoid cracking his own skull. The grain was then tossed in the air; if no timely breeze was present to blow away the chaff, a sheet flapped by two men created one.

Simple tools used on fields filled with dead trees could not be expected to produce a large crop; in fact the first corn crop was seldom as much as fifteen bushels an acre. As time passed and the fields were better cultivated the corn crops on the more fertile Ohio and Kentucky land averaged forty to fifty bushels an acre, with some yielding as high as seventy-five. Even at best, however, work was hard and yields were low. Tools remained poor and no proper rotation of crops was practiced; in fact the same crop was grown year after year on the same field. Chemical fertilizers were unknown and manure was generally unavailable because the animals were allowed to roam freely.

The dominant western crop was corn, which was planted in check-rows about three feet apart. Seven or eight kernels were planted at each intersection, and all but two or three were weeded out when they started to grow, at which time there was one additional plowing. Ultimately the corn was picked, shucked, and shelled by hand. For home use it was either ground in a handmill or treated with homemade lye to produce the ubiquitous hominy. If marketed it never brought over twenty-five cents a bushel. Sometimes it was shipped as kernels, but more frequently it was ground into meal, packed into small barrels, and loaded on flatboats for shipment to New Orleans.

Although corn was the important western crop, such grains as wheat, oats, barley, rye, and buckwheat were grown in considerable amounts. Wheat was the usual cash crop of the Northwest. Tobacco was widely cultivated, particularly in Kentucky; much of it was used in the West, but shortly after 1800 several thousand hogsheads were floated down the river each year. Hemp was exported both raw and as rope; every western town of importance had one or more ropewalks. Flax was grown primarily for home use, but a marketable excess was sold mainly as rough cloth. A considerable variety of poor fruit was produced, particularly peaches, possibly because Westerners were told that peach trees became productive within two years. A large share of the peach crop was transformed into brandy, which sold commonly at a dollar a gallon. Vegetables were produced for home use, with a few sold to the residents of the towns.

Western livestock was never impressive. Oxen, horses, beef cattle, pigs, and sheep were kept for home use. Many times they were branded and allowed to forage for themselves, which indicates why their quality was generally poor and tended to deteriorate, and why fences were necessary for the cultivated fields. The pig was supreme from the standpoint of numbers, and furnished the meat staple of the West. Surplus hogs were marketed as ham and salt pork, but at times were driven across the mountains to be fattened in Pennsylvania for the eastern market. The raising of blooded horses was becoming a recognized Kentucky industry, but semiwild horses remained so common that they furnished skins for export.

As usual the West, and particularly Ohio, raised many cattle. Ordinarily they were branded and allowed to roam freely, only returning to be milked and to obtain salt. Some of the milk was made into butter for sale in New Orleans. Herds of cattle were often driven to nearby forts or over the mountains to be fattened for market, but the profit seems to have been questionable. With the passage of time, fences were built, special food was used, and improved stock was introduced. By this time Ohio served as a feeding ground for stock coming from farther west. This typical frontier cycle was to be repeated in later years as population moved westward.

MERCHANDISING

The western family's agricutural surplus was ordinarily bartered for articles it wanted, and little money changed hands. The family with extra cloth or corn or pigs took them to the nearest store and traded with the merchant for salt, spices, iron implements, window glass, cloth, or whatever else it wanted. Even in the early days the western stores had a surprising array of commodities, ranging from coffee to flutes and from nails to Havana cigars. This variety increased rapidly with time.

The business of the frontier merchant was by no means simple and uncomplicated. Ordinarily he had but little capital, and consequently did most of his business on credit. The articles he sold came from some eastern city, usually Philadelphia, but possibly Baltimore, Richmond, or elsewhere. These goods were purchased on credit, which meant that the merchants of Philadelphia financed a large part of western business. Eastern merchandise was hauled over the mountains by wagon and bartered for western products, which were then loaded on flatboats and floated down the river to New Orleans, where they were resold, frequently to the West Indies but sometimes to other parts of the world. Often this sale was again barter, as for sugar or molasses, which was then sailed to the eastern seaboard, thus completing the circle.

This circular trade meant that the great majority of the movement of western business within the United States was from east to west. Manufactured articles moved in this direction, for but few of the western bulky products could stand the high freight charges for the eastward trip, particularly since most of them were also produced in the East. Consequently most of the wagons returned empty. Furs and whiskey were prominent among the few articles that were shipped east. Obviously both East and West were anxious for improved transportation, which was expected to reduce costs and to increase the traffic both ways.

Exports from the trans-Appalachian West moved west and south, since that was the direction in which the rivers flowed. Not until after the War of 1812 was there a cheap way to reverse the trip; before this time the keelboat was too expensive for widespread use, and overland traffic was almost impossible. The usual method of hauling goods was by flatboat, which could move only with the stream. For example, a flatboat would be built on the Ohio, loaded possibly with 300 barrels of corn meal, and placed in the charge of a supervisor and four boatmen. After about a month the boat would reach New Orleans, where the meal was sold and the boat broken up and the wood sold. The men then returned overland.

MONEY

The lack of currency always seriously hindered western business. What little money there was came largely from new migrants, from New Orleans sales, and from the army as it bought supplies and paid its members —which was one reason why every western community was delighted to have an army post. Even these small amounts of currency tended to be drained back to the East, with the result that the average Westerner seldom saw even a few dollars in cash during the course of a year. Barter was necessary but far from completely satisfactory; paying the schoolteacher in corn or the Yankee peddler in pork was at best cumbersome.

The necessity for an expanded medium of exchange encouraged the use of anything that came to hand. Foreign coins, and particularly Spanish, were in common use; a "piece of eight" was roughly equivalent to an American dollar; "four bits," to a fifty-cent piece; and "two bits," to a quarter. Westerners also circulated a great variety of eastern banknotes, many of very dubious validity. Likewise they began to circulate currency of their own, issued by such organizations as the Kentucky Insurance Company (1802) and the Miami Exporting Company (1803). Such currency was not well backed, and its existence showed clearly the pressing western need for more circulating medium. This problem was to remain for many years in spite of numerous efforts at solution.

MANUFACTURING

As the West continued to develop, many of the functions that at first were performed by individual families were taken over by commercial enterprises. Among the earlier industries were mills for grinding corn, salt manufactories, distilleries, flour mills, tanneries, ropewalks, boat yards, sawmills, textile mills, glass factories, paper mills, shoe factories, and tobacco-processing concerns. The desirability of and even necessity for professional production in these fields were quite evident, even though most of the new shops were small, consisting of little more than the master and a handful of apprentices and workmen. In time some of these enterprises became important in favorable places, as did iron at Pittsburgh and pork packing at Cincinnati. Consolidations, with price-fixing tendencies, began to appear by the 1820s in such fields as salt, iron, cotton, glass, and transportation. Water furnished the early power, but the steam engine began to be used before the nineteenth century was very old.

Obtaining the necessary labor was always a difficult problem for the western manufacturer. Most men moving to the West were farmers, and even those who called themselves artisans were not highly skilled and tended to become independent farmers. At times workmen were bribed to come from the East, and at times women and children were used, but in any case both apprentices and skilled workmen were hard to find. The result was that wages, both money and real, were high, and that early nineteenth-century strikes had more than normal success in comparison with eastern and European strikes of the same period.

In addition to the employees of manufacturing enterprises, the towns contained a host of independent professional and business men. As the communities grew there appeared the usual collection of doctors, lawyers, ministers, and teachers, with the lawyers and ministers outnumbering their professional colleagues. Shopkeepers and clerks furnished a perceptible part of the population. Blacksmiths, shoemakers, tinkers, seamstresses, and tailors were soon performing functions difficult for the untrained man. Some of them were itinerant, taking the job to the customer, which was a desirable procedure with a sparse population unconnected by good roads.

GOVERNMENT

One occupation that was not generally accepted as a full-time job was that of the politician. Many men considered politics an avocation, even a sport. Any average adult male was assumed to be competent to fill any public office within the gift of his fellow citizens, and in the early communities the politician might also be a farmer or lawyer, land speculator, trader, or miller. Quite naturally the West accepted the most democratic egalitarianism then in existence, for Westerners were in fact more nearly equal than any other society in the world. Little wonder that in the 1790s they accepted Jefferson's agricultural democracy and that later they became enthusiastic supporters of Jackson. Only very gradually, and after the government became much more complex, did the West begin to think of politics as a full-time and moderately specialized occupation.

The earliest of the western governments were frequently extralegal, if not actually illegal, since they were self-constituted organizations within the limits of existing state or nation. Their occasion was the failure of eastern government to bring law and order as fast as settlement expanded. Watauga, Nashville, Cleveland, and the state of Franklin come quickly to mind, but there were hundreds of other cases. Even in the Northwest Territory counties were formed slowly, and many communities established their own organizations before the properly constituted authorities began to function.

The need for governmental organization was particularly evident in the newer and wilder sections of the country, which gave ocular proof that the West attracted the lawless and dissolute as well as the sober and industrious. Without direct law enforcement the strong and well-armed man could dominate his region, and bullies were never lacking to take advantage of more timorous men. Personal violence, ranging from fist fights and gouging matches to punctilious duels, were common in the West for a long time.

BANDITRY

Best-known evidence of western lawlessness were the bandits who preyed along the routes of travel, as they were to continue to do until the disappearance of the frontier. Western criminals were sometimes eastern criminals who had just escaped justice, but were often the restless and adventurous who found outlawry more interesting and exciting—and only a little more dangerous—than cutting trees and plowing virgin soil. Some were fascinated by adventure, but others were simply trying to avoid continuous hard work.

Several of the early nineteenth-century bandits attained enough notoriety to keep their names alive, even though often in a rather legendary form. Colonel Fluger, commonly known as "Colonel Plug," kept a tavern near Cairo, Illinois. His chief stock in trade was his wife, "Pluggy," who bestowed her favors freely on boatmen and traders while her husband robbed them. James Girty, nephew of the notorious Simon Girty, claimed without serious dispute that he could beat any man in the West; one of his paramours provided an explanation by asserting that his chest was solid bone. Micajah and Wiley Harpe, usually called Big and Little Harpe, roamed Kentucky and Tennessee, robbing and murdering in a casual and insensitive fashion. Legend has it that Big Harpe was ultimately killed by a posse and that his head was removed and nailed to a tree as a warning to other evildoers, thereby giving the name to Harpe's Head, Kentucky.

Most notorious of the western bandits of the early nineteenth century was John A. Murrell, "The Great Land Pirate," who operated during the 1820s and 1830s. Murrell was both picturesque and able. Tall, muscular, handsome, and an excellent leader of men, he was everything that the outlaw leader of fiction should be. His early crimes were simple holdups or horse thefts, but later he preferred to steal Negroes, whom he ordinarily sold and recovered several times before he finally killed them to destroy any possible incriminating evidence. His greatest achievement was the formation of the Mystic Clan, which he organized on his many trips along the Ohio and Mississippi and was a secret criminal organization specializing in Negro stealing. It had secret grips, code, passwords, and all the other fraternal symbols. At its height it contained possibly 1500 members, of whom a small inner group was cognizant of all the more important plans; and rank and file did specified jobs for which they were paid. It also had the luxury of a legal staff, with lawyers retained at strategic points to be ready to defend any member accused of a crime.

Murrell's early successes led him to conceive the idea of a general slave rebellion in the South to create a Negro empire of which he would be emperor. Unfortunately Murrell was but human and liked admiration and praise. He talked too much to a spy, was captured, brought before the court on the charge of stealing Negroes, convicted, and incarcerated. While in prison he contracted the "prison sickness" and died at forty-three.

NEW STATES

The earliest governmental interests of the West centered largely on the actions of the eastern states, but attention was later turned to the legislation of Congress. The provisions of the Northwest Ordinance and those of its counterpart in the Southwest had to be tried in practice. The performance of a governor with practically dictatorial powers, the change to partial self-rule, and the ultimate transformation to a state of the Union were all matters of intense interest to the Westerner.

Actually it was not a western but a New England state that became the fourteenth member of the Union. Northern New England remained a frontier approximately as long as Ohio. The Vermont district had long been in dispute between New Hampshire and New York, with both making land grants in this intervening area. Upon the outbreak of the Revolution Ethan Allen and his Green Mountain Boys engineered an independence movement that cynics have held was concerned primarily with land speculation. At any rate, independence was achieved in 1777 and maintained throughout the war, including negotiations with Congress and intrigues with England. Ultimately Vermont adopted the new federal Constitution and was admitted to the Union by Congress in 1791. This event at least recalls the existence of a frontier that stretched from Maine through central New York, and that was the New England equivalent of Kentucky and Tennessee.

Following Vermont in the procession of new states came Kentucky and Tennessee, as described earlier. Neither was a typical "public land state" any more than Vermont had been, because in each case the available land had been practically exhausted before Congress took control. Kentucky never came under direct congressional regulation before its admission as the fifteenth state in 1792, but Tennessee experienced the territorial form of government before it was admitted as the sixteenth state in 1796.

OHIO

The experiences of Ohio in its progress toward admission to the Union were more significant than those of its predecessors, since Ohio represented more nearly the usual process of development that was to take place in the great majority of the future states to the west. Governor Arthur St. Clair arrived in 1788 at Marietta, which was the only settled community in present Ohio. The remainder of the officials appointed by Congress under the terms of the ordinance of 1787 were three judges and a secretary of the territory, one Winthrop Sargent. St. Clair created one county immediately and others as settlement progressed. A code of laws was promulgated, courts were established, and efforts were made to increase the land open to the whites by purchases from the Indians.

The affairs of the Northwest Territory never proceeded smoothly. Governor St. Clair, Scottish-born, was an intelligent and well-educated man, with a degree in medicine. He had high ideals of public service, but his aristocratic federalism conflicted sharply with the prevailing Jeffersonian republicanism of the territory. Wealthy by virtue of marriage, formerly President of Congress, he despised democracy and described himself in the West as "a poor devil banished to another planet." This attitude partly explains why he was so frequently absent from the seat of government—in the East, or treating with the Indians, or prosecuting an Indian war. During his absences the secretary acted in his place, and Sargent was even more objectionable than St. Clair. Ultimately Sargent was advanced to the governorship of the newly created territory of Mississippi in 1798.

The second stage of government became possible for the Northwest Territory when a census of 1798 showed the requisite 5000 adult white males. Governor St. Clair immediately called for the election of a legislative lower house of twenty-two, which met the following year. This body nominated ten men, of whom five were picked by the President of the United States to form an upper house. St. Clair and his legislature never saw eye to eye. Frequently he acted on his own initiative, to the loudly expressed rage of the representatives. In turn he found much of their legislation displeasing and vetoed it. He obtained the nomination of his son to be the territorial representative in Congress, but William Henry Harrison won the election. Ultimately St. Clair's irritation overcome his discretion and he publicly criticized both Congress and the President; whereupon the President removed him.

The growth of the population of the Northwest Territory led many people to think of statehood, but for this purpose some reduction in boundaries was necessary. After many suggestions and much discussion, Indiana was finally sheared away in 1800, with the dividing line the present Indiana-Ohio boundary, except that it was continued north to the international boundary. The section that is now a part of Michigan was later removed, but the boundary was sufficiently uncertain to cause a near war. The new Territory of Indiana included at first all the remainder of the Old Northwest, and to this lordly domain was added, for a short time in 1804–1805 the vast bulk of the Louisiana Purchase, exclusive of Louisiana. Gradually this mass was reduced by eliminating the region west of the Mississippi (1805), Michigan (1805), and Illinois (1809), thus producing the present boundaries of Indiana.

As for the future Ohio, a strong statehood movement received added impetus from the disputes between the legislature and St. Clair. Congress from 1801 was quite willing to have more Republican votes, and on April 30, 1802, passed an enabling act to permit the region to construct a constitution and apply for admission. (This enabling act was the first of a long series passed for later areas farther west.) Under its terms Ohio formed a constitution, and early in 1803 was admitted by Congress to the Union as the seventeenth state. Not surprisingly the new Ohio constitution gave the governor no power of veto.

Ohio furnished the prototype for other states that were later to be carved from the public domain. It participated successively in the three stages of government outlined by the ordinance of 1787. The territorial legislature had the seemingly inevitable quarrels with the governor. Surplus lands were removed to make new territories. A state constitution was formed under the authority of an enabling act and the state was admitted to the Union. At this point a few states varied from the pattern by not waiting for the enabling act, but the general process soon became so standardized that only exceptions from it seem worthy of notice.

READINGS

POLITICAL. See the regional and state histories listed for Chapter 8 under Caruso, Bond, Havighurst, Clark, Davenport, Downes, Utter, Roseboom and Weisenburger. See also Thomas P. Abernethy, *From Frontier to Plantation* (1932), concerning Tennessee; Charles H. Ambler, *A History of West Virginia* (1933); John D. Barnhart, *Valley of Democracy* (1953), giving Ohio a Turnerian interpretation. Two pertinent biographies are Frazer E. Wilson, *Arthur St. Clair* (1944) and Alfred B. Sears, *Thomas Worthington: Father of Ohio Statehood* (1958), detailed.

ECONOMIC. The above political accounts also contain economic material. For regional accounts see Harriette L. S. Arnow, *Seedtime on the Cumberland* (1960); Everett Dick, *The Dixie Frontier* (1948); James M. D. Miller, *The Genesis of Western Culture: The Upper Ohio Valley, 1800–25* (1938). City histories listed in the previous chapter apply, as does the readable Harold Sinclair, *The Port of New Orleans* (1942). Louis C. Hunter, *Studies in the Economic History of the Ohio Valley* (1934) is a well-written monograph. Travel accounts always contain much economic material, as do John W. Harpster (ed.), *Pen Pictures of Early Western Pennsylvania* (1935); John E. Wright and Doris S. Corbett, *Pioneer Life in Western Pennsylvania* (1940); Solon J. and Elizabeth H. Buck, *The Planting of Civilization in Western Pennsylvania* (1939); Daniel Drake, *Pioneer Life in Kentucky* (1948); Harry Toulmin, *The Western Country in 1793* (1948); Reuben G. Thwaites (ed.), *Early Western Travels* (31 vols., and atlas, 1904–1907), particularly Vols. III and IV. Best on the larger story of the development of cattle, hogs, and sheep are, respectively,

Charles W. Towne and Edward N. Wentworth, *Cattle and Men* (1955) ; Charles W. Towne and Edward N. Wentworth, *Pigs* (1950) ; Edward N. Wentworth, *America's Sheep Trails* (1948).

BANDITS. Accounts of outlaws are always questionable, but worth consideration are Robert M. Coates, *The Outlaw Years* (1930) and Ross Phares, *Reverend Devil* (1941), concerned with Murrell. Walter Blair and F. J. Meine, *Mike Fink* (1933) is good on the semilegendary river man.

CHAPTER 10

REPRODUCING A CULTURE

W esterners in the years near 1800 did not devote their entire time and energy to earning their living and to providing a government for themselves. Even the most ambitious and hard-working needed periodic relaxation, while the majority consciously desired to cultivate an intellectual and emotional interest in literature, the arts, and religion. In such aspirations Westerners were distinctly children of the East; practically none thought of a characteristic and unique western culture, and one easy way of making a Westerner fighting mad was to accuse him of begin deficient in any of the traits that distinguished the East. The only difference he was willing to accept with pleasure was one that implied his superiority. Buildings must be as impressive, canals as long, women as charming, penitentiaries as depressing, horses as fast, and parties as magnificent as those in the East.

In the development of interest in sports, the arts, education, and religion, the West was under certain definite and obvious disadvantages. The fact that population was sparse and generally deficient in money and leisure made the development of the arts extremely difficult, even in the towns. Furthermore, few Westerners were thoroughly familiar with the more important contemporary intellectual contributions of the East or of Europe. Migrants were not drawn from the leisured and cultured classes, but from the less prosperous farmers and artisans. Although they were endowed with perfectly adequate native intelligence, they lacked the background, time, and funds that could have provided an excellent education and encouraged wide reading. Many of them were actually illiterate, and their children were equally handicapped.

LITERATURE

Although Westerners were generally deficient in literary interests, there were many exceptions. European visitors periodically marveled when they visited a rough, new log cabin in the wilderness and discovered a collection of books, newspapers, and magazines, plus a frontiersman owner who could talk long and informatively on national and international politics. Thousands of families had at least the minimum of the Bible, *Pilgrim's Progress,* and the poems of Milton. Other well-known English authors included Goldsmith, Pope, Shakespeare, Scott, and Maria Edgeworth; Byron was the first of the romantic poets to become popular. As early as 1788 the town of Lexington, Kentucky, with a population of no more than 700, had at least six merchants who handled books, and although schoolbooks were the most numerous, there were also volumes on religion, law, physics, and the classics. Most books originated in Philadelphia, even though the West itself did more publishing than might have been expected.

Of the western literary productions almanacs and newspapers were the most widely circulated. The almanac by no means confined itself to the calendar and the weather, but printed all kinds of advice and information, from the proper season for planting various crops to medical advice and moral precepts. The first to receive wide circulation was the *Kentucky Almanac,* which started publication in 1794.

Newspapers appeared quite early in most western towns, but their mortality rate was frightful: subscription lists were small, and many of the subscribers forgot to pay. The first paper west of the mountains (except in New York State) was the *Pittsburgh Gazette* (1786), which was soon followed by *The Kentucke Gazette* (1787) at Lexington. First in the Old Northwest was the *Centinel of the North-Western Territory* (1793) at Cincinnati. Early newspapers were usually of four pages. Their contents were almost entirely national and European news, partly because the editors felt that everyone in a small western town knew all the local gossip, but more because of the ease with which a paper could be filled with items clipped from the eastern and European press. Nearly every western paper was issued weekly; the daily paper was unknown. More frequent issues were impossible because of the lack of good communication to obtain news, the paucity of subscriptions, and the shortage of advertising.

Western books and magazines were scarce but not unknown. The first book printed west of the mountains was the third volume of *Modern Chivalry,* published at Pittsburgh in 1793. The author, Hugh Henry Brackenridge, was a prominent resident of Pittsburgh. The story was a long and rambling account of the troubles of an illiterate Irish servant, Teague O'Regan, who perpetually was being rescued from distressing and precarious situations by his master, Captain Farrago. *Modern Chivalry* is no masterpiece of fiction, but it does contain interesting comments on western life at that time. Much more widely sold and read was that eminently practical book, Zadock Cramer's *The Navigator,* of which the first edition appeared in 1801. The most important early publishing center west of Pittsburgh was Lexington, Kentucky.

Most of the other western literary productions consisted of a variety of highly ephemeral religious and political pamphlets. The first magazine to be published in the West was *The Medley, Or Monthly Miscellany,* begun at Lexington in 1803. Probably the earliest poem to be both written and published in the West was *The Kentucky Miscellany,* written by Thomas Johnson some time before 1800; Johnson disliked Kentucky heartily and made his views known with more force than beauty.

Lack of funds and interest meant that libraries were few and small. Many a family had a handful of books, but a collection of as many as a hundred was rare. Booksellers made a precarious living in the larger towns. Here and there a subscription library was established—Lexington in 1795, Belpre in 1796, and Cincinnati in 1802; the famous "Coonskin Library" of Athens County, Ohio, was opened in 1804.

EDUCATION

Lack of writing and printing could be traced largely to a meagerness of education. Few people were able to write effectively; more important, few could read with sufficient ease to make reading a pleasure. Most farmers of the early nineteenth century approved of education in theory, but felt skeptical of the practical advantages of anything more than an irreducible minimum. Education beyond the three R's seemed an unnecessary luxury at a time when every penny loomed large. Furthermore, Westerners (like Easterners) quite generally agreed that the operation of schools at public expense meant an unjustified increase of taxes. To their minds it seemed obvious that parents should pay for whatever education they wanted their children to have. The orators' panegyrics about the necessity of an educated population were accepted by the mass of farmers as true, but with various practical limitations.

Every school was private, and the teacher was paid by the parents of his students. Since the parents had little or no cash, the teacher frequently received his compensation in the form of pigs, vegetables, and corn. Ordinarily he "boarded around," staying for a short time at the home of each of his students. Such a life did not attract capable and interested teachers, particularly since teachers were poorly paid on the common assumption that anyone who could read and write was thoroughly competent to teach. The teaching profession had no important standing in the community and therefore was a haven for many misfits, men without steady occupations who found schoolteaching the path of least resistance. However, it also attracted a more desirable group of young New England men who used it as a means of becoming acquainted with the country while saving a little money before they began their chosen work.

Instruction, usually limited to the three R's, was given to children only when they could not be employed usefully on the farm, which meant a few weeks or months in the winter for the older children and a little additional summer work for the younger ones. Many children never attended school at all. The "little red schoolhouse" was an institution of the future, for the best that the West could afford in 1800 was a small, log, single-room schoolhouse. The children were ungraded and studied aloud simultaneously, after which they recited the lessons from memory. Texts were scarce and father's books were considered good enough for little John. The diversity of population sometimes meant that no two books in the school were alike. Paper was scarce and consequently little used; its substitute was slate, on which marks were made with a piece of soapstone. The summit of education for most children was the knowledge of the elementary rules of reading, writing, spelling, and ciphering.

Secondary and higher education in the West were almost nonexistent prior to 1800. Here and there were a few seminaries (sometimes called colleges) for either boys or girls. For the girls they offered polite "finishing" courses in such departments as fancy needlework, deportment, and painting. For the boys they offered the classical subjects necessary for entrance to an eastern college. The only institution of higher education in the West prior to 1800 was Transylvania University at Lexington. Its requirements were not high, and it had a hard struggle to continue its existence; eventually it was to become important. Between 1800 and 1810 a few other institutions appeared, such as Jefferson College and Washington College (later united) in Pennsylvania, Ohio University (Athens) and Vincennes University in the Old Northwest, and Cumberland College in Tennessee.

SOCIAL GATHERINGS

Western life was frequently lonely, each rural family being fairly isolated physically and self-sufficient economically, but there were few people who desired continual solitude. Moreover, a number of tasks could not be performed by the family without outside help. The result was that the West grasped eagerly every opportunity for common action, including some that were not really essential. Work was combined with play so that the work was lost to view in the general fun and merrymaking. Such an occasion as a logrolling, house-raising, cornhusking, maple-sugar gathering, a wedding, a funeral, harvesting, quilting, fulling, sewing, or weaving attracted the entire neighborhood. The singing school and the spelling bee brought similar gatherings.

Announcement of a community enterprise brought everyone who was within traveling distance. The men spent the day in raising the house, husking the corn, or doing whatever had been planned while the women prepared an immense feast. Neither sex was mute during these activities. Then everyone ate and drank all he could, told jokes (often crude), gossiped, and debated politics and religion. In the evening the older folk continued their conversations while the young people danced to the music of a fiddle. Square dancing was the rule, with some stentorian-voiced male calling off the figures. Although dancing was rather general in the back country, it had opponents; some of the more religious felt it to be immoral, and in this attitude they were supported by most of the churches.

Western parties tended to be boisterous, earthy, even crude. These were vigorous and hard-working people who had not as yet arrived at the Victorian period. Kissing games were frequent, and when a cornhusker found a red ear he could kiss the girl of his choice; the kiss was not a perfunctory peck, and it was rumored that the foresighted boys brought red ears with them to the party. Love-making was frequently coarse, vigor replacing finesse when youthful couples strolled off into the moonlit woods. A wedding produced riotous fun and pointed jokes. Frequently the happy couple was put to bed in the loft to the accompaniment of ribald remarks while the party continued downstairs. When to the natural relief from backbreaking toil was added the consumption of too much whiskey the result might approach a riot. Westerners lived close to the basic facts of nature, and were not oppressed by the prudishness of a later generation.

DRAMA

One amusement largely absent from the West was the drama. A few theaters were constructed before 1810, as at Pittsburgh and Cincinnati, but there were no regular professional companies of actors. Amateurs presented a few plays, as at Lexington before 1800, but the performances were bad. Many people throughout the country felt that the theater was basically immoral, and an even greater number held that professional actors, and certainly actresses, led lives of sin. The general feeling that the theater had a contaminating effect on women influenced the amateur actors to use men in all female parts. The performances may have been highly moral, but they had no other virtues to recommend them.

ATHLETIC CONTESTS.

The West was always interested in athletic contests, which it commonly combined with gambling. Horse racing was highly popular, with race tracks in operation at various towns, both North and South, before 1800. Shooting matches, foot races, and wrestling all had their devotees, each of whom usually had a stake on the outcome of an event. The stake was usually more than the bettor could afford, which of course made the affair more exciting. Each contest was accompanied by copious drinking, and sometimes the drinking occurred without the excuse of the contest. Shooting was possibly the most utilitarian of these sports, and each Westerner was proud of his prowess with a gun. Although the shooting was actually not remarkably good from a modern standpoint, it was next to miraculous when the heavy gun, the poor powder, and the small and often irregular shot are considered.

Athletic contests were frequently highly objectionable from the point of view of a later and more squeamish generation. Rough-and-tumble fist fights had no Marquis of Queensberry rules. The contestants kicked, butted, bit, and gouged, and the loss of an eye, an ear, or a finger was not uncommon. Even making allowances for the tall stories that the West liked to impose upon credulous Easterners, the fact still remained that the West was rough and uncouth, and that its fun was boisterous.

RELIGION

Among the various cultural developments in the West none was more important than the growth of religious denominations. The best-informed guess is that in 1800 less than half of western families were affiliated with any church. This was due in considerable part to obstacles other than irreligion. Money to build and repair churches and to pay ministers was hard to obtain. In fact, ministers themselves were difficult to find: all divinity schools were in the East, and a graduate needed considerable fervor and missionary zeal to forgo a comfortable living in the East for the hardships of the frontier.

A special western disadvantage was the multiplicity of sects that made the formation and support of any single church more difficult. In the East these various sects tended to concentrate geographically, but in the West a dozen or more might be represented more or less equally in a single small community—not only larger churches, such as the Methodist, Presbyterian, Congregational, Roman Catholic, Episcopal, and Lutheran, but also such small groups as the Moravian, Dunkard, United Brethren in Christ, Anabaptists, Quakers, and Shakers. Few groups had sufficient strength to build their own churches and support their own ministers, and the idea of a community church would have been viewed generally with horror.

The religious lag of the West greatly distressed thousands of people, both East and West. In the East, men feared that irreligion would grow in the West, infect the East, and thus destroy one of the foundations of the Republic. To avert this potential tragedy, proselyting groups were formed. Home missionary societies mushroomed during the 1790s, including notably the Missionary Society of Connecticut (1798), the Massachcusetts Missionary Society (1799), and the Boston Female Society for Missionary Purposes (1800). Various "female cent institutions" collected a cent a week from each member. These societies sent a considerable number of men on missionary tours of the West. In addition, tract societies provided religious pamphlets and books without charge, and Bible societies distributed the "Word of God." Each denomination of any size devoted part of its funds to work in the West.

Thousands of Westerners were similarly concerned with the dangers of irreligion, for they had been reared in religious eastern homes and wanted their children to have the benefit of church teaching. They realized that although worship could be an individual matter, for most people group worship was important, and they made every effort to organize and maintain churches in the West.

Religion meant much more to the Westerner than the fears of many Easterners suggested. Considerable numbers of Westerners were church members, and the various denominations exercised considerable control over the morals of their members; any man leaning toward such temptations as lying, slander, cheating in business, fighting, or illicit sex adventures might be deterred by the considerable chance of being ejected from church membership if he succumbed. Then, too, most churches supported education, rgardless of the educational background of their own clergy. They were responsible for the founding of many western colleges that presumably would prepare students for the ministry.

The church had special importance in giving meaning to the hard western life. The hazards and hardships of frontier farming became more tolerable to one who believed that God watched over him and would make him successful. Hence a devout Christian could feel that the destruction of the Indian, an unbeliever, was a victory of right over the powers of darkness. The Westerner was no "turn the other cheek" type of Christian, but believed in a more positive, vigorous, and aggressive brand of Christianity.

Organized religion also offered the Westerners social and emotional outlets that were highly important. On Sunday the whole family walked or rode to church to spend the entire day. Sunday school was followed by a morning service, then dinner, and finally an afternoon service. Although sermons were long and seats hard, the singing of hymns gave a joyous occupation to the lungs; hymns were "lined out" two lines at a time, since many people could read neither words nor music. The noon dinner provided an opportunity to hear the latest news of crops, politics, and new babies. Furthermore, religious emotionalism gave a welcome release from the hard and prosaic task of making a living. Few Westerners thought of frontier life as providing any emotionally stimulating experiences.

A church with real hopes for success in the West should have had an optimistic faith, with stress on the importance of the individual. It should have provided social and emotional content. It should have had an organization adapted to the widely scattered western population. Further, it needed a clergy that could speak the language of the crude and hard-working West. The refined and sophisticated product of the eastern theological seminary was no doubt eminently satisfactory to an educated and intelligent audience, but his appeal to a relatively uneducated and uncultured West was slight.

METHODISTS

One church well fitted for western needs was the Methodist as reorganized after the Revolution to give the American branch relative independence. The best-known and most effective leader was Francis Asbury, usually called by the unmerited title of Bishop. He disregarded his feeble body and much sickness to travel widely, preaching and praying. Under his guidance Methodism became an important part of the religious life of the United States. Methodism crossed the mountains in the early 1780s. The Western Conference, organized in 1800, included some 2500 members in Kentucky and Tennessee; an additional 350 members belonged to three circuits north of the Ohio; and Methodist ministers had pushed into Missouri. By 1811 western Methodists numbered 30,000 (including 1500 Negroes) and were at least as numerous as any other denomination.

The Methodist doctrines of free will, free grace, and individual responsibility appealed to the Westerner. Furthermore, the church organization was admirably adapted to the conditions of the West. Instead of devoting his entire time to the care of one church, a minister might "ride circuit," thus distributing his attention over a considerable region. During his absence from any one community the work was continued by lay members, called "exhorters" or "local preachers." These laymen both preached and conducted religious services. Methodist ministers tended to be particularly effective because the church was willing to use forceful men regardless of their education. Such men talked in the strong and vivid language of the frontier, and although they might be confused by the subtleties of theological disputation and be entirely ignorant of Latin and Greek, they could paint the terrors of hell in compelling terms, and could call upon the sinner to repent with a vigor, earnestness, and pathos that put their more learned brethren to shame.

The circuit rider ordinarily went on horseback, and his circuit required continuous traveling for four or five weeks. He preached daily at noon in any convenient gathering place, such as a cabin or a clearing. His salary in 1784 was sixty-four dollars a year, out of which he paid his own traveling expenses, but in 1800 his salary was advanced to eighty dollars and traveling expenses for himself plus an allowance for his family. This stipend often took the form of agricultural products, and was frequently supplemented by entertainment and gifts from parishioners. The circuit rider usually wore a straight-breasted waistcoat, a high collar, and a plain necktie. Suspenders were a luxury. His hair was allowed to grow to his shoulders, according to the western custom of the time; barbers were rare, and the man with long hair, or his wife, could do any needed trimming.

The Methodist circuit rider threw his influence in the direction of civilization and culture in spite of his own crudities and lack of education. Often he carried books in his saddlebags, and lent them to the people with whom he stayed. On many occasions he was the only visitor a family would entertain for months at a time, and to such a family he would bring the news of the outside world—tales of wondrous cities, new styles in dress and social intercourse, marvelous mechanical improvements, and neighborhood gossip. His advent was awaited eagerly, for he was more informative than the newspaper.

BAPTISTS

The chief frontier rivals of the Methodists were the Baptists, who believed in immersion and in close communion. Great freedom was allowed the individual churches, which varied widely in their practices. Instead of having a regular circuit system the Baptists licensed local preachers and encouraged very small congregations. Like the Methodists, they were more interested in fervor than in education for the ministry, and favored rapid evangelization by emotional pleas. Also like the Methodists, they established their first trans-Appalachian churches in the 1780s and then expanded rapidly, until by 1800 they had crossed the Mississippi.

The Baptists were the unwilling parents of the Disciples of Christ, commonly known as "Christians" or "Campbellites." The originator of this new sect was Thomas Campbell, who migrated from Scotland to western Pennsylvania in 1807, but the important leader was the founder's son Alexander. The Disciples favored a "purer," more primitive Christianity to combine the true believers of all churches. After flirting with the Presbyterians they joined the Baptists (1813) and grew within that church. Ultimately, in the late 1820s, they withdrew from the Baptist Church to produce, rather ironically, a new sect. Their belief in poverty and self-sacrifice did not prevent them from trying to take all the church property they felt belonged to them.

PRESBYTERIANS AND CONGREGATIONALISTS

Third in size among western Protestant sects was the Presbyterian, which was handicapped by the gloomy doctrines of Calvin, the lack of an effective frontier organization, the insistence on an educated clergy, and a reluctance to accept revival methods. On these issues occurred two southwestern schisms in the years immediately after 1800. The "New Lights" raised doubts about the doctrines of election and predestination, but soon died. The Cumberland Presbyterian Church (1810) seceded largely on the educated ministry issue, holding that piety was more important than book learning and that high educational qualifications meant a deplorable lack of ministers in the West. The parent church tried to fill western needs by promoting western colleges, but this procedure was too slow for many impatient Westerners.

Closely allied with the Presbyterians were the Congregationalists. These two churches were in such community of feeling that in 1801 they adopted a plan of union by which they collaborated in founding new churches and then allowed these churches to decide for themselves whether their services, church rules, and ministers would be Presbyterian or Congregational. The general result of this cooperation was the development of Presbyterian rather than Congregational churches. Congregationalism became more important when an increased flood of New Englanders carried it to Michigan, Wisconsin, Iowa, Minnesota, and other regions of the Far West.

EPISCOPALIANS

The Episcopal Church had more difficulties in appealing to the West than any of the larger Protestant sects. As an integral part of the Church of England it had suffered severely during the Revolution because it was connected in the popular mind with upper-class Tories. The English connection had been broken with the Convention of 1789, but the old reputation lingered. Furthermore, the scarcity of its ministers, due in part to the high educational requirements, the lack of a system of itineracy, and the reluctance to use emotionalism, all made work in the West more difficult. Even the growth of a strong evangelical, Low Church group that accepted the universal possibility of conversion rather than predestination did not correct the situation entirely.

The slowness of Episcopalian expansion was evident to everyone. Here and there was a man, such as Philander Chase, who worked effectively in Ohio after his arrival in 1817 and his elevation to bishop the following year, but such a man was rare. In 1820 there was only a handful of ministers west of the mountains, with none in Indiana, Illinois, Tennessee, or Mississippi. During this same year the Domestic and Foreign Missionary Society of the Protestant Episcopal Church was organized, but it did little work until after its reorganization fifteen years later. In 1840 the Missionary Society was helping to support 64 western ministers, or over a third of those west of the mountains (152). The smallness of the Episcopal strength is indicated by the fact that its total number of western ministers in 1840 was approximately equal to the number of Baptist clergy in the one state of Missouri.

ROMAN CATHOLICS

The Roman Catholics did the earliest missionary work in the region west of the Appalachians. Jesuit priests had labored long among the Indians and with the French and Spanish settlers, but these efforts were of practically no influence on the American West of 1800. Catholicism expanded from east to west in the period after the Revolution in the same way as did other faiths. The Diocese of Bardstown (Kentucky) was established in 1808 and Joseph Flaget arrived to take charge of it three years later. By 1815 there were probably 10,000 Catholics among the white settlers west of the mountains. Later migration was to increase Catholic membership, to the great distress of many Protestant Americans who questioned whether Catholicism was not worse than paganism.

CAMP MEETINGS

The frontier community had a definite need for vital religious experiences that could not be satisfied by the occasional preachings of a peripatetic Methodist minister. Frequent emotional outpourings were necessary to alleviate the deadly seriousness of daily life. All believers must at times be assembled to gain consciousness of common purpose and strivings. The frontier needed some religious expression that would weld isolated families into a sense of emotional unity. The institution that ultimately met this need was the camp meeting. In its original form as an emotional expression of religious strivings, the camp meeting was not distinctively western, but in its increased use and in the typical form that it later assumed it was a western contribution to the religious life of the nation.

As early as 1796 James McGready, a Presbyterian minister inspired by eastern revivals, arrived in Kentucky. McGready was personally unprepossessing and had a coarse, tremulous voice, but he produced a curious and unearthly effect that was extremely impressive. He held a series of emotional meetings in which hell was pictured frequently and vividly, and in which much weeping and ecstasy occurred. The unusual effectiveness of these meetings aroused widespread interest among Westerners who desired the advance of religion.

Among the people attracted to hear McGready were the McGee brothers—William, a Presbyterian, and John, a Methodist. The McGees heard McGready in 1799 and were so impressed that they held similar meetings throughout the West. Of William it is related that "he would sometimes exhort after the sermon, standing on the floor, or sitting, or lying in the dust, his eyes streaming, and his heart so full he could only ejaculate, 'Jesus! Jesus!'"

Emotional religious meetings had an immediate and profound appeal for Westerners. Soon the attendants became too numerous to be accommodated by the small country churches. Tents and cabins were found necessary, with tents probably first used in 1800. The length of the meetings increased until it became common to occupy an entire weekend from Friday until Tuesday. The largest of such meetings, and the one that may be said to have marked the height of the "Great Revival," was at Cane Ridge, Kentucky, in August 1801: the attendance was variously estimated at between ten and twenty thousand. Although the Great Revival had ended by 1805, the camp meeting continued to be used frequently and successfully.

Whole families traveled twenty, thirty, or even a hundred miles to attend a camp meeting. They brought with them tents, food, cooking utensils, clothes, and even furniture. Upon their arrival they raised their tents or constructed rude log cabins on the edge of the cleared space that was to be used for the larger meetings. Furniture for these living quarters was crude and cooking was done over open fires.

The main meetings were held in the large clearing at the center of the camp ground. A high platform at one end served as a pulpit, with eight, ten, or even more ministers serving in relays. Most of the participating clergy were Methodists but there was a sprinkling of Baptists and Presbyterians. Seats for the congregation were usually the halves of split logs arranged in parallel rows. Between the congregation and the platform was a litter of loose straw placed there to support the knees of repentant sinners. Meetings were held morning, afternoon, and evening, pine torches providing illumination after dark. Along the sides of the cleared space smaller meetings in tents were usually held simultaneously with the large meeting.

The camp meeting stressed the mystical and emotional appeal of religion. Songs by the congregation and prayers were prefaces and interludes to the main business of exhorting. The appeals included lengthy descriptions of the horrors of hell, with less stress on the glories of heaven, and included many admonitions for sinners to repent. Frequently they were punctuated by shouted "Amens" and "Yes, Lords" and "Glories" from the members of the congregation and other clergy.

Bombarded by soul-harrowing discourses, some of the "sinners" came forward to repent of their sins, and the ministers "labored" with them individually. Flaming calls for repentance inspired even the purest woman or most innocent young girl to feel a conviction of deadly sin that must be acknowledged and repented. Adolescent girls seemed to be particularly affected by threats of hell and damnation. The response of a few people was contagious, and soon the whole meeting was raised to a pitch of hysteria, particularly because the ministers knew by experience the psychological appeals that would produce maximum religious exaltation. Conditions for emotional release were most favorable at night, when the wild flare of the torches contrasted dramatically with the blackness of the surrounding forest and when the description of other worldly subjects was particularly impressive. Of almost equal effectiveness were the small meetings in the tents, where the hot, stuffy air and the exhortations for repentance were a combination difficult to resist.

The intensity of the emotional strain produced by a camp meeting was shown by the convulsive and involuntary actions of those people most affected. They leaped, ran, jumped, laughed, sang, sobbed, shouted, and swooned; the better the meeting the larger the number of the "slain." Some beat the ground in agony; others barked like dogs or emitted the "holy laugh." Many twitched in every joint with the "jerks," reputed to be so contagious that even scoffing onlookers were similarly affected. Trances and visions, in which conversations were held with Christ or His apostles or the dear departed, were not unusual. The more powerful the reaction the more the Lord had worked, and the more the sanctification of the person affected.

The emotional displays of the camp meeting were desired, and plans were laid carefully to produce them, but other results of the gatherings were achieved less consciously. The camp meeting was incidentally an occasion for meeting friends and neighbors, and for discussing subjects of common interest. Families came in part to see other families, and in intervals between meetings and while food was being prepared over the open fires, gossip was exchanged and old friendships were renewed. The small children played together during the day, and it was not unknown for the elders to miss meetings to discuss crops or the latest candidate for the legislature.

The social intercourse of the camp meeting was generally good, but at times it had its less desirable aspects. People not interested in the religious exercises would come for the excitement and human companionship, and their presence would detract from the sincerity of the worship. Other hangers-on would also be attracted by the meeting. Large numbers of people required an immense supply of food, necessitating the establishment of a number of small stores on the edge of the grounds. Among other merchandise, these stores frequently handled whiskey, which attracted a rowdy element from the nearby towns. Sometimes friction between the religious and nonreligious elements ended in a free-for-all fight. The Westerner, even the religious Westerner, was not docile.

The camp meeting encountered another difficulty in the tendency of some of the young people to confuse human and divine love and to obey too literally the injunction to "love thy neighbor as thyself." Some meetings found it necessary to post a guard at night to prevent young couples from wandering into the surrounding woods. In the emotional orgy of a meeting women at times threw themselves upon the ground in suggestive attitudes, tore open their clothes, and hugged and kissed everyone they met. The overemphasis on sex was undoubtedly linked closely with the emotionalism of the whole camp meeting. Observers commonly noted that adolescent boys and girls were most subject to religious exaltation, and it is easy to believe that at times sex was not sublimated, but took direct and earthy means of expression.

In spite of minor difficulties, the camp meeting was useful to the West both as a social meeting place and as an occasion for the emphasis of religious idealism. It provided a socially accepted vehicle for the expression of emotions that frequently were given no outlet in life on the frontier. Friendships were made or renewed, common problems discussed, courtships begun or continued, information and experiences exchanged, and the inhabitants of the region given a feeling of unity and religious fellowship that helped to make more bearable future months of isolation. Many of the people were influenced to lead more socially desirable lives, although of course there was the inevitable backslider who was "saved" at each successive meeting. In consequence, the camp meeting must not be considered as a picturesque but unimportant western eccentricity; rather, it was an institution that added necessary elements to western life.

READINGS

SOCIAL. The nonpolitical readings of the previous chapter are almost all applicable to this one; to the state histories add Francis P. Weisenburger, *The Passing of the Frontier, 1825–50* (1941), which concerns Ohio. Particularly interesting are Arthur K. Moore, *The Frontier Mind* (1957), an interpretation based on Kentucky, and James McD. Miller, *The Genesis of Western Culture* (1938). Frank L. McVey, *The Gates Open Slowly* (1949) is detailed on Kentucky schools. John F. McDermott, *George*

Caleb Bingham (1959) is a good biography of the West's most eminent artist. Thomas D. Clark, *The Rampaging Frontier* (1939) treats western humor.

RELIGION. Most diligent and useful of the religious historians has been William Warren Sweet; his *The Story of Religions in America* (1930) and his *Religion in the Development of American Culture, 1765–1840* (1952) are good for background. On missions consult Wade C. Barclay, *History of American Missions* (1949); confined to the West is Colin B. Goodykoontz, *Home Missions on the American Frontier* (1939). Baptists: William W. Sweet (ed.), *Religion on the American Frontier. Vol. 1: The Baptists* (1931), largely documents. Catholics: Theodore Naynard, *The Story of American Catholicism* (1941); Joseph H. Schauinger, *Cathedrals in the Wilderness* (1952), with biographies of Kentuckians. Congregationalists: William W. Sweet, *Religion on the American Frontier. Vol. 3: The Congregationalists* (1939). Disciples of Christ: Winfred E. Garrison, *Religion Follows the Frontier* (1931); Winfred E. Garrison and Alfred T. DeGroot, *The Disciples of Christ* (1948); William G. West, *Barton Warren Stone* (1954). Episcopalians: William W. Manross, *A History of the American Episcopal Church* (1935) and *The Episcopal Church in the United States 1800–1840* (1938); Clara O. Loveland, *The Critical Years: The Reconstruction of the Anglican Church in the United States of America, 1780–1789* (1956). Methodists: Wade C. Barclay, *Early American Methodism* (2 vols., 1949) is long and informative; William W. Sweet, *Methodism in American History* (1933), *The Rise of Methodism in the West* (1920), and *Religion on the American Frontier, Vol. 4: The Methodists* (1946); good special studies are Elizabeth K. Nottingham, *Methodism and the Frontier* (1941), which concerns Indiana, and Walter B. Posey, *The Development of Methodism in the Old Southwest* (1933); two useful biographies are Herbert Asbury, *A Methodist Saint* (1927), which is interesting on Francis Asbury, and Helen H. Grant, *Peter Cartwright* (1931), based largely on the subject's writings. Presbyterians: William W. Sweet (ed.), *Religion on the American Frontier. Vol. 2: The Presbyterians* (1936); Walter B. Posey, *The Presbyterian Church in the Old Southwest* (1952); Dwight R. Guthrie, *John McMillan* (1952). Shakers: Julia Neal, *By Their Fruits* (1947) describes Shaker communities in Kentucky. William W. Sweet, *Revivalism in America* (1944) and Bernard A. Weisberger, *They Gathered At the River* (1958) are general accounts of revivals; Charles A. Johnson, *The Frontier Camp Meeting* (1955); Catharine C. Cleveland, *The Great Revival in the West, 1797–1805,* (1916) remains the most useful on that event.

CHAPTER 11

WAR IN
THE NORTHWEST

T he surging of white population into the West during the opening years of the nineteenth century was impressive, but did not touch the greater part of Indian land. In the Old Northwest the whites occupied little more than the cessions of the Treaty of Greenville. The Indians were generally hostile to the advancing Americans and friendly to the British, who retained a considerable interest in the area in spite of their evacuation of posts south of the border. The British desired to retain the lucrative Great Lakes fur trade, and were glad to keep aggressive American frontiersmen as far as possible from Canada. The Indians preferred trading with the British to trading with the Americans, and felt no danger from Canadian expansion, whereas the Americans were becoming more menacing year by year. They had been overawed temporarily by the Wayne campaign, but the memory of white military power was now fading, and again they had hopes of resisting white aggression successfully, and even of expelling the intruders by force.

INDIAN GRIEVANCES

The Indian had many rankling and irritating grievances to arouse his hatred of the whites. The contact of the two civilizations always meant the eventual supremacy of the white, with the decay and destruction of the red. The Indian of the Old Northwest realized increasingly that his total elimination was not far distant if he did not fight back. He could see clearly the increasing numbers of whites driving off his game and taking possession of his land. The federal government continued to give lip service to the fiction of Indian independence and landownership, but the Indian was more impressed by the rapidity with which the whites obtained any area they coveted. No opposition short of war seemed to have the least chance of damming the white flood.

The Indian was also increasingly resentful of the way in which he suffered at the hands of the white man. He was cheated at the trading posts. He was plied with whiskey until his reasoning powers were gone. He traded a year's catch of furs for a few trinkets and a little bad whiskey. He gave the trinkets to his wife and drank the whiskey, with the result that his season's work gave him only a dark brown taste and impaired health. And then the white man's diseases completed the havoc. Gambling and stealing were traits common to both races, but now they became for the Indian mean and degrading instead of remaining a part of the life of every self-respecting adult. The traits of the warrier now became those of the sneak thief. The white had taught him new and more expensive ways of eating and dressing; with his money gone for bad liquor, the Indian was often reduced to slinking about the white settlements and resorting to petty pilfering, which damaged his self-respect and could put him in jail. The crimes committed by the Indians were always punished if the culprits were detected, but those of the whites against the Indians might be overlooked. Furthermore, Indian women were comparatively easy prey for the aggressive frontiersmen. The result was the introduction and spread of venereal disease, which further sapped the strength of the Indians. No wonder they became increasingly hostile toward the whites.

The Indian who best exemplified the growing rancor toward white civilization was Tecumseh, probably the ablest leader the Shawnee ever produced. Tecumseh was born in 1768 of a Shawnee father and a Creek mother. His father was killed by a white hunting party, and his mother instilled vengeance in his youthful mind. As a young man he fought against St. Clair and then at Fallen Timbers against Wayne. He was married at the rather advanced age of twenty-eight, but soon separated from his half-breed wife; then he fell in love with a white girl, but refused to adopt the white ways upon which the girl insisted, and did not marry her. Tecumseh was five feet ten inches, although he looked taller. He was exemplary in habits and never drank liquor. Physically he was powerful in spite of a slightly bent leg that had been broken in a buffalo hunt and never set properly. His mind was keen and his speech convincing. His brother, called the Prophet, had been a drunken and worthless young man who had lost an eye in an accident, but after his conversion by the Shakers he was transformed, and was felt by other Indians to have magical powers.

Tecumseh watched the advance of the whites and the progressive deterioration of the reds with an ever-growing surge of anger. He was certain in his own mind that the land belonged to the Indian tribes forever, no matter by what show of legality it might be taken away from them, and that they could cling to their traditional ways of life. He concluded that the only possible method of opposing the white advance successfully was to obtain the cooperation of all the Indians and to have them act in concert. With this plan in mind he traveled widely, particularly in the first decade of the nineteenth century, talking with Indians both north and south in an effort to form an alliance against white aggression. In 1808 he and his brother had their headquarters at the confluence of Tippecanoe Creek and the Wabash; here was built Prophetstown, with its extensive agricultural fields and large herds—and no whiskey.

WILLIAM HENRY HARRISON

The white man who best represented the point of view diametrically opposed to that of Tecumseh was William Henry Harrison. Harrison was a frontiersman only by adoption: he was born in Virginia on February 9, 1773, to a family that had lived in Virginia for over a century. He was given a good education in the expectation that he would enter the medical profession, but military life attracted him more and in 1791 he joined the army. His command was ordered west, and arrived at Fort Washington just as the remnants of St. Clair's defeated army were returning. Harrison subsequently took part in Wilkinson's campaigns against the Indians and then distinguished himself at Fallen Timbers with Wayne. Returning to Fort Washington in 1796 he was given command of the fort with the rank of captain. Two years later he resigned because of lack of action.

Harrison spent much of his life in seeking remunerative positions through political influence. In 1798 he wangled the job of secretary of the Northwest Territory, but proved more interested in farming and distilling than in keeping records. The following year he took advantage of a factional fight in the Ohio Legislative Council and was elected as delegate to the United States House of Representatives. His victory was by the close vote of eleven to ten, and was probably due to the fact that his opponent was the son of the unpopular Governor St. Clair. In Congress Harrison was active in supporting a revision of the land laws and the division of the Northwest Territory to permit statehood to Ohio, playing an active role in the construction and passage of the land act of 1800 and in the formation of the Indiana Territory. Then once more he pulled all the political strings within his reach to obtain the appointment as Governor of Indiana.

When Harrison arrived at his new post early in 1801 he found himself with but few people to govern in spite of his nominal control of a large area. The total white population of the present states of Indiana, Illinois, Michigan, and Wisconsin was little more than 5000; the most populous town, Vincennes, had 700 residents. Consequently the new Governor had plenty of spare time in which to try a little farming, dabble in land speculation, and take an interest in the schemes of Aaron Burr. He was personally ambitious: as Governor of Indiana he desired to enlarge his constituency by buying Indian land for the benefit of white settlers. On the other hand, his immediate aim was to continue in office, and since he felt that Jefferson favored a policy of benevolent noninterference in Indian affairs he was content for the time being to sit idle and do nothing.

Harrison was soon free to follow his own desires by a plain intimation from President Jefferson that new land acquisitions would not be looked on with disfavor. Immediately (1802–1803) he entered negotiations with the Indians, and another million acres were added to the land available for white settlement. Other treaties followed, and the resulting Indian resentment was attributed by the Governor to British influence, which since the surrender of Detroit centered at Malden (Amherstburg) across the river. Harrison had some sympathy for the Indians, for they suffered from "unprovoked wrongs," but he was convinced that the only possible way to deal satisfactorily with them was to destroy them. He had visions of himself as a second Wayne, and read such classic war narratives as those of Herodotus, Thucydides, Caesar, and Sallust. He mapped out wonderful prospective campaigns, and felt that all he needed was an opportunity to exhibit his abilites as a strategist.

Harrison's attention was not called to Tecumseh until 1806, but the succeeding years saw the men come into closer and closer contact. In 1808, the year that Tecumseh took up his residence in Prophetstown, he had an interview with Harrison in which he promised peace if the United States did not make further treaties involving land cessions; if such cessions were made, Tecumseh threatened an English alliance and war. A similar interview was held the following year, but by this time events made peace impossible. Illinois Territory was created, leaving Indiana with its present boundaries. Harrison received permission from the Secretary of War to buy more Indian land; the purchase of 2,500,000 acres in the fall of 1809 increased the number and wrath of the hostile Indians. Rumors of war became current on the frontier.

TIPPECANOE

The new land purchase led Tecumseh in his conversations with Harrison in 1810 to insist more strongly that Indian land was held in common and could not be alienated by a few individuals. Harrison might well have commenced war at this time if the government had not been busy in West Florida, but he waited until August 1811, at which time he felt that his opportunity had come. Tecumseh, after an interview in which he had asked that no immediate action be taken, departed on a tour to the

South to talk with the southern Indians. As soon as he had gone, Harrison gathered 1000 men (mostly volunteers) and, with a well-planned campaign already formulated, prepared to annihilate his unsuspecting enemies. Possibly he was absent-minded—at least he forgot to report his plans to the President.

When Harrison left Vincennes on September 26, 1811, his objective was to crush Shawnee power by destroying Prophetstown. Moving directly up the Wabash he paused only long enough to build Fort Harrison on the present site of Terre Haute, and on the night of November 6 encamped on Tippecanoe Creek. Although he stated that he did not intend to attack Prophetstown, the Indians quite rightly feared treachery and under the leadership of the Prophet attacked the white camp early on the morning of November 7. In spite of the surprise, Harrison maintained his position. The white casualties were 61 killed and 127 wounded; the Indian losses were unknown. Both sides claimed victory, but popularly Harrison received the credit. He became a military hero largely because he had the foresight to dispatch messengers to the East immediately after the battle with reports of an overwhelming defeat of the Indians. In later years there was much controversy as to whether or not Harrison had actually won. He had avoided rout and repulsed the Indians; on the other hand he had found it necessary to retreat almost immediately, stopping only long enough to destroy Prophetstown. He was back in Vincennes on November 18.

The Battle of Tippecanoe had far-reaching effects, though somewhat different from those that Harrison had anticipated. Prophetstown did not disappear: the Indians immediately rebuilt it; Indian troubles did not stop: new depredations occurred at once. From a larger point of view, however, the Indians suffered greatly. Tecumseh lost some of his prestige, and plans for a general Indian alliance never again came so near to success as they had in the years just prior to 1811. The United States encountered no further resistance in expanding its land purchases to Lake Michigan after the War of 1812. For Harrison's personal benefit the encounter inspired the battle cry of "Tippecanoe and Tyler too" which was an important factor in his successful presidential campaign of 1840.

WESTERN WAR SENTIMENT

Scarcely had Harrison returned from his Indian campaign than the outbreak of the War of 1812 took the center of the stage. The stated causes of the war were freedom of the seas and the impressment of American seamen, but rather curiously the Northeast, which presumably should have been most concerned, was actually least in favor of the war. Sentiment for it came largely from the South and the West. These regions were especially bellicose, partly because of the temperament of the inhabitants, partly be-

Harrison and Tecumseh

cause of vigorous nationalism, and partly because of selfish economic interests. Both South and West had been suffering from a depression that had
started about 1808, and both resented English trade restrictions that hurt
the marketing of such raw materials as cotton, corn, tobacco, and hemp.
The West also blamed its Indian troubles on British incitement, and expected that a British defeat would give Americans the Great Lakes fur
trade and sap the power of the Indians. Then, too, the West had covetous
eyes on Canada and Florida; although waging two major wars at the same
time seemed foolhardy, at least Canada might be taken. England was the
traditional American enemy, as well as the stronger and more objectionable power.

War sentiment was brought to the boiling point in Congress by the
"War Hawks," mostly from the West and the South. One of them, Henry
Clay, became Speaker of the House. The War Hawks shouted long and

vaingloriously in the session of 1811 for a larger army and navy for "defense," and for the armed protection of American rights on the sea and elsewhere. Quite frankly they advocated the annexation of Canada and Florida, for were not these territories necessary for our defense and a "natural" part of the United States? The War Hawks were certain that these regions would benefit from being brought into the superior American civilization. Clay thundered that the Kentucky militia alone could conquer Canada.

The western war spirit just prior to 1812 showed vividly that the West was no longer thinking in terms of independence and foreign alliance. It had become belligerently and chauvinistically patriotic, sensitive to national insults and eager to expand United States influence in the world. The intrigues of the previous decade were ancient history. Now the West was growing so rapidly in population and exercising such an ever-increasing influence in the halls of Congress that it could attain its aims through the machinery of the federal government. The westward movement of population meant the eastward movement of separatist plans—first to New England and then later to the South.

HULL'S OPERATIONS

The West, having obtained its war, looked forward eagerly to the immediate conquest of Canada. The first campaign in the Northwest was undertaken by William Hull, then Governor of the comparatively new Michigan Territory, which had been created in 1805. Hull did not feel competent to undertake a military expedition, opposed his own appointment as leader, and finally accepted only under protest. His orders were to reinforce Detroit and then to invade Canada, with aid to be provided by an offensive movement at Niagara by General Henry Dearborn. From the very beginning Hull's plans went wrong. His boat containing supplies and orders for Detroit, which he sent ahead of his main advance, was captured by the British under Brock at Malden. On July 5, 1812, Hull and his army of 1600 men arrived at Detroit. A week later he crossed the Detroit River and entered Canada, issuing a proclamation promising real freedom to the British inhabitants of the region; he delayed, however, in his attack on Malden.

William Hull has been criticized severely for his failure to attack Malden when his effectives outnumbered the British three to one. It must be remembered, however, that Hull realized his own incompetence as leader of the expedition. Entirely lacking in military ability, by nature he was timid and fearful, leaning toward persuasion rather than force. He was opposed by Isaac Brock, a comparatively young man with a background of active military life, and the traditions of a British family of soldiers. In addition, Hull was hampered by the necessity of using part of his men to keep open his communications to the rear.

Hull suffered further by not receiving the cooperation he expected. The Niagara offensive failed, the eastern invasion of Canada did not materialize, and Lake Erie remained in English hands. In the West Mackinac was lost, and the troops from Fort Dearborn (present-day Chicago) were annihilated in their unsuccessful effort to join Hull. All these factors led him to decide that he was too weak to advance farther, and so he recrossed the river and returned to Detroit. In fact, he wanted to evacuate Detroit and retire to the Maumee, but his officers, led by Lewis Cass, effectively opposed any such retreat.

Hull's timidity encouraged Brock to cross the river and lay siege to Detroit. On August 15 he demanded the surrender of the city, and the next day, much to Brock's surprise, Hull acceded to the ultimatum. News of this ignominious capitulation soon reached the East, where it was received with amazement and chagrin. Without even attempting to defend themselves a considerable body of American troops that had been expected to capture Canada had been taken prisoner by a numerically smaller body of British. Hull was immediately court-martialed and sentenced to be shot, although his sentence was later remitted. His punishment not only was unnecessarily harsh but did not advance the American cause. The hostile Indians were lined up solidly with the British, and for the time being the frontier of defense had to be withdrawn to the line of the Wabash and Maumee. General James Winchester was sent with a relief army to recover some of Hull's losses.

HARRISON'S CAMPAIGNS

While these events were occurring in the north, William Henry Harrison was forced to remain in a position not at all to his liking. He had expected that upon the outbreak of the war he would be made a major general and given charge of offensive operations, for had he not shown his military acumen by his successful campaign against the Indians? When no such appointment was made, Harrison deserted his Indiana job and went to Cincinnati to use his political influence to obtain a high army command. He was successful in raising a body of Kentucky militia and in persuading his friend the Governor of Kentucky to commission him major general of the Kentucky militia. The appointment was curious in view of the fact that Harrison was not an inhabitant of the state.

Harrison's first offensive operation was to move on Cincinnati, where he found Brigadier General Winchester with a mixed army of militia and regulars, and with orders to reinforce Hull. Harrison thereupon browbeat Winchester and took control of the whole army. With the news of

Hull's defeat and with definite orders from Washington for Winchester to lead the relief army, Harrison was in an exceedingly embarrassing position, and found it necessary to say, possibly with his fingers crossed, that he would restore Winchester's army immediately. He interpreted this "immediately" to mean after the capture of Terre Haute, which had been taken by the Indians. Just at this time he received some measure of justification for his delay with the news that he had finally been appointed a brigadier general of the United States army, largely through the influence of his friend Henry Clay.

Harrison advanced upon Fort Wayne with his borrowed army, and entered it on September 12, 1812. The victory actually was barren, since the Indians had already departed. Winchester now demanded the return of his army, and even Harrison could no longer find a reason for refusal, since he was the junior officer. To add to his annoyance he received orders from the War Department to support Winchester with his Kentucky militia; such action would make him distinctly a subordinate, with little power of his own. Although Harrison had no choice but to obey, he kept control of his militia and decided to act independently and capture Detroit. Meanwhile the influence of Henry Clay had been at work in Washington, with the result that President Madison came to appreciate the merits of Harrison, and gave him complete charge of the armies of the West. It is not recorded what Winchester thought when these new orders reached him, but he had had a good army training, and obeyed the commands of his superiors.

As soon as Harrison took command he decided to divide the 10,000 men into three armies and advance toward Detroit at once. Both decisions were probably bad; the army should have been kept united and given more training before it undertook offensive operations. As it was, roads were either nonexistent or nearly impassable, supplies were poor and inadequate, the leaders were jealous, and the army showed its disaffection by desertions and threats of mutiny. Harrison thereupon became less sure of the desirability of an advance, and corresponded voluminously with the Secretary of War on the subject. While the troops under the immediate command of Harrison were thus loitering in October and November, the column under Winchester continued to advance—on the assumption that it was being supported by the rest of the army. On the Raisin River, January 22, 1813, Winchester was attacked by a small force under Henry Proctor, who had succeeded Brock in command of the British troops, and was defeated completely, in part because of a lack of expected support by Harrison. If Proctor had continued to advance he probably would have defeated the rest of the army under Harrison, but his force was so small that he grew timorous and hurried back to defend Malden.

Winchester's defeat caused Harrison to abandon his plans temporarily, and to retreat to the Portage River, where he established winter quarters. His explanation for the withdrawal was that the support of the West for his campaign had been lukewarm and ineffective. While the men were in winter quarters, the enlistments of many of the six months' militiamen expired, and most of them went home. Consequently Harrison found it necessary to postpone his advance still longer while he spent the summer of 1813 in raising new troops in Ohio and Kentucky. It was at this time that he learned that his rank had been raised to that of major general. Luckily for him his leaderless force was not attacked during his absence.

Activities on the northern frontier were resumed in the late summer. Both Proctor and Harrison advanced, and fought a number of indecisive skirmishes. Then came the news of Oliver Hazard Perry's victory on Lake Erie on September 10, 1813, and Harrison was encouraged to move more rapidly. In the latter part of September he embarked for Malden. When he arrived there on September 27 he found the town deserted. The greatly outnumbered Proctor had felt that discretion dictated a retreat rather than a battle. Harrison, after some hesitation, decided to follow his retreating enemy. By means of forced marches he overtook Proctor at the Thames River on October 5, 1813, where the numerically superior Americans defeated the British decisively. The Indian allies deserted the British cause, although Tecumseh remained to end his life fittingly on the field of battle.

After the Battle of the Thames, Harrison was again a hero and could enjoy the fruits of his victory. Returning by way of Detroit and the southern shore of Lake Erie, he eventually reached the East, where the "hero of the Thames" was given a proper reception of parades, banquets, speeches, toasts, and eulogies. American victories had been so infrequent that even the least of them was the occasion for enthusiasm that approached adoration of the victor.

Harrison returned to Cincinnati in January 1814, but finding that interest in the war had given way to boredom, resigned his army position. Although technically still going on, the war was at its end as far as the Northwest was concerned. The easy victories that had been expected at the opening of hostilities had failed to materialize. Hoped-for glory had been reduced to one small victory and a number of defeats, resulting in the loss of several posts in the Far Northwest. Since the war had brought no advantages and the conquest of Canada was now recognized as impossible, the West regarded a continuation of the hostilities as pointless.

EFFECTS OF THE WAR

The results of the War of 1812 were mixed in value. Several ignominious defeats had injured patriotic confidence. The expected conquest of Canada had not materialized. Men had been killed, property had been destroyed, and agricultural production had been reduced because of the absence of manpower. On the other hand, the power of the Indians had been broken. Tecumseh had been killed, and the possibility of a general Indian confederation had vanished. No further Indian outbreak was to occur until the Black Hawk War, a minor episode twenty years later. The subjection of the Indians inevitably meant new purchases of land in the succeeding years. Some of these cessions were engineered by Harrison, as was only fitting. In all, he bought some 33,000,000 acres.

The war was also responsible for the first real beginnings of settlement in Michigan, which from 1818 to 1834 included not only its present territory but also the region westward to the Mississippi. Returned soldiers advertised the opportunities in the vicinity of Detroit when they told their friends of their war experiences and observations. People from farther south moved northward in increasing numbers, although it was another decade before large-scale migration came to Michigan.

The development of Michigan was closely associated with the life and work of Lewis Cass. Cass had commanded an Ohio regiment in Hull's army in the early stages of the war. He opposed Hull's strategy and advocated the defense of Detroit, but his efforts were unavailing. In the general capitulation there he was taken prisoner, but was later paroled. His parole was removed in January 1813, at which time he gathered a new army and joined Harrison, whom he followed through the succeeding campaigns. When Harrison occupied Detroit, Cass was placed in command of the fort and the town.

Cass was appointed Governor of Michigan on October 29, 1813, and immediately set to work to rehabilitate his territory, which had seen such rough usage up to that time. For twenty years he was active in developing and advertising Michigan. He traveled widely, both on exploring trips and on missions to deal with the Indians, covering the territory as far west as the Mississippi. He was also instrumental in influencing Henry Schoolcraft to explore the area. In recognition of his abilities and services, Cass was appointed Secretary of War by Andrew Jackson in 1831.

The end of the War of 1812 marked the beginning of a definite stage in the development of the Old Northwest. The early hunters, trappers, and explorers had long been giving way to the advancing agricultural frontiersmen, but now, with the removal of the last Indian barrier, the way was opened for a still more rapid increase of white settlement. Frontier conditions were soon to be replaced by the peaceful development of a more stable society.

READINGS

GENERAL ACCOUNTS. Regional and state histories that cover the War of 1812: Clarence W. Alvord, *The Illinois Country* (1920) ; Frederick C. Bald, *Michigan in Four Centuries* (1954) ; John A. Caruso, *The Great Lakes Frontier* (1961) ; Logan Esarey, *A History of Indiana* (1915), which needs replacement; Louise P. Kellogg, *The British Regime in Wisconsin and the Northwest* (1935), very scholarly; and Milo M. Quaife, *Lake Michigan* (1944).

CAUSES OF THE WAR. The standard account has long been Julius W. Pratt, *The Expansionists of 1812* (1925), which stresses western causation based on land hunger and the Indians. Bradford Perkins, *Prologue to War* (1961) reverts to the older concepts; see also his *The Causes of the War of 1812* (1962). Reginald Horsman, *The Causes of the War of 1812* (1962) stresses trade factors, and minimizes western influences. The attitude of Clay may be followed in Glyndon G. Van Deusen, *The Life of Henry Clay* (1937) and Bernard Mayo, *Henry Clay* (1937).

FIGHTING OF THE WAR. Alec R. Gilpin, *The War of 1812 in the Old Northwest* (1958) is quite antiquarian. Henry P. Beers, *The Western Military Frontier, 1815–1846* (1935) is factual and pro-army. Harrison biographies include Freeman Cleaves, *Old Tippecanoe* (1939) ; Dorothy B. Goebel, *William Henry Harrison* (1926), good but heavily political; and James A. Green, *William Henry Harrison* (1941), too eulogistic. Tecumseh biographies include two very good biographies in Glenn Tucker, *Tecumseh: Vision of Glory* (1956) and John M. Oskison, *Tecumseh and His Times* (1938). Also pertinent are James W. Silver, *Edmund Pendleton Gaines* (1949), quite detailed, and Frank B. Woodford, *Lewis Cass* (1950).

CHAPTER 12

THE SOUTHWEST
AND JACKSON

A rough similarity existed between the Northwest and the Southwest before and during the War of 1812. Both regions were most thickly populated near the Ohio River, and became less densely settled away from the river banks. The Algonkin tribes harassed the northern frontier, while the southern tribes were only slightly less hostile in the South. The frontiersmen coveted English Canada in the North and the Spanish Floridas in the South. But here the similarity ceased. American leadership, action, and accomplishments in the South were entirely different from those in the North.

The history and situation of the Floridas were unlike those of Canada. The portion of the Floridas east of the Perdido River had been Spanish, and the portion west of that river French, until the end of the Seven Years' War (1763), when both areas went to England. Under English rule immigration was encouraged by liberal land grants and new settlements appeared. During the Revolution these settlements provided bases for expeditions into Georgia and havens for Tory refugees. At this time the northern boundary of the Floridas was the parallel of the mouth of the Yazoo River (32° 28').

The end of the American Revolution saw Britain in the role of the vanquished, and the Floridas were ceded to Spain. Spain would have preferred to keep the old English Yazoo line west of the Chattahoochee, but the treaty of peace drew the line along the 31st parallel to the Chattahoochee, down the Chattahoochee to its junction with the Flint, directly to the head of the St. Marys, and down the St. Marys to the coast. This line is the present northern boundary of Florida, but extended to the Mississippi.

A secret agreement with the United States, made at the same time, provided that if England retained West Florida its boundary should be 32° 28′, but this contingency did not arise.

After the Revolution the Spanish holdings in Florida and Louisiana were continual sources of irritation to the United States, for they included the control of the mouth of the Mississippi and other important rivers such as the Tombigbee, the Alabama, and the Apalachicola. For the time being the navigation of the Mississippi overshadowed all other considerations, taking preference both in private plots and in governmental negotiations. The results, as described earlier, were the Pinckney Treaty of 1795 and the subsequent purchase of Louisiana.

EFFORTS TO ACQUIRE THE FLORIDAS

The acquisition of Louisiana soon proved an altogether too meager morsel for the appetites of American expansionists, and agitation for the taking of the Floridas continued. The Americans who had settled on the Gulf Coast and the lower Mississippi preferred the United States to the Spanish government. The outlets of the principal southern rivers began to look more important as the Georgia and Tennessee settlements pushed toward the Southwest. The weak Spanish administration was a perpetual invitation to fugitive slaves as well as hostile Indians and outlaws of all kinds.

American desire for the Floridas went much further than mere dreaming. Pinckney made an effort to buy them in 1797 but failed. This failure, together with increased western irritation, brought frequent rumors of war in 1803–1806 and thus furnished part of the background for the Burr plans. After 1806 the talk of war decreased. Negotiations for the purchase of the Floridas were reopened, but Spain proved adamant. Thereupon Jefferson turned to France, for having bought one property from a country with dubious title he saw no reason why he might not again do business that way. His idea was sound, but in 1806 Napoleon asked more money than Congress was willing to appropriate.

Failure to buy the Floridas led people to consider other methods by which the region might be acquired. Most convenient and satisfactory was the supposition that at least West Florida had been included in the Louisiana Purchase. Truly, no one had thought of this possibility when the purchase was made, but when Napoleon's delightfully vague boundaries were reconsidered it seemed only reasonable to make them cover as much ground as possible. As early as 1803 Robert Livingston came to the conclusion that his earlier ideas of the boundaries of Louisiana were wrong and that the United States had also bought part of West Florida. In the next year Congress agreed with this pleasant theory and provided for the establishment of customhouses as far east as the Mobile River. Naturally Spain protested, and since the United States did not want war at this particular time, the objectionable act was held in abeyance.

ACQUISITION OF WEST FLORIDA

While the United States was making efforts to buy the Floridas, American citizens were filtering into the coveted region, and soon there were rumors that the settlers planned to revolt from Spain and either set up their own government or ask to be annexed to the United States. West Florida seemed particularly attractive because it included Gulf ports as well as land along the Mississippi. Jefferson talked of seizing the territory as far east as the Perdido, and Madison suggested to Governor Claiborne of Mississippi that Claiborne hint to a friend the desirability of a revolution in the Baton Rouge area, with subsequent annexation to the United States.

The rumors of trouble in West Florida were confirmed when a convention of settlers met in 1810. Although these men were thinking of a revolt and then annexation to the United States, and actually had prepared a declaration of independence, they at first declared their allegiance to the Spanish king and petitioned for a redress of their grievances. To no one's surprise the Spanish Governor failed to act; whereupon Philemon Thomas, as commandant of militia, took 104 men, seized Baton Rouge, captured the Spanish military commander, and declared West Florida independent. The "State of Florida" adopted a constitution based on that of the United States, designed a flag with a white star on a blue field, elected a president, and applied to the United States for annexation.

Here was the plum that the United States had so long desired, now ripe for the plucking. President Madison refurbished his claims to the territory and issued a proclamation declaring that the region as far east as the Perdido River was a part of the United States. He received the necessary support from Congress in the act of January 15, 1811. The western army was dispatched to the south and seized all of West Florida except Mobile, which was held by a fairly strong Spanish garrison. Upon the admission of Louisiana to the Union in 1812 it was given the portion of West Florida west of the Pearl River, and the remainder was added to the Mississippi Territory. This acquisition of West Florida was interesting in part because of its immediate effects, but more because it served as a startling parallel to later expansions of the United States.

EAST FLORIDA

After the acquisition of West Florida East Florida became the center of interest. President Madison decided that the pattern of events of the earlier acquisition might well be repeated, and sent to the scene of prospective expansion the elderly (seventy-two), short (five feet, six inches), stocky, red-haired, and aggressive George Mathews, brigadier general of Georgia militia and a former Governor of Georgia. He was instructed that he could accept any territory offered by local authorities or threatened by a foreign power, and he interpreted these instructions as giving him a free hand to take East Florida.

General Mathews established himself on the St. Marys River, where he collected "Florida patriots," largely from Georgia, many of whom had never been in Florida. The invasion of the "homeland" was begun in March 1812, supported by an American naval squadron, that cooperated reluctantly, and a regular army group, that required a change of commanders before it would act. Amelia Island and Fernandina were taken, and siege was laid to St. Augustine. Freedom was declared for East Florida, a constitution was adopted, and a flag was designed showing a blue soldier presenting a fixed bayonet against a white background. John H. McIntosh became Director of the Territory of East Florida. The obvious implication was early annexation to the United States.

Unfortunately for Mathews' plans, the administration then had a change of heart because of pressing war difficulties farther north. Mathews was dismissed on the pretext that he had exceeded his instructions—a repudiation that practically killed the old man, who died August 30, 1812, on his seventy-third birthday. After a brief period in which it seemed that Congress might authorize the military occupation of Florida, and after Andrew Jackson had been sent toward the border, more moderate counsels prevailed. American troops were removed on the promise of the Spanish Governor to grant amnesty to all rebels, and the "revolution" contracted to a few guerrilla groups that looted the countryside. The West Florida technique had failed in East Florida, and other measures had become necessary.

ANDREW JACKSON

In the Southwest the War of 1812 was notable principally because of the activities and rise to power of one man—Andrew Jackson. Jackson was Scotch-Irish by descent. In 1763 his parents had moved west to the Catawba region, where Andrew was born in 1765. His father died before Andrew's birth and his mother died when he was fourteen; hence for most of his life he was forced to depend on his own resources. He spent his youth and early manhood among rough and uneducated people, and it is not remarkable that he swore fluently, drank, chewed, dueled, gave way to violent fits of temper, and never commanded good English. In contrast to these less desirable traits he had the frontier virtues of straightforwardness, trustworthiness, truthfulness, self-sufficiency, and loyalty to his friends.

Andrew Jackson began his mature life with the study of law in

North Carolina, and in the latter 1780s moved to the Tennessee frontier, where he developed a successful legal business and entered local politics. He was a member of the state supreme court, and after 1802 held the rank of major general of militia. When the war with England began he immediately raised an army and offered his services to the government. His offer was accepted, and early in 1813 he received orders to move south and help capture Florida. His best route lay down the Mississippi, so he marched his troops to Natchez, preliminary to following the river to New Orleans. He was willing to promise with easy confidence the capture of Mobile, St. Augustine, Pensacola, or any other place that was desired. While at Natchez he quarreled with Wilkinson over the question of who was superior in rank, and then he quarreled with Thomas H. Benton because Benton thought Wilkinson was right. At a later time Jackson engaged in a tavern brawl with the Bentons (the future Missouri senator and his brother) and received a serious arm wound.

Jackson's orders to move south were part of a general plan that included three armies and was presumably designed to conquer all of the Floridas. The ostensible purpose was to prevent a Spanish invasion, Spain then being controlled by England. Whatever the general plans may have been, they were not put into operation, since the Senate would authorize no more than the occupation of Mobile. General Wilkinson obtained the honor of investing that city on April 13, 1813, thus rounding out the American control of West Florida.

By the time Jackson arrived in Natchez the government had changed its mind about the advisability of a Florida expedition, and ordered him to disband his troops. This order displeased Jackson intensely. Not only did it destroy his hopes of a successful military expedition; the volunteers would have to make their way as best they could over several hundred miles of wilderness, since no provision was made for returning the men to their homes. For a person of Jackson's temperament there was only one thing to do: not to obey orders. Disregarding his instructions, he marched his men home, making himself liable for the necessary expenses. It was a brave and humane act—bad military etiquette but good politics. Eventually he was paid for his expenses.

CREEK WAR

The return of Jackson to Tennessee coincided with a new outbreak by the Indians of the Southwest. These tribes had long resented white aggression, and now were heartened by Hull's defeat in the North. More important at the time, however, were internal conflicts, particularly between those who favored adopting white methods of life and those who preferred traditional Indian customs, and even the peace tour of Tecumseh could not allay the dispute. As part of this intratribal struggle on August 30, 1813, Creek primitives attacked the half-breeds at Fort Mims, which lay at the junction of the Alabama and the Tombigbee. In the ensuing battle the attackers were carried away by their martial enthusiasm, and ended by killing all the people of Fort Mims, white as well as Indian.

Almost before the last of the scalps had been torn from the heads of the slaughtered whites at Fort Mims, plans were made for a punitive expedition into the territory of the hostile Indians. As a matter of fact, such an expedition had been planned before and needed only the finishing touches. Three armies were to take the field—one from Georgia under John Floyd, a second from Louisiana under W. C. C. Claiborne, and a third from Tennessee under Jackson. The three divisions failed to cooperate according to plans, the generals quarreled over precedence, supplies were poor and insufficient, and the troops were disaffected. The Jackson column was by far the most important of the three.

The orders for Jackson to take the field against the Indians arrived while Jackson was confined to his bed as the result of his shooting fray with the Bentons. In spite of his illness he assumed command of the army at once, and conducted the early part of his campaign when he could scarcely sit on his horse. His plan called for a movement down the Coosa and Alabama rivers, and the establishment of permanent forts along the route. As Jackson progressed he found himself opposed by the Indians in continual skirmishing, with here and there a more important engagement that did not always turn out favorably for him.

Jackson's major difficulty was not with the Indians but with his own men. Most of them were new recruits, not anxious to fight the Indians at any time, but particularly reluctant to fighting on empty stomachs. From time to time, as portions of them started to desert, Jackson had to use one part of the army to keep the remainder from going home, and subsequently to use the second group to keep the first in camp. To preserve discipline he punished infractions of all rules severely, almost unknown with frontier militia. On one point, however, the men succeeded in having their own way. In the middle of the campaign the enlistments of most of them expired and they decided to go home. Jackson blustered and raged, but still the men went home. Left with only 1000 men, of whom most were enlisted for terms that would soon be over, he found it necessary to return to civilization to gather more troops.

By March 1814 Jackson again had 5000 troops at Fort Strother in present northern Alabama. Resuming his movement to the south he won decisive victories at Horseshoe Bend (March 27) and at the junction of the Coosa and the Tallapoosa; on the latter battlefield he erected Fort Jackson, where in August he dictated a treaty by which the Creeks ceded 22 million

Jackson in the South

acres of land, permitted military posts and roads, and agreed to keep the peace in the future. In the meantime his militia had been dismissed (April 21, 1814) and had marched home. The southwestern Indians had been crushed.

Jackson was rewarded for his successful Indian campaign with the major-generalship in the regular army left vacant by the resignation of Harrison. He made his headquarters in Mobile to be ready for either a re-currence of Indian trouble or an attack by the British. Having some leisure, he entered into an acrimonious dispute with the Governor of Florida over the return of fugitive Indians; he also built a fort west of Pensacola, which was clearly within Spanish territory. Finally, becoming impatient at the slowness with which the war was being fought, he asked permission of the War Department to take Pensacola, justifying his proposed action by the presence of British troops, whose capture he felt would be a "defense" of Spain. The War Department denied his request; whereupon Jackson cap-tured Pensacola in November 1814. Desk generals could not prevent Jack-son from doing what he considered desirable.

BATTLE OF NEW ORLEANS

By this time it had become fairly certain that the British contemplated a southern invasion, which would begin at New Orleans, and so as soon as Jackson had completed his occupation of Pensacola he hurried west to the hitherto defenseless New Orleans. Arriving on December 2, 1814, he displayed his usual energy in completing the defenses, in collecting supplies, and in recruiting and training soldiers. Unified action was obtained by placing the city under martial law. As Jackson's preparations were nearing completion, the British arrived, making a careful landing below the city. They were led by General Edward M. Pakenham, an able soldier who had seen service under Wellington.

After preliminary skirmishing the final attack on New Orleans was launched on January 8, 1815, and resulted in a complete victory for Jackson, who lost only six men while his opponents lost two thousand. The British advance was halted, Pakenham was killed, and soon the invading troops took to their boats and sailed away. It was a glorious victory for Jackson, who was thereupon toasted throughout the United States as the "hero of New Orleans." A picture of him riding a hypothetical white charger came to be a commonplace in the barrooms of the country. The glory of the feat was in nowise dimmed by the fact that it occurred two weeks after the signing of the Treaty of Ghent. Carping critics have insisted that Jackson's troops were superior in number and equipment and had their choice of a position to defend, while Pakenham's men were confused by the terrain. Even admitting these conditions, the credit that Jackson received for his effective handling of the defense of New Orleans was deserved.

After the victory of New Orleans Jackson continued to rule despotically. Military discipline was enforced vigorously and the very unusual punishment of death was given for desertion. New Orleans remained under martial law, and Jackson's word was supreme. Such a situation was endurable in time of imminent danger, but now that peace had returned, the people of New Orleans became restive. Collisions between civil and military authority were increasingly frequent and acrimonious. Jackson involved himself in disputes with many people, including a federal judge, D. A. Hall, Governor Claiborne, and the state legislature of Louisiana. The situation did not improve until the spring of 1815, when the army was restored to a peacetime basis. At this time Jacob Brown was placed in command north of the Ohio, Jackson in the Southwest, and Edmund Gaines on the Florida border. Jackson felt himself sufficiently relieved of military duties to travel in the East, where he was acclaimed as the outstanding hero of the late war, and where his exploits would help him become President.

FLORIDA TROUBLES

While Jackson was receiving a deserved ovation from his admiring countrymen, the Florida situation remained as troublesome as ever. Although active operations in that region had been curtailed for the duration of the war, the United States had by no means lost its interest in annexation. Now new sources of irritation made the acquisition of Florida still more desirable. The Indians who had been defeated farther north found an asylum in the Florida swamps, from which they emerged to harass the border settlements. Escaped Negro slaves also went to Florida, where they could not be recaptured. Both groups remained actively hostile, partly because of the activities of English traders who operated south of the borders of the United States.

The center of the Florida trouble was the so-called Negro Fort on the Apalachicola River. Here the escaped Negroes rallied and showed their disdain of their pursuers by desultory firing at the Americans on the other side of the river. This situation was no more pleasing to the Spanish Governor of Florida than it was to the Americans, so he gave permission for the capture and destruction of the fort. After a brief attack it was demolished by hot shot on July 27, 1816.

Negotiations for the purchase of Florida were resumed by President Monroe after the War of 1812. In the latter part of 1817 he felt so doubtful of the possibilities of peaceful purchase that he sent troops to the border to invade the territory if the occasion demanded. Gaines was ordered early in December to capture Amelia Island, which was a well-known rendezvous of smugglers, and Jackson was put in charge of border operations. When Gaines arrived at Amelia Island he found a body of American filibusters in control, and consequently his occupation was bloodless.

When Jackson took control of the border late in 1817 he had a not unreasonable feeling that the administration might be pleased if he conquered the desired territory. Before acting on his own authority he took the precaution of writing to Monroe, asking for at least tacit permission. Under normal conditions he would have written to the Secretary of War, but in this case he disliked the Secretary, even to the extent of forbidding his subordinates to obey any orders coming directly from the Department of War. This action was called treason by General Winfield Scott, whom Jackson immediately challenged to a duel, which Scott refused on religious and patriotic grounds. Jackson's letter to Monroe was never read by the President, who was ill at the time. The President's friend John Rhea, however, wrote to Jackson intimating that the President approved of the general's plans—or at least this was the tenor of the letter according to

Jackson's later statements. Unfortunately, Jackson had burned the original document before he quoted it to others.

With these hypothetical instructions Jackson raised troops in Tennessee and marched to a position near the site of the old Negro Fort, arriving in March 1818. Then, pursuing some fleeing Negroes, he crossed the border into Florida. Later he supported his action on the grounds that hostile Indians were given encouragement from Florida, and that the British in the region were a continual source of trouble to the United States. In this advance into Florida he pushed the Indians ahead of him, killing a few of them as well as executing two Britons who happened to be in his path. The latter act caused the United States some diplomatic trouble. Eventually Jackson captured St. Marks, and at the same time ordered Gaines to take St. Augustine. On his way home he made a final gesture by recapturing Pensacola, which had been returned to Spain.

Jackson's operations in Florida threw the government at Washington into turmoil. Spain was angry and asked that Jackson be punished and the captured territory returned. The negotiations for the purchase of Florida, which had been progressing fairly well, came to an end. Long Cabinet meetings debated whether or not Jackson should be upheld; Adams backed the general while Calhoun was his chief opponent. Congress was restive, and Henry Clay brought in a motion censuring Jackson for his precipitous action. Apparently Jackson himself was amazed and resentful at all this hubbub. In respect to the Cabinet he was completely in error, for he credited Calhoun with his defense and for many years hated Adams because of his supposed opposition. Jackson also missed the political significance of the move by Clay, and considered it a personal affront.

Eventually the Cabinet adopted a compromise position. Pensacola and St. Marks were returned to Spain as requested, but Adams intimated plainly that the presence of Florida as a constant source of irritation was bound to produce just such invasions unless Spain sold the territory to the United States. The soundness of this attitude was demonstrated later in Spain's sale of Florida, but at the time it served only to infuriate the irascible Jackson, who was certain in his own mind that he had obeyed orders. The compromise also displeased the people of the United States, who admired the spectacular exploits of the impetuous general. Monroe attempted to placate Jackson by a friendly letter, and the general public by an open communication to the *National Intelligencer*.

PURCHASE OF FLORIDA

The results of Adams' diplomacy came in the purchase of Florida in 1819, the Adams-Onís Treaty being ratified two years later. In addition to transferring title to Florida, the treaty also finally settled definitely the northern limits of Spanish claims in the Southwest. Starting at the mouth of the Sabine, the boundary followed that river to its intersection with the 32° north latitude, then due north to the Red River, up the Red to 100° west longitude, north to the Arkansas River, along the Arkansas to its source, north to the 42° of latitude, and thence along that parallel to the Pacific. In view of later developments it is interesting that not even Jackson desired to acquire Texas at this time.

After the acquisition of Florida, Jackson was finally and completely vindicated by being appointed Governor of the new territory. As he had in previous similar situations, he at once proceeded to involve himself in quarrels with many of the people with whom he had dealings; this time his chief opponent was the former Spanish Governor. Jackson's temper was further ruffled by the scarcity of offices that he could bestow on his relatives and friends. By October he had come to the conclusion that his health was not adequate for the governorship of Florida, and therefore resigned. Two years later he was offered a mission to Mexico, but refused because he thought the mission was not needed.

The series of events in the Southwest that terminated with the acquisition of the Floridas had many results: the United States acquired a considerable body of new territory, rounding out its possessions east of the Mississippi, and many people thought that the end of expansion had been reached; the Indians had been defeated and were to remain harmless for another generation; a new figure from the West, Andrew Jackson, had arisen to prominence and assumed an important role on the national stage, while two of his principal rivals, Henry Clay and William Henry Harrison, also Westerners, were brought into prominence by the war. Possibly most significant was the method used for expansion—a method that was to appear again and again with but minor variations.

READINGS

GENERAL ACCOUNTS. Best for the entire subject is Thomas P. Abernethy, *The South in the New Nation* (1961); a shorter but also a good account is E. Merton Coulter, *A Short History of Georgia* (1933). The Florida part of the story is covered in Kathryn T. Abbey, *Florida* (1941); Caroline M. Brevard, *A History of Florida* (2 vols., 1924–1925). Julius W. Pratt, *The Expansionists of 1812* (1925) describes the revolts in both East and West Florida; Rembert W. Patrick, *Florida Fiasco* (1954) is excellent on Mathews; Isaac J. Cox, *The West Florida Controversy, 1798–1813* (1918) is complete but not exciting.

INDIANS AND JACKSON. The best complete story of the Indian troubles is Robert S. Cotterill, *The Southern Indians* (1954); Angie Debo, *The Road to Disappearance* (1941) is excellent on the Creeks; Marion L.

Starkey, *The Cherokee Nation* (1946) is good on the Cherokee. Biographies of Jackson are almost endless, but among the useful ones in connection with the Indians are Marquis James, *Andrew Jackson, the Border Captain* (1933) and David Karsner, *Andrew Jackson* (1929).

DIPLOMACY. The best general account is Philip C. Brooks, *Diplomacy and the Borderlands* (1939); also useful, although detailed, are two older books, French E. Chadwick, *The Relations of the United States and Spain* (1909) and Hubert B. Fuller, *The Purchase of Florida* (1906). The Cox book, mentioned earlier, also applies in this connection.

CHAPTER 13

THE GREAT MIGRATION

The end of the War of 1812 cleared the way for a vastly increased influx of settlers from the East. As is true of all population movements, people were both propelled and attracted: they had to find their home conditions in the East less desirable than their prospects in the West. The causes of the migration and the location of the migrants are basic elements of the western story.

PROSPERITY AND MIGRATION

The period of the Napoleonic Wars was generally one of depression in America, particularly as Britain tightened her control over ocean shipping and as the United States replied with self-imposed limitations. New England shipping was badly damaged, while the markets for western and southern products declined frighteningly. The Northeast began to turn to manufacturing, but the shift was too small to be of immediate significance; the South and the West could only suffer and hope. Business was in the doldrums and life was hard.

Depression in the East could theoretically have meant an increase in the movement to the West by those brave souls who were willing to undertake a risk with the hope of even slightly increased economic opportunity, but actually no such expanded movement occurred. The costs of moving and of settling could not be dismissed lightly, and where was a man to obtain the necessary capital in hard times? The truth was that people found more difficulty in moving during hard times, and consequently migration slowed, although it never came to a complete halt.

The other side of the story was that the attractive pull of the West also declined in bad times when western agricultural prices fell, work was scarce, and wages were low. Particularly serious handicaps were faced by the migrant who planned to leave the East with a minimum of funds and to earn a stake in the West. Westerners wrote to their eastern friends advising them to defer moving until times were better. Any potential migrant found the West much less attractive in bad times than in good.

Several types of evidence support the generalization that the heaviest westward movements occurred during periods of prosperity. Census figures would seem to be a logical place to find such evidence, but they are disappointing because a decennial count has no useful correlation with the business cycle. Here and there a state has helpful figures, particularly when a western territory counted its inhabitants several times in the hope of obtaining statehood. The dates of the admissions of the various states are in themselves useful when ranged alongside the business cycle, since normally admission occurred at the time of the first big influx of people. Accounts of Westerners give clues to the time in which migration was heaviest, as do the toll receipts of roads and canals used heavily in travel to the West. Land sales can be tabulated, although with the reservations that all sales did not mean settlement and all settlement did not mean sales. But no matter the method used, the conclusion emerges that the great flow of migration came in prosperous times.

Although the depressed decade of 1805–1815 discouraged migration, it also contained seeds that germinated a little later into a large-scale growth of population. Various striking events gave the West effective advertising. The purchase of Louisiana, the Lewis and Clark and other explorations, the Burr episode, the boundary disputes, the Florida disturbances, the Indian wars, and the War of 1812 all helped to arouse interest in the West and its possibilities. Then, too, the West was becoming more attractive and accessible. The Indian menace was practically eliminated with the operations of Harrison and Jackson. The National Road was under construction and the first steamboats were appearing on western waters. More land was available with the new land purchases and surveys. Land was becoming cheaper because of the land bonuses given to the soldiers of the War of 1812. These grants were made in the form of scrip, which most soldiers sold instead of exchanging for land. The throwing of considerable amounts of land warrants on the market thus made available large quantities of good land at comparatively low prices.

The factors at work in the period prior to the close of the War of 1812 produced an increased movement to the West that came to a peak in the years 1818–1819 and ended with the panic of 1819. So great was the movement of population that it came to be known as the Great Migration. Over 1 million acres of land were sold in 1814, a total greater than the sales in any one previous year; the volume continued to increase until sales of approximately 3.5 million acres were recorded for each of the years 1818 and 1819. After 1819 the figures decreased.

ACQUIRING LAND

The land settled during the Great Migration was theoretically occupied under the provisions of the land act of 1800, which provided for local land offices, the auction system, and then private sale at two dollars an acre, with possible credit payments for the greater part of the purchase price. Surveys of the new land were made as rapidly as possible, and local land offices were opened as they were needed; by 1820 there were thirty-four western land offices, of which fourteen were in Ohio. The auction system did not prove profitable, since the average selling price remained very near the legal minimum.

In actual practice the settlers frequently paid little attention to government surveys and sales. All surveys were necessarily made slowly and systematically, and included all the land, no matter whether it was good or bad. Settlement, on the other hand, skipped the apparently poorer sections and took only the best land along the rivers. The result was that some of the settlement was always ahead of the surveys, and a large percentage of the new inhabitants took up unsurveyed land to which they had no legal right and trusted to luck that they would be able to buy it at a later time. Their number was increased continually by those who lacked funds and sought to elude the governmental land system.

The subdivision of the government that handled land sales prior to the War of 1812 was a bureau in the Department of the Treasury, but a more effective control of the public domain was provided by a law of April 25, 1812, creating a General Land Office. The new bureau remained, however, a part of the Treasury Department until it was transferred to the Department of the Interior when that department was organized in 1849.

LAND ACT OF 1820

The Great Migration brought to light glaring faults in the public land system that might have gone unnoticed if it had not been for the thousands of new citizens desiring homes and farms. Outstanding were the difficulties produced by the credit feature of the land act of 1800. Western farmers were always too optimistic, and wanted to buy all the land on which they could make the down payment. Frequently their optimism was unjustified, and they could not meet succeeding installments. Theoretically they should then have been dispossessed and their first payments forfeited. Actually it was difficult to evict thousands of farmers when they became obstinate and bitter; moreover, such a procedure was politically dangerous for the party in power. Not only the delinquent farmers but all of the West was opposed to dispossession and forfeiture, for each Westerner realized that at some time he might have the same sort of trouble. And, what would happen to the dispossessed families?

The credit situation became worse, with the number of defaulters increasing, when hard times swept the country during the Napoleonic Wars, the Indian troubles in the West, and the War of 1812. Not only was depression general but the use of a farmer militia meant that many farmers were in the army rather than cultivating their land. To add to these difficulties, the existence of a disorganized currency in the West made it hard to tell the well to do from the paupers, for wealth depended less on the amount of money than upon the institutions that had issued it.

The immediate result of western difficulties was a flood of petitions asking for congressional assistance. Congress responded by passing a long series of relief bills that aided particular persons or localities by postponing or remitting payments, or by allotting reduced amounts of land to correspond with the amount of money already paid. In spite of such relief, $21 million was still overdue and unpaid in 1820, and with the panic of 1319 the future looked dark.

The failure of Congress to modify the land act of 1800 earlier than it did was due in part to a very real division of opinion as to what should be done. The East continued to feel that western land was a trust fund for the nation, and should be made to produce the largest possible amount of revenue. Furthermore, many Easterners favored a high price for the land to discourage western migration so that the new manufacturing establishments of the East would not suffer from a lack of labor. The West, on the other hand, felt that the price should be decreased so that the people who worked the land and gave it value should be benefited. A further argument stressed that a reduced price would encourage settlement and thus add to the wealth and strength of the United States.

Out of this sea of conflicting interests and arguments eventually emerged the land act of 1820. The credit system was abolished by general agreement. The smallest unit to be sold was to be eighty acres. The auction system was to be retained, and was to be followed, as before, with private entry at the minimum price, but now the price was reduced to the compromise figure of $1.25 an acre. Defaulters under former legislation were to be aided by being given outright an amount of land corresponding to the money they had already paid.

The land act of 1820 was a real watershed in the history of the public domain because it changed the emphasis from the production of revenue for the federal government to getting land into the hands of actual settlers. The credit idea was never revived. The smaller minimum unit was found desirable and retained. On the other hand, the auction system continued to prove less and less satisfactory. The settler wanted the right to settle on the land before it was surveyed and then to be assured that a speculator could not bid it away from him at an auction. The most pressing demand of the West, however, continued to be low-priced land. These western desires came to be mixed with various sectional disagreements and conflicts in the generation after the passage of the land act of 1820, and were a continual source of trouble for Congress.

REGIONS OF SETTLEMENT

The greatest flow of settlers during the Great Migration followed the central route through either Pittsburgh or Wheeling and then down the Ohio River. The state of Ohio received more population than any other region, so that by 1820 its nearly 600,000 made it the most populous state west of the mountains. Farther to the west new families occupied southern Indiana and Illinois, followed the Mississippi both north and south, and pushed up the Wabash and the Missouri. To the north a string of settlements blossomed along the entire southern short of Lake Erie and as far west as Detroit. Detroit at the end of the War of 1812 numbered fewer than 1000 people; in 1820 the entire Michigan Territory (which included the present Wisconsin) contained less than 9000 persons. Migrants clung closely to navigable waters and wooded land, and hence did not touch central and northern Illinois and Indiana or the great bulk of the present Michigan and Wisconsin.

To the south additional migration flowed into Kentucky and Tennessee, so that by 1820 the former was almost as large as Ohio, while the latter had over 400,000 residents. In general the land extending north and south through the central section of the two states attracted most people. The real beginning of Memphis came in 1819, but any important growth waited until later. Still farther south the largest concentration of population was in Louisiana, where 150,000 people made it the fourth largest of the western states. Mississippi was settled almost exclusively in the southern part. Alabama had a sprinkling of farms covering most of the western half of the state, but with the greatest concentration in the region of the great bend of the Alabama River. West of the Mississippi, and in addition to the Louisiana and Missouri settlements, were a few residents in Arkansas Territory, particularly along the Mississippi and Arkansas rivers.

Even though the greatest part of the West of 1820 was but sparsely settled, the new states and territories west of the mountains had a total of some 2,225,000 people, which was almost a quarter of the total population of the United States. Here lies the reason for the ever-increasing power of the West in the federal government. In the House its votes might be deci-

Population Density, 1810

45 AND OVER INHABITANTS PER SQUARE MILE

6-44 INHABITANTS PER SQUARE MILE

2-5 INHABITANTS PER SQUARE MILE

LESS THAN 2 INHABITANTS PER SQUARE MILE

Population Density, 1820

45 AND OVER INHABITANTS PER SQUARE MILE

6-44 INHABITANTS PER SQUARE MILE

2-5 INHABITANTS PER SQUARE MILE

LESS THAN 2 INHABITANTS PER SQUARE MILE

sive, but in the Senate its proportional strength was even greater. Consequently the West had better than an even chance of obtaining any legislation that it really desired wholeheartedly. The great limitation was that the West was not always itself united. Clay and Jackson were both Westerners, but not necessarily in accord for that reason. The more highly developed states such as Ohio and Kentucky by no means always agreed with the smaller and younger communities.

THE NEWER SOUTHWEST
The most novel and distinctive characteristic of the Great Migration was the changing character of the people going to the Southwest, which was making this region far different from the Northwest. The change was due largely to two important developments. The first was the invention of the cotton gin by Eli Whitney in 1793 and its subsequent rapid development after 1800, which made practicable the large cotton plantation operated by slave labor. The second was the opening of large quantities of virgin soil in the Southwest by Jackson's successful operations against the Creeks. As a result of these two factors there was a westward push by the cotton planters with their slaves. The movement first became noticeable about 1810, and after that time grew very rapidly.

The new southern migration did not change radically the old pioneering process but, rather, brought it to a different conclusion. The first stage of development, both North and South, remained approximately equivalent: the trapper and hunter was followed by the agricultural pioneer who cleared the land and planted the first crop of grain. Sometimes the frontiersman had one or two slaves, but not ordinarily. After the land had been cleared and planted, similarities of its development in North and South ceased. In the North, diversified small farms brought a sprinkling of little towns and general prosperity. In the South, the first settler either bought more slaves and started the large-scale cultivation of cotton or else sold his holdings to a large eastern planter and moved farther west. No matter which procedure was followed, the result was large plantations with slave labor, a one-crop system, and no efforts to prevent soil exhaustion. Eventually the soil was depleted and the wise planter moved again, leaving behind him exhausted and deserted land. If he were prudent he left the plantation before the exhaustion of the soil made his farming unprofitable.

By the end of the War of 1812 the southern roads to the west were so crowded with planters and gangs of Negroes that there was a scarcity of provisions. The Negroes, sometimes shackled, traveled on foot while the planters rode. Most groups went overland, although a few moved to the lower Mississippi Valley either by ocean or by way of the Ohio and Mississippi rivers. The roads, as elsewhere, were very bad, often little more than bridle paths. The most important one in the Far South was the Federal Road, authorized by Congress in 1806, which ran from Athens, Georgia, by way of the Tombigbee settlement to New Orleans; in the east it connected Athens with Greenville, Charlotte, Salisbury, Fredericksburg, Washington, and Baltimore. A few slaves appeared in Kentucky and Missouri, and more went to Tennessee, but the main migration was to the lower South.

The majority of the planters who moved west came from the Piedmont region of the East rather than from the coastal plain, and carried to their new homes the customs with which they had been familiar. They soon constructed large, ramshackle "mansions" in which they dispensed typical southern hospitality. They raised almost exclusively the two important crops of cotton and corn, which meant that the plantation frequently depended on the outside world for even its necessary food and clothing. By far the most important single crop was cotton, which was high in price and hence particularly profitable in the period immediately after the War of 1812. The first plowing came in February, and the cotton was planted in March. Later the plants required thinning and frequent cultivation. Picking started late in August and went on into the winter. After picking, the cotton was ginned, although a certain number of impurities had to be removed by hand; it was then pressed into 350-pound bales. Because there was no fertilization of the soil and no rotation of crops, the land was soon exhausted.

The labor of the southern plantation was performed by Negro slaves, who were worked in large gangs under continuous supervision. Each slave was given clothing twice a year, in the spring and the fall. Exclusive of food, his total annual cost to his master was about twenty to twenty-five dollars. With full-time work he was supposed to be able to cultivate from five to six acres of cotton or corn, with the result that for each slave there was about a thousand pounds of ginned cotton. On some plantations the individual slave was given a limited area of land and allowed to cultivate it for himself. The planter seldom rolled in wealth; normally his profits were put back into the business to purchase new land and more slaves, so that he seldom had any reserve capital and was frequently in debt. When a dwindling yield threatened disaster in any one area, he might move his whole laboring force and his entire equipment farther west.

The most obvious characteristics of the southern system of agriculture were the increasing importance of cotton and the rapid exhaustion of the soil. In the decade 1811–1821 only one third, by value, of the crops raised west of Georgia came from cotton, but by 1831 the proportion had grown to one half and by 1834 to two thirds ($75 million). As for soil depletion, older communities, such as Virginia, had shown evidences of it as early as colonial times, and districts farther west soon exhibited the same tendency; hence a decrease of population and wealth in the older communities was by no means unusual.

Another characteristic of the southern system was a continued and increasing demand for slaves. The institution of slavery, far from dying as southern colonial leaders had expected, grew progressively stronger. The demand for additional western labor was filled in part by the increase of illegal slave trading, but more importantly by the purchase of Negroes from the worn-out farms of the East. Eastern slaveowners were confronted with exhausted lands and an oversupply of Negroes to be fed and clothed, whereas the West was willing to pay high prices for these surplus eastern slaves. The result was the development of a recognized and lucrative business of buying Negroes in the East, shipping them to the West, and selling them to western plantation owners. The traffic was so profitable that in some cases slaveowners were accused of breeding their slaves like cattle to profit by their sale.

To the Negro, being sold to the West was the acme of misfortune, and many humane owners refused to sell their slaves for the western trade. The West meant hard work, poor food, inadequate clothes, and an excessive amount of sickness. The swampy cotton plantations of Mississippi and the sugar plantations of Louisiana, where slaves died by the hundreds, were especially dangerous. The attitude of the Negro toward being moved was expressed by the popular old song "Darling Nellie Gray":

> One night I went to see her, but "She's gone!" the neighbors say,
> The white man bound her with his chain;
> They have taken her to Georgia for to wear her life away,
> As she toils in the cotton and the cane.

Free Negroes were not numerous in the West except at New Orleans, where they included many artisans and small shop owners. Generally they were quiet and peaceful, although a slave revolt in 1811 had made the whites fearful. Curiously enough, Negroes in New Orleans approved of slavery and themselves had slaves. City life produced some unusual situations for the Negro. Many mulatto girls became the mistresses of white men, and likely looking female slaves had a good market among the "sporting class." One result was a shortage of Negro women to marry Negro men.

METHOD OF SETTLEMENT

The process of hewing homes from the wilderness during the Great Migration was very similar to that of twenty years earlier. There was the same long and tedious trip to the West, the same effort to pick out good land near friends from home, the same clearing of a plot of land, the same community house building, and the same girdling of trees and planting. Amusements were still dances, house-raisings, singing schools, weddings, camp meetings, and husking bees. Life had changed but little since the first pioneers had followed Daniel Boone into the wilderness.

The crops of the newly settled lands in the Ohio Valley were, as before, chiefly corn, wheat, rye, oats, tobacco, hemp, and flax. Prices were comparatively high, but it was difficult to get the goods to market. Labor was scarce and expensive, and difficult tasks were done by community effort. The homemade clothing, as in an earlier period, was made of linsey-woolsey from the wool and flax grown on the farm. The materials from which clothes were made continued to be raised, carded, spun, woven, and sewed at home. Even shoes were still made at home by the frontier farmer, although the tanning of leather was coming more and more to be a commercial process. Both clothing and shoes were saved as much as possible, particularly in the summer.

Towns and centralized industry continued to develop slowly. Pittsburgh, with its manufacture of iron, glass, and rope, and its building of boats, still grew and prospered. Farther west, Cincinnati was attaining commercial importance, particularly with the development of pork packing; the farmers were learning that it was more profitable to drive their hogs to a central slaughtering and packing plant than to do the work themselves. St. Louis was coming into prominence as a center of the fur business and as a distributing point for the Far West. New Orleans, with the increase of the steamboat traffic, continued to maintain her commercial dominance. Other smaller but bustling centers contained water-driven lumber mills, grist mills, distilleries, and tanneries.

The growing towns were divorced to some extent from the rural countryside, even though their main function was as commercial centers. City dwellers usually came from the East rather than from the surrounding countryside. In fact they tended to look down on the country people, who in turn were becoming suspicious of city folk. City residents frequently specialized in their work, whereas the farmer continued to be a jack-of-all-trades. Cultural life in the cities became incomprehensible to many of the poorly educated of the country, and the prosperous lawyer or businessman increasingly sent his son to an eastern college and his daughter to an eastern finishing school. Class divisions, both within the cities, and between city and country, were clearly sharpening.

HEALTH

One of the most unsatisfactory conditions of western life was its lack of adequate medical facilities. During the first quarter of the nineteenth century there were few properly trained doctors west of the mountains. Competent physicians preferred to remain in the East rather than to undertake the poorly paid and hardworking life that was inevitable farther west. Western medical practice meant riding many miles over atrocious roads, day and night, in good weather and in bad, to serve a widely scattered and poor population. Good hospitals did not exist, and medical schools and publications were rare.

The West was not an exceedingly healthful region in spite of the outdoor life and hard work of its inhabitants. Accidents were common as long as hunting, felling trees, and fighting Indians were regular pursuits. Fever and ague were omnipresent in the river lowlands. Scarlet fever was frequent and at times epidemic. Yellow fever was prevalent in the New Orleans region during the summers, killing its hundreds and thousands. A typhoid epidemic caused numerous fatalities all over the West in 1816–1817. Cholera had periodic epidemics, the worst being in 1832 at the time of the Black Hawk War. In addition to these serious diseases the Westerner suffered from all the other common human ailments.

The earliest medical treatment on the frontier was given by any individual who possessed even the simplest knowledge of drugs and surgery. Every educated man was supposed to be competent to treat disease, and each family had its own supply of simple herbs such as calomel, jalap, and cinchona bark (containing quinine). The seventh son of a seventh son was presumed to have unusual healing powers; early morning dew was supposed to be excellent for the complexion. As for surgery, it was as gruesome as torture by the Indians. For example, the details of an amputation without anesthetics (ether and choloroform were not used until the 1840s) and performed with a butcher knife, a meat saw, and a hot iron are best left to oblivion.

The ministrations of the early pioneer doctor were little better than those of kind friends, for such a practitioner ordinarily had little formal education, and had learned his trade from his predecessors and by experience. His equipment, which he carried in his saddlebags, consisted of a few simple drugs, roots, herbs, calomel, a lancet, cupping glasses, and possibly a few other crude surgical instruments and a supply of leeches. He compounded all his own medicine, and a particularly bitter dose was concealed in a piece of apple or dough. The western physician had two principal cures for all diseases—calomel or jalap, and bleeding. Calomel (sometimes jalap) was prescribed for every known disease, and often given in such large doses that it caused intense salivation and loosening of the teeth. Bloodletting was almost equally universal, being ordinarily accomplished either by cupping or by the use of leeches. The leeches were put in a tumbler and the open end of the tumbler was then placed over the skin. Cupping consisted of opening a vein and covering the opening with a glass from which the air had been expelled by the burning of alcohol. Such bloodletting was done in reckless amounts, and was considered especially efficacious for any illness that involved a fever.

Early medical methods produced results that were marvelous in view of the size of the group that remained alive. Fresh air was taboo; in a case of fever or inflammation the patient was placed between feather beds and the doors and windows of the sickroom were tightly closed. Cautery was performed with a white-hot iron. Wounds were encouraged to discharge pus by being kept irritated with threads or a pea. Hemorrhages were treated by bloodletting.

Western doctors were bad and western health was poor, but these facts lose some of their force in view of generally poor American health and generally badly trained American doctors. Western epidemics were national and world epidemics, while peculiar western remedies were also general American remedies. Furthermore, the West had some of the nation's more progressive doctors. Dr. William Goforth introduced vaccination to the West at the early date of 1801. Dr. Sappington of Missouri popularized the use of quinine, particularly for malaria, in the 1830s with "Dr. John Sappington's Anti-Fever Pills." Dr. Crawford Long, a small-town Georgia doctor, probably made the first medical use of ether as an anesthetic in 1842 for the removal of a neck tumor.

Curiously enough, several notable medical operations were first performed in the West. Dr. Francis Prevost of Louisiana claimed the use of the rare Caesarean section in four cases prior to 1832, with three of them successful. The best-authenticated of the early Caesarean operations was performed by Dr. John L. Richmond in 1827 in rural Ohio. Dr. Richmond, who was also a Baptist minister, was called to the rude shack of a Negro woman late one night, and there he performed the operation by the light of candles and with only his pocket case of instruments; the child died, but the woman returned to work in twenty-four days. Most amazing of all was the ovariotomy performed by Dr. Ephraim McDowell of Danville, Kentucky, in 1809. Without special training or equipment, and of course without anesthetics, Dr. McDowell was the first man in the world to remove an ovarian tumor successfully; his operation marked the real beginning of abdominal surgery.

After about 1820 medical science west of the mountains gradually improved. Here and there promising young men attended the medical schools in the East, while more and better doctors moved west as the population grew large enough to support them. Medical schools were established in the West. The earliest of these schools was the medical department of Transylvania, which attained an excellent reputation by the 1830s. Other schools such as the Ohio Medical College (1819) and the Worthington Medical College (1832) helped raise the level of medical practice. Magazines such as the *Ohio Medical Repository* (1826), which later became the *Western Journal of the Medical and Physical Sciences* under the editorship of Daniel Drake, provided mediums for disseminating the latest scientific advances.

NEW STATES AND TERRITORIES

Advancing settlement brought agitation for statehood, since most Westerners desired greater self-government than existed under territorial organization. Each region followed the steps outlined in the Northwest Ordinance—congressional control, limited self-government, and finally statehood. In each case a congressional enabling act and a constitutional convention preceded admission to the Union. The state constitutions showed the democratic tendencies of the times, with limitations on executive power, removal of religious and property qualifications for voting, and the election of judges by the legislature. These trends were not original with the West, but had their fullest expression in that region.

North of the Ohio the western fruits of the Great Migration in terms of new states were Indiana and Illinois. Indiana Territory had come into existence in 1800, and with the arrival of settlers its size was reduced by the creation of the Michigan (1805) and Illinois (1809) territories. The second stage of territorial government came in 1805, and ten years later an Indiana census showed the 60,000 people necessary for statehood. The Indiana desire for statehood was satisfied by Congress in 1816. A strict adherence to the boundaries stated in the Northwest Ordinance would have meant that Indiana touched Lake Michigan at only a single point, but the extension of the northern boundary for ten miles at the expense of Michigan produced the lake frontage that now includes the city of Gary. Indianapolis, founded in 1819, became the state capital in 1825 for no better reason that that it was approximately the geographical center of the state.

The first Governor of Illinois Territory was Ninian Edwards, who remained in office until statehood. The second stage of territorial government was achieved in 1812, and a growing movement for statehood reached its goal in 1818, even though the population was then considerably less than the required 60,000. As had been done for Indiana, the new state was given a lake frontage—this time by extending the northern boundary some sixty miles; in consequence many Wisconsinites have long resented the fact that Chicago is in Illinois rather than in Wisconsin. North of Indiana and Illinois the country to the international boundary was reallotted several

United States, 1820

times, depending largely on southern conditions. From 1818, when Illinois was admitted, until Wisconsin became a territory, present Michigan and Wisconsin were combined as Michigan Territory.

South of the Ohio River the first new state of the nineteenth century was Louisiana, which had been populated largely before the Americans took control and hence should not be considered a result of the Great Migration. Its admission in 1812 was opposed bitterly by New England Federalists, who foresaw dire results if the entire Louisiana Purchase, with its semiwild people, were to be carved into states and admitted to the Union. The eastern boundary of the new state was extended to the Pearl River, thus including a part of West Florida, which had but recently been annexed by the United States.

Mississippi Territory had come into existence in 1798 to provide for the region between the 31st parallel and the mouth of the Yazoo, which had been evacuated reluctantly by Spain. The addition of the Georgia land cession of 1802 expanded the new territory to the present size of Mississippi and Alabama, except for the Gulf Coast, which was not added until 1812. After Jackson crushed the Indians, settlement increased, particularly in the rich black land of the Mississippi, the Gulf Coast, and the valleys of the Alabama and Tombigbee rivers. Expanding population brought a division of the territory in 1817, the year in which Mississippi became a state. Two years later Alabama followed into the Union; by 1820 the population of Alabama was about 128,000, which was over half again as large as that of Mississippi.

The last two states to be produced by the Great Migration were Maine and Missouri, admitted respectively in 1820 and 1821. Maine had been a part of Massachusetts, but in 1820 was separated from it by mutual agreement. Missouri, which had a more checkered career, had been something of an administrative problem, since for many years the St. Louis settlement had been the only important area of population west of the Mississippi. The entire Louisiana Purchase, exclusive of the prospective state of Louisiana, had been successively Louisiana District (1804) attached to Indiana Territory, Louisiana Territory (1805), and Missouri Territory (1812). In 1819, two years before Missouri became a state, Arkansas Territory was created to include not only present Arkansas but also the land west to the existing international boundary.

The application of Missouri for statehood called attention to the fact that with the admission of Alabama in 1819 the slave and free states each numbered eleven. This equality of sectional interests seemed important to the politicians of the time, for it ensured the South half of the votes of the Senate in a day when its influence in the House was declining. Consequently Congress, after a heated debate, accepted (1820) the admission of

Missouri and Maine as compensating states, but with the proviso that no later state formed from the Louisiana Purchase and north of the principal southern boundary of Missouri (36° 30′) should have slavery. This "Missouri Compromise" led to the immediate admission of Maine, but Missouri was delayed until the following year (1821). The delay was caused by Missouri's adoption of an extremely proslavery constitution to demonstrate its independence, which made a new compromise necessary. Missouri was the twenty-fourth state to enter the Union. Of the twenty-four states nine were west of the Appalachians.

The Great Migration was significant in carrying settlers to, and even beyond the Mississippi, although large areas remained unsettled farther east, both in the North and in the South. Half a dozen new states had been added to the Union, until the older West was no longer the frontier of settlement. Ohio, Kentucky, and Tennessee were soon to consider themselves old and well-settled regions, and to resemble seaboard communities more than they did a new frontier. The conquest of the continent had been well begun.

READINGS

NORTH. General accounts include Roscoe C. Buley, *The Old Northwest* (2 vols., 1950), a prize-winning book, but long and detailed; Albert L. Kohlmeier, *The Old Northwest* (1938) ; John A. Caruso, *The Great Lakes Frontier* (1961) ; Walter Havighurst, *Wilderness for Sale* (1956). More localized accounts include Clarence W. Alvord, *The Illinois Country* (1920) ; John D. Barnhart, *Valley of Democracy* (1935), good on Indiana and Illinois; Solon J. Buck, *Illinois in 1818* (1918) ; Floyd R. Dain, *Every House a Frontier* (1956), Detroit; Logan Esarey, *History of Indiana* (1915), continues to remain single best volume; Theodore C. Pease, *The Story of Illinois* (1949) ; William T. Utter, *The Frontier State* (1943)—Illinois; Charles Boewe (ed.), *Prairie Albion* (1962), contemporary Illinois settlement of 1817; Milo M. Quaife and Sidney Glazer, *Michigan* (1948). Richard C. Wade, *The Urban Frontier* (1959) is excellent on specific cities. Lewis D. Stilwell, *Migration from Vermont* (1937) is first rate; Stewart H. Holbrook, *The Yankee Exodous* (1950) is episodical.

SOUTH. The best general account is Thomas P. Abernethy, *The South in the New Nation* (1961). More specific accounts include Thomas P. Abernethy, *The Formative Period in Alabama, 1815–1828* (1922) ; Thomas D. Clark, *A History of Kentucky* (1937) ; Samuel C. Williams, *The Beginnings of West Tennessee* (1930) ; Floyd C. Shoemaker, *Missouri and Missourians* (5 vols., 1943). John H. Franklin, *From Slavery to Freedom* (1947) is the best history of the Negro.

MEDICINE. Medical histories generally give little attention to the West, but two interesting accounts are Madge E. Pickard and Roscoe C. Buley, *The Midwest Pioneer* (1945) ; Erwin H. Ackernecht, *Malaria in the Upper Mississippi Valley* (1945).

LAND ACT OF 1820. Best is Roy M. Robbins, *Our Landed Heritage* (1942, also in a paper edition) ; another satisfactory book is Benjamin H. Hibbard, *Public Land Policies* (1924).

CHAPTER 14

THE PERMANENT
INDIAN FRONTIER

T he increase of the white population between the Appalachians and
Mississippi presaged the elimination of the Indian tribes still
there. The Indians had been squeezed into smaller and smaller
areas with each white advance. Futile efforts had been made to keep whites
out of the Indian country and to persuade the Indians to adopt a settled
agriculture. Now the day was fast coming when these delaying measures
were obviously inadequate. The white wave was soon to overflow practically
the entire country east of the Mississippi.

THE NEW INDIAN HOME

Provision for the eastern Indians actually seemed a simple matter to
most Americans. West of the Mississippi lay millions of acres of wild land
that everyone felt would never be desired by white farmers, and hence
would be perfect as a home for the eastern Indians. Lewis and Clark described much of the region as "desert and barren." Pike likened the Southwest to the African deserts. In 1820 Stephen H. Long found the area
"wholly unfit for cultivation." In fact, even the plains areas east of the
Mississippi were viewed doubtfully. Southeastern Wisconsin was found to
be "laboring under permanent defects of coldness of soil and want of
moisture" (1817), while northern Illinois was described by Horace
Greeley as late as 1847 as having "the great, formidable, permanent" drawback of "deficiency of water." School geographies labeled the vast western
plains as "The Great American Desert," and almost everyone agreed that
they would support only prairie grass, buffalo, and Indians.

The idea of moving eastern Indians to the western plains went back as far as Jefferson, but without involving a conscious, long-run policy; eastern groups had no homeland acceptable to the whites and so they were moved west. This idea was gradually generalized. The Senate Committee on the Public Lands urged exchange of eastern for western land in its report to Congress in 1817, arguing that such action would remove the Indians from demoralizing white influences. Six years later Secretary of War Calhoun made the same recommendation to Congress. President Monroe followed similar reasoning in his congressional messages of 1824 and 1825. By this time an increasing number of treaties being made had removal as their objective. A law of 1830 accepted this procedure as general American policy. The objectors were mainly philanthropists, whose attitude was influenced by the large mission establishments, particularly in the South, that they would lose if the Indians went west.

New western homes for eastern Indians involved persuading eastern Indians to move and western Indians to make room for them, neither of which was simple to do. Above all, however, the developing policy was assumed to be the permanent solution of the Indian problem. The most important congressional act of 1830 authorized the President to make the necessary treaties and "solemnly to assure the tribe . . . that the United States will forever secure and guarantee to them, and their heirs or successors, the country so exchanged with them." Nearly every treaty had a similar provision; one of 1838, for example, gave the Cherokee "a permanent home, and which shall, under the most solemn guarantee of the United States, be, and remain, theirs forever." The "forever" that the United States so solemnly promised actually turned out in most cases to be less than a generation.

NORTHERN INDIANS

The removal of the northern Indians was relatively easy, since no strong and warlike tribes remained to oppose the will of the United States. A long series of treaties indicated that the eastern tribes accepted the necessity of moving. Another long series of treaties produced western land for them to occupy; most noteworthy was a St. Louis treaty of 1825 with the Kansa and Osage, which together with other agreements provided space between the Platte and the present Oklahoma for the Kickapoo, Delawares, Shawnee, Kaskaskia, Peoria, Miami, and others.

Farther north the Indians were a trifle more vigorous, but still comparatively peaceful and inoffensive. The earlier efforts, such as the Prairie du Chien agreement of 1825, were merely to get the Iowa, Sauk, Foxes, Sioux, and Chippewa to agree to boundary limitations. The negotiations at Prairie du Chien were among the most notable of western gatherings, with the white negotiators including such well-known men as William

Clark, Lewis Cass, Henry Schoolcraft, and Lawrence Taliafero. White advances soon made necessary further agreements, particularly a new Prairie du Chien treaty five years later.

BLACK HAWK WAR

The one outbreak that resulted from northern removals was the Black Hawk War, which has been better advertised than its importance warranted. The disturbing nations were the allied Sauk and Foxes, some 5400 strong, seminomadic, and noted for their fighting ability. Their resistance to the whites was entirely unjustified from a legal standpoint. By a treaty made with Harrison in 1804 and reaffirmed several times later they had sold their land on the east side of the Mississippi between the mouths of the Illinois and the Wisconsin, retaining only the right to use this land until it should be demanded by the white settlers. For two decades no whites encroached on their principal town near Rock Island at the mouth of the Rock River, but finally in the 1820s the first settlers came. Their number continued to increase yearly so that by 1830–1831 they were sufficiently numerous to be menacing. Relying on the old Indian treaty, they paid no attention or respect to their red neighbors, but plowed up Indian villages and graveyards to plant their fields of corn.

The Indians were surprisingly mild and docile in their reaction to white encroachment, particularly since the squatters had no more legal right to be there than the Indians had. Keokuk, the principal chief, counseled moving west of the Mississippi. The war chief Black Hawk, now sixty years old, wanted to resist and to remain in the country in which he had spent his whole life, but he was persuaded to go west with Keokuk and the rest of the tribe. Then Black Hawk visited Malden and was advised by the British that he could not be forced to leave. When he returned home he ordered the white settlers to depart. They immediately petitioned Governor John Reynolds of Illinois for assistance, and in response the Governor declared Illinois "invaded" and called for volunteers. Almost at once General E. P. Gaines of the United States Army moved to the scene of the trouble with 600 volunteers and 10 companies of regulars. As soon as Gaines arrived the Indians deserted their villages and fled across the Mississippi. The new treaty signed in the same year—1831—confirmed the old agreement of 1804.

Unfortunately for the Indians, they crossed the Mississippi too late in the year to grow crops of corn before winter, and in consequence they were soon near starvation. In this extremity some of them stole back across the river and pilfered some corn they had planted in the spring. Immediately there was another loud outcry from the settlers, who had visions of being murdered and scalped in their beds.

Conditions among the Indians went from bad to worse; whereupon Black Hawk concocted a wild plan for mitigating the suffering of his people. The main part of his project was to cross the river in the spring, join the friendly Winnebago, and jointly raise a crop of corn. Probably he also hoped to secure British aid in regaining his old village. Certainly he had a childish faith that he would not be harmed if he did not enter his old village.

To carry out these vague plans Black Hawk and 400 warriors with their families crossed the Mississippi in April 1832 and started up the Rock River toward the Winnebago country. Colonel Henry Atkinson immediately sent orders for him to return, but he refused. The frontier was once more in an uproar. Volunteers were gathered in Illinois amid scenes of wild excitement, with the men enlisting for adventure and fun. General Winfield Scott started from the East with some 1000 regulars, including the West Point cadet corps; these troops never saw action because of a cholera epidemic that held them at Fort Dearborn (Chicago).

The gathering of these hundreds of white soldiers worried Black Hawk, who had expected no such reaction. Then, too, his reception by the Winnebago was far from cordial, and no encouragement came from the British. In consequence he dispatched a small party with a flag of truce to arrange for a surrender. When the white volunteers saw the Indians they paid no attention to the white flag but started firing at once; some of the Indians were killed, the others were captured, and the whites made a wild scramble to take part in the complete destruction of Black Hawk's band. Black Hawk was naturally amazed at this reception of his flag of truce and decided that if he could not surrender he would at least die fighting; hence with 40 warriors he awaited the oncoming rush of the whites. When the whites came within range, the Indians rushed from the woods, uttering their death cries of defiance, and as soon as the Indians charged the white troops ran. Again the Indians were astonished at this new turn of events— so astonished that when they did start to pursue the fleeing troops, the whites were out of range.

After the white troops had returned to safety they told awe-inspiring stories of battling with 1500 to 2000 bloodthirsty and ferocious savages led by that military genius, the crafty Black Hawk. More troops were raised until they numbered about 4000. As for Black Hawk, he was elated by his easy and unexpected victory. The whites were, after all, not invulnerable, and so the Sauk and Fox warriors attacked the frontier at various unprotected spots, keeping the outlying settlers in continual apprehension.

One Indian victory did not make a successful war, and Black Hawk soon found it necessary to retreat before the superior white force. Up the Rock River he went, but his flight was hampered by the presence of women, children, the aged, and the sick, and provisions became scarcer each day. Finally the Indians were reduced to eating horseflesh and whatever barks and roots they could find along the line of march. As the situation became worse, Black Hawk's one thought was to return to the main part of the tribe, and so he crossed over to the Wisconsin River and descended it toward the Mississippi. Most of the women and children were put on rafts to float down the Wisconsin, while the warriors went on foot, always remaining sufficiently far in the rear to cover the retreat of their dependents.

The pursuing white army floundered and grumbled through the woods. Fighting Indians was an exciting occupation, but pursuing them through hundreds of miles of wilderness was anything but a holiday excursion. For a long time the troops moved rather blindly, depending largely on a general impression of the direction in which the Indians were going, but in the Four Lakes region of Wisconsin the whites finally discovered the trail and there was a small engagement with the Indians who were acting as a rear guard for the crossing of the river. As luck would have it, some of the whites troops blundered on a party of women and children floating down the river on rafts. The troops had great sport shooting at these open targets until the entire party had been either shot, drowned, or captured.

Eventually Black Hawk and the remnants of his party reached the Mississippi. Here he again tried to surrender, this time to the steamboat "Warrior," which happened to be passing. And again the whites failed to respect a flag of truce and fired on the Indians. About this time the white troops also reached the Mississippi and partly by accident discovered a band of 300 men, women, and children. The ensuing slaughter continued for three hours until all but 50 women and children had been killed. Black Hawk was captured, and the remainder of his force was taken back to Iowa; only 150 of the original 1000 Indians survived the expedition.

General Scott finally arrived and took command of the situation on August 7, 1832. Under his auspices a new treaty was signed, in which the Indians agreed to remain west of the Mississippi and in which they ceded a fifty-mile strip along the west bank of that river as expiation for their sins. Not surprisingly, other treaties and land cessions soon followed. Game was not available, the demoralized tribe spent altogether too much of its time drinking and gambling, and its numbers declined by over half. The Sauk and the Foxes were put on an Oklahoma reservation in 1867, and their land was allotted to individuals in 1891.

Black Hawk himself was taken east and exhibited as an object of curiosity to throngs of thrill-hungry Easterners. Elderly, hollow-cheeked, and pale, he turned out to be a great disappointment to those who had expected a fierce savage of bright copper color. He was released in June

1833 and went back to Iowa. His own comment on the episode was terse: "Rock River was a beautiful country. I loved my towns, my cornfields, and the home of my people. I fought for it. Now it is yours. Keep it as we did."

SOUTHERN REMOVALS

The removal of the southern Indians was much more difficult than the similar process farther north. The five tribes, which numbered possibly 60,000 and occupied some 18 million acres of land, resisted strenuously. Because relatively little demand existed, active efforts by the federal government to move them did not come until the 1820s even though such action had been promised Georgia with her cession of 1802. Pressure mounted during the 1820s when the normal flow of settlers was swelled on news of the discovery of gold. The consequent removal of the Indians was one of the least savory incidents in long story of unhappy racial contacts; the sorry details were repeated with monotonous and depressing regularity.

Many of the treaties for moving these tribes to the West included unexpected provisions for distributing at least part of the homeland to individuals of the tribe—a sort of allotment process half a century before the famous Dawes Act; in fact, some of the treaties were superficially only land allotment acts, with no mention of removal. However, the land was in reality only a sort of bonus for moving, and the government had no idea that any considerable number of Indians would remain in their homeland. In so far as land was allotted there appeared the same sort of fraud and injustice later apparent under the Dawes Act: many who should have received land did not, and vice versa. The Indian who received land often used it to pay an existing debt, or sold or rented it for a very small sum; seldom did his profit exceed the cost of a single spree. The general result only added confusion to the process of removal.

Up to this time the Choctaw of Mississippi had been consistently friendly to the United States in spite of various provocations, including several fraudulently obtained land cessions. They had a fairly high civilization during the 1820s, including the outlawing of whiskey, which might have served as a laudable example to the whites. Efforts by the whites during the 1820s to buy more land failed even when various chiefs were bribed. Mississippi thereupon became impatient and attached the Indian land to adjacent white counties (1829), thus making the Indians citizens of the state and subject to her laws.

Spurred by the action of Mississippi, the United States obtained a treaty of cession in 1830, but the circumstances were so unsavory that even President Jackson agreed that the document was fraudulent. The Senate rejected it, but more because of the cost than because of the fraud. At a new council in 1830 the Choctaw remained steadfast in their refusal to sell their eastern land even in the face of threatened military action. After this council had officially disbanded, the white commissioners bribed the few remaining Indians to sign the desired treaty, and this treaty was ratified by the Senate and proclaimed by the President.

In spite of Choctaw resentment, a considerable share of the tribe migrated in the years 1831–1833; others remained in Mississippi permanently. The whites did not wait for Indian departures, but seized land, cattle, homes, and other property at once. Most Indians started their migration with no more possessions than the clothes on their backs. They were cheated unmercifully by merchants and ship captains, and encountered blizzards, near starvation, and cholera and other diseases. In the West they found completely unimproved land, with no provision for their arrival, and were harassed by thieving settlers, dishonest traders, and wild Plains Indians. To the immense credit of the Choctaw was their construction of a fairly prosperous civilization that included churches, schools, newspapers, and a tribal government under constitutions of 1834 and 1838. Quite understandable was their law that provided death for any chief who agreed to a further land cession.

Chickasaw removal followed much the same pattern: unsuccessful efforts to purchase land, the extension of Mississippi laws in 1830, and white appropriation of Indian land and improvements. Cession treaties of 1830 and 1832 were never put into force because of the difficulty of obtaining western lands, but the treaty of 1834 gave the basis for the real migration that started in 1837. By this time the eastern Indians had become almost completely demoralized by white encroachments, whiskey salesmen, and the cholera. Arriving in the West, they were greeted by a smallpox epidemic and a drought; moreover, they were outnumbered by the Choctaw, who were not as friendly as they were expected to be. Subsequent Chickasaw history is not a subject for the sensitive investigator.

The Cherokee had also been advancing rapidly in civilization during the 1820s. They had become a settled agricultural people, adopting white ways of life and even a constitution (1827) based on that of the United States. Cherokee policemen maintained at least as good order as that maintained in the neighboring white communities, and taxes were collected at least as poorly. Most remarkable was the work of the Indian genius Sequoyah, son of a white trader and an Indian mother, who developed an alphabet of eighty-six symbols that made possible a written language. The *Cherokee Phoenix,* printed in both English and Cherokee, began publication in 1828.

An agricultural civilization meant Cherokee stability. Removal treaties could be obtained only by fraud, and then the Indians refused to move. Georgia became increasingly impatient, particularly after the gold discoveries of 1828, and in that year annexed the Indian lands, after which she provided for their distribution by lottery among white Georgians. As usual, miners and settlers did not wait for the law, which was scheduled to go into operation June 1, 1830, but began immediately to seize Indian land and property. President Jackson approved the Georgia action, feeling that if the Indians were placed under Georgia law they would soon see the desirability of moving, and he withdrew federal troops. The Indians on their part provided heavy penalties for anyone signing a treaty of cession, and appealed unsuccessfully to the federal government.

Even the Supreme Court of the United States became involved in the Cherokee troubles, and found difficulties of its own when it tried to define the status of the Indian. It finally labeled the Cherokee a "domestic, dependent" nation [Cherokee Nation v. Georgia (1831)], which meant whatever the Court wanted it to mean, and did not allow the tribe to appear as a litigant. In each of the cases appealed to the Court the state of Georgia refused to appear, and in each Georgia carried out the provisions of her own laws regardless of the Court's decision. In the best known of the cases [Worcester v. Georgia (1832)], which concerned two missionaries imprisoned by Georgia, the Supreme Court held the pertinent Georgia law unconstitutional. Georgia refused to recognize the decision, but avoided some unpleasantness by freeing the missionaries by executive clemency. The federal executive supported the actions of Georgia rather than the decisions of the court. President Jackson is reported to have remarked about the decision on the missionary case: "John Marshall has made his decision— now let him enforce it!" Even if the words are apocryphal, they accurately report his sentiments.

The Cherokee resisted white pressure, and defiantly refused to leave their homes. Treaties of 1834 and 1835, signed by a few Indians who had been bribed, were rejected by the tribe. A new treaty of 1835 was signed by some twenty men, none of whom was a chief, and then repudiated by the overwhelming majority of the tribe. The federal government, apparently despairing of anything better, ratified the document and declared it to be in force.

The mere assumption that a fraudulent treaty was binding did not move the Indians west; consequently General Winfield Scott was sent in 1838 with 7000 regulars to do the job. Detachments were ordered to round up the Indians; all too frequently, as a party of white soldiers surprised and surrounded an Indian family, white adventurers stood ready to grab the property that was about to be abandoned. Because this particular summer was unbearably hot many of the removals were postponed until fall. Winter removals proved even more unfortunate: more than a quarter of the 16,000 migrants died en route, and the remainder ended their trip in poverty and squalor, and suffering from disease.

Creek removals paralleled those of the Cherokee. The Creeks had been the most advanced of the southern tribes at the advent of the whites, with a settled agriculture and a reasonably stable government. Land cessions had been forced by Jackson at the end of his southern campaign, but no later ones were signed except through bribery, and the signers were frequently put to death. Conscientious President Adams disapproved of the fraud during his presidency, and was denounced vitriolically by Georgian authorities. Georgia then appropriated Creek territory. Whites overran the Indian country, seizing land and property, and debauching the natives. In the process, however, Georgia got rid of the Creeks.

All the eastern Creeks finally accepted a removal treaty in 1832, and started to move west the next year. Traders and contractors took advantage of them, and the militia fired on them—presumably by mistake. Some 1500 of the Indians were so angered that they went on the warpath, harrying outlying western settlements. Immediately 11,000 troops were sent under General T. S. Jesup to put down the insurrection. Although most of the Creeks were corralled and sent west, a number evaded the soldiers; during the 1850s an additional 4000 were removed, part of them in irons. As a result of its troubles the Creek population was cut almost in half within a generation.

SEMINOLE WAR

A few of the Creeks who disliked the idea of moving west escaped to Florida, where they joined their racial brothers, the Seminole. These Seminole had always been exasperating, not only because they occupied desired land, but also because they raided outlying settlements, killing and plundering, and offered an asylum for escaped Negro slaves. After the American acquisition of Florida a treaty was concluded in 1823 by which the Seminole agreed to withdraw to the poorer lands, but this treaty was not always observed, and the Floridians desired ardently the removal of the Indian population.

A Seminole removal treaty was signed in 1832, although probably the majority of the tribe opposed it. In accordance with its terms, a band of prospective migrants gathered at Tampa in the winter of 1832–1833. While there they heard of an Indian raid and consequently dispersed because of fear of white retribution. Then followed ten years of sporadic warfare between the United States Army and a handful of half-starved, poverty-stricken Indians. In defense of the army's performance it should be added that the Indians could find their way through the almost impentrable swamps, emerging only for short raids, and that pursuit was extremely difficult. The best-known Indian leader was Osceola, who ulti-mately died in captivity. A succession of white generals included E. P. Gaines, T. S. Jesup, Zachary Taylor, G. C. Macomb, and W. J. Worth. Even though they were not above treachery, their results were not impressive.

The last real battle of the Seminole War occurred in 1842, at which time Taylor estimated that less than 3000 Indians had been removed at a cost to the federal government of $20 million and the lives of 1500 soldiers. These figures did not include the serious damages suffered by the Floridians. When hostilities finally ended, some 500 Seminole, whose descendants are today in Florida, still remained.

WESTERN CONDITIONS

The removal of the Indians of the Old Southwest was not an accomplishment in which Americans can take pride, but at least it opened the remainder of the South to cotton culture. As for the Indians, they ended their mournful hegira in present Oklahoma, where they were any-thing but happy. The Plains Indians, including the Osage, Kiowa, Comanche, and others, objected strenuously to their new neighbors, and the southern tribes fought back to the best of their ability. The federal govern-ment forced cession treaties on the western Indians to provide room for the eastern arrivals, established new forts to preserve the peace, and sent expeditions to overawe the plains tribes. Several Indian councils, notably those of 1842 and 1843, sought to create amity between the old and new inhabitants of the present Oklahoma. Although they were a real contribu-tion to the settlement of grievances and the creation of friendships, they by no means eliminated all frictions.

Not least of the difficulties confronting the migrant Indian was that of leaving an agricultural way of life to enter a plains country without houses or barns or stock, and where the plow had not as yet broken the tough prairie sod. For the time being the Indians were entirely dependent on the bounty of the government as it trickled through the sticky fingers of private contractors. The Indian seldom received what the government had authorized, and the government was far from generous in any case. Then, too, illegal traders entered the Indian country where they found the natives all too willing to trade anything they possessed for a few hours of forgetfulness. Furthermore, and quite unexpectedly, white settlers found the country attractive and became a perpetual source of friction.

Rumors of fraud and mismanagement in the West reached the War Department, which sent Major Ethan Allen Hitchcock to investigate (1840). The major filled nine fat notebooks with circumstantial stories of bribes, falsified accounts, short weights, spoiled meat, and similar deplorable situations. His report was duly filed, but the department took no action—some said because too many prominent men would have been involved. When Congress became insistent in demanding this information, the War Department discovered very conveniently that the report had been mislaid.

THE PERMANENT FRONTIER

With the removal of both northern and southern tribes, except for a few isolated and fairly harmless groups, the Indian problem east of the Mississippi had been solved. The resulting Indian frontier was not a vague general region but a definite line that could be drawn on the maps of the 1830s. Starting from a point on northern Lake Michigan, it struck across Wisconsin to the Mississippi, with a little dip for the Menominee. It followed the Mississippi to the northern boundary of Missouri in 1830, but moved west in Iowa during the decade because of the Sauk and Fox cessions. Then it followed the northern boundary of Missouri and the western boundaries of Missouri and Arkansas to the Red River. West of this line lived some 350,000 Indians in 1840; possibly the ancestors of some 100,000 of them had once lived east of the Mississippi.

The permanence that this frontier was expected to have was demonstrated by the provisions made for marking and guarding it. A road from the mouth of the St. Peters to the Red was ordered surveyed by Congress in 1836, and although the surveys were not made, some of the road was actually constructed and a long line of forts built to guard the frontier. An Indian commission suggested the creation of a no man's land between Indians and whites, to be controlled by rangers. General Gaines, who commanded in the West, proposed in 1838 the creation of permanent stone forts that would at least outlive the century, but before his recommendations received favorable attention the frontier line had again advanced. This time the shortage of undesired land to which the Indians might be pushed necessitated a new and different "solution."

The administration of Indian affairs was strengthened during the early 1830s. General supervision was given to the office of Commissioner of Indian Affairs, with the commissioner responsible to the Secretary of War. The entire country was divided into three superintendencies, and under each superintendent were numerous agents and subagents who dealt directly with the Indians, settling disputes, allotting rations, and presumably avoiding the necessity of using the army to keep peace. The agency was not a new institution, but the functions of the agent were stated more specifically and carefully.

Among the functions of the Indian agent was the licensing of traders who could enter the Indian country. A new Indian Intercourse Act of

Permanent Indian Frontier, 1825–1845

1834 made more stringent the licensing provisions for traders and the regulations excluding whiskey. Presumably all unauthorized persons were expected to stay east of the permanent frontier.

Some hope existed that in time the Indians would be persuaded to adopt the ways of white civilization, although a number of critics insisted that settled agriculture could not develop until the Indians were given individual rather than tribal ownership of their lands. The annuities provided by the federal government had long included agricultural and other implements, sometimes at the request of the tribes themselves. Furthermore, the government had for many years aided missionaries in the establishment of schools and churches; thirty-eight schools were thus assisted in 1825 at the cost of $200,000, and the aid became more regular and extensive as the years passed. Many of the mission establishments had been moved west with the Indians and were concentrated particularly in the Southwest. The Congregationalists and the Presbyterians, acting mainly through the American Board of Commissioners for Foreign Missions, were most active, but other denominations also participated.

WESTERN ARMY

The main work of controlling the Indians remained basically in the hands of the army. Starting in 1837, the entire region west of the Mississippi was constituted the western department and was placed under the control of Gaines, so that administration of the entire frontier was unified. The American army of the period grew from some 6000 men in 1830 to 11,000 in 1841. Even though most of the men were stationed on the frontier, they did not constitute an impressive force for 1500 miles of border. Many of them were down-and-outers or immigrants trying to learn English. Their arms were rather nondescript and sometimes they had no uniforms. Supplies, such as overshoes and mittens, were often lacking. Altogether the army was seldom very intimidating.

Besides the army of the western department, a special western force was created in the 1830s to meet the peculiar problems of the frontier. A corps of rangers was raised under the authority of a law of 1832, but lacked both uniforms and discipline; the next year it was replaced by a regiment of 600 mounted dragoons. These men were never very impressive in appearance, but they did good work in the wilderness; they comprised a good quarter of the western army. The colonel of the regiment was Henry Dodge, the lieutenant colonel was Stephen Watts Kearny, and one of the second lieutenants was Jefferson Davis.

The western army spent a large share of its time in the various forts. Most important in 1830 were Forts Howard (Green Bay), Winnebago (Portage), Snelling (St. Paul), Crawford (Prairie du Chien), Armstrong (Rock Island), Leavenworth (Leavenworth), Gibson (on the Arkansas River in the present northeastern Oklahoma), Jesup (Natchitoches), and Jefferson Barracks (St. Louis). During the decade a number of changes were made, including the establishment of several new posts among the Civilized Tribes of the Southwest. The busiest of the forts was Fort Gibson, which ordinarily contained the largest complement of men.

A western fort, ordinarily built by the soldiers, was usually constructed of pickets, although sometimes of stone, and typically had two-story towers at diagonal corners. Inside the walls were the barracks for the men, homes for the officers, kitchen, dining hall, offices, school, storehouse, magazine, guardhouse, and hospital. Ordinarily a small civilian community sprawled near by, and a fur-trading post was not uncommon.

The frontier fort was impregnable to attack from the outside, even when badly manned and equipped. The wide spacing of the forts, however, made reinforcements difficult.

Life in the fort was outstandingly monotonous, particularly in the winter, when the little community might be completely isolated for months at a time. Routine filled most of the day from reveille at daybreak to the reading of orders and taps at night. In addition to the regular drilling, cleaning, and guard duty the soldiers spent most of their time in farming and construction work, for soldier labor erected most of the buildings and grew vegetables and other crops as well as hay for the horses. During the summer the soldiers' diet might be palatable, thanks to vegetables from the post garden, but during the rest of the year the staples were bread and soup, neither very good. Special delicacies in food and drink and wearing apparel might be purchased from the authorized post sutler, but prices were high and pay was low.

The chief diversion of the army was gambling, whether on cards, horses, checkers, or even the weather. Whiskey was a possible means of relieving the tedium, but in 1832 the War Department became abstemious in behalf of the soldiers and stopped their whiskey rations; a soldier's pay did not permit him to get drunk many times a month. A post library had some possibilities, but the few books were badly chosen. For the officers and their wives there was the usual round of dinners, teas, dances, and calls, but the West Point graduates curtailed their own enjoyment by a rigid insistence on the dignities of rank. Amateur theatricals were common, but women were excluded from the boards; men donned their wives' clothes and squeaked the female parts with more ardor than artistry. A school generally catered to the children of the post, and the sutler devoted part of his income to such worthy projects as school, library, and the care of widows and orphans.

The few army amusements alleviated but slightly the dreariness of life, which was made even less bearable by the frequency of sickness; the youth and resiliency of the men averted a high mortality rate. The inevitable results of boredom were many infractions of the rules, and desertions. From an army of 6000 in 1830 there were some 1250 desertions. The situation was not improved by the severe punishments visited on men for such minor offenses as a missing button or imbibing too much whiskey. An iron yoke, stocks, confinement on bread and water, hard labor, stoppage of pay, or extra guard duty while possibly carrying a log or a bag of shot, was common. Whipping was still in vogue, being done by the drummers taking turns. The man was stripped to the waist, tied to the flagpole, and whipped with a knotted instrument made of nine leather thongs.

The monotony of the life at a western fort made any alternative seem attractive, and even Indian outbreaks were viewed with some enthusiasm. Periodically a detachment was sent into the wilderness to remind the aborigines that the United States was not a pacific nation and had the power to enforce its desires. Such an expedition tried to remove causes of friction and to obtain promises of good behavior. Its commander had to be a man of both energy and discretion, who could double as explorer, strategist, and diplomat. The limited number of his troops and the wildness of the country counseled extreme care, for even with great diligence he might lose much of his command through Indian attacks, accident, starvation, and disease. His negotiations with the Indians required both moderation and firmness, with his small force hardly permitting aggressive domineering. Among the western expeditions of this type, those of Colonel Henry Dodge and his dragoons during the mid-1830s were notable. Dodge covered a large share of the country from the Arkansas to the Red, and west as far as the Rockies.

Other special army details were also necessary. Sometimes a detachment was used to enforce the decision of an Indian agent, as, for example, to bring to the agency a native accused of theft or murder; such a mission had dangerous possibilities, since lack of tact might drive an entire tribe into open hostilities. From time to time men were sent on exploring expeditions. Sometimes detachments were used to guard the overland traffic; the Santa Fe trade was thus protected in the years 1829, 1834, and 1843. This work was comparatively dull, since it meant long hours of slow travel in the dust kicked up by the traders' mules. Even such a trip, however, had advantages over the dull routine of the fort.

The idea of a permanent frontier was delightful in theory but somewhat disappointing in fact. The Indian problem was not solved but merely moved across the Mississippi, where all the old difficulties soon reappeared. The Indians never succeeded in living in permanent peace either with the whites or with each other. Indian agents found themselves without adequate power to control their charges, and even the support of the army was sometimes insufficient.

The worst trouble with the so-called permanent frontier was that it failed to divide. Traders and trappers, both licensed and illegal, flowed across the border, and the Indian agents were powerless to stop them. Explorers and traders traversed the plains country in increasing numbers. Even worse, the "desert" proved much less forbidding than had been expected. Before the outbreak of the Civil War settlers had begun to seep into the Indian country all the way from Minnesota to Texas. The frontier that had looked so permanent and useful in the 1830s had definitely outlived its usefulness by the 1850s, and treaty obligations proved no effective barrier to the advance of the American nation.

READINGS

GENERAL ACCOUNTS. James C. Malin, *Indian Policy and Westward Expansion* (1921) is a good monograph, but see also William C. MacLeod, *The American Indian Frontier* (1928) and Everett N. Dick, *Vanguards of the Frontier* (1941), quite readable. Useful biographies are Brainerd Dyer, *Zachary Taylor* (1946) and James W. Silver, *Edmund Pendleton Gaines* (1949).

ARMY LIFE. Eugene Bandel, *Frontier Life in the Army, 1854–1861* (1932) is contemporary; Henry P. Beers, *The Western Military Frontier, 1815–1846* (1935) is monographic on campaigns; Louis Pelzer, *Marches of the Dragoons in the Mississippi Valley* (1917) is scholarly; Francis P. Prucha, *Broadax and Bayonet* (1953) deals with the Mississippi Valley, but his *American Indian Policy* (1962) is more general; Edgar B. Wesley, *Guarding the Frontier* (1935) is a good monograph; Theodore C. Blegen and Philip D. Jordan (eds.), *With Various Voices* (1949) contemporary accounts of Fort Snelling; Marcus L. Hansen, *Old Fort Snelling, 1819–1858* (1918) is particularly good on soldier life; Bruce E. Mahan, *Old Fort Crawford* (1926) is interesting.

BLACK HAWK WAR. The best complete account is William T. Hagan, *The Sac and Fox Indians* (1958), but see also Theodore C. Pease, *The Frontier State 1818–1848* (1918), which concerns Illinois. A biography of Black Hawk, Cyrenus Cole, *I Am a Man* (1938) is overly eulogistic; more illuminating is Donald Jackson (ed.), *Black Hawk: An Autobiography* (1955), which was dictated.

SOUTHERN REMOVALS. The general story is covered well by Robert S. Cotterill, *The Southern Indians* (1954). Most work has been done by Grant Foreman in his books *Advancing the Frontier, 1830–1860* (1933), *The Five Civilized Tribes* (1934), *Indian Removal* (1932), *Indians & Pioneers* (rev. ed., 1936), and *The Last Trek of the Indians* (1946); they are informative but not well written. Mary E. Young, *Redskins, Ruffleshirts, and Rednecks* (1961) studies eastern Indian allotments. Useful state histories include those of Abbey, Brevard, and Coulter cited in the Readings for Chapter 12, and Sidney W. Martin, *Florida During the Territorial Days* (1944). For the receiving end the accounts are a bit dull: Edward E. Dale and Morris L. Wardell, *History of Oklahoma* (1948); Grant Foreman, *A History of Oklahoma* (1942); Edwin C. McReynolds, *Oklahoma* (1954).

INDIVIDUAL SOUTHERN TRIBES. Marion L. Starkey, *The Cherokee Nation* (1946), excellent; Morris L. Wardell, *A Political History of the Cherokee Nation* (1938); Henry T. Malone, *Cherokees of the Old South* (1956) stops with the removals. Minor parts of Cherokee history are presented in Althea L. Bass, *Cherokee Messenger* (1936); Edward E. Dale and Gaston Litton, *Cherokee Cavaliers* (1939); Grant Foreman, *Sequoyah* (1938); scholarly; Ralph H. Gabriel, *Elias Boudinot* (1941). Angie Debo, *The Rise and Fall of the Choctaw Republic* (1934), and *The Road to Disappearance* (1941) are both good, the latter being concerned with the Creeks. See also Edwin C. McReynolds, *The Seminoles* (1957).

THE WILDERNESS ROAD THROUGH THE CUMBERLAND GAP. From W. C. Bryant (ed.), *Picturesque America,* 1872. Situated on the border of Kentucky, Tennessee, and Virginia, the Gap was named by Thomas Walker, who went through it to the West in 1750, but for centuries earlier this pass through the Appalachian Highlands had been in use by Indians—and buffalo. In 1775 Daniel Boone blazed a trail across it to the Kentucky River, and for the next half century the Wilderness Road, extending from eastern Virginia to the interior of Kentucky and then to the Ohio River and beyond, was a principal route to the early West. (New York Public Library)

(*Above*) CONESTOGA WAGON. This freight carrier, adapted to transporting heavy loads long distances, originated among the Pennsylvania Dutch, but it first came into general use on the overland routes across the Alleghenies after the Revolution, when new roads to the West were being built. The wagon was designed to be higher at the ends than in the middle so that its contents would not spill out on hills. The under parts were characteristically painted blue, the upper parts red. It was a forerunner of the Prairie Schooner. (Baltimore and Ohio Railroad)

(*Below*) PLAN OF AN AMERICAN NEW CLEARED FARM, 1793. An engraving by McIntyre from Patrick Campbell, *Travels in the Interior Parts of North America*, 1793. The caption reads: "1, a birch canoe poled by an Indian; 2, a birch canoe poled by squaws; 3, a baboose, or Indian child; 4, a log fence; 5, worm fences; 6, post and rail fence; 7, Virginia rail fence; 8, dwelling house and wings; 9, barracks or Dutch barn; 10, barns roofed with singles; 11, shade for cattle to ly in winter; 12, shade for winning Indian corn; 13, fold for confining cattle at night & in which they are milked; 14, a dwelling log house covered with bark, 15, an Indian dog."

STAGES IN THE CULTURE AND MARKETING OF TOBACCO. From William Tatham, *An Historical and Practical Essay on the Culture and Commerce of Tobacco*, 1800. (*Above, from top down*). A tobacco house, with the leaf hung on a scaffold at right, prizing tobacco at left; tobacco hung in open sheds to dry; tobacco packed in hogsheads for shipment; inspection of tobacco in the warehouse. (*Opposite*) Transporting tobacco by double canoe, by upland boat, by wagon, and by rolling hogsheads equipped with wooden hoops. (New York Public Library)

(*Above*) THE ERIE CANAL AT LOCKPORT, NEW YORK, 1836. Lithograph by J. Bufford after a drawing by A. Wilson. Extending from Buffalo on Lake Erie to near Albany on the Hudson, the Erie Canal, completed in 1825, opened a water route from the Great Lakes to the Atlantic Ocean. At Lockport, by deep cuts and five ascending and five descending locks, it was taken through one of its most difficult stretches. (The New York Historical Society)

(*Below*) A CAMP MEETING, 1830-1835. Lithograph by Kennedy and Lucas after a painting by A. Rider. The camp meeting revival was a form of religious-social entertainment, bringing people together, often joining them in a concerted release of pent-up emotion. (The New York Historical Society)

(*Above*) CAMPUS MARTIUS, 1791. From *American Pioneer*, 1842. This palisaded area known as Campus Martius was the first settlement, in 1788, in the new Northwest Territory, at Marietta. By 1800 Marietta, which was named in honor of Marie Antoinette of France, had taken on the appearance of a village. (New York Public Library)

(*Below*) OLD FORT DEARBORN, 1857. For a third of a century, from 1803 to 1836, Fort Dearborn on the Chicago River, on the site of present Chicago, guarded the midwestern frontier. (Phelps Stokes Collection, New York Public Library)

(*Opposite, above*) A FLATBOAT ON THE OHIO. From William A. Crafts, *Pioneers in the Settlement of America*, 1877. On reaching the Ohio, many emigrants floated down the river in flatboats or keelboats. Flatboats were built of planks and were sometimes partly roofed over. They were too awkward to propel upstream, so they were generally broken up at the end of a journey and used for building. (New York Public Library)

(*Opposite, below*) A KEELBOAT WORKING UPSTREAM. From *Harper's Magazine*, 1853. Keelboats were longer and narrower than flatboats, and had a shallow keel for stability. The fastest and most easily managed of the pre-steamboat river boats, they could be rowed, if small enough, sailed, or poled. They were adapted to upstream as well as swift downstream transportation, and were widely used to carry passengers. (New York Public Library)

KANSAS, 1853. The greater number traveling overland to the gold fields in '49 went by the Oregon Trail. The village of Kansas, at the junction of the Kansas and Missouri rivers (site of present Kansas City), was important as an outfitting and starting point for the route. (Phelps Stokes Collection, New York Public Library)

Captain Lewis & Clark holding a Council with the Indians

A Canoe striking on a Tree

Captain Clark & his men building a line of huts

An American having struck a Bear but not killed him escapes into a Tree

(*Opposite, above*) EMIGRANTS COMING INTO LOUP VALLEY, CUSTER
COUNTY, NEBRASKA, IN 1886. (*Below*) A SOD DUGOUT IN THE LOUP
RIVER COUNTRY OF NEBRASKA, 1892. Photographs by S. D. Butcher. After
passage of the Homestead Act in 1862, many settlers homesteaded land in
western Kansas and Nebraska or bought from the railroads, which at this
same time were selling their land grants at attractive prices. (Nebraska State
Historical Society)

PLOWING ON THE PRAIRIES BEYOND THE MISSISSIPPI. An engraving after a
sketch by Theodore R. Davis. From *Harper's Weekly*, 1868. Plowmen with
heavy oxen and breaking plows generally broke the tough prairie sod.

BREAKING UP A LOG JAM ON THE CHIPPEWA RIVER, WISCONSIN. From *Leslie's Illustrated Weekly*, 1871. Logs were hauled from the cutting ground to water and then floated down the river to the mill, here and there forming log jams on the way. The caption explains that the jam here is not being broken up in the usual way, by prying and lifting the logs with handspikes and poles; operations are facilitated by the application of steam power and the use of cables to jerk out individual logs, thereby loosening many others. (New York Public Library)

CHAPTER **15**

STAGECOACH
AND STEAMBOAT

T
he West of the early nineteenth century had no more perplexing problem than transportation. Most attractive were the rivers, but they had obvious limitations. Rivers flowed only in one direction. They often lacked water in the fall and froze in winter, and were remote from much desirable land. Consequently road travel was important from the time when the earliest trapper plodded over a blazed trail.

Any American road before 1790 was unpaved, and typically exhibited two deep ruts in dry weather and a sea of mud in wet. Streams usually had to be forded, although there was an occasional undependable ferry. After 1790 a few roads were improved along the lines suggested by the Englishmen McAdam and Telford. Such roads were not hard-surfaced but had ditches for drainage, bridges over the streams, and a roadbed of various-sized rocks that were supposed to produce a firm surface with the passage of traffic.

WESTERN ROADS

Early western roads achieved the distinction of being even worse than eastern roads. Starting usually as Indian trails, they followed the uplands as much as possible. The whites blazed the trails (notched trees along the side) because they were poorer woodsmen than the Indians, and the paths became wider with more use. Here and there a few logs were placed side by side to enable passage over the worst mudholes, and now and then a crude and erratic ferry seemed to the harassed traveler a gift from Providence. The average road was a partially cleared path on which the traveler weaved back and forth among the stumps and felled trees, trying to avoid

211

the mudholes, which were rumored able to swallow horse and rider at a single gulp.

Building good roads was almost impossible because of the great distances and lack of funds. The federal government felt responsible only for military roads in the territories. States legislated concerning some of the main highways, but grandiose plans came to nothing because of inadequate funds. Private businessmen now and then opened a toll road, which possibly was subsidized by the federal government. Counties and townships did most of the actual road building; taxpayers usually worked out their taxes on the roads, but with apparently much less enthusiasm than when they worked for themselves.

In spite of the difficulties, a few main roads were at least partially improved before the War of 1812. Among the best known was Zane's Trace from Wheeling, Virginia, to Limestone (later Maysville), Kentucky. Its construction, aided by a congressional grant of 1796, consisted of felling the larger trees—but not removing their stumps—and clearing away the brush. Zane's Trace connected with a road to Lexington and then to Nashville. From Nashville to Natchez was the famous Natchez Trace, used largely by flatboat men returning from New Orleans. Among other main highways was one directly over the mountains to Nashville, and another through Georgia to New Orleans, as mentioned earlier.

Western roads seldom could accommodate anything as luxurious as a stagecoach. Passengers ordinarily rode in a farm wagon with the seats placed crosswise, and sometimes covered by a canvas top and curtains. Freight was carried in a Pennsylvania or Conestoga wagon. The Conestoga was distinctive in being tipped upward at each end, reputedly to avoid losing freight on the hills. A sixteen-foot box was covered by a twenty-four foot canvas top, the whole rig being hauled usually by six horses. The blue underbody, the red upper, and the white top produced a vivid and patriotic display on the road. The poorer road would hold nothing more than a wooden cart with two wide wooden wheels; the usual traveler was the man on horseback, his entire baggage contained in a pair of saddlebags.

ROADS BETWEEN EAST AND WEST

Bad western roads distressed all Westerners except those in New Orleans, who profited. Farmers, merchants, and bankers looked longingly at eastern markets and at the more direct route to Europe if only transportation were improved. They also looked yearningly at manufactured goods that could not be hauled economically. Even more distressed were Easterners, and particularly manufacturers, importers, and merchants, who

Zane's Trace, the Natchez Trace, and the National Road

were saddened as they saw western business floating down the river. The
project of highest priority for both East and West was an improved road
connecting the two sections, and as is frequent in such cases, the yearning
crystallized as a continuing demand for Congress to act.

Congress was perfectly willing to aid an East-West road provided
the economy-minded administration did not have to advance cash. It provided in the Ohio Enabling Act of 1802 (as modified in 1803) that 5 percent of the proceeds of Ohio land sales should be dedicated to roads, three
fifths to be spent for roads within the state, and two fifths for roads from
elsewhere to the borders of the state. Similar provisions were made for other
states as they were later admitted to the Union. The 3 percent fund soon
permitted Ohio to build several roads, particularly to connect Lake Erie
and the Ohio River; other states with smaller land sales were less lucky.
The 2 percent fund was allowed to collect in the federal treasury for future
use on an East-West road.

THE NATIONAL ROAD

The route of the new East-West road, as stated in the law of 1806, was picked ouly after intense competition among dozens of communities with high aspirations for future commercial importance. Baltimore was chosen for the eastern terminus, although the actual construction was to begin at Cumberland. For the western terminus Wheeling won over many competitors, of which the strongest were Pittsburgh and Steubenville. Albert Gallatin of Uniontown, Pennsylvania, had sufficient influence to swing the road out of a direct line to go through Uniontown and Washington. Immediately Maryland, Pennsylvania, and Virginia authorized the construction. The first contracts were let in 1811, but actual construction did not come until the end of the War of 1812. By 1818 the mails were being carried over the road from Washington, D.C., to Wheeling. The total cost was $1,700,000 or an average of $13,000 a mile, which was probably excessive.

The right of way of the National Road (often called the Cumberland Road) was thirty feet wide in the mountains and sixty-six feet elsewhere. Bridges were of solid masonry. The roadbed was raised in the center, with a ditch on each side to drain off the water, and was composed of stones broken by hand hammers wielded by workmen paid a dollar a day. The lowest stratum of the road was made of stone broken to pass through a seven-inch ring, while the top stratum had stones that passed through a three-inch ring. A layer of stones was put in place and after traffic had packed it down, another layer was added. The process was repeated until the desired depth was reached.

The National Road was a great improvement, but it had serious deficiencies. Heavy traffic produced bad ruts that melting snows and heavy rains turned into deep gullies; at times portions of the mountain construction washed out completely. The eastern part of the road actually wore out before the western section was completed, and soon the whole road needed repair. Congress met the situation by passing a law authorizing the collection of tolls to provide funds for repair, but to the dismay of friends and users of the road President Monroe vetoed the bill on the basis of rather complicated constitutional reasoning that Congress had the power to build and repair the road but not to collect tolls. Congress then refused to make appropriations from general funds, and a decade was spent in constitutional wrangling while the road continued to deteriorate. Ultimately Congress provided for the repairs and then (1831–1834) turned the road over to the states through which it ran; these states thereupon erected tollhouses and used their collections for repairs.

TRAVEL ON THE NATIONAL ROAD

The National Road was immediately crowded with immigrants, salesmen, farmers, freighters, stages, and cattle being driven to market. Both Wheeling and Baltimore grew in size and importance, with rosy hopes for the future. To care properly for the growing traffic considerable amounts of equipment were necessary, and in consequence there appeared large freighting and coaching companies. The most important of the stage lines was operated by the National Road Stage Company; its chief competitor was the Good Intent Line.

A stage was ordinarily drawn by four horses, which were changed about every twelve miles. The stage itself had three seats, of which the front one faced the rear and the middle one had a strap for its back. Each seat held three passengers; another place, beside the driver, was much coveted in fair weather. The driver sat on top in front, and the baggage was placed in a "boot" in the rear. Leather straps were the only springs, and leather curtains were but partially successful barriers against rain and cold. A coach ride over the Alleghenies, with the coach rattling and jolting over the ruts and around the corners, with magnificent vistas in the distance and frightful chasms in the immediate foreground, was an experience not easily forgotten.

The aristocrat of the road was the stage driver. Every small boy along the road knew the drivers by name, and achieved an imperishable halo of glory if one of the drivers condescended to speak to him. The importance of the driver did not depend on his pay, which was ordinarily twelve dollars a month and keep, but on his courage and skill. He drove rapidly and well, averaging ten miles an hour, which was excellent for the sharp grades and abrupt turns of a mountain road. Driving was a dangerous occupation even under the most favorable conditions, but on a dark night, or in a heavy rain, or on icy roads it was so hazardous that only the most competent or the most foolhardy man would dare to undertake it.

Stage fares were collected by the hotel landlords, who acted as agents for the various companies. The landlord gave a bill of lading to the driver, and this list told the next landlord the names of the passengers and the distances for which they had paid. The fare varied somewhat from year to year, with the average a little over six cents a mile. The price of the trip from Baltimore to Wheeling was usually a little less than twenty dollars.

The distance covered by a stage each day tended to increase, but of course varied with the time of the year and the condition of the highway. During the 1830s the trip from Washington to Wheeling could be made in a continuous thirty hours, although the usual time with stops at night was two and a half days. By then the construction of the road had been continued farther west, reaching Columbus, Ohio, in 1833 and being graded, but not surfaced, into Illinois. By 1837 the trip from Washington to Columbus could be made in forty-five and a half hours, to Indianapolis in sixty-five and a half hours, and to St. Louis in ninety-four hours. The usual times to these places were, respectively three days, sixteen hours; six days, twenty hours; ten days, four hours.

Freight, like passengers, was handled mostly by large companies, although farmers with their teams and wagons offered competition during the slack farming seasons. The usual wagon was of the Conestoga type. Wheels were continually made wider, for it was found that the broader tire was more satisfactory on a gravel road. Brakes were poor, and on heavy grades saplings were sometimes fastened around the rear wheels or heavy logs were tied to the back of the wagon. The average load was about 6000 pounds, although there is a record of as much as 10,375 net pounds carried by one wagon in 1835. Wages of the wagoner were paid by the trip. The freight rate between Cumberland and Wheeling varied from $1.25 to $2.25 per hundred pounds, and the average daily trip was about fifteen miles. Unlike the stages, the wagons always stopped at night; the same horses were used throughout a trip.

Taverns lined the whole route of the National Road at frequent intervals, even in the mountains. Drivers of wagons were not given rooms in these hotels, but had to sleep either on the barroom floor or outside. Here and there were so-called "wagon houses"—rude shacks for the use of the teamsters; the teamster furnished his own bedding and food, and did his own cooking.

HAZARDS OF ROAD TRAVEL

The National Road, in spite of its drawbacks, was immeasurably superior to the average western road, which improved but little with the passing of the years. A so-called road was often no more than a single track through the woods, and at best an unimproved double track that was almost impassable in the early spring. A traveler on the road between Nashville and Memphis in 1831 reported: "Frightful roads. Precipitous descent. No regular highway. The road is only an opening cut in the forest. The stumps of the trees are not completely cut away, so that they form so many impediments over which we jolt."

Bad roads meant high freight rates. The Illinois farmer of 1820 would have lost money in hauling his corn even twenty miles at the cost of 50¢ a hundred pounds. One region might have a near famine while a neighboring area had an unmarketable surplus. One consequence was that prices varied tremendously from place to place. Wheat sold for 25¢ a bushel in Illinois in 1825 and for $2.00 on the eastern seaboard, corn varied from 10¢ to $1.75 a bushel.

Coach travel was undertaken only by the hardy or under the pressure of dire neccessity. The usual main road had one or more coach lines, but often there was no regular schedule and the passenger might wait days or even weeks for a connection. Travel might continue both day and night, but the traveler ordinarily stopped overnight. The usual day's trip was between twenty and fifty miles, although it might be as long as a hundred miles; the fare was six to seven cents a mile. An ordinary day's trip might begin as early as three or four in the morning and last until ten in the evening or even later, with stops only for meals. Three or four days exhausted even the strongest traveler, who would then be glad to stop for a week or more to regain his strength.

A stage had to follow the meanderings of badly located roads, but it also had to dodge back and forth to avoid being "up against a stump" or "stumped." In dry weather the coach lurched, swayed, and bumped over the rutty roads, enveloped in dust from the horses' hoofs; at the end of a day many a traveler nursed a headache produced by bumping the roof. In rain, the leather curtains offered but little protection, and the passengers were thoroughly soaked. The coach plowed through the water, with now and then a detour through a neighboring field to avoid a particularly menacing mudhole. If the coach stuck in the mud the male passengers used fence rails or saplings to pry or push the vehicle to a drier spot.

Accidents were commonplaces of western travel. When the coach swayed with the bad road the passengers swayed in the opposite direction, but sometimes the coach lost its balance and fell on its side. The passengers then crawled out of the wreckage as nonchalantly as possible, bound their wounds, righted the coach, and proceeded on their way. The breaking of an axle or a wheel was more serious, even though the driver carried materials and implements for repairs. If the men could not make the necessary repairs, the driver would set out on foot for the nearest settlement while the passengers invited themselves to stay for the night at the most convenient log cabin.

The smaller streams were forded. Timid passengers might alight and walk, with appealing scenes of gallantry as the men carried the younger, more attractive, and lighter members of the opposite sex through the water. Floods might mean days of waiting until the water subsided; a premature effort at fording might result in the coach being washed down the stream. Ferries were operated on the larger rivers, but probably the ferryman had to be called from his farmwork. The coach was carried on the first trip of a ferry, and the passengers on the second.

TAVERNS

The usual stopping place for a stage was a tavern. The horses were raced for the last few rods, the horn was tooted, the brakes were set with a grinding roar, and the driver leaned back on his reins pulling the horses to a sliding stop in a cloud of dust. The tavern might be anything from a commodious frame house to a small log cabin where the traveler slept in the same room with the landlord's family. The keeper of the inn met his guests at the door, showed them to their rooms, and presided at meals, where he led the conversation. The largest and most attractive room was the bar, in which the men gathered. Normal decorations would be a wooden clock, a map of the United States, a map of the state, a framed copy of the Declaration of Independence, a looking glass with brush and comb attached, and a few engravings or woodprints.

The rooms of the western inn were usually large and bare. Frequently the washing facilities were a pump and a tin basin outside the backdoor. Real luxury was a shallow tin pan, pitcher, and bucket in the room, the traveler using whatever water was in the pitcher since there was no personal service. Bedding was usually scanty and filthy. A room often had several beds that were filled without regard to sex or previous acquaintanceship, except that a bed was not allotted to a man and woman unless they were married. In the smaller inn the first floor might be given to the ladies, while the loft was occupied by the men. The ordinary price for accommodations was a dollar a day for board and lodging.

Tobacco and liquor were everywhere. There was a cud of tobacco in nearly every male cheek, and the chroniclers have reported that spitting was done with a fine disregard of consequences; the floors, coaches, boats, and great open spaces were all convenient receptacles for surplus juice. Drinking was equally universal among the men. The better hotels had long wine lists, but the smaller establishments concentrated on the cheap and potent whiskey, which was even used at meals in place of water.

Meals were served at regular hours and were eaten by everyone together, with breakfast usually at seven thirty, dinner at two, and supper at seven. Everything was put on the table at once in large dishes, and the guests helped themselves; a servant girl passed the tea and coffee. Immense quantities of food were consumed rapidly and silently. Tablecloths were common, napkins rare. Spoons were frequently of silver, but knives and the two-pronged forks were likely to be steel, with horn handles. Eating with a knife had to be a fine art to avoid accident.

Western food varied with the type of tavern, the region, and the time of year. In the North the traveler might expect such viands as venison steak, bread, butter, honey, tea, coffee, beefsteak, eggs, apple sauce, corn bread, fat pork, chicken, and potatoes. In the South the common bill of fare included such items as beef, turkey, venison, chicken, sweet potatoes, corn cake, ham, and bacon. Pork was ubiquitous in both North and South. Whenever feasible the food was fried in grease, and meat often was practically swimming in it. Coffee was poor, and any sugar served was usually brown. The one typically American dish was corn on the cob. Characteristically lacking were green vegatables, which were scarce in the summer and rare in the winter. New Orleans was one of the few places where the traveler might hope to be served such vegetables as radishes, peas, asparagus, lettuce, and spinach.

EARLY WATER TRAFFIC

Roads were desirable for the West, but only when water was not available. The water traffic on the Mississippi and its tributaries was the most significant western transportation until well after the middle of the nineteenth century. Before 1790 almost all water travel was by canoe, which ordinarily was a dugout and seldom a bark canoe. The dugout, hollowed from the trunk of a tree, was usually about 20 feet long. It could be constructed by four men in four days. A few were as large as 30 feet, with a beam of $3\frac{1}{2}$ feet, and carried a square sail. Most of them were divided into four compartments formed by allowing portions of the tree trunk to remain as partitions. The front and rear divisions were used for paddling and steering, respectively, while the center divisions contained the cargo. When used for commercial purposes the canoe was handled ordinarily by Indians or by French from Canada or Louisiana, with the French Creoles being noted as hard-working, happy, and carefree; their songs rang joyously in the silence of the river and the neighboring forest.

Several modified forms of the canoe were called pirogues. The ordinary type of pirogue was a canoe with a square stern. Two canoes lashed together and floored over, and frequently using a sail for motive power, represented another type. West of the Mississippi were two other kinds of boats. The Mackinaw boat resembled a large rowboat possibly 50 feet long, with the cargo carried in a watertight compartment in the center; four oarsmen sat in the front to row, while the steersman sat on an elevated perch in the rear. An even more peculiar craft was the bullboat, which looked something like an inverted rimless hat, possibly 30 feet long; made of caulked buffalo hides stretched over a willow frame, it had the virtues of lightness, easy construction, large capacity, and very shallow draught. The bullboat was navigated by two men with poles and consequently was slow-moving.

The increasingly popular boat of the whites was the flatboat, which obviously was flat-bottomed. Although flatboats varied a great deal in dimensions, common varieties were anywhere from 20 to 100 feet long, and 8 to 15 feet wide; the depth was seldom over 3 feet, but might be much more. The crudest of the boats were little more than good-sized rafts, and when used by migrants might support a barn for the cattle and a small cabin for the family. A boat used for a comparatively short commercial trip might be partially roofed, but the New Orleans boats were completely covered and somewhat more sturdy.

Each flatboat had four oars, but not to furnish the motive power. On each side was a 30-foot oar to get the boat to shore or out into the current; because of their appearance the boat was sometimes called a "Kentucky broadhorn." In the stern was a 40- to 50-foot oar used for steering, and in the front a smaller oar called gouger to aid the steering in unusually rapid water. Since the flatboat depended on the current for motive power and speed it moved slowly except during those moments when it shot the falls of the Ohio at Louisville. The favorite aid to navigation was Zadoch Cramer's *The Navigator*. Ordinarily the boat was tied to the bank every evening, since sand bars and other obstructions made it dangerous to travel at night.

The passengers on a flatboat had their living quarters aboard, with bunks instead of beds. Food was prepared in a rude fireplace. Migrants took aboard all their possessions, including their livestock, and one of the humorous sights of the river was a cow riding peacefully on the deck of a flatboat. A migrating family broke up its boat at the end of the trip and used the boards and nails for the construction of a home on land. When a cargo was sold at New Orleans the boat was ordinarily torn apart and sold, with the men returning overland by the Natchez Trace.

The principal upriver craft was the long, narrow keelboat, which usually measured about 50 feet in length and 7 to 10 feet in width. Being designed for longer use than the flatboat, it was better constructed, with pointed ends and a regular keel, which gave it its name. The draught varied from 20 to 60 inches, depending on the rivers on which it operated. In spite of this small draught the boat could carry between 20 and 40 tons of freight, which was protected from rain and sun by a roof.

The keelboat used every possible method of propulsion. Three to six oars on each side permitted rowing. A square sail of some hundred square feet was rigged to a 33-foot mast and used in a favorable wind. A cordelle or towrope, could be stretched from the top of the mast to the shore, with an auxiliary line to keep the boat from yawing; it was also used to tow the boat through turbulent waters. This form of progress was slow and arduous, with twenty to thirty men scrambling over the rocks and through the water to drag the boat upstream; at times it was even necessary to employ a block and tackle. Because of the difficulties of towing, the method was used only when absolutely necessary. Whenever the water was sufficiently shallow the boat was propelled by poles, and for this purpose a 15-inch platform was built on each side of the deck. Half of the crew took their places on each side. Each man thrust his pole into the bed of the river, put his shoulder against the socket at the end of the pole, and walked from fore to aft; as each man arrived at the stern he took out his pole, walked to the bow, and repeated the trip.

The only advantage of keelboats was that they could transport fairly heavy cargoes upstream. Trips were long, exhausting, and expensive, and so were practical only for valuable goods that would not spoil in transit. Since most western products were cheap and bulky they could not be carried by keelboats. Incidentally, the model boat of the river was the galley, with dimensions of approximately 45 by 12 feet; it was propelled exclusively by oars and carried only passengers and mail.

River traffic grew rapidly as white immigration to the West increased. Down the river went such heavy and less perishable commodities as flour, potatoes, salt pork, bacon, linen, corn, and cordage. Up the river came such articles as molasses, sugar, coffee, and tea all of comparatively large value in small bulk. An observer of 1810 counted 197 flats and 14 keelboats passing the falls of the Ohio within two months. Six years later a traveler from Natchez to Louisville met 2000 flats within twenty-five days. One scholar has estimated an average of 3000 flatboats a year on the Ohio River between 1810 and 1820; certainly by the end of the War of 1812 the river was covered with these slow-moving crude crafts floating with the current.

River traffic necessitated a "floating population" to furnish the labor on the flatboats and keelboats, and on the waterfronts. These river men, "half horse, half alligator" were poorly educated, restless, strong, rough, and tough. The semilegendary Mike Fink boasted that "I kin outrun, outhop, outjump, throw down, knock down, drag out, and lick any man in the country. I'm a Salt River roarer. I love the wimmen and I'm chock-full of fight." Men of the breed of Fink collected in such river towns as Cincinnati, Louisville, Natchez, and New Orleans. They roistered up and down the river, drinking, fighting, and making love, but they also created folklore and folk songs that have continued to live.

EARLY STEAMBOATS

Early western river traffic was slow; even more distressing, it could not move upstream without tremendous expenditures of capital and labor. The immediate answer was the application of steam to river transportation. Robert Fulton demonstrated the commercial possibilities of the steamboat in his trip on the Hudson with the "Clermont" in 1807, and he and his backer, Robert R. Livingston, obtained a legal monopoly of steamship transportation in the states of New York and Louisiana. If this power could have been maintained it would have meant control of a large proportion of all the shipping of the United States. The breaking of the monopoly, including the case of Gibbons v. Ogden (1824), made constitutional history.

One of the earliest efforts of the Livingston-Fulton monopoly was to introduce and develop the steamboat in the West, since western commerce was large and the control of Louisiana was strategic. In May 1809 Nicholas Roosevelt was sent West to sound out steamboat possibilities. For Roosevelt the trip was a honeymoon as well as a business venture, so he built a flatboat at Pittsburgh, fitted it with luxurious appointments, and floated leisurely down the river. At each town he discussed his plans with the leading citizens. He spent three weeks at Louisville for here were the dreaded falls, and the old-timers were naturally skeptical of the ability of the proposed new machine to move against the current. The end of Roosevelt's journey was New Orleans, from which city he returned to the East by ocean, reaching New York in January 1810.

Roosevelt's report to the monopoly was apparently favorable, for in 1811 the steamboat "New Orleans" was built at Pittsburgh. The "New Orleans" was 138 by 26½ feet, burned wood, and cost $38,000. Whether it was a side- or a stern-wheeler is still argued. It was launched in March 1811 and started down the river in October. On the second day it arrived at Cincinnati, where the people admired it but were not convinced that it could move upstream. The following day the vessel arrived at Louisville, where it inspired a big reception and dinner. Some of the leading citizens were taken on a short ride to demonstrate the boat's possibilities, and for the first time the skeptical were convinced that progress could be made against the current; they were impressed even though the maximum upstream speed was only about 3 miles an hour. After waiting for high water the boat shot the rapids at Louisville and continued downstream, arriving on January 10, 1812 at the city for which it was named. Its life was short, for while engaged in regular trips between New Orleans and Natchez it struck a snag and sank on July 14, 1814. Despite the briefness of its career, the "New Orleans" demonstrated the possibilities of steamboat traffic on western waters.

THE WESTERN STEAMBOAT

The advance of the steamboat was very rapid. Competition was introduced with the defeat of the Livingston-Fulton monopoly after a long court struggle. Steamboat machinery was improved so that better speeds could be maintained. The side-wheeler was common on the Ohio and the Mississippi, but the stern-wheeler was the usual boat on the narrow and winding Missouri. Keels gave way to flatbottoms, which were so necessary for western rivers. More decks were added and the decorations were elaborated. By the 1820s the river boat had reached the general form it was to maintain during succeeding decades. It navigated practically every western river as well as the Great Lakes, where the first American boat was the "Walk-in-the-Water" (1818).

Every steamboat carried its freight, machinery, and fuel at water level. The engines burned wood, producing multitudes of sparks and necessitating frequent refueling. The woodcutters' homes on the banks of the river soon became landmarks. Some of the wood was carried on board by the deck passengers, who traveled at lower rates and usually slept on the rear of the first deck. The second deck, the domain of the cabin passenger, had sleeping quarters, a dining room, a men's room and bar, and a ladies' parlor. The ladies' parlor was always in the rear—not because the ladies were considered unimportant but because the frequent explosions of the boilers in the front of the boat made the stern the safest place aboard. The top or hurricane deck was occupied by the pilothouse and the officers' quarters, and was commonly known as the texas in later years.

The cost of steamboat travel varied with the amount of competition, but tended to decrease. In 1819 a cabin passage from New Orleans to Natchez was $30, to the mouth of the Ohio $95, and to Louisville $125; the return trip from Louisville to New Orleans, being with the current, cost only $75. A deck passage was, of course, much cheaper, since such passengers furnished their own food and bedding, slept on the deck, and helped carry the wood. By 1832 the traveler could make the trip from New Orleans to St. Louis for $25 and return for $20; the deck passage either way was $5. Freight was also cheaper, with a common rate of 62.5¢ a hundred pounds from New Orleans to St. Louis in the 1830s.

Along with decreased fares went increased speeds. In 1817 the "Enterprise" made a record run of 25 days, 2 hours, and 4 minutes from New Orleans to Louisville; by 1825 the "Tecumseh" was holding the record for this trip with 8 days and 4 hours; in 1853 the "A. L. Shotwell" covered the same distance in 4 days, 9 hours, and 30 minutes. Every boat was proud of its speed and cherished any record it made. Each new record soon became common gossip up and down the river.

The effort to make new speed records was one of the many factors producing frequent accidents. Part of the trouble, however, was due to nature and not to man. Even with the most careful navigation the Ohio and the Mississippi were dangerous rivers. Snags and sawyers were omnipresent and difficult to avoid. A snag could, and often did, rip the wooden hull so that the boat would sink in a few minutes; effective snag removal did not begin until the late 1820s. In the summer and fall both rivers were low, and in a channel changed by shifting sandbars it was easy to go aground. In the spring the floods, carrying large quantities of debris, created other hazards.

Serious accidents were also caused frequently by mechanical failures. Western steamboats used dangerous, high-pressure boilers to get more power with less weight. The metal of the boilers was sometimes poor and burst under the high pressure of steam or lack of water. When the captain wanted a high speed a Negro might be ordered to sit on the safety valve to maintain an abnormally high pressure of steam—the pressure always went up, and sometimes the Negro and most of the passengers with it. Then, too, the wooden boats were highly combustible and the sparks pouring from the smoke stack often set fire to the boat. This danger was increased when greater speed was obtained by the addition of such substances as pitch, oil, turpentine, and lard, which produced a hotter fire and more steam, but also evoked a greater shower of sparks.

Another common cause of accidents was racing, carried on for the most part by the sporting southern element. Each captain considered his own boat the best on the river, and when rival claimants met they frequently tested the merits of their respective crafts. Some of these races were accidental encounters, but some were planned long in advance, with each captain placing a wager on his own boat. The races were particularly spectacular at night, the lights of the two steamers showing against the blackness of the surrounding darkness, and the open furnace doors bringing into strong relief the muscular bodies of the firemen, stripped to the waist, as they rushed wood to the insatiable fires. The engines roared, the paddles churned, whistles shrieked, and the passengers gathered at the rail to lay odds on the outcome. Masses of sparks shot out of the funnels as heavy black smoke indicated the addition of lard or turpentine. Not infrequently the boat would catch fire or the boilers would burst from the increased pressure, and the spectacle would end in tragedy.

The most noted race of them all came after the Civil War (1870), when the "Robert E. Lee" and the "Natchez" sped up the river from New Orleans to St. Louis. The "Lee" stripped for action, had made special preparations for refueling, with the result that it won the race even though the "Natchez" was probably the faster boat under ordinary conditions. Mile after mile they raced neck and neck, their progress followed all over the country by telegraphic dispatches. They arrived at St. Louis within a few minutes of each other, having covered the 1278 miles in 3 days, 8 hours, and 14 minutes, or at an average speed of 14⅙ miles per hour, including stops.

The possibilities of disaster were illustrated in a few of the more notable accidents of the time. The "Brandywine," while racing 30 miles above Memphis on April 9, 1832, caught fire and a hundred people were lost. The "Ben Sherrod" was racing the "Prairie" on May 8, 1837, when it caught fire, and shortly later its boilers, together with some gunpowder and liquor in the cargo, exploded; the "Prairie" failed to stop to rescue the survivors, and some two hundred people lost their lives. The "Moselle" was just leaving Cincinnati on April 25, 1838, to race down the river against time when all four of its boilers burst simultaneously, throwing bodies and debris a quarter of a mile; there were eighty-nine known dead and fifty-one missing.

The height of the steamboat business came during the 1850s, at which time the Mississippi and the Ohio were the most important rivers, although the Missouri and other tributaries carried some part of the business. This was the period of huge, many-decked boats embellished with gingerbread scrollwork and bright paint. Rich carpets covered the floors and elaborate glass chandeliers multiplied the brilliance of the many lights, while luxurious furniture rivaled that of the best hotels in the land. Excellent food was prepared by a corps of cooks and served by a host of well-trained black waiters. Elaborate bars and long wine lists were provided for convivial guests. Orchestras and brass bands added the romance of gay music to the scene. After the Civil War the splendor of the steamboat waned as the traffic on which it was based was diverted rapidly to the expanding railroads and taken directly to the East.

The development of the steamboat during and after the 1820s made it the home of many activities that in an earlier time had been confined entirely to dry land. Photographers bought their own boats and worked the river towns. Patent-medicine vendors followed a similar procedure in presenting vaudeville acts as part of the sales pitches for their nostrums. Gamblers, saloonkeepers, and prostitutes also took to the river, either running their own boats or exploiting the opportunities available on regular commercial craft. "Showboats," with the dulcet strains of their calliopes and their bright lights beckoning, brought to many river towns their only touch of the drama; in spite of the smallness of the showboat theater and the poorness of the players, the showboat filled a very real need in the emotional life of the West. Even preachers sometimes navigated their own boats to bring salvation to the river population—which certainly needed it if any group ever did. Add to these itinerants the immigrant, the migratory worker, the river man, and all the other people who found water transportation desirable, and the diversity and size of the river traffic can be partially understood.

BOAT CREWS

Navigation of the river boats was in the hands of comparatively well-trained and experienced men. Most skilled was the pilot, who sometimes received as much as $1000 a month. He was in absolute command of the movements of the boat except that the captain ordered the time to start and stop. The knowledge of the Mississippi pilot can be estimated justly only when it is remembered that he had to know intimately 1500 miles of the most changeable river in the world. The channel varies continually with the shifting of sand bars; even the banks and cutoffs shift. There were no lights or buoys as there are today; consequently the pilot had no guide except his own vision and experience.

The captain of the boat, frequently a part owner, was absolute master of the ship although he could not give orders to the pilot concerning navigation; he acted as host to the passengers, much as did the proprietor of an inn. Of slightly less importance was the engineer, who was absolute ruler of the machinery, obeying only the tinkling orders of the directing bell. A mate and a clerk had their chief duties in accepting and reckoning the charges on freight. A semiofficial person on most boats was the barkeeper, who usually made good profits by operating his bar as a concession. In early days simple drinks were favored, with whiskey ranking first and the mint julep second in popular favor, but later times brought more elaborate concoctions. Possibly also to be considered semiofficial were the professional gamblers who traveled on many boats; not infrequently they paid part of their profits to the captain.

Roustabouts did the common labor of cleaning the boat, carrying the wood, stoking the furnace, and loading and unloading cargo. A few of them were old river men who had drifted to the steamboats when the slower-moving vessels were driven off the rivers, and there were considerable numbers of Irish immigrants who were employed during the 1830s and later. By far the largest group, however, and the one that eventually monopolized this kind of work was the Negro. Happy and carefree, the Negro gave much of the tone to the life of the river, and, like preceding boatmen, left a permanent record with his folklore, poetry, and songs.

READINGS

GENERAL. By far the best account of transportational developments, although not limited to the West, is George R. Taylor, *The Transportation Revolution* (1951). Other useful accounts include Seymour Dunbar, *A History of Travel in America* (1937); Archer B. Hulbert, *The Paths of Inland Commerce* (1920); Charles H. Ambler, *A History of Transportation in the Ohio Valley* (1932), detailed; Everett Dick, *Vanguards of the Frontier* (1941), west of the Mississippi; Ulrich B. Phillips, *A History of Transportation in the Eastern Cotton Belt to 1860* (1908). State and regional histories normally deal with transportation; for them, see the Readings for Chapters 6 and 13. See also Leland D. Baldwin, *Pittsburgh* (1937), which is very good.

ROADS. Philip D. Jordan, *The National Road* (1948), good in every way; Jonathan Daniels, *The Devil's Backbone* (1962), episodical on Natchez Trace; Norris F. Schneider, *Y Bridge City* (1950), good on Zane's Trace; Alvin F. Harlow, *Old Post Bags* (1928), on mail.

WATER TRANSPORTATION. General accounts, including more than the West, are Fred E. Dayton, *Steamboat Days* (1925), detailed; Garnett L. Eskew, *The Pageant of the Packets* (1929). Presteamboat transportation is described excellently in Leland D. Baldwin, *The Keelboat Age on Western Waters* (1941). Early river men appear in Walter Blair and Franklin J. Meine, *Mike Fink* (1933) and their *Half Horse, Half Alligator* (1956). Ohio River outlaws are described in Otto A. Rothert, *The Outlaws of Cave-in-Rock* (1924).

STEAMBOATS. By far the best account is Louis C. Hunter, *Steamboats on the Western Rivers* (1949). Emphasizing the Mississippi are Herbert and Edward Quick, *Mississippi Steamboatin'* (1926), somewhat fictional; Lyle Saxon, *Father Mississippi* (1927), with many quotations; Florence L. Dorsey, *Master of the Mississippi: Henry Shreve* (1941), readable; Philip Graham, *Showboats* (1951), good; William J. Peterson, *Steamboating on the Upper Mississippi* (1937). For the Missouri the classic account is Henry M. Chittenden, *A History of Early Steamboat Navigation on the Missouri River* (2 vols., 1903), but easier to read are Stanley Vestal, *The Missouri* (1945) and Joseph M. Hanson, *The Conquest of the Missouri* (1946), centering around one man. More recent is William E. Lass, *A History of Steamboating on the Upper Missouri River* (1962). For the Great Lakes see Harlan Hatcher, *The Great Lakes* (1944) and Milo M. Quaife, *Lake Michigan* (1944).

CHAPTER **16**

CANAL BARGE AND
RAILROAD LOCOMOTIVE

T he desire for improved transportation gripped nearly all Americans. Westerners were sure that lower freight rates would give them profitable access to eastern markets. Easterners felt equally sure that better communications would open profitable markets for their own products. Although these ideas of economic salvation were not realized in their rosiest forms, there is no question that improved transportation was profitable for the entire country. A whole series of enthusiasms swept across the country. Improved roads helped a little. Steamboats were fine, but limited by the availability of navigable rivers; certainly no rivers connected East and West. In consequence, enthusiasm turned to new possibilities, first canals, and then railroads.

EASTERN PLANS

Eastern merchants were emphatically unanimous in favoring improved transportation to the West, but completely at odds over routes. Each seaboard town from Maine to Florida had its own dream of a route that would make it great and opulent. Most of these dreams were shattered when the federal government gave Baltimore the nod for the National Road. Rival cities groaned unhappily, for even if they could raise the necessary money their own routes would be less attractive; for example, Boston and Charleston were almost hopeless. New York and Philadelphia both had roads to the West, but neither merited any boasting. Even Baltimore itself was not completely happy: it realized that high stage and wagon rates were sending business down the Mississippi, with New Orleans in real competition to become the leading American port. In fact, all eastern cities realized that improved roads were not the complete answer to the problem.

The great transportation innovation of the 1820s and 1830s was the canal, which seemed at the time the ultimate achievement. The canal would move traffic smoothly and cheaply, and each community closed its eyes to inconvenient if not insuperable obstacles and dreamed of itself as the center of a national network of canals. The wilder enthusiasts vapored about canals linking navigable bodies of water to connect the Atlantic and the Pacific, ignoring such obstacles as the Rocky Mountains. Public-spirited citizens gave and solicited funds, governments helped, and even the loafer at the grog shop came to speak learnedly of locks and water levels. This excessive enthusiasm ultimately was squelched by the panic of 1837. When men recovered a measure of their financial stability, their eyes turned toward the newer railroads.

NEW YORK'S PRIMACY

The canal that fanned a small blaze of enthusiasm into a holocaust of forest fire dimensions was the Erie Canal, the greatest engineering project of its day. Here was a canal, 364 miles long, to connect the Hudson River with Lake Erie at a time when all the canals of the United States covered less than 10 percent of this distance. It was to run through a wilderness with no existing traffic along much of its route and little available from farther west. Financing was a problem in itself. Moreover, workers were difficult to obtain, even with the newly arrived Irish immigrants, and at times, fever and ague almost brought work to a stop. The many people who chuckled sardonically at this visionary plan were far from stupid.

The Erie Canal was begun at Fort Stanwix (Rome) in 1817 and was opened for traffic in 1825. The opening was marked by a tour of Governor De Witt Clinton and his party from Buffalo to Albany, and then by steamship to New York. Each town along the way celebrated with parades, bands, dinners, speeches, toasts, and fireworks. Finally at New York City, on November 4, 1825, a keg of Lake Erie water was emptied into the Atlantic Ocean to symbolize the wedding of those two bodies of water.

The Erie Canal was in some ways unimpressive, being little more than a large ditch, forty feet wide at the top, twenty-eight feet at the bottom, and four feet deep. Locks were only ninety by twelve feet, which meant that the largest boat they could handle could carry only about a hundred tons of freight. And yet the effects of the Erie Canal were almost incalculable, exceeding the hopes of its most ardent supporters. It was significant in the development of central and western New York, being directly responsible for such cities as Herkimer, Utica, Syracuse, and Lockport. Buffalo grew mightily, particularly with the harbor improvements that

Canals and Canalized Rivers, 1850

began in the 1820s. The canal was also vitally important in the early growth of the Great Lakes country, including Michigan, Wisconsin, Minnesota, Iowa, and northern Ohio, Indiana, and Illinois. It brought an immense amount of business to New York City, thus helping vitally in producing the supremacy of that port. Almost at once its facilities were overtaxed, and enlargement began within a decade of the opening. For a visionary scheme it had decidedly practical results.

PHILADELPHIA COMPETES

Philadelphia viewed with apprehension and alarm the building of the Erie Canal by its chief commercial rival, New York. Rather despairingly, Pennsylvania made a survey (1824–1825) of possible water routes across the state, but even the strongest optimism could not carry water across the mountains. The ultimate solution was a marvelous combination of canals, inclined planes, and newfangled railroads. Work was started in 1826 and completed in 1834, with the state shouldering the entire cost of $13,500,000, or almost twice that of the Erie Canal.

The Pennsylvania System was a mechanical marvel that attracted visitors in large numbers. In general its route was that of the later Pennsylvania Railroad. From Philadelphia to Columbia on the Susquehanna was one of the nation's early railroads, with the heavy grade at either end surmounted by an inclined plane on which the cars were raised and lowered by a rope attached to a stationary engine; in the early years horses were used to move the cars on level stretches. From Columbia a canal with 18 dams, 33 aqueducts, and 101 locks followed the Susquehanna and Juniata rivers to Hollidaysburg. The mountains of the next 37 miles were surmounted by inclined planes with stationary engines; between the mountains were stagecoaches, which were soon replaced by horse-drawn railroad cars, which were in turn replaced by steam locomotives. At Johnstown the traveler again boarded a canal boat that encountered 64 locks, 10 dams, 2 tunnels, and 16 aqueducts before it arrived at Pittsburgh. The total length was 363 miles.

The Pennsylvania System was exceedingly ingenious but not very practical. High costs of building and maintenance necessitated high rates, while the speed was not impressive. Improvement came with the introduction of sectional canal boats that could be loaded piecemeal on railroad cars, but this improvement was not enough. Income was inadequate to maintain the interest on the bonds the state had issued for its construction, and the state was delighted to turn over the whole white elephant to the Pennsylvania Railroad, which was chartered in 1846.

OTHER EASTERN CITIES

The Baltimore area also was worried by the Erie Canal, and consequently chartered the Chesapeake and Ohio Canal (Virginia in 1824, Maryland in 1825) to connect the navigable portions of the Potomac and Ohio rivers. The project was considered so important that President Adams threw the first shovel of dirt on July 4, 1828. Unfortunately the work progressed so slowly, that Cumberland was not reached until 1850, and there the work stopped permanently. As a delayed and only partially completed project it was never financially successful.

Other cities could show even less success. Boston could never imagine how to run a canal across the Berkshires. Richmond managed to inspire a canal as far as Lynchburg, but plans to cross the mountains to the Kanawha River never materialized. Charleston toyed with the idea of a canal to the Mississippi Valley, but got no further than talking. By the 1830s it was clear that the only city to gain through canals was New York, which in turn meant that every competitior looked anxiously for any form of transportation that would surpass canals. In time the answer was railroads.

WESTERN PLANS

Eastern canal enthusiasm was no greater than that displayed by the West. Each western community saw one or more canals as its outstanding chance for future greatness and wealth. Although every town with any imagination saw itself as the center of a vast network of canals, the principal planned projects were designed to connect the Great Lakes with the Ohio-Mississippi system. Involved would be eastern connections that already existed with New York, could easily be made with Philadelphia by way of the Pennsylvania System, and with Baltimore by way of the Chesapeake and Ohio Canal if it were ever completed. What was sought was an easy and cheap flow of goods between the East and most of the West.

The overwhelming difficulty facing the West was a lack of funds with which to build canals. Individual subscribers were solicited successfully, but were frequently too optimistic in their subscriptions, and in any case were not wealthy. States borrowed freely, but their credit was limited. The federal government received earnest appeals. When Henry Clay proposed federal help for internal improvements as part of his American System, he was expressing the opinion of much of the West. Unfortunately both Madison and Monroe had constitutional scruples about using federal money for local projects. Adams was more generous, and considerable aid was given during his administration. Jackson, too, had constitutional scruples, as shown in his Maysville veto (1830), but was quite willing to approve bills that were interstate in their application and hence to his mind were constitutional.

Western canal building was also limited by the very enthusiasm that characterized it. Each community was certain that its future prosperity depended on having canal facilities and, realizing the limited nature of the funds available, opposed any project not immediately to its own benefit. The obvious way to obtain action was to combine several plans in a single proposal, closing one's eyes to the financing and sometimes even to the necessary water. The existence of too many projects made delay inevitable in completing any one of them.

OHIO

The first western state to build canals was naturally Ohio, the most populous. Inspired by the building of the Erie Canal, Ohio investigated (1822–1825) possible routes, mostly to connect Lake Erie and the Ohio River. Two canals were authorized in 1825. The first was to run from Portsmouth on the Ohio north along the Scioto, east to the Muskingum, and then follow the Muskingum and Cuyahoga to Cleveland. The second was to follow the historic Maumee-Miami route from Cincinnati on the

Ohio to Toledo on Maumee Bay; largely because of this project Ohio was willing a little later to fight a war (see Chapter 17) for the possession of Toledo. These plans represented a magnificent gamble in view of their estimated cost of $5,700,000, which was approximately a tenth of the value of all taxable property in the state, and even the most optimistic knew that actual costs always ran higher than estimated.

The work on the Scioto-Muskingum route, commonly called the Ohio Canal, began on July 4, 1825. Governor De Witt Clinton of New York came west to help celebrate the occasion by digging the first spadeful of dirt at Licking Summit, near Newark. Labor was scarce, but by November 2000 men were at work; German and Irish immigrants were imported to keep the labor supply from diminishing in size or increasing in price. Preliminary cost estimates were found to be too low, and some of the contractors absconded; in spite of such setbacks the whole 333-mile project from Cleveland to Portsmouth was completed in 1832. It had approximately the dimensions of the Erie Canal, and on the whole was built both well and cheaply.

The other Ohio project, commonly known as the Miami Canal, was also begun in 1825. It was opened from Cincinnati to Dayton in 1829, after which work went more slowly because the Ohio Canal was considered more important. The Miami Canal was finally completed to Lake Erie and opened for traffic in 1845. In addition to these two state projects there were several private ventures, some of which were aided by the state. None was very important.

INDIANA

Indiana, like Ohio, had canal schemes before 1820, but they did not assume vital importance until after Ohio began work. All the difficulties hampering Ohio were magnified in Indiana because Indiana had fewer people and less wealth; the total taxes collected in Indiana in 1827 were $33,000. Congress gave some slight assistance through its land grant of 1827, but main dependence was placed on a $15 million state bond issue. Of this imposing sum, about $2 million was embezzled, $4 million was lost in worthless securities, and much of the remainder was frittered away.

The principal route upon which the Hoosiers looked with favor was from the navigable portion of the Wabash northeast to Lake Erie near Toledo—another historic portage route. A small part of the route lay within Ohio, which gave permission in 1829 to build, and then backed out of her agreement and had to be repersuaded. Work was begun in 1832, but was bungled from the beginning. Money was spent haphazardly, management was inefficient, and the Irish laborers were continually embroiled in fights between the partisans of Northern and Southern Ireland.

In spite of these various troubles, the Wabash and Erie Canal was finished in 1842 and opened the next year from Lafayette to Toledo, 215 miles. Work was then pushed south, so that by 1853 boats could go all the way to Evansville. Several other projects were complete failures, but for a time in the early 1850s the main canal carried much traffic, while the Whitewater Canal in southeast Indiana was a fair success. Business then declined, particularly with the opening of the Wabash Railroad in 1856. The floods of 1875 stopped all traffic and the canal was never repaired.

OTHER WESTERN CANALS

Illinois also had its pet project in the Illinois and Michigan Canal, designed to connect Lake Michigan with the navigable portion of the Illinois River. The idea was old, but not until 1820 was the route surveyed and a tract of land donated by Congress. One of the results of the surveys was the plotting of the town of Chicago near Fort Dearborn in 1830. Actual construction of the canal began in 1836, and it was opened for use twelve years later.

These four canals in the states immediately north of the Ohio River were the most important projects completed in the West. Of the smaller canals, most significant were the two miles of the Louisville and Portland around the falls of the Ohio at Louisville; it proved moderately profitable after its opening in 1830. A modest original investment by the federal government grew to complete control by 1874. Other minor enterprises ranged from the portage canal at Portage, Wisconsin, built in the 1840s, to a number of waterways in the vicinity of New Orleans. For every canal built there were a hundred plans for others, and every western state toyed with at least eight or ten projects that it considered important.

Most of the canals completed between 1820 and 1840 were in the Northwest rather than in the Southwest. The sparser population and lesser wealth of the South had their effect, as well as the prevalence of the plantation system, which eliminated the urban centers so necessary for canal promotion. Furthermore, the rivers of the South were more navigable than those of the North, being frequently slow and deep, and allowing steamboat navigation practically to the front door of the plantation.

CANAL TRAFFIC

To the modern observer the outstanding characteristic of canal traffic was its slowness, for the usual speed was between 2 and 4 miles an hour. This leisurely pace was satisfactory for the transportation of heavy nonperishable freight to a fairly stable market, but was not so desirable for most other cargoes. Passengers were reasonably comfortable, at least as compared with travel on a stagecoach, and those who were interested in the country through which they passed had plenty of time to enjoy the scenery.

Most canal boats were painted in bright colors, and, except for those devoted entirely to freight, could be classified as either line boats or packets. The line boat carried only local traffic and did not provide sleeping accommodations; the usual charge was 1 cent a mile without food and 2 cents with food. The packet was larger and finer. It furnished both food and bed, and traveled both night and day, so that it could cover some hundred miles a day. The cost, including food, was about 5 cents a mile, which was much less than the rate charged by the stages.

Boats carrying passengers were arranged somewhat alike. In the front was a tiny cabin with five or six bunks for the crew. Next came a small room used by the women for washing and dressing. Then there was a women's cabin, where the lady traveler could retire from the prying eyes of the male passengers, and where all the women slept at night. In the center of the boat was a large central apartment, which might be as long as 45 feet. In the day it was used as a general assembly room in which the passengers could entertain themselves or doze, and in which smaller parcels were kept (the larger baggage was stacked in deck). Here meals were served on planks supported by wooden trestles. At night the cabin served as the sleeping quarters for the men. Bunks were suspended on iron brackets, of which the ends on one side were pushed into the wall and on the other hung by ropes from the ceiling. Such shelves were each 6 by 3½ feet, and were arranged in tiers of three so that there was very little room between them. When all the bunks were filled the surplus men slept on the tables or floor. Small straw mattresses and filthy blankets completed the equipment; these bedclothes were piled in a corner of the room in the daytime and were seldom washed. Behind the large room were a bar and the kitchen; the cook generally doubled as bartender, and worked both day and night. The usual crew consisted of a captain, two steersmen, two drivers, and a cook; the drivers and steersmen alternated in 6-hour shifts. Just which of these dignitaries had any duty in caring for the wants of the passengers is not clear.

Most of the passengers spent the fine days on deck, talking, playing games, sewing, reading, painting. From time to time some would get off the boat and obtain exercise by walking along the towpath and chatting with the driver. The principal hazard of deck travel was the bridges, which were encountered every mile in some areas and still more frequently in the towns; these bridges were so low that everyone had to duck to avoid being knocked into the water. On bad days most people went below to the cabin, which was close and stuffy under the best conditions, and almost insupportable in warm weather. Ventilation was unknown, and some of the travelers preferred the rain to the cabin. Some of the passengers might be highly objectionable to the others, for standards of personal cleanliness were not always high. Sometimes a traveling minister would seize the opportunity presented by a captive audience to hold a religious meeting.

One of the amusements of canal boat travel was to watch the manipulation of the vessel, which was usually drawn by one to three horses or mules. The towpath was on only one side of the canal and so when two boats met, one of them would let its towline go slack so that the other could pass over. When the towpath crossed the water, considerable agility was necessary on the part of horse and driver. The horse would first go under the bridge and then gallop over it to arrive on the other side of the canal before all the slack of the line was taken up by the drift of the boat. Now and then a horse was too slow and was pulled into the water. Mules found a bridge a disastrous place on which to balk.

The canal was an exceedingly important factor in the development of the West, even though its period of dominance was brief. It afforded cheap and safe, although slow, transportation. Even when canals did not show a profit they helped to advance the economic well-being of the communities they served. Prices for farm products improved while the cost of imported articles decreased. Many towns traced the beginnings of their commercial importance to the influence of the canal.

One of the greatest services of the canals was to bring population into new areas. Often their very construction brought settlements of canal employees along their banks. When completed they attracted more people because of the improved transportational facilities, which involved an increase of land values. They carried thousands of settlers to the West, increasing the flow of migration with their promise of better transportation.

As with similar enthusiasms, the canal mania was carried to excess. Plans were always greater than the completed projects. More work was started than could be finished. Excessive loans were floated to complete waterways that had no chance of financial success. Many canals were built far in advance of any possible usefulness. The overexpansion helped to produce the financial panic of 1837 from which the canals never recovered.

The desire for canals represented the peak of a movement for better transportation that included all types of internal improvements. The emphasis was placed on canals because they were the latest and most desired form of transportation. Other projects, such as building roads, removing obstacles from the rivers, marking river channels, and placing lighthouses and buoys on the lakes, also received sympathy and support. While the canal was at the height of its popularity an even newer idea found expression in the first experimentation with railroads. Eventually the railroad overshadowed its predecessor.

RAILROADS APPEAR

The transportation innovation of the late 1820s was the railroad, but most Americans had only the vaguest idea, if any, of what it was. Here and there a mining tramway existed, but the story is told that when the people of Baltimore first decided to build a railroad they sent a man to Europe to discover what it was. The attractiveness of the idea is easy to understand. Here was a new means of transportation that could be used anywhere, regardless of mountains or water supply, and that would permit a horse to draw a larger load more rapidly than was possible on a regular road.

The difficulties of building railroads in the United States were intimidating. Distances were tremendous, and there were few concentrations of population so desirable for successful railroads. Costs of construction far exceeded those of roads and canals, and no one could conceive that it would be profitable to parallel such a body of water as the Hudson River. Methods of construction involved speculations that ranged from the permanence of granite blocks to the resilience of wooden trestles. The tracks themselves were first made of wood, which was then topped by iron strips. Later they were replaced by completely iron rails of various designs; a steel rail was too expensive to use until after the Civil War, when the cost of steel declined. Even the width, or gauge, of the track was a subject for argument, with preferences ranging from 3 feet 6 inches to 6 feet. In addition to differences in gauges were variations in time standards—standard time was not adopted until the 1880s—and it is easy to understand why the interchange of traffic between railroads was impossible, and why even passenger connections were difficult.

Equipment was also a matter of uncertainty. Some of the cars at first resembled stagecoaches, but soon became more like oblong boxes. Such matters as specialized cars, brakes, signaling devices, lighting, and heating were unsolved problems. Even motive power was a question mark. The first engine was a horse, used now and then on a treadmill inside the car, but other devices, including sails, were tried. Obviously the final solution was the steam locomotive, with the first one a stationary engine on a flat car, and subject to such frequent breakdowns that many people thought a horse would be more satisfactory. The development of an effective steam locomotive was far from a simple problem. In short, the amazing thing about early American railroads is not the slowness but the rapidity with which they were built.

BUILDING FROM EAST TO WEST

Quite naturally the eastern cities, aspiring eagerly for western business, looked hopefully at the new gadget. First to enter the competition was Baltimore, which saw the National Road being outmoded, and quite properly had little hopes for the Chesapeake and Ohio Canal, which did no more than provide a branch line for the city. On the same day that President Adams inaugurated work on the Chesapeake and Ohio Canal (July 4, 1828) the venerable Charles Carroll of Carrollton, last surviving singer of the Declaration of Independence, performed a similar service for the Baltimore and Ohio Railroad, which was designed to reach the Ohio River and thus bring western business to Baltimore. Its first few miles of track, opening the following year, inaugurated commercial railroading in the United States, but were attractive mainly to travelers who enjoyed the novel ride. Construction proceeded slowly, but by 1853 the Baltimore and Ohio had reached the Ohio River near Wheeling.

Other cities that had suffered, but not in silence, as they saw western business moving toward New York on the Erie Canal, also picked up hope. Charleston, although remote from the Ohio Valley, was inspired to speculate that it could at least short circuit a share of the western business that was floating down the Savannah River. The Charleston and Hamburg Railroad was built to the Savannah River, and when its 136 miles were opened in 1833 it was the world's longest railroad under single management. To the north, Boston revived its hopes of being a terminus for western business and built westward through Worcester, opening a line as far as Albany in 1841. Unfortunately there was no bridge at Albany, and most shippers and travelers preferred steaming down the Hudson to bumping over the mountains to Boston.

Philadelphia was in a difficult situation when railroads entered the picture. With the construction of the Pennsylvania System the state had strained its resources beyond the breaking point and had no funds to replace the canal system, even though realizing that it was losing in the competition for western business. The ultimate solution was to charter the Pennsylvania Railroad in 1846 and turn over to it the old canal property. By combining railroads already in existence and adding others, the Pennsylvania Railroad was able to open its complete line to Pittsburgh in 1852, at the same time looking to expansion as far as the growing metropolis of Chicago.

New York was slowed in its railroad construction by the excellence of its water facilities. By 1842 seven independent railroad lines paralleled the Erie Canal, their main advantages speed and the fact that they did not freeze in winter. Their drawbacks were that they were not well run and that the connections between them were bad. No railroad paralleled the

Railroads, 1860

Hudson River until 1851. The small lines through central New York State united in 1853 to form the origin of the present New York Central. In addition, the Erie Railroad completed its line through the southern tier of New York counties to Lake Erie in 1851; so that New York had two railroad outlets for western business.

WESTERN RAILROAD HOPES

The West contracted the eastern railroad enthusiasm in a virulent form. Western optimists envisioned their economic salvation if only their local communities could receive the new form of transportation. Whereas steamboats were limited to navigable rivers, and canals to available water supplies, now every town could hope to be on a railroad. Even a community in the middle of the prairie might entertain the beautiful picture of itself as an important railroad center.

The main problem of the West in building railroads, as it had been in building canals, was money. Individual subscribers had much enthusiasm but little capital, and bankers, including those of the East and of Europe, were properly suspicious of large investments where traffic was mainly a gleam in the eyes of speculators. Even a partial exemption from taxation, as promised by Ohio, produced no rush to buy railroad stocks and bonds. As for the federal government, it remained hobbled by current interpretation of the Constitution, and before 1850 the best it could do for western railroads was to lower the import duties on iron used for rails.

Local and state governments did the best they could for their electorates. Local governments frequently bought railroad stocks and bonds, and even more frequently provided lands for depots and yards; after all, they were vitally interested in obtaining railroad facilities. Some states— for example, Georgia and Michigan—built and operated their own railroads that they later sold to private groups, often at very low prices. Railroads were included in a number of general acts designed to promote construction of internal improvements. An Ohio law of 1837 permitted the state to purchase a third of the capital stock of any railroad after the other two thirds had been subscribed by private parties; promoters found such "subscriptions" easy, and ultimately made off with some $3 million. An Indiana law of 1836 brought great state expenditures but produced only a few miles of grading. An Illinois law of 1837 projected some 1300 miles of railroads, which would have reached practically every crossroad in the state, but brought negligible results. Such plans were a mistake as viewed with later knowledge, but they were in accord with the actions of eastern states, to say nothing of later western states beyond the Mississippi. The newer West may well have been particularly optimistic, but it still followed the general American pattern.

The plans of the 1830s had little practical effect, with only a few random miles here and there, as in Michigan, Kentucky, and Louisiana. Then followed the depression starting in 1837, and even aspiring Westerners shelved their plans. One traveler in Illinois in 1845 described that state's longest railroad in this fashion: "This rail-road . . . is another of the links of that endless chain that was to bind the State in love together, but has bound them in debt forever. It is already so dilapidated that mules have been substituted for locomotives, and as it fails to pay expenses, it must shortly go out of business for want of repairs."

HOPES REALIZED

When prosperity returned in the 1840s the West was ready to embark on a vast program of railroad building that was not to slow down until the depression of 1857. The North had a greater concentration of population, including cities, than the South, and hence did more building of railroads, but both sections of the country eagerly threw their resources into expanding their networks. At the outbreak of the Civil War Ohio was said to be better covered with railroads than ony other state in the Union.

Some of the newly built railroads were designed to connect the larger cities, although, from the standpoint of the farmers, the feeder lines were equally important, since any long wagon haul of corn or wheat or cotton was economically impractical. Examples of such roads were those between Springfield and Sandusky, Ohio (1848), Cleveland and Cincinnati (1850), and Louisville and Nashville (1859). Each city, of course, was anxious to become the center of as many lines as possible. Here was the real chance for such a place as Indianapolis, which depended on road travel. Here also was the opportunity for bustling, aggressive Chicago, which had less than 5000 residents in 1840, under 30,000 in 1850, and then jumped in the next decade to 109,000. One of the reasons for the growth of Chicago was the spiderweb of so-called granger roads—the Chicago & Northwestern; the Chicago, Rock Island & Pacific; and the Chicago, Burlington & Quincy. The Rock Island was the first to reach the Mississippi (1854) and to bridge it (1855). In contrast, the city of St. Louis continued to depend more on the river and hence gradually lost ground to its ambitious Lake Michigan rival. The injury to river business of the Civil War was a hard blow; by 1870 Chicago population almost equaled that of St. Louis, and within another decade had far surpassed it.

EAST-WEST CONNECTIONS

Probably more important than the connecting of large towns was the completion of through lines from the east coast to the Mississippi. Such connections were made in the 1850s, although frequently a particular route would not be under a single management. The completion of the Michigan Central and the Michigan Southern across Michigan to Chicago in 1852, plus the building of the Lake Shore to the east (1854) and the Rock Island to the Mississippi gave both the New York Central and the Erie railroads the connections by which freight might be carried entirely by rail from the Atlantic to the Mississippi. The Pennsylvania opened its complete line to Chicago in 1853; the Baltimore & Ohio made connections with St. Louis shortly afterward.

While several lines were traversing the North, the South was having more difficulty, even though the merchants of Charleston, Richmond, and other such cities were as eager for railroads as were their northern counterparts. With tremendous labor a series of connecting roads was finally completed from Charleston through Hamburg, Atlanta, and Chattanooga to Memphis; the final connection was made in 1857. Farther south a line was being built from Savannah through Macon, Columbia, and Montgomery to Vicksburg, but it was not completed before the outbreak of the Civil War.

The importance of railroads to the outcome of the Civil War was considerable and obvious. The North was well served in bringing raw material from the West with the New York Central, Erie, Pennsylvania, and Baltimore & Ohio, even though much effort was necessary to keep the eastern terminus of the Baltimore & Ohio in northern hands. The one southern line suffered in comparison and grew worse as railroad iron and equipment became almost impossible to obtain. The Sherman campaign, which was extremely injurious to the southern cause, was railroad-inspired.

In long-run terms the South also suffered. The corn and wheat of the Northwest, the bulk of which had formerly moved down the river to New Orleans, went increasingly by railroad to northeastern ports. New Orleans, which had outcompeted even New York in 1840, began to fade. The North had not only better transportation but also better markets, as a result of its growing cities and its improved connections with Europe.

ILLINOIS CENTRAL

One western railroad, the Illinois Central, deserves special mention because of its sectional implications and because it gave a preview of conditions and problems that were later to become widespread. The Illinois Central represented the culmination of an old movement to build north and south in Illinois, say, from Galena to Cairo. As usual, funds were lacking, and appeals were made to the federal government. When Stephen A. Douglas entered the Senate in 1847 he sponsored such a line with personal motives that were both political and economic. Intensive logrolling brought an expansion of the plan to carry the railroad to Mobile to attract southern support. The reward for the Douglas political astuteness was a federal law of 1850 by which alternate sections of land within six miles of the track went to a railroad that was to originate somewhere between Galena and Chicago and run to Mobile; actually the northern terminus became Chicago. The grant was in fact made to the two states, Illinois and Alabama, since there was no public land in the intervening states.

Illinois chartered the Illinois Central in 1851 and transferred to it the federal land grant, while providing that in lieu of taxes the state should receive 5 percent of the gross operating revenue of the railroad—a very profitable deal for the state. Work started immediately and was pushed strenuously because there was a time limit beyond which the road would not get the land grant. The difficulties of construction were immense: both labor and railroad iron were imported from Europe, and the labor camps were characterized by drunkenness, rowdyism, and sickness; a cholera epidemic was particularly disheartening. In spite of these troubles the road was completed, and completed well, to Cairo in 1856, at which time George B. McClellan was the chief engineer.

The land for the Illinois Central was acquired and sold as rapidly as possible. Under the terms of the grant the railroad had to wait for its land until the government had sold its alternate sections at $2.50 an acre, or twice the usual minimum price. As each section of the road was completed and as the government sold its land, the railroad received its grant, with the first installment coming in 1854. The land was advertised widely both in the United States and in Europe. It was sold at prices that averaged about $10 an acre and on fairly liberal credit terms. Considering the costs of sale and the difficulties of collection, prices were quite moderate. Soon settlers were flowing into the area, with such towns as Champagne and Centralia booming. The most important aspect of the Illinois Central grant, however, was that it opened the way to future federal grants, first to states, and then to individual railroads. The pattern of at least part of the future had emerged.

READINGS

GENERAL. See references listed in the Readings for Chapter 15.

CANALS. Alvin F. Harlow, *Old Towpaths* (1926) and Madeline S. Waggoner, *The Long Haul West* (1958) read easily. More limited are Ernest L. Bogart, *Internal Improvements and State Debt in Ohio* (1924); James W. Putnam, *The Illinois and Michigan Canal* (1918); Harlan Hatcher, *The Great Lakes* (1944) and *The Western Reserve* (1949), covering the Ohio Canal; Grace L. Nute, *Lake Superior* (1944), describing the Sault Canal. Noble E. Whitford, *History of the Canal System of the State of New York* (2 vols., 1906), is comprehensive. James W. Livingood, *The Pennsylvania-Baltimore Trade Rivalry 1780–1860* (1947) is excellent.

RAILROADS. The best brief, general railroad history is John F. Stover, *American Railroads* (1961). See also John W. Starr, *One Hundred Years of American Railroading* (1928); Stewart Holbrook, *The Story of American Railroads* (1947); and Martin D. Stevers, *Steel Rails* (1933). Ulrich B. Phillips, *A History of Transportation in the Eastern Cotton Belt to 1860* (1908) needs revision. Stanley J. Folmsbee, *Section-*

alism and Internal Improvements in Tennessee (1939) is satisfactory. For the Illinois Central see Carlton J. Corliss, *Main Line of Mid America* (1950) ; Paul W. Gates, *Illinois Central Railroad and Its Colonization Work* (1934), a careful study; Howard G. Brownson, *The History of the Illinois Central Railroad to 1870* (1916). For the main eastern roads see George H. Burgess and Miles C. Kennedy, *Centennial History of the Pennsylvania Railroad Company* (1949) ; Samuel M. Derrick, *Centennial History of the South Carolina Railroad* (1930) ; Edward Hungerford, *Men and Iron: The History of the New York Central* (1938), *Men of Erie* (1946), and *The Story of the Baltimore & Ohio Railroad* (2 vols., 1928) ; Charles W. Turner, *Chessie's Road* (1956), the Chesapeake & Ohio.

CHAPTER 17

A DELUGE OF PEOPLE

T he flood of settlers that had ebbed after the panic of 1819 again swelled to magnificent proportions during the prosperous period of the late 1820s and early 1830s. The land sales of one year, 1835, were over 12 million acres, or twice as much as those for any previous year; the year 1836 registered sales of 20 million acres. Then history repeated itself as the flood of arrivals receded with the panic of 1837.

The trans-Appalachian West grew rapidly, not only in absolute numbers, but also in comparison with the remainder of the United States. The West's 2.2 million in 1820 became 3.7 million by 1830 and 6.4 million by 1840, a rate of growth almost twice that of the United States as a whole. Westerners in 1820 were something less than a quarter of the whole American population, but twenty years later they were a third. Ohio, Kentucky, and Tennessee, among the ten most populous states in all three census periods, were joined by Indiana in 1840.

The rapid growth of western population brought no great increase in the number of organized states and territories between 1820 and 1840. The only significant changes after the organization of the Florida Territory in 1822 were the creation of the states of Arkansas and Michigan and the territories of Wisconsin and Iowa. However, by 1840 there were eleven states west of the mountains, which together with western population gave the West a considerable power in national politics, provided it could speak with a single voice.

In spite of the increased foreign immigration of the period, the western migration of the 1820s and 1830s was composed predominantly of American-born farmers. Irish immigrants tended to stay in the East, where they worked as unskilled laborers, but a good many toiled on western roads and canals and then settled in the regions in which they had worked. An increasing flow of Germans went to the Ohio Valley and as far west as Missouri and Wisconsin, where they were joined by early Scandinavian migrants. In spite of such foreign elements, however, the American West remained largely native born.

THE OHIO VALLEY

The center of western population remained in the Ohio Valley, where lived a good half of all Westerners. Kentucky grew only moderately, but the states north of the river boomed. Ohio almost tripled between 1820 and 1840, Indiana increased more than fourfold, and Illinois over eight times; in fact Illinois tripled within the single decade of 1830–1840. Not only were the river bottoms occupied, but people pushed into the prairie land of central and northern Indiana and Illinois.

Part of the population increase of the Ohio Valley represented not an expansion of the agricultural frontier but an increase in the size of cities, since the valley contained an important share of western metropolitan centers. Pittsburgh continued to dominate the upper valley in spite of the pretensions of Wheeling, but by the 1830s its title "Gateway to the West" had lost some of its pertinence because of the completion of the National Road farther south. Pittsburgh was known increasingly as a manufacturing center. "This city of smoke and mud, and ugly pavement" was all bustle and dirt and confusion, with commercialism rampant and ambitious businessmen grabbing their meals on the run. Shipbuilding, a major industry, included the construction not only of a considerable proportion of western steamboats but also of ships destined for the ocean trade. Coal mining and iron smelting were responsible for the general pall of smoke that was the despair of housewives; reputedly Pittsburgh residents never saw white snow. Among the numerous Pittsburgh manufacturing industries were glass, rope, cotton cloth, hardware, paper, liquor, and books.

Farther down the valley were Louisville and Cincinnati, with the latter the more important. Louisville had become dominant in Kentucky, even though its commercial growth was slightly slowed by the canal that eliminated the necessity of transshipping goods around the falls of the river. The city had a varied assortment of young industries, but was most important as a distributing and shipping center. Here the state's agricultural products, particularly tobacco, were brought for shipment on the hundreds of steamboats that plied the Ohio. And here it was that the people from the back country did their shopping in the many stores of which Louisville was justly proud.

The commonly recognized "Queen of the West" was Cincinnati, seventh American city in 1830 and sixth in 1840, when its 46,000 residents displaced Charleston in the national ranking. Cincinnati was one of the

Population Density, 1830

45 AND OVER INHABITANTS PER SQUARE MILE

6-44 INHABITANTS PER SQUARE MILE

2-5 INHABITANTS PER SQUARE MILE

LESS THAN 2 INHABITANTS PER SQUARE MILE

Population Density, 1840

45 AND OVER INHABITANTS PER SQUARE MILE

6-44 INHABITANTS PER SQUARE MILE

2-5 INHABITANTS PER SQUARE MILE

LESS THAN 2 INHABITANTS PER SQUARE MILE

most attractive of western cities, with clean, paved streets bordered by trees, well-tended houses, and good stores. Most visible architecturally was "Trollope's folly," a bazaar constructed speculatively by Mrs. Frances Trollope, one of the least loved of American visitors; it exhibited Greek, Roman, and Moorish influences. Cincinnati commerce boomed, the stores were well filled, and steamboats crowded the wharves.

The principal industry of Cincinnati was pork packing, which assumed such proportions that the city was frequently dubbed "Porkopolis." The squeal of pigs was the city's dominant sound—partly because Cincinnati, like other American cities, allowed pigs to roam the streets freely as scavengers. Cincinnati had the first packing house west of the mountains in 1818, and twenty years later some 182,000 hogs were packed in a single year. Pork packing involved the best contemporary division of labor, and utilized "everything but the squeal." One man drove the pig into a small pen, another knocked it on the head and stuck its throat, two more hauled the carcass away, and then another two immersed it in boiling water. After another man had removed the bristles in about a minute and a half, stretchers were put between the legs, and still two other men disemboweled, beheaded, and halved the animal. All these operations were completed in about three minutes and a half, so that the pig was dismembered almost before the last grunt had died away. After cutting, the pig was allowed to cool and then packed in brine for shipment.

But Cincinnati was not devoted entirely to business. It was also an important literary and cultural center. The books, magazines, and newspapers that flowed in a steady stream from its presses included several daily newspapers. The city counted among its residents outstanding western authors and painters as well as numerous professional groups. Schools, hospitals, and libraries were comparatively plentiful and good; moreover, the city was the western center for such philanthropic organizations as the American Sunday School Union.

Cincinnati during the 1820s and 1830s with the greatest center of the increasing German immigration that was coming in large numbers to central and southern Ohio. Cincinnati had German newspapers, clubs, and singing societies; German was spoken commonly on the streets, and peasant costumes could be seen here and there.

The growth of the Ohio Valley meant that by the 1830s the older sections along the river could no longer be considered as a frontier, unless one talks of literary, educational, medical, or other frontiers. In most of the ordinary cultural traits it was more akin to the East than it was to the newer regions farther west, and consequently it leaves the frontier picture.

NORTHERN OHIO AND MICHIGAN

To the north, migration flowed in vast quantities along the Great Lakes, filling such cities as Erie, Cleveland, Sandusky, Toledo, and Detroit; Cleveland, for example, had a population of 1000 in 1830 and 6000 in 1840. Continuing west, migrants pushed into Michigan, northern Indiana and Illinois, Wisconsin, and even as far as Iowa. The numbers of west-ward-bound migrants kept on increasing impressively as the travelers filled the boats and crowded the roads. During the year 1833, 60,000 people left Buffalo by water for the West, the next year saw 80,000, and the succeed-ing years brought still more. These figures did not include the greater number going by land: no one felt it was worth his while to count the wagon trains.

The city of Buffalo boomed with the opening of the Erie Canal, the improvement of its Lake Erie harbor, and the vastly increased migra-tion; by 1840 it numbered 18,000. The buildings that rose on every hand were usually large and cheaply constructed, with an extraordinarily large number of hotels; they included, however, a theater that was considered one of the finest of the West. The streets were crowded with immigrants, land speculators, runaway slaves and their pursuing masters, Indians who were often drunk, merchants, canal drivers, and other elements of the heterogeneous population. Buffalo provided fine opportunities for the energetic and ambitious, particularly the speculators, but it was no place for a lady alone on the streets at night.

The great northern area of opportunity during the 1830s was Michigan, which was particularly attractive to Yankee migrants, who arrived in great numbers.

> Then there's old Varmount, well, what d'ye think of that!
> To be sure, the gals are handsome, and the cattle very fat:
> But who among the mountains 'mid cloud and snow would stay,
> When he can buy a prairie in Michigania?
> Yea, yea, yea, to Michigania.

Detroit, the gateway to Michigan, remained as late as 1840 a rather small town with a population of about 9000, but it had large ambitions. It bulged with immigrants and merchants who stretched the accommodations for food and lodging to the breaking point. Streets were wide and unpaved, and sidewalks no more than a few random planks; in rainy weather a caller avoided being mired by driving his carriage directly to the front door of the house he was visiting. Detroit was a city of the future, and as such attractive only to the man who kept his eyes on the new churches, banks, stores, newspapers, and homes, and transported them into a glorious future.

Many visitors saw only the drab present rather than the hoped-for future: "O Detroit, what a barren and inhospitable City thou art! Thou shalt sit enthroned as the Queen of Muddy Streets, through which do saunter thy gaunt lean cows, which after feeding upon what thy generous inhabitants cast from their kitchen doors are killed and quartered to be cooked—but to be eaten—aye there's the rub—that is frequently an impossibility. Gristle, skin & bone, pervade thy very marrow & boiled, baked, or fried one's teeth suffer in the attack."

Michigan settlers came largely from New York and New England and concentrated in the southern third of the state. All of the inland towns in this area had been established after the War of 1812 and now they grew magnificently. Farther north such frontier settlements as Grand Rapids and Saginaw received their first growth in the 1830s. Land speculators practically monopolized available building lots. To the west the new towns of St. Joseph and New Buffalo considered themselves rivals of Chicago, with the speculators dreaming of the happy day when their towns and cities would outdistance the Illinois upstart. The Michigan boom was sadly injured by the panic of 1837, and then revived a little, only to collapse completely when depression finally hit the West with full force in 1839.

MICHIGAN STATEHOOD

The growth of Michigan naturally led its inhabitants to talk about statehood. The census of 1830 had shown a population of only 32,000, but a new census four years later showed three times that number, which was more than sufficient for statehood. Assuming quick and easy congressional approval, a constitutional convention was called in 1835, and after arduous labors produced a document that was accepted by the voters. So assured did the inhabitants of Michigan feel of immediate statehood that they elected state officers and put them to work.

The admission of Michigan did not come promptly, being delayed by a boundary dispute with Ohio. The southern boundary of Michigan as stated in the Ordinance of 1787 was a line directly east from the tip of Lake Michigan. When Ohio had been admitted to the Union there had been some doubt as to where, if at all, such a line would strike Lake Erie. The matter did not at the moment seem very important, and merely as a precautionary measure the constitution of Ohio included a provision that, if the line did not hit the western end of Lake Erie, it could, with the consent of Congress, be changed to strike the most northerly cape of Maumee Bay.

The actual survey of the Michigan-Ohio boundary showed that it did in fact miss the western end of Lake Erie. Moreover, the Toledo region was growing rapidly with the prospective building of the Wabash Canal. In consequence Ohio claimed the alternate line of her constitution, and

Michigan promptly refused, positively and belligerently, to consider herself bound by a provision of the Ohio constitution. Both Ohio and Michigan rolled up their sleeves for a fight. Ohio raised troops and started them north toward the disputed area. Michigan likewise raised troops and sent them on what turned out to be a delightful junket while the legislature voted funds for "defense." Ohio surreptitiously held court in the disputed area; whereupon Michigan patriots kidnaped some of the officials.

A potential civil war brought the intervention of President Jackson, although he was embarrassed by his desire to obtain the friendship of both sides in the coming presidential elections. In this dilemma he followed good political practice by asking a truce, during which a federal commission would investigate the conflicting claims. The commission in time proposed a compromise that Michigan felt was dictated by the electoral votes of Ohio: Ohio was to receive the line she wanted, while in return Michigan was to receive the upper peninsula, which she did not in the least want. Presumably the only people who should have been dissatisfied were the few residents of the Wisconsin region, but their votes were insignificant, and by this time they should have been accustomed to losing territory to a neighboring state.

The proposed "compromise" was utterly unacceptable to Michigan and was rejected with considerable heat at a convention that met at Ann Arbor in September 1836. Incidentally, the extralegal state government continued to operate during these troubled times. After the delegates to the September convention returned to their homes a small, unauthorized group of men anxious for statehood convened at Ann Arbor in December 1836 and voted to accept the compromise. Congress must have breathed a great sigh of relief when it heard of this latest vote, for immediately it turned a blind eye on the credentials of the members of the group and hastily admitted Michigan to the Union on January 26, 1837.

NORTHERN INDIANA AND ILLINOIS

Part of the settlers who had moved west by way of the Great Lakes ended on the plains of northern Indiana and Illinois, where they merged with other streams of settlement from the south. The result was the appearance of thousands of new farms and the establishment of such cities as Galesburg, Springfield, and Chicago. The land rejected by early settlers as unfit for farming proved to be the most productive of the entire area.

Many of these new settlements came into existence on the relatively treeless prairies, and hence the pioneers faced a whole new set of problems that were later to become familiar beyond the Mississippi. Solutions were not found immediately, but at least the problems were recognized. The absence of trees eliminated the labor of girdling and chopping, but increased the difficulties of the first planting; at least four oxen were required to drag a plow through the tough prairie soil, with a cost of something like two dollars an acre, or more than the usual cost of the land. The scarcity of trees also made it difficult to build houses and barns, fence the land, and find fuel. For the time being, old frontier techniques were continued but at a greatly increased cost because of the necessity of hauling wood long distances.

The wonder city of Illinois was Chicago, lying on Lake Michigan at the mouth of the Chicago River. The region had been fortified because it was on a trade route that ascended the Chicago River, portaged to the Illinois, and finally won through to the Mississippi. At the opening of the year 1830 the future Chicago consisted of one abandoned stockade, a handful of cabins, and large wastes of sand.

The Chicago boom started with the plotting of the city in 1830 by the canal commissioners, and almost immediately the land speculators seized both reins and whip. Reports had it that although the town contained some 2000 inhabitants in 1834 it had enough surveyed building lots to provide for a population of 300,000 without crowding. Every male inhabitant bought and sold town lots, and eagerly transmitted the gossip of how someone else had made a profit of 20 to 30 percent within a few days or 100 percent or more within a few weeks. Every speculator could show amazing paper profits, and all the inns and stores were crowded with men just on the point of making their fortunes—at least until the pinprick of the panic of 1837.

Before the panic of 1837 Chicago had attracted some 6000 residents with the customary variety of houses, stores, churches, taverns, banks, and newspapers, not to mention a considerable variety of industrial enterprises. Many people felt assured of the future greatness of Chicago, and, judging by the outcome, their prophetic vision was much better than that of many others who were equally certain of the future opulence of towns that never actually matured. Optimism was in the Chicago air, even though older and more important cities such as Cincinnati, St. Louis, and New Orleans as yet saw no reason for alarm.

WISCONSIN

North of Illinois, Wisconsin was receiving its first important settlements. Two areas had the preference. The first was the typical farming frontier stretching from Milwaukee west through Waukesha and north to Appleton. As was true of Michigan, a considerable number of the new residents came from New England and New York, but Wisconsin also received many foreign-born, particularly German, Swedish, Danish, and Norwegian. The Scandinavians were particularly enthusiastic about the new country, and their letters to their friends back home brought an ever-increasing flow of Scandinavians—first to Wisconsin and then to Minnesota and Dakota.

As on other frontiers, Wisconsin was a happy hunting ground for the land speculator. In most regions he was the first pioneer, occupying good agricultural land, mill sites, and town sites. These early claims were generally respected without benefit of the law, and claim jumping was viewed askance even if done by a man who really wanted to farm. Later arrivals had to choose between paying for land already claimed, taking inferior land, or going to a more remote district.

The activities of the speculator were not considered bad as long as tremendous areas of the state were unoccupied. Men went west to improve their conditions, and any sign of either farming or commercial activity was considered a hopeful portent of the future. Wisconsin wanted more people, and quantity was more immediately important than quality. It was the earliest state (1852) to give official encouragement to immigration, being followed by Iowa, Minnesota, Dakota, and other territories and states. Pamphlets were published in various languages, and an agent in New York tried to route the settlers to the region he represented. Unfortunately many of these migrants were badly swindled before they arrived at their new homes.

The metropolis of the infant Wisconsin was Milwaukee, which had its first speculative boom in the years 1835–1837. Quite appropriately its first newspaper (1836) was titled the *Advertiser,* and devoted its main efforts to attracting settlers. The Milwaukee of 1836 had less than 1000 inhabitants but great expectations. Houses were being built feverishly, living quarters were at a premium, wages and other prices were high, and speculation was rife. In other words, it was a typical frontier town.

The second important area of settlement in Wisconsin was the lead district that straddled Illinois and Wisconsin, stretching roughly from Galena, Illinois, to Mineral Point, Wisconsin. The lead appeared near the surface and was comparatively pure; hence it could be extracted easily from pit mines and then smelted before being moved down the river to St. Louis and New Orleans. Desultory mining had existed for many years as far west at Dubuque, but the real development dated from the early 1820s. By 1826 there were an estimated 1600 miners in the region; during the following year there was a boom that was not equalled until the discovery of gold in California.

The lure of lead drew prospective miners mainly from the West and the South, but also attracted considerable numbers of Irish and French. Trial holes were dug all over the landscape, and rumors of new finds resulted in the overnight appearance of such mining camps as New Diggings, Hard Scrabble, Coon Branch, Fair Play, Platteville, Mineral Point, Dodge-ville, and Blue Mounds. The miner first discovered a promising claim, then dug and smelted his own ore; he usually lived in a cave dug in the side of a hill. Now and then he attained wealth, but, as in most mining booms, the majority of searchers lived largely on hope. These mines were the lure that brought farmers to the Rock River region and hence were responsible indirectly for the Black Hawk War, in which a good many miners fought.

The imminent admission of Michigan as a state led Congress to split off the western section as the territory of Wisconsin in 1836. It included not only the present state but all the land farther west between the Mississippi and the Missouri, and from Canada to the northern border of Missouri; this region west of the Mississippi had been a part of Michigan in the years 1834–1836. In 1838 Wisconsin was cut to its present limits except that it continued to retain the region northwest of Lake Superior. The infant territory created in 1836 could boast some 22,000 inhabitants; its governor was Henry Dodge. The location of the territorial capital was a matter of bitter rivalry between Mineral Point and Milwaukee; a compromise was finally arranged that produced the town of Madison in the wilderness of the Four Lakes region. Wisconsin attained statehood in 1848, and Minnesota became a territory in the following year.

IOWA

West of the Mississippi settlement began to flow into the present Iowa during the 1830s. Earliest interest had been in the lead region near Dubuque, but with Indian land cessions after the Black Hawk War the way was opened for normal frontier advance. Population first flowed into the area near the Mississippi, with the growth of such towns as Keokuk, Burlington, Davenport, and Dubuque. Quite properly the oldest of them, Dubuque, had the first newspaper—the *Du Buque Visitor* in 1836. The rapidly increasing flow of hopeful Hawkeyes resulted in the opening of two local land offices, at Dubuque and at Burlington, in 1838. The Iowa prairies provided no obstacle to the expansion of population, and Iowa City was founded as early as 1839.

Governmentally, Iowa had at first no independent existence, being only a small part of the vast region lying between the Mississippi and Missouri rivers and north of the state of Missouri. Its growth created problems because it was so remote from the center of administration at Madison; when the territory of Wisconsin was formed in 1836 it had 11,687 people east of the Mississippi and 10,564 west of the river. Under these circumstances the obvious solution was to create the territory of Iowa (1838), with Burlington as the temporary capital and Robert Lucas of Ohio as governor. Statehood was not to be long delayed (see Chapter 27).

KENTUCKY AND TENNESSEE

South of the Ohio River the slowing growth of Kentucky was almost as striking as the rapid expansion of the states to the north. Kentucky's diversified agriculture might have been expected to attract the same stream of settlers that appeared on the other side of the river, but several factors changed the outcome. Negro slavery deterred both Northerners and immigrants from abroad. The absence of public land brought a preference for the open spaces farther south. The very diversity of agriculture seemed unpromising to Southerners interested in raising cotton. The consequence was that Kentucky grew slowly. Although in 1820 she was a close second to Ohio for the lead in western population, by 1840 Ohio had twice as many residents as Kentucky, and Indiana had almost come abreast of her southern neighbor.

Tennessee was quite different from Kentucky in that the fertile western part of the state remained open for settlement after 1820. The planters flooding into this section produced a great boom in Memphis, which was the first important town south of St. Louis. Memphis did a flourishing business as a shipping and distributing center. Farmers, traders, and migrating Indians crossed the river at this point. Cotton and other agricultural products were heaped high on Memphis docks waiting to be moved by river steamer. Planters, Indians, trappers, gamblers, and prostitues rubbed elbows in the streets in typical western fashion.

THE LOWER SOUTH

Farther south the population of the new territory of Florida made little growth, the settled areas being confined entirely to the northern parts of the territory. Neither oranges nor tourists were yet conceived as the basis of permanent prosperity. To most people, Florida was a region of marshy land, imposing wastes of sand, scrubby trees, and hostile and dangerous Indians, for the Seminole troubles did not end until after 1840. In spite of insufficient population Florida desired statehood, formulated a constitution, and applied for admission in 1838. The plea was refused.

The great bulk of southern migration moved into western Georgia, Alabama, Mississippi, and Louisiana. The older of these states, Georgia and Louisiana, almost doubled in the years from 1820 to 1840, but the newer ones, Alabama and Mississippi, increased fivefold. The new settlements of the lower South primarily attracted planters moving their slaves in order to cultivate cotton, although Louisiana also had a very considerable sugar industry. A few of these migrants moved by water, either around the tip of Florida to the Gulf or by way of the Ohio and the Mississippi, but most of them started from Virginia or the Carolinas and moved overland through Georgia. Every night brought the twinkle of lights as the slaves prepared their evening meals over their campfires. Eastern planters who moved to the West frequently bought out the holdings of earlier frontiersmen who had cleared the land and who then continued farther west.

If current accounts may be believed, the southern frontier was even more boisterous and lawless than the northern. Indian troubles attracted the dissolute and vicious, who found a splendid opportunity to seize Indian land and improvements as the natives were forced to move west. Furthermore, the fact that the towns were comparatively small, isolated, and badly policed made them splendid refuges for the lawless. As usual, land speculators were as much in evidence as they were in the North.

Cotton culture in a region with navigable rivers that permitted shipping directly from the front doors of the plantations discouraged development of the hundreds of small, bustling communities so characteristic north of the Ohio. The larger commercial centers depended on water for their transportation. For the eastern portion of the Deep South, Augusta and Savannah were both important outlets, since with existing forms of transportation Augusta's position on the river was but little inferior to that of Savannah. Farther to the west most of Alabama and a portion of Mississippi were tributary to the city of Mobile; the growing business of the rural regions was beginning to crowd the unpaved streets and wooden sidewalks of the Alabama metropolis. Mobile still contained a fair number of French- and Spanish-speaking residents, but the dominant class was now Anglo-American.

Western Mississippi, Louisiana, and, in fact, the whole area bordering on the Mississippi looked to that river for its transportation. Such cities as Vicksburg, Natchez, and Baton Rouge drew the business of their back countries. Of these towns Natchez was the best, but not the most favorably, known because of its appeal to the more rowdy element of the river.

The dominant western city of the 1820s and 1830s was unquestionably New Orleans. Its location was such that it was expected to control the business of the two thirds of the nation drained by the Mississippi and its tributaries, and few people doubted that New Orleans was destined to become and remain America's most important city. Its importance and prospects of growth attracted great numbers of people who aspired to get rich with the country, and the population of New Orleans reached the neighborhood of 100,000 by 1840.

Steamboats from the upper Mississippi and the Ohio lined New Orleans wharves, where they nudged ocean-going vessels from all over the world. As early as 1821 the city exported some $16 million worth of western products in the course of the year, while silks, French wines and brandies, British cutlery, rum, coffee, and other exotic imported products jammed its warehouses. Before the Civil War annual exports passed the $100 million mark in spite of the bad river channel that inspired much moaning but no action. New York could well look to its laurels.

The most obvious drawbacks of New Orleans were its swampiness and its high morbidity, with the two of course related by more than the reputed necessity of weighting coffins to keep them underground. New Orleans suffered from all the usual western ills, but in addition was a notorious center of yellow fever. The mosquito was considered a great nuisance but was not connected in the popular mind with the disease. Every inhabitant who could find time and money went north during the "sickly season."

New Orleans continued to remain quite foreign in appearance, being somewhat Spanish, but more French. French architecture was in evidence, French was spoken commonly on the streets, a French theater operated successfully, and a magnificent Catholic cathedral served the Spanish-French population. Across Canal Street was the American section of the town, slightly cleaner, and more bustling, with its own theater and hotels and stores. Some of the streets were paved; ultimately paving stone was brought from the North as ship ballast. Most of the houses were constructed of wood, and some were covered with stucco.

New Orleans was famous for its gaiety, which visitors often identified with wickedness. Sailors gambled and brawled in the saloons, poolrooms, and gambling halls of the waterfront. Pickpockets jostled each other on the streets. In 1836, in a city of some 60,000 there were 543 licensed saloons, cabarets, and taverns, plus an unknown number of others not licensed. Brothels were numerous. The gaslights of the theaters glittered brightly, and the St. Charles Hotel, opened in 1837, was considered the most imposing building west of the mountains. The institution of slavery permitted the wealthy and more leisured inhabitants to engage in a round of balls, dinners, and masquerades.

Part of the city's reputation for sin came from its use of Sunday as a day for shopping, visiting, attending the theater, and giving parties. Northerners who arrived on business, and particularly conscience-ridden New Englanders, called these activities desecrations of the Sabbath, and were sure that they indicated general depravity. Northern visitors also frequently expressed doubts of the virtue of Creole ladies, even though their evidence was extremely scanty. New Orleans women were noted for their dark, voluptuous charms; their soft, languorous drawls were enchanting to all but the most captious critics, who professed to detect a deplorable lack of animation. When feminine charms were combined with the peaceful and romantic beauty of a moonlit river they erased even the unpleasantly monotonous music of the clouds of mosquitoes.

In addition to the Creole women New Orleans had many mulatto girls who seemed quite attractive to the white men. A whole section of the city was devoted to small, attractive houses inhabited by white men and mulatto (usually called quadroon) girls. The couples were prevented from marrying by both law and social custom. If the white man married one of his own race, the quadroon received the house and furniture; reputedly the girl seldom contracted a new alliance, and not infrequently committed suicide. As for the white ladies, they met this delicate situation by ignoring it.

MISSOURI AND ARKANSAS

West of the Mississippi the great population center north of Louisiana was the state of Missouri, including the important city of St. Louis. The number of residents increased fourfold between 1820 and 1840, as settlers from both north and south of the Ohio River spread themselves over the greater part of the state, and as foreign immigrants began to arrive. German migrants in particular came in considerable numbers even though they were frequently unhappy in a region that was aggressively proslavery. Older towns such as Cape Girardeau, Ste. Genevieve, Carondelet, and St. Charles retained considerable numbers of French Catholics, but the newer towns were entirely Anglo-American, and even the older towns were so overrun by English-speaking people that they began to lose their former ways of life.

The city of St. Louis dominated the Missouri area and much of the trans-Mississippi West, even though its population in 1840 was little over 16,000. Old and well established in comparison with most cities of the newer West, it looked down with disdain on such young upstarts as Memphis, Milwaukee, and Chicago. Any St. Louis resident was completely confident that his home town, situated near the confluence of the Mississippi and the Missouri had command of the business of both of those rivers, and that its control of the fur trade was a harbinger of a similar dominance of any business that developed in the upper Mississippi and Missouri valleys. Like other boom towns of the period, its wharves were jammed with steamboats, its stores crowded with purchasers, and its streets filled with the heterogeneous population of the West.

Naturally the business section of St. Louis was close to the river, and this part of the town was badly drained, filthy, and almost smothered by millions of flies. Some sections of the city showed evidence of French settlement, including an imposing cathedral, a Catholic college, and the Convent of the Sacred Heart. Other parts of the city were entirely American, with broader streets and many new buildings, including one of the finest theaters west of the Appalachians.

Lying between Missouri and Louisiana was the territory of Arkansas, which had been but sparsely populated upon its creation in 1819. In early territorial days Arkansas had extended as far west as the international boundary, but by 1828 it had been reduced to its present limits. The settlement of Arkansas proceeded but slowly, in part because of the considerable swamps and mountains. As more easterly states were occupied, the overflow entered Arkansas, settling primarily along the Arkansas, White, Black, and Red rivers, which was certainly a colorful collection. Development was hastened by the construction (1821–1833) of a military road between Memphis and Little Rock and by the removal in the early 1830s of the obstructions to navigation in the Arkansas River. The person responsible for the clearing of the Arkansas was Henry M. Shreve, a steamboat man even better known for his work in clearing the Mississippi.

Newly arrived Arkansans were not numerous but were vigorous in self-expression. A demand for statehood produced a convention at Little Rock in 1836; a constitution was formulated and an appeal for admission directed to Congress. Statehood came immediately, with Arkansas offsetting the northern state of Michigan. The population of Arkansas in 1840 was slightly under 100,000, but spread so thinly that few areas could boast of as many as six inhabitants per square mile.

With the admission of Arkansas and Michigan, and the formation of the territories of Wisconsin and Iowa, the eastern half of the United States had almost assumed its present political form. East of the Mississippi only Florida and Wisconsin remained eligible for statehood. In the first tier of trans-Mississippi states, Iowa remained to be admitted, and Minnesota was still a matter for the future; otherwise settlement had reached the longitude of the great bend of the Missouri.

READINGS

NORTH. See Buley, Havighurst, Holbrook, Wade, Esarey, Quaife and Glazer cited in the Readings for Chapter 13. Eugene H. Roseboom and Francis P. Weisenburger, *A History of Ohio* (1953); Francis P. Weisenburger, *The Passing of the Frontier 1825–1850* (1941), Ohio; Elbert J. Benton, *Cultural Story of an American City*, Part II (1950), Cleveland. William V. Pooley, *The Settlement of Illinois from 1830 to 1850* (1908); Paul W. Gates, *Frontier Landlords and Prairie Tenants* (1945), monograph on Illinois; Rebecca Burlend, *A True Picture of Emigration* (1936), contemporary on Illinois; Earnest Calkins, *They Broke the Prairie* (1937), popular on Galesburg, Illinois; Bessie L. Pierce, *A History of Chicago* (3 vols., 1937–1957), scholarly; Henry J. Smith, *Chicago's Great Century* (1933), journalistic; Milo M. Quaife, *Lake Michigan* (1944); William Nowlin, *The Bark Covered House* (1937), contemporary on Michigan; William F. Raney, *Wisconsin* (1940), text; Louis Pelzer, *Augustus Caesar Dodge* (1908), governor; Joseph Schafer, *Wisconsin Lead Region* (1932) and his *A History of Agriculture in Wisconsin* (1923); Bayrd Still, *Milwaukee* (1948), scholarly; H. Russell Austin, *The Milwaukee Story* (1946), episodic; David T. Nelson (ed.), *The Diary of Elizabeth Koren, 1853–1855* (1955); Ole M. Raeder, *America in the Forties* (1929), his letters; John Plumbe, *Sketches of Iowa and Wisconsin* (1948), contemporary. Cyrenus Cole, *Iowa Through the Years* (1940), short; Irving Richman, *Ioway to Iowa* (1931); Earle D. Ross, *Iowa Agriculture* (1951). Two good accounts of Norwegian immigration, largely in the Northwest, are Theodore C. Blegen, *Norwegian Migration of America, 1825–1860* (1931) and Carlton C. Qualey, *Norwegian Settlement in the United States* (1938).

SOUTH. Francis G. Davenport, *Ante-Bellum Kentucky 1800–1860* (1943); Thomas P. Abernethy, *From Frontier to Plantation in Tennessee* (1932); Samuel C. Williams, *The Beginnings of West Tennessee* (1930); Sidney W. Martin, *Florida During Territorial Days* (1944); Fayette Copeland, *Kendall of the Picayune* (1943), New Orleans; Harold Sinclair, *The Port of New Orleans* (1942); John G. Fletcher, *Arkansas* (1947), mostly after the Civil War. See also Clark, Abernethy, Shoemaker cited in the Readings for Chapter 13.

CHAPTER 18

THE MONEY PROBLEM

T he western prosperity of the early 1830s, with its orgy of speculative investments in transportation innovations, its rise of land
and commodity prices, its flood of immigration, and its high hopes
for the future, came to an end with the panic of 1837. The resulting economic collapse damaged the West more than had any similar preceding
event, and focused the attention of the whole country on the financial conditions of the West as an important factor in American prosperity.

The West was handicapped throughout its history by a lack of both
cash and credit. The West of the early nineteenth century, as in later years,
was a debtor area. The migrant to the new lands of the frontier was not a
rich man, and he needed capital even for his original settlement. A horse
and wagon had to be bought, provisions acquired, land purchased, a house
built, and the family supported until the first crop was harvested. The
usual frontiersman obtained most of these funds in the East. Possibly he had
saved some money or had some property that he could sell, or relatives or
friends might advance him the needed capital; otherwise, he might work
some years in the West and acquire land before he returned East to claim
a bride or to move his family. In any case his method of obtaining funds
was largely a personal matter and did not involve commercial banking institutions.

CREDIT BY MERCHANTS

After the migrant to the West arrived at his new home, any further
financial requirements were satisfied in part by credit from local merchants.
Surplus corn, tobacco, furs, honey, or pork could be traded for tools or
cloth, and often purchases might be made on credit. Western merchandising was a complicated and hazardous occupation. The merchant might

travel both to New Orleans and to the eastern coast to arrange sales, purchases, and credit; his hardware normally came from Pittsburgh. His stock was considerable, ranging from cotton cloth to flutes, and from sets of Shakespeare to Bateman's Drops. The freight charges were high, amounting to possibly a third of the final cost. The merchant himself frequently lacked ready money and was lucky if he was near an army post where the men were paid in cash. Currency might well be lost in transit, and bills of exchange on the East were hard to obtain. These difficulties of western storekeepers measured their services to the struggling communities of the West. They were an important source of western credit, which in turn was advanced in part by eastern firms.

Some western desires could be satisfied by the merchants, but others could not. Each settler was hopeful of the future and wanted more money to buy additional land, acquire new machinery, construct new buildings, and buy seeds and stock. He could hardly borrow from friends and neighbors, since one man was nearly as poor as another. Even the most prosperous Westerners looked sadly and enviously at such commercial enterprises as factories, packing plants, canals, and railroads—not to mention such community necessities as churches, courthouses, and jails. For all these desirable trappings of civilization new sources of credit must be found.

EARLY BANKS

The first transmontane settlers came west at the time of the Revolution, when organized commercial banking was as yet unknown in the United States. The only lending of money was done by men who had a surplus of ready cash and were willing to lend it to trusted individuals. The first refinement of this simple operation came when people realized that paper credit was not always redeemed immediately. An order to pay the bearer a specified amount of money might pass from hand to hand for many years without being redeemed, thus serving in itself as currency. This practice afforded the basis for much of the later banking activities of the world. It meant that a person or a company might issue paper promises to pay definite sums of money to the holders of the notes and feel confident that no large share of them would be presented for payment at any one time, thus avoiding the necessity of maintaining a cash reserve equal to the face value of the notes. Furthermore, these paper tokens might be loaned the same as money.

Discovery of the first simple principles governing paper credit led to the establishment of several kinds of banks in the United States in the period immediately following the Revolution. The first Bank of the United States (1791–1811) acted as financial agent of the federal government as well as doing private business of its own. Local banks were incorporated by the states, with each bank having its own unique charter provisions, since general and uniform banking laws were still a thing of the future. Finally, since there was no prohibitory legislation, private persons and groups of persons could engage in banking at their own discretion; sometimes such private enterprises were so small that the entire bank could be moved from place to place in a trunk. Members of both of the last two groups frequently carried on other businesses at the same time. The rapid growth of banking in the United States is evident from the fact that the three banks in existence in 1789 increased to twenty-six by 1800; in 1811, which was the year that the charter of the Bank of the United States lapsed, there were eighty-eight such institutions.

WESTERN BANKS

The attitude of the West toward banks and banking was dictated by the desire for more credit. As far as the Westerner was concerned, the one important service of a bank was to issue large quantities of paper money and to lend it to anyone who wanted it. The idea of requiring adequate security for a loan was approved, but only in theory; everyone was optimistic about the future, feeling that wealth was just around the corner and that repayment of any loan, no matter what its size, would be painless. In this frame of mind the Westerner naturally objected to the repayment of a loan at any specified date. If wealth lay just ahead, then it was cruel as well as unbusinesslike for the bank to remove the steed on which its patron was galloping down the broad path to prosperity. The function of the bank was to increase the money in circulation and not to recall any of it. Finally, the West carried its well-known democratic concepts into bank management. Just as the average man should be able to fill any post in the government, so should he be able to operate a bank satisfactorily.

On the basis of these simple beliefs the West began to acquire banks of its own during the first decade of the nineteenth century. The Lexington (Kentucky) Insurance Company (1802) did a banking business. The Miami Exporting Company (Cincinnati, 1803) was organized to finance New Orleans trade, but soon confined its business to commercial banking. The Bank of Michigan and the Bank of Kentucky started operations in 1806. The very famous Nashville Bank opened its doors in 1807 and continued operations until the panic of 1819. Other small banks appeared throughout the West. Most of the organizations were short-lived, but all succeeded in issuing large quantities of paper money before their respective demises.

The checks on the transactions of the early western banks were few and comparatively ineffectual. Some reliance could be placed on the honesty and good businesss sense of their promoters, but this control was somewhat vitiated by the proprietors' lack of banking training and experience. A more effective and immediate check was exercised by the Bank of the United States, which felt some responsibility for banking conditions all over the country. This bank followed the policy of collecting the paper money of banks that were rumored to be unstable, and then presenting a considerable amount of such paper for immediate payment in cash; the bank then either gave convincing proof of its stability or was forced to admit its insolvency and close its doors. Even the threat of such action was sufficient to make many of the smaller banks follow a comparatively conservative policy.

The only real limitation upon irresponsible operations by the smaller banks disappeared when the first Bank of the United States was not re-chartered in 1811. The small banks then saw their opportunity and multi-plied like rabbits, even after the chartering of the second Bank of the United States in 1816. By 1820 there were in the United States 307 banks, of which the West had at least its fair share. In the one year 1818 Kentucky authorized 40 banks with a total capitalization of $8 million, and other states were almost as generous. The country was deluged with a flood of paper money, for which the West gave loud cheers and asked for more. The answer of the small banks was that if all the large banks were elim-inated still more paper money could be issued. This statement was undoubt-edly quite correct, even though students of the subject both then and later deplored the removal of the last check on irresponsible banking.

When the disappearance of the first Bank of the United States was followed immediately by the outbreak of the War of 1812, banking condi-tions became more and more confused. With the suspension of specie pay-ment all over the country the last vestige of control over the smaller banks disappeared. The field of banking was thus opened wide to all comers, with the result that hundreds of men decided that the easiest way to amass riches was to print their own money. As long as public confidence remained, any sort of paper currency could be circulated, at least for a short time.

As might have been expected, many of the new banks were badly managed by their amateur owners. Usually a company was organized on the basis of a small cash subscription; then paper money supplied the deficit of gold, or working capital was raised by loans on the company's crisp, new stock. Metallic currency was a rarity and was kept mostly for purpose of display. Paper money was backed by little or no specie reserve. Most of the bank's loans were "frozen assets," long-term loans that could not be called in case of sudden need. Short-term or call loans were of little use in the West, where the farmers needed money for at least a year at a time; conse-quently, banks had little option but to tie up their money in fairly perma-nent form. Even worse, many of the loans were based on the scantiest of security, with the banks accepting the farmer's own optimistic statement about the value of his land. As security, land was reasonably satisfactory in prosperous times, but became practically worthless with economic depression and falling prices. In such a period the bank might call the loan, but then it received the hostility of the borrower and his friends and was probably left with a large amount of unsalable cheap land on its hands. Its only choice was to allow the loan to continue indefinitely, with slight prospect that payment would be made even in the remote future, and the excellent chance that the bank would go bankrupt in the mean time.

The evils inherent in western banking practices were worsened by a considerable amount of fraud. The "saddlebag bank" was notorious. A man would ride his horse into a small town with his saddlebags crammed with beautiful crisp new bank notes. He would then set up an office and lend his paper money to all the neighboring farmers on easy terms and with but little security. After collecting all the promissory notes available he disposed of them to the store owner or the innkeeper at a discount for ready cash and decamped with the proceeds. The local note holder was thus left with the job of placating the irate farmers when they discovered that their attractive new bank notes were practically worthless.

Another common type of fraud was counterfeiting. All bank notes were poorly printed and easily copied, thus offering great temptations to the dexterous man who possessed a printing press, was desirous of easy wealth, and was not over burdened with scruples. The number of notes that were counterfeited became so great that anyone handling large sums of money bought a frequently revised "counterfeit detector," which described the most common frauds. The situation became so bad that all bank notes were looked upon with suspicion. Usually they were accepted at par only in the community in which they were issued; at other places they were discounted, with the size of the discount depending on the reputation of the issuing bank and its distance from the place of presentation. Many notes would not be accepted at any value if taken far from home.

THE SECOND BANK OF THE UNITED STATES

Conditions were so bad that well-informed people did not question the need for the ameliorating influence of a federal bank; hence the second Bank of the United States was chartered in 1816 for a period of twenty years. The new bank sought to obtain the resumption of specie payments, in which effort it was finally successful, and, like its predecessor, to keep an eye on the smaller banks throughout the country. It also engaged in a vigorous policy of expansion, establishing eleven branches within a few years, and issuing much paper currency of its own.

The West was by no means enthusiastic over this new federal fiscal agency. The pressure of the second Bank of the United States immediately caused some of the less sound western institutions to close their doors, and the Westerners who held the notes of these defunct organizations could be pardoned for not viewing with pleasure this increase of sound banking. Furthermore, all the influence of the central bank was exerted to decrease the issue of paper made by the smaller and less stable institutions, with the result that the West found its supply of currency diminished and its credit contracted. When the Westerner considered that all of the West was in debt and needed money, and that no one had any doubts as to eventual prosperity, it seemed to him both tragic and unreasonable that the whole credit structure should be contracted.

The obvious villain of the scene from the standpoint of the West was the second Bank of the United States, which was the prime mover in the much-deplored contraction of credit. Consequently the West did all it could to curtail the power of the bank. Between 1816 and 1819 the states of Ohio, Kentucky, Tennessee, Maryland, North Carolina, and Georgia made efforts to tax the branch banks out of existence. Unfortunately for the success of their attempts the Supreme Court was not imbued with the western spirit and judged the tax legislation to be unconstitutional in the cases of *McCulloch* v. *Maryland* (1819) and *Osborn* v. *United States Bank* (1824).

Then came the crash of the panic of 1819, and the West saw the national bank as the chief cause of this tragedy. Although the debacle had in fact resulted chiefly from the bad banking and extravagance of the preceding years, the West was not interested in complicated explanations involving itself. It wanted simple and logical reasoning, together with a scapegoat: everything had been fine before the chartering of the second Bank of the United States, now conditions were bad; therefore the bank had obviously done the damage. The debtor part of the West was very bitter on the subject. Kentucky tried to relieve the situation by passing stay laws to prevent the collection of debts by the banks, but after a bitter political struggle that affected even the courts the more conservative element won; the laws were declared unconstitutional by the state courts.

When the worst effects of the panic of 1819 disappeared and prosperity returned during the 1820s the West lost some of its resentment against the national bank, but there remained an undercurrent of hostility and distrust. Certainly the bank never attained any considerable popularity in the West. Many persons—Andrew Jackson was one—continued to harbor a grudge that was to produce bitter fruit some fifteen years later.

SPECULATION

The new period of prosperity reached its highest point with the migrations of the middle 1830s. New communities came into existence, property values increased, trade expanded, and the West looked toward the future with renewed hope. Along with the general expansion went an in-

crease in the number of banks; by 1834 there were 506 banks operating
under state charters, and three years later this number reached 788. The
amount of paper money per capita in circulation, which had decreased from
$6.96 to $6.69 between 1820 and 1830 now rose to $9.86 in 1835 and
$13.87 in 1837. With the expanding currency went an increase of prices
that pleased the Westerner because the enhanced value of the products he
sold more than offset the increased cost of his purchases. Furthermore, high
prices were a boon to all debtors with goods to sell; each $100 borrowed in
1825, for example, had a greatly decreased real value when it was returned
ten years later, due to the general rise of prices in the meantime.

As prosperity continued to grow, the energy and enthusiasm of the
West knew no bounds. Everyone was confident of the future and bought
all the land he could. Immense speculations took place in farms, town sites,
city lots, and water sites. New homes, barns, stores, theaters, schools,
prisons, and wharves were constructed. The greater part of this expansion
was of course based on credit, and again the credit took the form of long-
term loans that could not easily be liquidated, But no one was worried.
Times were good and would be better. A small investment today would
return a fortune tomorrow. No speculation was too wild or hazardous to be
inviting.

Individuals transmitted their enthusiasm to their respective states,
and each state launched an immense program of public improvement. Canals
were dug, rivers dredged, railroads constructed, harbors marked, roads
built, and educational facilities expanded; in every way preparation was
made for a glorious future. The South was a trifle less involved than the
North, but more from a lack of credit than from a lack of desire. Nearly
all the public works throughout the country were constructed on the basis
of borrowed capital, with each state issuing its bonds to be sold at a discount in the East or in Europe. The total figure of American state loans
by 1839 was at least $170 million. The West had again illustrated its con-
fidence in the future by bonding itself far beyond its prospective capacity
to pay.

JACKSON AND THE BANK

The only important brake on western banking optimism was the
pressure of the second Bank of the United States, which held bank notes
of country banks and forced their issuing institutions at least to approach
solvency. The older and more developed portions of the West, as represented by Henry Clay, approved this concession to sound banking, but the
majority of the younger West felt otherwise. A decrease in central control
would permit a greater expansion of credit, with more paper money for
everyone, and the West felt that such a development would benefit all poor

people. Before the general feeling of the West could become effective, however, it needed crystallization by a popular leader.

The man who finally dramatized western hostility and made the national bank appear as the ogre that gobbled up little children was Andrew Jackson. Jackson remembered vividly the panic of 1819, and as President of the United States was in a position to put his prejudices into practical effect. Emotionally he was antagonistic to all banks, his opposition to the second national bank being based on a few immediate and specific grievances. His hostility to the bank was encouraged and strengthened by rising businessmen who were anxious to decrease the financial power centering in Philadelphia. His dislike of the bank increased when it refused to make appointments that he desired, but the charge that the bank was using its power to oppose Jackson politically was not justified until the fight was in full swing.

Four years before the expiration of the bank's charter Jackson made it known that he was implacably opposed to renewal. As a result the issue became political, with Clay and the Whigs supporting the bank and Jackson and the Democrats opposing it. A recharter bill was passed by Congress in 1832 and immediately vetoed by Jackson in a vigorous message; whereupon the rechartering of the bank became one of the most hotly contested points in the election of the same year. Jackson won the election and interpreted the victory as a vindication of his policy in respect to the bank. In 1833 he followed his victory by removing the governmental deposits that were in the national bank—even though he had to change Secretaries of the Treasury twice to do it—and by placing the deposits in "pet banks" in various parts of the country. This removal curtailed the power and usefulness of the national bank, which declined to insignificance by the time its charter expired in 1836. Jackson had "slain the octopus" and the American people were "free."

STATE BANKING

The opposition of Jackson and the West to the second Bank of the United States did not mean they were necessarily opposed to all large banks or even to government banking. They hated this particular institution because it performed functions they did not like. Considerable feeling existed that the development of a proper system of credit was a legitimate government function, and several of the western states themselves engaged in banking ventures before, during, and after the 1830s. The results were partly good and partly bad, but at least the ventures showed that the West was not opposed to government banking.

State owned and operated banks were established mainly in the Northwest. Indiana was unlucky in establishing its first bank in 1819, the year of the depression, and it had a short life. Another state bank chartered in 1834 was quite successful, weathering the depression of 1837 to attain banking leadership of the state. A third bank was established later. Illinois also planned three banks, but with very sad results. The first was chartered in 1819 but not even organized. The second, incorporated in 1821, was run so badly that it lost half a million of state funds before its charter expired a decade later. The third was chartered in 1835 but its early growth was stunted by the panic of 1837, which brought insolvency; it passed away in a long death agony during the 1840s. Missouri chartered a bank in the depression year of 1837 and gave it a monopoly position; the bank weathered its early difficulties successfully and was sound and prosperous during the 1840s and 1850s.

The southern states tended to subsidize private banking rather than to establish state banks. Louisiana, Mississippi, Florida, and Arkansas all furnished such aid during the 1820s and 1830s. The usual plan was for the state to subscribe to the capital stock of one or more private banks, although sometimes it made further guarantees of other bank securities. The state subscriptions were financed by state bonds, which were sold mainly in the East or in Europe.

Western state banks were on the whole successful as compared with the many contemporary private enterprises that were notoriously badly managed and were frequently insolvent. This success was particularly noteworthy in view of the strong political pressure to make state banks more lenient in their lending policies and thus to speculate in the future of the country. The use of state credit to furnish capital for private banks was not nearly so fortunate, with the banks thus aided seeming to spend more time in trying to cheat the state than in doing regular banking business; the inevitable results were poor banks and enormous state debts. In general this period of state banks and state aid, and of specially chartered private corporations, came to an end during the 1840s and 1850s, when general state laws provided for uniform incorporation and at least a minimum of regulation.

Even though state banks were reasonably conservative, they were few in number and therefore slight in influence. Other banks were less careful, especially when the restraining influence of the second Bank of the United States decreased as deposits were removed in 1833 and its charter lapsed in 1836. Less control plus the demands created by a rampaging prosperity brought new banks into existence daily, and each one issued large quantities of paper currency. Everyone had more money than he had ever had before. Prices rose steadily for the benefit of the debtor who had something to sell. Internal improvements were constructed on a magnificent scale, giving plenty of employment and putting much money into circulation. By 1839 the West had spent on such improvements possibly $50 million, of which the greater part had been borrowed from the East or from Europe.

FEDERAL FINANCES

The wave of prosperity brought the federal government more revenue than it had ever before collected. Land sales reached a staggering total, with the greatest receipts in history. The compromise tariff of 1833 brought unusually large receipts. For one time in its history the federal government had more money than it well knew how to spend.

The flow of money into the treasury of the United States was so large in the early 1830s that Congress became embarrassed. Legislative ingenuity in spending failed to keep pace with the flow of funds into the treasury, with the result that the legislators became worried. Some suggested that the surplus be spent for internal improvements, others talked of lowering the tariff or the price of land, while still others proposed giving the unused funds to the states. Each legislator had his pet scheme for disposing of the extraordinary receipts.

The result of congressional cogitations was the passage of the Distribution Bill in 1836. The act provided that the Secretary of the Treasury should take the balance that he had on hand (excluding a reserve of $5 million) and divide it among the states according to population. Payments were to be made in four quarterly installments. In theory these payments to the states were loans, and were technically called "deposits," but in practice no one expected that the federal government would ever ask for their repayment. They have in fact never been returned.

With the passage of the Distribution Bill the Secretary of the Treasury immediately notified the "pet banks" to turn over the governmental funds they had on deposit to make the payments to the states. Then the trouble began. Most of the banks had lent all their available cash to patrons and when they tried to recall these loans a cry of distress went up all over the country. Many debtors were forced into bankruptcy and the whole credit structure of the country showed signs of strain. The banks managed to meet the first and second payments in January and April 1837, but by that time they were in serious difficulties and on May 10 they stopped specie payments. This precautionary measure enabled them to meet the third installment on July 1, but the fourth was never paid.

The financial difficulties of 1837 were increased by an earlier maneuver on the part of Jackson. Jackson had always had an emotional preference for hard money rather than the paper variety, and had disliked the payment for large speculative land purchases with paper money borrowed from the banks. He tried unsuccessfully to persuade Congress to prohibit the practice, and ultimately (July 11, 1836) issued his famous "specie circular," an executive decree requiring that all payments for public lands be in gold and silver coin, with certain possible exceptions for actual settlers. This order produced an immediate rush by land purchasers on the banks for specie. As this money was paid to the government for land it was shipped east to the treasury, thus depleting the specie of the West and disorganizing the currency of the country. Land purchases fell drastically in amount since borrowed paper could no longer be used. Even more serious results became evident when the banks attempted to find the money to carry out the terms of the Distribution Bill.

PANIC OF 1837

The financial difficulties of the country came to a climax with the suspension of specie payment in May 1837. The unsteady pyramid of currency and credit had long needed only a slight touch to cause it to tumble, and now that touch had come. Suspension by the banks brought a temporary eclipse of the earlier optimism about the country's future, and people became suspicious, economical, and conservative. Few bank notes remained at par, and many of them were refused under any circumstances. The banks became cautious, calling their notes as they became due, and refusing to make new ones. The resulting contraction of credit was a severe blow to all debtors, and western farmers were particularly hard hit; many of them could not pay their debts, and in consequence lost the products of years of labor through foreclosures. Moreover, the Westerners were also adversely affected by a contraction of credit by the business houses with whom they dealt. Merchants tried to settle outstanding accounts and were reluctant to establish new ones. This was a bitter blow to the western farmer, who long had been accustomed to living largely on credit.

The results of the depression of 1837 were visible not only in the affairs of the banker, merchant, and farmer, but also in the business of government; the receipts of both federal and state governments declined as land sales fell to a minimum and the prices of all taxable property went down. With the exception of immediately necessary work, construction of public improvements came to an end; partially completed canals and roads were deserted, and machinery was allowed to rust beside the abandoned work. Many of the states that had issued large amounts of bonds based mainly on overoptimism now found themselves hopelessly in debt. Often they had but little to show for their large expenditures, and found difficulty even in raising the money necessary to pay the interest on the bonds. Taxes were hard to collect since most people were in debt and property values had gone down. In this extremity some of the states avoided their immediate financial troubles by exercising their sovereignty in stopping payments of their bonds.

One of the most easily visible effects of the panic of 1837 was the widespread unemployment that developed, particularly in the East, during the late 1830s and early 1840s. The closing of factories and the cessation of work on public improvements meant loss of jobs to many. The number of unemployed was swelled by the addition of the clerical employees of businesses that had found retrenchment necessary, by jobless farm laborers, and by farm owners who had lost their farms. The contrast with the prosperity of the early 1830s was startling, and the future looked black.

Rather surprisingly the panic of 1837 was at first not very severe in the West, and after the first necessary readjustment there came a period of improvement in which it seemed as though the West would weather the storm. This return of optimism proved premature, for a second collapse, coming in 1839, pushed the West into the depths of financial confusion. Prosperity did not return until well into the 1840s.

The panic of 1837 was but one of a long series of similar cataclysms that swept over the United States at fairly evenly spaced periods. Among them, the panics of 1819, 1837, 1857, 1873, and 1893 were the most important of the nineteenth century. Each panic was preceded by a crescendo of prosperity, enthusiasm, and optimism that found expression in public and private construction, rising land values, improvements in transportation, full employment, and large profits. Ultimately the prosperity bubble was pricked, with the prick frequently coming from abroad, since most periods of depression were world-wide. Then came a period of gradual recovery, leading to another boom and another recession. The tendency to feel that these people caused their own troubles and should have known better should be modified with the realization that the much greater social controls developed in the succeeding years still did not prevent men from being alternately optimistic and pessimistic.

READINGS

NATIONAL CONDITIONS. The classic account of the national bank is Ralph C. H. Catterall, *The Second Bank of the United States* (1903), but see also Bray Hammond, *Banks and Politics in America from the Revolution to the Civil War* (1957). For the panic of 1837 see Reginald C. McGrane, *The Panic of 1837* (1924) and *Foreign Bondholders and American State Debts* (1935). Every biography of Jackson covers the bank troubles, as do John S. Bassett, *The Life of Andrew Jackson* (2 vols., 1911); Marquis James, *Andrew Jackson* (1937). Also pertinent are Alonzo B. Hepburn, *A History of the Currency of the United States*

(1915) and Murray S. Wildman, *Money Inflation in the United States* (1905).

WESTERN CONDITIONS. Special, detailed studies include John R. Cable, *The Bank of the State of Missouri* (1923); George W. Dowrie, *The Development of Banking in Illinois, 1817–1863* (1913); Logan Esarey, *State Banking in Indiana, 1814–1873* (1912); Stanley J. Folmsbee, *Sectionalism and Internal Improvements in Tennessee, 1796–1845* (1939); Fred D. Merritt, *The Early History of Banking in Iowa* (1900); James M. Primm, *Economic Policy* (1954), Missouri. Interesting accounts of retail trade are Thomas D. Clark, *Pills, Petticoats and Plows: The Southern Country Store* (1944); Lewis E. Atherton, *The Pioneer Merchant in Mid-America* (1939) and *The Southern Country Store* (1950).

REGIONAL ACCOUNTS. The regional history usually contains some discussion of money, banking, and depression. Such accounts are listed in the Readings for Chapters 8, 13, and 17.

CHAPTER 19

CULTURAL ADVANCE

T he West of the 1820s and 1830s included both frontier communities struggling to conquer a wilderness and older towns that considered themselves rising cultural centers. Population ranged from illiterate criminal fugitives to the leisured few who read the latest European periodicals and tried their hands at poetry. Cities of the Ohio Valley boasted daily newspapers, theaters that presented the outstanding stars of the American stage, and authors of more than local repute, while newer settlements in Michigan, Wisconsin, and Arkansas were composed almost exclusively of hard-working farmers who thought themselves lucky if they were able to keep their families from starvation.

The general cultural level of the West was low, even allowing for the well educated and well informed. Large numbers of people were illiterate and hence unread, with no other thought than making their fortunes. Speech was crude and actions were direct. Jokes were coarse and amusements rough. The frequently seen pistol-carrying, swearing, tobacco-chewing, whiskey-drinking Westerner cared little for the polite usages of eastern society. Many Easterners and a few Westerners feared that this reversion to the primitive would in time contaminate the entire nation.

RELIGION

Western deficiencies in religion were widely deplored by Easterners, who felt that the Westerner was notably less religious than he, in the sense of belonging to and attending church, and of observing the Sabbath. Religiously minded Easterners, and particularly New Englanders, were sure that the West was on the road to perdition and might well carry the East with it. One minister quite typically reported that the people of Green Bay in 1836 "seemed to be agreed in only one thing and that was to blaspheme

275

God and indulge in all kinds of wickedness." Irreligion, according to the godly, led inevitably to improper speech and action, immorality, the degradation of women and the family, the failure of democratic institutions, and the collapse of patriotism. No descendant of Puritans could view these dire possibilities without serious concern.

Many Protestants also felt that the lack of religion was no worse, and possibly was less bad, than the acceptance of the rapidly growing Catholic Church. New Catholic clergy were arriving, and Catholic schools and churches were being opened. European missionary societies were pouring money into the American West. Irish and German Catholics were flooding into the Mississippi Valley. Many Protestants were filled with foreboding and saw deep-laid plots to undermine American democracy; this alarm was soon to be translated into political action.

In spite of Protestant fears, the Catholics actually faced serious difficulties. The flood of Catholic arrivals could have little hope for help from a predominantly Protestant America, and suffered from a lack of funds. A typical priest wrote that his little church "can scarce accommodate all who come to worship," and that he found difficulty in raising funds for a larger church with its expensive equipment. Moreover, the Protestant minister might hold such a lay job as farming, but the Catholic priest had no such option.

The western irreligion that so alarmed the East was in part more apparent than real. The West may have attracted the irreligious and shown a lack of attention to the church, but in fact the appearance of disinterest was probably in the main the result of sparse population, poverty, and a diversity of sects. Even a basically religious Westerner who was struggling to attain wealth parted reluctantly with the dollars necessary to build a church and maintain a minister.

MISSIONARY WORK

The obvious way of reclaiming the West was through home missionary work by pious Easterners, although extensive work was also undertaken by such groups as the American Education Society (1815), American Bible Society (1816), Sunday School Union (1825), and American Tract Society (1826). The most important home missionary group was the American Home Missionary Society (1826), in which Congregationalists and Presbyterians cooperated. Other similar groups included a Presbyterian Board of Missions, an American Baptist Home Mission Society (1832) which replaced an earlier ineffective organization, a Methodist Missionary and Bible Society (1819), and an Episcopal Domestic and Foreign Missionary Society (1821). Least active of these was the Methodist, since the entire church was organized on a missionary basis. These organizations combined and directed earlier state and local societies, which were now affiliated, although in some cases they continued their own independent work.

New methods appeared with the new societies, which tended to use their funds to provide settled pastors for regularly organized churches rather than to send missionaries on western tours. For example, the American Home Missionary Society encouraged appeals by western churches and then normally granted an applicant church $100 a year, which was presumed to be a quarter of the salary of a minister; in time the church was expected to assume the entire salary. Each society sent out agents to encourage mission interest and collect funds, and to visit the aided churches to give advice and assistance. By 1835 the American Missionary Society had a budget of some $100,000 that went to over 700 representatives. Hundreds of churches were thereby brought into existence or their continuance was made possible. Various mission groups, like the "Illinois band," the "Iowa band," and the "Kansas band," helped the church to follow the population frontier rather closely; these groups happened to have all been from Andover Theological Seminary.

The home mission movement was not without its opponents in the West. A certain number of Westerners resented being considered a mission field. Some of the western clergy were also dissatisfied. The Baptists had a bitter internal war on the subject during the 1820s, with ministers holding that the doctrine of predestination made a mission movement silly if not outright impious. Eastern replies suggested that the real opposition was based on the fears of badly educated western ministers that they would be overshadowed by better-trained Easterners.

The missionary movement was connected closely with education. A lack of qualified western ministers reflected the absence of proper educational institutions, and to rectify this situation the churches founded a large proportion of western schools and colleges. Funds were raised in the East for western schools that would educate poor boys for the ministry. Best known was the American Society for Educating Pious Youth for the Gospel Ministry (1815) organized by the Congregationalists and Presbyterians, and becoming later the Education Society. A Ladies' Society for the Promotion of Education in the West (Congregational) took form in 1846, largely through the efforts of Catharine Beecher. It was designed to help western education, but also to assist energetic unmarried girls to migrate to the West.

ELEMENTARY EDUCATION

Westerners approved education in theory, but their main interest was in the elementary variety, with some suspicion of the higher subjects. The elementary school generally remained private, with parents paying possibly a dollar or two a year for each of their children; the usual session was 13 weeks of 6 eight-hour days. Presiding over the ordinary ungraded one-room school was a man whose lack of training limited him to the most elementary subjects. Among the many shortages of the western school were proper textbooks, the children using a miscellaneous collection that had belonged to their parents. Most popular were Noah Webster's spelling book, Jedidiah Morse's geography, and Lindley Murray's grammar, all of which had originated before 1800. The famous McGuffey readers were first published at Cincinnati in the late 1830s and in time became highly popular, being used by the majority of children of the last half of the nineteenth century.

The proportion of children who attended school even for a short time in any one year was low. It was estimated that in 1840 only one eleventh of the western population of school age was in school, while the eastern proportion was one sixth. In 1829 it was reported that of 2114 children of school age in Bullitt County, Kentucky, only 160 were in school; in the same year it was said that sixty families in the county had no member who could either read or write. Educational facilities were in general greater north than south of the Ohio, but were deplorable in both areas. The state of Ohio apparently had the best educational record, possibly because it had the largest population.

Interest in education grew rapidly in the West during the 1820s, with particular emphasis on furnishing free (not compulsory) public education to all those who might wish it. By 1830 a few cities such as Cincinnati, Louisville, Lexington, and Detroit boasted public schools, although of course insufficient to take care of the total population of school age. Public schools increased rapidly so that by 1840 Ohio, Illinois, and Michigan had at least the beginnings of state systems of education. By 1837 Cincinnati proclaimed proudly that it had ten public schools attended by 3300 of the 5500 children between six and sixteen. The salary list of $14,000 a year provided for forty-three teachers; male principals received $500 and their assistants $300; female "mistresses" received $250 and their assistants $200. The average cost per child per year was $8, considered an almost extravagant amount.

Elementary education received impetus from the growth of a class of professionally minded teachers. These men and women considered teaching to be a profession comparable to that of law or medicine, and not, as in the past, a stopgap until more profitable work could be found. They organized the Western Literary Institute and College of Professional Teachers in 1831, published the proceedings of the society, and founded an educational periodical, the *Common School Advocate*. Educational problems were discussed, new methods given publicity, and increased educational facilities urged. At no time during the period, however, were western teachers specially trained for their profession; the first normal school of the United States was opened in Massachusetts in 1839.

SECONDARY AND COLLEGE EDUCATION

Possibly 400 secondary schools, generally called academies, existed beyond the mountains in 1840. Almost all of them were private, for although the public high school movement developed in the East during the 1820s and 1830s, it reached the West slightly later. The usual secondary school either trained boys for college or "finished" the girls; none was coeducational. The work they gave was much less advanced than that offered by the modern high school. Entering students were frequently as young as ten or twelve and never had more than a common school education in the elementary subjects. Although a large proportion of the curriculum of the academies was devoted to the classics, their graduates had little more than the equivalent of what the modern secondary school offers for the first two years of study.

The peak of the educational system was the college or university; here Transylvania University at Lexington, Kentucky, reigned as the most influential school of collegiate rank in the West. Transylvania was founded as a seminary in 1783, and although it nominally became a college before 1800, it was really little more than an academy until Horace Holley became its president in 1818. Under his guidance Transylvania became the outstanding college of the West, with a faculty that included the best-known men in their fields. By the 1830s the medical department had become so strong as to overshadow the rest of the university.

Other colleges came into existence to challenge the leadership of Transylvania in the generation after 1815. The Presbyterians were particularly active, and in fact they controlled Transylvania until 1823, when they withdrew to found Centre. Presbyterian-founded colleges included the University of Pittsburgh, Indiana College (later the University), Muskingum, Wabash, Knox, and Ripon. In conjunction with the Congregationalists the Presbyterians were responsible for such institutions as Western Reserve, Beloit, and Illinois College. Other denominations did their part. The Baptists founded Shurtleff; the Eposcopalians, Kenyon; the Catholics, St. Louis University; the Methodists, Augusta, Allegheny, McKendree, Lawrence, and Indian Asbury (later De Pauw), while also taking over Transylvania in 1841. State universities such as Missouri and Michigan were opened. Of considerable importance was Miami University (Oxford, Ohio), opened in 1824 under the presidency of R. H. Bishop, a former member of the Transylvania faculty; William Holmes McGuffey was at one time on the Miami faculty.

Western colleges were generally small and poor, with one or two buildings for both classrooms and dormitories, two or three professors, and a handful of students. A considerable number of students actually did preparatory work instead of pursuing studies of collegiate rank. The instruction was generally poor, although a few good men drifted West from the better eastern institutions, notably Yale and Princeton. The rank of professor carried little social prestige and its possessors were mostly recruited from the ministry; most men preferred farming or some other "useful" occupation to any form of teaching.

In addition to the regular colleges there were several western professional schools by 1840. Half a dozen medical schools existed, of which the largest were the medical department of Transylvania, Louisville Medical College, and the Medical College of Ohio at Cincinnati. Three law schools presented the principles of Blackstone and Coke, and again Transylvania had the largest enrollment. Ten theological schools prepared candidates for the ministry; seven of these were Presbyterian, two were Baptist, and one was Episcopalian. The largest was Lane Seminary (Presbyterian) at Cincinnati, of which Lyman Beecher became president in 1832. A secession from Lane on the slavery issue led to the establishment of Oberlin, near Cleveland, which soon became practically as large as its unwilling parent. Oberlin was particularly notable as being the first college to admit both men and women as candidates for degrees.

BOOKS AND LIBRARIES

Educational progress in the West was continually hampered by the lack of cheap and easily available books. The publishing business of the West was of slow growth because of the difficulty and expense of obtaining necessary materials, and because the sparseness of western population made sales comparatively small. Prior to 1820 the publishing center of the West was Lexington, but most western books were actually printed in the East; after 1820 Cincinnati became the dominant literary center.

A lack of books meant a lack of libraries, both public and private. Here and there were libraries for the use of subscribers, but these were not open to the general public. Among the oldest of such libraries was one at Lexington, which was opened before 1800 and contained approximately 4000 volumes by the 1830s. Similar libraries in Cincinnati, Louisville, and other western cities could not boast as many books; anything over 1000 volumes was considered a noteworthy collection. Most of the colleges had libraries of their own, but they were small, consisted largely of textbooks, and were little used; the most impressive in 1840 was that of Lane Theological Seminary, which contained 10,000 volumes, and was the largest library in the West.

OTHER TYPES OF EDUCATION

A less formal educational feature of the West during the 1820s and later was the lyceum, of which at least one existed in each of the larger towns. The lyceum was an association whose members were interested in the discussion of what they considered important problems, and had as its principal activity the presentation of a series of lectures during the winter. The subjects for discussion might vary from the abolition of capital punishment to the occupation of the Oregon country. Of much interest during that time was phrenology, particularly because of its advocacy by Charles Caldwell, a member of the medical faculty of Transylvania; through his teachings Henry Ward Beecher and others were converted to this new medical "science."

First-rate work in the sciences was by no means unknown in the Ohio Valley of the 1820s and 1830s. William McClure and Robert Dale Owen did able work in geology; McClure has been described as the father of American geology. The American-born Thomas Say had been best known in entomology. John James Audubon, natural son of a Haitian Creole woman and a Frenchman, was in business in Kentucky for some years; his epochal *Birds of America,* published in 1826, brought him fame and fortune. Quite unique was C. S. Rafinesque, Transylvania professor, who did creditable work in practically every science, not to mention sorties into the arts and social sciences. Some quarter of a century before Darwin he wrote (1833): "There is a tendency to deviations and mutations through plants and animals by gradual steps at remote irregular periods. This is a part of the great universal law of perpetual mobility in everything."

Regional history aroused much interest even when the region was young. John Filson wrote a narrative of Kentucky, although not well. The ethnologist Henry Schoolcraft studied and wrote about Indian culture. A general interest in local history was demonstrated by the founding of such societies as the Vincennes Historical and Antiquarian Society (1808), the Antiquarian and Historical Society of Illinois (1827), the Historical Society of Michigan (1828), the Historical Society of Indiana (1830), the Historical and Philosophical Society of Ohio (1831), and the Kentucky Historical Society (1838).

Both politics and religion greatly interested the West. Political opinions were expressed with great vigor and intense partisanship, with such western politicians as Andrew Jackson, Henry Clay, William Henry Harrison, and Davy Crockett having their strong followers and their bitter opponents. Similarly, a discussion of religion always drew an interested crowd. Of particular note were the debates of Alexander Campbell, founder of the Disciples of Christ, especially his meeting at Cincinnati in 1829 with Robert Owen, who was visiting the United States to further his utopian experiment at New Harmony, Indiana; Owen supported the proposition that all religions were bad and contrary to human nature. The Owen-Campbell debate continued for hour after hour, day after day, with lengthy, theoretical arguments that frequently were irrelevant, but the audience remained solemnly attentive until the end—certainly a tribute to the West's interest in religion. More exciting were the Lyman Beecher diatribes against the advance of Popery. The West also came to listen to the feministic radicalism of "Fanny" Wright, who was then involved in an experimental community at Nashoba, Tennessee, to raise the standards of the Negroes. Westerners disapproved of Miss Wright's beliefs but paid her respectful attention.

The lyceum and the lecture had an important rival in the museum. Each larger town had a museum where the visitor, for a small fee, could see Indian relics, old coins, collections of animals and plants, mummies, clothes and utensils from the Far East, and wax figures of the great rulers, statesmen, soldiers, and criminals of the world. Particularly notable was Dorfeuille's museum in Cincinnati, where on the top floor was a "pandae-monium of hell," in which were dwarfs that grew into giants, imps of ebony with eyes of flame, large reptiles devouring youth and beauty, cakes of fire, and mountains of ice; the surrounding railing, connected with one of the new electrical machines, gave a shock to anyone who leaned on it. Most visitors satisfied their consciences that this exhibit was educational and taught an excellent moral lesson.

The museum was closely allied to various types of traveling exhibitions. Minstrel shows were coming into favor, and a few of them toured the West. Traveling manageries attracted many of the curious, and particularly when they were supplemented by the gyrations of acrobats. Automations, of which the automatic chess player was best known, were viewed with interest. Balloon ascensions were high in popular favor. The greatest of American showmen, Phineas T. Barnum, was beginning his career by tours through the West. All such amusement, however, was periodic in nature, and enjoyed by comparatively few citizens.

MUSIC AND OTHER FINE ARTS

The music of this new and growing West was usually primitive. The piano was rare, and the common instruments were the flute and the fiddle, the latter being much more popular. The fiddle (it did not attain the aristocratic name of violin in the West until later) was essential to all dances; the musician, almost always self-taught, frequently made his own instrument. Any attempt to cultivate good instrumental music was rare, although as early as 1807 a group of young men in Pittsburgh organized an Apollonian Society, and gave acceptable renditions of compositions by Haydn, Pleyel, Mozart, and Handel.

Vocal music was used largely as a means of amusement for social groups. Few people could read music; consequently most songbooks were printed with only the words and the names of the tunes or with "patent notes" that showed their pitch by their shapes. Singing classes were popular, particularly with young men and women. Any one with even the vaguest knowledge of music would act as teacher, give the pitch, and sing the tune, after which the others would repeat the song. Singing in the churches was by the unaccompanied congregation. An organ would have been considered sacrilegious, even had there been funds to pay for one.

If western music was in its infancy, the other fine arts were new-born. A few Westerners with artistic leanings, such as S. N. Clevenger and Hiram Powers, did a little sculpturing, but they were self-taught and their work was crude. It was Hiram Powers who made the figures for the representation of hell in Dorfeuille's museum, and this work proved so arresting that a patron of the arts subsidized him to study in Europe. Eventually Powers produced some fairly good work, but his best-known figure, the "Slave Girl" probably attracted more attention for its nudity than for its artistry.

Architecturally the best building was the despised and derivative log cabin, which adapted western materials to western needs; certainly it was better than an octagonal house of fifty-seven rooms or an experimental concrete house, both of which appeared in Wisconsin during the 1840s. Homes and public buildings with pretensions toward style copied eastern forms, and the East was in the throes of a Greek temple craze. Most distinctive and challenging was Mrs. Trollope's bazaar at Cincinnati, which was described by an eyewitness as "Graeco-Moresco-Gothic-Chinese." Luckily it was early covered with whitewash.

Painting had a slightly better reception than architecture or sculpture. A few artists, such as Charles Lesueur and Karl Bodmer, visited the West, or moved to it, painted western scenes, and taught some appreciation of pictorial art. George Catlin, who came from the East, did hundreds of Indian portraits. Now and then a foreign artist would settle in a western city and give lessons in his art, but although the West always entertained him hospitably, it could not waste much time in viewing or acquiring this effeminate talent. The most that the average Westerner would concede for painting was that a talented daughter of a well-to-do family might do worse than paint pictures on velvet.

A few Westerners braved the absence of popular appreciation of art by teaching themselves the rudiments of painting, and then trying to exist on the dollar a head that farmers were willing to pay for pictures of their wives. Some evidence of an increasing interest in art came with the founding of the Academy of Fine Arts in the frontier town of Chicago in the late 1830s. Such proofs of a growing artistic appreciation were, however, but faint clouds in the sunny sky of western materialism. Even in the East the prospective painter could not obtain proper instruction or materials, while in the West the business of making a living left little time for nonessentials. The few picture galleries were nearly all in the museums, and were sorry collections of paintings.

The West furnished a fair market for cheap portraits because of the unavailability of the camera. A landscape could now and then find a purchaser. Quite popular was the panorama, which at its most impressive might be a picture of the entire Mississippi, painted on three-quarters of a mile of canvas that could be rolled past the patrons. There was no western demand for still-life pictures, and portraits of nudes were banned by all polite society as fit only for barrooms.

Most important of western painters of the period was the Missouri artist George Caleb Bingham. Largely self-taught, he succeeded in making his living by doing portraits at some fifty dollars a head, including portraits of Clay for a political banner. In time he became sufficiently prosperous to visit the East and Europe. Best remembered are his descriptive paintings of local elections, pioneers, and river life, which are excellent both as paintings and as historical evidence. Very possibly he was correct in his not very modest claim: "I am the greatest among the disciples of the brush, which my native land has yet produced."

DRAMA

The art that obtained the most secure foothold in the early West was the drama. Amateur theatricals were presented in Lexington before 1800, and appeared very early as part of the amusements of such towns as Pittsburgh, Cincinnati, Detroit, and St. Louis. Military garrisons in the West spent spare moments in producing their own plays in which soldiers usually took the feminine roles, with results considerably worse than those of the modern all-male college production. Theaters did not exist in the early days; hence any large vacant room might be equipped with a rough stage and furnished with crude seats. Candles gave the necessary light, one or two small rooms provided dressing facilities for the entire cast; the scenery was entirely homemade. Plays produced under these circumstances were designed primarily for the amusement of the families, friends, and acquaintances of the amateur actors.

The first professional company to visit the West was recruited in Montreal and Quebec and opened in Lexington, Kentucky, in 1810 with the tragedy "Jane Shore." It was followed by other companies, notably those headed by Samuel Drake and N. M. Ludlow. The life of the traveling player was arduous and uncertain, for western towns were small and far apart, and the size of their audiences was uncertain. Sometimes the town fathers considered the drama an immoral influence and tried to close the theatres by heavy taxation. Audiences were mostly men, with a sprinkling of prostitutes, and rowdies were not averse to hurling overripe vegetables or breaking the furniture if displeased by either the play or the acting. Such reactions were often justified.

The theaters of the West remained poor and few before 1820. A traveling company might play one night in a regular theater, the next in a billiard hall, then in a brewery, in a vacant store, in the hall above the courthouse, or even in a clearing in the woods. The trip between stops was often long and always over bad roads. Poor receipts caused many a company to disband, leaving its members penniless in the wilderness. The chance of a western actor's becoming a star in the East was remote.

The western theater began to make progress in the late 1820s and 1830s, due largely to the efforts of the rival producers James Caldwell and Sol Smith. Caldwell favored New Orleans, but also worked more northern towns such as Natchez, Nashville, and St. Louis. Sol Smith preferred Kentucky but also made trips north into Ohio and south into Georgia, Alabama, and Mississippi, and had a theater in St. Louis. He was probably the best known and most popular comedian in the West.

The best theatrical town in the 1820s and 1830s was New Orleans, with both an American and a French theater. Even grand opera was produced: "The Barber of Seville," "The Marriage of Figaro," "Cinderella" (the English version of Rossini's opera), and others. Cincinnati was next to New Orleans in dramatic importance, particularly after the opening of Caldwell's new theater in 1832. This structure cost $40,000 and held between 1300 and 1500 people. It was decorated elaborately and was lighted with lamps instead of candles. Its magnificence was dimmed only by a new St. Louis theater of 1837, which even though not completed because of the panic was the most impressive ever attempted in the West. The stage was fifty-five feet wide and seventy-three feet deep, and the auditorium could hold 1400. The seats and floor could be removed to accommodate the equestrian performances so popular at the time.

Each theatrical company had a large repertory; otherwise, because of the smallness of most western towns, it would have been forced to move almost continuously. A certain amount of variety was achieved by the starring system then in vogue. Outstanding actors and actresses appeared with one company after another in a limited number of plays. In this way the West was able to see such famous performers as Junius Brutus Booth,

Edwin Forrest, Charles Kean, James H. Hackett, Jane Placide, Ellen Tree, Fanny Elssler, "Jim Crow" Rice, and the Ravel family. Edwin Forrest, the most popular native-born actor, usually appeared in Shakespearean roles. Fanny Elssler, an Austrian dancer, was greatly admired, but charged such high fees that theater managers were sometimes lucky to make expenses at her performances.

The usual dramatic performance consisted of a three- or four-act play followed by a one-act farce, with singing and dancing specialties between the acts to keep the audience from becoming restless. Acrobats, such as the Ravel family, drew good houses. Equestrian companies, all the rage during the 1830s, soon lost their appeal. A fake dancing match arranged by Barnum in New Orleans about 1840 drew large and partisan crowds. Infant prodigies such as Master Burke were favorably received, and several of them toured the country profitably.

Most of the plays presented to western audiences were English in origin. Those of Shakespeare had the most performances, and particularly "Richard III," "Othello," and "Hamlet." Quite popular also were the plays of Thomas Morton, particularly "Town and Country," "Speed the Plow," and "A Roland for an Oliver." Efforts by American actors such as Edwin Forrest to encourage American playwrights had only limited success, although "Metamora," written by J. A. Stone for Forrest, was well received. During the 1830s there were staged a few costly spectacles, including a battle in the war with Tripoli and the eruption of Mt. Vesuvius, as well as a wild horse in "Mazeppa," dogs, camels, monkeys, a Hercules, pugilists, and fireworks. These expensive treats were enjoyed by the audiences but were not popular with the poor western producers.

NEWSPAPERS AND MAGAZINES

The most common reading material of the West was the newspaper, and a printing press was one of the first nonessentials to be brought to a new community. Before 1800 newspaper subscription lists were small, advertising was limited, paper, ink, and type were expensive, deliveries uncertain, and news hard to obtain, so that all papers were weekly and depended largely on the printing of public notices for their support. After 1800 they grew more and more rapidly. In 1790 there had been but one newspaper to each 75,000 people, but by 1840 the ratio had increased to 1 to 12,000, and the daily paper (six days a week) had become well established in larger cities such as Cincinnati. With all this growth, however, newspaper printing remained a hazardous business, and the mortality rate among publishing companies was high.

In addition to the newspaper there was the monthly magazine, usually literary or religious, but sometimes scientific. Usually it depended on exchange material, but several editors tried to encourage original western stories, sketches, and incidents. Timothy Flint failed in this attempt in his *Western Magazine and Review* (1827–1830). William Davis Gallagher did a little better in *The Western Literary Journal and Monthly Review* (1836), but best of all was James Hall's *Western Monthly Magazine* (1833–1836), possibly because he did most of the writing himself.

POETRY AND FICTION

Western poets were universally banal and uninspired. Probably the best was W. D. Gallagher, but even he could ruin fresh western themes with his dry and conventional treatment. Quite popular in the West was Richard Emmons, whose great work *The Fredoniad: or, Independence Preserved. An Epick Poem on the Late War of 1812,* published in 1827, received warm praise and earned a moderate financial return. To the modern reader, however, it is no better than the terrible *Columbiad* of Joel Barlow.

The two outstanding western authors of the 1820s and 1830s were Timothy Flint and James Hall. Flint was born in Massachusetts, attended Harvard, and entered the ministry. He went to the West in 1815 partly to improve his very poor health, and there he undertook missionary work. For twenty-five years, in spite of ill health, he lived a very active life, traveling in the West, in the East, and in Europe; he died at Natchez in 1840. Among his many literary labors were the editing of the *Western Magazine and Review,* the editing of the far western travels of James Ohio Pattie, and a life of Boone. Other writings included an autobiography, descriptive essays, and several novels. Flint based his work almost entirely on frontier themes, but unfortunately he had a romantic imagination and an instinct for melodrama, so that he cannot be trusted to depict western life objectively.

Much more important than Timothy Flint was Judge James Hall, the foremost western writer of his day. Hall was born in Philadelphia in 1793 and had just begun the study of law when the War of 1812 broke out. He joined the army, participated in the Niagara campaign, and fought against the Barbary pirates. Finally in 1820 he returned to Philadelphia, and after further law study moved to the famous Shawneetown in Illinois, where he became prosecuting attorney for twelve counties. His title of judge was not an honorary one: he held the office of circuit judge for twelve years. In his spare time he edited at least two newspapers, the *Illinois Gazette* of Shawneetown and the *Illinois Intelligencer* of Vandalia.

One of Hall's greatest contributions to the literary development of the West was his editing of the *Illinois Monthly Magazine* at Vandalia in 1830–1832. This, the first literary journal in Illinois, emphasized western material, of which Hall himself wrote the greater share. It was responsible for preserving many western figures such as Mike Fink. In 1833 Hall moved his periodical to Cincinnati, renaming it the *Western Monthly Magazine,* and continuing to stress original western contributions in order to increase western literary self-consciousness. It was he who discovered Harriet Beecher (Stowe).

Hall did not confine his literary efforts to editorial work. Novels, short stories, descriptive works, and texts flowed from his tireless pen in the prodigiously productive years 1828–1848. He was undoubtedly the greatest single advertiser and popularizer of the West, and did more than any one other man to develop a real western literature. His graphic accounts of western life and customs were rivaled only by Albert Pike's *Prose Sketches and Poems Written in the Western Country* (1834), A. B. Longstreet's *Georgia Scenes* (1835), Mrs. C. M. Kirkland's *A New Home— Who'll Follow* (1839), and J. G. Baldwin's *The Flush Times of Alabama and Mississippi* (1853). The best Indian stories came from the pen of William J. Snelling.

EASTERN LITERATURE IN THE WEST

The usual reading of the West was the literature of the East and of Europe. British publications were widely reprinted and read, since they were in the correct language, involved well-known names, and were not protected by copyright. The West bestowed its favor on the sickly sentiments of Felecia Hemans and Hannah Moore, both of whom were well known in both East and West. Byron had a large and devoted following in the West as well as in the East in spite of some doubts about his personal morals; works like *Beppo* and *Don Juan* were reprinted west of the Alleghenies within a year of their publications in England (1818 and 1819). Best and most favorably known was Sir Walter Scott, whose works were republished and read eagerly in the West as fast as they appeared; western writers such as Hall, Flint, and Gallagher were influenced by Scott.

Eastern writers also had their western readers, but western taste was generally bad. Holmes, Whittier, and Longfellow were creating reputations, but Hawthorne, Emerson, and Poe were almost unknown. Irving had some following but Cooper was viewed with distrust, most people feeling that his stories would have been better if he had known more of the West. Bryant was known but little and liked less.

EASTERNERS USE WESTERN THEMES

Eastern literary figures did not overlook the West as a rich source of material not only for works of travel and description, but also for short stories and novels. The situations particularly appealing to them were wilderness travel and Indian conflicts. Utilizing the travel theme, such books as Paulding's *Westward Ho!* (drawn largely from Flint), and R. H. Dana's delightful *Two Years before the Mast* were outstanding.

Washington Irving, the dean of American writers, was attracted to western material partly through his friend John Jacob Astor. He wrote historically and descriptively rather than as a novelist. His *Astoria, Captain Bonneville,* and *Tour of the Prairies* were all published during the 1830s and dealt with the trans-Mississippi West. The first is the best of these, although the others are interesting for their style and for their descriptions of the western plains. All three are readable, but none is among the best of Irving's work.

Eastern writers generally found tales of Indian life and warfare more appealing to readers than stories of travel and exploration, which was also the attitude of the American public. George Catlin drew large crowds when he exhibited his collection of Indian portraits and curiosities. T. L. McKinney's *The Indian Tribes of North America,* largely pictorial, was reputed to have yielded a profit of $100,000 to its publishers. Innumerable plays used the Indian as either hero or villain. Best known was the prize play *Metamora* by John Augustus Stone, with Edwin Forrest monopolizing the part of Metamora from the opening of the play in December 1829. Realism flew out the wings as Forrest ranted, orated, and gesticulated, but thousands of Americans hung on the words of Metamora as this fearless lover of nature pursued his tragic life until he finally perished with his wife and child.

As for the novelists of the period, few before 1850 failed to produce at least one Indian story. Starting with Philip Freneau and Charles Brockden Brown, each author found occasion either to praise or to condemn his red-skinned brother. The main problem was whether to picture the Indian as a noble and tragic son of nature or as a lurking, cruel, bloodthirsty savage. A few of the efforts, such as Longfellow's *Hiawatha,* still retain currency, but most have disappeared. Among the best was James Kirke Paulding's *Koningsmarke, The Long Finne* (1823), written in a light vein, but giving a credible picture of the Indian as a human being.

Among the best-liked works of their own day were the novels of Robert Montgomery Bird and William Gilmore Simms. Bird's great work was *Nick of the Woods, or the Jibbenainosay* (1837), a dark tale of violence and bloodshed in Kentucky immediately after the Revolution. The Indians were the villains and the Jibbenainosay was an avenging white who slaughtered them right and left. Simms did a more plausible job, particularly in his novel *The Yemasee* (1835). The scene is laid in the Carolinas of the early eighteenth century and the book abounds in fights and hairbreadth escapes, and yet the Indian is given a sympathetic treatment as a social being with loves and hates, virtues and vices, who is being over-whelmed by a civilization more powerful than his own.

The writer whose Indian stories have had the greatest power of survival is James Fenimore Cooper. The five volumes of his *Leatherstock-ing Tales,* dealing with the lives and contacts of Indians and frontiersmen, appeared between 1823 and 1841. Cooper had lived in central New York State as a boy and considered himself an authority on the frontier even though he actually had known no Indians except the deteriorated vestiges of once-powerful tribes, and had never revisited the scenes he described. Although Cooper was a dogmatic and intolerant man who quarreled with nearly everyone in sight and his criticisms of American institutions brought him much unpopularity, his frontier stories lived.

In spite of certain errors of fact, Cooper's tales are not bad pictures of the frontier. They are primarily both masculine and juvenile in content and appeal; Cooper's women are always wooden and unconvincing, and his descriptions of love affairs are mawkish. The Indians tend to be types rather than individuals. Either they are everything that is good and noble and true or they are a composite of man's less admirable traits. Possibly these very literary and psychological defects are the basic causes for the popu-larity of the volumes, both then and later. Many a small boy since the middle of the nineteenth century has marveled at the feats of the frontiers-men, has shuddered at the dangerous situations, has felt relieved at the miraculous escapes of his heroes, has applauded the good Indians and been angered by the bad.

Although the early nineteenth century made considerable use of frontier themes, much remained to be done. The emphasis on travel and Indian troubles meant that large masses of material were unexplored. The western thriller had not as yet appeared; its reputed originator, E. Z. C. Judson, published his first book in 1845, but it did not deal with the West. Even more important, there was as yet no fiction that the modern critic would consider realistic.

READINGS

GENERAL. The varied material of this chapter is included in such regional accounts as Everett Dick, *The Dixie Frontier* (1948); Roscoe Buley, *The Old Northwest* (2 vols., 1950); Francis G. Davenport, *Ante-Bellum Kentucky* (1943); Henry C. Hubbart, *The Older Middle West, 1840–1880* (1936). See the Readings for Chapters 8, 13, and also 17.

RELIGION. Particularly valuable are the works of William W. Sweet, *The Story of Religions in America* (1930), *Religion in the Devel-opment of American Culture* (1952), *Religion on the Frontier* (4 vols., 1931–1946), largely documents, *Methodism in American History* (1933), and *The Rise of Methodism in the West* (1920). Other useful studies include John F. Cady, *The Missionary Baptist Church in Indiana* (1942) ; Colin B. Goodykoontz, *Home Missions on the American Frontier* (1939) ; Theodore Maynard, *The Story of American Catholicism* (1941) ; Elizabeth K. Nottingham, *Methodism and the Frontier* (1941), Indiana; Walter B. Pusey, *The Development of Methodism in the Old Southwest* (1933).

LITERATURE AND THE ARTS. Careful surveys are Dorothy A. Dondore, *The Prairie and the Making of Middle America* (1926) ; Lucy L. Hazard, *The Frontier in American Literature* (1927) ; Ralph L. Rusk, *The Literature of the Middle Western Frontier* (2 vols., 1925). Albert Keiser, *The Indian in American Literature* (1933) is excellent although filled with quotations. Good biographies are Frederick W. Allsopp, *Albert Pike* (1928) ; John T. Flanagan, *James Hall* (1941) ; John E. Kirkpatrick, *Timothy Flint* (1911) ; John D. Wade, *Augustus Baldwin Longstreet* (1924). James A. Shackford, *David Crockett* (1956) investigates primarily the legend; the Crockett autobiography is readily available. Gwladys Spencer, *The Chicago Public Library* (1943) is scholarly. William G. B. Carson, *Managers in Distress: The St. Louis Stage, 1840–1844* (1949) is limited and detailed, but gives a good picture of the western theater. Rexford Newcomb, *Architecture in the Old Northwest Territory* (1950) contains many pictures. See also the writings of the authors mentioned in the chapter.

CHAPTER 20

BEYOND THE
MISSISSIPPI

M igrating frontiersmen found new problems as they moved west of the Mississippi. After passing the land immediately adjacent to the river they found themselves on seemingly endless plains, flat or gently rolling, of the kind about which they had felt skeptical farther east. Annual rainfall became less and less until it averaged under ten inches a year; beyond the ninety-eighth meridian eastern methods of agriculture became thoroughly hazardous if not impossible. Vegetation became limited largely to tough grass, which grew shorter and sparser with the miles. Trees were confined almost entirely to the river valleys, and the sound of the frontiersman's ax, so common in the East, faded away. Here the typical sounds were the thundering of buffalo herds as they swept across the plains and the fearsome crackling of prairie fires as they blackened the vegetation.

The Great Plains rose gradually as the traveler went west, ultimately giving way to the snowy peaks of the Rocky Mountains, which stretched from Canada to Mexico. Whereas the Appalachians had once been extremely troublesome, now they looked small and friendly compared with the intimidating peaks of the Rockies. The dangerous crossing of the Rockies led to the uninviting country of the Great Basin, dominated by the Great Salt Lake. Here the rainfall was so inadequate that part of the country was a complete desert, and the salt water of the lake was cheering in appearance but unappetizing in fact. To the north the Snake River was a welcome relief—until the rapidity of the current and the cragginess of the banks brought the realization that it was anything but a parallel to the Ohio River in the East.

After plodding over the Great Basin, the weary traveler heading for California then encountered the majestic High Sierras, a barrier which some failed to cross. Descending to the valleys of the Sacramento and San Joaquin rivers, the traveler had the feeling of entering heaven. Farther north he could float down the Columbia through increasingly well-watered country; one branch of the Columbia, the Willamette, flowing generally from south to north, provided conditions nearly like those of the East. In general, the western halves of the present states of Washington and Oregon received reasonable amounts of rainfall, and the coastal strip even more. In California, except for a few areas, the rainfall was inadequate by eastern standards.

PLAINS INDIANS

The Indians west of the Mississippi varied greatly in culture from the lowly "diggers" of California to the highly civilized Hopi, but the most important groups of the plains had rather similar cultures. They were generally less agricultural than the eastern Indians. The open, treeless, semiarid plains offered far less encouragement to farming than did the well-watered country farther east, and in addition the western plains supported a seemingly inexhaustible food supply in the buffalo. The Indians depended for the greater share of their necessities of life on this animal. Its meat, which was preserved by smoking or drying, was the Indians' principal food. Its skin, after being tanned, with its brains used as the tanning agent, made clothes, shoes, tents, and blankets; its bones furnished implements such as knives and hoes, and at times bows, or children's sleds. Its tendons were used for thread and bow strings. Even its entrails provided a part of the Indian domestic economy; the intestines were used in making sausages and the bladder was made into a water bag.

Since the buffalo moved across the plains in huge herds, the Indians too were generally nomadic even though they also had a little agriculture. The usual Indian domicile was the temporary wigwam or tepee constructed of a framework of slanting, crossed poles covered with joined buffalo skins. Permanent wooden houses were rare. For traveling the Indian used a travois, an arrangement of poles with one end lashed to a horse and the other dragging on the ground; on these poles were fastened the tepee materials, clothing, sleeping robes, and cooking and eating utensils; frequently a young child or two perched on top. Horses were a necessity, and were used much more here than farther east. They were small and shaggy, the descendants of horses earlier introduced by the Spanish to the south. Every Indian was a good horseman; his children were taught to ride almost as soon as to walk. The greatest use of the horse, except for traveling or fighting, was in hunting buffalo. In the usual buffalo hunt, horsemen rode into the herd and shot their quarry at close range. A miscalculation probably meant death under the hoofs of the frightened animals. Because arrows were hard to make and hence scarce, they were recovered at the end of a hunt; it was considered unfortunate if an arrow only wounded a buffalo, for then the arrow was lost. Buffalo hunts sometimes took the form of driving the animals into a corral where they could be killed at the hunters' leisure. At other times the beasts were driven over a cliff and thus slaughtered by the hundreds.

Many of the activities of the western Indians were similar to those of their eastern brothers. Chiefs obtained their offices by popular choice, and had but vague powers. War was the principal business of the men. These tribes were extremely powerful; their bows were probably more effective than muzzle-loading guns. Scalps taken in war proved that the brave had come sufficiently close to the enemy to touch him, while horse stealing conferred honor that was second only to touching the enemy. Prisoners were rarely tortured, but they were usually either enslaved or adopted into the tribe; women were frequently married.

The division of labor between the sexes was practically the same in the West as in the East. The men hunted, fished, and fought, while the women did the rest of the work. In spite of white sentiment to the contrary, the position of an Indian woman was comparatively good. She had rights that her husband had to respect; often she participated in ceremonial dances and tribal councils. Children belonged to the clan of the mother, and were well treated; unlike white children, they were seldom given physical punishment. Their play and education were combined; the girls played with dolls and kept house, and the boys engaged in make-believe buffalo hunts and battles.

Marriage customs were similar over the plains, even though they varied in detail. A girl presumably remained chaste before marriage, though there were some slips. She normally married young in a ceremony that involved some sort of purchase. Polygamy was accepted universally but was practiced in most tribes only by a few of the wealthier men. Divorce occurred normally on the desire of the husband alone, though here and there either party could take the initiative. Infidelity by the wife was frequently punished by the amputation of the end of her nose by her husband. Infidelity by the husband was punished by the relatives of the wife; in fact, the usual treatment of any crime was by vengeance. Women were ordinarily considered unclean during their menstrual periods, when they frequently lived by themselves in small temporary shelters. Childbirth seemed not very painful, and was not allowed to interfere with the mother's regular activities. No assistance was given except in the case of the first-born child. Immediately after the birth the woman washed herself and her new baby in the nearest stream, even if she first had to chop a hole in the ice, and then went back to her normal household work.

Medical care was furnished by medicine men, who mainly sought to drive out the wicked spirits by elaborate ceremonials, although they also used simple herbs and sucking. Infection was beyond the power of the Indian doctor; white men's diseases such as measles, smallpox, and syphilis brought frightful mortality: the smallpox epidemic that swept the plains in 1837 killed over half of several tribes. Surgery was so primitive that a broken arm or leg was seldom set properly, and there was no assurance that the limb could be used in the future.

Utensils and weapons varied widely, depending on the materials available and on the customs of the particular group. Vessels might be simple wooden, horn, or bone receptacles, or they might be glazed clay with elaborate designs. Material for clothes, blankets, and tents ranged from poorly tanned buffalo hides to well-woven cloth and waterproof blankets. Bows, arrows, lances, clubs, shields, and knives varied from tribe to tribe.

Each Plains Indian tribe had elaborate dances and ceremonials, many of which were long and complex. They were designed to ward off evil spirits or propitiate good ones, to ensure that the corn would grow well, the rain would fall, the buffalo would be plentiful, the young men brave, war successful, disease and accident absent, and that all the other things the Indian desired would come true. Frequently a dance was a mimicry of the thing desired, as in a pantomime buffalo hunt, and took the form of short, jerky steps, together with a vertical movement of the body. Most of the dances were only for men, a few were specially for women, and some were for both sexes. Usually the dance was accompanied by singing and instrumental music; the drum was the most common musical instrument. The drummer and the singer made no effort to agree on their rhythms; each did a solo, with results that were weird and unearthly to the visitor accustomed to the musical traditions of the white man. In addition to all sizes and shapes of drums, the Indians used a varied assortment of rattles and simple whistles. More rare was the flute, which was a variation of the whistle and was made by only a few tribes. The flute was used only for love songs, and even then but rarely; few white men ever heard it in its original Indian use.

The western Indians loved funny stories and practical jokes. They had strong family affection and were reasonably loquacious. They reveled in games of all kinds. A child had a sled and a hoop, bow and arrows, dolls, and other similar delights; he had dozens of games, including skating and snapping the whip. Adults also had many sports, including several ball games, kissing games, guessing contests, and various dice games; the dice were probably marked plum pits or bones. Both men and women participated in the games, and betting was universal.

Each Indian tribe had its legends of spirits, mythological heroes, and animals who talked with humans, as well as fabulous tales of the origins of particular kinds of animals, parts of the country, and the human race. Many good and bad spirits were thought to inhabit the world; usually the Indians accepted a supreme good spirit and a happy hunting ground. Great credence was placed in dreams and visions. Most tribes had their mythological "culture heroes," about whom long tales were told. Other stories explained the making of the world, the appearance of people, the creation of the buffalo, and similar mysteries. Ordinarily such tales were told only at night, and then by a commonly accepted storyteller, who made an elaborate ceremony of the narration.

In spite of their general similarities the Plains Indians were by no means a homogeneous people. Although they were grouped into tribes through similarities in descent, language, and geography, the tribe practically never acted as a unit; smaller groups within the tribe exercised complete freedom of action. Each tribe occupied a fairly definite portion of the plains, although periodic migrations changed the picture from time to time. Some tribes were traditionally friendly with each other, while others were ordinarily hostile. The idea of the Plains Indians acting together as a single unit does not correspond with the facts.

INDIVIDUAL TRIBES

One of the most highly civilized, friendly, and peaceful tribes in the West was the Mandan, living on the Missouri in the present Dakotas. Travelers almost inevitably spent at least a few days with these hospitable people. The Mandan were a branch of the Sioux. Probably at one time they had been numerous, but by the early nineteenth century they had been reduced to two small villages. They fought but little, and were more agricultural than their neighbors. They carried the usual Indian cleanliness to an extreme; almost daily they bathed in the river and they used a primitive sort of steam bath in which water was thrown over hot stones in a small hut, after which the bather dived into the river.

A Mandan house was round, some forty to sixty feet in diameter, and unusual in being both large and permanent. Four large center poles supported the roof. The walls, constructed of logs, were vertical at the bottom and tapered at the top. The entire structure was covered with mud. It was sufficiently strong to support the entire family on pleasant days. The ground inside the house was dug down about two feet and then trampled hard. The fire was in the center and the smoke escaped through a hole in

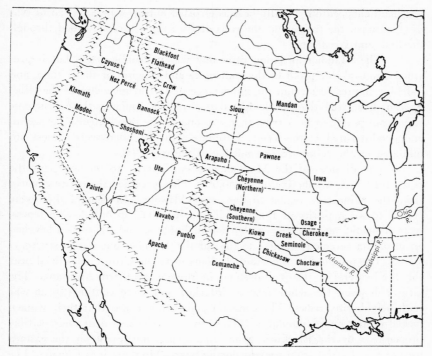

Indian Tribes, 1840

the roof. Such a house was sufficiently large to be the home of between twenty and forty persons.

The Mandan had in general the customs and beliefs of other Plains Indians, but they were noted particularly for a spring ceremony that was the most elaborate of any of its type on the plains. This ceremony honored the falling of the water in the river after the spring floods, celebrated the appearance of new vegetation, and initiated the young men into full membership of the tribe. Songs and ceremonies occupied four days, and on the fourth day all young men to be initiated were gathered in a central lodge. Each in turn had portions of the skin of the chest or back, upper arm, lower arm, upper leg, and lower leg lifted, incisions made, and splints introduced. Then the youth was hoisted by ropes attached to the splints of the chest or back until his feet left the ground; weights were hung to all the splints, and he was revolved until he fainted. Meanwhile everyone in the building shouted to sustain the group morale and to drown the young man's groans. After the initiate fainted he was lowered and allowed to recover consciousness. Then he was taken to one side of the room and the little finger of his left hand chopped off. Finally he was escorted outside where he ran or was dragged until the weights at the ends of the splints tore the wood through the flesh and freed him.

The Mandan initiation ceremony was unusually cruel, but it provided unmistakable proof of the endurance and stoicism of the initiate, and indelibly impressed on him the importance of full membership in the tribe. It also illustrated the paradoxical nature of the Indians: these gruesome rites were practiced by a tribe that was one of the most friendly, peaceful, and good-natured in the West. Ultimately the Mandan were almost annihilated by the yellow fever epidemic of the late 1830s.

On all sides of the Mandan, but particularly to the west, lay the powerful Sioux, numbering about 50,000. They occupied the entire country from the Minnesota region to the upper Missouri. In general they were typical of the majority of Plains Indians: they lived in buffalo-skin tepees, were nomadic, and excelled as horsemen, hunters, and fighters. They had an initiation ceremony similar to that of the Mandan but not so severe.

The proudest of the Plains Indians were the Crows, who lived near the headwaters of the Yellowstone in present southern Montana. The Crows despised the white men as inferiors and were continually at war with neighboring tribes. The common plains rumor was that their women lacked proper moral standards. The Crows were exceeded in their warlike propensities by the Blackfeet, who lived to the northwest on the eastern base of the Rockies from present northwestern Montana into Canada. The Blackfeet, the most aggressive and warlike of the Plains Indians, were noted for their ferocity, cruelty, and consistent hostility to the white man. They practiced no agriculture, but lived entirely by hunting; they were somewhat unusual in the extent to which they practiced polygamy and in the largeness of their families.

In the central plains region lived several very powerful tribes. The Cheyenne (in permanent alliance with the Arapaho) had been pushed west from Minnesota by the Sioux. During the 1830s they had split into two groups, with the northern Cheyenne occupying the upper branches of the Platte River and the southern Cheyenne the upper Arkansas. Both were typical Plains Indians. In present western Nebraska were the Pawnee, another typical plains group. The Pawnee have received unusual attention because one of their ceremonies included a human sacrifice and was practiced as late as 1838. In the spring a young girl, a virgin, was shot, and her flesh and blood were used in an elaborate symbolic ceremonial to fertilize the fields of corn. South of the Pawnee lived the Osage, a small tribe roaming over the region that is now western Kansas and eastern Colorado; its hereditary chieftainship was one of the tribe's few unusual characteristics. Farther west, centering in the present Utah, were various Shoshonean tribes, known commonly as "Root Diggers" or "Snakes" (the name coming from the Snake River). They were generally poor, miserable, and dirty, living mostly on roots because game was scarce and their land was not easily cultivated. Usually they were peaceful. The tribe known as Shoshoni, however, was a normal plains tribe.

In the Rocky Mountain region and along the Pacific Coast were many tribes that by the early nineteenth century were for the most part small, poverty-stricken, filthy, and degraded. They lived chiefly on fish and roots, with now and then a delicacy such as grasshopper pie. Their principal accomplishment was the weaving of baskets, of which some were so well constructed as to hold water. Some of the northern tribes flattened the heads of their children by strapping a board on the top of each new baby's skull (though this practice was not followed by the tribe known to the whites as Flatheads.) Notable exceptions to the characteristic natives of this area were the Nez Percés, who lived on the lower Snake River and its tributaries and were an extremely able and dignified people.

Two of the most feared tribes of the plains, the Apache and Comanche, lived to the south in the present Arizona, New Mexico, and western Texas. The difficult country in which they lived possibly accounts for their simple form of living and their tendency to act individually rather than in groups. They were wild, uncivilized, cruel, fierce, and warlike peoples. Prisoners were enslaved and sometimes tortured; if women, they were almost always raped. Both tribes were migratory, having no regular agriculture and no permanent villages.

Two minor groups in the South were notable for their high civilizations. The Pueblo Indians, living for the most part in present New Mexico, were the remnants of a highly organized and prosperous tribe; their stone, sometimes adobe, houses, excellent implements, and irrigated fields all indicated a former state of opulence. West of them, on the lower Colorado, were the Navaho. Although the Navaho did not have permanent homes they raised various grains and fruit, herded cattle, sheep, mules, horses, and asses, and wove excellent blankets and coarse woolen goods.

These were the Indians the white frontier encountered as it pushed from the Mississippi toward the Pacific. They were proud and effective warriors, and their numbers, plus their lack of permanent villages, made them difficult to conquer. Their ways of life gave little promise that they might be converted into farmers after the white model. There was no region farther west into which they might be shoved.

EXPLORING LOUISIANA

The Indian trans-Mississippi West was known but vaguely at the time that most of it was acquired by the United States with the purchase of Louisiana. Although the present Texas and the Southwest had seen some Spanish exploration and settlement (see Chapter 23) the remainder to the north was known only vaguely as a region of great plains, beyond which were high mountains. Quite naturally, various adventurers were lured by the vast unknown. Jefferson had been scientifically interested in the West for many years before he had any thought of buying the territory. While Minister to France he talked in 1786 to the migratory John Ledyard, an inveterate wanderer of considerable ability who was happy only when seeing new places and people. The two men planned that Ledyard would cross Siberia to Kamchatka, then sail across the Pacific, and finally make the overland journey through the Louisiana territory. Ledyard started across Russia in 1786, traveling mostly on foot; eventually he was stopped and turned back by Russian officials; he then went to Africa, where he died in 1788.

Other plans to explore the Far West soon followed those of John Ledyard. Captain John Armstrong made the attempt in 1790, but was thwarted by the Indians. André Michaux, the French botanist, started west in 1793, but was delayed by his involvement in the Genêt intrigue and did not travel beyond the Mississippi. Michaux was backed by America's most important scientific body, the American Philosophical Society, which acted on the recommendation of Jefferson. Other persons considered the long overland trip to the Pacific, but none of these projected expeditions was completed within the territorial limits of the United States before 1800.

LEWIS AND CLARK

The interest in the Far West, particularly Jefferson's, made it almost certain that when Louisiana became United States territory during Jefferson's presidency exploration of the whole area would be encouraged. Actually even before the purchase of Louisiana Jefferson had requested and received permission from Congress to organize an expedition to explore the region west of the Mississippi (January 1803). For its leader he chose Captain Meriwether Lewis (born 1774) and William Clark (born 1770). Lewis had been Jefferson's private secretary and Clark was a brother of the famous George Rogers Clark. These men were personal friends, and both were acquainted with the ways of the wilderness. Lewis started west shortly after his appointment, arriving at Pittsburgh in the summer of 1803. Both here and farther down the Ohio he gathered men and supplies.

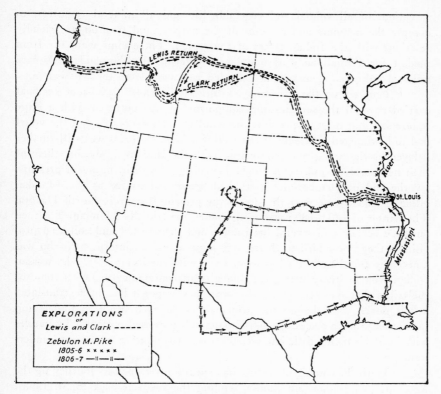

Exploration of the Louisiana Territory

The party spent the winter of 1803–1804 in Illinois nearly opposite the mouth of the Missouri.

The expedition actually started on Sunday, May 13, 1804, when the ascent of the Missouri River was begun. The party was composed of some thirty men, of whom about half were drawn from the army; the others had enlisted for the duration of the trip; in addition there were sixteen men to run the keelboat. Each man was expected to keep notes of all he observed, and oilskin wrappers were provided to protect the notes from the elements. In fact the entire expedition had been planned with great care, which extended to provision of a vast variety of necessary equipment and proper training of the men.

The general aims of the Lewis and Clark Expedition, as stated in the instructions, were primarily scientific. The men were to explore the land, rivers, and mountains from the Mississippi to the coast, to make observations of all animal and vegetable life and all mineral resources, to observe the manners and customs of the natives, and to promote friendly relations with the Indian tribes of the region. These aims were far from modest for a small body of white men entering the thousands of square miles of unknown country that extended westward from the Mississippi.

Progress up the Missouri was necessarily slow. A 55-foot keelboat carried most of the supplies and equipment; it was outfitted with a large square sail, but most of the time the wind was not favorable and the vessel had to be dragged upstream at the end of a rope. Progress was still further delayed by the necessity of conferring with the Indians, informing them of their new masters, and trying to obtain their good will by means of presents. By the end of October the party had progressed as far as the Mandan villages, which were near the site of the present Bismarck, North Dakota. The winter of 1804–1805 was spent among the friendly Mandan. The men built a stockade and several log cabins, and then rested and collected provisions; they also added to their party a guide and an interpreter, who was a necessity for the trip farther west. Even with the interpreter, who was an Indian woman, there was great difficulty in communicating with some of the tribes that were encountered. Sometimes a speech had to be translated a half dozen times before the principals could even begin to understand each other. Such a procedure, particularly when carried out badly by natives with insufficient linguistic knowledge, was not conducive to accurate understanding.

With the coming of spring the expedition resumed its journey up the Missouri in pirogues and canoes, sending the keelboat back to St. Louis. The party left the Mandan villages on April 7, and on April 26 arrived at the mouth of the Yellowstone, where some difficulty was experienced in determining which was the main stream. The next leg of the trip had its worst period in the month that it took to portage the Great Falls of the Missouri, but eventually the party arrived (July 25) at the three forks, which diplomatically were given the names of Jefferson, Madison, and Gallatin. Any one of these three branches, which combine to form the Missouri River, offered almost equal possibilities for the continuance of the journey, and consequently considerable time was spent in exploring all three. Finally the most westerly, the Jefferson, was chosen, and the party followed it and then the Beaverhead to about the present Dillon, Montana. Then the men abandoned the river and prepared to make the next stage of the trip by land.

Lewis and Clark were in an unenviable position when they left their canoes and started forward on foot. They were then nearly two thousand miles from civilization, having crossed an untracked wilderness with its perils of starvation, accident, and disease. They had traversed an unfriendly wilderness in which an unwise gesture might well have meant annihilation by the Indians. All these difficulties remained to be met again on the return trip, but the hardest part of the journey still lay ahead of them if they were to reach the Pacific. The unknown Rocky Mountains had to be crossed in the face of approaching winter; supplies were running low, native guidance was poor, and hostile Indians occupied the country they were approaching. The decision to push farther west in the face of these obstacles required the highest courage and resolution.

The pesdestrian part of the trip was begun in August under the leadership of unwilling guides who had to be watched to prevent their desertion. Snow fell by September 3, making the mountain passes exceedingly dangerous. On September 7 the party was near the present Idaho line at Grantdale, Montana, and from there it followed the Lolo Creek and Lolo Pass (Nez Percé Pass) through the mountains. Frequently the men floundered in the snow; most of the time they were wet and cold, and provisions were so scanty that hunger was the ordinary condition. In late September they passed the mountains and struck a branch of the Clearwater, where they built five canoes. The remainder of the westward trail followed the Clearwater, the Snake, and the Columbia, including a portage at The Dalles on the Columbia. The main objective of the expedition was attained when the Pacific Ocean was sighted on November 7, 1805.

Reaching the Pacific Ocean was a notable accomplishment, but from the standpoint of Lewis and Clark, a good half of the work remained to be done. The homeward trip still bristled with obstacles, and additional exploration was much to be desired. For the time being, the men constructed winter quarters (called Fort Clatsop) at the mouth of the Columbia, where they suffered through the fog and rain, and made preparations for the return trip. The eastward journey began on March 23, 1806, with the party retracing the path that had been followed westward through the mountains. Difficulties in obtaining food increased with the depletion of trading goods, and Lewis and Clark posed as doctors to secure the needed supplies. After the mountains had been crossed the group was divided, half going north with Lewis and then descending the Marias River, while the other half under Clark followed the Yellowstone. The two parties were united at the mouth of the Yellowstone on August 12, and from this point the trip down the river was comparatively easy. The Mandan villages were passed on August 14, and on September 23, 1806, the party was back in St. Louis.

The Lewis and Clark Expedition was the first trip by white men overland through the present continental United States to the Pacific Ocean. The magnitude of the feat was in no wise lessened by the even more marvelous trip of Alexander Mackenzie, who had reached the ocean through

Canadian territory a full decade earlier, on July 22, 1793. It marked the beginning of accurate knowledge concerning the Far West, for the journals kept by the men were gradually published. Unfortunately some of the diaries were lost, but those that remained gave the only reliable facts thus far collected about the Far Northwest.

The expedition was also notable for the remarkably effective way in which it had been handled. Thirty white men had been taken without serious mishap through 6000 miles of wilderness inhabited by potentially hostile Indians. For this service, Lewis was rewarded with the governorship of Louisana Territory, a post he held until a bullet cut short his life in 1809. Clark entered the fur trade, and was Governor of Missouri until it became a state. He then became Superintendent of Indian Affairs at St. Louis, holding the job until his death in 1838.

OTHER EXPLORERS

The expedition of Lewis and Clark was but the first of a long series of governmental efforts to obtain complete and accurate information concerning the country west of the Mississippi. Even before Lewis and Clark were well started, Congress authorized (1804) the exploration of a number of the rivers of the Great Plains—the Panis (Platte), the Paduca (Kansas), the Morsigona (Des Moines), and the St. Peters (Minnesota). Parties were picked for surveying each of these rivers but, although all of them did some work, the total results were disappointing. Most important were William Hunter and George Dunbar, both well-known scientists, who led a small party up the Ouachita of Louisiana in the winter of 1804–1805; they covered this river satisfactorily, but did not reach the Red River, in which Jefferson was particularly interested. A short time later (1806) Thomas Freeman ascended the Red River some 600 miles before he was turned back by a superior Spanish force.

ZEBULON M. PIKE

Of the minor expeditions the most important were the two under the command of Zebulon Montgomery Pike, a young army officer who did his exploring under the orders of James Wilkinson, commander of the western army. By orders dated July 30, 1805, he was instructed to ascend and find the sources of the Mississippi, survey Indian conditions, and locate possible military routes. On his way north he stopped at the present St. Paul, Minnesota, where he bought a considerable tract of land just south of the falls of the Mississippi as a site for a future military post. Resuming his journey, he was much troubled by the difficulties of travel, for it was then midwinter. He found Canadian traders in control of the area, and made the noble and futile gesture of ordering them to pay duty on all goods brought across the international boundary, and to refrain from selling liquor to the Indians. Considering the smallness of Pike's force, its distance from effective support, and the nonexistence of an ascertainable boundary, such orders must have sounded ludicrous to Canadian ears.

Pike continued from Sandy Lake to Leech Lake, where he arrived February 1, 1806. Here he ended his advance to the north, since he mistakenly considered Leech Lake the source of the Mississippi. His return to St. Louis was slow and uneventful. The results of this first expedition of Pike were disappointingly meager. He had found what he thought to be the source of the Mississippi; he had bought land that was later to furnish the site of an important army post; he had made futile gestures toward the North West Company; but he had added little information to the slowly growing body of knowledge about the West.

Immediately upon his return (April 1806) Pike received new orders to explore the headwaters of the Arkansas and Red rivers. Leaving St. Louis on July 15 with twenty-two men, he ascended the Missouri and Osage rivers and then crossed overland to the Arkansas River, which he followed through what is now southern Kansas. His plan was to ascend the Arkansas, cross to the Red, and descend the latter stream to its junction with the Mississippi. The farther west he moved the nearer he came to Spanish territory, and although the exact boundary line was as yet undetermined, the Spanish government became alarmed. A force of 600 Spanish dragoons under Lieutenant Don Facundo Malgares was therefore dispatched to keep Pike and his party out of Spanish territory. Pike heard rumors of this hostile Spanish expedition and so stopped and built fortifications on the site of present Pueblo, Colorado. Incidentally he took the time to start (but not complete) the ascent of the peak that now bears his name. As it happened his fears of the Spanish force proved groundless, for Malgares never found him.

In December Pike took a small part of his force and started south, ostensibly to find the source of the Red River. The weather was bitterly cold, he had but the vaguest idea of where he was going, and the men had to fight a grim struggle with snow and hunger. Eventually they came to a river that Pike later said he thought was the Red, and built a stockade. The building of the stockade was a very wise precaution in view of the fact that the river on which it was constructed was actually the Rio Grande and the party was probably within Spanish territory. Unfortunately the rude fort did not provided sufficient protection; when a hundred Spanish troops appeared on the scene, Pike was forced to give himself up as a prisoner.

After their capture of Pike the Spanish had the perplexing question of what should be done with him. If his party was considered hostile, the penalty might be severe; but if the presumed invasion of Spanish territory was actually an accident, then the invaders should be treated more leniently. The Spanish captain felt incapable of deciding the case and so took Pike first to Santa Fe and then south through El Paso to Chihuahua. Meantime Pike was making copious notes of the country through which he passed, hiding them carefully so that they would not be confiscated. At Chihuahua it was decided to return Pike to the United States, and so he was escorted by way of San Antonio to Natchitoches and there handed over to the United States troops (July 1, 1807). During this return trip he again took voluminous notes. The net result was that Pike, although not carrying out his orders to explore the Red River, brought home a great amount of information that added to American knowledge of the Southwest and stimulated interest in the Texas region.

All these governmental expeditions, as well as many private ventures, helped to push back the frontier of knowledge concerning the Far West. The main tribes of Indians were enumerated and their characteristics described. The animal and plant life of the western plains was reported. The principal geographic features became known, although much remained to lure other explorers to risk their lives in the wilderness.

READINGS

GENERAL ACCOUNTS OF INDIANS. See the Readings for Chapter 7. Every history of any state or region has at least one chapter on the local Indians, and every travel account of the period deals with them. Special treatments of the Plains Indians are George E. Hyde, *Indians of the High Plains* (1959); Robert H. Lowie, *Indians of the Plains* (1954). the importance of the buffalo to the Indian is well covered in E. Douglas Branch, *The Hunting of the Buffalo* (1929).

SPECIFIC INDIAN TRIBES. Apache: Charles L. Sonnichsen, *The Mescalero Apaches* (1958), excellent; Ross Santee, *Apache Land* (1947), interesting but episodic; Ralph H. Ogle, *Federal Control of the Western Apaches, 1848–1886* (1940), reads moderately well. Blackfeet: both John C. Ewers, *The Blackfeet* (1958) and James W. Schultz and Jessie L. Donaldson, *The Sun God's Children* (1930) are fine descriptions. Cheyenne: George B. Grinnell, *By Cheyenne Campfires* (1926), stories, *The Cheyenne Indians* (2 vols., 1923), and *The Fighting Cheyennes* (1915, 1956) are all good; Donald J. Berthrong, *The Southern Cheyennes* (1963), fine; Thomas B. Marquis, *A Warrior Who Fought Custer* (1931), interesting on the Northern Cheyenne. Comanche: Rupert N. Richardson, *The Comanche Barrier* (1933), competent; Ernest Wallace and E. A. Hoebel, *The Comanches* (1952). Crow: Robert H. Lowie, *The Crow Indians* (1935); Frank B. Linderman, *American* (1930), *Red*

Mother (1932), and Glendolin D. Wagner and William A. Allen, *Blankets and Moccasins* (1933), all concern individuals. Kiowa: Mildred P. Mayhall, *The Kiowas* (1962), fair; Wilbur S. Nye, *Bad Medicine & Good Tales* (1962), Indian stories. Navaho: Ruth M. Underhill, *The Navahos* (1956), anthropological approach. Osage: John J. Mathews, *The Osages* (1961). Sioux: four very good books describe individuals: Mari Sandoz, *Crazy Horse* (1942); Henry H. Sibley, *Iron Face* (1950); John G. Neihardt, *Black Elk Speaks* (1932); Luther Standing Bear, *My People the Sioux* (1928). See also two excellent books by George Hyde, *Red Cloud's Folk* (1937) and *A Sioux Chronicle* (1956), and Stanley Vestal, *Sitting Bull: Champion of the Sioux* (1932).

EXPLORATION. John Bakeless, *The Eyes of Discovery* (1950), through Lewis and Clark. John B. Brebner, *The Explorers of North America, 1492–1806* (1933, 1955) tries to be popular. Jeanette Mirsky, *The Westward Crossings* (1946), semipopular. Abraham P. Nasatir (ed.), *Before Lewis and Clark* (1952) concerns upper Missouri 1785–1804. Grace L. Nute, *Caesars of the Wilderness* (1943) describes two early French explorers.

LEWIS AND CLARK. John Bakeless, *Lewis and Clark* (1947), good in every way; Ethel Hueston, *Star of the West* (1935), journalistic. Good shorter accounts are included in Bernard De Voto, *The Course of Empire* (1952); James Monaghan, *The Overland Trail* (1947). Burton Harris, *John Colter* (1952) concerns a member of the expedition. The original records can be consulted in Reuben G. Thwaites (ed.), *Original Journals of the Lewis and Clark Expedition* (7 vols., 1904–1905); Nicholas Biddle (ed.), *The Journals of Lewis and Clark* (2 vols., 1962); Bernard De Voto (ed.), *The Journals of Lewis and Clark* (1953); Donald D. Jackson (ed.), *Letters of the Lewis and Clark Expedition* (1962).

PIKE AND MACKENZIE. Excellent in every way is W. Eugene Hollon, *The Lost Pathfinder: Zebulon Montgomery Pike* (1949). Quite satisfactory on Mackenzie is Mark S. Wade, *Mackenzie of Canada* (1927); Mackenzie's journal is reprinted in Walter Sheppe (ed.), *First Man West* (1962).

CHAPTER 21

THE FUR TRADE

A wilderness drew traders and trappers as well as explorers, since wild country was valuable chiefly for its furs. Lewis and Clark met trappers on the Great Plains and Pike found them near the source of the Mississippi. The Daniel Boone type of frontiersman was the one who ordinarily first surveyed the country and whose reports encouraged later occupation. The trapper thus was important both because of the business he represented and because of his position in the vanguard of white settlement.

The first large-scale American business on any new frontier was the collection of furs, whether by catching the animals or by trading with the Indians. Fine furs, such as beaver, otter, mink, and fox, were specially desired, but coarse pelts, such as buffalo, bear, and deer could be used for lap robes and heavy coats. Buffalo tongues, buffalo and bear tallow, and a few other commodities could be marketed.

SPANISH AND FRENCH

The Spanish, who were the first European arrivals in the New World, had little interest in the fur business in the early days. They dreamed of precious metals and stones, and trading for furs seemed a less profitable and more prosaic business. From time to time Spanish trappers and trading companies were licensed, but for many years they remained relatively unimportant. Not until Spanish power in North America had nearly vanished did the trappers and traders of Spanish extraction attain any considerable importance.

It was the French who were responsible for the development of the American fur business as a large-scale enterprise. They worked up the St. Lawrence and through the Great Lakes to the Mississippi Basin, establishing trading centers as far afield as Kaskaskia, Cahokia, and Vincennes. The French adapted themselves quickly and well to both trading and trapping. They isolated themselves in the wilderness, apparently happy, and were on the most friendly terms with the Indians, often marrying Indian girls and rearing half-breed progeny. Even after French political power had disappeared in North America the French trader and trapper continued to set the tone for the fur business of the West all the way to the Pacific Coast.

ENGLISH

With the elimination of France from North America, England fell heir to the control of the fur traffic of the new country. The business was transacted largely by English and Scotch merchants who used Montreal as their main American trading center and London as their chief distributing point. London set the fur prices of the western world. In spite of English control, most of the men engaged in the fur trade in America were not Anglo-Saxon but French, and the French influence remained dominant in the wilderness.

The most important of the English fur trading companies was the Hudson's Bay Company, chartered in 1670 with absolute power over the vast and vague region of the Northwest that was tributary to Hudson's Bay. The "Great Company" made an enviable record of fair treatment of the Indian, insisting upon the principles of one price, no rum, and no violence. In spite of minor lapses in the application of these precepts in special conditions, the dealings of the Hudson's Bay Company were on the whole commendable.

Chief among the other but less important English companies interested in the fur trade was the North West Company. A group of Scottish Montreal merchants headed by Benjamin and Joseph Frobisher and Simon McTavish originated the company in 1790 in a tentative agreement made permanent in the winter of 1783–1784. The company's general field of operations was from the Mandan country to the Pacific and from the Hudson's Bay territory to Louisiana. At the height of its power it employed some 2000 men. It not only had trading posts like those of the Hudson's Bay Company, but also equipped expeditions to trade with the Indians in the more important Indian villages.

The proximity of the regions worked by the North West Company and the Hudson's Bay Company threw the two into a conflict that began almost with the organization of the younger concern. Geographical concepts were vague, so there was real doubt as to the proper limits of the jurisdiction of each company. Competition between them sometimes included such devious and objectionable practices as the excessive use of whiskey in trading, stealing furs, and inciting the Indians against rivals. In 1811 a settlement sponsored by Lord Selkirk at the present Winnipeg was encouraged by the Hudson's Bay Company as a buffer between the rival organizations; the object was attained, but at the expense of the settlers. Eventually, in 1821, the North West Company was absorbed by its older competitor and good trading methods were restored.

The most productive fur area in the West until a generation or more after the Revolution was the Great Lakes region. Here were the English and Scottish traders, whose operations were pushed north, south, and west so rapidly that Alexander Mackenzie actually succeeded in reaching the Pacific Coast as early as 1793. Here also were the Spanish and French, operating from Vincennes, Kaskaskia, Cahokia, and St. Louis, and also pushing up the valley of the Missouri. Finally, here were the American traders who had come over the mountains with the hope of participating in the rich fur business farther west. With the appearance of the Americans, the greatest competition for western furs was between the English and American traders. This rivalry was largely responsible for the refusal of England to surrender her Great Lakes posts at the end of the Revolution, and also explained in part the campaigns around Detroit in the War of 1812.

FEDERAL REGULATION

One of the early problems faced by the federal government under the Constitution was the regulation of the western fur trade. The fur traders were the only white men seen by many Indians, and their behavior had a considerable effect on the attitude of the Indians toward white government. Unrestricted competition among private white fur buyers had unfortunate effects. The first attempt to deal with the problem was a long series of laws providing for the licensing of private traders and for the exclusion of all other persons from the Indian country. A trader was to be licensed only if he could show a good moral character and give a bond that he would not sell liquor to the Indians. These provisions looked fine on paper but were never enforced effectively, the small traders being a greater problem than the large companies. Licenses were easy to obtain, unlicensed traders were not ejected, and liquor sales and other undesirable practices continued to be widespread. The lack of necessary law enforcement personnel was decisive, and the Indians continued to be cheated unmercifully by many white traders.

A new attack on the problem came when the federal government itself entered the fur business, establishing its first "factory" in the Indian country in 1796; a total of twenty-eight government trading houses were in operation at one time or another before the experiment ended. The hope was that a nonprofit-making organization providing first-rate goods at moderate prices would help the Indian, improve Indian-white relations, and force private traders to adopt better practices to meet the competition. At first the selling of liquor and the use of credit were outlawed. Although the first objective was at least approached, the second proved impossible. Private traders were still permitted, but with the expectation that their number would decrease and that they would merely supplement the government system.

The small government establishments were never very successful. Their prices forced those of the private operators somewhat lower, but in the process the government was faced with steady losses. Among the reasons for this lack of success were the poor locations of government posts, the inability of the "factors" to travel widely among the Indians, less specialized and less efficient employees, bad judgment in the purchase of trading goods, poor furs that were improperly handled, and excessive credit to bad risks, including white soldiers of neighboring garrisons.

Private hostility to the government operations first became important after the War of 1812. The outstanding opponent was the American Fur Company, which went to the extent of encouraging Indian hostility toward the United States. It undercut the government on the staples it sold and advanced the prices of other articles; it lobbied vigorously. Among the politicians opposing government in business were Lewis Cass and Thomas Hart Benton, both friends of, and influenced by, John Jacob Astor of the American Fur Company. Cass was Governor of Michigan, which had much fur trade and hence many traders. Benton's home state was Missouri, where the city of St. Louis was the most important western center of the fur business. Political opposition was successful, and the government venture was abandoned in 1822, at which time there were nine government factories and 126 licensed traders. The license system was continued, as were the violations.

The Americans, since they entered the fur trade rather late, found the most lucrative business monopolized by the English and Scottish companies. The long overland trip across the Appalachians was a serious handicap when competitors were using the easier St. Lawrence route; marketing and distributing facilities were underdeveloped until after 1800.

ASTOR

The most important single figure in the development of the fur business of the United States was John Jacob Astor, who was as far from being a frontiersman as can be imagined. Astor was born in Germany in 1763, and at sixteen left home to join a brother, in the musical instrument business in London. During the winter of 1783–1784 he realized a long ambition by migrating to the United States. His only assets were seven flutes. He found work first as a baker's helper and then as an assistant to a fur merchant. After learning the fur business he set up shop for himself, combining fur trading with the sale of musical instruments; eventually he dropped the musical side of his enterprise. At first he gathered most of his own furs in central New York State and bought the rest in Canada, but gradually he developed an efficient collecting organization and was able to confine most of his attention to merchandising. About 1800 he expanded his operations to the Great Lakes region.

Along with his growing fur business Astor combined trading with China, which was an excellent fur market, and by the beginning of the century had ships of his own engaged in trade with the Far East. Astor's strength and energy seemed inexhaustible, and everything he touched turned to gold. By the early 1800s he was one of the richest and most powerful men in the United States.

Then came the purchase of Louisiana, and Astor's mind was fired with the possibilities of the fur business in this new and unworked country. Why should he not expand his operations and monopolize the new region for himself? A vision appeared of a huge company with posts on the Great Lakes, and then along the Missouri and Columbia rivers to the ocean. He dreamed of furs being taken to China to exchange for teas, silks, and spices, which would be returned to the United States to complete the circle of transactions. Included in the business would be the supplying of the Russian posts that stretched along the Pacific Coast of North America. Truly it was an ambitious dream, including a territory as large as an empire and embracing the entire world in its operations.

Astor's first move was to consolidate his existing position and obtain new capital by organizing the American Fur Company (1808) to control the region of the Great Lakes. Two years later he chartered the Pacific Fur Company, which was to be used in furthering his plans in the Far West. In practice it was difficult to distinguish the operations of these two companies since Astor controlled both, and used their funds, supplies, and men interchangeably.

ASTORIA

The realization of Astor's dream of a series of forts along the Missouri and Columbia rivers was entrusted to the Pacific Fur Company. Partners were added to control field operations, and given approximately half of the stock. Astor himself advanced the necessary funds ($400,000) and agreed to assume any loss incurred within the first five years. Traders and *voyageurs* (boatmen) were hired from the North West Company.

The first planned fort of the projected chain was the most westerly one at the mouth of the Columbia. Two parties were to participate in its construction, the first to go west by sea and the second by land. The former started in 1810 on the trip around the Horn in the vessel "Tonquin," commanded by Captain Jonathan Thorn, an able navigator but a stern, forbidding, and arbitrary disciplinarian. Thorn's attitude may have been successful in normal situations but it did not appeal to the extremely individualistic fur traders, who had ideas and wills of their own. The result was a series of misunderstandings and disputes, mostly personal, that marred the trip.

The "Tonquin" arrived at the mouth of the Columbia early in 1811 but had much difficulty in entering the river, losing a small boat with all on board before the entrance was finally effected. Upon entering the Columbia, Thorn discovered that the overland party had not arrived. After sailing up and down the river to pick a good place for a trading post the men disembarked and built a small fort they named Astoria in honor of the principal partner, John Jacob Astor. The "Tonquin" and its crew left Astoria on June 1, 1811, to trade with the Indians along the coast. A surprise attack by the natives killed most of the crew; whereupon the remainder blew up the ship. The four men who escaped in a small boat were eventually killed.

Meantime the overland group under the leadership of Wilson Price Hunt had left New York in July 1810. Hunt first went to Montreal to engage *voyageurs* for the long trip, but difficulties were thrown in his way by the older companies and he had to do some of his hiring as he proceeded west. His route from Montreal was by way of Lake Huron and Lake Michigan, overland to the Mississippi, and then down that stream until he arrived at St. Louis in September. Ascending the Missouri to near the present St. Joseph, he established a permanent winter camp and then returned to St. Louis to obtain additional supplies and an interpreter.

It was the middle of April 1811 before Hunt and his latest recruits joined the main group, and the whole party started up the Missouri. The plan was to ascend the river to the mouth of the Yellowstone, or as far as it was navigable, and then cut overland to a branch of the Columbia. Part way up the Missouri the men heard rumors of Blackfoot hostility and therefore changed their plans. Leaving the Missouri in present South Dakota, Hunt led his party through the Black Hills and ultimately across the Rockies to the headwaters of the Snake, which was descended by canoe until the river became impassable. The one large group was found to be unwieldy and so was divided into four, each group to seek its own route to the Pacific. Each of these small parties experienced terrible hardships and privations in its wanderings, and several men died. The last of the survivors reached Astoria on February 15, 1812.

The arrival of the overland party, together with the additional supplies brought by the ship "Beaver," infused new spirit and vigor to the settlement at Astoria. The fort was strengthened, cabins were built, fish were caught and dried, trading was done with the Indians on the coast, and detachments were sent to deal with the tribes of the interior. Then came rumors of war between the United States and England, and the Astorians decided (1813) that, because of their isolation and England's control of the sea, their capture was only a question of time and they might as well abandon the fort.

Before Astor's men departed, a force of North West Company traders arrived. To both groups the arrival seemed opportune. Many of the Astorians were Canadians, and in the fall of 1813 were easily persuaded to sell their post, particularly when they heard rumors of an approaching English warship. Some of them joined the North West Company. The Astorians were pleased to sell their property instead of having it captured by a British man-of-war, while the North West Company was glad to buy out a competitor at a moderate price. Within a month of the sale the British warship "Raccoon" arrived and "captured" Astoria. The commander was greatly disgruntled when he saw the insignificance of the small wilderness fort he had crossed half the world to conquer.

The loss of Astoria ended Astor's plans in the Far Northwest, and he dissolved the Pacific Fur Company. The failure of the enterprise was not due to any fault in the overall plan and only in small degree to the outbreak of the war. The decisive factors were the lack of adequate communications with the East, the failure to construct the series of forts originally planned to link East and West, and the mismanagement of the two groups sent into the field.

AMERICAN FUR COMPANY

After his failure in Oregon, Astor concentrated his attention on the regions farther east. His operations in the Great Lakes country were strengthened until they became a monopoly; his control in the upper Mississippi Valley was almost as great. One estimate of the Astor company was expressed by Zachary Taylor, who commanded infantry in the upper Mississippi Valley in the 1820s: "Take the American Fur Company in the aggregate, and they are the greatest scoundrels the world ever knew." Later scholarly researchers have a different judgment, and have generally praised the company. In the matter of liquor, for example, the company preferred not to use it but finally lowered its high standards to be able to compete effectively with smaller and less scrupulous operators; individual employees had always disregarded company policies.

The American Fur Company sent agents into the Missouri Valley in 1822, and during the same year established the headquarters of the western department at St. Louis. Gradually the employees of the company worked farther and farther up the valley, consolidating with or crushing competitors until it was supreme. In 1829 it established Fort Union at the mouth of the Yellowstone. Its boat, the "Yellowstone," which ascended the river to Fort Union in 1832 and later to Fort Benton, was responsible for the opening of steamboat business on the upper Missouri. Astor himself retired from the company in 1834, when its business was at a peak, but the American Fur Company remained dominant in the Missouri Valley for another decade.

The establishment of the western headquarters of the American Fur Company at St. Louis was one of many indications of the increasing importance of that city as the center for the trans-Mississippi fur business. St. Louis, with its strategic position on the Mississippi just below the mouth of the Missouri, was the natural outfitting point for traders and trappers and the logical place for them to market the furs they brought back. Here, quite understandably, were the headquarters of many companies doing business in the Far West.

MISSOURI FUR COMPANY

The earliest important company with its main headquarters at St. Louis was the St. Louis Missouri Fur Company, commonly known as the Missouri Fur Company. This firm was started by prominent St. Louis men in the winter of 1808–1809, and included many of the best trappers, traders, and hunters in the West. Its first trading expedition, leaving St. Louis in 1809, was an imposing body: 150 men with their necessary supplies, materials for the establishment of four or five permanent posts, and outfits for equipping several smaller subparties. It ascended the Missouri River and built its first post on the Bighorn River. Then it continued farther west, constructing a second fort at the three forks of the Missouri; here it was attacked by the Blackfeet, who killed some twenty-five whites and caused the rest to abandon the fort. Farther west, a third post was established on the Snake River.

This first expedition of the Missouri Fur Company seemed pursued by an evil fate, for it met one misfortune after another. The attack by the Blackfeet was followed by other Indian encounters, physical obstacles proved unexpectedly difficult to overcome, some of the furs were accidentally burned, and all the forts eventually had to be abandoned. Nevertheless, the expedition showed a small profit. The Missouri Fur Company, like similar groups of the period, was reorganized frequently; in fact most of the fur companies changed their names and personnel so rapidly that it is almost impossible to follow consecutively the history of any one group.

ROCKY MOUNTAIN FUR COMPANY

The Missouri Fur Company ended its precarious existence in the early 1820s, and was succeeded by the Rocky Mountain Fur Company. The succession was not in any sense formal, but the same men who composed the earlier group were also active in the later. The principal leaders of the new company were William H. Ashley, who had been born in Virginia, and Andrew Henry, who had come originally from Pennsylvania. Henry controlled operations in the field, while Ashley spent most of his time in St. Louis arranging the financial affairs of the company, purchasing supplies, hiring men, and disposing of the furs.

The first expedition of the Rocky Mountain Fur Company was announced by a little notice in *The Missouri Gazette & Public Advertiser* for February 13, 1822. One hundred "enterprising young men" were invited "to ascend the Missouri to its source, there to be employed for one, two, or three years." The expedition, which was away for two years, included some of the most famous trappers of the West. Among them was Jedediah Strong Smith, who later was responsible for the exploration of a large share of the hitherto unknown Southwest. There also was James Bridger, soon to become one of the best known of the mountain men. Not least was Hugh Glass, whose exploits were later described in the poems of John G. Neihardt. Glass, according to the usual tale, was at one time left for dead after an encounter with a grizzly bear, and crawled some two hundred miles without a gun, food, or adequate clothes to reach the nearest white habitation. Because of these many famous trappers, the first expedition of the Rocky Mountain Fur Company was notable in the history of the fur trade.

The later history of the Rocky Mountain Fur Company is difficult to follow since, like similar organizations, the company frequently changed its name, and at times lapsed completely or used no name at all. The title commonly given it is more a convenience than an exact designation. The company's field of operation was the upper Missouri Valley and the mountainous region beyond. A large part of its business was done in what is now the southern part of the state of Idaho.

HUDSON'S BAY COMPANY

The chief competitor of the Rocky Mountain Fur Company in the Far Northwest was the Hudson's Bay Company, which had continued to push southwest after its absorption of the North West Company. Its chief agent in the Oregon country was John McLoughlin, who had established himself at Fort Vancouver, opposite the mouth of the Willamette, in 1825, and who became sufficiently powerful in the twenty years of his residence to deserve the title of "the King of Old Oregon." McLoughlin's power was absolute and he wielded it with choleric vigor. At the same time he was wise, generous, and hospitable, so that his monarchy was of the benevolent variety. Every traveler and trader who visited the region stopped at Fort Vancouver, where he was invariably well treated. The one exception was Hall J. Kelley, whom he mistook for a cattle thief, but to whom he nevertheless gave shelter and care.

McLoughlin as representative of the Hudson's Bay Company was engaged in a three-cornered fight with the American Fur Company and the Rocky Mountain Fur Company for control of the Oregon region. In spite of the bitterness with which this contest was waged, McLoughlin's business dealings were fair and honorable; he treated the Indians generously and his own trappers justly. The profits of the fur trade of the region were only moderate, and one reason for maintaining the post was the desire of the Hudson's Bay Company to have an outpost to halt the advance of American trappers. Because of this situation McLoughlin was encouraged in his policy of trying to make the post self-sufficient. He fenced his fields, conducted a varied agriculture, raised stock, and built comfortable homes. When the first real agricultural settlers came to Oregon, McLoughlin was their friend, adviser, and helper—services for which he was later ill repaid. His control of Oregon was one of the brightest spots in the history of the fur-trading West.

NATURE OF THE FUR TRADE

The activities of the fur-trading companies were conditioned by the obvious fact that although furs originated on the North American continent the business was essentially European. Most of the furs were obtained in trade with the Indians, European-made articles being given in exchange. The furs themselves found their largest market in Europe, and European demand determined the American price. Even the traders, camp keepers, boatmen, and other participants in the trading were usually French and Spanish rather than American. The French language was in more common use than the English, and many of the terms of the business were French in origin.

The fur trade was also characterized by the large amount of credit involved in most transactions, and by the considerable element of hazard that produced either large profits or large losses. A period of approximately four years elapsed from the time the manufactured goods were shipped from Europe until the furs were returned and sold; almost every operation occurring in the interim was based on credit. The sale of goods, transactions of the middlemen, trading with the trappers and Indians, transportation, preparation, and sale of the furs were all normally credit operations. This emphasis on credit, when added to difficulties and dangers inherent in the business, produced a highly speculative industry. An annual profit of 50 percent was not unusual, and frequently the figure was much higher. On the other hand the operations of any single year might result in total loss, often including the sacrifice of human lives.

PERSONNEL OF FUR TRADE

The personnel of the fur trade of the West was both interesting and distinctive. The most important individual was the "bourgeois," who was head of the permanent trading post and frequently a partner in the business, for employee ownership of stock is not a new device. The position required considerable administrative ability, for it was the bourgeois who performed such functions as hiring hunters and trappers, supervising the trading, ordering the necessary goods and supplies, and setting the prices. Next in rank was the "partisan," who commanded field operations and held a rendezvous if there were no permanent post in the region. The first lieutenant of the bourgeois was the clerk, who was second in authority at the permanent post, taking complete command when his superior was absent; sometimes he held stock in the company.

In addition to the managerial force, an army of men performed the heavy manual labor. First of all there were two main types of white trappers —those who were hired by the year and those who had no direct connection with any particular company. The man hired by the year was paid a wage of about $400, for which he would give his entire catch to the company, while the "free trapper" disposed of his furs annually for whatever they would bring. Of lower social rank than the members of either of these groups were the camp keepers, each of whom received approximately $200 a year. The camp keepers performed all their duties in camp, where they tended the stock, and cleaned and dressed the furs. Another large group was that of the *voyageur,* who was usually a French Creole from Canada or Louisiana, and who did the arduous work of handling the boats. At the larger posts were artisans, such as blacksmiths and carpenters. Unskilled labor went by the name of *mangeurs de lard* (pork eaters) and came principally from Canada. Not least in importance were the Indians who gathered a considerable proportion of the furs and traded them annually.

The most interesting and picturesque of these groups was the white trapping fraternity, which included such well-known men as Kit Carson, Jim Bridger, Jedediah Smith, Ewing Young, Bill Williams, and William Wolfskill. The white trappers were gaunt, brown, gloomy, taciturn men, with a dry native humor. Physical courage was essential for their existence; human life was not valued highly. They were the direct heirs of the Boone tradition, and knew the forest as intimately as the town dweller knew his front yard. They lived largely in the wilds, going to a trading post but once a year to exchange the season's catch for the necessities of life and for the ornaments so dear to their hearts. Most of them were improvident and were usually in debt to the trader, although it should be added that the trader's high prices, faulty measurements, and inaccurate bookkeeping contributed to this situation. The trapper spent his earnings immediately, and then bought on credit as long as the trader would trust him. By winter he was penniless and found it necessary to go back to work.

The trapper favored a costume which was a curious mixture of Indian and white habiliments. Ordinarily he wore a light-blue cotton shirt, and over it a knee-length leather hunting shirt. Sometimes he wore breeches, but just as frequently he wore a breechcloth and allowed his thighs and hips to remain bare. Indian leggings and moccasins protected the feet and ankles, while a handkerchief turban warded off insects and added a touch of color. Decorations were at a premium and included colored porcupine quills, feathers, and beads to fasten to his clothes, and feathers to thrust into his hair. His ammunition bag was attached to a belt that hung over his left shoulder in such a fashion that the bag came close to his right hand. In his belt were a knife, a hatchet, tobacco, sugar, and salt. A buffalo robe served for bed and cover, while a saddle made a high and hard pillow. Most of the trappers were excellent horsemen and very proud of their horses and equipment; the saddle and other gear were painted, embroidered, or decorated with feathers, beads, or silver. In the winter the trapper frequently lived in a rude hut, with an Indian wife to keep him amused and do his hard work. His language was a medley of bad English, French, and Spanish. Rather curiously he had no interest in minerals except for decorative purposes; deposits of gold and silver were common knowledge, but no self-respecting trapper ever seriously considered descending to the ignoble work of mining.

TRADING POSTS

The permanent posts of the fur trade were notable landmarks in the wilderness of the West. Ordinarily they were rectangular or square, with sides between 100 and 400 feet in length. The walls were formed of pickets 12 to 18 feet high and 4 to 8 feet thick except in the South, where adobe walls were more common. Frequently a wooden path designed for defense was bracketed some 4 feet from the top. At diagonal corners were two blockhouses, each 15 to 18 feet square, two stories high, and surmounted by a roof. The blockhouse jutted out from the walls, so that it could command a clear view of the sides of the fort. The ground floor was designed for the use of cannon, while the upper story had peepholes for rifles. The strength of the blockhouse was attested by the fact that none

The Fur Trade

was ever attacked successfully by the Indians. Somewhere in the picket wall of the fort was a heavy wooden door, well buttressed, and usually with a small wicket to permit a view of the person desiring admittance without opening the main gate. Indians were admitted only in small groups.

The buildings inside the stockade included barracks for the men, a storehouse, shops, the trader's house, and the clerk's house. Often there was a garden just outside the wall, and sometimes it too was barricaded. Livestock were ordinarily kept outside the walls, but in times of danger they were brought inside. Life at the fort was slow and monotonous, but exciting moments came with the arrival of a caravan of goods from the East, a skirmish with the Indians, a hunting trip, or the departure of a trading expedition. In addition to the larger and more important posts were a number of smaller and less powerful stations scattered here and there throughout the West.

The alternative of the permanent trading post was the rendezvous, of which the first was held by Ashley in 1822 and the last by the American

Fur Company in 1839. Its greatest use was in the region that is now southern Idaho and western Wyoming. The rendezvous was a specified gathering place for trading and had its principal advantage in obviating the necessity for a permanent post with a large personnel. A locality was chosen that had a good supply of grass and water, and to it would come the trappers, the Indians, and the traders from the East with their goods. The caravan left St. Louis early in the spring and arrived at the meeting place in late June or early July. Here it would stay and trade for the year's catch until either the furs or the goods were exhausted. Articles in special demand by both the Indians and the trappers were blankets, cloth, trinkets, beads, mirrors, jewelry, salt, sugar, tobacco, guns, ammunition, knives, and large quantities of liquor. Athletic contests, gambling, and drinking would occupy all of the days and most of the nights, and everyone was merry. Eventually the caravan would start its return trip in time to arrive in the East before winter.

Trading at all the posts was in goods and seldom in cash; the unit of value was the beaver skin. Manufactured goods were overvalued and furs undervalued (from the standpoint of the trader), and whiskey was plentiful; consequently the trapper was ordinarily in debt and the Indian was impoverished. This situation was on the whole favorable to the trader, who was thus assured that the trappers would be forced to work hard the next year, and that they would be likely again to do business with the same trader to whom they were in debt.

The fur trade reached the peak of its importance in the United States during the 1830s, after which it declined in relative significance even though not in total value. The cream of the American fur supply had been skimmed, and advancing settlement was eliminating the trapper.

READINGS

GENERAL. Hiram M. Chittenden, *The American Fur Trade of the Far West* (2 vols., 1954) is the classic account; Paul C. Phillips, *The Fur Trade* (2 vols., 1961) is encyclopedic; Clarence A. Vandiveer, *The Fur Trade* (1929); Richard E. Oglesby, *Manuel Lisa and the Opening of the Missouri Fur Trade* (1963) is good on the early period; Bernard De Voto, *Across the Wide Missouri* (1947) concerns mostly the fur trade; Harold A. Innis, *The Fur Trade of Canada* (1930) and Wayne E. Stevens, *The Northwest Fur Trade, 1763–1800* (1928) are scholarly. Regional histories almost always cover the fur trade; see the Readings for Chapters 24, 26, 34, 37. Government policy may be followed monographically in George D. Harmon, *Sixty Years of Indian Affairs, 1789–1850* (1941); Ora B. Peake, *A History of the United States Indian Factory System* (1954); Francis P. Prucha, *American Indian Policy, 1780–1834* (1962).

OREGON AND THE HUDSON'S BAY COMPANY. Accounts of the company are John S. Galbraith, *The Hudson's Bay Company* (1957), scholarly; and Robert E. Pinkerton, *Hudson's Bay Company* (1931). See also Robert G. Montgomery, *The White-Headed Eagle* (1934), biography of McLoughlin; and D. Geniva Lent, *West of the Mountains: James Sinclair and the Hudson's Bay Company* (1963). Oscar O. Winther, *The Old Oregon Country* (1950) covers the subject. Original narratives include Edwin E. Rich (ed.), *Letters of John McLoughlin* (1941) and *Peter Skene Ogden's Journals* (1950); *Peter Skene Ogden's Snake Country Journal 1826–27* (1961); Alexander Ross, *Fur Traders of the Far West* (1956); George Simpson, *Fur Trade and Empire* (1932).

ASTOR. Good biographies are Harvey O'Connor, *The Astors* (1941); Kenneth W. Porter, *John Jacob Astor* (2 vols., 1931), scholarly; Arthur D. H. Smith, *John Jacob Astor* (1909), reads easily. The Stuart journal is reprinted in Kenneth A. Spaulding (ed.), *On the Oregon Trail* (1953) and Philip A. Rollins (ed.), *The Discovery of the Oregon Trail* (1935).

TRAPPERS. Good general accounts are Robert G. Cleland, *This Reckless Breed of Men* (1950); Bernard De Voto, *The Year of Decision* (1943); Harvey Fergusson, *Rio Grande* (1933); Stanley Vestal, *Mountain Men* (1937). Grace L. Nute, *The Voyageur* (1931) is excellent. Good individual biographies are J. Cecil Alter, *James Bridger* (1962); Levette J. Davidson and Forrester Blake (eds.), *Rocky Mountain Tales* (1947), Bridger stories; Alpheus H. Favour, *Old Bill Williams* (1936); Blanche C. Grant (ed.), *Kit Carson's Own Story of His Life* (1926); Dale Morgan, *Jedediah Smith and the Opening of the West* (1953) and *The West of William H. Ashley* (1963); Maurice S. Sullivan, *Jedediah Smith* (1936) and *The Travels of Jedediah Smith* (1934), diaries; John E. Sunder, *Bill Sublette* (1959); Stanley Vestal, *Jim Bridger* (1946) and *Kit Carson* (1928).

FORTS. Particularly good are David S. Lavender, *Bent's Fort* (1954) and Le Roy R. Hafen and F. M. Young, *Fort Laramie* (1938).

CHAPTER 22

FAR WESTERN
EXPLORATION

Interest in the trans-Mississippi West increased steadily after the purchase of Louisiana. Explorers such as Lewis and Clark and Pike brought back fascinating reports of vast plains, snow-covered mountains, salt lakes, and other marvels of nature. Stories of the picturesque trappers and traders began to seep back to civilization, and many Americans watched the Astor enterprise with admiration. Farmers began to cross the Father of Waters and to look at the country beyond with mingled hope and awe. Even before 1840 a few hopeful white men saw agricultural possibilities in a region as remote as the Pacific Coast.

Increasing interest in the Far West brought concern over the Louisiana boundaries that had seemed of such little consequence at the time of the purchase. The boundary between the United States and Canada was discussed in a desultory fashion, but hardly seemed vital as long as the questionable country was visited only sporadically by a few trappers. For a time there was talk of having the boundary follow the watershed of the Missouri, which was reasonable geographically. Ultimately (1818) it was found easier to agree on a straight line along the 49th parallel from the Lake of the Woods to the Rocky Mountains; such a line was at least comparatively easy to find and mark. The boundary west of the Rockies was not specified in the treaty of 1818, partly because no one knew just how much territory was included in the Louisiana Purchase, and partly because both England and the United States had claims based on exploration and occupation and could not agree on a compromise. Provision was made that the Oregon country be left open to joint occupation for a period of ten

323

years. In 1827 this provision was continued indefinitely until one of the parties should give notice of the termination of the treaty.

The boundary between the Louisiana Territory and Mexico was settled in 1819 in the Adams-Onís Treaty. The line as it was then drawn excluded the present American Southwest from Louisiana to the Pacific coast. Possibly the Texas region might have been included if the United States had been sufficiently insistent.

The defining of western boundaries was necessary, but it was much less interesting to the general public than efforts to obtain accurate information about the soil, climate, physical features, flora and fauna, and native inhabitants of the Far West. The desire to obtain such information, coupled at times with the hope of monetary reward, lured a continuous procession of explorers across the continent, so that by the late 1830s the outstanding features of the Far West were reasonably well known to anyone who had the desire and energy to learn of them.

The observations made by these explorers were remarkably keen and accurate, considering the difficulties of traversing an unknown wilderness and the usual lack of precise scientific instruments; many of the observations were made without the aid of any instruments and represented only the experienced guesses of the explorer. The most obvious error of most explorers was the assumption that all of the western plains were semiarid or desert places that could never support a white agrarian population. This mistake was easy to make, since an explorer judged the fertility of the soil almost entirely from the nature of the vegetation growing on it. Because the trans-Mississippi country had but few trees, it was reasonable to deduce that the soil was very inferior.

The expeditions going to the Far West were of every possible variety, but for purposes of convenience they can be divided into three general groups. The first was the government party, moving under instructions from Washington, and usually commanded by a man who was interested in western exploration; its guide was ordinarily a Westerner who had a firsthand knowledge of at least a portion of the country to be traversed. The second type was the trader who was motivated largely by the hope of personal gain, but who also in many cases was inspired by a desire for adventure in unknown parts of the country. The third group included the miscellaneous remaining expeditions of men going west to make their fortunes from salmon fishing, for the pure love of adventure, from scientific curiosity, or for any one of the several reasons that lead men to perform new and dangerous exploits.

STEPHEN H. LONG

The most noteworthy governmental explorer in the years shortly after the War of 1812 was Stephen H. Long, a member of the Corps of Topographical Engineers. This organization had been formed in 1777 but had grown rather slowly. Its eventual dominance in western exploration, based on work done largely by men trained at West Point, came after the appointment of Colonel John J. Abert as its head in 1838. Long made his first trip in 1817, when he ascended the Mississippi River and built Fort St. Anthony at the junction of the Mississippi and St. Peter's (Minnesota) rivers. The expedition had little importance except that the fort it established later became Fort Snelling and was on the site of the city of St. Paul.

Two years later Major Long was given command of the most pretentious expedition to be sent to the Far West since the days of Lewis and Clark. Its aims were both military and scientific, including a demonstration of power meant to impress the Indians as well as the exploration of the region of the Missouri River. The military section, under the immediate command of Colonel Henry Atkinson, spent the winter of 1819–1820 at Council Bluffs. In spite of extensive plans the troops never advanced far beyond this point.

The scientific part of the expedition, under the direct command of Long, included a botanist, a zoologist, a geologist, an assistant naturalist, a painter and sketcher (for there were no cameras), and a topographical engineer in addition to the laborers necessary for moving the equipment and supplies. It was transported in the "Western Engineer," a specially constructed 75-foot vessel that was one of the first steamboats to navigate the Missouri. The boat had its machinery hidden, and its bow was built to resemble a serpent's head; when the fires were burning the smoke issued from the snake's nostrils. The vessel was better at frightening the Indians than at carrying men and supplies.

The scientific party made its way slowly up the Missouri, making observations as it went; it, too, spent the winter of 1819–1820 at Council Bluffs. By this time Congress was becoming impatient: the cost was great and the accomplishments were small. A congressional investigation led to the cutting off of financial support and the expedition came to an end, which was unfortunate in view of its well-qualified personnel.

Long's failure did not prevent his being placed in charge of a new expedition in 1820 that was designed to explore the Platte, the Arkansas, the Red, and other rivers of the region. This was the same general task that had earlier been given to Pike. Long left St. Louis in June 1820 and made a leisurely trip up the Platte, arriving at the site of the present

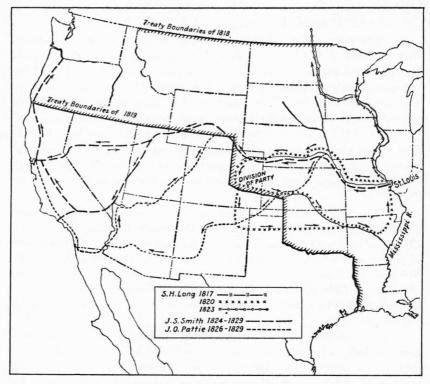

Western Exploration, 1815–1830

Denver on July 5. He failed to locate the headwaters of the Platte, but he viewed the peak that now bears his name. Turning south he sent half his party home by the Arkansas; with the remainder he made a halfhearted effort to find the source of the Red River and then descended the Canadian River. By October he was back in St. Louis, having accomplished little and having added almost nothing to the knowledge of the region he had traversed. Like Pike, he classified the plains as a country unsuitable for farming.

In spite of Long's meager results to date he was called upon to make another expedition in 1823; this time he was to explore the region between the Mississippi and the Missouri. Possibly because of his previous experiences he was to accomplish more of importance on this expedition than he had in his three former expeditions combined. His party included a zoologist, a mineralogist, a geologist, and a landscape painter, all of whom he recruited in the East. The group left Philadelphia on April 25 and went west by way of Fort Wayne, Fort Dearborn, and Prairie du Chien, adding a few soldiers en route.

The real start of the expedition was from Fort Snelling. During almost all of the trip the force was divided, part going by boat with the luggage and the remainder exploring the shore; at night the parties joined to camp. The expedition moved down the Mississippi and then up the Minnesota, making careful observations along the way. The sources of the Minnesota and the Red River of the North were explored; then the party started the descent of the Red toward the town of Pembina in present North Dakota. Near Pembina the international boundary was located and marked.

Major Long's orders were to leave the Red River at the international boundary and follow the forty-ninth parallel on his return trip to the East. Actually he found these orders impossible to follow because of the swampy nature of the ground and so he continued along the Red River into Canada as far as Lake Winnipeg. Then he crossed to Lake Superior and followed the Great Lakes as far as New York State. He arrived again in Philadelphia on October 26, 1823. The results of the expedition were satisfactory, including as they did a large amount of information about a hitherto comparatively unknown part of the country.

OTHER GOVERNMENT EXPLORERS

Although Major Long was the most outstanding of the western military explorers of the period 1815 to 1840, he was but one of many. Leavenworth, Atkinson, Dodge, and other western commanders who dealt with the Indians ranged far afield to collect both fact and rumor concerning unknown parts of the country. One of the best known of their expeditions was the demonstration of Colonel Henry Leavenworth against the Missouri River Indians in 1823, which resulted more in securing geographical information than in intimidation of the Indians. Fort Leavenworth, named after the Colonel, was established in 1827. Colonel Henry Atkinson led an Indian peace commission up the Missouri River in 1825; with his 476 men he made a great display of military force and obtained treaties of peace with the Indians whom he visited. In this trip he traveled to 120 miles above the mouth of the Yellowstone, but established no permanent posts. In the 1830s Colonel Henry Dodge led several Indian expeditions, of which the most important (1835) ascended the Platte and South Platte, coming back along the Arkansas and then cutting overland to St. Louis.

Probably the expeditions of Henry R. Schoolcraft, the Indian agent at Mackinac, should also be classified as military. The most important of Schoolcraft's several trips was that of 1832. With a party of thirty, including a geologist and a missionary, he skirted Lake Superior and ascended the

St. Louis River. Portaging to the Mississippi Basin he eventually arrived at Sandy Lake, where there was an important trading center that had been visited by Pike a quarter of a century earlier. Continuing his trip he came to the farthest limit of previous exploration at Cass Lake, discovered and named by Lewis Cass. Here he reduced his party to those best able to continue the arduous trip upstream. Finally their hardships were rewarded by the discovery of Lake Itasca, that will-o'-the-wisp source of the Mississippi. Schoolcraft's discovery was important in itself, but it was overshadowed by his literary contributions to a greater understanding of the Far West. Schoolcraft had an immense knowledge of Indian ways and customs and a facile pen; his writings greatly expanded the information the East had concerning the western country and its inhabitants.

The best known of all military explorers in time became John C. Frémont, the "Pathfinder of the West." His first trip, a nonmilitary one, to the West was an exploration of the Minnesota River in 1838. At this time he was only twenty-five, bright, quick, clever, handsome, and impetuous. The party of which he was a member was commanded by the eminent French scientist J. N. Nicollet, who gave Frémont much of the information and training he was to put to use on his later trips in the 1840s.

These and other minor military expeditions increased vastly the information about the plains region of the Far West before 1840. The main rivers, such as the Missouri, Platte, Minnesota, Arkansas, and Red, had been examined and described. The outstanding physical characteristics of the plains had been recounted. Obviously the data still contained large gaps that would require many years to fill, but the essential information had been stated. But very little was known about the region west of the Rockies, unless vague rumors were to be given credence. No military expedition followed Lewis and Clark across the mountains until after 1840, partly because the United States held no exclusive possessions on the coast.

FUR TRADERS

Almost as important as the army men, and often ahead of them both geographically and chronologically, were the fur trappers and traders. The fur trade constantly opened new areas because of the normal expansion of the business, the push of settlement, and the depletion of eastern fields. The necessary expansion was by no means always unpleasant, for many of the trappers found pleasure and satisfaction in the exploration of new parts of the country. Frequently the trappers and traders went much farther than business required and often lost both time and money in their operations. The lure of unexplored wilderness has always called a certain type of man, whether he be a Marco Polo, a John Ledyard, a Robert Perry, or an Alexander Mackenzie.

The most active and able of the trader-explorers was Alexander Mackenzie, a Scotsman operating in Canada. Fifteen years before the purchase of Louisiana and the exploration of Lewis and Clark, Mackenzie descended the river that now bears his name far enough to see the whales and the ice sheet of the Arctic Ocean at 69° 14′ north latitude (1789). Four years later he embarked on the adventure of reaching the Pacific Ocean overland. Ascending the Peace River he then crossed the mountains and descended the Fraser, finally painting his name on a rock on the coast on July 22, 1793. This feat was one of the most remarkable in the annals of the West. Mackenzie's small party was frequently without food, wet, surrounded by wild beasts, and facing unknown natives. The trip was a monument to Mackenzie's endurance, to his mastery over men, and to his driving personality.

Other Canadian traders followed Mackenzie into the wilderness. David Thompson operated between Lake Winnipeg and the Mandan villages after 1795. He crossed the Rocky Mountains to the Columbia River in 1805, just failing to meet Lewis and Clark. Between 1807 and 1809 he traveled widely in the Oregon country. Donald McKenzie explored the Columbia and ascended the Snake River into present Idaho in the years just following 1818. Alexander Ross traversed much of the present northern Idaho in 1824. Peter Skene Ogden was also in the Idaho region during the 1820s, and later claimed to have discovered the Great Salt Lake in the winter of 1824–1825; probably the first white man to see the lake was Jim Bridger in 1825, although the matter is still in considerable doubt.

Traders of the Canadian companies moving southwestward were met by American traders moving to the northwest. Representatives of such companies as the Missouri Fur Company, Rocky Mountain Fur Company, and American Fur Company were pushing north and west from St. Louis during the early nineteenth century, with the Pacific Fur Company going the entire distance to the coast to establish Astoria. The American groups were particularly strong in the valley and near the headwaters of the Missouri, and in the southern Idaho region, where many a rendezvous was held in the 1820s and 1830s. Their greatest single discovery was the mountain route since known as South Pass, which was probably first used by the party of Robert Stuart returning from Astoria in 1812. This pass in present southern Wyoming is by far the best crossing of the mountains, since it has only a gradual grade all the way. After its discovery and popularization nearly all travelers to the Far West used it, and but few people traversed the more arduous passes near the headwaters of the Missouri.

The one great region that the traders had failed to explore by the middle 1820s was the Far Southwest beyond the mountains. This portion of the country was of course outside the boundaries of the United States, but international boundaries never hampered the men searching for furs. More important to the trapper, it was an arid region of mountains and deserts, difficult to traverse and supporting relatively few fur-bearing animals. Moreover, it was far from any navigable rivers; the Colorado was impassable and the Rio Grande flowed through the inhabited part of Mexico. There seemed every reason why trappers would have no interest in this part of the country.

JEDEDIAH STRONG SMITH

In spite of the obvious drawbacks of the Southwest, several trappers became interested in it during the 1820s—probably more because of the excitement of prospective exploration than because of the opportunities for profitable trapping. The most important was Jedediah Strong Smith, who was responsible for the first exact information about the Far Southwest. In many ways Smith was an unusual man. He came from a New England family at a time when most traders were southern or western in origin, and he was deeply and sincerely religious. He drifted west in search of opportunity, and ultimately was attracted to St. Louis by the lucrative possibilities of the fur trade. He was a member of the first expedition of the Rocky Mountain Fur Company in 1822.

Smith accompanied William H. Ashley on the annual caravan of the Rocky Mountain Fur Company in 1826, but when Ashley stopped in present southern Idaho, Smith continued west. Following in general the later route of the San Pedro, Los Angeles, and Salt Lake Railroad, he eventually entered California, where he stayed through the winter. Early in 1827 he returned by the present Union Pacific route, leaving most of his party in California to await his return. He attended the rendezvous of 1827, where he joined two other men in buying out Ashley's business, and then persuaded his partners to commence trapping in the Southwest.

Upon the completion of his business at the rendezvous Smith rejoined his party in California and started north along the coast. The trip proved unexpectedly difficult and dangerous, and a surprise attack by the Indians brought disaster. Only Smith and two others escaped with their lives; the furs which they had worked a year to collect were gone. After many trials and a vast amount of wandering Smith finally reached Fort Vancouver, where he was well received and kindly treated by John McLoughlin. In fact, McLoughlin went much further than the laws of hospitality required, recovering and paying for Smith's furs; in return Smith promised not to compete in the Oregon country. After Smith had rested he set out on his return trip by way of the Missouri. At St. Louis he decided to give up trapping and to enter the Santa Fe trade. He met his death on the Santa Fe Trail at the hands of the Comanche in 1831.

Smith's travels and adventures in the West were worthy of a Homer. Traveling thousands of miles through an unknown wilderness, penetrating forests full of wild animals, crossing raging torrents, paddling his canoe into unknown dangers, plodding across weary miles of sand, crossing snow-capped mountains, and continually evading hostile savages, his exploits in the decade that he spent west of the Mississippi verge on the miraculous. His own statement of motives is illuminating: "I of course expected to find beaver, which with us hunters is a primary object, but I was also led on by the love of novelty common to all, which is much increased by the pursuit of its gratification."

THE PATTIES

Two other trappers should be classed with Smith in the exploration of the Southwest during the 1820s. Sylvester and James Ohio Pattie, father and son, roamed over the present states of New Mexico, Arizona, and California during the years 1824–1830 mining copper, hauling supplies, trapping, hunting, and fighting Indians (who nearly killed James on several occasions). In 1827 they gathered a small party and started down the Colorado River toward the ocean. Eventually they were forced to leave their boats and go overland, but the country was inhospitable and they nearly died of privation. Food gave out and they ate their horses. Water gave out and their mouths became so parched that they could speak only with the greatest difficulty. Sylvester, the eldest, collapsed first and begged to be left behind so that the rest of the party might be saved, but his son refused and they staggered on their way, partially supporting the old man.

When the Pattie company finally arrived at San Diego it received anything but a friendly greeting from the Spanish governor. The whole party was thrown into prison and fed spoiled food. Prison was unbearable for men who had been accustomed to vigorous outdoor life and who had just passed through a period of terrible hardship, and the older Pattie soon sickened and died. Shortly after his death a smallpox epidemic broke out on the coast; James Ohio, who was a Jack-of-all-trades, offered to vaccinate everyone if he and his party were set free. The Spanish accepted his offer and he vaccinated thousands of whites and Indians up and down the coast. For this service he was given his freedom, and eventually he made his way back through Mexico to the United States, where he arrived penniless and in bad health. His travels, as edited by Timothy Flint, are a fascinating story of adventure and suffering.

PRIVATE EXPLORERS

The western explorations of governmental parties and of fur traders were but a few of the many trips to the region west of the Mississippi. Other travelers included private adventurers, observers, missionaries, sick men looking for health, and scientists in search of specimens. These men were largely responsible for the increase of eastern knowledge of the West, for they often kept and later published journals of their travels. Brief résumés of the travels of a few of these private adventurers will give an idea of what they accomplished.

John Bradbury, an English scientist primarily interested in botany, traveled up the Missouri River in 1809–1811 to make scientific observations; he published an interesting and illuminating account of his trip. Colonel John Shaw started in 1809 to go from Missouri along the 37th parallel to the coast; although he was turned back by the Indians before he attained his objective, he succeeded in reaching the mountains. The two years after his return (1809–1811) Shaw spent in exploring a large part of Missouri and Arkansas. H. M. Brackenridge, an amateur botanist, published a good account of his trip up the Missouri River in 1811.

The best known of the many botanists who explored the Far West was Thomas Nuttall, who made numerous trips to the Northwest after 1810. Nuttall was the true scientist of fiction, and many stories are told of his care of specimens. After a hard day's work, when the entire company was wet, hungry, and exhausted, Nuttall would spend hours over the campfire classifying and labeling with painstaking care the specimens he had collected during the day. At one time the party was caught in a sudden, savage storm on the Missouri and was saved from destruction only by Nuttall's presence of mind in grabbing a shrub on the bank, thus keeping the boat from being blown into the river; Nuttall's account of the incident consisted mostly of a classification of the shrub.

Only a few of the western travelers can be mentioned. Henry R. Schoolcraft explored for pleasure as well as for business and in 1818–1819 made an extensive tour through the Ozark region of Missouri and Arkansas. Prince Maximilian of Wied, one of many titled visitors, went a considerable distance up the Missouri in 1833–1834; his account of his observations was interesting, but even more valuable were the paintings made by the excellent artist who accompanied him. Another painter, George Catlin, made several tours through the West in the 1830s and drew hundreds of pictures, mostly of the Indians. An entirely different type of man was Father Pierre De Smet, a Jesuit priest who did very effective missionary work during the 1830s, particularly in the Idaho-Wyoming region. J. N.

Nicollet, a scientist mentioned previously, made extensive surveys of the Mississippi and Missouri valleys between 1836 and 1840.

Another private adventurer, disproportionately publicized by the writings of Washington Irving, was Captain B. L. E. Bonneville. Bonneville received a leave of absence from the army from 1831 to 1833 to engage in trading. He outfitted at Independence and then journeyed over the Platte River route, trading as far west as present Idaho. As a commercial venture the trip was a failure; as a scientific enterprise it was unimportant, because the ground covered by Bonneville had been well known for two decades, and he had neither the knowledge nor the training for accurate scientific observation.

NATHANIEL J. WYETH

The most spectacular of all the private trading expeditions were those of Nathaniel J. Wyeth, a solid and substantial New England ice merchant. Wyeth's interest in the West was inspired mainly by the enthusiasm of Hall J. Kelley, a New England schoolmaster who was so greatly impressed with the future of the Oregon country that he planned to settle a group of colonists on the Columbia River. Wyeth liked Kelley's proposals and so gathered a group of his friends and neighbors to join the venture. Every Saturday night these prospective Westerners met at Wyeth's house and made grandiose plans for their trip across the continent and for the operations they expected to pursue when they arrived at the coast. In general they projected a trading expedition, but just what or where they would trade was left delightfully vague. Of course they expected to barter with the natives, but why not also do business with the white inhabitants of California, the Hudson's Bay Company, the Russian traders? Some talked also of salmon fishing on the Columbia.

Wyeth's group eventually grew tired of waiting for Kelley's larger plans to materialize, and decided to go ahead on its own. The total membership of the Wyeth group was twenty-one, mostly farmers and artisans. Each man wore a sort of uniform, including a coarse woolen jacket and pantaloons, a striped woolen shirt, and rawhide boots. Equipment included food, clothing, axes, beads, and trinkets. For the trip across the plains there were three amphibious monsters, part wagon and part boat. These transportational novelties were carefully fitted and caulked canoes with removable wheels, so that they could be used on both land and water. They were given the name "Nat-wye-thium" in honor of the leader of the expedition.

The Wyeth party decided that before it started its travels it needed some real wilderness experience to acclimate itself to western life, and so spent ten days on an island in Boston Harbor. The people of Boston came in large numbers to view this curious group of far western explorers.

The actual start for the West came in March 1832, when the party left Boston for Baltimore by water. At Baltimore the men rode on the newly opened track of the Baltimore and Ohio Railroad to the end of the line. The remainder of the journey over the mountains proved long and arduous, largely because of the necessity of dragging the wagon-boats over the hills. At one place the innkeeper refused to give the travelers rooms, alleging fear of Yankee shrewdness; possibly the curious appearance of the party with its remarkable method of transportation played some part in his decision. Upon reaching the Ohio River the party continued its trip to St. Louis by boat. Here the wagon-boats were sold, since every Westerner advised Wyeth and his followers that such vehicles could not be pulled over rough ground, or through forests and mountain passes, or paddled over the rapid streams of the West.

The expedition crossed the plains under the guidance of an old fur trader. From time to time some members became so discouraged they went home. Eventually the more persistent reached present southern Idaho, but by that time everyone was thoroughly disheartened, and all would have started home except that the return trip was more difficult than continuing west and taking ship to Massachusetts. In consequence Wyeth and eleven others eventually arrived at Fort Vancouver on the Columbia River, where the party was completely disbanded. Wyeth was back in Boston before the end of the year, defeated but not discouraged.

Wyeth certainly possessed the virtue of persistency: he immediately planned a second trip, which he made in 1834. He benefited from his former experiences, and although the expedition was a financial failure, it did not end as disastrously as the first. Wyeth trapped, and fished for salmon, but without profit. He built Fort Hall on the Snake River in present southern Idaho, and this fort was an important outfitting point for many years. Eventually he gave up his western dreams and returned to Boston, where he re-entered the ice business and died a fairly wealthy man.

As a result of these and many other expeditions by the end of the 1830s the Far West had become fairly well known. It was still considered generally uninhabitable, but it was no longer an unexplored wilderness. As the reports of government-sponsored explorations were printed, the journals of private travelers published, and the tales of the trips of the fur traders told and retold, the average Easterner came to have fairly accurate notions of the main physical features of the Far West. In addition, these many expeditions were a training ground for a considerable number of guides who later were able to lead other parties to the newer parts of the country with but a fraction of the difficulties encountered by their predecessors. The Far West was becoming known.

TRAFFIC ACROSS THE PLAINS

The main distributing center for business to and from the Far West was St. Louis, which was strategically situated for commerce in the Missouri Valley, on the South Pass route, and to Santa Fe. For the usual traveler, however, the actual outfitting and jumping-off place was farther west, nearer the great bend of the Missouri. The town of Franklin, opposite present Boonville, was the busiest of such centers until 1828, when the river changed its course, and washed the town into oblivion. Its successors were most notably Independence and Westport (present Kansas City), but other towns participated in the business.

Traffic across the plains started in the spring as soon as there was grass on which to graze livestock and the ground was firm enough to support wagons. To be ready for the earliest possible move, traders, trappers, soldiers, interpreters, hunters, guides, boatmen, and missionaries crowded the Missouri River towns for several weeks in the early spring. By the 1840s the addition of settlers migrating to the Pacific Coast brought a chaos of tents, livestock, wagons, and equipment, making bedlam of the towns. Whereas the bulk of early travel went over the Santa Fe Trail, now the Platte River route, with its connections to both California and Oregon, took precedence.

Parties traveling across the plains varied in equipment and personnel depending on their size and aims. Traders bound for a mountain rendezvous or for Santa Fe carried an irreducible minimum of clothes and food, since they conserved all possible space for trading goods. A few staples such as flour, bacon, coffee, sugar, and salt were used to supplement a diet that depended mainly on game shot along the route. The army expedition carried more food, although it hoped to vary its meals with game; if engaged in an elaborate survey, both the personnel and the equipment were exceedingly varied. Settlers carried the largest amount of personal possessions, since they needed household furnishings similar to those of their predecessors in the Ohio Valley. Their covered wagons were filled with everything that the owners felt could be hauled across the continent, but the frequency of errors in judgment was attested by the discarded equipment that soon lined the road.

Motive power was a matter of considerable differences of opinion. Horses were fastest, but were most easily exhausted; they were most useful in the fur trade. Mules were more sturdy but not quite as fast; they were preferred in the Santa Fe trade, where speed was desirable but where long arid stretches made horses a poor gamble. Oxen, slow but hardy, were the pick of most settlers and freighters. The difficulties of travel necessitated more than one team for a wagon. Ordinarily the Santa Fe traders used eight mules; settlers, four or six oxen, with other animals in reserve for emergencies.

Travelers usually moved in groups to be able to cope with the natural and human dangers that might be encountered. A fur caravan might have fifty to a hundred men, with three or four times that many horses and mules. Other parties might range from five wagons to a hundred or more, the larger groups becoming more prevalent as settlers increased in number. The smaller party could move faster and was less troubled by internal dissension, but the larger group was safer.

The usual practice was for individuals and families to leave the Missouri River as they felt the urge in the early spring and then to stop at Council Grove in present eastern Kansas to organize parties for the rest of the trip, whether to Santa Fe, California, or Oregon. Semimilitary organizations were created, and the various jobs such as cooking, gathering wood, feeding the stock, and standing guard were allocated.

The average day of travel on the plains was anything but exciting— a plodding, dusty trip broken only by lunch and by short rest periods in the middle of the morning and the middle of the afternoon. A camp site had to have grass and water, and if possible the caravan stopped early enough to complete all necessary chores before dark. The wagons were arranged in a circle and a guard was set, but the horses were brought into the circle only in time of Indian danger. The usual day's trip was possibly fifteen miles, but the distances covered ranged widely from the two or three miles made by settlers confronted with adverse conditions to the thirty or forty miles made by professionals. Sundays were often used for rest and repairs.

The prevailing impression of plains travel was the slow pacing of countless miles in the scorching heat of the sun, the caravan enveloped by clouds of dust and the travelers suffering from parched, irritated throats. Fear of hostile Indians was much less pressing than worry over the necessary minimum of water, grass, and game. A severe storm might flood the camp and stampede the animals. Sickness was common, particularly the internal upsets created by an improper and monotonous diet. Accidents might come from an undesired contest with a bear, a snake, a mule, or a horse, by a misstep on a mountain, or from a bursting gun. The necessary human repairs were then as rough as wagon repairs. A snake bite might bring incision and searing with a hot iron, with the sufferer first fortified by whiskey taken internally; some men confined the treatment to the whiskey. An amputation might be performed with a butcher knife and a meat saw, but gangrene ordinarily cut short the sufferings of the victim.

Not the least of the dangers of plains travel was the Indian menace. Although Indians normally were friendly and hospitable, there were important exceptions. Young Indians sought dignity and older men reputation by joining war parties to steal horses and collect scalps, neither of which feats received the approval of the whites. In addition, the Indian was sensitive to personal slights and believed in personal retribution for any damage to himself or his family. When seeking revenge he was not always careful to harm the same white man who had harmed him.

The whites were not without sin in the relations between the two races. White traders cheated the natives, white hunters drove off their game, and white government took their land. Like the Indians, the whites were not discriminating as to whom they punished for any trouble. An Indian raid frequently brought retribution to someone, but very possibly not to the person or group creating the original disturbance; all Indians looked very much alike to white eyes. In fact most Westerners were convinced that the only desirable Indian was one who had ceased to breathe, and many were willing to help along the good work. Not infrequently a white took a shot or two at a stray Indian just for target practice.

Indian attacks were made but seldom on large white parties. Most Indians were armed with bows and arrows and were not anxious to face white guns. Small white parties, however, might have their possessions stolen or even at times be attacked. The resulting engagement might be bitter and bloody, with each side employing every stratagem that generations of frontier warfare had developed. Mutilation of the dead was common for both Indians and whites, for plains warfare followed no strict military code.

Indian troubles tended to increase as the years passed. The first explorers and trappers found the various tribes generally peaceful, but as racial contacts increased so did frictions. In part the conflicts were caused by the less desirable and more headstrong of each race, but in part they were the inevitable outcome of an aggressive culture moving into control of a region occupied by a proud and warlike people. A completely peaceful removal of the Indian control of North America was difficult to imagine.

READINGS

SECONDARY TRAVEL ACCOUNTS. James C. Bell, *Opening a Highway to the Pacific, 1838–1846* (1921), scholarly; Robert C. Cleland, *A History of California* (1922); Gloria G. Cline, *Exploring the Great Basin* (1963), very good; William E. Connelley, *History of Kansas* (5 vols., 1928), long; Leland H. Creer, *Founding of an Empire* (1947), Utah; Harrison C. Dale, *The Ashley-Smith Exploration* (1918), monograph, 1822–1829; Gordon C. Davidson, *The North West Company* (1918);

Everett N. Dick, *Vanguards of the Frontier* (1941), reads well; William H. Goetzman, *Army Exploration in the American West* (1959), detailed; Le Roy and A. W. Hafen, *Old Spanish Trail* (1954); James Monaghan, *The Overland Trail* (1947), Wyeth; Dale L. Morgan, *The Great Salt Lake* (1947) and *Jedediah Smith and the Opening of the West* (1935), very good; Allan Nevins, *Frémont* (1939); Stanley Vestal, *The Missouri* (1945); Mark S. Wade, *Mackenzie of Canada* (1927); see also biographies of the fur traders in the Readings for Chapter 21.

ORIGINAL ACCOUNTS. Albert J. Dickson (ed.), *Covered Wagon Days* (1929), central route in the 1860s; Matthew C. Field, *Prairie and Mountain Sketches* (1957), Wyoming in 1843; Harlin M. Fuller and Le Roy R. Hafen (eds.), *The Journals of Captain John R. Bell* (1957), Long expedition; John F. McDermott (ed.), *Up the Missouri with Audubon* (1951); Lloyd McFarling, *Exploring the Northern Plains, 1804–1876* (1955); Philip P. Mason (ed.), *Expedition to Lake Itasca* (1958), Schoolcraft; Henry R. Schoolcraft, *Narrative Journal* (1953); Walter Sheppe (ed.), *First Man West* (1962), Mackenzie; Reuben G. Thwaites, *Early Western Travels* (31 vols. and atlas 1904–1907), Vols. V–VI, XIII–XVII, XXII–XXX.

THE OVERLAND STAGE. From John W. Clampitt, *Echoes from the Rocky Mountains,* 1889. Except for the "hurdy-gurdy" girls, who were hired by saloon keepers to dance with all comers, women were seldom seen in frontier towns, as is evident from the interest shown these two passing through in the stagecoach.

RAILROAD BUILDING ON THE GREAT PLAINS. From *Harper's Weekly,* 1875. During construction, the workers lived in portable villages, or camps, near or at the end of the tracks. These usually consisted of a string of boxcars equipped with bunks, and boxcars, tents, or portable shacks for eating, with similar shelter for the usual camp following of land speculators, petty merchants, saloon keepers, and prostitutes. Many a "hell on wheels," as such towns came to be called, left no trace when they moved forward with the railroad construction. On the site of others a community remained after the departure of the railroad workers, forming the nucleus of future towns such as Julesburg and Cheyenne.

(*Opposite, above*) LOADING CATTLE ON THE KANSAS-PACIFIC RAILWAY AT ABILENE, KANSAS, 1871. From *Leslie's Illustrated Weekly,* 1876. An early cow town, Abilene was established in 1866 as a depot to which Texas cattle were driven for shipment by rail to Kansas City. (New York Public Library) (*Below*) ON THE TRAIL. Drawing by Frenzeny and Tavernier from *Harper's Weekly,* 1874. Shows the manner in which cattle lined out while on the move.

(*Above*) Custer's Seventh Cavalry Attacking the Cheyenne. Custer served through the Civil War and later engaged in
western patrol duty and Indian fighting. He took his last stand
against the Indians at Little Bighorn, in present Montana, in 1876.
(Gilcrease Institute, Tulsa, Oklahoma)

(*below*) Indians Destroying Railroad Tracks near Russell,
Kansas, 1869. Painting by I. Goglin. (Kansas State Historical
Society)

(*Above*) TRADING ON THE PLAINS.
From *Leslie's Illustrated Weekly,*
1871. (*Right*) WHITE TRAPPER
OF THE ROCKY MOUNTAIN WEST.
Sketch by Frederic Remington from
Century Magazine, 1889. Furs
were the basis of the first large-
scale American business on any new
frontier, and were obtained by
trading with the Indians and by
hunting and trapping. Coarse furs
such as buffalo, bear, and deer were
used for lap robes and heavy coats.
(New York Public Library)

BUFFALO HUNTER OF THE 1870s. From *Harper's Weekly,* 1874. In the 1860s great herds of buffalo still roamed the western plains, but by the 1870s buffalo robes had become popular and millions of the animals were slaughtered for the hides alone. By 1884 the herds had been all but exterminated.

LEADVILLE, COLORADO. From *Frank Leslie's Illustrated Newspaper*, April 1, 1897. A boom town 10,500 feet above sea level in the Colorado Rockies, Leadville was prominent in mineral circles during the '80s and '90s. (Denver Public Library Western Collection)

GREAT SALT LAKE CITY, 1867. A contemporary lithograph. The caption reads, in part: "The city covers an area of about 9 square miles and is probably the most beautifully laid out and finest watered city in America. The streets are very wide, with rows of shade trees on each side, and water cool and pure from the mountains capped with eternal snow running through nearly every street and garden. Every block is filled up with fruit trees, shrubbery and flowers, making the city look like an immense orchard. The mountains in view vary in distance from 40 to 150 miles. The suburbs of the city reach the shore of the lake. This singular body of water is 55 miles wide by 85 long and is intensely salt. There are four considerable rivers emptying into it without any visible outlet. The scenery around the lake is grand and sublime." (Phelps Stokes Collection, New York Public Library)

LOCAL AND TERRITORIAL.

GREAT EXPRESS ENTERPRISE!

From Leavenworth to Sacramento in Ten Days!

Clear the Track and let the Pony Come Through?

In our telegraphic columns a few days ago, there was an item stating that it had been decided by the Government to start an Express from the Missouri river to California, and the time to be ten days; but we were not aware that our fellow-citizen, Wm. H. Russell, Esq., was at the head of the enterprise, until we were shown the following dispatch. Its importance can be readily perceived:

> WASHINGTON, Jan. 27th, 1860.
> To JOHN W. RUSSELL—Have determined to establish a Pony Express to Sacramento California, commencing the 3rd of April.—Time 10 days.   WM. H. RUSSELL.

(*Left*) PONY EXPRESS ANNOUNCEMENT. From the Leavenworth *Daily Times,* January 30, 1860. The general impatience for speedier communication across the continent led to establishment of the Pony Express. In April 1860 it began carrying mail on a central overland route between St. Joseph, Missouri, and San Francisco in ten days. Only the specially designed mail pouches attached to the saddle made the entire trip. Ponies and riders were relieved at intervals to assure no slacking of speed in a schedule that reduced by twelve days the time required to carry mail to the West by overland stage on the southern route. (Kansas State Historical Society) (*Below*) CONSTRUCTION OF THE TELEGRAPH LINE ACROSS THE PLAINS IN THE EARLY SIXTIES. From John W. Clampitt, *Echoes from the Rocky Mountains,* 1889. As the transcontinental telegraph stretched westward from the Missouri River and eastward from the Pacific, the Pony Express was left an ever shorter distance to cover. The telegraph line was connected at Salt Lake City on October 26, 1861, making the Pony Express obsolete.

MULE CAR IN SALT LAKE CITY, 1872. (*Below*) PREPARING TO
LAY MULE CAR TRACKS.

FORT LARAMIE, 1853. From *Leslie's Illustrated Weekly,* 1871.
Established by fur traders in 1834, Fort Laramie, at the junction of
the Laramie and North Platt rivers, became the trade center for a
large area, serving both Indians and white trappers. By the 1840s the
growing emigrant tide demanding protection from the Indians led
the government to purchase the post and convert it to a military fort.
It was an important station on the Oregon Trail. (New York
Public Library)

Mission of St. Mary among the Flathead Indians. From J. P.
De Smet, *Oregon Missions and Travels over the Rocky Mountains in
1845–46,* 1847. This mission in the mountains of eastern Oregon
(present Montana) was one of a number founded in the region
between 1840 and 1850 by the Jesuit Father Pierre De Smet. (New
York Public Library)

(*Above*) SUTTER'S FORT, 1849. From J. M. Letts, *A Pictorial View of California*, 1853. Built in 1841 by the Swiss John Augustus Sutter on the site of what is now Sacramento, the fort served as headquarters of a great ranch that Sutter held under a grant from the Mexican government, and was a stopping place for army officers and early settlers. Gold was discovered nearby on January 24, 1848. (Phelps Stokes Collection, New York Public Library)

(*Below*) SACRAMENTO CITY, 1849. Lithograph by William Endicott after a sketch by G. V. Cooper. The city was laid out in the spring of 1849 about a mile and a half from Sutter's Fort and was a thriving community before the end of the year. (Phelps Stokes Collection, New York Public Library)

A Camel Train Encampment near Carson Valley, California, 1856. From Vischer, *Pictorial of California,* 1868. At the
close of the Mexican War in 1848 the United States acquired additional territory to the west, and the need to establish fast express
routes across the arid portions of the land led Congress in 1855 to
appropriate money for the purchase of camels. Seventy-six were
brought from the Near East to Texas, and twenty-eight were taken
from there to California to carry mail and express across the desert.
The method proved impractical, and within the next few years the
camels could be found carrying freight to and from the mines in
Nevada or doing farm work. A few were sold to circuses and
zoological gardens. (New York Historical Society)

CHAPTER 23

MEXICO ATTRACTS

A merican advances toward the west met not only a wilderness to be conquered and red men to be brushed aside, but also another European frontier—that of Spain. Along the southern fringe of the United States lay the "Spanish borderlands," where the clash of civilizations became a three-way affair.

Spanish occupation of the Americas had begun in the Caribbean as the result of an error plus an accident. The error was a consequence of Columbus's lack of geographical knowledge, and the accident was the place of his landing. The result was that Spain occupied first the West Indies and Mexico, and then used Mexico as a base for expansion to the north. Within half a century much of the Caribbean area had been overrun, and venturesome Spaniards had explored the northern continent as far as Kansas. By 1540 Spanish expeditions had touched the present states of California, Arizona, New Mexico, Texas, Louisiana, Arkansas, Oklahoma, and possibly Missouri. Such men as Cabeza de Vaca and Hernando de Soto should rank with men of the caliber of Alexander Mackenzie and Lewis and Clark.

Most imposing of the early expeditions was that led by Francisco Coronado in the years 1540–1542. Coronado's main power lay in some three hundred horsemen, many of them titled Spanish adventurers, elaborately caparisoned in suits of burnished armor, and carrying swords and lances. In addition there were a smaller number of foot soldiers, and hundreds of servants and friendly Indians, together with artillery, livestock, and provisions. A portion of this impressive array finally advanced as far as present Kansas. Although Coronado failed to find the precious metals that were the main object of his search, and though his expedition returned bedraggled and discouraged, the boundaries of geographical knowledge had

339

been pushed back one step further. The magnitude of the achievement can be appreciated only if one realizes that it came within fifty years of Columbus's discovery of the continent, and over half a century before the English tried to establish their first permanent settlement at Jamestown.

SPANISH ADVANCE

Stories of fabulous amounts of gold, silver, and precious stones, including the famous but imaginary Seven Golden Cities of Cibola, lured Spanish adventurers northward. Such rumors died hard, but were succeeded by other inspirations to adventure. Were there not other sources of wealth, and were there not pagan souls to be saved from eternal damnation? Other expeditions, both lay and cleric, plodded the weary, sandy miles to the north. The church and the state, cross and sword, went side by side; soldier and settler often combined in a single person. Small Spanish settlements began to appear from the easternmost St. Augustine (1565) to the far reaches of the Pacific Coast.

The most easily attainable and most desirable region west of the Mississippi and north of the present Mexico was the valley of the Rio Grande in present New Mexico. Here in 1598, under Juan de Oñate, settlers came to establish the first permanent white settlement west of the Mississippi; San Juan, north of the present Santa Fe, was founded nine years before Jamestown. A little later (1609) the village of Santa Fe was established to become the capital and metropolis of the area. The succeeding years brought an increasing flow of friars, soldiers, and settlers, although not in sufficient numbers to break the solitude of most of the wilderness. The Rio Grande settlements grew with moderate rapidity, in part because the colonists married natives and produced numerous offspring. Farther west, hopeful priests, cattlemen, soldiers, and miners trickled into the present southern Arizona.

The Spanish control of the Southwest was thin, but at least it was unchallenged until the Spanish authorities were startled in 1685 by the arrival of a French expedition headed by Robert Cavelier, Sieur de La Salle. La Salle had been searching for the mouth of the Mississippi, and had ultimately ended at Matagorda Bay in Texas, where he landed and built Fort St. Louis. From Matagorda he set out to find the Mississippi, which seemed very elusive for so large a body of water. After tremendous hardships before and during the attempt to reach the Mississippi overland, La Salle was murdered by his men in 1687. The La Salle expedition was a failure, but it frightened the Spanish, particularly when it was followed by the establishment of Louisiana (1699), by further exploration, and by the establishment of Natchitoches (1714) on the Red River. Spain's reply was to send new expeditions of her own, and to found Nacogdoches to offset Natchitoches. Unfortunately for Spain, few troops and settlers were available and the Indians were hostile. For a number of years there were clashes between Spanish and French forces on the north and east boundaries of Texas. In a sense the situation was ludicrous—infinitesimal forces were fighting for a wilderness of little value to either side. The trouble ended when Spain acquired Louisiana in 1763.

Even as France was losing its hold in the East, a new threat appeared in the West with the advance of Russia down the Pacific Coast. Although this expansion never reached the Golden Gate, it inspired Spain to increase her colonization program. The priesthood took the initiative, backed by the army. Father Junípero Serra led the clerical group, Gaspar de Portolá the military. They built a mission at San Diego and then moved north, visiting the sites of what would be Monterey and San Francisco. In 1770 the settlement of Monterey was begun, although by this time many of the original party were dead. San Francisco was established the year of American Independence, 1776.

The occupation of the Pacific Coast north to San Francisco was the last important expansion of Spanish power in the American West. Thereafter Spain was to revert to a defensive that was soon to become a final stand to maintain her existence in North America. Spain's ultimate failure was based on the fact that there were not enough Spaniards west of the Mississippi to hold the country against aggressive outsiders. By the late eighteenth century there were probably not over 15,000 people of white blood in the American Southwest, two thirds of these being in the Rio Grande Valley of New Mexico. Many of these were at least half Indian, and the likelihood of their uniting in effective resistance to the Anglo-Americans was small.

SPANISH CIVILIZATION

The Spanish empire was theoretically the private property of the king, but in practice was controlled by two Spanish bodies—the Council of the Indies, with legislative and administrative duties, and the House of Trade, which enforced colonial trade restrictions. In Spanish America the top official was the viceroy, of whom there were several; in descending order the hierarchy went from the governor to the alcalde (mayor) in the individual town. On paper the organization seemed efficient but in practice it tended to creak at the joints because complete control from the top was cumbersome in a period of slow communication. Furthermore, the Spanish bureaucracy had a reputation for inefficiency and graft that was notable in a period in which competitors for that honor were legion.

Control of the sparsely settled wilderness depended largely on the army, which was stationed in presidios (garrisons) throughout the Southwest. Best known were the garrisons at San Antonio (1718), El Paso (1683), Santa Fe (1609, replacing San Juan), Tucson (1776, replacing Tubac), San Diego (1769), and San Francisco (1776). The great paucity of soldiers attested both a lack of funds and a touching and unjustified faith in Spanish arms. Twenty or thirty soldiers were considered a good-sized force, but some posts had no more than five to ten. Twenty soldiers could hardly overawe Indian tribes numbering thousands. Indian outbreaks and depredations were almost continuous throughout the entire area. Worst was the Pueblo revolt of 1680, which brought death to one sixth of the white population of New Mexico and drove the remainder to El Paso, but at many other times and places life was precarious for the Spanish "conqueror."

Even more conspicuous than the military in the new communities were the Franciscan, Dominican, and Jesuit priests who in many cases, as at El Paso, arrived before the soldiers. Not infrequently High Mass, a Te Deum, and a salvo of cannon fire were the opening ceremonies for a new town. Church and state were indivisible, with the state preserving order to permit the saving of souls, and the church civilizing and Christianizing the natives to produce good, loyal subjects of His Catholic Majesty.

The work of the church centered around the approximately sixty-five missions at which were congregated Indian converts or potential converts. Here the good friars worked and taught and prayed to save the pagans from eternal punishment. The results were impressive when stated in the number of those baptized; as early as 1630 the New Mexico missions claimed 60,000 converts. Unhappily this success came not entirely from the attractiveness of the Gospel and its preachers, but also from the lure of Spanish goods and the power of Spanish arms. From time to time the Indians discarded their allegiance to the Prince of Peace to engage in theft, arson, and murder; when Spanish military power lapsed most Indians reverted to their original ways of life.

The head of a mission was by no means interested exclusively in matters spiritual. He desired to make the Indians into settled agriculturists as a way of reinforcing their Christianity; he wanted to make a success of the sizable economic and social unit that he headed. Large herds of cattle and horses, flocks of sheep and goats, great fields of grain, considerable numbers of artisans, and hundreds of Indian workers presented problems to challenge the keenest business intellect. Missions produced their own food, and much of their clothes and tools. They not only traded but also functioned as inns, hospitals, and schools. The missions of California in particular waxed fat with their broad acres of wheat and fruit, and with horses, sheep, mules, and cattle numbered in the thousands. They did not overlook vineyards and wine making, and distilleries were far from rare.

Successful large-scale business must be credited to these factory-farm-church establishments.

Alongside each mission was an Indian town or pueblo, for the fathers felt they could do their best work if the Indians were concentrated so that they might be supervised more easily. In New Mexico these towns already existed as a part of the native culture, but elsewhere they had to be produced by a mixture of cajolery and force.

White settlers were sometimes grouped in towns, but frequently lived as isolated ranchers. White settlement was encouraged from time to time by the Spanish administration, and sometimes was forced, as when soldiers were required to bring their families and to remain in the north. The usual town grew near a presidio or mission or both, and was highly dependent on them. In many cases the whites intermarried with the natives. Outside the towns were numerous cattle ranches. Land seemed inexhaustible and was donated in immense tracts. Cattle, too, were cheap because there was no easily available market for them. The average rancher lived in a crude log or adobe cabin, where he dispensed open-handed hospitality.

The golden age of the Southwest was approximately the years 1790 to 1810. Missions and towns were beyond their first crude youth and now worried mainly about hostile Indians. Many of the missions were highly prosperous. Spanish administration had become routine and was not particularly severe. France had been eliminated from North America. The Russian menace had proved less terrifying than its advance notices. The bulk of United States population was far distant, and the acquisition of Louisiana promised to channel American energies away from the Spanish possessions. The few American visitors and settlers in the Spanish Southwest seemed no more than the casual sparks from a locomotive headed in a different direction.

INCREASING DISORDER

The peaceful stability of the years around 1800 was not to last. A series of revolts starting in 1810 brought increasing domestic disorder, which the successful Mexican revolution of 1821 did not end. Garrisons were reduced and the few remaining troops were paid but irregularly. Instead of a concrete wall against internal and external troubles they became a barrier of tissue paper.

Wavering internal control was matched by shaky external protection. Early in the nineteenth century pirates in the Gulf of Mexico were bold and vigorous. Their principal rendezvous was Barataria, which was within 50 miles of New Orleans, and there is reason to believe that the New Orleans merchants encouraged piracy as a means of obtaining cheap supplies. The audacity of these pirates is illustrated by their plans to seize and

loot Pensacola, and to invade Florida and sell it to the United States. Outstanding among the pirates were the Lafitte brothers (the name has been
spelled variously), particularly Jean, six-feet-two, dark, handsome, and
unsmiling.

The Barataria retreat was made untenable by United States naval
forces in 1814 and many of the pirates were thrown into the New Orleans
calaboose. As luck would have it their services were needed in the defense
of New Orleans and in time they were pardoned by President Madison.
After the war they found little happiness in legal trade and soon reverted to
piracy. Jean Lafitte took over Galveston in 1817 and there he made piracy
a well-organized and efficiently managed business. He was so strong that
Americans arriving overland generally felt that the wise procedure was
to make their peace with Jean Lafitte.

AMERICAN FILIBUSTERS

Americans near the Texas frontier looked at the lax Mexican control with hope. In Texas were numerous herds of cattle and horses and
millions of acres of fertile lands within easy distance of Gulf ports. To the
west lay trapping opportunities soon to be exploited by the Patties and
others of their stamp. In Texas, but particularly along the Rio Grande,
were dozens of isolated settlements eager for American products, for the
various Mexican revolutions had interrupted their slender communications
to the south. And if trade went to Texas and New Mexico, why not to
California and even to present Mexico itself? In addition, California
offered a supply of hides and furs, together with an opportunity for the
outfitting of American ships. Energetic and optimistic Americans viewed
each of these opportunities enthusiastically.

The earliest American infiltration of Spanish territory was mainly
by individual traders and by raiding expeditions. Even before 1800 various
Americans sought trade with the Indians or whites, some trying to tap the
Sante Fe trade; their fortune was universally bad, their goods were consistently confiscated, and they themselves often ended in jail. Most spectacular were the operations of Philip Nolan, horse trader (and thief), friend
of Jefferson, and protégé of Wilkinson. His last expedition came in 1800,
when with a small party he trapped wild horses as far west as the Brazos
River. Discovered and attacked by Spanish soldiers, he was killed and his
men were imprisoned. Spanish power was not tremendous, but it could still
cope with a handful of adventurers.

Other Americans were not intimidated by Nolan's fate and continued their raids into Texas. Wilkinson's name seemed to be connected
with an extraordinary number of them. Wilkinson boasted of his connections with Nolan; later he was involved in the Burr plans, which looked

toward the Southwest. He gave the orders that led Pike to traverse large parts of New Mexico and Texas. He encouraged various dissidents. His son was a member of the Gutiérrez-Magee expedition and his nephew James Long led still another party.

The Gutiérrez-Magee expedition of 130 men invaded Texas in 1812 in the name of Mexican patriotism. Bernardo Gutiérrez de Lara just missed obtaining official American support for the revolution in which he was engaged. His partner, Augustus Magee, resigned his commission in the American army to participate in the venture, thus bringing to mind similar incidents in East Florida about the same time. The growing army surged ahead, defeated an opposing force, and occupied San Antonio, although by this time Magee had died. Internal dissension and a loyal Spanish army brought the collapse of the movement, with neither side showing mercy in the fighting. Reports indicated that ninety-three Americans escaped from a force that at its maximum included at least five times that number of Americans plus many Mexicans and Indians.

Not daunted by this disaster, James Long, formerly a surgeon in the United States Army, planned an invasion in 1819. Recruiting some fifty volunteers at Natchez he advanced on Nacogdoches, captured the town, and declared Texas free. He tried to obtain the assistance of Jean Lafitte, but Lafitte clung to piracy as safer and more lucrative than filibustering. Long maintained a precarious independence for two years. Upon his defeat he suffered the usual punishment of being shot; his men were imprisoned.

American filibustering in Texas received no governmental support. In fact, the Florida treaty of 1819 specifically excluded Texas from the United States, even though plausible claims might have been advanced for at least part of the area, and the Long expedition was in considerable part a protest against this governmental action. At the time of the Long expedition it must have seemed to anyone east of the Appalachians, including the King of Spain, that American colonization and acquisition of Texas were such a remote possibility as hardly worth consideration.

SANTA FE TRADE

Conditions west of the Sabine changed markedly in 1820, when, as a result of a Spanish revolution, foreign settlement in the empire was permitted. Hardly had this news reached America than a successful Mexican revolution (1821) ended old colonial restrictions. The way was opened for American trade and settlement, depending only on the attitude of the Mexican government, which was never strong, particularly in the remote North.

The most important trade to develop was that with Santa Fe, that is, with the New Mexican settlements of the area and extensions to California and Mexico. The Santa Fe trade began in 1821 with the successful venture of William Becknell. During the next few years only a scattering of traders ventured the trip; their success led to large yearly caravans, which continued until the railroad arrived over half a century later.

The Santa Fe trade was based on commodities of fairly large value and small bulk because of the expense of the trip across the plains. Usually included were woolens, cottons, silks, velvets, shawls, looking glasses, and hardware. These goods were carried in Pittsburgh or Conestoga wagons, each drawn by eight to twelve mules or oxen and holding three to seven thousand pounds of merchandise. The return trip brought mules, horses, beaver skins, and bullion.

The Santa Fe trade prospered in spite of numerous difficulties. In the path of the trader lay treeless and waterless plains, and one real desert. Streams had to be forded. The Indians, particularly the Comanche, were dangerous. The import tax at Santa Fe was always annoying, being sometimes as high as 60 percent of the value of the imports. A flat rate of $500 a wagon, which was introduced in 1839, encouraged the traders to use large wagons. Bribery of customs officials was an ordinary part of the business: usually a third of the tax went to the government, a third to the official, and the other third was retained by the trader. In spite of these various handicaps the trade prospered; an average trip brought a gross profit of 10 to 40 percent.

The total value of the trade was not as much as might have been expected. The average per year between 1822 and 1843 was $130,000— the largest single year (1841) amounted to $450,000. The trade was stopped by Santa Anna in 1843–1844, but then revived; the caravan of 1846 was valued at $1,752,250. The business continued important through the Civil War.

Each year the caravan from the United States moved west as soon as the ground was passable, and returned before the coming of snow; travel was at the rate of about fifteen to eighteen miles a day. Most of the goods passed through St. Louis, but the usual outfitting point was some town farther up the Missouri. Each man carried for food approximately fifty pounds of flour, fifty pounds of bacon, ten pounds of coffee, twenty pounds of sugar, and some salt. These supplies, supplemented by a little game, were supposed to be adequate for the trip to Santa Fe.

The start from Independence, Kansas City, or any other outfitting town was a helter-skelter affair, for each driver left whenever he was ready. The Indians of the region were not hostile and the plains were not dangerous, so precautions were unnecessary. To provide for the dangers farther west a rendezvous was held at Council Grove (in present Kansas). Here all the men making the trip gathered to rest, repair their wagons, and fatten their stock. The company was then organized for mutual protection and assistance; officers were elected to command the entire caravan, provide for both day and night guards, select the men to do the cooking, and take complete control in case of trouble. After this organization the group moved out of Council Grove in a body, and the difficult trip began.

The trail from Council Grove went directly west to the great bend of the Arkansas River, a distance of 270 miles from Independence. Then it followed the river to its crossing at the 392-mile mark. From this point either of two routes might be followed. Most caravans cut overland from the Arkansas across the Cimarron desert to the Cimarron River (a branch of the Arkansas), then up the Cimarron and finally cross-country to Santa Fe. The optional route continued up the Arkansas River as far as Bent's Fort, which was located near the present La Junta, Colorado. Here it turned directly south to Santa Fe. The second route was safer but longer, so most of the traders went by way of the Cimarron. At Santa Fe the traders sold their merchandise on the streets until their stock was gone or winter approached. Then the caravan started the return trip, hoping to arrive at the Missouri River before the first snowfall.

The trade with Santa Fe was indicative of the eventual disintegration of the permanent Indian frontier. The government was drawn into the anomalous position of supporting the permanent frontier and at the same time giving direct aid and encouragement to the Santa Fe traders. By a law of 1825 the Santa Fe road was marked within the limits of the United States, although unfortunately the markings were placed on the little-used route by Bent's Fort. Fort Leavenworth was established in 1827 for the principal purpose of restraining Indians who might interfere with the Santa Fe trade. Military escorts were provided at government expense in 1829, 1834, and 1843 to protect the traders as far as the United States boundary; this assistance was not given more frequently because the value of the trade hardly justified it, and also because the worst part of the route was in Mexican territory.

The significance of the Santa Fe trade was greater than its monetary value indicated. Its romance and adventure appealed strongly to a nation that had received its concepts of the West from Cooper and Irving. Fighting Indians and forest fires, shooting buffalo and other game, fording rivers, crossing deserts, attending Spanish fandangos, and eating chile con carne all seemed exciting. Then too there was the romantic appeal of the dusky Mexican beauty with her high combs, her long black cigaret, and her alluring eyes and figure. Dirt and vermin were invisible over a space of a thousand miles.

The Santa Fe trade demonstrated the ease with which the United States might conquer the Southwest. Any illusion of Mexican military power could not be maintained in the face of the observations of the traders.

Furthermore, the Sante Fe traders helped in some measure to dispel the idea of a Great American Desert. The whole effect of the trade was to begin the disintegration of the permanent Indian frontier and to turn American attention toward the Mexican territory of the Southwest.

AMERICAN SETTLERS IN TEXAS

If the Santa Fe trade suggested Mexican weakness, the beginnings of American migration to Texas proved the point beyond contradiction. In the van was one Moses Austin, Connecticut Yankee by birth, who had pursued an elusive fortune to Pennsylvania, to Virginia, and to Missouri before he finally turned to Mexican lands as a last resort. His application coincided with the newly liberalized policy of the Spanish government and a grant was approved (1821) on condition that he bring 300 families.

Moses Austin died before he could profit by his new-found good fortune, but his work was continued by his son Stephen, who after considerable effort succeeded in obtaining the reaffirmation of his father's grant by the new Mexican government. His land lay between the San Jacinto and Lavaca rivers on the Gulf side of the trail from Nacogdoches to San Antonio. Within the grant Austin had supreme power to distribute land, lay out towns, administer justice, and exercise the other necessary functions of government. He immediately offered attractive terms to prospective American colonists, and by the end of the decade attracted some 5000 who lacked the hard cash to pay the minimum of $1.25 an acre charged by the United States.

At the same time that Stephen Austin was in Mexico City lobbying for the confirmation of his grant, other Americans, including James Wilkinson and Haden Edwards, were seeking grants of their own, and the Mexican Congress was debating some kind of general land legislation. In 1824 it finally laid down a few general rules but delegated most power to the individual states; the next year the state of Coahuila and Texas acted very liberally by providing *empresario* grants much like the one Austin had received. Each *empresario* was to receive a large free tract of his own if he brought a proper number of colonists, while each colonist was to receive one labor (177 acres) for agriculture and twenty-four labores for grazing. The cost was extremely small, and payment was spread over six years. Tariffs were removed from agricultural implements, and all taxes were to be remitted for six years and then halved for the next six years. The introduction of slaves was prohibited except in the Austin colony, but this provision was soon modified.

The Mexican policy took concrete form in the next few years with large grants to such men as Green Dewitt and Haden Edwards, so that Texas became a patchwork of claims. This policy was definitely dangerous to Mexican control of Texas, and the danger increased with its success. Although more people brought more power and wealth, and hence more revenue, the examples of East and West Florida might well have caused Mexico to be more cautious. The day was coming when she would rue her policy bitterly.

American farmers found Texas desirable. By 1827 their number was possibly 10,000, three years later it had doubled, and by 1835 it had reached 35,000. Most of them were from the southern states, particularly Kentucky and Tennessee, but some came from as far as New England, and a few hailed from Germany and Ireland; there was no slavery conspiracy, as later claimed. Theoretically they were all loyal Catholic citizens of Mexico, but actually both their patriotism and their Catholicism were scarcely skin-deep. Catholic priests and Mexican soldiers were greeted with apathy. Some of the late arrivals married Mexican girls, which indicated not Pan-American unity but the scarcity of women and the larger land grant available to a married man. Here and there settlers spoke openly of their desire for United States control, but most of them followed Austin's lead in preserving at least technical loyalty to the Mexican government.

One straw in the wind was the Fredonia revolt of 1826–1827, even though it was a small affair with little general Texan support, and soon collapsed. Haden Edwards had been awarded an *empresario* grant that included Nacogdoches, and immediately had trouble with earlier settlers, largely Mexican, over their claims. On appeal to the government the older claims were upheld and the Edwards grant was canceled; whereupon Edwards established a revolutionary government with the usual constitution and the equally usual appeals to the United States for assistance. The United States turned a deaf ear and the revolt was suppressed by a Mexican army aided by some of the Austin colonists.

The Fredonia trouble was itself unimportant, but it underlined a situation that was giving more and more concern to informed and intelligent Mexicans. Spanish and Anglo-Saxon cultures did not mix happily. Particularly in government and religion were there wide and deep differences. Each people looked at the other with suspicion and even hostility. Each felt the other inferior. The explosion came daily closer as the American predominance in numbers increased year by year.

A prominent Mexican analyzed United States policy in 1830:

> They begin by introducing themselves into the territory they covet, upon pretense of commercial negotiations or of the establishment of colonies. . . . These colonies grow, multiply, become the predominant part of the population; and as soon as a support is found in this manner, they begin to set up rights which it is impossible to sustain in a serious discussion. . . . These pioneers originate, little by little, movements which

complicate the political state of the country in dispute. . . . When things have come to this pass, which is precisely the present state of things in Texas, diplomatic intrigue begins.

The validity of the final assertion in this statement was illustrated by the fact that the United States had acquired an interest in Texas that had been absent in 1819. President Adams had tried to buy the region, and although he had to be content with a treaty that did no more than recognize the Sabine River boundary, the Mexicans may be excused for fearing that action would be taken through United States-born citizens of Texas.

MORE SEVERE MEXICAN POLICY

Mexican fears produced a severely restrictive policy in 1830. Further immigration from the United States was prohibited. *Empresario* grants were to be canceled as soon as legally possible. Foreign ships were admitted to Mexican coastal trade in the hope that Mexican trade would be encouraged at the expense of the traffic with New Orleans. Texan military garrisons were reinforced in 1830 and 1831. Finally, an effort was made in 1832 to encourage immigration from non-American countries.

The Mexican reforms came too late to be effective, even had they been conscientiously administered. A handful of poorly paid and inadequately equipped Mexican soldiers could not guard a thousand miles of land and water frontier against United States settlers. Trade continued to go to New Orleans in spite of a tariff and shipping preference. Immigrants from other countries did not arrive. The only tangible accomplishment was to irritate the colonists so that even formerly loyal supporters of Mexico began to grumble at the many restrictions. And this result was produced without stopping United States migrants; the administration of the law was lax, and immediate exceptions were made for the Austin and Dewitt colonies; in 1833 the prohibition on immigration from the United States was repealed completely.

Texas troubles increased during the early 1830s. Internally, more American settlers made belligerent demands for their "rights." Externally, President Jackson made a new offer of $5 million for Texas, and also asked for California. Jackson's representative was the swashbuckling and vainglorious Anthony Butler, who suggested wholesale bribery as the road to success; Jackson's morality was affronted, and he recalled Butler.

Just when Butler's mission was becoming obviously hopeless (1832) a friend of Jackson appeared on the scene in the person of Sam Houston; this coincidence in time may of course have been an accident. Houston had been born in Virginia, but had grown up in Tennessee and served with Jackson in the War of 1812. He had then entered law practice and politics; his public offices included a major-generalship in the militia and membership in Congress. At the age of thirty-four (1827) he was elected Governor of Tennessee and two years later he married. Unquestionably he seemed headed for a long and distinguished career.

Within three months of Houston's marriage he threw up his job as governor, deserted his wife, and fled to the Indian country, where he adopted Indian ways including an Indian wife, and drank enough to distress his new friends. Houston never explained his actions, and most guesses have involved his relations with his wife. During the three succeeding years he was twice in Washington and entertained by Jackson at the White House. When he crossed the border into Texas he was a marked man, not only because of his past career and his friendship with the President, but also because of his appearance and personality. Well over six feet tall and built in proportion, handsome, with a deep, rich voice and an attractive manner, he was immediately outstanding. At once he became the leader of Texan groups favoring independence and there can be little question that thereby he was following Jackson's desires, whether or not they had been expressed explicitly.

During the very year of Houston's arrival occurred a small Texas revolution, although there is no connection between the two events. The abortive uprising came from an unpopular administration of customs restrictions, and coincided with a successful revolution by Santa Anna in Mexico. Santa Anna immediately sent an army to Texas; in addition Austin returned from Mexico with promises of reforms if the Texas revolutionists accepted the new Mexican administration. The rebels, impressed more by the promises than by the army, laid down their arms, threw their hats in the air, and gave three cheers for the "liberal" Santa Anna.

The only indication of Santa Anna's presumed liberalism was the repeal of the prohibition of United States immigration; but the Texans wanted self-rule. Discontent increased when Santa Anna (1834) dropped even the pretense of liberalism, dismissed his Congress, and took all power in his own hands. As Texan mutterings increased, the new dictator decided that military chastisement would be salutary and at the same time would increase his own prestige.

TEXAS REVOLUTION

Events moved rapidly to a crisis. General Martín Perfecto de Cos entered Texas in September 1835. A month later a Texas convention created a provisional government headed by a known advocate of independence and gave Houston command of the army, but did not declare independence. Cos was defeated and driven out. Santa Anna then took personal command; he crossed the Rio Grande on February 12, 1836, and on March 2 Texas proclaimed her independence.

When Santa Anna crossed the Rio Grande he had an army of some 6000 and visions of military fame. In numbers he was clearly superior to any possible opposing force, and he tended to overlook poor equipment and morale. He designed his campaign to ferret out and destroy all rebel forces. No quarter was to be given and no prisoners were to be taken. Texas was to be given a taste of Mexican authority that would not soon be forgotten.

The situation of the Texans was precarious. Although hardy and self-reliant as individuals, they were variously armed and equipped, and without formal discipline. They numbered possibly 1000 but were divided into several small groups. Sam Houston was theoretically in supreme command, but in practice his orders were no more than suggestions or requests.

Santa Anna took full advantage of Texan division. A force of about a hundred Texans was annihilated at San Patricio, with survivors of the battle being executed. A force of 182 men under W. B. Travis was trapped at San Antonio, which Houston had ordered abandoned; the heroic defense of the Alamo ended only with the death of the last defender. Four hundred men under J. W. Fannin were surrendered at Goliad. They surrendered on the promise that they would be permitted to go home; whereupon they were marched out in three small groups and massacred at the order of Santa Anna. Apologists insisted that rebellion should be punished by death, but most people were horrified.

These slaughters had at least the effect of unifying the Texan command by killing all rivals to Houston. In addition, Santa Anna, flushed with victory, became increasingly less cautious. Most important, Texans were inspired to desperate resistance for they clearly had no option between victory and death. The battle cries of "Remember the Alamo!" and "Remember Goliad!" were heard increasingly as Houston and his 350 men started retreating eastward, gathering recruits as they went.

Mexican victories and the Houston retreat brought the question of whether the United States would interfere. Throughout the Union public meetings demanded federal action, and sent supplies, munitions, and men to aid the rebels. President Jackson undoubtedly prayed for Texan victory. He followed the campaign closely and sent to the border an American army under Gaines, who he perhaps hoped would follow the Jackson Florida precedent. More positive action was a distinct possibility if Houston had been defeated, but in fact the United States government maintained proper neutrality except that it winked at the aid given by American citizens to the rebels.

Houston's retreat was at first an inescapable necessity, but later seemed to become a habit. An enlarged and better-disciplined army still brought only retreat. Even when Santa Anna's self-confidence and lack of military ability led him to divide his army, and when Texan forces outnumbered Mexican, Houston still refused to do battle. Many of the Texans became bitter and sullen, some of them went home, and Santa Anna overran the capital of the new republic.

Ultimately Houston and Santa Anna confronted each other on the San Jacinto River near Galveston Bay. The Texans were at first the more numerous, but Houston waited until Santa Anna was reinforced. Then, against the advice of some of his staff, Houston made a frontal rather than a flank attack on a superior position on April 21, 1836. Judged by results, the Houston campaign had been masterful, for it achieved total victory. Apparently the Mexicans were taken by surprise because Mexican military traditions did not envisage the possibility of an attack by an outnumbered army on a superior position. Houston's reports of the engagement claimed more Mexican casualties than Santa Anna had troops, but there was no doubt that the Texans had won an overwhelming victory at little cost. Santa Anna was himself captured, but demonstrated his plausibility by persuading his captors to release him on his promise to use his influence toward the acceptance of Texan independence. This promise he later repudiated—after all, it had been extorted by force.

TEXAN INDEPENDENCE

With Houston's victory at San Jacinto, Texan refugees who had crowded the roads to the East began to return. The constitution that had been drawn up at the time of the declaration of independence was placed before the people and ratified. The temporary president was superseded by one regularly elected, who naturally was Sam Houston, the hero of the hour. A minister was sent to the United States and a proposal for annexation was adopted by an almost unanimous popular vote. The anticipated course of events was perfectly clear to the world.

Annexation struck an unexpected snag in the person of President Jackson. Long desirous of acquiring Texas, he now not only proved cool toward the idea of annexation but also very lukewarm even about recognition. Possibly he feared trouble from Mexico and England, but more likely he was influenced by domestic political considerations. At any rate he passed the buck to Congress, which replied in kind by authorizing him to recognize Texas whenever he thought it desirable. Among Jackson's last official acts were the reception of the Texas minister and the sending of a chargé d'affaires to Texas. After his retirement from the presidency he became an ardent annexationist, while Van Buren continued his predecessor's official policy of caution.

The issue of the annexation of Texas became mixed with the slavery question. Two pamphlets of the abolitionist Benjamin Lundy developed the idea that Texas was a den of the blackest iniquity, and that its settlement and revolution constituted a deep-laid plot by slaveholders to add more slave territory to the United States. With the issue thus confused a decade of congressional debate was necessary before Texas could be admitted even by the narrowest of votes.

Balked in her desire for annexation, Texas withdrew the proposal and tried to make independence succeed. In this effort she had not only the usual difficulties of any postrevolutionary country, but also a small population (some 55,000 in 1840) and a lack of variety in resources and occupations. The presidency would undoubtedly have been a permanent possession of Sam Houston had it not been for a constitutional provision prohibiting a man from succeeding himself. After his first term he was succeeded by Mirabeau Buonaparte Lamar, and after his second term by Anson Jones, during whose administration annexation finally took place (1845).

One of the earliest problems of Texas was to obtain world recognition of its independence, for recognition would promote foreign trade and make foreign loans easier to obtain. Recognition by the United States was soon followed by that of England and France. As for Mexico, the best offer Santa Anna ever made was home rule if Texas returned to her Mexican allegiance.

Relations with Mexico were far from peaceful. Immediately after the Battle of San Jacinto, Houston had trouble persuading his army not to rush down to Mexico to find more Mexicans to thrash. In fact, the army, unruly and demanding, remained something of a problem. Shortly after independence, groups of Texans crossed the border and made an unsuccessful effort to foment a revolution in Mexico. Texas in 1841 tried to conquer Santa Fe, since it claimed the land to the Rio Grande, but the expedition was mismanaged and its members ended in Mexican jails. Mexico retaliated the next year with an effort to reconquer Texas, and succeeding years saw further raids from both sides. Incidentally, Texas also had a small navy that did as it pleased, refusing to obey orders it did not like.

The Indians presented still another problem as they raided across the borders. Treaties were made with some of the tribes, and certain groups were expelled forcibly. Most troublesome were the Comanche, who refused to be cowed by Texas military might. Ultimately Texas developed a policy similar to that of the United States. Garrisoned forts protected the less-populated areas. All Indian trade was put under governmental supervision (1843), and sales of liquor and firearms were prohibited.

The greatest internal problem was the raising of money, which would have been difficult under the best conditions but was well-nigh impossible as the panic of 1837 tightened its grip. Property taxes were levied, but no one had money to pay them. Tariffs were enacted but were unproductive as long as trade languished. Efforts to float loans in the United States and Europe were lamentable failures. Bonds were issued for public sale, but found few purchasers even with interest at 10 percent. Paper money was issued, but the confidence in Texan finances was so small that its purchasing power soon fell to about a tenth of its face value.

The most valuable possession of Texas was her land, and Texas devised a land system that she retained after entering the Union, for the federal government never took over control. Land sales were meager, but gifts could be made to worthy causes. The revolutionary soldiers were paid partly in land. Transportation was subsidized by land grants. An impressive school system was given regal land subsidies. Immigration was encouraged by liberal gifts, and the *empresario* system was revived. The result was an influx of many settlers, not only from the United States but also from the various German states, and from England, France, and elsewhere; the population of 1846 has been estimated at 100,000.

The decade of independence was not a satisfactory period for Texas. Only a few citizens, such as the second president, M. B. Lamar, had ever wanted a separate existence for Texas. Most Texans continued to think of the United States as their country, and to some extent everyone marked time until the expected goal was achieved in 1845.

READINGS

EXPLORATION. Satisfactory general accounts are Philip W. Powell, *Soldiers, Indians, & Silver, 1550–1600* (1952); Herbert E. Bolton, *The Spanish Borderlands* (1921); Bernard De Voto, *The Course of Empire* (1952); W. Eugene Hollon, *The Southwest* (1961). Good accounts of individuals include Morris Bishop, *The Odyssey of Cabeza de Vaca* (1933); Herbert E. Bolton, *Anza's California Expeditions* (5 vols., 1930), Vol. I is the biography and the other four are documents, *Coronado* (1949), (ed.) *Pageant in the Wilderness* (1950), *Rim of Christendom* (1936), Kino; Arthur G. Day, *Coronado's Quest* (1940); José M. Espinosa, *Crusaders of the Rio Grande* (1942), De Vargas; Cleve Hallenbeck, *Alvar Nuñez Cabeza de Vaca* (1940); George P. Hammond and Agapito Rey (eds.), *Don Juan De Oñate* (2 vols., 1935); Herbert I. Priestley, *Tristán de Luna* (1936); Rufus K. Wyllys, *Pioneer Padre* (1935), Kino.

SANTA FE TRAIL. The classic account is Josiah Gregg, *Commerce of the Prairies* (1954); see also Maurice G. Fulton (ed.), *Diary and Letters of Josiah Gregg* (2 vols., 1941–1944). Robert L. Duffus, *The Santa Fe Trail* (1930) is interesting, as is Stanley Vestal, *The Old Santa Fe Trail* (1939). Original narratives, in addition to Gregg's, are Stella M. Drumm (ed.), *Down the Santa Fe Trail, 1846–47* (1926), and particularly good; Archer

B. Hulbert (ed.), *Southwest on the Turquois Trail* (1933); John E. Sunder (ed.), *Matt Field on the Santa Fe Trail, 1839–1841* (1960). Related material is included in Kate L. Gregg (ed.), *The Road to Santa Fe* (1952), surveys of 1825–1827; David Lavender, *Bent's Fort* (1954); Max L. Moorhead, *New Mexico's Royal Road* (1954), the road from Santa Fe into Mexico.

TEXAS. Herbert E. Bolton, *Texas in the Middle Eighteenth Century* (1915) is the classic account of the Spanish-French conflict. Of the histories of Texas, Rupert N. Richardson, *Texas* (1943) is probably best; Ralph W. Steen, *The Texas Story* (1948), scholarly; Owen P. White, *Texas* (1945), more informal. Shorter accounts are included in W. Eugene Hollon, *The Southwest* (1961); Paul Horgan, *The Great River* (2 vols., 1954), Rio Grande; Ray A. Billington, *The Far Western Frontier* (1956); Rupert N. Richardson and Carl C. Rister, *The Greater Southwest* (1935). Lyle Saxon, *Lafitte the Pirate* (1930) has much on Texas. Ross Phares, *Cavalier in the Wilderness* (1952) concerns an early trader. Filibustering is treated in Harris G. Warren, *The Sword Was Their Passport* (1943). Best on Austin is Eugene C. Barker, *The Life of Stephen Austin* (1925), *The Austin Papers* (3 vols., 1924–1928), *Mexico and Texas, 1821–35* (1928), lectures. Ohland Morton, *Terán and Texas* (1948) is a good monograph.

TEXAS REVOLUTION AND INDEPENDENCE. Best on the revolution is William C. Binkley, *The Texas Revolution* (1952); Carlos E. Castañeda (transl.), *The Mexican Side of the Texas Revolution* (1928) is interesting; Lon Tinkle, *13 Days to Glory* (1958) concerns the defense of the Alamo. For Houston, see Marquis James, *The Raven* (1929), which reads well; Llerena Friend, *Sam Houston* (1954), factual; Amelia W. Williams and Eugene C. Barker (eds.), *The Writings of Sam Houston* (8 vols., 1938–1943); Donald Day and Harry H. Ullom (eds.), *The Autobiography of Sam Houston* (1954), a synthetic autobiography. For Santa Anna see Wilfred H. Calcott, *Santa Anna* (1936) and Frank C. Hanighan, *Santa Anna* (1934), which is entirely hostile. Best on the independence period is William R. Hogan, *The Texas Republic* (1947), but see also Joseph W. Schmitz, *Texan Statecraft, 1836–1845* (1941); Stanley Siegel, *A Political History of the Texas Republic, 1836–1845* (1956), detailed; Robert P. Gambrell, *Anson Jones* (1948), last president; Noel M. Loomis, *The Texan–Santa Fé Pioneers* (1958), excellent on expedition of 1841.

CHAPTER 24

DESTINY BECKONS

D ramatic Texas developments did not monopolize the attention of the many Americans who were looking for the reputedly greener fields in the distance. An increasing number were casting their eyes toward the Pacific Coast and even farther. The interests and aspirations of a youthful America seemed limitless.

CLAIMS TO THE PACIFIC COAST

The Pacific Coast of North America had long been one of the minor stakes in the game of world imperialism. Spanish, English, and French explorers had touched various points in their wide-flung efforts to understand and conquer the world. By the late eighteenth century the only real competitors were Spain and England, and in spite of the availability of thousands of miles of wilderness the two nations collided on Vancouver Island at Nootka Sound (1790). Spain was clearly outclassed, and could no longer claim a north Pacific monopoly. In fact her farthest actual advance was San Francisco Bay, and in time (1819) she transferred to the United States any possible claims north of the present northern boundary of California (42°).

A new competitor began to appear on the horizon in the late eighteenth century with Russian expansion from west to east. The Danish-born Vitus Bering jumped the ocean in 1725 on the first of his trips to North America, and soon was followed by Russian traders who made their headquarters in Alaska. Near the end of the century the Russian-American Fur Company was organized to control the business of the new world. The company continued to edge southward until it established Fort Ross (1812), not far north of San Francisco Bay. This advance furnished part of the inspiration for Spain to occupy California and also helped to produce

357

the Monroe Doctrine, but in fact these responses were utterly out of proportion to the very small menace that the Russian advance produced.

The last nation to make its appearance on the Pacific Coast was the United States. American interest first manifested itself when profit-seeking Boston merchants projected a three-cornered trade in which Yankee cutlery, textiles, and trinkets would be taken to the Pacific Coast to be traded for furs, which would then be traded in the excellent Chinese markets for such products as tea, spices, and silks for the American trade. Although Americans were not the first to develop this business they soon dominated it.

The first Boston ships destined for the northwest trade were sent by an association of Boston merchants in 1787. One of them, commanded by Captain Robert Gray, was the first American ship to circumnavigate the globe, and was received with tremendous enthusiasm when it returned to Boston in 1790. Gray immediately re-outfitted and sailed for the West, where he entered the Columbia River (1792) slightly ahead of the English Captain George Vancouver. Gray's voyage provided the basis for later American claim to Oregon, even though a Spaniard had actually predated both Gray and Vancouver by several years.

Very soon American ships dotted the coastal waters from Alaska to Mexico. Theoretically such vessels could not enter Spanish ports, but in practice the shipmasters could always discover complaisant officials who found that a little gold made them very nearsighted. American ships were more warmly welcomed after various Mexican revolutionary movements almost eliminated Spanish trade between Mexico and California.

The main interest of the early years was seal and otter pelts, which were available all along the coast, and were traded for the manufactured goods and knickknacks so attractive to the isolated coastal communities. The ship captains also seized the opportunity to scrape the hulls of their vessels and to re-outfit them with meat, grain, vegetables, and water; the only place more favored for such business was Hawaii. Seal and otter were virtually extinct by about 1820; and although other furs were traded in the northern country, the visitors to California were increasingly whalers and hide and tallow ships. The hide and tallow business was the descendant of the fur business in California; during the 1820s and 1830s its principal center was San Diego. The business was legal under Mexican law if port duties were paid, but admittedly many ships evaded these taxes at least in part. The hides from the large California herds were ultimately made into shoes in New England. The classic account of this business as it existed during the 1830s is Richard Henry Dana's *Two Years before the Mast*.

Following close on the heels of the explorers and traders who traveled by sea came the explorers, traders, and trappers by land. Down from the north swept the Canadian companies, with Alexander Mackenzie in the van. Then from the east came the Americans, with Lewis and Clark in the lead. The failure of Astoria left the Hudson's Bay Company in complete control of the Oregon country. The center of the fur trade was Fort Vancouver, opposite present Portland; the original fort was constructed by McLoughlin in 1825. Farther south the California area was monopolized first by Spain and then by Mexico.

Aggressive American trappers did not long accept quietly their exclusion from the Pacific Coast. To the south, the Patties, Smith, and others crossed the Sierras in spite of their uncertain California welcome. To the north, the American fur companies competed on the fringes of the Hudson's Bay Company's domain, while a scattering of such men as Smith, Young, and Wyeth visited Fort Vancouver, although they did not try to complete actively with the company in its own field.

DIPLOMATIC NEGOTIATIONS

The United States government was not entirely unconcerned with the westward expansion of the interests of its citizens. In the early years official Washington was in no position to challenge Spanish control of California since that control was based on at least a small settled occupation, but Oregon was another matter. Oregon was occupied by only a few fur traders, and had very considerable advantages. It was closer to the Orient than was California; the first assumption was that the Columbia River would be the best outlet, but when the difficulties of navigating that river became evident, interest shifted to the Puget Sound area. Furthermore, the Oregon country contained rich resources of fur and land; timber and minerals were not important at that time.

The first official act of the United States was an agreement with England (1818) whereby the Canadian boundary of 49° was continued west to the mountains, with the Oregon country remaining open for joint occupation for ten years. Here Great Britain made a mistake. Relying on her existing fur monopoly and on the complete absence of Americans, she underestimated the rapidity of American expansion. The Adams-Onís Treaty of the following year put a northern limit to Spanish claims at 42°, the present northern boundary of California; thus the United States could argue that she fell heir to all Spanish claims farther north. Then came the Monroe Doctrine, which was aimed partly at Russia, followed by an agreement with that country in 1824 limiting Russian expansion from the north to 54° 40′. By these treaties the contested region was limited to the area between 42° and 54° 40′ west of the Rockies.

Congressional interest in Oregon became evident by 1820, and after that year a succession of measures appeared, usually aimed at improving and guarding the route to Oregon. Senators Linn and Benton were most active, and one can hardly overlook the fact that both men came from Missouri, which had the greatest immediate interest in Oregon. Although legislation at times came close to passage, no laws actually emerged from congressional discussions. There was doubt about the value of the country, the distance was great, and the costs were very large. Many people felt that the Pacific Coast was so remote that it would in time become an independent nation.

Congressional interest produced no positive action except to encourage the State Department to try to obtain at least part of the Oregon country outright when the agreement of 1818 neared its ten-year expiration date. The United States suggested a continuation of the 49th parallel to the coast, but Great Britain refused. Ultimately the old joint occupation agreement was continued indefinitely, but with the provision that it might be abrogated by either party on twelve months' notice.

Diplomatic and congressional maneuverings were but the reflection and not the substance of American interest in the Pacific Coast. The important fact was that more and more Americans were envisioning opportunities in the Far West and seeking to embrace them. These optimists were at first a few traders, trappers, and more or less casual travelers, but then included more permanent settlers engaged in commercial, agricultural, and religious occupations. As their number increased, United States policy reflected the change.

American interest until well into the 1840s was more in Oregon than in California. California was Spanish while Oregon was open to Americans, but this factor should not be overestimated in view of the contemporary Texas situation. Of greater practical importance, Oregon had more fur-bearing animals, more fish in her rivers, and more well-watered agricultural land—and was closer to the Orient. The overland road to Oregon was possibly a trifle easier than that to California. Most important, however, was the somewhat accidental factor of successful advertising, including an appeal to religious interest.

HALL J. KELLEY

The first great ballyhoo artist of Oregon was the Boston schoolmaster Hall J. Kelley, who was so neurotic that many considered him insane. He had very poor vision, and eventually became almost blind, which may largely explain why he was highly nervous, extremely sensitive, diffident, and so excitable that at times he lost the power of speech. Deeply religious, he almost completely lacked a sense of humor, and was increasingly obsessed by a feeling of persecution. He released part of his nervous tension by writing texts from which he profited moderately, but he lost his savings in unfortunate investments.

Kelley's first interest in Oregon came from reading an account of the Lewis and Clark Expedition. The more he read the more excited he became, until the failure of Astoria seemed to him a world-shaking tragedy. By the 1820s Oregon had become a mania with him, and he spoke and wrote voluminously about his one great love: Oregon was supreme for climate, soil, fishing, fur traffic, missions, trading, or what have you—"no portion of the globe presents a more fruitful soil, or a milder climate, or equal facilities for carrying into effect the great purposes of a free and enlightened nation." Kelley made elaborate plans for a great colony, and memorialized Congress for aid. Disciples appeared slowly; and ultimately, as already described, Kelley's most important convert, Nathaniel Wyeth, became impatient and started ahead with his own small group.

Kelley finally and regretfully abandoned his plans for a large settlement, and late in 1832 started west with a small party by way of New Orleans, Vera Cruz, and San Diego. Whether through bad management or bad luck he finally arrived at Monterey penniless and alone. There he joined Ewing Young and several others to drive a herd of cattle to Fort Vancouver. En route most of the cattle were lost and Kelley contracted malaria. His reception at the fort was conditioned by McLoughlin's belief that he was a cattle thief; although he was housed, fed, and doctored, he was not entertained with McLoughlin's usual hospitality, and he felt himself to be persecuted. Kelley returned to Boston by sea to spend the rest of his life in writing justifications that were frequently incoherent and sometimes completely incredible, as when he claimed that "the colonization of Oregon was both conceived and achieved by me."

The Kelley effort at colonization was a complete fiasco, but the Kelley writings did much to stimulate a rapidly growing American interest in Oregon. Books and articles about Oregon flowed from the press in increasing numbers. Lyceum lectures on Oregon were popular. Even by the early 1830s there was considerable sentiment that the acquisition and occupation of Oregon was only a matter of time.

OREGON MISSIONS

A new interest in Oregon came in 1831, when a little party of four Blackfeet and Nez Percés traveled to St. Louis to see the white man's civilization, and possibly to inquire into the religion of the "black robes." Even a small interest in the white man's religion was little short of startling, since the Indians had usually been anything but receptive. The story of "the wise men from the West" appeared first in the Methodist *Christian Advocate* for March 1, 1833, and was then given wide circulation in the religious press. Money was solicited and missionaries were enlisted for the new and promising venture. Rather curiously, the first fruits of a reputed request for Catholic missionaries in the interior was a Methodist mission that operated primarily for the whites in the Willamette Valley.

Interest in Oregon missions was not new. Earlier reports on the country had stressed the need for them, and appeals were numerous during the 1820s. Acting on these suggestions, and especially on the recommendations of Hawaiian missionaries, the American Board of Commissioners for Foreign Missions (Presbyterian, Congregational, Dutch Reformed) had sent the Reverend Jonathan Green to make a survey in 1829. Mr. Green did not touch the present Oregon but he saw enough of the coastal Indians to deplore their moral conditions and to recommend missions. The American Board felt, however, that it had more profitable uses for its limited funds, and took no immediate action.

Vague hopes for a nebulous future mission were crystallized into action by the Indian pilgrims. First in the field was a small party of Methodists headed by Jason Lee and his nephew Daniel. Crossing the plains with the Wyeth party in 1834, Jason wrote home: "I rejoice that I am counted worthy to bear the news of salvation to these poor red men of the west, and I would not abandon the enterprise and return home for all the honors of Cesar, Alexander, and Boneparte united, and all the temporal pleasures of the civilized world in addition."

Upon his arrival at Fort Vancouver Jason Lee lost some of his enthusiasm with the McLoughlin advice that work among the Blackfeet was not hopeful and that he had better stay near the coast. The Methodist mission was finally set up in the Willamette Valley near present Salem. In spite of the handicaps of the wilderness, a lack of workers, and sickness, the missionaries constructed necessary buildings, planted crops, and established a school. Early realizing the ineffectiveness of work with Indian adults, attention was confined largely to the children and to local French-Canadians who had formerly been employed by the Hudson's Bay Company.

Jason Lee felt his greatest handicap was a lack of workers, and wrote fervent pleas for assistance. Finally he went east himself (1838), and through his efforts obtained several small groups and then a larger party in 1840, at which time several branch establishments were created. The later arrivals included teachers, farmers, and artisans as well as missionaries, but even with their help the results were not impressive.

The American Board was not far outdistanced even though suffering from a lack of both funds and qualified missionaries. The elderly and ailing Reverend Samuel Parker was sufficiently eager for the "conversion of the world" but the Board doubted his qualifications and ultimately appointed him reluctantly. Mr. Parker arrived at St. Louis too late in 1834 to join the annual overland caravan, and so waited until the next year, when he was joined by another seeker after health, Dr. Marcus Whitman. When the two men got as far as the Green River they decided they needed more help; Parker continued to Fort Vancouver and then went home by ship while Dr. Whitman retraced his steps.

A new trip west in 1836 was something of a honeymoon trip for Dr. Whitman, who brought his bride back with him. Also in the party were Reverend and Mrs. Henry H. Spalding and a mechanic. Spalding was an Oberlin man, conscientious, pious, and hard working, but lacking in humor and inclined to be critical of others; his wife was not in good health. The party took the first wagon to go west as far as Fort Boise, but the rough country prevented the ladies from riding in it most of the time; Narcissa Whitman preferred her sidesaddle.

After consultation with McLoughlin the Whitman party established a station at Waiilatpu (near present Walla Walla). As reinforcements arrived new stations were soon started at Lapwai (near present Lewiston) and Tshimakain (near present Spokane). Unfortunately the representatives of the Prince of Peace could not themselves live in peace and amity, much of the blame being due to Spalding's jealous and critical nature; the new stations were designed in part to divide the belligerent ministry. Then, too, the Indians proved disappointingly unreceptive to the Gospel or any other phase of white civilization. Conversions were notably lacking, and braves could not be persuaded to stick to one wife and to give up hunting in favor of agriculture, which to them was squaws' work.

The Board was discouraged by the bickering of the missionaries and by the lack of conversions; on several occasions it was on the point of abandoning one or more missions. Dr. Whitman's ride east in the winter of 1842–1843, as a result of which legend has held that he persuaded Tyler and Webster to "save" Oregon, actually induced the Board to save the mission. The central mission was finally destroyed by the Indians in 1847 during an uprising in which the Whitmans, along with a quarter of the mission population, were killed. The other missions were abandoned a little later.

Shortly after the establishment of the Whitman mission the Catholics entered the field (1838). They worked with both the Indians and the whites; McLoughlin himself was a Catholic. Best known of the Catholic workers was the Jesuit, Pierre Jean De Smet, who came to the mountains in 1840. His field work was not particularly important, but his many popular writings and his raising of money were exceedingly significant. In December 1843 the Columbia mission was made a vicariate apostolic.

The work of the Oregon missionaries may have been of slight importance in the evangelization of the world, but it was highly effective in helping to advertise Oregon. Even the family that confined its reading to the *Christian Advocate,* the publications of the American Tract Society, and the annual reports of the American Board could hardly avoid knowing about, and being interested in, Oregon.

JOHN C. FRÉMONT

Last and greatest of the popularizers of Oregon was John C. Frémont. Frémont's title of "the pathfinder" was hardly merited, even though he traveled widely in the West. His great contributions were the vivid and exciting accounts of his travels that appeared over his name but were actually written by his wife Jessie, daughter of Senator Benton of Missouri. These books not only stimulated a desire in men to go to the Far West, which at the time meant Oregon, but also described the best route and the proper equipment.

Frémont's first expedition left St. Louis in June 1842, guided by that famous trapper and hunter Kit Carson, then thirty-three years old. Carson had been born in Kentucky, but as a boy had been brought by his family to Missouri, where he was apprenticed at the age of fifteen to a saddle maker. He soon ran away to join the Santa Fe traders, and later traveled widely over the West, going even to California. He probably knew more about the western country than any other one man. Under his guidance the Frémont expedition went west over the well-known South Pass route and as far as the Wind River. The party made few discoveries, but when Frémont returned to Washington he wrote (rather, his wife wrote) a compelling and attractive description of his adventures and the country he had traversed.

Frémont undertook his second expedition (1843) with an unusually large and well-equipped body of men. His superior, Colonel J. J. Abert, doubted the wisdom of so much military preparation and particularly the presence of a twelve-pounder brass howitzer, so he ordered Frémont back to Washington. The Abert letter was opened by Jessie, who held it and wrote to her husband to leave as soon as possible, which he did; incidentally, the cannon was later abandoned. Near the headwaters of the Arkansas the Frémont party was joined by Kit Carson and an attempt was made to find a pass directly to the West. With the failure of this effort the party went north and used the South Pass route. Farther west Frémont examined the Salt Lake area, and it was his later written description that was largely responsible for the Mormon choice of this region. From Salt Lake he swung north as far as the Whitman mission and Fort Vancouver, and then turned south, making in February a marvelous crossing of the Sierras near the present Virginia City. Continuing south through California he eventually returned by approximately the route Jedediah Smith had used earlier in going to California. After many adventures and narrow escapes he was back in St. Louis in 1844.

Frémont found himself a hero when he returned to Washington. Congress had printed 100,000 copies of the report of the first expedition, while additional copies were being sold by private publishers. The report of the new expedition was soon written, and proved even more popular than its predecessor. The whole nation wanted to follow the exciting adventures of Frémont and his party, with some of the readers packing their belongings and starting overland for Oregon. Frémont's clear and accurate description of the proper route caused his reports to be used as handbooks by the immigrants.

FARMING MIGRATION TO OREGON

As Oregon increased in attractiveness more and more westward-moving farmers were interested. Population began to move to Oregon, at first slowly and then more rapidly. The first of these settlers went in 1839 under the leadership of T. J. Farnham, and thereafter at least a few people went each year. The first considerable group made the trip in 1842, when eighteen wagons and over a hundred persons were piloted by Elijah White, formerly a missionary and now a sub-Indian agent for Oregon. The next year a group of a thousand settlers was accompanied by Dr. Marcus Whitman. The annual migration of 1844 was smaller, but in the next year nearly 3000 migrants left Westport and other Missouri River towns; in 1847 the number was between 4000 and 5000.

Immigrants to Oregon followed the well-known Platte River or South Pass route. The starting point was Westport, Independence, or some similar town, and here the migrants provided themselves with wagons, mules or oxen, and provisions for a trip of some four or five months. If the party left Independence it followed the Santa Fe Trail for a short distance and then struck north, with the routes from the other towns entering at various places along the line of march. The trail ran a little west of north, and after reaching the Platte River followed that stream, eventually reaching Fort Laramie, a distance of 667 miles from Independence. Here a stop was made to rest both the human beings and the livestock, repair the wagons, and buy necessary extra provisions. Leaving Fort Laramie the trail followed first the Platte and then the Sweetwater. At 947 miles South Pass was reached—a beautiful pass with an even grade that presented no obstacles to wagon traffic. Leaving South Pass the trail followed branches of the Green River and then the Green River to Fort Bridger (at 1070 miles). Here it struck northward to Fort Hall (at 1283 miles) and then followed the Snake to the Columbia (at 1835 miles) and the Columbia to the ocean.

The South Pass route was by far the best way across the plains and Rockies, and after the later 1820s was used by practically everyone going to the Far West. The worst part of the whole two thousand miles, in terms of terrain, was the Idaho region, where the rocky country, the hills, the forests, and the lack of good water and grass in certain sections made the trip exceedingly unpleasant and at times dangerous. Farther east, in the plains region, physical obstacles were comparatively less important. Bad river crossings offered certain dangers, and in time vegetation became scarce with the passage of many caravans. The traveler also had to plan for a possible shortage of food, sick livestock, accidents to persons or wagons, and similar misfortunes. The threat of hostile Indians was met by group migration and in a manner similar to that used in the Santa Fe trade. Each night the wagons were placed in a circle, and when danger threatened the tongue of one was placed under the body of the next to form an embrasure. Sometimes a rope was tied around the wagons, and the stock driven inside the enclosure. A guard was posted both day and night to report any sign of hostile Indians. Actually remarkably little blood was shed in conflicts with the Indians.

The new settlers of Oregon found themselves in a position that was both isolated and somewhat embarrassing. They were under the joint control of two governments, neither of which had acted to produce even the semblance of law and order. Since the settlers were American in origin they turned to the United States as early as 1838 and asked for recognition and some sort of government. Congress was now embarrassed in its turn, for it was hard to say just what government should be given to a region that was under joint control, and decided that the easiest solution was to do nothing. In the meantime McLoughlin and the Methodist missionaries furnished a certain amount of order and legal procedure. In 1843 the settlers became tired of waiting for congressional action and followed good frontier precedent by organizing a government of their own.

The increase of the population of Oregon brought a rapid intensification of American sentiment for aggressive action in respect to the Northwest. A growing official interest was demonstrated when Lieutenant W. A. Slacum was sent to the Pacific Coast in 1836–1837 to obtain information for President Jackson; he was followed by Lieutenant Charles Wilkes in 1838 for an extensive survey that lasted almost five years. When Lord Ashburton arrived in the United States in 1842 to try to settle the outstanding differences between Britain and the United States he discussed Oregon among other matters. Webster was at first willing to accept the Columbia River as a permanent boundary, but when Wilkes returned with his report that sand bars blocked the mouth of the Columbia and that the good harbors were farther north on Puget Sound, Webster shifted his demands to a continuation of the line of the 49th parallel. Since Ashburton would not accept this boundary, the final settlement, the Webster-Ashburton Treaty, did not mention Oregon.

EARLY CALIFORNIA

Interest in Oregon did not mean that Americans entirely forgot California. They were quite aware of its varied attractions, including its climate, and even in the early days it was considered a healthful resort for invalids. As one trapper-booster proclaimed: "There never was but one man in California who had the ague. He was from Missouri and carried the disease in his system. It was such a curiosity to see a man shake with the chills that the people of Monterey went eighteen miles in the country to watch him."

The greatest advantage of California over Oregon was that it was inhabited by whites, which meant greater trade, more opportunities for outfitting ships, larger herds of cattle, more agriculture. Doctors and other professional men had immediate business; merchants also benefited by settled communities. The accompanying drawback was that a white population meant an existing government that at times was definitely unfriendly. Although the Americans were normally well received, there were occasions when the government felt the other way and jailed newcomers.

The people of California were themselves an attraction to Americans from the East, since their distinctive costumes and manners labeled them as quaint or picturesque. The rancher was impressive in rich jacket, velvet or silk vest, velvet or satin breeches slashed at the knee, and all decorated with quantities of gold and silver braid and embroidery; a broad red sash and a wide sombrero gave the finishing touches. Women's clothing, in comparison, was plain, but the lady, when dressed in her best, was loaded with jewelry, including conspicuous combs if she were married. Visiting New Englanders were shocked by the absence of sleeves and corsets, and completely horrified when the women smoked cigarets. These clothes and manners provided the inspiration for ribald stories to be told to companions at home concerning the immorality of California women; such stories did nothing to deter other young men from going west to see these strange things for themselves.

Governmentally, California was left largely to her own devices, particularly after Mexican independence, when home troubles were sufficient to occupy the complete attention of national politicians. Most of the time a Mexican appointee held office as governor, but the outcome of a local revolution was ordinarily regularized by Mexico. On one occasion California proclaimed a short-lived and rather meaningless independence. Between 1820 and 1846 California was blessed—or cursed—by fourteen administrations.

Latin governments have long been the object of the condescending smiles or jeers of Anglo-Saxons. The many parades, bombastic proclamations, revolutions instead of elections, and maneuvers instead of battles have seemed amusing, and have been blamed primarily on the Latin temperament and on governmental inexperience. Instead, the revolution may be considered as only a more dangerous and hence an exciting substitute for an election. A succession of revolutions, however, would have been extremely depleting in manpower and wealth if fought to the bitter end; hence the Californians quite intelligently made only a pretense of fighting, after which victory was conceded to the stronger side. The Battle of Cahuenga Pass in 1845, for example, brought only the killing of one horse and the wounding of one mule, even though it was the decisive battle in a successful revolution.

From the standpoint of landownership the period of Mexican control was important. Many new land grants were added to the few made in Spanish days so that the entire state became a mass of claims. Further confusion was added with the secularization of the missions and the dispersal of their land. Wealth-hungry men had long looked covetously at the prosperous missions, but before 1833 had been able to make only minor inroads. Decrees of that year and the two succeeding ones removed the property of all twenty-one missions from the hands of the friars, who retained only their religious functions. By law half the land went to the mission Indians individually and half went to state trustees, but somehow it slipped rapidly into the hands of individual whites. Between secularization and land grants most of the state was claimed by individuals, and the basis was laid for great bitterness after acquisition by the United States and an influx of American settlers. Ultimately a United States law put the burden of proof of landownership on men who had obtained their land before the American occupation—proof that was always difficult and sometimes impossible to obtain.

AMERICAN MIGRATION TO CALIFORNIA

California of the early nineteenth century had political turbulence but social and economic peace. The ranchers dispensed a crude but generous hospitality and the small villages slumbered in the sun. Into this calm there arrived a scattering of foreign settlers, with the first Americans appearing in 1816. The number of arrivals in any one year was small, probably never exceeding 50 before 1840. The best estimate for California in 1840 gives 380 foreigners, of whom possibly 50 had come overland and the rest by sea.

The influence of these strangers, however, was out of proportion to their numbers.

Several American groups in California may be distinguished. Sailors had deserted their ships, searching either for health or for economic opportunity. A scattering of trappers had settled permanently west of the mountains. These two groups were of little importance except as their numbers increased American influence. Some did trapping, either in the interior or along the coast; others became cowboys (*vaqueros*) or even ranchers. More important were a few individuals who came to California to take advantage of specific opportunities. These men became agents for the hide and tallow trade, entered commercial business, or acquired ranches. They adopted Mexican citizenship, embraced the Catholic faith at least nominally, spoke Spanish, attended fandangos, and even took native wives. Within this small group was soon vested control of the majority of California business and the ownership of much California land.

Several Americans were pre-eminent. Most important was Thomas O. Larkin, who arrived in 1832 and soon became the leading merchant of Monterey; not only did he become wealthy, but he was first American consul in California, Polk's secret agent in promoting annexation, and in general a center of American influence. Isaac Graham founded a successful distillery near Monterey; always a troublemaker, he and his band of American riflemen were decisive in the success of the California revolution of 1836. John Marsh was a Harvard graduate, intelligent and well educated, but miserly and misanthropic. He sought his fortune in ranching, but he was also known as a doctor even though he had no formal medical training; his importance lay largely in his continuous urging of American immigration.

The greatest of the American influences was probably John A. Sutter, who was born in Germany of Swiss parents and grew up in Switzerland. His ambition and ability were more than counterbalanced by an overactive imagination, an openhanded generosity, and a spirit of adventure that combined to bring him a shotgun marriage, five children, and a staggering mountain of debts. When his varied obligations proved impossibly oppressive he made a hurried departure, leaving just ahead of a warrant for his arrest.

Arriving in America in 1834 at the age of thirty-one, Sutter found himself drawn to a German community in Missouri. After acquiring many friends and even more debts he decided to try his fortune in California. On his trip overland he manufactured an impressive background and reputation for himself. After visiting Fort Vancouver for a time he found that the most available transportation led him to Hawaii and Alaska. It was not until 1839 that he finally reached California.

In California Sutter was taken at his own evaluation. He acquired Mexican citizenship, large tracts of land, and borrowed capital. He has been described as small and bald, with a neat mustache and polite manners. In the Sacramento Valley he created an impressive establishment that he called New Helvetia. An adobe fort, the necessary buildings, shops, fields, herds, orchards, and vineyard constituted a regal domain. Unskilled labor was performed by the Indians under compulsion, but there were also many white artisans of various skills. Sutter himself lived on the best of food and drink, surrounded by his faithful retainers, and dispensing hospitality in keeping with his self-admitted importance. He had his own coinage, his own artillery, his private army of Indians in blue and green uniforms trimmed with red, and even the rank of captain in the Mexican army. Unfortunately his one military adventure was on the wrong side of the revolution of 1845, in which he experienced hurt pride even if not material damage.

Sutter's main importance was his relations toward the Americans, whom he always favored. His fort was the first settlement reached by the usual overland traveler, and Sutter in California was just as hospitable as McLoughlin in Oregon. He was generous and helpful to Frémont on several occasions, and to the groups of immigrants that started to arrive from over the mountains in 1841. For these services he was badly paid. Later arrivals stole his property, and Frémont always viewed him with suspicion and even dislike.

The real American invasion of California began in 1841 with the first group of permanent settlers to come overland. First was the John Bidwell group of thirty-two; significantly, the larger part of the original Bidwell party seceded to go to Oregon. Other small parties also arrived later during the same year. These newcomers had no desire to adopt California ways of life, and their increasing number foreshadowed the end of Mexican control of California. No additional immigrants arrived during 1842, but each later year saw more Americans top the Sierras. In 1845 some 250 arrived, drawn largely by the glowing reports of Frémont and L. W. Hastings. The migration of 1846 included Sam Brannan and 200 Mormons arriving by ship, and was the largest influx before the gold rush.

Migrants to California followed several routes, including the Santa Fe Trail or the long swing around the Horn, but their usual path was the Oregon Trail as far as Fort Hall, where they swung southwest. Passing north of Salt Lake they followed the Humboldt River to the Humboldt Sink. Early travelers then took the route of the Carson River, Walker Pass, and the Stanislaus, but the favorite route from 1844 went by way of the Truckee River and the Truckee Pass.

The trip to California was long and arduous. Even during the early years wagons could be taken to Fort Hall with comparative ease, but then came the arid stretches of present Utah and Nevada, where water and grass were infrequent, where equipment wore out, where supplies ran short, and where tempers became frayed. Finally appeared the intimidating masses of the High Sierras, with no crossing like the famous South Pass over the main ranges of the Rockies. Progress was slow, difficult, and dangerous. A late start from the East, delays en route, or early winter in the mountains might bring snow that could easily be fatal. Most tragic was the fate of the Donner party, which was snowbound at Donner Lake in the winter of 1846 and was reduced to cannibalism before a fraction was finally rescued. Little wonder that the green vegetation of California looked like heaven to the weary immigrant as he surmounted the last mountain range.

By 1846 California contained possibly 700 Americans, 100 British, 7000 Spaniards, and 10,000 Indians. Although the Americans were still a small minority they were sufficiently numerous to give pause for thought to any Mexican administrator who was familiar with the past history of American expansion, particularly with the events in Texas during the preceding decade.

READINGS

GENERAL AND TRAILS. Good general histories of the Pacific Coast are Norman A. Graebner, *Empire on the Pacific* (1955) and John W. Caughey, *History of the Pacific Coast* (1933). Routes across the plains are described in James C. Bell, *Opening a Highway to the Pacific, 1838–1846* (1921); William H. Goetzmann, *Army Exploration in the American West* (1959); Bernard De Voto, *The Year of Decision* (1943), which reads well. The overland trail is described in James Monaghan, *The Overland Trail* (1947); George R. Stewart, *The California Trail* (1962), excellent; Francis Parkman, *The Oregon Trail* (1943), contemporary. Standard on Frémont is Allan Nevins, *Frémont* (1939); see also Charles Preuss, *Exploring with Frémont* (1958).

OREGON. Useful general accounts include Oscar O. Winther, *The Great Northwest* (1947) and *The Old Oregon Country* (1951); David Lavender, *Land of Giants* (1958); Bernard De Voto, *Across the Wide Missouri* (1947) and *The Course of Empire* (1952). Early travel to Oregon is described in Bern Anderson, *Surveyor of the Sea* (1960), Vancouver; Daniel Henderson, *The Hidden Coast* (1953), Wilkes; Le Roy and Ann Hafen (eds.), *To the Rockies and Oregon, 1839–1842* (1952); Eleanor Allen, *Canvas Caravans* (1946), a trip made in 1852; Archer B. Hulbert (ed.), *The Call of the Columbia* (1934) and (ed.), *Where Rolls the Oregon* (1933); Ross Cox, *The Columbia River* (1957), contemporary. McLoughlin can be followed in John S. Galbraith, *The Hudson's Bay Company* (1957); Richard G. Montgomery, *The White-Headed*

Eagle (1934) ; Burt B. Barker (ed.), *Letters of Dr. John McLoughlin, 1829–32* (1948) ; Edwin E. Rich (ed.), *Letters of John McLoughlin* (1941). Kelley is well covered in Fred W. Powell, *Hall Jackson Kelley* (1917) and (ed.), *Hall J. Kelley on Oregon* (1932).

MISSIONARIES. William N. Bischoff, *The Jesuits of Old Oregon* (1945), simple account; Clifford M. Drury, *Diaries and Letters of H. H. Spalding* (1958), *Elkanah and Mary Walker* (1940), many quotations, *Henry Harmon Spalding* (1936), *Marcus Whitman, M.D.* (1937), detailed, and (ed.), *First White Women over the Rockies* (2 vols., 1963), wives of the missionaries; Archer B. Hulbert (ed.), *The Oregon Crusade* (1935) ; Archer B. and Dorothy P. Hulbert (eds.), *Marcus Whitman, Crusader* (3 vols., 1936–1941) ; Reuben G. Thwaites, *Far Western Travels* (31 vols. and atlas, 1904–1907), Vol. XXVII, De Smet.

CALIFORNIA—GENERAL ACCOUNTS. John W. Caughey, *California* (1953) ; Robert G. Cleland, *A History of California* (1922), *Pathfinders* (1929), travelers to California, *From Wilderness to Empire* (1944) ; Rockwell D. Hunt and Nellie V. de G. Sanchez, *A Short History of California* (1929) ; Oscar Lewis, *California Heritage* (1949), mostly pictures; James A. B. Scherer, *Thirty-first State* (1942).

CALIFORNIA—EARLY ACTIVITIES. Lightly written is Felix Riesenberg, Jr., *The Story of California's Spanish Mission Trail* (1962). Sea trade is described in Donald M. Brown (ed.), *China Trade Days in California* (1947) ; Adele Ogden, *The California Sea Otter Trade* (1941) ; Raymond A. Rydell, *Cape Horn to the Pacific* (1952). The cattle business appears in Robert G. Cleland, *The Cattle on a Thousand Hills* (1951) and *The Irvine Ranch* (1944) ; Victor E. A. Janssens, *Life and Adventures in California* (1953), contemporary, 1834–1856. William W. Robinson, *Land in California* (1948) tries to disentangle a complicated situation. The Donner party can best be followed in George R. Stewart, Jr., *Ordeal by Hunger* (1960) and (ed.), *The Opening of the California Trail* (1953). Outstanding early residents are described in Reuben L. Underhill, *From Cowhide to Golden Fleece* (1939), Larkin; George P. Hammond (ed.), *The Larkin Papers* (4 vols., 1951–1953) ; Rockwell D. Hunt, *John Bidwell* (1942) ; Julian Dana, *Sutter of California* (1934), dramatic; James P. Zollinger, *Sutter* (1939), excellent.

CHAPTER **25**

SPOILS TO THE STRONG

N ew and attractive vistas were opening before delighted American eyes during the 1840s. Americans had long been optimistic about their future and not at all loath to help make their dreams come true, but there had seemed to be insuperable limits to the expansion of population. The presumed existence of a Great American Desert in the plains area, the Spanish occupation of the Southwest, and the English dominance in the Northwest had convinced many people that the ultimate limit of American population was somewhere near the great bend of the Missouri River. Now the flow of settlers across the plains to the Pacific Coast, together with the obvious weakness of Mexico, gave new horizons to American aspirations.

MANIFEST DESTINY

Population expansion and an active desire for more territory went hand in hand, with some doubt as to which was leading the other. Manifest Destiny was the current ideal, with the term itself coming into common use during the mid-1840s. More and more Americans were convinced that the United States must inevitably own and occupy the entire region from the Mississippi to the Pacific coast, including not only existing possessions but also the entire area from Texas to the Pacific and north through Oregon. A vocal minority had even bolder visions and talked of all of North America and such neighboring islands as Cuba; even Hawaii was not outside the orbit of American interest.

The American expansionist felt deep in his heart that the United States was the finest civilization the world had ever produced, and that his nation was destined by the will of God to carry the blessings of democratic institutions and Christianity to less enlightened people. In the words of the

373

time, the United States "is destined to manifest to mankind the excellence of divine principles; to extend on earth the noblest temple ever dedicated to the Most High—the Sacred and the True." In fact "we should be recreant to our noble mission, if we refused acquiescence in the high purpose of a wise Providence." The idea of self-defense was seldom mentioned, and material advantages were stressed less than religious and moral ones.

The idealistic object of fulfilling a high mission as foreordained by the Deity was sometimes buttressed by specific claims to desired territory. In the case of Oregon the joint occupation agreement was in itself a recognition that the United States had plausible title to the drainage basin of the Columbia River. As for Texas, American claims had been abandoned with the treaty of 1819, but now the independence of Texas made annexation a distinct possibility, and after annexation the most extreme of the Texan claims could be adopted. For the Far Southwest there were no plausible claims.

The trend of American official opinion became clear as efforts of the late 1820s to buy Texas were expanded in the next decade to include the entire Southwest. Apparently American public opinion was not at this point prepared for drastic action, since both Jackson and Van Buren were cool toward Texan annexation. John Tyler expressed a more vigorous policy when he succeeded to the presidency on the death of William Henry Harrison, but even as late as 1844 the Senate rejected decisively a treaty for the annexation of Texas.

The annexation issue took the center of the stage in the campaign of 1844. The Democrats nominated the expansionist James K. Polk, and the party platform favored what it called the reannexation of Texas and the reoccupation of Oregon. Public opinion responded to this spur so obviously that Henry Clay, the Whig candidate, hedged on his original opposition to expansion until even his best friends had doubts as to where he stood. The great stress of the campaign turned out to be Texas, with Oregon receiving little consideration by either party.

The Polk victory, which included Democratic majorities in both houses of Congress, made certain that further American expansion was just around the corner. Tyler at once pressed an earlier proposal that Texas be annexed by joint resolution, which would avoid the necessity of the two-thirds Senate majority required for a treaty. This time annexation won, even though by a very narrow margin. On December 29, 1845, the laws of the United States were finally extended formally over Texas, and in the following year Texas members were sitting in Congress.

The annexation of Texas was manifestly an unfriendly act toward Mexico, which had never recognized Texan independence, and the Mexican Minister in Washington immediately demanded his passport and left for home. The next years saw Mexico periodically threatening to reconquer Texas, and war with Mexico seemed constantly possible even though both countries had some misgivings about taking up the sword.

OREGON

When Polk entered the White House the more pressing part of his expansion program had already been completed, and he was faced with a potential war with Mexico. He still desired to settle the Oregon dispute satisfactorily, but he did not want to risk two wars at the same time. The English negotiations that had been begun during the previous administration were continued by James Buchanan, the new Secretary of State. Buchanan was not influenced by the increasingly violent demands of the extremists and suggested the compromise boundary of 49°. The British representative refused because, although he had been authorized to accept 49°, he had been instructed to insist on free ports to the south of that line. The British negotiator then suggested arbitration, which Buchanan refused.

Polk put pressure on the British government in his annual message to Congress in December 1845. Stating vigorously the American claim as far north as 54° 40', he asked Congress for power to give notice of the abrogation of the joint occupation agreement, which was promptly voted. By this time the British Foreign Office was in a conciliatory mood as its bargaining power was being progressively weakened by the influx of American settlers by the hundred into the disputed area. In fact, the Hudson's Bay Company had already recognized the approaching end of its Columbia River business by moving its main station to Vancouver Island in 1845.

The new British proposal accepted the 49° line, but stipulated that the entire Vancouver Island should remain British. This proposal was sent by Polk to the Senate without recommendation. The Senate passed a favorable resolution; whereupon a treaty embodying these terms was signed and ratified (1846). Although these provisions were not as favorable to the United States as some people had hoped, they actually represented an American victory. The American government had long desired the 49° boundary, and presumably had made the larger demands partly for political advantage and partly for bargaining purposes.

The acquisition of Oregon did not produce immediately the stability of government that the people of the Northwest desired, for Congress was dilatory. Not until August 13, 1848, was Oregon made a territory, and its first governor, Joseph Lane of Indiana, did not arrive until the next year. At this time the white population of Oregon numbered approximately 9000. The original Oregon Territory included all the country west of the mountains between 42° and 49°. The first division occurred because the people north of the Columbia were so desirous of a government of their own that they talked of statehood. The division of the territory was accepted by Congress in 1853 when the northern half of the territory was cut off and given the name Washington; Isaac A. Stevens was the first governor. When Oregon was admitted as a state in 1859 Washington was given all the country not within the present limits of Oregon. The present boundaries of Washington were established when Idaho was made a territory in 1863.

TEXAS AND THE MEXICAN WAR

While the fate of Oregon was still in the balance, Texan troubles went from bad to worse. Not only was the United States confronted with the inevitable hostility arising from the annexation of territory claimed by a neighboring state, but the exact limits of the annexation were in bitter dispute. Mexico had long insisted that the western boundary of Texas was the Nueces River, which had its outlet in Corpus Christi Bay. Texas insisted that its proper boundary was the Rio Grande, thus including a large section of New Mexico. Naturally the United States accepted the more favorable statement and sent General Zachary Taylor with an army to occupy the region in dispute. A border clash seemed only a matter of time.

Sending an army seemed to promise direct and drastic military action, but Polk at the same time made another effort to obtain his desires by means of bullion instead of bullets. John Slidell was sent as United States Minister with authority to release Mexico from paying admittedly valid claims if she would recognize the Rio Grande boundary. Furthermore, Slidell could offer $25 million and possibly more for the entire Southwest, which included approximately the region later obtained at the end of the Mexican War. Finally, if this latter proposal were not acceptable, $5 million could be offered for New Mexico. Unfortunately Slidell arrived in Mexico at an exceedingly unpropitious moment, for a revolution was in progress and neither side could risk the popular displeasure that would result from land cessions. In consequence Slidell was not even received, and in disgust he left Mexico in March 1846.

With the failure of the Slidell mission, Polk was in a quandary over the proper course to pursue. He definitely wanted to acquire the Southwest, not only for itself but also to block England. He felt that England might encourage an independent California hostile to the United States, or herself take California in payment of debts owed her by Mexico. However, there seemed no way but by war, and Polk was a peace-loving man. There was also considerable doubt whether Congress would be willing to declare and support a war for the acquisition of further slave territory. Polk presented the disturbing problem to his Cabinet and lengthy discussions ensued. Ultimately (May 9) the entire Cabinet with the exception of Bancroft agreed that the only solution was war. Polk was left to determine the ways and means of starting such a conflict.

Even while the Cabinet was holding its discussions Taylor had moved his army as far as the Rio Grande and had seized ships carrying supplies to the Mexicans on the other side of the river. These actions were quite understandably labeled aggressive by Mexico, which at the moment was willing to risk an American war under the delusion that she had a good chance of victory in consideration of the division of American opinion. A Mexican detachment crossed the Rio Grande in April 1846 with orders to harass the Americans. Almost immediately there was a small clash of patrols, unimportant except that it was a good pretext for war.

The news of the engagement on the Rio Grande happened to reach Washington on the very day that the Cabinet had decided on war, and even though Polk was a religious man and May 10 was a Sunday, he devoted himself to a war message that was delivered to Congress the next day. The message recited the wrongs suffered by the United States and the aggressions of Mexico, which were capped by the invasion of the United States and the spilling of American blood on American soil. "War exists . . . by the act of Mexico herself." Congress reacted properly and declared war. The entire country was aroused. The Mexican invader must be repelled. On to Mexico City!

Even after war had begun, Polk made one final effort to achieve his goal by peaceful means. It so happened that Santa Anna was then out of power and in exile; through a representative he promised that if he were slipped past the American blockade he would favor American desires. Polk was undoubtedly somewhat credulous to accept this proposal, but he was not sufficiently naïve to withdraw the army. As might have been expected, the return of Santa Anna to Mexico merely added another Mexican general to be defeated.

CONQUEST OF CALIFORNIA

One of the first operations of the war was the dispatch of an overland expedition to capture Santa Fe and California; unquestionably the American negotiator at the end of the war would be in a stronger position if the United States were already in possession of the territory desired. The command of the overland expedition was given to Stephen Watts Kearny, an able and experienced officer. Kearny had started his army career as a private, and had fought through the War of 1812. After the war he saw considerable action in the West, learning the ways of the plains and their Indian occupants. He was a kindly man but a strict disciplinarian, which sometimes distressed the militia.

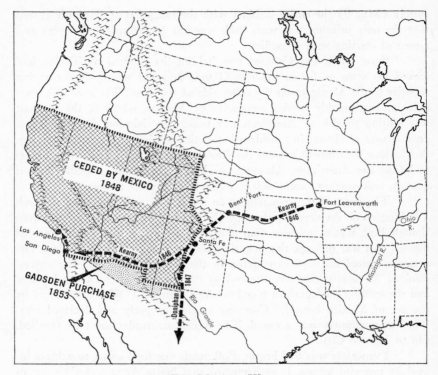

The Mexican War

Kearny was stationed at Fort Leavenworth when he received his orders to move west, and his rank was raised from colonel to brigadier general for the occasion. He immediately sent supply trains ahead, and then departed with 1658 dragoons and 16 cannon. On August 18 he entered Santa Fe without opposition. For six weeks he acted as governor, keeping his men well in hand and being conciliatory toward the local residents, even to the extent of attending Catholic Mass in spite of the fact that he was an Episcopalian.

When Kearny left Santa Fe he established a civil government with Charles Bent as Governor; the choice was a good one, but unfortunately Bent was murdered early in 1847. Kearny obviously expected the conquest of California would be easy because he took only 300 men, leaving the majority with Colonel A. W. Doniphan, who was soon relieved by General Sterling Price and moved south to reinforce Taylor. Not far from Santa Fe Kearny met Kit Carson, who was riding to Washington with the news that California had already fallen. Upon receiving this information Kearny sent back two thirds of his troops and continued with the remaining hundred, arriving near San Diego in December 1846.

Following Kearny across the plains came the so-called Mormon Battalion, which had been enlisted from the ranks of the Mormons, who were just then starting their exodus across the plains. Leaving the Missouri River on July 20 the Mormons limped into Santa Fe between October 9 and 12. There they got their second wind for continuing their march to San Diego, where they arrived late in January 1847 under the command of Philip St. George Cooke. The 1400-mile march was an impressive accomplishment even though the battalion had no influence on the course of the war.

The situation that confronted Kearny when he reached California was complicated. The story is difficult to reconstruct in spite of the tremendous amount of research that has been done on its actors and actions. Particularly speculative are the motives and instructions of the American stars in the drama.

A preview of California's annexation came on October 19, 1842, when Commodore T. A. C. Jones, assuming that war had begun between the United States and Mexico, followed his orders for that contingency and seized Monterey. The next day he decided that his impression of war was in error, so he returned the town with apologies and sailed away. His actions made clear, however, the expectations of the American government and the feebleness of Mexican control of California.

The California pot began to simmer when Polk assumed the presidency in 1845. His confidential agent in California was T. O. Larkin, who had been United States consul since 1843. Larkin was given the rather equivocal suggestions that he should not plot against the existing California government, but that an independent California would be welcomed as a part of the United States. Larkin's rather reasonable response was to plot a revolution scheduled for 1847 or 1848. The revolutionists were to include not only recent American arrivals but also native Californians.

The second marionette operated by a string pulled in Washington was Commodore John D. Sloat, who was sent to the Pacific Coast with orders to seize Monterey in the event of war with Mexico; if he also had other and secret orders they remain unknown. The seizure orders were standard for the navy, and designed not so much to help win the war as to forestall possible British action. Not long after Sloat left for the West Commodore Robert F. Stockton was sent after him (October 1845) with sealed orders for Larkin.

A third actor in the coming drama was John C. Frémont, who probably had hopes of becoming the star of the production. Frémont was sent across the plains in the summer of 1845 ostensibly to explore the sources of the Arkansas, Rio Grande, and Colorado rivers, the Great Salt Lake, and the Sierra Nevada and Cascade mountains. The official orders of Colonel John J. Abert did not mention California. Later there was much dispute as to the exact meaning of the Frémont orders, and also whether he had additional secret orders or at least suggestions, coming possibly through his father-in-law Thomas Hart Benton, who had been in the inner circles of the Polk administration. Frémont's own evidence is inconclusive, since he apparently wavered between conflicting impulses, and his later recollections were somewhat different from the statements he made at the time. But whatever the instructions, there is no question as to the nature and accomplishments of the party.

Frémont's expedition had several curious characteristics, of which the first to become obvious was its unusual size and composition. Sixty-two men picked for their marksmanship and devoting their spare time to target practice were surely excessive for an avowedly peaceful exploration, even in a hostile wilderness. Then, too, they did no exploring on their way west, not even mapping the Oregon Trail, although this was one of their stated purposes. The party headed straight for California by the most practicable route, dividing into two parties to cross the mountains. Frémont himself was at Sutter's Fort early in September and from this point rode down to Monterey, where he had a long and confidential talk with Larkin. Presumably this conversation did not deal entirely with the beauties of California scenery, and certainly Frémont's official instructions gave no authorization to enter a foreign country.

Instead of replenishing his supplies and leaving California, Frémont obtained permission to settle down for the winter. The only restriction was that he should not approach the coast. When spring arrived he still showed no signs of leaving—in fact he moved closer to Monterey and started to construct a fort. By this time Governor José de Castro had become justifiably suspicious of Frémont's intentions and ordered him to leave Mexican territory; whereupon Frémont refused and began to fortify his position. In March 1846 one of his men raised the United States flag, but in justice to Frémont it should be added that probably the flag was not raised as a result of his personal orders.

Just as an armed clash seemed probable Frémont apparently changed his mind, for he started north. At first his progress was slow and defiant, with his well-equipped and rested force making only some 6 to 8 miles a day, but after passing Sutter's Fort he moved more rapidly. Castro boasted of having driven out the Yankees. Just beyond the California border Frémont again seemed hesitant, for he slowed down and developed an intense interest in the painstaking exploration of a hitherto completely unattractive region. It almost seemed as though he were waiting for something or somebody.

While Frémont was loitering in the north there appeared in California one Lieutenant A. H. Gillespie of the United States Marine Corps, who spoke fluent Spanish and had traveled across Mexico disguised as an invalid merchant. Gillespie brought new instructions from Buchanan for Larkin and Frémont. As published later these instructions were completely innocuous and certainly not worth the long trip to California; the curious aspect of the mater was that Gillespie had considered the messages so damaging that he had learned them by heart and destroyed them before traveling through Mexico.

When Gillespie arrived at Monterey Larkin immediately boarded his boat and the two men talked long and earnestly. Then Gillespie hurried to find Frémont. As Frémont told the story almost half a century later, he heard that Gillespie was coming and galloped back 45 miles in a single day to meet him, for "then I knew the hour had come." The two men spent a long evening before the campfire, but what they said still remains a mystery. The next day Frémont turned south.

The maneuverings of American officials coincided with a series of apparently unrelated events in California. The American settlers had grown progressively more hostile to Mexican rule and had started to talk revolution as the only means by which they could run their own affairs. Upon Frémont's return they did their plotting in his camp, but Frémont discouraged such talk; possibly his own plans were different. In spite of this discouragement some thirty-five settlers, of whom the best known was William Ide, declared their independence (June 14, 1846) in an oratorical proclamation, and raised the Bear Flag of revolt.

The first stages of the revolution were considered by many native Californians as nothing but thievery by disaffected nomads, but the movement was taken more seriously after the occupation of Sonoma and the capture of several loyal Mexican citizens. Frémont talked to Ide and other revolutionists, but decided to maintain something that he could at least call neutrality. He did no actual fighting but he gave the rebels advice and guarded their prisoners, which was certainly an unusual form of neutrality.

The ultimate importance of the Bear Flag revolt was negligible. In early June, with the news of the war with Mexico, Sloat landed and took possession of Monterey; he was soon replaced by Stockton. Frémont enlisted most Americans, including the Bear Flaggers, in his "California battalion." Next Frémont and Stockton advanced jointly to the south and captured Los Angeles. The main American force then returned north to celebrate its victory by getting drunk, leaving a small detachment under

Gillespie to hold Los Angeles. California had thus been conquered easily and almost bloodlessly, and it was this news that was carried east by Kit Carson and that influenced General Kearny to send most of his troops back to Santa Fe.

The only real fighting in California came after it supposedly had been conquered. Native Californians, finding the Gillespie rule of Los Angeles distasteful, revolted and drove him out of the city. Just at this time Kearny appeared on the horizon and was attacked by the Californians. The tired Kearny troops did the best they could, but their casualties were high and they were lucky to avoid complete annihilation; Kearny, with doubtful accuracy, reported the engagement as a victory. Luckily Stockton and Frémont returned and, with the support of the Kearny forces, were able to re-establish American control in southern California.

The noisiest of the California battles was waged at the end of the war between Frémont and Kearny as to who should be in supreme command. Stockton had placed Frémont in control and then sailed away. On the other hand, Kearny bore orders from Washington giving him the top command; in any case he outranked both Frémont and Stockton; Stockton was a commodore, a rank equivalent to a colonelcy in the army. Moreover, communications from both General Scott and the Secretary of the Navy gave control to Kearny. After a spirited exchange of insults, Kearny started home, taking Frémont along as a virtual prisoner. Frémont was then tried by court-martial and found guilty of mutiny, disobedience, and unbecoming conduct. The President approved this sentence but remitted the penalties the court imposed. Frémont was so angered by what he felt to be injustice that he resigned his army commission. Much of his later activity reflected no credit on his abilities as an explorer, a businessman, or a public servant, even though his presidential candidacy showed his continued popularity. His historical reputation suffered particularly from his unsuccessful and almost disastrous fourth exploring expedition, from his doubtful financial ventures, and from his unsatisfactory record in the Civil War.

TREATY OF GUADALUPE HIDALGO

The conquest of California was but a small part of the campaigns of the Mexican War. The first really important action was the southerly advance of Zachary Taylor, including the capture of Monterrey and the repulse of a larger army under Santa Anna. Taylor, however, was no military genius, and his limited successes were due more to the failures of Santa Anna and the poor training and equipment of the Mexican army than to his own abilities. The one positive advantage of the Taylor campaign was that the "Hero of Buena Vista" attained enough popularity to make him President of the United States.

Polk was not only displeased with what he considered Taylor's inconclusive operations, but distressed by the boom of Taylor for the presidency; hence he turned to General Winfield Scott, who landed at Vera Cruz in 1847. Scott defeated a new Santa Anna army, and after a completely victorious campaign entered Mexico City on September 14, 1847. At this point he could dictate whatever terms of peace he desired.

Before the Scott operations were completely successful, Polk sent a representative to Mexico to try to conclude a peace. For this mission he chose Nicholas P. Trist, chief clerk of the State Department, and a worse choice could hardly have been made. Trist was a man of integrity, scholarly and industrious, but of mediocre ability, chronic indecision, and great stubbornness. He had meticulous regard for the niceties of behavior, and was a virtuoso with the pen. His instructions were to obtain Texas, New Mexico, Upper and Lower California, and the right-of-way across the Isthmus of Tehuantepec. For this territory he might offer $30 million plus the cancellation of some $3 million of American claims. The least he was authorized to accept was a line up the Rio Grande to El Paso and then due west to the coast; for this he could offer $15 million.

Trist's first trouble was with Scott, for the two men disliked each other on sight and for a time refused even to speak, confining themselves to writing home long letters of justification. Eventually they became close friends and Scott arranged an armistice to permit negotiations. Santa Anna encouraged the discussions because he hoped to get the $30 million to use on his army, but ultimately the armistice collapsed, Santa Anna fled the country, and Scott took the city of Mexico.

Polk was displeased with the Trist negotiations since he found on the one hand the Whig opposition to the war growing and on the other hand a growing sentiment that Mexico disgorge more of her territory. Polk's own desires were growing and ultimately he ordered Trist to come home. Trist disobeyed this order on the grounds that he saw a chance for a treaty and kindheartedly did not want to cause more Mexican confusion or hurt Mexico more than absolutely necessary. The treaty he signed in 1848 fulfilled his minimum first orders by the acquisition of Texas, New Mexico, Arizona, California, and the region to the north for $15 million plus claims up to $3.25 million.

When the treaty that Trist had negotiated arrived in Washington Polk was very angry and at the same time embarrassed. His term was coming to an end and he had renounced a second one. Opposition to the war raised questions as to whether Congress would vote adequate funds for its continuance. In consequence he tried to avoid at least major political tragedy and sent the treaty to the Senate, where it was ratified. As later events showed, the Treaty of Guadalupe Hidalgo marked the beginning of the end of American continental expansion. Subsequent additions were the small Gadsden Purchase of 1853 and the purchase of the detached Alaska in 1867.

LATER FILIBUSTERING

The end of continental expansion can be recognized today, but at the time it was not apparent. During the years after 1850 the old preliminaries of expansion continued to occur as American settlers flowed across both the northern and southern boundaries and as filibusters went to the south; the only difference from the pattern of earlier years was that these activities did not result in annexation. Most famous of the filibusters of the 1850s was that "man of destiny," William Walker, slight, gray-eyed, dapper, cultured, and soft-spoken. With an "army" of thirty-three men he established in November 1853 the Republic of Lower California, with the usual embellishment of president, flag, and constitution, and then "invaded" Mexico. The invasion failed, and Walker retreated to the United States, where he was haled before a court for the violation of Mexican neutrality. That the old American expansionist spirit was not dead is suggested by the story that the jury took but eight minutes to bring in a verdict of not guilty.

Walker's next project showed greater ingenuity and produced greater success. In 1855 he sailed to Nicaragua, landed, and seized control of the government, which he operated for two years. His ultimate defeat and execution can be traced not so much to Nicaragua patriots as to the efforts of "Commodore" Vanderbilt, whom he had antagonized. Walker's untimely death was particularly sad when it is realized that he might well have been an American hero of the stature of Sam Houston if only he had lived a little earlier and so have fitted into the ideology and desires of the United States.

Most fantastic of the expansionists were the Knights of the Golden Circle, organized at Lexington, Kentucky, in 1854. The golden circle at which they aimed was a magnificent slave empire, centering at Havana and with a radius of some 1200 miles, that would include southern North America, northern South America, and everything between. The order had the three degrees of Knights of the Iron Hand (military), Knights of the True Faith (financial), and Knights of the Columbian Star (governmental). It was credited with having helped to inspire such men as Walker. The Knights planned a Mexican invasion in 1860, but these plans fizzled, and the order itself finally disappeared during the Civil War.

COMPROMISE OF 1850

As a result of the Treaty of Guadalupe Hidalgo the United States was endowed with an immense new domain for which some governmental provisions had to be made in view of the considerable white settlements.

Texas, of course, was already a state, but her boundaries remained uncertain; New Mexico and California struggled along under military government; and the Mormon community of Utah (see Chapter 26) existed under a government of its own devising. The problem of acceptable governments was made more acute by the slavery issue, which Congress debated acrimoniously. Before the debate ended, President Polk's term of office had expired, President Taylor had died, and President Fillmore had assumed office.

The congressional debate concerning the government of the new territories involved complex factors and was highly significant for the future, but the men and women of the Southwest were hardly willing to sit passively and twiddle their fingers while congressmen and senators made oratorical reputations for themselves. The great interior basin, approximately present Utah and Nevada, was organized by the Mormons in 1849 as the state of Deseret, with the usual constitution and state officers. Statehood seemed unlikely for this area, not only because the population was inadequate but also because of considerable doubt as to whether Congress would be willing to tolerate polygamy, which soon was to be linked with slavery as "twin evils."

The settlements of the upper Rio Grande had been organized by Kearny as the territory of New Mexico, which theoretically included the white population of Arizona; in fact, distance prevented any real control. A revolution early in 1847 was suppressed by the military; in the course of it Governor Charles Bent was killed, which at least saved some future unpleasantness, since Kearny had had no power to establish a territorial government. During the congressional debate after the Mexican War the people of New Mexico petitioned for territorial government and then on their own initiative formed a state constitution (1850) that was accepted by the voters 8371 to 39.

The New Mexico situation was further complicated by boundary difficulties. The New Mexicans wanted a government of their own that would include the residents of Arizona, who were not pleased with the idea. More important, Texas had long claimed the area as far west as the Rio Grande, and that claim had at one time been accepted by the United States government. To reinforce her title Texas had organized the county of New Mexico and had sent county officials who had been prevented from functioning by the army. Incidentally, there still remained the unsettled problem of whether Texas herself should be divided into several states.

Californians were even more insistent upon an improved local government than were her eastern neighbors. American settlers had not been enamored of Mexican rule and were almost equally displeased with army control; moreover, their number had increased vastly with the gold rush. On a local level, most towns continued the office of *alcalde,* but here and there communities set up their own governments. On the state level the desire for a more responsive and effective government became so strong that the military governor finally bowed to the popular will and called a convention to devise a state government; he felt that, if he could not prevent such a convention, he might as well have the glory of calling one.

The California convention met at Monterey in September 1849. The place of meeting was in itself an indication of the fact that it was more a creature of the old than of the new order. Three quarters of its members had arrived in California before the gold rush, and included not only such men as Larkin and Sutter but also a sprinkling of native Californians. The resulting constitution, ratified overwhelmingly by the electorate, produced a frame of government and also the present boundaries of the state. The first governor was Peter H. Burnett. The first legislature met at San Jose in December 1849, and among other actions elected John C. Frémont and W. M. Gwin as United States senators. Here was a full-fledged and active, although extralegal, government confronting the United States Congress.

The debate from which the Compromise of 1850 emerged was notable as the last important appearance of the three men who had so nearly dominated the American political scene during the preceding generation— Henry Clay, Daniel Webster, and John C. Calhoun. The final compromise was proposed by the aging Clay, supported by Webster, particularly in his famous Seventh of March speech, and opposed by Calhoun, who, as usual, couched his arrogant demands in soft words. The original compromise was contained in a single bill but failed of passage because of the combination of opponents. Ultimately the ideas in it were embodied in separate measures and passed.

The Compromise of 1850 provided for the admission of California under the constitution that was already in operation, which meant as a free state. Texas was paid $10 million to accept suitable boundaries, and of course remained a slave state. New Mexico, including present Arizona, became a territory, with statehood sixty years away. Utah also became a territory, with statehood to be delayed some forty-five years, primarily on the polygamy issue. In addition, slave trade was prohibited in the District of Columbia and a more stringent fugitive-slave law was enacted.

The Compromise of 1850 has long been recognized as a turning point in American history. In the East the old compromising spirit was ebbing rapidly with the passing of the conciliatory generation and the arrival of more aggressive younger men. In the West the formation of new states and territories marked very clearly the breakdown of the old concept of a permanent Indian frontier: no longer could men believe that the limits of white settlement had been reached at the great bend of the Missouri. Equally important, the total continental boundaries of the United

States had been attained except for the small area of Gadsden's Purchase and the noncontiguous Alaska. The old and aggressive expansionism of the past, which had pushed the United States from the Atlantic to the Pacific, was to recede for over a generation, after which it was to reappear only in terms of overseas aspirations. Much of the continental United States remained to be populated, but only a little remained to be acquired.

READINGS

MANIFEST DESTINY. Albert K. Weinberg, *Manifest Destiny* (1935) compiles the arguments. Laurence Greene, *The Filibuster* (1937) treats Walker. The Oregon situation can be followed in Melvin C. Jacobs, *Winning Oregon* (1938); see also M. Margaret Jean Kelly, *The Career of Joseph Lane* (1942).

TEXAS AND THE MEXICAN WAR. Nathaniel W. Stephenson, *Texas and the Mexican War* (1921) is a good, brief account; Alfred H. Hill, *Rehearsal for Conflict* (1947) reads easily; George L. Rives, *The United States and Mexico, 1821–1848* (2 vols., 1931) is scholarly, as is Juston H. Smith, *The War With Mexico* (2 vols., 1919); general histories of Texas are listed in the Readings for Chapter 24. Eugene I. McCormac, *James K. Polk* (1922) is detailed. Taylor is treated in Brainerd Dyer, *Zachary Taylor* (1946); Holman Hamilton, *Zachary Taylor* (2 vols., 1941); Silas B. McKinley and Silas Bent, *Old Rough and Ready* (1946). John D. Fuller, *The Movement for the Acquisition of All Mexico* (1936) concerns the years 1846–1848. Paul N. Garber, *The Gadsden Treaty* (1929) is concerned, as is Averam B. Bender, *The March of Empire* (1952), with frontier defense in the years following 1848.

CALIFORNIA. For general accounts see the Readings for Chapter 24 under Caughey, Graebner, Cleland, Sanchez, Scherer. Information concerning the Kearny trip appears in Dwight L. Clarke, *Stephen Watts Kearny* (1961), a scholarly defense; George W. Ames Jr. (ed.), *A Doctor Comes to California* (1943); Robert L. Duffus, *The Santa Fe Trail* (1930); Erna Fergusson, *New Mexico* (1951); George R. Gibson, *Journal of a Soldier under Kearny and Doniphan* (1934); Blanche C. Grant (ed.), *Kit Carson's Own Story* (1926); William C. Kennerly, *Persimmon Hill* (1948), Doniphan; David S. Lavender, *Bent's Fort* (1954). Parts of the California story appear in Werner H. Marti, *Messenger of Destiny* (1960), Gillespie; Reuben L. Underhill, *From Cowhides to Golden Fleece* (1939), Larkin; George P. Hammond (ed.), *The Larkin Papers* (5 vols., 1951–1955); Joseph T. Downey, *Filings from an Old Saw* (1956), contemporary; William H. Ellison, *A Self-Governing Dominion, 1849–1860* (1950), statehood; Fred B. Rogers, *William Brown Ide, Bear Flagger* (1962) and (ed.), *A Navy Surgeon in California, 1846–1847* (1957);

Robert V. Hine, *Edward Kern and American Expansion* (1962), artist with Frémont; Allan Nevins, *Frémont* (1939). A later fourth expedition of Frémont is well covered in William Brandon, *The Man and the Mountain* (1955); Hine, noted above; Solomon N. Carvalho, *Incidents of Travel* (1954), contemporary; Le Roy and Ann Hafen (eds.), *Frémont's Fourth Expedition* (1960).

CHAPTER **26**

KINGDOM OF THE SAINTS

E ven as Taylor and Scott were driving into Mexico a new type of
migration was crossing the plains to the Far West as the Mormons
began in 1846 their magnificent trek to escape the unhappiness
that had been their lot in the Mississippi Valley. This religious group represented an unusual type of frontier experience, and demonstrated that at
least some of the country traditionally called "desert" could in fact be
used by white farmers.

MORMON ORIGINS

The Mormons, or more properly the members of the Church of
Jesus Christ of Latter-Day Saints, belonged to a recently developed
Protestant Christian sect. The prophet and originator was Joseph Smith,
who had been born in 1805, the son of a poor Vermont farmer. Smith grew
to maturity in central New York State, a region that was unusually affected
by religious emotionalism. Even at an early age Joseph Smith spoke of
seeing visions and receiving revelations.

Mormonism was based not only on revelations to the prophet, but
also on the sacred Book of Mormon, which reputedly was dug from the
ground near Palmyra, New York, in 1827 by Smith, acting upon revelation.
The Book of Mormon was engraved on golden plates, and its authenticity
was attested by a "cloud of witnesses"; it could be read directly in English
by the use of spectacles that contained the magical stones Urim and Thum-
mim. The book was a historical narrative, starting about 600 B.C. and telling how certain lost tribes of Israel had wandered to America, where the
bad Lamanites (Indians) had destroyed the good Nephites about A.D. 400;
incidentally, this theory of the origin of the American Indians was reasonably common in the United States. Ultimately the only remaining Nephites

were the distinguished prophet Mormon and his son Moroni; Mormon wrote the bulk of the book describing the wanderings and fate of the Nephites, and his son completed the work. Smith's divinely revealed mission was to reconquer America, "the promised land," from the wicked Lamanites.

The faith taught by the Book of Mormon was generally democratic and optimistic. Free will was emphasized, with salvation free to anyone who repented and obeyed God. Eternal punishment was to be visited only on those who had heard the truth and rejected it, and not on those, such as small children, who had no choice. As the Mormon faith developed, God was a real person who existed in both time and space; the traditional idea of the trinity was rejected in favor of three separate personalities. Man was eternal, with a waiting soul coming into the world whenever a child was born. Progress continued after death through three degrees of glory.

After the publication of the Book of Mormon, Joseph Smith and his friends sold it from door to door. Purchasers were not easy to find in the comparative poverty of central New York, but some of the readers became believers and ultimately a formal church of six members was established on April 6, 1830. The new Saints were disturbed by the skepticism of doubting neighbors and consequently some of them followed Smith in 1831 to establish a homogeneous group of their own at Kirtland, Ohio, near Cleveland. All property, as revealed to Joseph Smith in the Order of Enoch, was transferred to the church, with enough being lent to each individual for his own use; this practice was to be continued later. A magnificent temple, which even today remains impressive, was built. Houses were constructed, farms put under cultivation, and stores and a bank opened.

Extensive missionary work, a characteristic of the Mormons from early days, provided the basis for a later spectacular increase in numbers. Indian missions were obviously desirable in view of the purposes of the faith, but in addition there were missions for white Americans, and before the end of the decade the work was extended to Europe. Missionaries were sent in pairs as part of their religious duties and were highly successful, particularly in England. Thousands of European converts soon were streaming to the New World to expand the number of the Saints. England alone sent 4000 converts in the years between 1840 and 1846.

Most important of the early converts was Brigham Young, who saw the light in 1832, although at this time he had never seen Joseph Smith. Young resembled Smith in having been born in Vermont and reared in New York. By trade he had been a joiner, house painter, and glazier. By nature he had a forceful and attractive personality, a ready tongue, and excellent judgment concerning men and affairs. His most important early

The Mormons

work was as a missionary, and he had tremendous success in England. He was sufficiently prominent to be named a member of the Council of the Twelve Apostles in 1835, but he never came into close contact with the prophet.

The Mormons were never happy in Kirtland. Gentile (non-Mormon) neighbors were suspicious and frequently hostile, accusing the Mormons of sacrilege, immorality, and polygamy—all denied indignantly by the Mormons. Even more important, the Mormons were rent by internal dissensions as various individuals claimed personal revelations that rivaled those of the prophet, each tending to become the nucleus for a small group of malcontents. Then, too, the panic of 1837 brought serious distress. Smith's investments in land, industry, and banking began to show signs of strain; in fact the prophet agreed that his best abilities were not in the field of business.

The solution of the Kirtland difficulties was to move the community farther west—actually an old plan that had been in Smith's mind at least as early as his first western trip in 1831. The new "promised land" was Zion, Missouri, known to the gentiles as Independence, and to this place the Mormons had been moving during the 1830s in larger numbers than to Kirtland. Unfortunately the people of Missouri proved no more hospitable than those of Ohio. In 1833 the Saints were driven out of Independence and went to the Missouri counties to the north. Here it was that the prophet came when conditions in Kirtland became intolerable in 1838. But again the gentiles proved hostile, and mobs destroyed Mormon life and property. The crisis came in 1839, when the governor of Missouri not only refused to act against the mob but said: "The Mormons must be treated as enemies and must be exterminated or driven from the State if necessary, for the public good."

NAUVOO AND JOSEPH SMITH

The new Mormon haven was the town of Commerce, renamed Nauvoo, which lay on the Illinois side of the Mississippi, about halfway between Fort Madison and Keokuk. An impressive city was planned, and, as was true of each such settlement, one of the earliest activities was the beginning of the construction of a magnificent temple; as events materialized this temple was never completed, and even the partially built section was later destroyed. Necessary homes and public buildings were erected and farming was begun. The people worked very hard, and the community almost immediately had an appearance of prosperity. Thrift, religious earnestness, and contentment were evident to even the most casual eye.

The Mormon community of the 1840s, both religious and lay, was dominated by the striking personality of Joseph Smith. Although Smith considered himself a prophet, he laid no claim to divinity or even to personal perfection. Handsome and naturally impressive, he was over 6 feet tall and carried his 200 pounds easily and well. He had a magnificent physique, which he delighted to exhibit by wrestling with any and all visitors. A man of strong passions and lusty with life, he loved his friends and hated his enemies, worked hard, ate heartily, and sometimes drank to excess. His versatile mind embraced activities that ranged from the translation of Egyptian papyri to managing the combined grocery store and hotel named the Nauvoo House. His most magnificent gesture was to run for the presidency (1844) on a platform of territorial expansion, abolition, a national bank, and penal reforms; Mormon missionaries did his campaigning. With all these activities he never lost an almost childlike love of display, whether of his own mental powers and religious authority or of his impressive uniform, lavishly embellished with gold, lace, and brass buttons, which he wore as head of the Nauvoo Legion.

The Mormons always placed great stress on the importance of the individual, but also held that the individual could attain his maximum stature only by working with others to develop the highest temporal and spiritual values. Each person should live an honest and abstemious life, avoiding such things as coffee, tea, tobacco, and liquor. A man should work hard and be frugal; poverty was a sign of sin. Property should not be considered a goal; all property really belonged to the church and was permitted to individuals only on the tolerance of the church. In fact the church was active in all phases of life, including economic endeavor, philanthropy, and amusements. The individual went through elaborate rituals upon entering the church and upon getting married, performed some sort of special mission for the church, and paid tithes throughout his life on all income of any kind. These ideals were not far different from those of other Protestant faiths, but the Mormons were distinctive in the extent to which they applied their religion. They could not lay it aside on weekdays and then parade it on Sundays.

While the church was extremely paternalistic it was also benevolent and democratic, at least in theory. Every male member of the church was also a member of one of the two priesthoods, and each higher office was elective; the catch in this procedure was that a church-preferred slate of candidates received almost unanimous votes. No individual was neglected and no individual could go unclothed, unhoused, and unfed if he were willing to work. Child labor was opposed, but every adult was supposed to work.

The basic Mormon social institution was the family, not only to promote morality and to care for children, but also because the Mormons believed that for a woman marriage was a necessity for salvation. Herein lies an important reason for the introduction of polygamy into a society that had a surplus of women. Also involved is the basis for the development of two kinds of marriage, of which one was for eternity only and did not include physical cohabitation on this earth. The family was the only proper place for sex expression, and large families were much to be desired. The husband was head but not master of his family, for his wife was an individual and not a slave. In fact women were treated very well. They were allowed to vote in the early Salt Lake settlement, and Utah later became one of the first states to have woman suffrage.

Most discussed of Mormon practices was polygamy, which was based on a revelation to the prophet, but of course it had also been common in Old Testament times. Although the practice was denied publicly until after the migration to Utah, the original revelation had presumably come to Smith in 1831. Not until Nauvoo did the prophet divulge his revelation to a few of the leaders, by whom it was received with considerable consternation, since it violated deeply ingrained ideas of morality. Polygamy was but little practiced in Nauvoo except by Smith, who had a total of at least twenty-eight wives, and whose affections apparently were not entirely confined to even this considerable family.

Plural marriage among the Mormons has very properly been described as "Puritan polygamy." A second marriage was undertaken only after much prayer and also after consultation with and acceptance by the first wife. Elaborate ceremonies emphasized the gravity of the occasion.

Licentiousness and sensuality were frowned upon whether inside or outside marriage, and adultery was punished severely. Marriage was a serious duty, both temporal and religious. By plural marriage the surplus women, many of them from England, were given the security of homes of their own, and an opportunity for salvation, while the number of children in the community increased desirably. Of course only a relatively small proportion of Mormon men could afford more than one wife; one estimate is that about 10 percent of Mormon families were polygamous in the 1860s. The husband with more than one wife was supposed to treat his wives equally, but did not always do so. Frequently a man married sisters, possibly at the same time. Ordinarily the wives were good friends and enjoyed the companionship of living together and sharing the work. In fact the women gave little evidence of having any objections to polygamy.

Regardless of the possible justifications for polygamy, the gentiles near Nauvoo considered it as evidence of moral turpitude, and held that it was a fitting concomitant of the sacrilege of calling "Joe" Smith a prophet. These Illinois farmers may conceivably have been a little jealous of the pleasures they pictured in polygamy; they were certainly envious of the prosperity of the industrious Mormon community. In politics they also resented the Mormons. Nauvoo, at 15,000 in 1845, was the largest city of the state, and since the Mormons voted as a unit they held the political balance of power in the state and were able to obtain special favors. The enmity of the gentiles soon produced mob violence in the form of fires, thefts, malicious destruction, and personal attacks. Ultimately Joseph Smith and his brother Hyrum were charged with inciting a riot that had involved the burning of a critical newspaper, the *Expositor*. Ostensibly for their own protection they were placed in the Carthage jail, but a mob found only token resistance when it stormed the jail and murdered the two men in 1844.

BRIGHAM YOUNG AND THE MOVE WEST

The murder of Joseph Smith inspired several rival claimants to compete for his power as head of the church. Most picturesque was James Jesse Strang, who later had himself crowned "King of Beaver Island" in northern Lake Michigan. Most able and ultimately successful was Brigham Young, who luckily returned from a missionary tour at the psychological moment. Young first obtained the confidence of most of the Mormons and then consolidated his power by excommunicating rival pretenders. Several small groups, including one headed by Joseph Smith III, son of the prophet, went their own way, claiming to be the real depositories of the true faith.

Brigham Young faced problems as serious as ever confronted any leader. The death of Smith had removed the central figure of the group and hence reduced its cohesion. Internal dissension continued to be trouble-some even though the excommunication of rival leaders made it less effective. The hostility of the neighboring gentiles threatened annihilation unless the entire group were moved again. But where could the Mormons go? And could they find the depths of courage once more to abandon the fruits of years of hard work and start life again in poverty?

Young's answer to his problem was to start the evacuation of Nauvoo in February 1846, in the heart of the winter and with only a tentative objective in view. Groups of Mormons, led by a small party under Young, crossed the ice of the Mississippi and struggled through the roadless mud of Iowa. These people were leaving a settled and prosperous community with little more than the clothes on their backs and the few possessions that could be packed in wagons. Their farms and homes were conceded to acquisitive Illinois farmers; their furniture, crockery, and other personal possessions became the toys of future generations of Illinois children. Embarking toward the setting sun, they were hazarding their very lives for the attainment of an ideal—the right to live and work and worship God as they pleased.

The migration of 1846, like every Mormon undertaking, was organized thoroughly and effectively. Small groups went ahead to establish temporary camps, where cabins were frequently built and crops planted for the benefit of later arrivals. Then came the larger parties, which included the old and young, the sick and the infirm, for by fall the gentiles had ejected the last of the Mormons from Nauvoo. Even with the best possible planning, however, provisions soon became scarce. Some of the young men worked for the Iowa farmers along their route, others sold the products of their work; a brass band gave concerts to raise their own morale as well as to gather funds. But even at their best, conditions were desperate. Only the magnificent faith of the people kept them moving as they went slogging through Iowa mud, pelted by spring rain, subsisting on a meager and monotonous diet. Many a Mormon man or woman breathed his last on the Iowa prairie, and many a Mormon baby was ushered into the world on a blanket placed under a wagon box.

The principal winter quarters for the cold weather of 1846–1847 were near the present Omaha, although other Mormon communities were scattered throughout the surrounding countryside. Here it was that the Mormon Battalion was recruited for the long march to San Diego in accord with an agreement with President Polk by which the Mormons were to demonstrate their loyalty, and in return were assured—according to their understanding—of protection in the West. A forest of tents and crude cabins kept out at least a part of the elements. Food was scarce, and even the crude tools of frontier life were frequently lacking. The poor dict and exposure brought a dreadful mortality, so that at times the living had difficulty in providing burials for the dead. Brigham Young and other leaders exhibited day by day the tremendous courage that alone ensured the survival of the group.

WESTERN COLONIZATION

The Missouri River was but the first step in the march to a Zion that would be far distant from the troubles with hostile gentiles; there is no evidence, however, that the Mormons tried to get outside the boundaries of the United States. Early in 1847 Young received his first and only revelation, which was that the Saints should continue their march west. In April he took the road again, this time at the head of a party of 148, which included 3 women and 2 children; the bulk of the party was composed of young men of a variety of skills needed to establish a new community. Guided by Frémont's writings, Young followed the usual Platte River— South Pass route, except that he took the north rather than the more frequently used south bank of the Platte. From Fort Bridger he cut directly to Salt Lake, where he announced, "This is the place." Immediately the party set to work to start building houses and planting crops in preparation for later arrivals. As for Young, he again turned his face east to meet and direct later emigrants.

Although the Salt Lake area was described to eastern Saints in glowing terms, the actuality was exceedingly drab. The lake was beautiful but useless except for bathing parties. The land was treeless, and in fact had almost no vegetation except sagebrush. The ground was hard-baked by the sun. Everywhere was desolation and wasteland. Irrigation was necessary before the first crops could be planted with any hope of a harvest. The first buildings had to be closely packed and arranged as a fort to provide against possible attacks by hostile Indians.

Other parties immediately followed the pioneers, although it was five years before the entire population of Nauvoo reached Salt Lake. Each party was well organized, and experienced no more than the usual trials of wilderness travel. Part of the migrants were foreign converts, largely from England, who arrived by the thousand. Mormon agents planned their trips, met them on arrival (New Orleans in the early years), and supervised their overland journey. Special rates were provided. A Perpetual Emigrating Fund, started in 1849, lent money to the migrants who were poverty-stricken; after reaching Utah they were supposed to pay back from their earnings these advances plus interest, and thus furnish funds for similar loans to later travelers.

To reduce the cost of the trip across the plains, the experiment was tried in 1856 of having some of the migrants pull handcarts across the plains.

Five people were assigned to each cart, with the body of the cart some 3 to 4 feet long. The total baggage per person could weigh only seventeen pounds. Other belongings and supplies were carried in regular wagons. The distance per day was between 10 and 20 miles. Tragic results occurred when groups started the trip so late that they were caught in winter weather. By the time the experiment was abandoned in 1860 ten companies had made the trip, with 2962 people pulling 653 handcarts.

The Mormon settlement was not confined to Salt Lake City even in the early years. Ninety-five communities were established during the years 1847–1857, stretching 1000 miles north and south, from Idaho to south of the Colorado River, and 800 miles east and west, extending as far west as the Pacific Ocean. Settlers for each "stake" were picked by the church authorities and went as a religious duty. Such careful attention was given to the general plans, the leadership, a proper distribution of skills, and necessary supplies, that there should be little surprise that the communities generally survived. Plans existed as early as 1849 for lines of settlement to San Francisco and Los Angeles. The latter objective led to the establishment of a community at San Bernardino, California, but the church difficulties of 1857 brought its abandonment.

ECONOMIC DEVELOPMENTS

The first years in the Salt Lake Valley were a time of extreme hardship for everyone. As new arrivals appeared by the thousand food became so scarce that it had to be rationed. The building of houses was unusually difficult because all the wood had to be hauled with tremendous labor from the neighboring mountains. Clothes, tools, furniture, and other equipment were of the scantiest, for these consisted only of what had been salvaged from Nauvoo and hauled by wagon over the plains. Even Nature seemed hostile when the first crop failed because of the lateness of the planting. The crop of 1848 started well, but soon its destruction was threatened by the arrival of swarms of locusts, and salvation came only with the providential appearance of large numbers of gulls, which today are commemorated by a statue in Temple Square.

The future prosperity of the Mormon community depended primarily on irrigation, for agriculture was impossible without an adequate supply of water. Irrigation canals were among the earliest ventures, being built and operated cooperatively under the supervision of the church; as early as 1865 they included over 1000 miles of ditches. Irrigation meant comparatively small farms, intensive cultivation, and closely packed communities. In Salt Lake City, for example, each resident was given a town lot and a farming lot; the farming lot of an artisan was quite small and near the city so that it could be used for garden crops. Everyone was guaranteed the right to the necessities of life if he were willing to work, with newer immigrants often laboring at public works. No one has ever accused the Mormons of lacking industry.

In agriculture, as was true of every phase of Mormon life, Brigham Young had a dominant role. He urged new immigrants to bring all sorts of seeds, small trees, and shrubs. He sent parties to California to collect seeds and stock. He encouraged better agricultural processes by offering prizes for the largest crops of flax, hemp, wheat and other grains to be grown on a single half acre. Sometimes he was unsuccessful, as with such newer crops as cotton, silk, and sugar beets.

Young also appreciated quite early the necessity for developing as nearly a self-sufficient economy as possible, since connections with the rest of the United States were not only difficult but awakened unpleasant memories. Iron mines were discovered and developed, but the manufacture of nails, other hardware, and machines was not successful. A sugar mill was also unsuccessful, producing nothing better than molasses. Cotton was introduced in the "Dixie" of southern Utah. Successful industries included tanneries, flour mills, lumber mills, potteries, and a woolen mill. Many industries, such as the manufacture of cloth, remained primarily in the home. The medium of exchange included a few locally minted gold coins but was mainly paper currency backed by gold dust; in general, however, Young discouraged Mormons from prospecting for gold. A special effort was made to attract a proper variety of artisans, and Utah soon boasted men who could make boots and shoes, watches, caps and hats, paper, carriages; in addition there were stone masons, cabinetmakers, and other skilled workmen.

Mormon enterprises were frequently inspired and not infrequently owned by the church. The tendency toward cooperative community endeavor developed at some places into outright communism, but this trend proved to be transitory. Merchandising was a particularly difficult problem. With the arrival of gentiles, the newcomers tended to monopolize retail selling; the common explanation was that Mormon merchants were expected to give unlimited credit to their fellow church members. The permanent answer was the cooperative store, the Zion's Co-operative Institution (Z.C.M.I.) being organized in 1868 at Salt Lake City. For Mormons there was no distinct division between religious and nonreligious activities; the church had a vital part in all aspects of life.

Transportation and communication were also important matters because even with the greatest efforts the Mormons could not in fact become completely self-sufficient or be entirely indifferent to events of the outside world. The church early encouraged a Mormon freighting company that made connections with the East; later a mail route was established. When the transcontinental telegraph was strung in 1861 the Mormons were interested, and five years later completed their own connections. With the arrival of the Union Pacific, Brigham Young obtained a contract for building part of the line in Utah, and this contract he sublet to other Mormons. Salt Lake City was disappointed in not being on the main line of the Union Pacific, and consequently had to build its own branch, which was completed in 1870; in 1883 connection was made with Denver by way of the Denver and Rio Grande Western Railroad.

SOCIAL DEVELOPMENTS

The tremendous importance of material progress overshadowed but did not eclipse social interests. Education was always a matter of concern to the Mormons, and schools were opened even in the first year in Utah; these, like all Mormon schools, were coeducational. The elementary schools long remained private, primarily because Young was opposed to the use of taxes for the support of schools. Higher schools were slow to open because only the most elementary education seemed vitally necessary for a community that had but little surplus capital. In time academies were established and in addition theological training was given. A college had been founded at Nauvoo, and the University of Deseret functioned at Salt Lake City for a few years starting in 1850, but this first effort failed, and the university was not reopened until 1867. Considered as a whole, Mormon educational efforts were not impressive unless allowance is made for the tremendous difficulties faced by the early Mormon educators.

The amusements favored by Young and the church were drama, music, and dancing; as always the church was itself an integral part of most developments. As early as 1855 the church built a community center that was partly a theater. A magnificent theater was opened by the church in Salt Lake City in 1862, its elaborate decorations demonstrating the skill of local carpenters and painters. The actors included visiting companies and stars as well as local players, and Brigham Young could watch his own daughters perform on the boards. He thoroughly believed in the values of drama, music, and dancing, and felt, moreover, that they were closely related to religion; dances were generally opened with prayer. Music was common both inside and outside the church, with numerous choirs, bands, and orchestras. The performances not unexpectedly varied in quality.

Other cultural activities of the Mormons were less impressive. One or more newspapers were always published, with preference going to the *Deseret News,* which struggled desperately for its existence during the two decades after its founding in 1850. Magazines were scarce, books were even scarcer, and decent libraries were almost nonexistent. Poetry was encouraged, but its quality was no better than mediocre. Considerable interest went to lectures that ranged in subject material from science and farming to history and morals. Museums were reasonably numerous. Artists were rare. Literary, musical, and other societies had somewhat tenuous existences. Here, as in all phases of life, the attitude of the church was the decisive factor as to what activities would succeed and what would fail.

One of the early advantages of Utah to the Mormons was that it was completely their own world, untroubled by skeptical or hostile gentiles. The first arrivals in considerable numbers from the outside world came with the gold rush of 1849, but these Argonauts proved helpful rather than damaging; they stopped but briefly and had money and manufactured goods they were anxious to trade for provisions, an exchange that was mutually profitable. But increasingly during the 1850s and 1860s, and particularly with the opening of the Union Pacific, other gentiles moved into the Salt Lake area in search of wealth. Their reception was not cordial, since the Mormons were clannish, and had good reason to be suspicious of outsiders. The establishment of cooperative stores was one method of curtailing the business that went to gentile traders.

The Mormon hostility to non-Mormons was illustrated most extremely in the Mountain Meadows Massacre. In 1857, at the height of Mormon troubles with the federal government, a party of 140 Arkansas settlers passed through Salt Lake City on the way to California. At Mountain Meadows it was attacked by Indians, some of whom were disguised Mormons. The emigrants prepared for defense by arranging their wagons in a corral and digging a protective trench. A group of Mormons then appeared and persuaded the beleaguered travelers to give up their arms and be escorted to safety. After the immigrants were disarmed they were all murdered in cold blood except for seventeen children who were too young to remember. This cruel act of butchery has been admitted by the Mormons; the only argument about it concerns the extent of the participation, if any, of Brigham Young. The least possible complicity that can be claimed for him is that he had knowledge after the act but made no effort to apprehend and punish its perpetrators.

GOVERNMENT

Law and order in early Utah might have been comparable to that of California and Oregon except that the Mormons were an unusually orderly and obedient people, and that the church was a strong, controlling force. Almost at once the church made and enforced civil as well as religious rules. Enforcement was easily possible because the church not only could impose religious sanctions but also had the power of economic life and death.

As for civil government, the United States delayed in making provision and hence the Mormons, like other Westerners, set up a state government of their own. A convention met at Salt Lake City in 1849 and wrote a constitution for the new state of Deseret, modeling the document along the usual American lines. The infant state was not modest; it included within its borders all the land between the Rockies and the Sierras, and south of Oregon. The constitution was at once put into effect, and to no one's surprise Brigham Young was elected the first governor. A delegate was sent to Washington to request Congress to recognize the new state, but Congress decided in the Compromise of 1850 to make Deseret only a territory, with the name of Utah. Its limits were reduced, but still included approximately the present Utah and Nevada, with parts of Colorado and Wyoming. Later legislation continued to cut the territory until it attained its present boundaries.

Brigham Young was given the appointment as territorial governor, but the fact that the other federal officers were gentiles immediately created trouble. Some of the new appointees were definitely inferior and tactless men. A couple of them (and their wives) thought of the Mormons as a "gang of licentious villains," and peeked through doors and windows to see what these peculiar people were doing. One judge left his wife at home and brought a Washington prostitute, who at times sat with him on the bench. But even the best possible officeholders could not have avoided all difficulties. The Mormons were sensitive, suspicious, proud, and dictatorial; under no conceivable circumstances would they have accepted the gentiles lovingly. The result was that even the best-intentioned federal officers found great difficulty in performing their duties.

A crisis in federal relations came in 1857 when a territorial judge fled from Utah shouting that his life was in danger, and roaring diatribes against the Mormons, who, he said, were flouting federal authority with impunity. This incident occurred just as the practice of polygamy was receiving nation-wide disapproval. The church had publicly accepted polygamy in 1852, and four years later the national Republican platform had linked polygamy with slavery as twin evils; apparently more people deplored polygamy than objected to slavery. With considerable public sentiment backing him, Buchanan decided to send a non-Mormon governor, backed by an army ready to enforce federal authority. The new governor was Alfred Cumming of Georgia, grossly fat, jealous of his power, and a difficult man with whom to do business. An army of 2500 was under the command of Colonel Albert S. Johnston, who later attained fame in the Civil War.

As the army moved across the plains the Mormons prepared for defense, with Brigham Young breathing defiance to the United States, which he labeled somewhat inelegantly "a stink in our nostrils." Outlying settlements were abandoned and their inhabitants drawn back to the neighborhood of Salt Lake City. Salt Lake City itself was prepared for evacuation and destruction if capture threatened. The Danites, a Mormon militia, harassed Johnston by capturing wagon trains, stampeding livestock, and burning the grass. As Johnston approached, Young threatened to destroy Utah and to fight the invaders to the last man.

The federal army spent the winter of 1857–1858 in camp not far from Fort Bridger. It was marked by rowdiness, gambling, fighting, and drinking, together with disobedience and some desertions. Cumming and Johnston disliked each other thoroughly. Ultimately mediation persuaded Cumming to visit Salt Lake City personally and without the troops; his position was recognized by Young. When the troops entered the city in the summer of 1858 there was no opposition; quite diplomatically they camped outside the city, and in a short time were returned East. The Utah "rebels" were pardoned by the President. The entire episode had cost the federal government $15 million, but the general situation remained unchanged, with the same frictions as before.

The "Mormon problem" remained unsolved for a generation after the regrettable "Mormon War." No Congress could be found to accept an American state with polygamy while polygamy was frowned upon by the great bulk of American citizens. Public opinion was dominated by a flood of pornographic literature of the same general appeal as the *Police Gazette*. Wildly impossible tales related how women were held in white slavery and how Brigham Young and other Mormon elders indulged in orgies at the Endowment House. Numerous "confessions" of ex-wives appealed to the prurient and morbidly curious. Many good Christians professed to see Salt Lake City as little better than an immense house of prostitution.

The Mormons of course quite properly answered their accusers that polygamy was an ancient and well-recognized form of family organization, used extensively in Old Testament days, and that it was highly moral, decreasing rather than increasing the amount of prostitution. Such answers were completely ineffective because most Americans did not see them, and in any case would have rejected them. Furthermore, polygamy was becoming less desirable for the Mormons themselves. The surplus of women was disappearing. Outside opposition was harder to bear as communication and transportation improved, and particularly because it delayed the desired statehood.

Starting in the 1850s Congress passed a long series of laws designed to eliminate polygamy. The first laws were too weak to be effective; moreover, their active enforcement was held up by the Civil War. With increasing experience Congress was finally able to pass effective legislation in the Edmunds Act of 1882. Plural marriage was forbidden, and living with more than one wife at the same time was made punishable by fine and imprisonment. All children born before January 1, 1883, were to be considered legitimate and those born in plural marriage after that date were to be held illegitimate. The real teeth of the act came in the provisions that no person practicing polygamy could vote, hold office, or perform jury duty, and that a presidential commission should be the final judge as to the beliefs of the voters, elected officials, and jurymen.

The Edmunds Act was enforced so vigorously that within five years five hundred Mormons had been jailed under its terms. The church then saw the handwriting on the wall, and the president of the church officially banned polygamy by an order of September 25, 1890. Polygamy of course did not actually end overnight, if for no other reason than that conscientious citizens were not willing to desert their wives, even though they were plural. Congress recognized the practical death of polygamy by passing an enabling act for the territory in 1894. Two years later Utah was admitted to the Union.

READINGS

GENERAL. Among the many general accounts of the Mormons a few of the more useful are Nels Anderson, *Desert Saints* (1942), scholarly; Leonard J. Arrington, *Great Basin Kingdom* (1958), particularly good on economic factors; Leland H. Creer, *Utah and the Nation* (1929); Gustive O. Larson, *Prelude to the Kingdom* (1947), quite sympathetic; William J. McNiff, *Heaven on Earth* (1940); Thomas F. O'Dea, *The Mormons* (1957), particularly good on beliefs; Ray B. West, Jr., *Kingdom of the Saints* (1957). Kirtland is treated in Harlan Hatcher, *The Western Reserve* (1949); Nauvoo is described in Theodore C. Pease (ed.), *The Frontier State* (1918); Missouri experiences are covered in Stanley Vestal, *The Missouri* (1945). Original accounts are George R. Bird, *Tenderfoot Days in Territorial Utah* (1918); Robert G. Cleland and Juanita Brooks (eds.), *A Mormon Chronicle* (2 vols., 1955), very good on period 1848–1876.

PORTIONS OF THE STORY. Juanita Brooks, *The Mountain Meadow Massacre* (1950) and *John Doyle Lee* (1962), by a Mormon. Paul D. Bailey, *Sam Brannan and the California Mormons* (1943), interesting. Norman F. Furniss, *The Mormon Conflict 1850–1859* (1960) is excellent on the Mormon "War"; Le Roy R. and Ann W. Hafen (eds.), *The Utah Expedition, 1857–1858* (1958) has many documents. Le Roy R. and Ann W. Hafen (eds.), *Handcarts to Zion* (1960) contains a good historical sketch. William Mulder, *Homeward to Zion* (1957) concerns Scandinavian Mormons; see also William Mulder and A. R. Mortensen (eds.), *Among the Mormons* (1958). Brigham H. Roberts, *The Mormon Battalion* (1919) is written by a Mormon, as is Levi E. Young, *Isn't One Wife Enough?* (1954), a sociological study. Erwin G. Gudde (ed.),

Bigler's Chronicle of the West (1962) concerns a member of the Mormon Battalion.

BIOGRAPHIES. Young: Frank J. Cannon and George L. Knapp, *Brigham Young* (1913), good, friendly; Susa Y. Gates, *The Life Story of Brigham Young* (1930), by a daughter; Milton R. Hunter, *Brigham Young the Colonizer* (1940); Morris R. Werner, *Brigham Young* (1925), reads easily. Smith: Harry M. Beardsley, *Joseph Smith* (1931); Fawn M. Brodie, *No Man Knows My History* (1945), excellent; John H. Evans, *Joseph Smith* (1933), very sympathetic. Strang: Milo M. Quaife, *The Kingdom of St. James* (1930); Oscar W. Riegel, *Crown of Glory* (1935), reads well.

CHAPTER 27

FROM PRE-EMPTION
TO HOMESTEAD

T he troubles and excitement in Texas, California, Oregon, and
Utah during the 1840s and 1850s attracted so much attention
that there is danger of overlooking the more prosaic advance of
ambitious farmers occupying nearby agricultural land. Most westward-
moving migrants were of the traditional, fortune-seeking type. They pressed
along steadily, adding one area after another to the settled portions of the
country, but making no transcontinental treks, fighting no revolutions, and
establishing no new religious communities. The volume of this normal westward push increased rather than diminished during the stirring events in
the Southwest and on the Pacific Coast.

AGITATION FOR LAND-LAW CHANGES

Settlers who started farming in the 1840s and 1850s had the advantage of a new land law that was passed in 1841 as an effort to eliminate
the difficulties of the law of 1820. One objectionable feature of that law to
the Westerner was the auction system that forced the firstcomers to bid
against later arrivals who might have more money and at least push up
the price. The Westerner delivered stirring, emotional speeches about the
wealthy eastern speculator who could buy the land literally from under the
feet of the worthy western farmer who had been improving wild land as a
home for himself and his family. In sober fact the situation was frequently
different from this stereotype. Although some of the first arrivals in any
region were men who had no expectation other than of making a living by
farming, a great many others were speculators in at least the sense that
they claimed more land than they expected to use, and hoped to sell the sur-

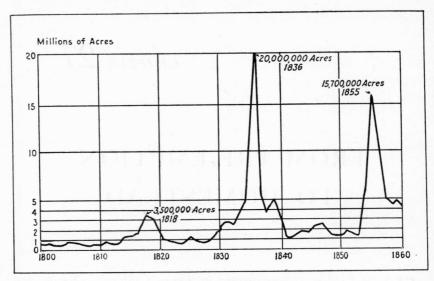

Land Sales, 1800–1860

plus to later arrivals. In other cases, however, the firstcomers never had any intention of farming, but expected to profit from selling their claims to farmers who came later. Westerners did not, then, object to speculation as such. They did object, however, to a system that might force land prices higher than they could pay, and that permitted a well-to-do and nonresident Easterner to bid land away from the man who had reached it first.

The West wrestled with the land situation both by appeals to Congress for new laws and by direct action. The direct action came through extralegal "claims associations" composed of farmers and speculators who had taken up land ahead of the auction and wanted to be sure to be able to purchase it at the minimum price when it was offered for sale. With the usual American passion for organization, each such group wrote a constitution, adopted bylaws, and elected officers. The most active officer was the secretary, who recorded the claims of the members.

When an auction was announced an interested association sent a bidder, usually the secretary, to act for all members. As each parcel was offered for sale the bidder consulted his little book of records; if the land were claimed by a member the agent bid the minimum of $1.25 an acre. Now and then some bumptious or uninformed outsider bid on a member's land, which meant bad luck for the outsider. Some night they might receive a forcible invitation to be the guest of honor at a ducking, a whipping, or a tar-and-feathers party. Competitive bidding was thereby discouraged. The association also settled conflicting claims between members, and failure to accept a committee award might bring the destruction of improvements or even physical harm to the noncooperator. The land association was one of the many organizations in the history of the frontier that solved problems immediately and effectively in the absence of regularly constituted authorities.

Westerners had no real desire to operate outside the law; hence they flooded Congress with a sea of petitions designed to obtain the kind of land legislation they preferred. Western agitation for land reform in the years after 1830 was particularly hopeful because of the political situation. The Presidents, starting with Jackson, were generally interested in western problems, Jackson and Harrison being identified with the West in the popular mind. Congress also tended to be responsive, particularly the Senate, many of whose members were from the new states.

The power of the West in Congress was further enhanced by a sectional split between Northeast and Southeast, which enabled the West in some cases to exercise the balance of power. Not that the West followed a consciously opportunistic policy; rather, it represented a third section of the country that might attain any particular goal by combining with either of the other two, or that might receive favors from supporting a measure in which either Northeast or Southeast was interested. On many issues the West itself was not united, but when it had a generally accepted program it had a reasonable chance of victory.

Congressional legislation concerning the public domain was delayed because land disposition was connected with those equally moot problems of tariff and federal aid to internal improvements; another reason for the delay was the difficulty of agreeing on any one proposal. From the welter of debate there emerged with some clarity the five possibilities of handling the disposition of land: cession, graduation, pre-emption, distribution, and an increase in prices. Most pleasing to the West was the idea of ceding the public lands to the states in which they lay. Senator Benton, as an influential Westerner, gave it his rapturous support, but practically all the East was opposed; South Carolina's John Calhoun once favored the plan in a desperate effort to gain western support for legislation he considered really important.

Next to outright cession, the West's favorite plan was graduation, which was Benton's pet. The idea of graduation was to reduce the price of unsold land year by year, and thus supposedly dispose of the poorer land to the less affluent purchasers. The East was unsympathetic since it visualized a progressive decline in federal revenue and an increased flow of industrial labor to the West. More moderate was the proposal for pre-emption, by which the bona fide settler could buy land at the minimum price before auction. The West liked the idea, but considered it at best a half loaf; the East was either noncommittal or tepidly favorable. Pre-emption, like some of the other proposals, could be combined with other plans.

A fourth proposal, sponsored by Henry Clay as part of his "American system," was to retain existing land laws but to distribute the proceeds of land sales to the various states according to population. The idea appealed to the Northeast because its population would entitle it to most of the money and because the whole plan included a high tariff. The Southeast opposed the idea on the same reasoning. The West was interested because it provided some money for internal improvements even though it did not involve any basic land reform. Distribution became law in 1836, but the plan came to an early death with the panic of 1837 (see Chapter 18).

Possibly most appealing to the Northeast was the idea of raising land prices or even stopping completely all land sales; the latter proposal, as suggested by Senator S. A. Foot of Connecticut, produced the Webster-Hayne debate, which did nothing to clarify the land situation. Although such a plan was appealing, it involved political suicide, for it would push the West into the arms of the Southeast; hence it was not pressed.

While Congress was debating a permanent land policy, pre-emption was actually going into effect slowly and unobtrusively. The federal government had long recognized the impossibility of ejecting thousands of squatters as the law indicated, or of forcing them to bid in actual competition for their farms. Consequently Congress accepted the situation, and in a series of laws beginning in 1830 gave the right of pre-emption to particular regions within definite time limits. The passage of a general pre-emption law seemed only a matter of time.

PRE-EMPTION

The land issue was revived in Harrison's Log Cabin and Hard Cider Campaign of 1840, during which the Whigs talked pre-emption in the West and distribution in the East. With the Whig victory a measure combining these two propositions was finally forced through Congress in a bitter fight that saw the votes cast almost entirely on party lines. Necessary to ensure its passage was an amendment providing that there would be no distribution if the tariff went over 20 percent; this provision was deadly poison to distribution since the tariff of 1842 proved to be well over 20 percent.

The law of 1841 has been known commonly as the Pre-emption Act. Its distribution feature provided that 10 percent of land proceeds go to the states in which the land lay, and that the remainder, minus administrative costs, be divided among the states according to the number of senators and representatives each had in Congress. In addition, 500,000 acres

were given to each of the public-land states. The pre-emption section provided that a man could settle on the public domain before it was surveyed.
When the land was surveyed and offered for sale, a settler, upon evidence
of having cultivated the land he claimed, could buy a maximum of 160
acres at the minimum price without auction, except that no man could
qualify for a pre-emption claim who thereby would own over 320 acres. A
settler was not prohibited from selling his claim immediately to another,
but an amendment of 1843 prohibited any man from making more than one
pre-emption claim.

The adoption of pre-emption was a landmark in the history of the
public domain, for it established the principle that an actual settler should
be given special privileges and consideration. Incidentally, Benton's idea of
graduation was adopted in 1854, but apparently with no considerable advantage to the small farmer. The West greeted pre-emption favorably, but
was by no means enthusiastic since Westerners felt that Congress deserved
little praise for a long-delayed act of simple justice. Agitation continued for
cheaper—preferably free—land, and also for larger and larger grants to
aid internal improvement. When the pressure became sufficiently great,
Congress acted.

MIGRATION AND NEW STATES

While Congress continued to debate further modifications of the
land laws, settlement moved steadily west. Migration had been large during
the 1830s and had produced the states of Arkansas and Michigan, and the
territories of Wisconsin and Iowa. It had declined with the panic of 1837
and then again increased during the 1840s. From 1840 through 1850 came
the states of Texas and California, and the territories of New Mexico,
Utah, and Oregon, as already described, as well as important developments
farther east.

One of the products of the migration of the 1840s was statehood
for Florida, although Florida represented a byway rather than a main
road. The area was not yet acclaimed for its citrus fruit or sunshine, and
few Americans felt any enthusiasm for the Florida swamps inhabited only
by hostile Seminole. Migration during the 1820s and 1830s had resulted in
many communities all the way from Apalachicola to Key West, the concentration being largely in the northern areas. A statehood movement produced a constitution in 1838 and the beginnings of a compromise capital
at Tallahassee the next year, but Congress was unsympathetic. Not until
1845 was Florida admitted to the Union, and then only to balance the
northern state of Iowa. The Florida population of 1850 was 87,445, and
was still concentrated almost entirely in the north and north central sections
of the state.

The main migration to the West during the 1840s and 1850s went to or near the fringe of the frontier. In the South, although there was movement to Mississippi and Louisiana, there was much more to Missouri, Arkansas, and Texas. Missouri increased over 75 percent during each decade, but Arkansas and Texas each increased over 100 percent in each decade. In spite of these impressive percentages the increase in the Southwest was less than that of the Northwest; this lag was accentuated during the 1860s, presumably because of slavery and the Civil War.

Part of the migration to the Northwest in the two decades after 1840 was to the older states of Illinois and Michigan, but the bulk was to the newer regions of Iowa, Wisconsin, and Minnesota. As usual, the peak of the migration came during prosperous times, in this case just prior to the panic of 1857. The new arrivals included an unusually large percentage of the foreign-born—notably Germans, particularly in Wisconsin, but also Norwegians, Swedes, Danes, Dutch, and others, mostly from northern and western Europe.

Iowa was the first of the new states of the upper Mississippi Valley after 1840. The first important white population had come after the Black Hawk War and had occupied the eastern fringe along the Mississippi, giving rise to the various river towns. Optimistic farmers started immediately to push farther west but there was little predictable pattern of settlement since the comparatively open plains suggested no obvious route or place of settlement. These pioneers had the usual frontier disregard for Indian landownership, especially since the Indians were by then impotent. Settling ahead of land surveys, they organized claims clubs to protect their holdings when the government finally caught up with settlement. The Indian cessions of 1837 and 1842 merely recognized existing white occupation. Early Iowa settlers grew considerable amounts of wheat, but the hog-corn economy so typical of later Iowa was evident as early as 1840.

In government the Iowa region had been attached successively to Michigan and Wisconsin; in 1838 it became a territory in its own right. At that time it included most of the present Minnesota and considerable parts of the Dakotas; its capital was Iowa City. Early talk of statehood was somewhat muted because of the increased costs involved. A constitutional convention finally met in 1844 and produced a constitution agreeable to the people of Iowa. Congress, however, refused to accept the boundaries that Iowa had drawn for herself with a lavish hand. A considerable wrangle over the boundary issue finally ended in a compromise and Iowa was admitted to the Union on December 28, 1846; eleven years later the capital was moved to Des Moines. Iowa's population growth was magnificent; the 43,000 of 1840 increased to 192,000 in 1850, and to 675,000 in 1860.

Wisconsin antedated Iowa in becoming a territory but attained

Population Density, 1850

45 AND OVER INHABITANTS PER SQUARE MILE

6-44 INHABITANTS PER SQUARE MILE

2-5 INHABITANTS PER SQUARE MILE

LESS THAN 2 INHABITANTS PER SQUARE MILE

MINNESOTA TERRITORY

WISCONSIN

IOWA

UNORGANIZED

OREGON TERRITORY

UTAH TERRITORY

CALIFORNIA

NEW MEXICO TERRITORY

TEXAS

Minneapolis

Milwaukee

Chicago

St. Louis

Kansas City

Bent's Fort

Santa Fe

Fort Hall

Salt Lake City

San Francisco

San Diego

Houston

New Orleans

United States, 1850

statehood later. Early arrivals tended to congregate in the mining districts of the south and in the lake towns of the southeast, but an ever-increasing number pushed north and west into the grain country, while a few hardy souls settled along the Mississippi and on the shores of Lake Superior. Vast reaches of the northern and western parts of the territory remained comparatively unpopulated for many years. The total growth of population was spectacular—from 30,000 in 1840 to over 300,000 in 1850; the next decade brought another increase of 150 percent.

Wisconsin was apparently less anxious for statehood than were some other areas, for it took no positive action until Congress passed an enabling act in 1846; among other factors, many Badgers were irritated by the fact that their territory had lost to Illinois and Michigan two important areas that should have been hers under the Ordinance of 1787. In time a constitutional convention was held and the results were ratified by the people. Wisconsin was admitted as a state on May 29, 1848, leaving the Minnesota area without a government, but this defect was remedied the next year by the creation of the territory of Minnesota.

By the time the new states and territories of the 1840s were joined by the products of the Compromise of 1850 the organized territories of the United States had assumed the appearance of a horseshoe. The eastern leg was formed by Minnesota, Iowa, Missouri, and Arkansas. The southern base comprised Texas and New Mexico. The western leg included California, Utah, and Oregon. White settlement, of course, was sparse in many areas, the Rio Grande and Salt Lake Valley settlements being the only important ones between Texas and California. The remainder of the trans-Mississippi West continued to be the hunting grounds of the Indians.

KANSAS AND NEBRASKA

The most trouble-provoking of the white advances of the 1850s was that into the present Kansas and Nebraska, particularly that into Kansas. The great bend of the Missouri had long been the springboard for travel to the Far West. Outfitting and distributing centers lined the river, and farmers began to occupy the country to the west. Theoretically this region was closed to the whites as Indian country but actually the Indians did not make an effective barrier. Advancing whites brought Indian treaties of cession, notably the treaty of 1854, which ceded all land between 37° and 42° 40′, or present Kansas and southern Nebraska.

The main troubles of Kansas and Nebraska were not disagreements between Indians and whites but between whites and other whites. Even before Kansas and Nebraska had enough settlers to disturb the coyotes they entered national politics. As early as 1844 Stephen A. Douglas of Illinois began his advocacy of the territorial organization of Kansas and

Nebraska to pave the way for a transcontinental railroad, and with an eye on the honey of public approval to satisfy the bee of presidential aspirations that was buzzing in his mind. His main obstacle was not the solemn promises of the government of permanent Indian possession of their lands, but the fight between North and South over slavery. The ultimate solution proposed by Douglas was "popular sovereignty," by which he meant the repeal of the Missouri Compromise, with permission to each new territory to decide for itself whether or not it wanted slavery. His plan ultimately was enacted in 1854. Kansas as then constituted stretched west to touch Utah. Nebraska included roughly the immense area between the Missouri River and the Rockies north of Kansas.

Early Kansas settlers were largely the ordinary frontier element coming from near at hand and engaged in the endless search for economic advancement. Predominating were swarms of speculators who utilized military land warrants, or bought Indian lands or railroad grants, frequently on credit, with the hope of selling their land profitably to real settlers. Quite naturally many of these early arrivals came from Missouri and combined proslavery sentiment with their land speculation. To offset these proslavery influences the zealous abolitionists of New England organized an Emigrant Aid Society, which subsidized abolitionist settlers, even to the extent of furnishing them rifles. The abolition center was Lawrence and the proslavery center Atchison. Curiously, the abolitionist belief in human rights did not as yet extend to the Indian. The main fight was in Kansas rather than in Nebraska because even the most ardent proslavery man could not imagine Nebraska as anything but free.

The political history of Kansas during the middle 1850s was a depressing story of fraud and violence. Elections were frequently controlled by parties of armed men stationed at the polls, and in at least one case there were twice as many votes as there were qualified voters. Successive elections might produce almost unanimous votes on opposite sides, depending on which party dominated the polling places and did the voting. A steady stream of governors tried to achieve some semblance of order, but their successes ranged from moderate to negligible. At one time two rival legislative groups had simultaneous meetings.

Most disturbing for the future was the increasing disorder and violence, with bands of armed men using the territory as a rendezvous and the slavery issue as a pretext for depredations redounding to their personal and immediate advantage. For a time the conflict was so widespread that it was labeled the "Wakarusa War." On May 21, 1856, a Missouri mob sacked the town of Lawrence, and a reprisal in the form of a free-state march toward Topeka was so alarming that the governor asked for federal troops. Among the least creditable episodes was the Pottawatomie massacre in which the mentally unbalanced John Brown and his four sons, on the plea that they were fighting for liberty, killed and mutilated five men and stole their horses (1856).

Ultimately statehood became the vital issue, and in 1857 a pro-slavery constitution was adopted at Lecompton; the free-state men were suspicious of the governor and hence abstained from voting either for delegates to the convention or on the ratification of the constitution. This constitution was submitted by Buchanan to Congress (1858) and accepted by the Senate, but amended by the House to require another popular vote. This vote rejected the constitution by a ratio of about 10 to 1. A new constitution was then prepared at Wyandotte, and Kansas was admitted as a free state in 1861. The population of Kansas by the census of the preceding year was 107,206.

Nebraska, the "twin" of Kansas, was not the occasion for similar trouble: even the most moral and conscientious New Englander saw no reason to rush to "save" a territory that would obviously be saved in any case. A few settlements along the Missouri River plus even fewer along the Platte comprised almost the entire population of the 1850s; the figure given by the census of 1860 was 28,841. Congressional leaders who desired a few extra votes obtained the passage of an enabling act in 1864, but Nebraska residents promptly rejected increased responsibilities and expenses. The legislature of 1866 received a new proposal for statehood unenthusiastically and passed it along to the electorate, of whom only some 8000 voted, with a favorable majority of a scant 100. A constitution was then formulated and accepted by Congress, only to meet the veto of President Johnson. Congress showed its current respect for the judgment of the President by passing the bill over his veto in 1867. By 1870 the population of Nebraska had reached 112,993.

MINNESOTA

Although the struggle over Kansas occupied the center of the stage during the 1850s, the growth of Minnesota actually involved greater numbers of persons. The early white settlement that centered at Fort Snelling, at the junction of the Mississippi and the Minnesota rivers, was very small, for as late as 1850 the federal census showed only 6000. As Wisconsin approached statehood Congress toyed with the idea of government for this handful of whites west of the Mississippi, but apparently any action was at least partially stymied by a difference of opinion as to the spelling of the word "Minnesota." At any rate, Minnesota was left without a government when Wisconsin was admitted. A convention met at Stillwater and sent H. H. Sibley to Congress to present a memorial asking for the provision of a government. Congress solved the problem of how to treat a representative of a territory that did not exist by paying him as a delegate of the defunct territory of Wisconsin. Minnesota became a territory in 1849, with boundaries that extended as far west as the Missouri River and with Alexander Ramsey as the first governor.

Almost all of Minnesota was Indian country until the big accession from the Sioux treaty of 1851. Other agreements followed, so that within the succeeding decade nine tenths of the present Minnesota were opened for settlement. In accordance with age-old frontier practice, the whites frequently took up land before the Indians had sold it. Theoretically the Indians were paid for their cessions, but the joker in the usual treaty was a provision that before any money would be paid to an Indian all traders' claims against him should be satisfied. The Indians were perpetually in debt and the traders kept the accounts, so there can be little wonder that very little treaty money ever reached Indian hands.

The rush to Minnesota in the 1850s was spectacular even for the American frontier. An unending procession of wagons poured into the territory, land being occupied much faster than it could be surveyed, and towns being planned hopefully at every promising location. St. Paul was the expanding metropolis, with the usual preponderance of land speculators, and with "gambling houses too numerous to mention." An actual count of the territory in 1857 showed 150,000 residents, an increase of 144,000 or 2400 percent in seven years. With the depression of 1857 the tide slackened somewhat, and the census of 1860 showed 172,000.

Minnesota attracted considerable numbers of foreign-born, particularly Danes, Swedes, and Norwegians, and, like Wisconsin before it, gave official encouragement to such settlers from abroad. But the great attractions, as always, were the wonders described by the older immigrants to their friends back home. Their letters spoke glowingly of the absence of social classes and of the higher pay. They also advanced the remarkable claims that the United States was practically free of crime, drinking, profanity, and Sabbath-breaking. Fabulous stories were told of common pastures with cows free for everyone to milk, of grass so high that it concealed all of the cattle but the horns, of freedom from taxes, and of rivers that ran syrup.

Minnesota had sufficient population by the middle 1850s to warrant statehood, but the inhabitants showed no interest in that status. They changed their minds when they realized that as a territory they could not borrow money to build railroads, but that as a state they could. Congress passed the necessary enabling act in 1857. A constitutional convention found the Democrats and Republicans so bitter toward each other that they held separate meetings, but they ultimately compromised by accepting the same constitution, which was then adopted by the people of the territory. In Congress the Southerners lost a fight to exclude a new northern state and Minnesota was admitted on May 11, 1858. Just as the admission of Wisconsin had left Minnesota dangling, so the admission of Minnesota left unorganized the region between the western boundary of the state and the Missouri River; finally it was included in Dakota Territory upon the latter's organization in 1861. By that year all of the West, with the exception of the present Oklahoma, had been divided into organized states and territories.

CHANGING INDIAN POLICY

The advancing white frontier, together with the vast increase of overland traffic, was the handwriting on the wall for the Indians and their "permanent frontier." The western Indians had already been compressed to make room for eastern tribes, and now they saw white farmers pouring into the country west of the Mississippi, while hundreds of white travelers crossed the plains to Santa Fe, Salt Lake City, California, and Oregon. They could feel no thrill of gratitude for a "permanent frontier" that presumably was established for their benefit but actually was enforced by the whites as a barrier only to the Indians, the whites being free to go wherever their fancy dictated. Quite understandable was an increasing sulkiness and resentment by the Indians, with more and more talk of making some final stand before they were completely annihilated.

The federal government had accepted honestly the idea of the permanent frontier, and had made real efforts to maintain it, but now troubles were increasing as "the Great American Desert" was proving to be far from a desert. Increased plains travel brought a desire to obtain a safe right of way to the Far West, which in turn meant a better control of the Plains Indians. Even more important, white farmers and miners were invading the Indian country, and the government was confronted by the practical difficulty and the political impossibility of excluding them. Possibly the Indians could be pushed back still further and ultimately be concentrated in some completely undesirable part of the country.

A change in the Indian policy of the federal government appeared during the early 1850s, when commissioners were sent to make new treaties with the western tribes. Sometimes additional land was acquired, but the usual treaty provided only for the right of white travelers to cross the Indian country and for the United States to mark and construct roads. Such treaties continued to be negotiated by the Indian Bureau, which from 1849 was a part of the Department of the Interior rather than of the War Department.

Several of these treaties of the early 1850s were of particular importance because they supplied the background of later disputes and war.

Among these agreements was one with the Sioux of Minnesota (1851) by which the Sioux made more land available to white settlers. The northern Plains Indians, including the Cheyenne, Arapaho, Sioux, Assiniboin, Arikara, Crows, Grosventres, and Shoshoni agreed (1851) to permit the United States to build, fortify, and use a road or roads across the plains, and not to molest travelers. The southern Plains Indians, particularly the Apache and Comanche, signed a similar agreement (1853).

These treaties made clear once more that the primary concern of the federal government was the protection of the whites, and that in any conflict between the two races Indian hopes and rights would take second place. In justice to the Indians it should be added that during the succeeding years they observed their treaty obligations scrupulously. The conflicts that occurred were due almost always to the whites, and particularly to their habit of regarding every Plains Indian as necessarily hostile.

GIFTS OF LAND BY CONGRESS

The same years that saw such important changes in the political map of the West witnessed an equally important revolution in the laws concerning the disposal of the public domain. Expanding settlement, meant new members of Congress who brought substantial backing for any number of ingenious plans as to how the federal government could give away its land in desirable ways. And the federal government, prodded by land-hungry Westerners and by speculators from all over the country, was but mildly reluctant to accede to such demands, for here was an easy type of bounty that might be used to lure votes without increasing taxes. Best of all was the argument that the wealth and prosperity of the country were thereby enhanced.

One class of the population favored by the government was the soldiers, for Congress was both thankful for the services of our brave defenders and mindful of their votes. The soldiers of each major war were given land warrants, and in 1850 a general act included Indian wars, so that practically any former soldier could obtain his 160 acres free. Then various near-soldiers, including teamsters and chaplains, were added (1855), and finally the navy was included (1857). In the early years specific land had been set aside to satisfy these claims—first in Ohio, and then in Michigan, Illinois, and other areas; eventually (1842) the claims could be located anywhere.

Military warrants provided the recurring basis for a tremendous amount of speculation, even though prior to the law of 1852 they could not be legally transferred; but they were sold always freely and in large amounts. Their price varied with time and place, the common price of 1857 being about 60 cents an acre. One expert has estimated that not over one in five hundred of the warrants was actually located by the soldier or his heir. No new grants were made after 1855 because at the time of the next major war land was free to everyone, but soldiers were given special privileges, such as the ability to homestead 160 acres of the alternate sections of railroad grants, as compared with the 80 acres available to other people, and a shorter term of cultivation before final title.

Education was likewise the occasion for munificent grants. Starting with Ohio the states received gifts of land to aid all kinds of education, from primary school through college, although with limitations on its disposal. Aid to higher education was at first sporadic, but was regularized in the Morrill Act of 1862; each state received land in proportion to its representation in Congress, with a maximum of 1 million acres, the proceeds to be used to establish and support agricultural and mechanical colleges. Direct money aid began in 1890.

Internal improvements, particularly roads, canals, and railroads, were a third occasion for lavish gifts of land. Grants for specific improvements really became imposing after the Illinois Central grant of 1850 opened the way for large-scale giving. In addition to specifically designated gifts, certain other donations were expected to be used largely for public improvements. The Pre-emption Act gave half a million acres to each public-land state. The Swamp Land Act of 1850 gave outright to each state the swamp land within its borders, and reputedly much land looked swampy to state authorities for the first time; some 80 million acres were transferred under the terms of this act.

These and other magnificent gifts of the land heritage of the United States were justified publicly as advancing the nation's prosperity, but cynical commentators have long noted that speculators were active in the passage of the laws, harvested a considerable share of the land, and pocketed a goodly portion of the resulting profits. The results of the work of early speculators such as John Cleves Symmes are well known. Quite clearly the military warrants were used primarily for speculation, and there seems little doubt that Benton's graduation measure was of greatest importance to speculators collecting large tracts. Railroad grants were at times manipulated to the disadvantage of actual settlers. Educational grants received notoriously bad handling and soon appeared in private hands with little revenue to the state or the schools. Swamp lands were no better, since they also gravitated rapidly to the speculators, with little revenue to the state and no reclamation of the supposed swamps. All these gifts were at least disappointing, either in getting land to actual settlers or in providing revenue for public improvements. Whether they were dictated by the speculators or merely used by these gentlemen for their own advantage remains a subject for investigation, but the ultimate results are unquestioned.

THE HOMESTEAD ACT

The various grants, no matter how munificent, did not satisfy the West. What the West desired was free land for settlers, and this proposition it kept before Congress almost continuously throughout the 1850s. The often repeated arguments in its favor were that such a measure would encourage the development of the United States by making it possible for every ambitious American to acquire a farm of his own, and that the increasing prosperity and resulting taxes would more than compensate for any immediate loss of revenue from land sales. As time passed, free land seemed to become a natural right to which each American was entitled by the mere fact of being alive.

Western ambitions came closer and closer to realization as eastern conditions changed. Increased immigration was taking care of the northern need for industrial labor and Irish immigrants were more tractable than New England farm boys. The frontier was becoming so remote in distance that it drew but little from the eastern seaboard; the new frontier of the 1850s drew more from the farms of the Mississippi Valley than from those of the East. Eastern manufacturers were at the point of desiring markets even more than labor, and the expanding West meant a vastly increased market.

The demand for free land was buttressed by the arguments of a growing eastern labor and reform movement. Led by such men as Horace Greeley, numerous articulate minorities insisted that free land was one of the essentials for a rich and contented democracy. They not only extolled the general advantages of an expanding population, but argued that free land provided an outlet for the restless, the ambitious, the oppressed of the East. If industrialists offered low wages and bad working conditions, their employees could escape to the opportunities of the West. This argument was not justified, at least in short-run terms, but it appealed to many.

Various homestead bills, designed to assure free or at least very cheap land, were considered by Congress during the 1850s. Ultimately one of them passed both houses in 1860, only to be vetoed by Buchanan, who sympathized with the southern opposition. During the same year the Republicans linked free land with a high tariff to appeal to both East and West, and with the Republican victory free land was assured.

President Lincoln finally signed in 1862 the Homestead Act, which provided 160 acres of free land from the public domain to each American adult or head of a family who was a citizen or had declared his intention of becoming one; the only cost was a small fee of $10. The one important qualification was that each settler had to prove five years of continuous residence and cultivation before receiving final title. After six months of residence he had the option of commuting his claim and obtaining immediate ownership upon the payment of $1.25 an acre. Although these provisions were modified slightly in the succeeding years, the law remained the basic feature of the American land system. It superseded but did not eliminate the Pre-emption Act, which was not repealed until 1891.

The Homestead Act was the best advertised of many laws that threw the public domain open to land-hungry Americans more freely than had ever been done in the past. Although homesteading has been traditionally conceived as the most important method used in acquiring land after 1862, it actually was not (see Chapter 36). Regardless of the method, however, the next generation saw the great bulk of agricultural land that did not require irrigation transferred to private hands. The rapidity of the process exceeded anything that had gone before: the second half of the continent was occupied, even though sparsely in many spots, in a tenth of the time that the first half had taken. Inevitably there was much selfish grabbing, fraud, and waste. Whether a more deliberate process would in the long run have brought more desirable conclusions is one of the historical questions that can never be answered finally.

READINGS

LAND LEGISLATION. Roy M. Robbins, *Our Landed Heritage* (1942) is best, but Benjamin H. Hibbard, *A History of the Public Land Policies* (1924) is satisfactory. Two special studies are Raynor C. Wellington, *The Political and Sectional Influence of the Public Lands, 1828–1842* (1914) and George M. Stephenson, *The Political History of the Public Lands, from 1840 to 1862* (1917).

INDIVIDUAL STATES. Wisconsin: See the Readings for Chapter 17 under Raney, Still, Austin, Schafer; Merle E. Curti, *The Making of an American Community* (1959), illuminating; Theodore C. Blegen (ed.), *Frontier Parsonage* (1947), the 1850s; Clarence A. Clausen and Andreas Elviken (eds.), *A Chronicle of Old Muskego* (1951), diary. Minnesota: Theodore C. Blegen, *Minnesota* (1963), very good, *The Land Lies Open* (1949), *Grass Roots History* (1947), immigration, *Norwegian Migration to America, 1825–1860* (1931), *Norwegian Immigration* (1940); Theodore C. Blegen and Philip D. Jordan, *With Various Voices* (1949); Grace L. Nute, *Lake Superior* (1944), *Rain River Country* (1950), very good; Mary W. Berthel, *Horns of Thunder* (1948), St. Paul; Margaret I. Snyder, *The Chosen Valley* (1948), interesting; Arthur J. Larsen (ed.), *Crusader and Feminist* (1934), Jane Swisshelm; Merrill E. Jarchow, *The Earth Brought Forth* (1949), agriculture. Iowa: William J. Peterson, *Iowa* (1941); Irving B. Richman, *Ioway to Iowa* (1931); Cyrenus Cole, *Iowa Through the Years* (1940); Roscoe L.

Lokken, *Iowa Public Land Disposal* (1942), factual; *A Century of Farming in Iowa* (1946), good; Thomas H. McBride, *In Cabins and Sod Houses* (1928). Florida: Caroline M. Brevard, *A History of Florida* (2 vols., 1924–1925); Sidney W. Martin, *Florida During Territorial Days* (1944); Dorothy Dodd (ed.), *Florida Becomes a State* (1945), documents. Kansas: General histories are James C. Olson, *History of Nebraska* (1955), good, William F. Zornow, *Kansas* (1957), clear and factual; William E. Connelley, *History of Kansas* (5 vols., 1928); Samuel A. Johnson, *The Battle Cry of Freedom* (1954), good on the Emigrant Aid Company; Paul W. Gates, *Fifty Million Acres* (1954), scholarly; James C. Malin, *John Brown and the Legend of Fifty-Six* (1942), voluminous, and *The Nebraska Question, 1852–1854* (1953); Louis Howland, *Stephen A. Douglas* (1920); Allen Johnson, *Stephen A. Douglas* (1908).

SPECIAL TOPICS. Lewis E. Atherton, *Main Street on the Middle Border* (1954) and *The Pioneer Merchant* (1939) concern retail trade. Wyatt W. Belcher, *The Economic Rivalry Between St. Louis and Chicago, 1850–1880* (1947), a fine study; Stewart H. Holbrook, *The Yankee Exodus* (1950), New England migration; Carlton C. Qualey, *Norwegian Settlement* (1938).

CHAPTER 28

FORTY-NINERS
AND FIFTY-NINERS

Prospectors and miners have always been among the advance guard of the white frontier. The searcher for mineral wealth has never been overawed by wild aborigines or by the wilderness, including mountains and deserts. The lure of great riches has obscured dangers that otherwise might have seemed insuperable. It was white miners who precipitated the removal of the southern Indians and who played a big part in the Black Hawk War.

The most exciting metal pursued by the white man was gold, whether in the Indian country of Georgia or in the snowy wastes of the Yukon. Gold has large value in small bulk and has been the standard by which other values have been measured; even more important, it can be found uncombined in nature and hence prospecting for it presents an opportunity to even the poorest person. The ambitious drugstore clerk, the unemployed carpenter, or the dispossessed farmer has at least a chance for the lucky strike that will make him wealthy for life.

IRON AND COPPER

Although gold is fascinating, iron and copper are actually more important for a high-speed industrial civilization. Discoveries of large amounts of these metals came during the 1840s. Most significant for the future were the findings in 1844 by William A. Burt of the Lake Superior iron deposits. By the end of the decade this ore had been carried to Pennsylvania to be married to Pennsylvania coal; the offsprings of this union were to be important elements in the growth of American civilization. Large-scale operations did not come, however, until the 1880s.

423

The practical working of the Lake Superior copper mines dates from 1846, although the existence of copper in the region had long been known and some of it had been extracted earlier. Metal worth millions was removed before the Civil War, for the mines were of almost incredible richness. One miner in 1857 found a single lump of ore that weighed 420 tons and yielded 75 percent of refined copper. The famous Calumet & Hecla Consolidated Mining Company, formed in 1871 by the merger of companies that had started work in the 1860s, by 1930 had produced over 3 million pounds of copper and had paid dividends of over $170 million. Operations of this kind, of course, needed considerable capital, and a list of the stockholders of the Calumet & Hecla was full of the socially and financially elite of Boston.

CALIFORNIA GOLD RUSH

Mineral discoveries in Michigan and Minnesota were soon overshadowed by the most dramatic and best-advertised mining boom in American history. The detonating spark came on January 24, 1848, when James W. Marshall found traces of gold in the tailrace of a mill he was erecting for John A. Sutter on the south fork of the American River. Sutter tried to keep the discovery a secret, with prescience as to the effects it would have on himself and on the agricultural empire he had built in the Sacramento Valley. But very soon the cry of "gold" was heard on the streets of San Francisco, with samples of the finds passed from hand to hand. Soon there was wild enthusiasm all along the coast and even overseas in Hawaii. A mad rush for quick and easy wealth led sailors to desert their ships, cattle tenders to leave their herds, farmers to abandon their plows in the fields, and merchants to close their stores. Overland travelers who heard the news were deflected from Oregon to California.

The gold fever infected the East late in the year—even the President mentioned it in a message to Congress—and thousands of young men planned to leave their current occupations, which now seemed humdrum, to seek the new El Dorado. Stores featured mining supplies that ranged from picks and shovels to Spanish grammars. Frémont's reports received renewed circulation as travel guides. Potential miners swaggered down the streets in hip boots and talked grandly of placers, fandangos, pound nuggets, and Spanish beauties. Their expectation—seldom realized—was that a few months of mining would produce sufficient wealth for an eastern palace, blooded horses, and a trip to Europe.

Hopeful gold seekers streamed west during 1849, sometimes individually, but also frequently as groups elaborately organized under such names as "Ophir" or the "California Mining Company." The organized group came usually from New England, and was based on equal contributions

Mining Centers

and equal profits; once the group reached California the plan for common work and the division of profits was usually abandoned. With typical Puritan zeal and morality, each company had a full complement of officers and strict rules concerning such matters as swearing and Sabbath-breaking; unfortunately these moral rules tended to lose force as Boston receded in the distance. The association was so popular that Eliza W. B. Farnham, who later became well known as a feminist, planned one for 130 women. The Farnham plan failed, and it must be admitted that, aside from the wives who accompanied their husbands, most of the California-bound women in the early days were anything but fitting companions for God-fearing New England boys.

Many of the eastern migrants went to California by water. If by way of the Horn, the tedious six months' trip, with its monotonous diet of salt meat and hard bread, tended to fray the tempers of all but the least impatient of the young men. Even assiduous Bible reading, religious services, and long hours communing with a diary did little to alleviate the monotony. Reading, games, and music were possible occupations, and ingenious minds spent countless hours inventing variations of popular songs:

> Oh! California,
> That's the land for me,
> I'm going to Sacramento
> With my washbowl on my knee.

The sea route could be made shorter but even more uncomfortable by crossing the Isthmus of Panama by land. The Pacific Mail Steamship Company had established water connections on both sides of the isthmus just before the gold rush, but accommodations were never adequate: the ships were overcrowded and dirty, and the food was poor. Travel across the isthmus was difficult, dirty, costly, and dangerous to health, for cholera, dysentery, and yellow fever were rampant. The coast cities of Panama and Colón were so filthy that most miners rejected their dubious hospitality in favor of camping. Conditions were somewhat improved early in 1855, with the completion of a railroad across the isthmus. Nevertheless, some travelers chose the longer route through Nicaragua because of the overcrowding of Panama.

The majority of the Argonauts went to California overland, which was both shorter and cheaper. A variety of routes passed through Mexico or the southern United States. Mexican routes were poor choices, partly because Mexicans remembered very vividly their recent unpleasant experiences with the United States. Various Texas routes generally combined at El Paso and continued by way of the Gila River. Farther north other routes joined at Santa Fe, from which place the traveler might either swing south or follow the old Spanish trail.

The most popular overland route to the mines was the well-known Platte River Trail, which probably saw more traffic than all other routes combined. Amateur travelers often suffered severely on the trip: the trail was marked by dead animals, jettisoned supplies, discarded furniture, and the graves of the weak, the improvident, and the unlucky. West of the Rockies there were several alternatives. Most migrants followed the Humboldt River, which they usually reached by way of either Fort Hall or Salt Lake; from the Humboldt there were several possible choices, all poor, for crossing the Sierra Nevada Mountains. Some of the travelers swung southwest from Salt Lake to Los Angeles, but a few of them made the sad mistake of taking the unpleasant and very dangerous route through Death Valley.

The great metropolis of the gold country was San Francisco "the boisterous," the center of all sea traffic as well as the business of the mines. Here the prospective miner waded through seas of mud or drifts of dust, garbage, and filth. Saloons, gambling halls, and brothels in profusion welcomed the convivial, and normal moral values seemed lost. As one traveler reported, "virtue plodded through the streets bearing burdens, while prostitutes, lauded and caressed, became the leading conservators of social life, fanning its ephemeral brightness by a magnificent display of their presence and deceitful smiles." A quarter was the smallest coin in circulation; gold dust was the more usual medium of exchange. Prices left the Easterner aghast: he paid $10 to $20 a week for a bug-infested bunk in a tent or $250 a month for a room to himself.

A San Francisco filled with the foot-loose, not only from the United States but from all over the world, with the riffraff of four continents from Valparaíso to Hong Kong, and with extraordinary amounts of loose gold, was bound to be rough and rowdy. Between 1849 and 1856 there were a thousand homicides, not to mention less spectacular crimes. Regular police were ineffective, so committees of citizens took over control of crime. A vigilance committee of 1849 soon "reformed" itself into a particularly vicious criminal gang; its successor of 1851 worked four years before it could claim the suppression of even the most violent and lawless.

GOLD MINING

The center of the gold fields was the scene of the first discoveries, but from this point the miners spread in every direction with incurable optimism. Mining camps were established and died with bewildering rapidity. Dozens of camps such as Poker Flat, Slumgullion, Delirium Tremens, and Hell-out-for-noon-City had their brief days.

> Once more on Hangtown's hills we delve,
> On Murderer's Bar we mine,
> At Nigger's Tent and Boston Jim's,
> You Bet, Red Dog, Port Wine.

The early miners were seeking uncombined gold either as nuggets to be pried out of the rocks or as fine particles to be washed from the beds of streams. Simplest of the methods of obtaining the smaller grains of gold was to rock a pan containing the gold, mud, sand, and water until only the gold and sand were left, and then fan off the sand. Early improvements merely increased the size of operations: a large cleated box replaced the pan, possibly a sluice provided the water, and mercury caught the gold. Such an operation required two men, and there was a tendency to develop group operations, even to the extent of damming a river so that the gold might be collected from its bed. Hydraulic mining was used as early as 1852, but no basic change in the processes was involved.

Crude mining methods were profitable only when gold was very plentiful. The output of 1849 was about $10 million; it rose to a peak of over $80 million in 1852. Although stories were common of miners making

$1000 or more a day, the average miner in the early days was fortunate to collect as much as an ounce ($16) a day; a little later $2 a day was more likely. Such a return could hardly be considered a fortune or even a decent living in terms of existing California prices. The real profiteers were the real-estate men, the merchants, and the gamblers. As soon as easily worked deposits were exhausted in a particular area the bulk of the miners left for more promising fields and the mining was taken over by companies that used stamp mills to crush the ore and mercury to extract the gold; even these processes were not particularly efficient.

LIFE OF THE MINERS

Save for the glamorous excitement of finding gold, the life of the miner was arduous, drab, unpleasant, and monotonous. He lived in a crude tent or cabin, sat on a cracker box, darned his own socks, and ate a heavy, monotonous succession of simple meals he prepared from poor but expensive ingredients. Washing of either person or clothes was frequently neglected. Working most of the time in the cold water rushing down from the Sierras, eating an unbalanced diet, and being without doctors, miners had a high morbidity rate.

Since sheriffs did not keep pace with the mining camps, the miners had to provide and enforce their own laws. Simple rules were soon adopted for the making and holding of claims; in 1866 these rules were written into the laws of the United States. Minority groups were given little consideration: the Indians were killed, the Mexicans were usually driven out, and the Chinese were permitted to work only claims abandoned by the whites. Crime was rare in the early days, but increased rapidly as the scourings of the world poured into California. The usual camp then organized its own law enforcement in the form of a vigilance committee that used the primitive punishments of whipping, exile, or death; jails were not available. Such a system frequently involved some sort of jury trial but still remained haphazard and not entirely just. The one thing that can be said for it was that it provided at least a moderate amount of order in an otherwise completely lawless community.

The recreation of the miners was necessarily circumscribed and tended toward the rough and crude. The absence of women was particularly deplored; there were stories that men would walk miles to see a homely, white-haired grandmother, or even to see her clothes hanging on the line. The thousands of prostitutes coming to California not only from the East but from South America, Europe, and Asia, tended to concentrate in the larger towns; some of the smaller mining camps actually drove them out. The favorite place of entertainment for the miners was naturally the saloon, where men not only could drink themselves into a transient delusion of success, but could chance their earnings on roulette, faro, or poker, or sometimes dance with the hurdy-gurdy girls (ordinarily not prostitutes) provided by the house. Drinking and gambling were connected inseparably with mining life, even for the men who had resolved to keep the highest moral standards when they left home.

Wherever miners gathered there were songs to the accompaniment of fiddle or flute, or even to beatings on tin cans and dishpans. Inevitable were such old and nostalgic favorites as "The Last Rose of Summer," but there were also innumerable varieties, some not fit for polite ears, of such current favorites as "Joe Bowers from Pike":

> My name is Joe Bowers,
> I have a brother Ike;
> I come from ol' Missouri—
> Come all the way from Pike.

The usual version told a story of Joe kissing his girl good-by; whereupon she immediately married the red-haired butcher and had a redheaded baby.

The influx of miners strengthened the statehood movement, which had been active from the end of the Mexican War (see Chapter 25). For a time a military governor headed a semicivil government, but then a constitutional convention was called; it was composed mainly of nonminers. A state government was put into operation, and was legalized by Congress in the compromise of 1850, when California was admitted to the Union as a state.

Hordes of hungry men prospecting for gold brought a tremendous demand for food of all kinds. Native cattle- and sheepmen who hitherto had had difficulty in obtaining sufficient funds to buy the gold braid for their jackets suddenly found themselves rolling in wealth. This new wealth unfortunately proved only temporary. The expansion of the eastern agricultural frontier and improved transportation made the California market more competitive, while bad times on the coast, and particularly the drought of 1863–1864, sadly depleted the herds. But although the cattle boom was temporary, the expansion of agricultural crops proved permanent. Wheat production increased spectacularly through the 1850s, with the utilization of such laborsaving machinery as the McCormick reaper, while the magnificently diversified California climate made possible an unusually wide variety of other crops.

The mining industry, even though it declined both relatively and absolutely during the late 1850s, left a permanent mark on San Francisco, which was the natural metropolis for shipping and finance, and which, as other booms developed, provided the main transportation and banking facilities. San Francisco remained for many years not only the feverish center of the highly speculative trading in mining stocks, but the most important commercial center of the coast and the source of the financing of much of the commercial enterprise of the Far West.

LATER GOLD RUSHES

The decline of California gold production, and particularly of the placer variety, meant that the state had a large and exportable surplus of miners. Some of them returned to the East, others turned to ranching and farming, but many were held captive by the lure of the golden metal and followed that elusive magnet to other promising regions. California gold had been found in the streams, and the natural deduction was that it might be found in other streams in other places or in the mountainous areas from which the water had originated. Here were two possibilities that many men felt to be worth investigation.

As prospectors spread through the West there came rumors of rich finds here, there, and the other place. All the way from New Mexico to Washington, and even from far-off Alaska came fascinating tales of rich and easily available deposits. Foot-loose miners rushed from one reported find to the next, with only a small portion either becoming rich and retiring, or staying permanently in the new community. Gold prospecting was a will-o'-the-wisp that nearly always promised more than it paid. One of the results was a scattering of ghost towns that had once been teeming with boisterous miners intent upon the search for quick wealth.

As might have been expected, the first new finds came in the immediate vicinity of California. Wandering prospectors had discovered traces of gold in the present Nevada as early as 1849, and a few of them had been willing to forgo the reported riches of California for the seemingly meager supply of Nevada gold. The peak of the early placer mining in 1855 showed production of only a little over $110,000. A few miners recognized the existence of silver, but it was less valuable, and in any case for the moment was beyond the reach of the individual miner with his scant equipment and lack of capital. Gold remained king.

Rumor had long indicated rich mines to the south, in New Mexico and Arizona, but the actuality of the 1850s seemed disappointing. Most of the deposits were copper and silver, which were difficult metals to exploit at that time. Of the scattering of gold finds reported, the most important were on the Colorado near the mouth of the Gila, and in the region from Tucson to the south, including particularly Tubac. Tucson became the best known of the mining communities, attaining the title of "paradise of devils," which was a description not won lightly in the mining West of the 1850s; it was reported that in 1860 only two of the residents of the Tucson cemetery had reached there through natural causes. The Apache ravaged this area, and permanent development came only after the Civil War.

To the north the most important find was at Colville, which was a Hudson's Bay Company post near the international boundary in the present northeast Washington. The resulting rush of 1855 was disappointing in its results and was expiring when there came news of easily available wealth on the Fraser River in Canada, with a resulting stampede in 1858. A succession of later finds in the Far North culminated forty years later in the spectacular and well-known Yukon rush.

Many miners had hopes for the northern American Rockies, particularly along the Columbia, the Snake, and their tributaries. Their search in this region was aided by the construction by the federal government of a road from the East across the mountains from Fort Benton by way of Mullan Pass to the Columbia River. Built between 1859 and 1863 at a cost of $230,000, this road made more accessible the entire area of the northern Rockies.

A succession of booms in the region of the Snake River started with gold discoveries on the Clearwater in 1860 and the establishment of Lewiston, Oro Fino, and Pierce City. The miners naturally disregarded the fact that this country had been guaranteed to the Nez Percé Indians, and considerable trouble resulted later for the federal government. Following the Clearwater boom came a mad rush to the Salmon River (1861). One result of these booms was that the territory of Idaho (including present Montana and Wyoming) was created in 1863 to provide a government for the district.

Pushing east over the Bitter Root Mountains, the miners started a succession of booms in the Montana region. The existence of gold in this part of the country had long been known by the trappers, who were uninterested in the information; throughout the 1850s the only mining had been on a desultory and unimpressive scale. The first important mining was done in 1862 by James and Granville Stuart; later years saw successive waves of mining enthusiasm break over the soil of Montana.

Three general regions of Montana, fairly close together, attracted the majority of interest. The Stuart discoveries were in the vicinity of Bannack City. Next came the Alder Gulch and Virginia City region, which was opened in 1863. Finally, in 1864, came Last Chance Gulch, later given the more melodious name of Helena. The population that poured into these three districts again made necessary a rearrangement of western territory for governmental purposes, since the government of Idaho could not care adequately for people living across the mountains near the headwaters of the Missouri. Montana, with its present boundaries, was made a territory in 1864; at the same time the unwanted region, later to become Wyoming, was given back to Dakota.

COLORADO

The northern and southern gold rushes were cast into obscurity by developments in the central region. In present Colorado gold had long been known to exist, but discoveries of 1858 provided the shock that started an avalanche of hopeful miners toward the land of Pike's Peak. The first arrivals tended to collect in two main centers. The first was El Paso, near the present Colorado Springs. The second was at the junction of Cherry Creek with the South Platte, where the small villages of Montana, Auraria, Highland, and St. Charles soon coalesced to form Denver City.

The news of gold deposits near Pike's Peak was welcomed enthusiastically in the East. The panic of 1857 had produced thousands of men who were anxious to try new methods of bettering their fortunes if only too much capital was not needed, and the new gold discoveries were much more accessible than previous ones. The result was a vast trek of fortune-hunting prospective miners in 1859. Estimates have it that some 100,000 crossed Nebraska during that year. The newcomers were gambling with fortune and their frame of mind was expressed by their now-familiar slogan: "Pike's Peak or Bust!" In spite of the relatively short distance to Colorado, the roads were soon lined with mute evidence of mistaken zeal, of insufficient knowledge, and of mistakes in judgment.

The Colorado mining boom produced a whole series of new towns, such as Golden, Boulder, Black Hawk, Central City, Idaho Springs, and Georgetown; the metropolis remained Denver, which could boast the *Rocky Mountain News* as early as 1859, and which had its youthful cockiness enhanced by such distinguished visitors as Horace Greeley and Henry Villard. Government was a difficult problem in which Congress was not helpful. Big talk of statehood ultimately simmered down to the creation of the territory of Jefferson in 1859, without the blessing of Congress. The congressional debates on this self-invited, boisterous newcomer were confused and made sterile by the slavery issue, so that it was not until 1861 that the territory of Colorado came into existence, its boundaries approximately those of the present state. The Colorado placer boom proved of short duration, since the comparatively small quantity of free gold could not satisfy a horde of inexperienced miners. The quartz rock was rich in minerals of all kinds, but their extraction required expensive machinery. Many of the newcomers soon followed the lure of gold to other parts of the West. Others settled down to the safer and more prosaic business of farming or raising stock. Still others were completely disillusioned and returned to the East, their wagons bearing the significant phrase: "Busted, by gosh!"

A collapsed placer mining boom left Colorado in economic doldrums; population actually declined during the 1860s. Late in that decade, however, with the coming of the railroad (1870), better transportation gave renewed hope. Farmers began arriving in large numbers, including such organized group migrations that produced Greeley, Longmont, Evans, and Green City. More people brought greater prosperity, and again there was a renewal of interest in statehood. Colorado was admitted to the Union in 1876 as the centennial state.

NEVADA

The height of the Colorado boom coincided with the discovery of what was probably the richest ore-bearing region of the United States—the Comstock Lode of Nevada. The name came not from the discoverer but from one of the early claimants, Henry T. P. Comstock, who had the nick-name of "Old Pancake" because he was too lazy to bake bread, and who obtained his claim through fast talk, a blind horse, and a bottle of whiskey. He thought so little of his property that he sold his claim within two months for $10,000. Although Comstock threw away millions by this sale he was not in fact acting stupidly; up to this time all Nevada mining had been of the placer variety and there was no way of knowing that a vast store of wealth lay a few feet underground. But by late 1859 it was dis-covered that a sample of the "blue stuff" (quartz), hitherto discarded as worthless, assayed at $1595 in gold and $4791 in silver per ton. A new era had opened.

The first big rush to Nevada came from California late in 1859 as thousands of young and old, feeble and strong, men and women, trudged over the High Sierras to the new El Dorado. Over 20,000 people arrived within a few months, with population centers taking form at Virginia City and Carson City. For the first time people had become silver crazy: the golden sun was sinking and the silver moon was rising.

The search for silver posed many new and perplexing problems. Everyone knew that silver could be found in quartz rock, but not all quartz contained silver. Furthermore, quartz ledges ran in seams that were not uniform in size or quality; rich surface indications might disappear a little farther down the seam, or a poor seam might develop rich ore under the surface. The result was that the miners dug exploratory shafts all over the countryside. Enthusiastic miners might even start digging in the street of a town or under a house: in the search for quick wealth no land was sacred.

Extensive prospecting by hit-or-miss methods produced much waste and wild fluctuations in the prices of claims. Hundreds of abandoned shafts were mute evidence of the days, weeks, months of wasted labor. Mining claims, as represented by their stock, were subject to vigorous speculation, for they were sold and traded freely, or even given to friends. Every man could show a varied assortment of from ten to a hundred different kinds of mining stock of various potentialities. The prices of these securities fluctuated with tremendous leaps as rumors passed from person to person. The shares of the Alpha mine, for example, which sold for $1570 in February 1868 could find but few buyers at $33 in September of the same year.

The process of quartz mining that was typical of Nevada was entirely different from the earlier gold operations in California. The miner might work for a large company, which meant that he had $4 a day fairly regularly. If he did prospecting on his own he might be outfitted on credit —possibly for half of his returns. His search was entirely different from that of his predecessor, who merely looked for free deposits of gold, and he might take months and cover hundreds of miles. Whenever he saw quartz that seemed promising he examined it with a magnifying glass for possible specks of uncombined gold and silver. If this examination were satisfactory he pulverized a specimen, washed the light matter away and dissolved the rest in nitric acid, which precipitated chloride of silver. This was dried and then heated with a little soda in a hollowed piece of charcoal by the flame of a candle. The result was a button of pure silver that showed in a rough way the richness of the original specimen. Sometimes, instead of using this method, the prospector only collected samples and carried them back to experts for assaying. In any case, if the prospects were good a claim was marked and work started; if not—and this situation was more usual—the prospecting expedition was continued.

The individual miner was highly dependent on the big company if he were to make money, for the treatment of quartz on a sufficient scale to be profitable required large amounts of capital to obtain the necessary machinery. Consequently he either sold his claims to the large company or dug the quartz and then took it to the large company for smelting; in the latter case he frequently paid what he considered an unreasonable price for the service.

A few of the Nevada mines were fabulously productive. The Gould and Curry mine took out $9 million of ore in the two years 1863 and 1864; the original investment in land, buildings, and machinery had been $200,-000, and the dividends were a handsome $2.9 million. The Ophir mine extracted $15 million of metal, but returned only $1.4 million in dividends. In the period 1859–1880 the total cost of operating all Nevada mines has been estimated as $62 million; the extracted bullion had a value of $306 million, and the declared dividends were $118 million. In considering these figures, however, one should remember that for each successful individual or company there were dozens who lost everything.

Outstanding success for an individual miner might be a sign of diligence and intelligence, but was just as likely to be the result of very good luck. Prospecting was often a matter of almost pure chance. Often the miner traded stock in his own rather dubious potential mine for other attractive speculations such as "Root Hog or Die," "Dry Up," "Grizzly Hill," "Wake Up Jake," "Let Her Rip," "You Bet," or "Gouge Eye." If one of these ventures turned out to be rich he dug down into his collection of securities until he unearthed the right one, and then cashed in on his good fortune.

Miners who made their fortunes from lucky strikes were notoriously easy to separate from their money. "Sandy" Bowers furnished an excellent example. Bowers was an ordinary miner, married to a washerwoman, when he made a rich strike that netted him more money that he had ever imagined existed in the world. Immediately he built a house costing $407,000, and entertained lavishly. Then he spent three years in Europe, during which time he bought almost everything except the Tower of London. Upon his return to Virginia City he hired a hotel and held open house for the entire town. When the mine's ore was finally exhausted (about 1868) Bowers was penniless and went back to prospecting while his wife told fortunes.

The rich strike was unusual, and for most miners life in Nevada had the characteristics of every mining rush. The men worked hard, lived poorly, and kept up their hopes by exciting amusements and the anticipation of future wealth. Coarse, cheap, heavy clothing was the rule, with buttons reduced to the absolutely necessary minimum to avoid unnecessary sewing. Each man was his own cook; the limitations of his own cooking ability and of the available food meant that his staples were flapjacks, beans, bacon, and coffee of rather less than epicurean appeal. Housing long remained a difficult problem because of the lack of wood. In the early days tents furnished the usual accommodations, wood being used only for cooking; many a man conserved fuel in the winter by living in a cave in the side of a hill.

As in California, the chief forms of amusement were drinking and gambling. The best-known saloon was the Jones Canvas Hotel at Virginia City, a tent of eighteen by forty feet; the bar was an old sluice box; tin cups served as glasses. The gambling halls were well patronized, and could easily be recognized by the streams of profanity, shouting, and smoke that issued from their doors. The usual undesirable element of desperadoes, bad men, claim jumpers, gamblers, and prostitutes put in its appearance almost at once. These gentry were accepted so calmly that a killer such as Sam Brown could stab a man in cold blood and then peacefully go to sleep on a convenient billiard table without interference. Now and then a group of wandering players was given a cordial reception as it performed in some saloon or store. The first theatrical performance given in Virginia City took place on September 29, 1860.

Prices in Nevada, as in other boom regions, were both high and fluctuating. Typical was brown sugar at 50 cents a pound, rice at 45 cents, butter at $1, nails at $1, and whiskey at 50 cents a glass. The result was that a considerable part of the wealth of the mines went to the freighters, the storekeepers, and the gamblers. Mining was a tremendous gamble, in which only a few won.

READINGS

GENERAL ACCOUNTS OF MINING. Best is Rodman W. Paul, *Mining Frontiers of the West, 1848–1880* (1963), but also useful are Thomas A. Rickard, *A History of American Mining* (1932); George F. Willison, *Here They Dug the Gold* (1931), Colorado; William S. Greever, *The Bonanza West* (1963); Glenn C. Quiett, *Pay Dirt* (1936); Harold E. Briggs, *Frontiers of the Northwest* (1940), readable; Clark C. Spence, *British Investments and the American Mining Frontier* (1958), tells the financial story; Ray A. Billington, *The Far Western Frontier* (1956), short.

CALIFORNIA. General histories are cited in the Readings for Chapter 24. See also John W. Caughey, *Gold Is the Cornerstone* (1948); Owen C. Coy, *Gold Days* (1929); Octavius T. Howe, *Argonauts of '49* (1923); Rodman W. Paul, *California Gold* (1947). Several good accounts exist of the travel to the California gold fields, as Owen C. Coy, *The Great Trek* (1931); R. B. Harris, *The Gila Trail* (1960); Oscar Lewis, *Sea Routes to the Gold Fields* (1949), entertaining; James Monaghan, *The Overland Trail* (1947); John H. Kemble, *The Panama Route 1848–69* (1943), scholarly. Individual travel accounts include John R. Browne, *A Dangerous Journey: California 1849* (1950); Robert Eccleston, *Overland to California on the Southwestern Trail* (1950); George W. B. Evans, *Mexican Gold Trail* (1945); Vincent Geiger and Wakeman Bryarly, *Trail to California* (1945), diary; Heinrich Lienhard, *From St. Louis to Sutter's Fort, 1846* (1961), just before the gold rush; Elizabeth Page, *Wagons West* (1930); John E. Pomfret (ed.), *California Gold Rush Voyages, 1848–1849* (1954).

INDIVIDUAL ACCOUNTS OF THE MINING AREAS. These accounts are legion: Charles A. Barker (ed.), *Memoirs of Elisha Oscar Crosby* (1945); Doyce B. Nunis (ed.), *The Golden Frontier* (1962), various activities 1851–1869; Joseph G. Bruff, *Gold Rush* (2 vols., 1944); Franklin A. Buck, *A Yankee Trader in the Gold Rush* (1930); John W. Caughey (ed.), *Rushing for Gold* (1949) and (ed.), *Seeing the Elephant* (1951); Robert G. Cleland (ed.), *Apron Full of Gold* (1949), a woman '49er;

Carvel E. Collins (ed.), *Sam Ward in the Gold Rush* (1949) ; Le Roy R. and Ann W. Hafen (eds.), *Journals of Forty-Niners* (2 vols., 1954) ; Archer B. Hulbert, *Forty-Niners* (1931), synthetic diary; Joseph H. Jackson, *Anybody's Gold* (1941), mining towns; Francis S. Marryat, *Mountains and Molehills* (1952), concerns 1850; George W. Read (ed.), *A Pioneer of 1850* (1927) ; Benjamin B. Richards (ed.), *California Gold Rush Merchant* (1956) ; Walker D. Wyman (ed.), *California Emigrant Letters* (1952), '49ers; Erwin G. Gudde (ed.), *Bigler's Chronicle of the West* (1962), by a man present at first discovery.

OTHER PHASES OF CALIFORNIA LIFE. C. Gregory Crampton (ed.), *The Mariposa Indian War, 1850–1851* (1957) ; Edmond W. Cagey, *The San Francisco Stage* (1950) ; Carl B. Glasscock, *Lucky Baldwin* (1933), San Francisco banker; Elizabeth Margo, *Taming the Forty-Niner* (1955), amusements; William W. Robinson, *Land in California* (1948), scholarly; Mary F. Williams, *History of the San Francisco Committee of Vigilance of 1851* (1921) ; George R. MacMinn, *The Theater of the Golden Era in California* (1941) ; Thomas E. Harré, *Heavenly Sinner* (1935), actress Lola Montez; Helen Holdredge, *The Woman in Black* (1955), also Lola Montez.

NEVADA. Carl B. Glasscock, *The Big Bonanza* (1931) ; Oscar Lewis, *Silver Kings* (1947), readable; George D. Lyman, *The Saga of the Comstock Lode* (1943), interesting; Effie M. Mack, *Nevada* (1936), scholarly.

COLORADO. Robert G. Athearn, *High Country Empire* (1960), brief on rush to Rockies; Don L. and Jean H. Griswold, *The Carbonate Camp Called Leadville* (1951), interesting and informative; Percy S. Fritz, *Colorado* (1941) ; Le Roy R. Hafen, *Colorado* (1933), (ed.), *Colorado and Its People* (4 vols., 1948), (ed.), *Pike's Peak Gold Rush Guidebooks of 1859* (1941), (ed.), *Colorado Gold Rush* (1941), (ed.), *Overland Routes to the Gold Fields, 1859* (1942) ; Irving Howbert, *Memories of a Lifetime in the Pike's Peak Region* (1925) ; Donald C. Kemp, *Colorado's Little Kingdom* (1949), good pictures. On early Colorado settlement see also James F. Willard (ed.), *The Union Colony of Greeley, Colorado* (1918) and James F. Willard and Colin B. Goodykoontz (eds.), *Experiments in Colorado Colonization* (1926).

OTHER MINING AREAS. W. Eugene Hollon, *The Southwest* (1961), useful background on mining; Lola M. Homsher (ed.), *South Pass, 1868* (1960), Wyoming gold rush; Alice H. Ernst, *Trouping in the Oregon Country* (1961), interesting on amusements; Merrill G. Burlingame, *The Montana Frontier* (1942), not yet superseded; Paul C. Phillips (ed.), *Forty Years on the Frontier* (1925), journals of Granville Stuart; Larry Barness, *Gold Camp* (1962), entertaining; Andrew F. Rolle (ed.), *The*

Road to Virginia City (1960), Montana mining camps; James M. Hamilton, *From Wilderness to Statehood* (1957), Montana; Charles Lindsay, *The Big Horn Basin* (1932); Angus Murdoch, *Boom Copper* (1943), includes Michigan; Grace L. Nute, *Lake Superior* (1944), excellent on iron and copper; K. Ross Toole, *Montana* (1959), good; Oscar O. Winther, *The Great Northwest* (1947) and *The Old Oregon Country* (1951); Rufus K. Wyllys, *Arizona* (1950), brief.

CHAPTER 29

THE OVERLAND ROUTE

E arly residents of the Far West were almost completely isolated from their friends and relatives back East. Correspondence was a precarious business. Books, clothing, hardware, and other elements of civilization were as much as three thousand miles distant, while markets for western products were equally remote. Such conditions were unpleasant even for the fortune seeker who expected soon to return to the East, but were often intolerable for the man who realized that from either desire or necessity his stay was to be permanent.

EARLY COMMUNICATION WITH THE PACIFIC COAST

The best communication in the early days was by ocean, even though no planned service existed. The shipper of goods and the letter writer had the same problem: to find a boat going to the general area in which he was interested and then dicker with the captain. The journey around the Horn was time-consuming, and the captain took little responsibility for deliveries: the letter might never reach the addressee and goods might be dropped on the wharf to rot. Regardless of cost, such service was unsatisfactory. The Pacific Coast seemed as remote as Kamchatka or Capetown.

Transportation by land was even worse. Freight sent by wagon was slow, erratic, uncertain, and expensive; rarely were goods of sufficient value to be worth shipping. The delivery of letters depended on the kindness and memory of someone making the trip. Here and there along the overland trails was a primitive "post office," usually a deserted cabin or the crotch of a tree, where letters would be deposited in the hope that some future traveler would deliver them. No doubt some were delivered, but many merely served as reading material for other travelers.

OCEAN MAIL CONTRACTS

Regular communication depended on mail service, which was unprofitable unless subsidized by the government. The first mail contracts, utilizing the Panama route, were awarded in 1847. The successful bidders for the trip from New York to Panama organized the United States Mail Steamship Company, while those winning the Pacific section from Panama to San Francisco chartered the Pacific Mail Steamship Company. Both groups started operations in 1849, with the western part of the trip the first to be opened. The first boat, the "California," reached California along with the first big mining rush, and all the crew deserted for the mines except the captain and one cabin boy. The original monthly mail service became semimonthly in 1851 with a government payment of $724,-350 a year; the postage rate after 1855 was ten cents a half ounce. Passenger rates were high, a cabin from New York to San Francisco in 1849 costing $500, which of course did not include the trip across Panama. Not unexpectedly, the companies made large profits.

Both the eastern and western companies occupied the whole route and divided the business (January 1851). Cornelius Vanderbilt provided competition with his Accessory Transit Company, which in 1851 offered more comfortable boats by the Nicaragua route. Vanderbilt's partners double-crossed him and acquired his company while he was on a vacation in 1853. Upon his return all three companies paid him a subsidy to keep his fingers out of their pie. The three companies alternately maintained rates and fought each other bitterly.

The greatest improvement of the Panama route was the opening of the Panama Railroad in 1855; the fare for its 47 miles was a profitable 25 dollars. The advantage went mainly to the dominant Pacific Mail Steamship Company. Vanderbilt then regained control of the Nicaragua route, but his service was poorer, particularly because of his troubles with William Walker. Ultimately (1860) Vanderbilt controlled all the Atlantic business, and the Pacific Mail all the Pacific business; rates then rose. In time the transcontinental railroads were to bribe the steamship lines to avoid rate cutting.

Some efforts were also made to obtain mail service by the Tehuantepec route. An American concession, including the right to build a railroad, was given in 1853. Five years later came a mail contract at $250,000 a year, but the service was never satisfactory and was soon abandoned. Incidentally, although mail and passengers went through Central America, the great bulk of the freight continued to make the trip around the Horn.

OVERLAND MAIL ROUTES

The Panama route was an improvement, but it left much to be desired. It was long and slow, passed through foreign territory, required two reshipments, and was extremely circuitous for all points east of California. Westerners continued to agitate for more direct overland service. Little consideration was given to the most northerly possibility by way of the Missouri and Columbia rivers: this route was long, passed through few settlements, encountered hostile Indians, and included mountain passes that were impossible to use in winter.

The central route, in spite of dangerous deserts and mountains toward the west, was generally easy and well marked, had few hostile Indians, and benefited from passing the Mormon settlement. The southern route might either follow the 35th parallel from Santa Fe or, after the Gadsden Purchase, proceed along the Gila River. The southernmost of these options had the advantage of few mountains and no winter snow; on the other hand, it was long and indirect, and crossed much desert country.

The beginning of overland mail service came in 1848, when a contract was awarded for the trip between Independence and Salt Lake City; service to Santa Fe was begun the next year. Even these comparatively easy hauls proved difficult, and deliveries were slow and uncertain. Provision was finally made in 1851 for the western section of the central route, but two years later, because of the tremendous difficulties involved, the terminus was moved from the San Francisco area to Los Angeles. Travel remained difficult, however, and mule pack trains were at the best slow.

More western population increased the demand for coach service, while more progressive citizens talked of railroads. A few ingenious persons speculated that as long as much of the Southwest was known as a desert the right answer should be camels. The federal government was sufficiently impressed to detail an army officer to the Near East to buy the necessary camels, and seventy-five were delivered near San Antonio in 1856. To the disappointment of lovers of the picturesque, camels never became popular on the "American desert."

Whatever the means of transportation, more adequate geographical knowledge was essential to its success; between 1845 and 1853 at least twenty-five new expeditions penetrated the less known parts of the West, to say nothing of thousands of reports from immigrants and other travelers. The greatest single exploration of the West came in the years 1853–1855 under orders of Secretary of War Jefferson Davis, with the primary object of surveying possible railroad routes. Although these explorations produced a great deal of useful, detailed information, they discovered no new routes; those available were the northern, between 47° and 49°; the central, between 38° and 42°; the southern through Albuquerque and along the 35th parallel; and another southern along the 32nd parallel and following the Gila River. Davis, a Southerner, not unexpectedly concluded from the vast amount of evidence that one of the southern routes was to be preferred, but Congress failed to act on his recommendations.

BUTTERFIELD

A speculative railroad for some unspecified date in the future was far from satisfying to Westerners, who wanted immediate action. Their impatience produced results when in 1857 the Postmaster General called for bids on a fast and continuous service by road to the coast. The contract was awarded to a group of men including John Butterfield, one of the founders of the American Express Company, William C. Fargo of Wells, Fargo & Company, and William B. Dinsmore, later president of Adams Express Company. The federal payment was to be $600,000 a year for a semiweekly service taking not over twenty-five days for a single trip. When it opened the line started from both St. Louis and Memphis, converged at Little Rock, and then passed through Preston, El Paso, and Yuma on its way to San Francisco, a trip of over 2500 miles.

The Butterfield Overland Stage Company marked an important stage in the development of rapid communication between the East and the Far West. The first stages left opposite ends of the line in September 1858, the eastbound stage covering the road in twenty days, eighteen hours, and sixteen minutes, or well within the specified time limit.

The elaborate equipment of the company was expensive, costing about $1 million. Concord coaches were used, but with wide tires to make travel through the sand easier. Leather straps served for springs, and leather curtains excluded part of the inclement weather. The three seats were designed to hold nine passengers, although more were sometimes crowded into the space. The driver was perched on the top in front, with now and then a passenger or two beside him. Mail and packages were placed in the "boot" at back. An overflow of mail was frequently dumped on the side of the road to wait for a less crowded coach: passengers paid cash, whereas government mail was carried at a flat rate. Stages had to travel long distances with frequent changes of horses and drivers; stations were placed at intervals of between eight and twenty-five miles. "Swing stations" provided minimum care of the stock; less frequent "home stations" provided headquarters for company agents and served meals to travelers.

A trip on an overland stage was hardly a pleasure excursion. For over three weeks, day and night, the passengers jolted steadily on the most primitive of roads. Sleep on a moving coach filled with passengers was snatched if achieved at all. When the sun was shining the passengers

Overland Trails

roasted; during a rainstorm they were drenched; in dry weather the dust nearly suffocated them. Toilet facilities were nonexistent; hence bathing and shaving waited until the end of the trip. Little wonder the passengers drank large amounts of whiskey to keep up their courage. With little sleep, too much whiskey, and little water, overland travelers were a wild-looking group before the end of their trip.

One of the worst features of overland stage travel was the food. Of course each traveler might carry his own provisions, but food that could be carried in the hot sun for three weeks and then eaten without cooking was neither varied nor appetizing. The company provided food only at home stations, and even there it was far from tempting. The usual fare was rancid bacon, maggoty bread, and coffee that tasted like dishwater. The price for this unappetizing meal was sometimes as high as $1.50. The care of passengers was always secondary to the care of livestock: horses and mules were expensive to replace.

The drivers on the overland stage were sometimes drunk but always profane. The divisional superintendents, who were even worse, included a scattering of "bad men" who were making a little side money when their own business was dull. The fare varied with the amount of traffic and the business conditions of the country. A typical charge was that of 1859, which was $200 for the trip west and $150 for the return east, the difference represented the difference in the traffic in the two directions.

Butterfield did not confine his attention to passenger and mail service, but also did freighting. This portion of the traffic was the same as the freighting provided by others. The wagons, drawn by mules or oxen, lumbered across the plains with no effort at speed. There was no great rush to get freight across the continent: perishable commodities were not shipped. Many years were to pass before such products as fruits, vegetables, and dressed meat could be produced in the Far West for marketing in the East.

THE PONY EXPRESS

The Butterfield Overland Stage Company was the largest passenger and freight carrier on the plains in the late 1850s, but numerous other companies also operated, sometimes over many years and with United States mail contracts. Most important of these rivals was Russell, Majors & Waddell, the greatest freighting concern of its day, which operated along the central route. Its organization was much the same as that of its southern competitor. Its most important division point was Julesburg (in present Colorado), which was then the toughest town in the West.

The company of Russell, Majors & Waddell added further speed to the trip across the plains by introducing a pony express. For some years Senator William M. Gwin of California had urged upon William H. Russell the desirability of giving the people of California faster communication, and had suggested the possibility of a sort of horse telegraph system. Among the advantages claimed for the plan was the advertising of the central route, with possible mail contracts for Russell, Majors & Waddell. Russell was impressed with the idea, and after an unsuccessful effort to obtain governmental assistance decided to go ahead on his own. Stations were outfitted across the plains at ten-mile intervals, and Russell himself picked out hundreds of the fleetest horses he could find and a highly selected group of expert riders.

Public announcement of the pony express created a great sensation. Russell advertised his willingness to transport letters between St. Joseph, Missouri, and Placerville, California, at five dollars an ounce, and to do it in ten days, which was just half of Butterfield's best time. Later the fee declined to $1 a half ounce. Many observers doubted whether this speed would be maintained, particularly in the winter. This doubt was still unresolved when the route was opened on April 3, 1860, the day on which the first rider left St. Joseph; the next day another rider went out of Sacramento. The first trip was made in ten and a half days. The future was to show whether this time could be maintained, or even improved.

The success of the pony express rested primarily on the ability and endurance of the riders. Care was taken to choose only light men and boys, and to reduce the weight of their clothes and equipment to the smallest possible minimum. The mail was wrapped in oiled silk to protect it from the weather; a normal load was between forty and ninety letters, depending on their bulk. It is no wonder that the service was costly.

The rider was expected to average about 9 miles an hour, day and night, allowing no more than two minutes for changing horses. The usual "run" of a rider was between 75 and 100 miles, with a round trip twice a week. Sometimes, because of sickness or accident, runs were increased; at one time "Pony Bob" Haslam covered 380 miles with but nine hours of rest. The life of a rider was hard and dangerous; more than the usual courage and stamina were required for the fast riding on bad roads in all kinds of weather and in perpetual danger from the Indians. The pay of about $125 a month was considered high at the time.

The real test of the pony express and of the route over which it operated came in the winter of 1860–1861. The cold and snow perceptibly slowed the time, but still the men rode through; by the spring of 1861 they were averaging nine days for the trip. Even under extremely bad conditions, Lincoln's inaugural address was carried the 1600 miles between the ends of the "telegraph line" in seven days, seventeen hours.

The pony express proved that the central route was rapid and feasible for year-round travel, but in the process of the demonstration Russell, Majors & Waddell went bankrupt. The pony express failed to make money, which was expected, but it was completely ruined by the completion of the first telegraph line across the plains in October 1861. No longer was there any real reason for a pony express: the type of message it carried could be sent more rapidly and cheaply by telegraph.

Even more disastrous to Russell's hopes was the failure of his company to receive government mail contracts. When the Confederates at the beginning of the Civil War captured a portion of the route and property of the Butterfield Overland Stage Company, Russell and his partners expected that they would receive the overland mail contracts for the central route. Instead, Butterfield himself moved to the central route and continued operations until his contract expired in 1862. By that time Russell, Majors & Waddell had become bankrupt and had been forced to sell their interests (1862) to Ben Holladay, who was shortly to become dominant in overland transportation.

BEN HOLLADAY

Ben Holladay was one of the best-known figures on the plains during the 1860s. Badly educated, he was coarse, crude, and boisterous, with a taste for whiskey, gambling, and tall stories. He trusted no one, not even his wife, and his business and political morals were deplorable. On the other hand, he was congenial, lavish with his family, and beloved in the West as a champion of the underdog; he could be counted on to give land for a church or to grubstake a prospector. He lived with a flourish; he had an impressive mansion in White Plains, New York, but he spent his winters in Washington when Congress was in session. He traveled widely to inspect his properties. His private coach, drawn by blooded horses, was gold-trimmed, with silver door handles; it had coil springs, interior lights, a let-down bed, a food locker, and silver-topped decanters.

Holladay was born in Kentucky, but ran away from home as a youth, going to Missouri. Shrewd and energetic, he tried saloonkeeping, the job of postmaster, and running a general store before he gravitated to transportation; he freighted for Kearny and Doniphan during the Mexican War. His interest in transportation culminated in the purchase of Russell, Majors & Waddell in 1862. Holladay expanded rapidly: in 1866 he had over three thousand miles of stage lines under his control, plus vast amounts of freighting. In addition he had steamships running to Oregon, Panama, China, and Japan. Probably his was the greatest one-man business in the United States.

Ben Holladay's reputation throughout the United States was well illustrated in a story told by Mark Twain: American tourists were visiting the Holy Land, and one of the boys of the group was being told impressively how Moses had led the Israelites through three hundred miles of desert in forty years. After listening patiently for a while he could contain himself no longer: "Forty years? Only three hundred miles? Humph! Ben Holladay would have fetched them through in thirty-six hours."

Holladay's supreme ability was the organization and control of men. The main line of his overland route across the plains had three divisions: from Atchison to Denver, Denver to Salt Lake City, and Salt Lake City to Placerville. A superintendent had immediate supervision over each division. A conductor, or messenger, rode with each coach on the seat in front with the driver, his "beat" being about 200 miles. The presence of an authorized representative of the company prevented many of the unfortunate incidents that had taken place on the Butterfield line.

The driver was the most interesting man in the employ of the company, since it was he who held the reins of power. His characteristics were different from those of his predecessor who drove for Butterfield. Usually he was a reticent, somewhat retiring individual, who interrupted his driving only to chew and spit, and who almost never drank whiskey while on the job. Properly approached, he told fascinating stories of holdups, accidents, and Indian attacks, stories that grew with each retelling. The coach he drove was the usual Concord type, except that it was a fiery red, with yellow running gear and black trim, and on its door panels were painted western scenes. Each coach was drawn by four or six horses picked for speed and endurance.

The stations along the Holladay route were similar to those formerly maintained by Butterfield, and were placed at intervals of from 10 to 50 miles. The drivers were changed about every 50 miles at a home station. Even the home station was crude—a central building of rough logs and dirt floor. Ordinarily it included a blacksmith shop, living quarters for the drivers, and facilities for serving meals. All supplies had to be hauled by team. The worst men on the line were the stock tenders, who were usually undesirables, some of them with criminal records.

The price of the trip from the Missouri River to the Pacific varied widely because of the financial confusion of the period. Rates advanced along with other prices as the Civil War continued and paper money depreciated. In 1863 the fare from Atchison to Denver was $75, to Salt Lake City $150, and to Placerville $225. By 1865 rates had more than doubled, and a little later they were even higher.

The days of coach traffic across the plains were few. By the middle 1860s farsighted men such as Holladay saw the end in view as they watched the Union Pacific creep across the plains. Holladay did not wait for the end, but sold out to Wells, Fargo & Company in 1866. The completion of the railroad three years later ended most of the transcontinental coaching, but the stagecoach continued to operate for many years in regions to which the railroad did not extend. The Deadwood stage of the 1870s and 1880s was particularly famous, probably because of its use in Buffalo Bill's Wild West Show.

The stage was more picturesque than the other forms of transportation over the plains, but it was no more important than the freighting done both by individuals and by large companies. This business was conducted ordinarily in covered wagons drawn by ox or mule teams. It was estimated at one time that Russell, Majors & Waddell had 6250 wagons and 75,000 oxen in use; a little later Holladay was credited with having 20,000 wagons and 150,000 animals, including 600 thoroughbred horses. A big wagon held 3 to 5 tons of freight; a standard "train" included twenty-five freight wagons, a mess wagon, reserve animals, and spare parts. Ordinarily oxen were the motive power, but sometimes mules were used for greater speed. The usual six yoke of oxen per wagon might be increased to ten or twelve if conditions were bad. The bullwhacker and the mule skinner were particularly noted for their picturesquely profane vocabulary and for their prowess with a 30- to 50-foot lash, which they could crack to sound like a pistol shot.

RAILROAD PLANNING

The successor of the stagecoach was the railroad, which was well adapted to conquer the long flat stretches of the plains, and which offered by far the best solution to the special needs of the western farmer, stockman, and miner. The first trans-Mississippi railroads were constructed in the 1850s, when American railroads were still in the first quarter century of their history. Connections were just being made from the eastern seaboard to such midwestern cities as Chicago, St. Louis, and Memphis. The first bridge across the Mississippi was not opened until 1855. Population was sparse and capital scarce. The West lacked knowledge of the technical details of financing, construction, and operation, and was deficient in labor, whether skilled, unskilled, or managerial.

But Westerners were never long intimidated by obstacles, no matter how insurmountable they appeared to others. During the late 1840s and early 1850s enthusiasm for the railroad was aroused by the camp-meeting technique. Large and enthusiastic gatherings at such cities as Chicago, Iowa City, St. Louis, Little Rock, and Memphis stressed plans for a railroad to the coast, but the resulting interest also spurred the construction of local lines. Congressmen were urged to work for federal aid, and there was talk of state loans, county loans, city loans, town loans. Every possibility was canvassed hopefully. Railroads were supported as public improvements, much like the parks and museums of a later day. Their backers were considered public-spirited citizens. Not the railroad but the community was expected to profit. Costs of transportation would decline, property values would rise, profits of farmers would increase. The West would raise itself economically by its own bootstraps.

The basic requirement for the building of railroads was the collection of sufficient capital. The most obvious method of financing was to invite personal subscriptions, but although pledges were easy to obtain they were difficult to collect except in the form of land or labor. The West had little surplus capital, and the great bulk of funds had to come either directly or indirectly from the East or from Europe.

A second financial possibility was to utilize the credit of a small governmental unit, say, town, county, or city. A town, for example, would issue bonds to be exchanged for railroad stocks or bonds, and then these town bonds would be sold by the railroad in the East, usually at a large discount. To obtain such assistance, the railroad might play one town against another by surveying two or more routes even though the final line had already been decided upon. The towns thereby were encouraged to compete in offering assistance to obtain the road.

A third possibility was the state, which might use its bonds in the same way as the county or town. Missouri lent some $19 million in this way and lost almost all of it. Minnesota hurried her admission to the Union so that she could lend $5 million to prospective railroads; no railroads resulted, and ultimately Minnesota paid off her bonds at 50 cents on the dollar without providing for accrued interest. California gave some assistance to the Central Pacific. Texas probably had the best record, getting more railroads for her money than did other states; in addition, Texas had her own land-grant policy, for she controlled her own public domain.

Both states and smaller political units found difficulty in paying their bonds, particularly as many were twenty-year issues that came due during the depression of the 1870s. States were sovereign and hence could delay payment of their bonds or repudiate them. Towns and counties had no such option, and the courts held such debts collectible even if there had been minor irregularities in issuing the bonds. Most notorious was the hide-and-seek played by the officials of Yankton, South Dakota, to avoid payment. Conservative Easterners were so aghast at this display of what they considered the western temperament that they opposed statehood for the Dakotas. Ultimately, of course, the bonds were paid.

The fourth possible source of railroad funds was the federal government, which had earlier aided roads and canals. Cash loans would have been most welcome but were improbable. Land was different, and the West held that gifts of land would benefit the entire country by increasing western population and trade. Even the government would not lose, because alternate sections could be doubled in price, thus producing as much revenue as before. Congress remained reluctant because of sectional antagonisms until the Illinois Central grant of 1850 broke the jam. After 1850 all the first tier of states west of the Mississippi were given railroad grants, while specific projects farther west were aided.

All the grants of the 1850s were similar in terms. The railroad was given alternate sections within 6 miles on each side of the road, and if any of the land had been settled the railroad was allowed to make indemnity selections within 15 miles. The grants were to revert to the public domain if the aided roads were not completed within ten years. After 1860 grants were made only to such strategic roads as the Union Pacific, Santa Fe, Northern Pacific, Texas & Pacific, and Atlantic & Pacific; terms were usually more generous because of the lesser value of the lands farther west.

The administration of the railroad grants was in the hands of the General Land Office. As soon as a railroad filed its approximate route all the land within the indemnity limits was withdrawn from sale, so that settlers could not occupy regions that might be found to belong to the railroad. As fast as the road was located definitely, land selections were made, final patents were issued, and the remainder of the land was thrown back on the market.

The policy concerning railroad grants was a constant source of annoyance to prospective settlers. Large areas, frequently including much excellent land, were closed to settlement. The settler felt that he should have the right to take any unoccupied land, and often did so in spite of all restrictions. The situation was aggravated when the Supreme Court decided that the reversion clause of the grants did not work automatically, but needed special legislation by Congress. The result was that land grants were often kept off the market for many years even though the railroads gave no indication of building.

The last of the railroad grants was made in the early 1870s, for by then sentiment toward the railroads had changed, as was also evidenced by the granger movement. Approximately 180 million acres of the public domain were actually received by the railroads. The total value of these gifts, at the prices for which the land was sold, amounted possibly to $500 million.

RAILROAD BUILDING

Western railroad plans were of two general types. The first was the transcontinental project, which was completed later (see Chapter 35). Many roads that today are purely local at one time had hoped to build across the continent, while the transcontinental lines engendered enthusiasm that often resulted in local construction.

The second type of railroad project of the 1850s was designed to create state transportational systems, each state considering primarily its own interests and paying little attention to connections with neighboring states, except those to the east. Minnesota proposed several lines running east and west across the state, and others centering in St. Paul. Iowa planned almost every road to run east and west. The Missouri system, with the exception of a northern road across that state, centered at St. Louis, Arkansas roads at Little Rock, and Texas roads at Galveston Bay.

The first feeble beginnings of actual construction came in these states during the 1850s. Missouri, Iowa, and Texas acquired a few, short, weak lines. Farther west, in California a short mining road was built. These early efforts were halted by the panic of 1857, and before the resulting depression ended, the Civil War had further disrupted the finances of the country. Only two trans-Mississippi roads made important progress in these years. The Hannibal & St. Joseph was completed in 1859 between the two cities named in its title, thus connecting the Mississippi and Missouri rivers north of St. Louis. The Missouri Pacific, after many trials and tribulations, was finally finished from St. Louis to Kansas City in 1865.

The Civil War proved more destructive to the railroads of the Southwest than to those of the Northwest. Some of the Missouri and Texas lines were used for military purposes, and portions of them were destroyed on various occasions. When the war ended, the South had fewer miles of railroad than at the opening of hostilities. On the other hand the North, motivated in part by a desire to replace the Mississippi, continued to build. Such states as Wisconsin, Minnesota, and Iowa made reasonably satisfactory progress during the war period.

With the return of prosperity after the war, railroad plans and construction once more moved to the center of the stage. The second bridge across the Mississippi was completed at Clinton, Iowa, in 1865, and others followed. Three main groups of lines, as classified by their objectives, were being built. The first was the transcontinental group, to be discussed later; it was exemplified by the Union Pacific, completed in 1869.

The second group, the so-called granger roads, was being built from Chicago and St. Louis to the Missouri River. The two Missouri roads have already been noted. The Chicago & Northwestern, crossing the Mississippi at Clinton, was finished to Council Bluffs in 1867. The Chicago & Rock Island, crossing the river at Rock Island, reached Council Bluffs in 1869. The Chicago, Burlington & Quincy, crossing at Burlington, also arrived at Council Bluffs in 1869. The Illinois Central, crossing at Dubuque, was opened to Sioux City in 1870. The Chicago, Milwaukee & St. Paul, the other important road of the group, did not attain its objective, the Missouri River, until the late 1870s.

The roads in the third group were built to connect the Missouri River with the Gulf of Mexico. Two of the lines were completed in 1873. The Missouri, Kansas & Texas, commonly known as the "Katy," extended from the end of the Missouri Pacific at Kansas City south to Houston. The other line was really a combination of four roads that together joined St. Louis and Houston: the St. Louis, Iron Mountain & Southern in Missouri; the Cairo & Fulton in Missouri and Arkansas; and the Texas & Pacific and the International & Great Northern in Texas.

Also during this period immediately after the Civil War occurred the first important effort to create a large and effective railroad system. The sponsor was James F. Joy, a Detroit banker who was president of the Michigan Central and who had a financial interest in the New York Central. Purchasing the Chicago, Burlington & Quincy, he pushed it as far west as Fort Kearney by 1873. Then he added the Hannibal & St. Joseph, which he connected with the Burlington in the east, and from which he built branches in the west to Kansas City and Atchison. To these lines he added the Missouri River, Fort Scott & Gulf, but his intention of reaching the Gulf of Mexico was never realized. Joy's plans were wide-ranging and magnificent, but he had extended his investment too far for safety; when the panic of 1873 created a financial emergency the "Joy lines" collapsed with a resounding crash.

RAILROAD CONTROL

The buoyant and enthusiastic optimism with which the West viewed possible railroads during the 1850s underwent a radical revision twenty years later. The first unbridled and rapturous enthusiasm cooled, and finally turned to bitter opposition. The basic factor was disappointment that the hoped-for prosperity had not arrived; hence railroad mistakes and abuses tended to irritate the farmers more and more. Railroad construction and finance had both been notorious. Many of the roads had been built badly, with resulting poor service and numerous accidents. Financial mismanagement was the rule rather than the exception. Many of the roads had been built entirely for the sake of the profits to be derived from their construction, the original owners juggling the construction contracts so as to provide for themselves even though the roads were left hopelessly insolvent. Most of the misused money had been borrowed from states, towns, and private individuals who could ill afford its loss. When the debts contracted in the prosperity of the 1850s came due during the depression of the 1870s the debtors quickly developed a burning hatred of the railroads as the cause of their impoverishment.

The reversal of feeling toward the railroads came in part from a change in the railroads themselves. Frequently they had started as small, struggling, local concerns, freighted with the hopes and desires of their communities. Now they had grown into vast impersonal organizations, the Chicago roads becoming dominant as they constructed western additions or bought and consolidated local projects. Most of the western roads moved their headquarters, shops, and yards eastward. The executives frequently never saw the country through which their lines passed except through the windows of their private cars. This lack of contact resulted in the almost complete absence of mutual understanding. Transportation charges had gone down as expected, but market prices had also declined; hence the farmer had failed to benefit as he had hoped. In fact, the small producer actually suffered from the railroads because special rates, including rebates for large shipments and the favoring of competitive points over noncompetitive points, had given the large producer an even greater advantage than he had possessed before the railroad arrived.

Changing conditions lessened the West's enthusiasm for the railroads, and opposition made its appearance. State aid came to an end. State constitutions prohibited local gifts. No more land grants were made by the federal government. Congress debated and almost passed regulatory legislation; certain states put control measures on their statute books.

Growing hostility by no means halted railroad construction. After a work stoppage in the half dozen years after the panic of 1873 came a revival in the late 1870s and early 1880s that produced the largest amount of construction of any similar period in United States history. At the end of the period the railroad network of the West had assumed approximately its present form.

The change of the Far West from the stagecoach to the railroad did much more than increase the rapidity of the movement of passengers and freight. The whole concept of the West was modified. Gone were the lumbering oxcart, the covered wagon, the long and dangerous trip across the plains, the nightly stop with its gleaming campfires. Gone were the jolting stage, the periodic station, the driver with his cracking whip. Gone were the trapper, the trader, the hunter, and the explorer. In their places appeared the modern and efficient, but impersonal, steam locomotive. The result was eventually a transformation in the characteristics and state of mind of the West.

READINGS

ROAD TRAVEL. State and regional histories are pertinent; see the Readings for Chapter 22 for Cleland, Dick, Monaghan. See also Alvin F. Harlow, *Old Post Bags* (1928) and *Old Waybills* (1934); Oscar O. Winther, *Express and Stagecoach Days in California* (1945); W. Turrentine Jackson, *Wagon Roads West* (1952), scholarly. Smaller areas are treated in Grace R. Hebard and E. A. Brininstool, *The Bozeman Trail* (2 vols., 1922); Overton Johnson and William H. Winter, *Route across the Rocky Mountains* (1932), exploration; Charles Kelly, *Salt Desert Trails* (1930); Irene D. Paden, *The Wake of the Prairie Schooner* (1943), locates the California road; Agnes W. Spring, *The Cheyenne and Black Hills Stage* (1949), detailed.

ROAD TRAVEL—SPECIAL TOPICS. Butterfield: Roscoe P. and Margaret B. Conkling, *The Butterfield Overland Mail* (3 vols., 1947), detailed on route; Le Roy R. Hafen, *The Overland Mail, 1849–1869* (1926), scholarly; Waterman L. Ormsby, *The Butterfield Overland Mail* (1942). Russell, Majors & Waddell: Raymond W. and Mary L. Settle, *Empire on Wheels* (1949). Holladay: James V. Frederick, *Ben Holladay, the Stage Coach King* (1940), scholarly; Ellis Lucia, *The Saga of Ben Holladay* (1959), a trifle fictionalized. Wells Fargo: Lucius M. Beebe and Charles Clegg, *U.S. West* (1949), reads easily; Edward Hungerford,

Wells Fargo (1949), rather random. Camels: Harlan D. Fowler, *Camels to California* (1950), easy reading; Lewis B. Lesley (ed.), *Uncle Sam's Camels* (1929), journals. The Pony Express: Glenn D. Bradley, *The Story of the Pony Express* (1960); Arthur Chapman, *The Pony Express* (1932), good; Howard R. Driggs, *The Pony Express Goes Through* (1935). The Telegraph: Robert L. Thompson, *Wiring A Continent* (1947).

RAILROADS. The best general account is Robert E. Riegel, *The Story of the Western Railroads* (1926); see also Agnes C. Laut, *The Romance of the Rails* (2 vols., 1928). Exploration is covered in George L. Albright, *Official Exploration for Pacific Railroads, 1853–1855* (1921); there is good material in Leland H. Greer, *The Founding of an Empire* (1947). The congressional story is given in detail in Lewis H. Haney, *A Congressional History . . . to 1850* (1908) and *A Congressional History . . . 1850–1887* (1910); John B. Sanborn, *Congressional Grants of Land in Aid of Railways* (1899); Robert R. Russel, *Improvement of Communication with the Pacific Coast as an Issue in American Politics, 1783–1864* (1948). The railroad conventions are covered monographically in John G. Van Deusen, *The Ante-Bellum Southern Commercial Conventions* (1926) and Herbert Wender, *Southern Commercial Conventions, 1837–1859* (1930). Useful regional studies are Frederick Merk, *Economic History of Wisconsin* (1916) and James N. Primm, *Economic Policy* (1954), on Missouri. The Illinois Central Railroad has been treated in Howard G. Brownson, *History of the Illinois Central Railroad to 1870* (1916); Carlton J. Corliss, *Main Line of Mid-America* (1950); Paul Gates, *The Illinois Central and Its Colonization Work* (1934), scholarly. Histories of other railroads are scarce, but see John L. Kerr, *Missouri Pacific* (1928); Lewis Lewis and Stanley Pargellis, *Granger Country* (1949), C. B. & Q., mostly pictures.

CHAPTER 30

THE CIVIL WAR
IN THE WEST

T he era of gold rushes, Indian campaigns, stagecoaches, river steamboats, the pony express, and of planning for railroads was highly exciting to Americans of the 1850s. It was a time of inflation, of better prices—until 1857—and of harvesting the fruits of Manifest Destiny. The lengthening shadow of the "southern question" gradually dulled the frontier luster and, in 1861, the eruption of hostilities diverted national attention to the crisis at hand. During the war years there was a continued westward migration and a consciousness of that region's importance, but the ferocity of the conflict east of the Mississippi and the importance of its outcome prevented any serious development of new frontiers. Because events in the main theater of war were so dramatic, so critical, and so engrossing, historians generally have given them the attention they so justly deserve. By comparison, nothing appeared to be happening in more remote parts of the land. And so it has sometimes been recorded.

THE WESTERN PROBLEM

From an immediate military standpoint there was no reason why any concern should have been felt about the great trans-Mississippi West, for the side that won the war was bound to fall heir to that portion of the country. The West of 1861 was very sparsely settled, was without any satisfactory means of transportation, and was dominated by powerful Indian tribes who were happy that the whites were annihilating each other. Without cities to be captured, transportation systems to be destroyed, or populations to be defended it was obvious that military operations of the

455

traditional type would not be conducted. That this undeveloped back country would play no significant part in the war seemed apparent to the man on the street in both North and South.

However, some considerations made the West at least potentially significant. There was a possibility that Mexico, perhaps with the aid of some other nation, might take this opportunity to recover some of her lost possessions in the Southwest. The elevation of Austrian Archduke Maximilian—a puppet of the French—to be Emperor of Mexico strengthened this notion. The Pacific Coast, particularly mineral-rich California, was of interest to other countries. Great Britain, once attracted by Texas, remained alert to the possible benefits of an economic penetration of the Western Hemisphere. The warm sympathy that the English ruling classes showed for the Confederacy, and the growing desperation at Richmond as the war progressed, added to the concern of the North that the West might be a pawn in the international game. From the standpoint of larger strategy, both sides understood the impression that would be made upon world opinion if the great western reaches were added to the Confederacy. The new land, not well understood as yet by Americans, was an even greater terra incognita to Europeans, who would be impressed by the acquisition of so much territory even if it were still undeveloped.

CONFEDERATE INVASION OF NEW MEXICO

Behind any Confederate long-range, strategic considerations lay the more practical necessity of finding a source of bullion with which to buy foreign goods and to support a shaky domestic financial structure. Southern planners had some reason to believe that they could execute a successful invasion of northern-held mining country and capture valuable resources they sorely lacked. They knew that, after a brief period of indecision, the West had generally declared itself for the Union, but there remained pockets of resistance to such a loyalty. For example, one spring day in 1861 the Confederate flag flew briefly over a Denver store; even though it was ripped down by Union sympathizers, the southern faction was not dismayed. Pro-Confederate elements openly advertised for ammunition and percussion caps to be used in the "war against the government." There was open talk among southern-born miners that the Denver minting establishment of Clark and Gruber would be an excellent source of gold for the Confederacy. Such attitudes encouraged the Confederates to organize a raiding force and send it into the West.

In February 1861, Texas adopted an ordinance of secession and at once began to take over federal forts within her borders. Military posts in New Mexico territory were next on the occupation schedule. Accordingly, in July, Lieutenant Colonel John R. Baylor, C.S.A., led a body of troops into New Mexico by way of El Paso, and marched northward along the Rio Grande River toward Santa Fe. Within a month he had occupied most of the important population centers in the southern portion of the territory; shortly afterward Jefferson Davis proclaimed that the area should be organized as Arizona. Although this achievement brought the Confederacy nothing in the way of material riches, it was hoped that the move would be the first step in the conquest of Colorado and would perhaps open the way to California. An even more optimistic belief was that the Mormons, angered by the recent Utah expedition against them, would make common cause with the Confederacy.

Federal defense of New Mexico was placed in the hands of Colonel Edward R. S. Canby whose nineteenth United States Infantry was stationed at Santa Fe. Baylor's successful invasion of southern New Mexico had already cost Canby some of his men; and as Canby prepared to ward off further blows he found that he had less than 2500 men, that his forces were isolated, so far as any hope of reinforcements was concerned, and he was short of supplies. During the latter part of 1861 Baylor was appointed governor of Confederate Arizona and a fresh army, commanded by Colonel Henry H. Sibley, resumed the assault along the Rio Grande. "Sibley's brigade," which marched out of Texas about 3700 strong, comprised a force that appeared to be much stronger than that of the defenders. As Albuquerque fell, and Santa Fe was invested, Canby took his stand at nearby Fort Union and sent an urgent call to Colorado for help. Thus far the Confederate plan had succeeded admirably.

"GETTYSBURG OF THE WEST"

The first regiment, Colorado Volunteers, commanded by Colonel John P. Slough, marched nearly 175 miles in five days in response to Canby's plea. Pausing only a few days at Fort Union, Slough and his contingent of over 1300 men pressed on toward Santa Fe hoping to drive the Confederates from that city. On March 26, 1862, an advance element of the Volunteers, commanded by Major John M. Chivington (the presiding elder of the Methodist Episcopal Church in the Rocky Mountain district) encountered a group of Texans in the vicinity of Apache Canyon. The narrow defile, some seven miles in length, was the western end of Glorieta Pass; through it ran the trail to Santa Fe, about twenty-five miles to the west. In a bold stroke the "Fighting Parson's" men circled the enemy, destroyed a supply train of seventy-three wagons, bayoneted some six hundred mules and horses, and attacked rear elements of Texas troops. The main action, fought on March 28, was characterized by five hours of extremely bitter fighting. There the Union forces were driven back and so badly beaten that it was feared for a time Slough's Volunteers would

The Civil War in the West

mutiny. However, the Confederates assumed that it was Canby who had destroyed their supplies; and the belief that his large force lay between them and Santa Fe, coupled with the fact that they were now without supplies, caused them to withdraw. Sibley began a retreat into Texas, his forces seriously diminished and his striking power weakened.

Critics of Canby charged that he did not pursue Sibley, his brother-in-law, as relentlessly as he should have, but Coloradans contented themselves with the idea that this "Gettysburg of the West," as they called the Battle of Glorieta Pass, had saved the day for the Union in the Southwest. Actually, the invading force had about reached its limit. A federal force of 5000 men was prepared to march from Fort Leavenworth to New Mexico in the spring of 1862 while General James Carleton was en route from the West with his California Volunteers. As he moved eastward Carleton mopped up isolated pockets of Confederate resistance in Arizona. For example, at Tucson he took into custody one Sylvester Mowry, a former United States officer who was operating a mine in the vicinity and who was said to be supplying guns to southern raiders in the region. Then Carleton pressed forward, anxious to join Canby in New Mexico. Had Sibley stayed on he would have faced some 12,000 federal troops by autumn. Wisely, he left.

DEFENSE OF THE SOUTHWEST

Carleton arrived in September and assumed command of the Military Department of New Mexico. He immediately began to repair some of the older posts and to erect new ones to guard the avenues of approach. Fort Sumner was built in eastern New Mexico, between the modern towns of Vaughn and Clovis, and a temporary encampment was established at Las Cruces, near the Texas border, to ward off any further attempts at invasion. Although the Texans did not return, that possibility always remained; in fact Colonel Baylor received instructions from Richmond to recruit four battalions of rangers for such an effort. Before he could carry out his orders the war came to a close.

The reoccupation of New Mexico by Union forces ended any threat to Colorado. Small and widely scattered raids occurred during the next two years but, in the main, there was little work for the Colorado Volunteers who had done service at Glorieta Pass. In the autumn of 1862 a group of Southerners, including five members of the original Green Russell party that had made the initial Colorado gold discoveries, attempted to return home. Soldiers of the Second Colorado Cavalry arrested them. In February, 1863, they were released and, after taking an oath of allegiance—which, it is said, they kept—the men were permitted to go south. A second Confederate effort in the fall of 1862 also failed. William P. McClure, onetime Denver postmaster who had fled at the outset of the war, tried to re-enter Colorado, where he planned to recruit for General Sterling Price's Confederate army. This sally was cut short when Osage Indians, in the employ of the federal government, intercepted the party, killed all its members, and brought in the heads of the victims to show their employers they had carried out orders.

James Reynolds was the best known of the Confederate raiders in Colorado. Having threatened that he would pillage Denver as the Confederate guerrilla leader William Quantrill had pillaged Lawrence, Kansas, he returned to the mountains in the summer of 1864. With a force of about twenty-five men Reynolds plundered a wagon train on the Santa Fe Trail and then moved into Colorado's South Park region, robbing ranchers, miners, and stagecoaches—presumably to raise money for the Confederate cause. Before long a posse located the gang. Some of the members were captured and taken to Denver, where they were tried and condemned to be shot. The presence of southern sympathizers in the city, however, made an execution so risky that the men were ordered transported to Fort Lyon in the southeast corner of the territory. They failed to complete the trip. As the story went, the prisoners tried to escape and were killed, but it was generally understood in Colorado that the men were lined up along the way and executed.

UTAH'S WARTIME ROLE

The vast reaches of the West were connected by extremely weak transportation and communication threads. Hundreds of miles were served only by stagecoach and freight lines; a fragile telegraph wire, subject to disruption by Confederate raiders, by Indians, or even by buffaloes who scratched themselves on poorly placed telegraph poles, provided very unreliable service. It is no wonder that the Pacific Coast felt isolated or that Montana miners referred to the East as "the states."

The enormous task of guarding this lengthy roadway was given to Colonel (later General) Patrick E. Connor and his Third California Volunteers. With approximately 1500 men Conner was charged with keeping open the road, warding off the Indians, and keeping an eye on the Mormons. Although the latter saw some advantage in selling supplies to the Californians, who established headquarters at Camp Douglas near Salt Lake City, they were unhappy over the colonel's insistence that they first take a loyalty oath. Brigham Young said he would see the military in hell before he would subject his people to such an indignity, but there is no evidence to show that the troopers suffered from a lack of fresh vegetables.

Connor informed his superiors that Brigham Young had an active army of 8000 men that could be increased to 50,000 if necessary, and that in this hostile land the utmost diplomacy would have to be exercised by the Volunteers. He distrusted the Mormons, who, he asserted, publicly rejoice at federal reverses "and thank God that the American Government is gone, as they term it, while their prophet and bishop preach treason from the pulpit." The forces of Brigham Young and those of Connor lived under an uneasy truce, one that both sides knew might easily be shattered, and this realization was of concern to the federal troops. Yet the Californian permitted his men to engage in mining precious metals—something church leaders had discouraged among their own people—and even actively promoted such enterprises. He reasoned that it would keep his poorly paid men, many of whom were former miners, in a more contented frame of mind, and also that the mineral wealth so obtained would be useful to the Union. In his official correspondence he also indicated that a mining rush would settle the Mormon question peacefully because it would attract a large, non-Mormon population whose numbers would make unnecessary the maintenance of federal troops in Utah. As if this were not enough, Connor founded an anti-Mormon newspaper, the *Union Vedette,* to "educate the Mormons" in what he called "American views." Despite a great deal of publicity, in which Connor invested considerable sums of money, the anticipated boom did not take place. Other western mining regions were much richer and drew off most of the prospectors; Utah was so isolated that ore transportation costs were prohibitively high; and, finally, the church exerted so much pressure on its members that few Mormons joined the Californians in their search for gold. Until the coming of the railroad in 1869 none of the efforts of the Volunteer miners showed a profit.

Although the war did not stimulate Utah's mining industry it had a pronounced effect on the territory's efforts at economic independence. Just as the bitter conflict altered life in the northern states and in Great Britain, so did the disruption of the cotton trade have its influence on Utah. In 1857 and 1858 initial efforts were made to raise cotton in the southern part of the territory, what became known as "Dixie," but by 1860 the entire production of the territory amounted to only 160 bales. At the outbreak of war church leaders made a great effort to increase migration into southern Utah and did all they could to promote the "cotton mission." By 1863 enough was raised to allow a shipment of 74,000 pounds to "the states" at a price that ranged from $1.40 to $1.90 a pound. In Utah the price was set at $1.25 a pound and cotton was used as legal tender to pay bills or to make exchanges. The crops of 1864 and 1865 were a disappointment. By 1869, the coming of the railroad and the availability of cheaper southern cotton caused a rapid decline in this local industry. A cotton mill was built in 1867 and remained open until 1910, but the high cost of irrigating the crops made cotton culture in Utah prohibitively expensive.

Although Connor spent most of his time keeping an eye on the Mormons or promoting Utah mining he was called upon occasionally to stop Indian depredations along the overland trail. In 1863 there were scattered attacks, ranging from those made on travel in southern Utah to sporadic raids on the main routes. In that year Chief Washakie, a Shoshoni well known for his wisdom and friendship toward the whites, returned 150 stolen horses and mules, and shortly afterward Connor signed a peace treaty with this band at Fort Bridger. He also came to terms with a branch of the Ute and received pledges of peaceful cooperation in the Spanish Fork region of Utah. Further negotiations with the Shoshoni, Goshute, and Bannock relieved the pressure on wagon routes in southern Idaho. By an agreement reached in October 1863, some 8000 tribesmen agreed to remove pressure from white communications lines in return for annuities.

WARTIME CALIFORNIA

The problem of isolation, felt so keenly throughout the West, was particularly apparent in California. The mining rush of 1849 and after had brought to that area a number of foreign-born persons who were much more interested in economic betterment than in the sectional question that had so long plagued the eastern part of the United States. Both Europeans and Orientals maintained closer sentimental ties with "the old country" than with faraway Washington, D.C., a place that was only a name to most of them. Nor could the federal government expect much sympathy from the Californians of Spanish or Mexican descent. They had long resented the cavalier manner in which their lands had been taken over and the disdain with which the Americans treated them as a minority group.

Led by miners of southern origin large segments of the California population frequently complained of the laxity of Washington officials in providing the facilities of government. The U.S. mails were irregular, the federal court system was badly understaffed and painfully slow, and talk of transcontinental railroads had petered out in the late fifties as the sectional crisis mounted in the East. These and many less immediate grievances grew in intensity west of the Sierra Nevadas until older loyalties to the Union wore thin. Coastal residents, who generally associated the outbreak of war with the slave issue, found it difficult to become excited over a deadlock in which they felt they had but a small interest. Those in Lincoln's administration who felt concern about the threadlike connection that held golden California to its parent had adequate reason to worry.

The problem of disloyalty, of only a minor and transitory nature in such a place as Colorado, was much more evident in California. Newspapers in some of the more important cities were so hostile to the Lincoln administration that they were denied the use of the mails by the federal government. The injunction was lifted in early 1863, with certain exceptions, but by then at least one newspaper had been forced to suspend operations. The *Expositor* of Visalia, so unrelentingly hostile that it did not regain mailing privileges, was kept alive by contributions from the community. When troops were sent to suppress secessionists in Visalia, residents brazenly rode by a dress parade and loudly cheered for Jefferson Davis. Although they were promptly arrested, their confinement only stirred the opposition to more stubborn resistance. Meanwhile, all efforts to silence the *Expositor* of Visalia were in vain; it continued to attack President Lincoln openly and frequently. But when it referred to the state's volunteers as the "California Cossacks" the paper went too far. In March of 1863 soldiers stormed the paper's offices and threw all its equipment out into the street. The editors decided not to resume publication.

In another attempt to halt the spread of subversion teachers were required to take a loyalty oath. Those who would not sign were denied teaching certificates and no warrants for the payment of their salaries were to be authorized. Apparently Californians believed that the classroom was only one nest of subversion, for they also passed a law denying any attorney the right to practice unless he promised his allegiance to the Union cause. Any backsliding cost an attorney a fine of $1000. The state itself felt obliged to reassure the federal government of its loyalty, and on two occasions—in 1861 and in 1864—the legislature passed resolutions endorsing the Lincoln administration.

Punitive legislation and the use of troops drove the secessionist movement underground. Such organizations as the Knights of the Golden Circle (originally organized in Cincinnati) and the Knights of the Columbian Star were so active that they claimed secret membership within the Union League and among the California Volunteers. As was true of their eastern brothers, members held that the war was illegal, having been initiated by Lincoln without the consent of Congress, and they insisted that all they were guilty of was an unflinching support of the Constitution.

THE NORTHWEST

In addition to the men California contributed to the eastern theater of war, to the Carleton expedition into New Mexico, and to Connor's forces in Utah, the state sent volunteers into the Pacific Northwest. By the end of 1861 ten companies were dispatched to Oregon and Washington to replace regular troops recalled to duty in the East. Part of the men were stationed in northwestern Washington; others were sent to Forts Walla Walla and Colville in the eastern part of the territory. In addition to this force, local volunteers were raised in Oregon and Washington. The reward for enlisting was $31 a month, a bonus of $100 at the end of the three-year enlistment period, and a land warrant for 160 acres.

Although the principal contribution of these troops was patrol duty, much like that assigned to Connor's force, the existence of southern sympathizers on the Pacific Coast and their defiant attitudes prevented some of these companies from being sent east. The people of the Northwest were aware that the Canadian boundary was undefended. England's sympathy for the Confederacy, coupled with the potentially dangerous dispute over the San Juan Islands in the Vancouver area, kept the possibility of British intervention in that area uppermost in their minds.

In Oregon the local troops were used primarily to keep open routes of travel to the Idaho mines and to keep an eye on the Indians, who were growing restive over this traffic. New posts were established at Boise and near Klamath Lake in southern Oregon. Another post was constructed in

Nez Percé Indian country, near Lewiston, Idaho, and in 1863 a treaty signed with those Indians opened a considerable portion of the country to miners. For a mere $262,500 they accepted a much smaller reservation; the dissatisfaction thus generated within the tribe later led to trouble. The neighboring Snake Indians, having signed a treaty with General Connor the same year, remained generally quite.

The mining camps of Montana were born during the war years, and that territory felt almost nothing of the great conflict taking place in "the states." A remark of a miner dramatizes the distance that separated his kind from the war. When he saw an account of the firing on Fort Sumter in a newspaper then three months old, he noted, "Bad news from the states. The North and South are fighting." He made no comment, showed no emotional reaction, but simply made a record of the event. That the new territory, so remote and undeveloped, could play no part in the fighting was obvious. However, the presence of a large number of southern miners—some of whom could ride by the territorial governor's residence firing pistols and cheering for Jefferson Davis without fear of punishment—had an effect on the political development of the territory. Montanans voted the Democratic ticket, and continued to do so, with the result that the territory remained steadily with that political faith and waited patiently for twenty-five years after its birth (in 1864) for the Republican party to grant it statehood. During the latter years of the war millions of dollars worth of much-needed bullion passed down the Missouri River to Union coffers. What the young territory could not offer in manpower it gave in gold.

THE BORDER STATES

Although the far-flung mountain and coastal regions were not absolutely vital to the Union cause, those Westerners who lived closer to the seat of war were obliged to participate more actively. Missouri, whose outlook was western, did not belong to either the North or the South but, hanging in the balance, it was of importance to each side. Not only was it the most populous western state, but St. Louis was the greatest center of western trade and travel; its importance grew when the Butterfield route was moved north at the outbreak of hostilities. Superficially Missouri was southern, with legalized slavery and a governor (C. F. Jackson) who was clearly southern in his sympathies. On the other hand Missouri actually had very few slaves and contained a large number of Unionists, notably among the antislavery Germans of St. Louis. This complexity explains why, though the state legislature almost unanimously declined to secede (March 1, 1861), Jackson flatly refused Lincoln's request for troops for the Northern army.

Immediate and aggressive action by the wealthy and energetic Francis P. Blair made Missouri a Union state. St. Louis "home guards," mostly German, captured Jefferson City, put the state under martial law, and organized a loyal government. In reply, Jackson continued to insist he was the proper governor and in this capacity raised militia, called a state legislature into session, and on August 6 had Missouri declared a free and independent state. With aid from outside, Jackson forces overran most of the southern part of the state and defeated a Union army at Wilson's Creek on August 10.

Command of the Western Department of the Union Army was at this time most unfortunately in the hands of John C. Frémont, who at the least was dilatory and at the most was guilty of mismanagement, extravagance, favoritism, graft, and other sins. Moreover, Frémont made the mistake of issuing on August 30 a very drastic order, freeing all slaves and confiscating the property of rebels in a region he arbitrarily designated. At a time when every effort was being made to win the sympathies of doubtful border areas, such an order was catastrophic. This turn of events put Lincoln in a very difficult position, since he was obliged to discipline the Republican party's first nominee, a man who had married the daughter of Missouri's famous senator Thomas Hart Benton, and who was otherwise widely known. After some soul-searching Lincoln assumed the responsibility and on November 2 removed Frémont.

The political leaders of Missouri were able to maintain the connection with the Union, but there was a degree of geographical division. Western Missouri farmers did not agree with the sentiments of St. Louis businessmen and other eastern Missourians. Although no clear-cut distinctions between these two sections of the state can be made, the sympathies of those in the back country became apparent as the war proceeded.

Union forces took the offensive in 1862 and pressed Confederate defenders back into Arkansas. For the remainder of the war Missouri was in general under the control of the northern forces. A southern raid in 1863 penetrated as far as Springfield and another in 1864 advanced as far as Jefferson City, but neither had any real hope of adding the state to the Confederacy. Mainly they were bids for recruits, and here they failed most miserably, for more Missouri members of the southern armies deserted in order to go home than new recruits flocked to the colors.

Arkansas was of comparatively little importance to the war. She accepted secession, May 6, 1861, with but one dissenting vote. The military campaigns that touched Arkansas were concerned primarily with operations on the Mississippi River or in Missouri or Texas. Arkansas had little strategic value for either side.

Texas was in some ways the reverse of Missouri, for in Texas

Sam Houston, the Governor, was a Unionist whereas majority sentiment was southern. An irregular convention, boycotted by Union sympathizers, passed an ordinance of secession, February 1, 1861, by a vote of 167 to 7 and this action was legalized by the legislature over Houston's veto. Union property was confiscated and Union troops surrendered. A popular vote on secession late in February showed a 3 to 1 majority for that cause. Under these circumstances Houston was forced out of office.

JAYHAWKERS AND BUSHWHACKERS

In Kansas and western Missouri an informal or guerrilla warfare harried the population but did not materially influence the outcome of the war. Although a good many Kansans were less interested in the plight of the southern Negro than they were in the preservation of the Union, their leaders tended to be abolitionists. Some of the more enthusiastic residents, fearful that Missouri might join the Confederacy and effectively isolate Kansas, joined local regiments and marched on their neighbors. In the autumn of 1861 James Lane, recently elected to the United States Senate, and subsequently commissioned brigadier general, led an expedition into Missouri ostensibly to suppress secessionist activity there and to challenge the Confederate general, Sterling Price. He accomplished little more than confiscating a considerable amount of "secesh" poultry and collecting some 600 Negroes whom he brought back into Kansas. The foray, followed by several more into nearby Missouri, only antagonized the residents and drove many of them into the gray uniform. The "jayhawkers" served the Union badly at a time when Lincoln was trying to soothe feelings in Missouri and keep it in the Union. General Henry Halleck became so concerned about the raids that he predicted a few more would make Missouri as Confederate as eastern Virginia.

As Halleck anticipated, Missourians did not submit to such invasions peaceably. They repaid the visits with forays into Kansas that left a trail of blood, burned homes, and disrupted communities. These guerrillas who "took to the bush"—hence the name "bushwhacker"—carried on the same kind of irregular warfare practiced by the jayhawkers. The most famous of them was William Clarke Quantrill, who had come to Kansas a few years before the war and had ridden with the jayhawkers for a time. Early in 1862 he formed his own band of Missouri bushwhackers and began to plunder Kansas towns. From a modest force of less than 30 his following grew until he commanded a small army of approximately 300. Under the guise of serving the Confederate cause, Quantrill, the James boys, and Cole and Jim Younger, to mention only a few, entered careers that ended in undisguised banditry. Outlawed by the Union forces, Quantrill came in time under Confederate suspicion and was arrested. He escaped to Texas and in 1865 evolved the fantastic plan of dressing his men as Union soldiers, making his way to Washington, and assassinating Lincoln. He left a trail of blood and destruction as far as Kentucky, where he was killed in a surprise attack.

At first Confederate officials did not complain openly about the disruption of parts of Kansas, but they did not approve of the bushwhackers' methods. Feeling that the raids did more harm than good, southern authorities tried to persuade the guerrillas to join regular forces. This had little appeal to men who wanted to fight for plunder and who often were deserters from the Confederate Army. On the other hand, such men as Quantrill received open support from the people of western Missouri who approved of retaliating in kind to the jayhawk attacks. In addition to these grievances, there was a considerable resentment toward state authorities who tried to enroll sons of these Missouri farmers in the federal service. Although they had no real sympathies with the system of slavery, certain sentimental and cultural ties with the South remained.

THE RED RIVER CAMPAIGN

In the spring of 1864 federal forces embarked on an expedition in northwestern Louisiana aimed at an invasion of Texas. The purpose of the Red River campaign, as it became known, was to take advantage of Union sentiment among Texas Westerners and to open new sources of cotton to hungry New England mills. The idea was as old as the war itself, General George McClellan having recommended it to Lincoln as early as the summer of 1861. The invasion of New Orleans, supposed to produce cotton in quantity, was given precedence, and General Benjamin Butler's troops undertook that assignment in 1862. As a growing number of cotton spindles came to a halt, the pressure for a strike against Texas mounted. Lincoln, who viewed the Mississippi River as the "backbone of the Rebellion," found demands by representatives of the textile industry increasingly hard to put off. That he was able to do so until early 1864 was due in part to his personal abilities and to Union military successes in other parts of the South.

After elaborate preparations, nearly 30,000 men under the direction of General Nathaniel P. Banks and supported by Admiral David Porter's gunboats began the ascent of the Red River. Confederate General Richard Taylor's forces engaged a part of this army at Sabine Crossroads and again at Pleasant Hill (April 8 and 9, 1864) and sent it back down river. Meanwhile, General Frederick Steele's federal forces marched out of Arkansas in an attempt to execute a pincers movement, in conjunction with Banks's troops, only to be driven back upon Little Rock by Confederate cavalry divisions.

The Red River campaign, which General Sherman called a disaster, not only strengthened Confederate morale but had a direct influence on other operations. A. J. Smith's command of 10,000 men, drawn off to aid Banks, did not participate in the famed Georgia campaign and although this in all probability did not alter the outcome of that movement, it did diminish Sherman's army. Troops sent along with Banks also might have been assigned the task of reducing Mobile, whose capture was delayed nearly a year. Confederate troops scheduled to defend that port were diverted to General Joseph Johnston's army then facing Sherman's invaders. The expedition failed to liberate any cotton, the Southerners burning any that was in danger of falling into Union hands. Just as the Confederates had been denied the mineral resources of the Southwest, earlier in the war, so the federal side was unable to capture any appreciable amount of the South's major resource—cotton.

THE WARTIME ROLE OF THE WEST

In general, the remote and sparsely settled West experienced many of the war-born problems that confronted Americans farther east: divided loyalties, subversive activities, questions over civilian rights, shortages of certain supplies, and the general disruption of civil life brought on by such a struggle. However, there were additional difficulties that did not plague more settled parts of the land. The vast distances, served only by threadlike communications, magnified the remoteness in which Westerners lived. There was no rail connection with "the states" until after the war and the stagecoach and wagon routes were subjected to such additional pressures as increased Indian hostilities and the danger of Confederate raiders. The Pacific Coast states, aware that they dangled as colonial appendages in prewar days, found this status even more marked in time of war.

To hold this vast area of land until the major question was resolved between North and South put an enormous strain upon both the federal officials and the people of the West. Volunteer troops, generally unseasoned and not always reliable, were called upon to defend vast sections of the country, not only against the Indian tribes and the Confederates but against the possible invasion by outsiders. That the latter intervention failed to materialize did not lessen the concern of those who would have been involved and their constant vigilance provided a certain degree of strain.

By maintaining its control over the West the federal government could claim two important accomplishments: it retained the source of supply of valuable minerals that were vital to wartime finance and eagerly sought by the Confederates; and it presented the world with a diplomatic achievement—a demonstration of the loyalty of all the nation except eleven states in the American Southeast. To assess the importance of these accomplishments is, of course, very difficult and is filled with "what-might-have-beens." That both sides thought the West important is apparent in the efforts each made to control all or part of it.

READINGS

No satisfactory general study has been written about the role of the trans-Mississippi West in the Civil War. Ray C. Colton, *The Civil War in the Western Territories* (1959) treats only Arizona, Colorado, New Mexico, and Utah. Oscar Lewis, *The War in the Far West* (1961) is largely about California and contains little that is original. More ponderous than the Lewis volume, but one containing considerable information about the Pacific Coast during the war is Aurora Hunt, *The Army of the Pacific, 1860–1866* (1951). Her volume *Major General James Henry Carleton, 1814–1873: Western Frontier Dragoon* (1958) complements the earlier study and provides a good picture of the role of the California column. Flora Warren Seymour, *The Story of the Red Man* (1929) has a chapter entitled "The Civil War in the West."

The New Mexico campaign has been of recent interest to historians. William Clarke Whitford's older volume, *Colorado Volunteers in the Civil War* (1906), although still important, has been heavily supplemented by more recent works. Another basic work, Ovando J. Hollister's history of the First Colorado Regiment of Volunteers, first published in 1863, was reprinted as *Boldly They Rode* in 1949. Warren A. Beck, *New Mexico, A History of Four Centuries* (1962) has a chapter entitled "New Mexico and the Sectional Controversy." Martin H. Hall, *Sibley's New Mexico Campaign* (1960) is the best single volume about the Confederate invasion of New Mexico. Briefer is Robert L. Kerby, *The Confederate Invasion of New Mexico and Arizona, 1861–1862* (1958). Events leading to the outbreak of war are described in Loomis M. Ganaway, *New Mexico and the Sectional Controversy, 1846–1861* (1944). Max L. Heyman *Prudent Soldier: E. R. S. Canby* (1959) contains a chapter describing Canby's part in the campaign. Interesting also is W. W. Mills, *Forty Years at El Paso, 1858–1898* (1962). This work, introduced by Rex W. Strickland, provides additional reading on the Confederate effort in New Mexico.

There is little in print about the central plains and the Rockies during the war. Fred B. Rogers, a former army officer, wrote *Soldiers of the Overland* in 1938. It tells the story of General Patrick E. Connor's role. Something of Connor's impact on Utah may be found in Leonard J. Arrington, *Great Basin Kingdom* (1958). This excellent work also describes the impact of the war on Utah's economy.

A number of books discuss the events taking place in the "eastern" West, or along the border. Jay Monaghan, *Civil War on the Western*

Border, 1854–1865 (1955) reads well and is quite informative. More particularized is Richard S. Brownlee, *Gray Ghosts of the Confederacy: Guerrilla Warfare in the West, 1861–1865* (1958). Another very good work is Albert Castel, *A Frontier State at War: Kansas, 1861–1865* (1958). Castel also has written *William Clarke Quantrill: His Life and Times* (1962). See also Carl W. Breihan, *Quantrill and His Civil War Guerrillas* (1959). Stephen B. Oates, *Confederate Cavalry West of the River* (1961) explores a subject little written about. The Red River campaign is very well portrayed in Ludwell H. Johnson, *Red River Campaign: Politics and Cotton in the Civil War* (1958). Contemporary, and biased, is wartime Governor Samuel J. Crawford's *Kansas in the Sixties* (1911). It is useful in appreciating the political soldier's point of view.

CHAPTER 31

THE INDIANS AT BAY

The tribes of the high plains, those fierce, proud "horse Indians" so well remembered in countless pulp and celluloid westerns, were pressed back again and again by white invaders until they could retreat no more. The beginning of the end was the opening of such avenues of travel as the Santa Fe Trail that sliced through the Southwest, or the "California Trail" whose snakelike path followed the Platte River across the plains, crossed the Rocky Mountains, and took its travelers to the Pacific Coast. These were major developments, at first slender and tenuous, that broadened and sprouted branches until the open land the natives called home was finally locked in their grip. The Indians foresaw the development and predicted its outcome, but their lack of organization and the gradual nature of the white advance discouraged any all-out efforts to drive the strangers from the land. By the time they mounted their horses and made their appearance on the field of battle, it was too late. Fighting would occur, but the cause was lost from the outset.

During the latter half of the nineteenth century Americans talked a great deal about the "Indian problem." The problem was one of their own creation, not that of the natives. Americans generally lacked an understanding of the force and persistence of their own westward movement. Indian policy, as administrators developed it, was a piecemeal program that failed to take into account the degree of white pressure mounting against the western frontier. That the natives did not cooperate in the solution of the difficulty is perfectly understandable when one considers the ineptitude with which administrative minds approached the matter. Admittedly, hindsight is easier to acquire than foresight, but making that allowance, one must confess that even the most enthusiastic advocates of Manifest Destiny suffered from myopia with regard to Indian affairs.

WESTWARD BY TREATY

One of the most significant Indian treaties ever formulated by the American government was the far-famed agreement made at Fort Laramie in the autumn of 1851. By its terms the various Indians involved revealed their conviction that the white man had come west to stay, even if he asked no more than passage across their lands. The whites, on the other hand, confessed that the inviolability of "Indian country" was one of America's most short-lived myths. The results of pipe smoking at Fort Laramie set the stage for the final struggle of the plains Indians, one that was to continue for about forty years.

During the 1830s the removal of eastern Indian tribes to new trans-Missouri River homes was largely completed. By the end of that decade Americans talked about the "permanent" Indian frontier, a land that lay in the vicinity of the "Great American Desert," a place no white man in his right mind ever would covet. Yet the next decade witnessed an unparalleled outbreak of Manifest Destiny virus that sent thousands westward and generally familiarized the American reading public with descriptions of the "Oregon Trail," the "California Trail," and the "Mormon Trail." Each was a rush westward for various reasons, but whatever the cause they had one thing in common: each involved the movement of white settlers across Indian lands that invariably meant the shattering of what so recently had been established as a "permanent" Indian barrier. Sooner or later this traffic was bound to cause trouble.

The wagon roads would inevitably be followed by railroads and with them would come hordes of settlers. As early as 1849 Secretary of the Interior Thomas Ewing foresaw this development and predicted it would necessitate the protection of such routes against Indian depredations. Father Pierre Jean De Smet, the Catholic missionary who had traversed the West so thoroughly, also anticipated trouble in the future. In 1851 he expressed his belief that western Indians would soon experience the fate of the eastern tribes, that their lands would also be overrun by settlers. Even as he wrote, the Commissioner of Indian Affairs was worrying about moving farther west some of the removed eastern Indians "so as to leave an ample outlet for our white population to spread and to pass towards and beyond the Rocky Mountains." The expression of such sentiments forecast the necessity of the meeting at Fort Laramie and in the late summer of 1851 the representatives from some of the western tribes began to drift into that famous western outpost. They were prepared to "make talk."

Agent Thomas Fitzpatrick, of the Upper Platte Agency, acted as host and chief white negotiator. Old "Broken Hand," as he was called, had known the plains country ever since the twenties, when he came west with

William Ashley. In attendance also was David D. Mitchell, one-time employee of the American Fur Company, who was superintendent of the Central Superintendency. It was he who had advised Washington authorities to call the conference. Along with other whites, including the Jesuit missionary De Smet, a St. Louis newspaper editor, and a Missouri politician one day to be the state's governor, these men sat down with chiefs from the Sioux, Assiniboin, Arikara, Crow, Grosventre, Shoshoni, Arapaho, and Cheyenne. Jim Bridger, dean of the mountain men, served as an interpreter. After extended speeches by members of both sides, an agreement was reached. For the right of their people to make the westward passage unharmed the Americans promised to pay the Indian owners $50,000 a year in annuities for fifty years. These privileges were to include the building of military posts along western roadways. It was further agreed that any depredations by Indians or whites would be punished and that restitution of losses would be made. Tribal boundaries were marked off as additional insurance against collisions among the various signatories. The Indians then went to their various homes and the American negotiators submitted the treaty to the Senate for its approval. That body amended the document to read ten instead of fifty years, pending Indian agreement, but by now the natives were so scattered they could not be rounded up for the necessary quorum. Although the treaty was never ratified, the government paid annuities for fifteen years; in general, the Indians fulfilled their part of the bargain.

The negotiations at Fort Laramie gave official sanction to travel over the "Great Medicine Road" along the Platte River, but there was another western route that demanded equal consideration. The road to Santa Fe was still heavily traveled and at least two proposed railroads expected to pass that way. In the spring of 1853 Fitzpatrick arranged for a meeting at Fort Atkinson (near the present Colorado-Kansas line) with the Comanche, Kiowa, and Apache and in July he concluded an agreement with them for use of the route, including again the right to build forts and maintain military forces along the way. The latter stipulation required some persuasion on the part of Fitzpatrick, who reported that the Indians did not want military establishments in the area. He insisted, however, because "at no distant day the whole country over which those Indians now roam must be peopled by another and more enterprising race." This was, in effect, the point of the Indians' argument.

In addition to the Laramie and Atkinson treaties there were other pressures on the western tribes. The Kansas-Nebraska question loomed large, and those who were anxious to promote political status for the area wanted to extinguish its Indian titles. In 1853, Commissioner of Indian Affairs George Manypenny recommended the organization of what he called a "civilized government" in the new country. It was his belief that the opening of the area by "the enterprising and hardy pioneers" would be of benefit to both races, a point of view not shared by the original owners. Nevertheless, during the winter of 1853–1854, as Congress debated the controversial bill, government agents moved among the Plains Indians distributing money and harvesting titles. One result was the projection westward of a large wedge that tended to divide the tribes into two principal groups. The wagon-road treaties, the blossoming of transcontinental railroad plans, and the creation of new political subdivisions—all emerging nearly simultaneously in the early fifties—acted as a trip hammer against an Indian domain so recently regarded as forever fixed and secure.

THE FIGHTING FIFTIES

Even as Indian commissioners busied themselves extinguishing land titles in Kansas and Nebraska, trouble was brewing out on the high plains. In the late summer of 1854 a Mormon wagon train passed an encampment of Brûlé Sioux, not far from Fort Laramie, and the Indians killed one of the emigrants' cows. The loss was reported when the caravan reached the fort. Bear-That-Scatters, one of those who had signed the Laramie Treaty for the Brûlé Sioux, confirmed the story and offered to surrender the Indian, a Miniconjou camping with his band. Young Lieutenant Hugh B. Fleming declined the offer and decided upon a firmer course. John L. Grattan, a brevet second lieutenant fresh from West Point, and about thirty men were ordered to march on the Indian camp and bring back the accused.

The youngster in command discovered shortly that the cow killer's fellow Miniconjou would not surrender him, and in an effort to make a show of force he precipitated a fight in which the whole body of troops was wiped out. Severely handicapped by inexperience, by the angry haranguing of an intoxicated interpreter, and by the hostility of the Indians whose previous experience with white men had not been very satisfactory, Lieutenant Grattan became a victim of his country's efforts to solve the Indian problem by force: his mutilated body, bristling with twenty-four arrows, was mute testimony to the failure of such a program.

Agent John W. Whitfield, who arrived at Fort Laramie about this time, expressed surprise that an officer would try to bluff some 1500 Indians who surrounded him, especially in view of the fact that they had offered to pay for the cow. As Whitfield explained, any Indian who submitted to imprisonment would have been disgraced for life, and to avoid this he would gladly risk his life in battle. Such a reasonable approach was apparently lost on Lieutenant Fleming, who had sent Grattan to his death, for that officer promptly advised his superiors to send out a force sufficient to punish the offenders, arguing that this would cause neighboring tribes to remain peaceful. It was a notion that would cost the lives of a good many troops before plains warfare ended.

Widespread raiding occurred along the Platte route after the Grattan affair. Young tribesmen, out to make names for themselves, tended to ignore the advice of their elders and to strike at isolated travelers when the opportunity presented itself. In the autumn of 1854 a small band of Brûlé Sioux ambushed the Salt Lake mail stage, killed three men, and made off with $10,000 worth of gold bullion. In general, the Indians from the Platte Valley north to the Missouri River country were in a sullen mood, one that caused the War Department considerable worry.

In the spring of 1855 General Winfield Scott, the commanding general, ordered Colonel William S. Harney to conduct a campaign against the Indians with sufficient troops to punish with extreme severity any who accepted the challenge of battle. By August the colonel had gathered a force of some 600 men at Fort Kearny, Nebraska, and to the announcement that he was ready he added, "By God, I'm for battle—no peace." Quickly he moved up the Oregon trail looking for Indians who wanted to fight. On September 2 he found Little Thunder and his band of Brûlé Sioux encamped near the North Platte River in the vicinity of Ash Hollow. Lieutenant Colonel St. George Cooke (later famous as a Civil War general) placed four companies of men behind the Indian camp while Harney confronted Little Thunder with the demand that he surrender his unruly young men. When the chief declined to meet such conditions, an attack was launched on the camp. Harney later reported that they killed eighty-six, wounded five, and captured about seventy women and children at a cost of four killed and seven wounded.

After he had crushed Little Thunder's band, Harney moved on to Fort Laramie, where he laid down the law to other Sioux chiefs. In harsh terms he demanded that they surrender the braves who had struck the Salt Lake stage and that all stolen stock and property be returned. According to the colonel, his listeners "begged piteously to be spared" and promised to comply with all his demands. Not yet satisfied that the natives were duly impressed by armed might, Harney struck off for Fort Pierre, where he received delegations from several Sioux bands. At a peace conference held during early March 1856, nine tribes agreed to hand over all Indians who molested travelers, the chiefs giving their word that the agreement was to be carried out to the letter. In turn, the United States government promised to protect the Sioux against white incursions and to provide agricultural implements to those Indians requesting them. Not much time elapsed before both sides broke the agreement.

During 1856, as Harney concluded his agreement with the Sioux, army officials were increasingly irritated at the conduct of the Cheyenne, particularly the northern band that ranged along the North Platte River. During the summer of 1856 they raided that well-known road, killing men, women, and children. Almon W. Babbitt, Secretary of Utah Territory, was one of the victims. Spreading out from the Platte, they moved into Republican River country and impeded travel on that route. General Persifer F. Smith, in command of western troops, stated positively that "this tribe must be severely punished." Both sides knew there would be fighting when the grass grew in the spring and campaigning was renewed on the plains.

The men who received the assignment were Colonel Edwin V. Sumner and Lieutenant Colonel Albert Sidney Johnston, both of whom were to play important roles—on opposite sides—in the Civil War. Sumner divided his command, sending part of it under Major John Sedgwick in a circular movement to Bent's Fort, up along the Rockies to the South Platte and then eastward. Meantime Sumner scoured the interior of this arc Sedgwick was describing, searching for Cheyenne bands. Late in July he found about 300 of them along the Solomon River and promptly launched an attack. The Indians broke and ran, the troopers in pursuit. Only two men were killed and one officer, Lieutenant J. E. B. Stuart (later to be a famed Confederate officer), was wounded. The next day Sumner's men came upon a Cheyenne camp of some 170 lodges and nearly 20,000 pounds of buffalo meat, all of which they destroyed. The Indians fled from Sumner's reach and prepared to fight another day. This they would do, with great effect. As LeRoy Hafen wrote in *Fort Laramie:* "Thus ended the Sumner campaign against the Cheyennes. It has chastised a few Indians, embittered many more and overawed none."

THE CRITICAL YEARS: 1861–1865

By the time the United States was embroiled in the Civil War, the Indians of the high plains and the Pacific Coast region were becoming increasingly disturbed. The Indian mind was filled with bitter resentment at the arrival of caravans of emigrants, at the rumbling overland stages, at dozens of exploring parties, at railroad surveying crews, and at the succession of military expeditions. Most irritating of all were miners, who paid not the least attention to such scraps of paper as Indian treaties: where gold beckoned they went. A boom occurred here one day and a thousand miles away the next, any rush as likely as not in the heart of Indian country. Legally the miners had no right in any region reserved to the Indians, but the government seldom had either the troops or the desire to eject good white voters, no matter how turbulent; in fact it might well act for the miners' protection in the very probable event of trouble with the Indians. Quite understandably the Indians resented such intrusions wholeheartedly.

Of even more vital importance to the Indians were the hide hunters who methodically destroyed buffaloes, depriving the natives of their very livelihood. Early hunters and travelers had been prodigal of buffalo life, but the fewness of the hunters and the vastness of the herds had made the slaughter relatively unimportant. Now plains travelers were increasing, and they were all either hungry or imagined themselves mighty hunters. Railroad construction crews frequently depended on buffaloes for their meat supply, and by the late sixties special excursions from the East brought well-armed trainloads of men intent on shooting a few of the shaggy animals. In the seventeen months that "Buffalo Bill' Cody worked at supplying Kansas Pacific Railroad workers with meat he personally accounted for 4280 of the animals.

Even by the time of the Civil War the decrease of herds was evident, particularly in the Oklahoma area. After the war professional hunters armed with repeating rifles made the plains a slaughterhouse. Because of the ease with which a herd was approached, the hunter might kill as many as a hundred at a single stand; the carnage might be halted only by over-heated rifles or by the physical exhaustion of the two skinners who usually accompanied the hunter. By 1870 buffaloes were being killed at the rate of about a million a year, and by 1875 the southern herd was virtually exterminated. Less than a decade later the northern herds suffered a similar fate. By the mid-eighties a representative of the Smithsonian Institution had difficulty in finding twenty-five specimens to preserve. Saddest of all, much of the slaughter was not even very profitable economically: most of the meat rotted on the ground and the plethora of buffalo robes drove their prices to unprofitable levels. In time a minor subsidiary occupation developed—gathering the tons of buffalo bones that lay over the plains. One wonders how many buffalo died to bring five dollars a ton for the bones collected later.

The dwindling buffalo herds provided the handwriting on the wall for the old nomadic life of the Plains Indian. The buffalo had furnished food, clothing, tools, and weapons; its elimination made impossible the traditional life on the plains. Even without the many armed conflicts that were to occur before the end of the story the fate of the Indians was inevitable. In some future day he must accept woman's work: in the terminology of his conqueror, he must practice the agriculture of the white farmer.

Many Indians were aware of the precariousness of their situation as early as the 1860s. The old men shook their heads sadly and talked with regret of the good old days in which game had been plentiful and in which there had been no demoralization from the white man's whiskey and the white man's diseases. The young braves grew increasingly angry as they saw white encroachments and heard rumors of white atrocities. Every year more

Indians came to believe that if their race were to avoid annihilation it must soon make a stand against white aggression.

The era of the Civil War provided an excellent opportunity for the Indians to roll back the white man's advancing frontier. Those far-flung western settlements, cut off from more settled regions and very thinly protected, would have been hard pressed to withstand any organized military effort during the war years. With the bulk of the federal army heavily engaged in the East, and most of its armaments in use, the plains and mountain West was obliged to rely largely upon volunteer troops armed with such weapons as were available in their own communities. Yet the Indians remained remarkably calm while the big fight was going on among Americans in the East. Except for the uprising of the Sioux in Minnesota during 1862, the natives showed no disposition to attack white settlements in any great numbers.

THE MINNESOTA SIOUX OUTBREAK

The origin of the Minnesota affair was typical of the frontier misunderstandings that had made Indian-white relations so unstable in the past. Its background included the underlying Indian resentment against white expansion, the sharp dealing of the traders, the seduction of Indian girls by unprincipled white men, and the inspiration provided by overly large doses of the white man's "fire water."

On August 18, 1862, six whites were murdered by a small band of Indians near New Ulm, Minnesota. The murders were unpremeditated and represented no general major attack, but the survivors became panic-stricken and fled to the town, spreading exaggerated stories of a widespread Indian uprising. Most of the Minnesota Sioux seem to have been almost equally thunderstruck at the news of the murders. Knowing the ways of the whites, they concluded that they must either fight or flee toward the west. To remain peacefully in the lodges was to invite slaughter. In consequence of this reasoning, part of the Indians prepared for war while the remainder packed their belongings and left that part of the country.

The band that remained to fight was led by Little Crow and included some 1300 warriors. Not waiting for a white attack, it immediately began offensive operations against the outlying settlements of the Minnesota River Valley. Men, women, and children were killed to the number of 737; barns and houses were burned, and the frontier was thrown into a fever of apprehension. The young state government called for volunteers and asked for federal troops.

With surprising force the Sioux routed the troops, nearly captured Fort Ridgley, and came close to overrunning New Ulm. However, by September, volunteer troops under the command of Colonel Henry Hastings Sibley defeated the Indians. After rounding up over 1700 prisoners, the military staged a grand court-martial that condemned over 300 of them to death. Some were convicted of no other crime than being present at such battles as New Ulm or Birch Coulee, but Sibley was in favor of hanging the lot. Through the intervention of President Lincoln all but 39 of the death sentences were commuted. Toward the end of December, residents of Mankato, Minnesota, witnessed a mass hanging from a single scaffold, signifying the conclusion of this particular phase of western Indian warfare. Little Crow, who escaped the noose, was shot not long afterward by a settler and his son who were deer hunting.

The punishment of the Minnesota Sioux had been swift and terrible, but more was to come. In 1863 a punitive military expedition was sent against them and the rest of Little Crow's band met defeat. In the same year Congress confiscated all the Sioux land in Minnesota, and during the following year the dispossessed Indians were sent to Dakota, where they arrived too late to raise corn. Government supplies were few and poor, which meant a year of misery, with cold, disease, poverty, and starvation. If punishment could ever prevent further crime, then no new outbreak should have occurred after the disaster to the Sioux in Minnesota.

MASSACRE AT SAND CREEK

Another Indian-white engagement during the war years, one that had national repercussions, took place at Sand Creek in the southeastern part of Colorado Territory late in 1864. The conflict, which is still a subject of hot argument in Colorado, involved an attack of territorial volunteers on an encampment of southern Cheyenne said to be peaceful and friendly in which a large number of Indian men, women, and children died. The massacre underscored the general lack of understanding the two races had for each other and typified much of the ruthlessness displayed in the so-called Indian wars after the Civil War.

Central to the problem of the Indians was the federal government's policy of alternating peace with war. In this case the government had attempted to buy a considerable portion of the southern Cheyenne and southern Arapaho lands, the Indians signifying their agreement at the Treaty of Fort Wise in 1861. The new Indian home was to be a small tract of dry, sandy, almost gameless country in southeastern Colorado. The only virtue of the location was that it was so desolate and barren that it was unlikely to be the object of white cupidity.

The Treaty of Fort Wise made the Indians sullen and more resentful, and most of them refused to go to the designated land. War parties sniped at outlying settlements, plundered travelers, and struck at overland stagecoaches. Periods of ominous quiet were but uneasy interludes between frontier depredations. Governor John Evans of Colorado Territory, nervous over the Indian threat and hard-pressed by aggressive whites in his territory, ordered the "friendly" Arapaho and Cheyenne to report to Fort Lyon (formerly Fort Wise) in the spring of 1864. Some of the other tribes ranging Colorado's plains were told to report to posts designated by the governor. The implication was that the "friendlies" would be protected and those not reporting would be regarded as "hostiles," to be hunted down and punished.

The policy of separating friendlies from hostiles, to be practiced much more widely in later years, did not stop depredations against stage lines or attacks on isolated settlements. The territorial militia prepared for action and a first-class Indian war appeared to be in the making. Then, whether because of sober second thought or because winter was approaching, the Indians began flocking to the vicinity of Fort Lyon on Sand Creek. Their move was an anticlimax to troops who were anticipating the excitement and the glory of killing a large number of Indians. Furthermore, the whites had the uncomfortable feeling, coming from bitter experience, that the Indians would live peacefully on government rations during the winter, but in the following spring more Indian parties would be on the warpath. The majority white reaction was expressed by Major General Samuel R. Curtis, when he wrote from Fort Leavenworth: "I want no peace till the Indians suffer more."

Colonel John M. Chivington echoed the sentiment and marched his volunteers toward Fort Lyon. The colonel's subordinate, Major Jacob Downing, wrote: "I think and earnestly believe the Indians to be an obstacle to civilization, and should be exterminated." Meantime about 500 Indians under southern Cheyenne Chief Black Kettle were encamped peacefully at Sand Creek, under the impression that they had obeyed the governor's proclamation and were safe from harm. A white flag and an American flag were displayed to give evidence of their intentions.

Chivington and his troops reached Sand Creek late in November. Here they spied out the Indian village and prepared to win the glory for which they had enlisted. The attack of November 29, 1864, found the Indians completely surprised and unprepared. Their first reaction was to start to run, which gave the Colorado troops the opportunity to carry on the slaughter as they pleased. Both men and women were shot down, women were ripped up the body, children were brained, and every other conceivable mutilation was practiced. Here was Indian war at its worst: whites engaging in methods they had long condemned as uncivilized. When the carnage ended, the village had been destroyed and about a fifth of its inhabitants murdered. Black Kettle and the remnants escaped.

The action near Fort Lyon has often been labeled either the "Chivington massacre" or the "Sand Creek massacre"; Coloradans called it a punitive expedition and professed to be pleased with the results. They applauded when the victors returned to Denver with two women and five children as prisoners and agreed with Chivington's excuse for killing the young: "Nits make lice." The heroes of the battle also brought back to Denver over 100 scalps, some of which were stretched across the stage of a local theater by means of a rope, for between-the-acts viewing.

All in all it appeared to have been a satisfactory campaign, one that evened up the score for a number of past Indian crimes. Very shortly more treaties were signed with the natives—the Apache, Kiowa, Comanche, Arapaho, and Cheyenne, in particular—and more land was ceded. For the southern Cheyenne, victims at Sand Creek, the story was one of surrendering their last vestige of land in exchange for a home in Indian Territory, or what would ultimately be the state of Oklahoma.

THE POLICY DILEMMA

The wartime troubles in Minnesota and at Sand Creek dramatized the fact that the return of peace, certain to bring a fresh wave of whites westward, would be years of racial turmoil on the plains. As it had been before the war, the postwar era witnessed an undermanned army vainly trying to control thousands of shifting, ever-mobile bands of Indians. The plains military problem was primarily in the hands of General William Tecumseh Sherman, the war hero, who requested and was given command of the country lying between the Mississippi River and the Rocky Mountains. It was a task of monumental proportions: not only were the mounted tribesmen fierce, ever-dangerous enemies, but from the East came opposition both from the Department of the Interior—sponsors and guardians of the Indians—and from the humanitarians who saw the noble red man much as Cooper had envisioned him. This latter group, once fully occupied with the question of abolition, now devoted its literary talents to the plight of another minority and filled the eastern press with stories of injustice in the trans-Mississippi West.

In theory the Indian Bureau of the Department of the Interior had control of the Indians. In practice this was true only when the tribes were peaceful; when they got out of hand the army was called in to chastise the unruly, and this duplication of jurisdiction caused a good deal of friction between the two governmental departments. As a rule the Indian Bureau tried to be kind and beneficent, distributing goods, arms, and money, and settling Indian disputes in the hope that by kind treatment the Indian might be persuaded to be docile and peace loving. This policy irritated the War Department, which felt certain that the correct attitude toward the savages was a stern fairness, made effective by the frequent display of large and

heavily armed forces, and severe punishment of any Indian who trans-
gressed the white code of conduct.

Extremely controversial was the matter of arming the Indians. The
Indian Bureau believed that the Indians needed guns and ammunition to
kill the game necessary for their survival. But the army became vigorously
profane when the same guns were turned against the troops—and it was
particularly irritated when the guns of the Indians were better than those
of the soldiers. In behalf of the Indian Bureau it should be added that
comparatively few of the plains Indians ever had guns and that the few
repeating rifles they had usually came from white traders, not Indian agents.

The friction between Indian Bureau and War Department was
further increased by indefensible acts by representatives of each. Certain
Indian agents were notoriously inefficient and corrupt, lining their pockets
with the gains from distributing shoddy clothing and blankets, moldy flour,
and spoiled meat. Each unscrupulous agent created potential trouble for the
army. On the other hand the military sometimes interfered improperly—
often with such highhanded and dictatorial methods that peaceful agreement was impossible. Military expeditions often created more trouble than
they allayed, and an undiplomatic army officer could destroy within a few
hours the effects of years of painstaking work by a good Indian agent.

Differences between War and Interior Departments reflected a
national lack of agreement on the subject of solving the Indian problem.
Westerners, in particular, held that the only possible way to keep the
Indians in hand was to administer frequent and severe chastisement, and,
if necessary, to kill off enough of them to tame the others. The extreme
example of the application of this theory was Chivington's attack at Sand
Creek. Perhaps a majority of Easterners sympathized with the efforts of
the Interior Department. Their remoteness from the problem, their overall
ignorance of western Indian ways, and the great influence the humanitarians exerted over eastern minds explain this more peaceful point of view.
The arguments, pro and con, were a part of the general clamor that followed the close of the Civil War and the renewal of white-Indian conflict
in the West. Although scattered Indian battles beyond the Missouri frequently involved relatively few people and no significant amounts of land,
the question was national in scope. Today, decades later, thousands of words
are printed on the subject each year.

PLAINS WARFARE

As the Civil War drew to a close the western stage was set for a
drama that was to last for thirty years. With the coming of spring in 1865
and the approach of peace talks at Appomattox there was evidence that
full-scale violence would visit the high plains country. The Indians were

concerned at the demands for more territory that followed the cessions at Laramie in 1851, angered by such new transgressions as that of John Bozeman, who boldly marked off a short cut between the Oregon Trail and Montana, and then the final aggression of massacre at Sand Creek. When the northern Cheyenne heard about the treatment of their brothers at Chivington's hands they spread the word among their friends, the Sioux and the Arapaho. The word was out: violence would be answered by violence. As a taste of things to come, a band of northern Cheyenne waylaid nine whites who were making their way east, in January, 1865, and after dispatching them opened the dead men's baggage to find two scalps that had been taken in the Sand Creek affair. These veterans of the massacre were the first to pay for the fighting parson's attempts to solve the Indian problem. Their blood merely whetted the appetites of the braves, who were resolved that there would be no more Sand Creeks.

Widespread raiding now occurred along the line of communication between the Missouri River and the Rocky Mountains. In the early days of 1865 a Cheyenne party struck Julesburg, Colorado, and plundered it thoroughly. They streamed out of that little village trailing strips of cloth behind their ponies and brandishing captured articles of hardware. One piece of loot they found useless: an army paymaster's strong box yielded some $40,000 in currency, strange bits of colored paper they scattered across the prairie, letting the wind conduct a general disbursement.

Brigadier General Robert Mitchell assembled over six hundred cavalrymen and set out to punish the raiders, but after a fruitless march of several hundred miles he came home empty-handed. The Indians scattered widely, striking at isolated points, and then gradually withdrew northward to the Powder River country. Before they moved on they paralyzed travel along both branches of the Platte River, heavily attacked a group of soldiers at the Platte River Bridge (near present Casper, Wyoming), and frustrated the efforts of hundreds of soldiers.

Stung by these slashing attacks, a large body of troops commanded by General Patrick Connor plunged into the Powder River country in a determined effort to hunt out the warriors and punish them. An elaborate triple-headed strike was planned, a military vise in which the Indians would be caught and crushed. The story was one of rendezvous failure, uncoordinated attacks on scattered bands, and the near starvation of two of the three units invading that uncertain land stretching out toward Powder River. The whole expedition was a signal failure and for it Connor was handed the blame. It was not the failure of one man, or of his subordinate officers, but simply a victory of a raw and unconquered region, and its wily natives, over inexperienced Indian fighters who had much to learn about their business.

PEACE EFFORTS

Government officials, concerned over the expensive but futile efforts to hunt down Indians and mindful of voter pressure to cut back expenditures, decided on an alternative course of peace since war seemed so unrewarding. An expedition headed by General J. B. Sanborn, and bound for the Arkansas River country to fight the southern plains tribes, was called off. Treaty conferences were conducted on the Little Arkansas and at Fort Sully on the Missouri River in the autumn of 1865. By the first of these treaties the Cheyenne and the Arapaho signed away the remainder of their lands; by the other a portion of the Sioux merely agreed to cease hostilities.

General Grenville Dodge replaced Patrick Connor and was instructed to parley with the northern tribes, not to fight them. In June 1866, some two thousand Sioux, mostly Brûlé and Oglala, assembled at Fort Laramie to hear what the peace commissioners had in mind. At about the same time the War Department ordered Colonel Henry B. Carrington to move into the Powder River country to establish a line of posts that would protect travel on the Bozeman or Powder River Road. He and his troops passed through Fort Laramie about the time the commissioners were trying to talk peace to the Sioux. It is unnecessary to elaborate on the thoughts that passed through the minds of the assembled Indians. Red Cloud and Man-Afraid-of-His-Horses promptly withdrew from the deliberations and headed for home, ready to stop white travel across what was some of the best remaining buffalo country on the northern plains.

Carrington carried out his orders and three forts—Reno, Phil Kearny and C. F. Smith—appeared along the Bozeman Road. He made his headquarters at Fort Phil Kearny, named after the gallant Irish cavalryman who had lost his life in the recent war, and from this pivotal position (near the present town of Sheridan, Wyoming) he endeavored to carry out his assignment. From midsummer 1866 until late autumn his men labored at cutting logs, readying the headquarters post for winter, all of which went on under the careful scrutiny of the Sioux. From time to time the woodcutters were obliged to make a run for it as small war parties tried to intercept them. After a close call early in December, in which the men were saved only by a timely arrival of troops from the fort, it became clear that such escapes would not always be made. The Indians were tightening the noose around the hated little outpost that bristled in their very midst.

On December 21 distress signals from a beleaguered wood train stirred the men at Fort Phil Kearny into action, and young Captain William J. Fetterman, who had boasted that he could ride through the Sioux nation with eighty men begged for his chance to make the rescue. Cautious

Colonel Carrington acceded to the request but specifically warned his young cavalryman not to pursue the Indians over Lodge Trail Ridge. Fetterman saluted his acknowledgment of the instructions and led a force of eighty-one through the gates to what he imagined would be glory. The Indians—Cheyenne, Arapaho, and Sioux—stayed back in the hills and set up the oldest ruse in military history: the decoy. A few selected braves rode within rifle range and when the troops failed to nibble at the bait they became more daring. At some undetermined point Fetterman's resolve to follow orders yielded to temptation and he took up the chase—beyond Lodge Trail Ridge. Quickly the main Indian force snapped shut the trap and what amounted to an execution took place. In less than an hour Fetterman and his command lay dead, most of the troops in an area about forty feet square, the others scattered around it. By the time a relief party arrived the corpses lay frozen in grotesque shapes, presenting a grisly tableau of death. One of the surgeons in attendance wrote laconically: "We brought in about fifty in wagons like you see hogs brought to market."

Carrington at once dispatched the news east by means of civilian couriers who carried his message 236 blizzard-swept miles to Fort Laramie. His plea was simple: "Do send me reinforcements forthwith." Not only were additional troops sent but so was a replacement for Colonel Carrington, who spent most of the remainder of his life trying to vindicate himself. Although some army difficulties might be dealt with by a simple transfer of a commanding officer, it was not enough to silence the national outcry over such disasters. All across the country the cry that the only good Indian was a dead Indian was mixed with insistence by humanitarians that the heartless Indian policy was causing such understandable reaction by the natives. Both sides fired a good deal of verbal ammunition at the War and Interior Departments with the word "mismanagement" prominent in their salvos.

Once again violence on the plains brought renewed efforts at peace. In the spring of 1868 tribesmen and commissioners sat down to smoke the pipe at Fort Laramie. It had been less than two years since Red Cloud and the others had stalked out of that place, deeply angered at the government's resolve to fortify the Bozeman Road, and determined to oppose the move with all possible vigor. Red Cloud's demands were unchanged: close this short cut and oblige Montana-bound miners to use an alternate route. The abandonment was agreed to and troops were pulled out of the contested region. It is understandable why a "cause and effect" construction should be placed on this incident and that contemporaries as well as later students of western history should say that the mighty Red Cloud had turned back forces of the federal government. There were several reasons for the decision: the Union Pacific Railroad, then nearing completion, would allow fast and relatively cheap transportation to Corinne, Utah, from which point goods could be hauled into Montana by wagon over a well-used road that did not pass through the land of powerful, determined Indians; no organized public transportation, either freight or passenger, ever used the Bozeman Road, which was employed chiefly by emigrant parties and one-trip freighters; the number of federal troops required to keep the road open made it unreasonably expensive in terms of financial outlay and manpower. In short, the cutoff had pretty largely served its purpose by 1868. The Sioux were only a persistent annoyance.

WAR ON THE WASHITA

While the federal government was inclined to make peace where such a course seemed profitable, it continued to press the Indians in other quarters. In April 1867, General Winfield Scott Hancock maneuvered against Siuox and southern Cheyenne bands in Kansas and finally burned a village of about 250 Indian lodges along Pawnee Fork. The action not only outraged the Indians, who lost much property, but infuriated the Indian agents, who thought Hancock's campaign absolutely unnecessary. In fact, the badly timed and inept actions of the military are generally credited with setting off a whole series of Indian depredations that followed. As one example, the Indians lashed out so frequently and so severely at Kansas Pacific Railroad engineering parties that construction was virtually halted for over a month. All along the Smoky Hill Road across Kansas affairs became sufficiently turbulent to cut travel to a mere trickle.

In early 1867 there had been no war on the southern plains, only scattered raids here and there, but by autumn attacks had become so widespread and so bold that some solution to the problem had to be found. Again the government turned to the peace council in the hope of buying off the warlike plainsmen. In October 1867, General C. C. Augur, Kansas Governor Samuel J. Crawford, his lieutenant governor, and United States Senator Edward P. Ross (accompanied by newsmen, a photographer, and five hundred cavalrymen) met with the Cheyenne and Arapaho at Medicine Lodge Creek (Indian Territory), where a treaty was effected. The terms were familiar: white passage through the southern and central plains was guaranteed; railroad crews would be undisturbed; more Indian lands were ceded; new homes for the dispossessed would be provided on reservations. For this the government promised individual landholdings (320 acres per family head), issues of clothing, and $20,000 annually for the tribe for twenty-five years. Formalities concluded, some two thousand Cheyenne accepted presents from the commissioners (including ammunition) and headed south for winter camp.

During 1868 the Cheyenne warriors became restless and expressed their dissatisfaction with the recent treaty by renewing their practice of raiding. During August northern Cheyenne and Sioux came close to annihilating a small force under the command of Major George A. Forsyth along the Arikaree Fork of the Republican River in eastern Colorado. The Battle of Beecher's Island—named after Lieutenant Frederick H. Beecher who died in the siege—became a part of the annals of Plains Indian warfare.

The axiom that war follows the failure of peace was again demonstrated as troops took the field for a major campaign. One prong of an elaborately planned triple-headed strike was composed of eleven companies of the Seventh Cavalry, commanded by Lieutenant Colonel George Armstrong Custer, and elements of the Nineteenth Kansas Volunteers brought into service during the emergency.

Custer was probably the most picturesque and magnetic army officer of his day. Six feet tall, with the broad shoulders and narrow hips of the cavalryman, he wore his golden hair to his shoulders and moved with a swagger. Most unusual for the period, he used neither liquor nor tobacco and swore but seldom. The great and abiding goal of his life was glory, and in pursuit of it he was brave to the point of recklessness, a characteristic General William Tecumseh Sherman called "a good trait for a Cavalry officer." His career was brilliant but erratic. A graduate from West Point at twenty-one, Custer found in the Civil War the opportunity to achieve high rank in a brief period. As an Indian fighter in the 1860s he was a lieutenant colonel, although he is often referred to by his wartime rank of brigadier general of the volunteers. His command, the Seventh Cavalry, became one of the best and most famous units of its kind. Custer had that rare quality which, in spite of harsh discipline, attracted men who were willing to follow him to the death.

Custer left the rendezvous late in November, in bitter cold and in snow a foot deep, to search for Indians. He found Black Kettle's camp of southern Cheyenne along the Washita River, not far from the Texas border, and within ten minutes his troops had invested the place. Then the slaughter began. Over a hundred Indians, including the hapless Black Kettle, who had miraculously survived Sand Creek, fell before the troopers. Before neighboring Comanche, Arapaho, and Kiowa warriors could get into action Custer marched his men out of danger. Part of the young officer's fame for this action came from an exaggerated and much-publicized report he wrote, one in which little mention was made of the women and children who died at the hands of the troops. Nor was much said about the fate of Major Joel H. Elliott, whose detachment was surrounded and dispatched by the Indians. Captain Fred W. Benteen was so outraged at what he regarded as a callous abandonment of Elliott by Custer that he wrote a bitter but anonymous letter to the newspapers. It was the beginning of a famous enmity that survived even the controversial Custer. An even more unsatisfactory outcome of the engagement was the fact that it did not intimidate the southern Cheyenne, did not stop the raiding of the frontier, and was in no way decisive.

THE GREAT ENIGMA

In the spring of 1869 General U. S. Grant was inaugurated as President. His hopes for the troubled South, writhing in the agony of reconstruction, had been expressed in the words "Let us have peace." He felt the same way about the troubled frontier, a conviction that was shared by many Americans of his day. The early post–Civil War years yielded only turmoil in the West, where another American minority was struggling for its rights. Unfortunately for the Indians, they were powerful enough to fight for what they regarded as theirs and their willingness to exert that power was costly to them. Federal government authorities were perplexed over the apparent insolubility of a problem that frustrated them but was not sufficiently critical to call forth more of the nation's resources to combat it.

A historian who lived during those trying years described the situation as he saw it. In 1903 Hiram Martin Chittenden wrote in his *History of Early Steamboat Navigation on the Missouri River* (II, 355):

> History will exonerate the government from any but the purest motives in its dealing with the Indians. It may have been unwise in some of its measures; it was certainly weak in carrying its purposes into effect; but it always sought, with the light it possessed, the highest good of the Indian. . . . It was the problem of how to commit a great wrong without doing any wrong—how to deprive the Indian of his birthright in such a way that he should feel that no injustice had been done him.

The American government, having treated with the Indians at Medicine Lodge Creek and at Fort Laramie between 1866 and 1868, and having fought northern and southern tribes alike during that time, faced a disturbing dilemma as the decade of the seventies approached. After experimenting with both war and peace on the plains the government still had a problem that was no nearer solution; it was, in fact, growing worse. Unhappily, the fumbling was to go on for approximately a quarter of a century longer.

READINGS

THE DEVELOPING CRISIS ON THE PLAINS. LeRoy R. Hafen and Francis M. Young, *Fort Laramie* (1938) contains a great deal of material pertaining to the pre–Civil War period. Wilbur S. Nye, *Carbine and Lance* (1937) emphasizes old Fort Sill. Harold E. Briggs, *Frontiers of the North-*

west (1940) is general. See also Everett Dick, *Vanguards of the Frontier* (1941). Carl C. Rister, *Border Command* (1944) is good on Phil Sheridan's part in the early postwar campaigns. See also his *Southwestern Frontier* (1928). See Paul W. Gates, *Fifty Million Acres* (1954), Chapters 1, 2, and 6 on the land question. J. Cecil Alter's *James Bridger* (1925, 1962) tells something of the Indian pressure during the 1850s and 1860s. A good documentary account of pre–Civil War Plains Indian affairs is LeRoy R. and Ann W. Hafen, *Relatives with the Indians of the Plains, 1857–1861* (1959).

THE DISAPPEARANCE OF THE BUFFALO. Wayne Gard, *The Great Buffalo Hunt* (1959); E. Douglas Branch, *The Hunting of the Buffalo* (1929); Mari Sandoz, *The Buffalo Hunters* (1954); and Frank G. Roe, *The North American Buffalo* (1951). Donald B. Russell, *The Lives and Legends of Buffalo Bill* (1960) is the best book on the famed buffalo hunter. William Cody, *Autobiography of Buffalo Bill* (1920) gives a firsthand account.

INDIAN UPRISING IN MINNESOTA. Kenneth Carley, *The Sioux Uprising of 1862* (1961); Theodore C. Blegen and Philip D. Jordan, *With Various Voices* (1949); and Charles M. Oehler, *The Great Sioux Uprising* (1959) deal with the Minnesota campaign.

EARLY POST–CIVIL WAR DISTURBANCES. Captain Eugene F. Ware, *The Indian War of 1864* (1911, 1960) provides a firsthand account of troubles during the war that is useful in understanding the ensuing postwar struggle. More particularized is Dee Brown, *Fort Phil Kearny: An American Saga* (1962). A very informative reminiscence of an army wife who lived for a time at Fort C. F. Smith (Montana) is Merrill J. Mattes, *Indians, Infants and Infantry: Andrew and Elizabeth Burt on the Frontier* (1960). The most detailed account of trouble along the Bozeman Road is Grace R. Hebard and E. A. Brininstool, *The Bozeman Trail* (2 vols., 1922). A documentary account of the Connor campaign may be found in LeRoy R. and Ann W. Hafen, *Powder River Campaigns and Sawyer's Expedition of 1865* (1961). Custer's earlier exploits are briefly treated by Edgar I. Stewart in *Custer's Luck* (1955).

For a more extensive list of related readings see the bibliography for the next chapter.

CHAPTER 32

THE INDIAN
PROBLEM "SOLVED"

T he troubled condition of the plains moved Congress to engage in an extended study of the matter. Since the legislators were generally ignorant about Indian affairs and since the better-informed members were as badly divided in opinion as was the public at large, the first job seemed to be to collect information. As early as 1865 a joint committee of seven was appointed to investigate and to make necessary recommendations for legislation. Headed by Senator J. R. Doolittle of Wisconsin, the committee took its duties seriously and traveled widely over the plains, interviewing Indians, Indian agents, settlers, miners, army officers, and, in fact, every available person with information or a grievance.

The report of the committee of seven was presented in January 1867. Its conclusions were that Indian troubles were caused by white aggression and the overly vigorous actions of the army, and that the Indians were dying off rapidly. The report suggested a small permanent committee to investigate further and to make specific recommendations to Congress. These rather modest proposals brought no action, but the investigations of the committee had provided a vast fund of information upon which future action could be based. In spite of the seemingly inconclusive results a more vigorous and better coordinated policy was in the making.

PEACE COMMISSION

The rather tentative efforts of the 1865–1867 investigations led to the formation of a new commission composed of four civilians, including the Commissioner of Indian Affairs, and three generals. Congress stated its purpose: removing the causes of friction between the two races; securing the safety of the overland routes; discovering permanent homes for the Indians; and finding ways of promoting Indian civilization without interfering with the rest of the United States. Moreover, the new commission was not limited to investigation and recommendations, but could negotiate any necessary treaties to put its program into effect.

During 1867–1868 the commissioners criss-crossed the plains and negotiated treaties with practically all tribes. These agreements provided for various reservations throughout the West, the most important of which was Indian Territory. This region, essentially modern Oklahoma, was to house all the tribes of the southern and central plains. A large area west of the Missouri River (primarily in modern South Dakota) was given to the Sioux. It was this group of men (including General William T. Sherman, commanding the military Division of the Missouri) that agreed to the abandonment of the Bozeman Road.

The final report of the "peace commission" was sympathetic to the Indian, but recognized realistically that the Indians could not be permitted to roam freely over the plains, and that their concentration in reservations was necessary. The friction between the War and Interior Departments was noted, and the suggestion was made that a new and independent Indian Department be created to eliminate the resulting difficulties.

Soon after the report was made the troubles occurred that culminated in the Custer campaign on the Washita, and the commission then decided that complete control by the War Department would be the best solution. Noting that the Cheyenne and the Arapaho were raiding widely and that various treaties had been broken, General Sherman spoke for his colleagues when he said: "Spite of Indian Peace Commissions, and all our efforts to keep the rascals quiet, they have broke out simply because they can make more by war than Peace. We must not let up this time, but keep it going till they are killed or humbled." He advised the Secretary of War to cut off all annuities to hostiles and give the Indians the war they had asked for. "I propose to give them enough of it to satisfy them to their hearts' content," wrote the crusty general. The affair at Washita was an application of this line of thinking.

THE QUAKER POLICY

Just when the national debate about Custer's raid on Black Kettle's camp was at its height a new policy shift occurred. Grant took office in March 1869 and brought Sherman to Washington to fill the vacated position of general of the army. The President's stand on the Indian question did not agree with that of his old comrade in arms, Sherman, but rather looked toward pacification of the natives through peace overtures. Positions in the Indian service were filled by recommendations made by the various churches, the Quakers receiving a considerable proportion of the appointments; hence the name "Quaker Policy." Although the Indians registered no objections to the new approach it was not well received by all churchmen. The Catholics especially resented the small proportion of appointees awarded them and felt that the new policy was anti-Catholic.

The employment of church people to work among the Indians appealed to the humanitarians and particularly to the radicals in Congress who were heavily engaged in promoting Negro rights. The Indians were another minority, one whose problems appeared to be much more important immediately after the Civil War. In 1870, and a number of times later, delegations of Indians were brought to Washington to visit the Great White Father. As a rule they were put on display in one or more other eastern cities before being allowed to return home. During the visit of 1870 Red Cloud and about twenty other Oglala Sioux were shown military parades, naval cannon, warships and other examples of the white man's "thunder." Before returning home the visitors dined with the President and met with members of the Cabinet and the diplomatic corps. When Red Cloud declined an invitation to dinner extended by the wife of Admiral Dahlgren, on the ground that he was in Washington on business and not for pleasure, capital city society was titillated.

In another departure the old treaty system was abolished. By a law of March 3, 1871, the United States abandoned the fiction that the various tribes were sovereign powers. Agreements might still be made, but they were to be ratified by the entire Congress rather than merely by the Senate. The change was in the direction of political realism, since the Indians never had been foreign nations in the usual sense of the term; in practice the only important effect was to give the House a long-desired voice in any new Indian agreements.

Negotiating treaties for the creation of reservations was by no means equivalent to getting the Indians on the selected land and making farmers of them. Actually it was unlikely that they could be confined to the reservations as long as game was available on the plains. In the north the Sioux continued to roam as their desires dictated, with apparently not the least intention of migrating to their new home. Those confined to Indian Territory showed similar inclinations, spending their summers in war and hunting parties and then returning to the reservation for winter rations.

Although, the Indian problem obviously had not been solved by the mere creation of reservations, the temporary confusion and bloodshed should not be allowed to obscure the general trend of the time. Expanding settlements, together with more forts and soldiers, were inexorably pushing the Indians back toward their reservations; the day was coming when war and hunting parties would find no place to go. Moreover, the disappearance of game on the plains was rapidly eliminating the possibility of nomadic wandering. Not many years were to elapse before an Indian could avoid starvation only by staying on the reservation—if not to farm, then at least to draw his rations from the government.

With these basic conditions in mind, the Indian troubles of the seventies decline in importance. True enough, Indian disturbances were depressingly common but these were the last gusts of wind before the hurricane subsided. The comparative isolation of the various Indian tribes averted any possible chance of a general Indian war, and assured the ultimate complete victory of the whites. Many commentators of the seventies who saw the approaching end of all Indian troubles were well justified in their optimism, even though their predictions seemed silly when made in the welter of bloodshed.

MODOC REBELLION

The idea of negotiating with rebellious Indians, one that gained wide approval in the East during the early 1870s, had some serious drawbacks when put to a practical test. The disastrous result of diplomatic efforts with the Modoc of southern Oregon and northern California did not cause the peace advocates to abandon their theories, but it considerably modified their initial ardor.

A few months after Grant's inauguration in the spring of 1869 Alfred B. Meacham, a party worker and a great supporter of the general, was appointed Indian superintendent for Oregon. Meacham, a good Methodist and a long-time resident of the West, was regarded as well qualified to administer the President's "Quaker Policy." A good humanitarian, the new agent was properly appalled at conditions among his charges, and he at once set about uplifting their moral decline by issuing a number of prohibitions against such sins as polygamy, gambling, ghost-dancing, and slave-holding. The varying shades of color found among the Indian children suggested that the troops had anticipated the agent's desires for friendly association by some years and he made great efforts to terminate such outward evidences of friendship between the sexes of the two races. Before long there were a number of objections to Agent Meacham's program, which appeared to be aimed at keeping the natives in a condition of paternalistic subjugation. It is not surprising that this tribe reacted as other American Indians had, and balked the white man's efforts at civilization.

As always, in times of such trouble, there emerged a leader who became the spokesman for his people. In this case it was not the hereditary chief, who happened to be an old man, but a young subchief named Keintpoos, better known among the white settlers as Captain Jack. Meacham, who was somewhat taken in by Jack's initial display of cooperation, soon discovered that he was not as tractable as at first appeared, particularly when Jack led his band off the reservation and refused to return peaceably. For a number of months the situation was in a stalemate, for the military, weakened by troops drawn off to support Crook's campaigns in Arizona, did not feel strong enough to challenge the defiant Indians.

By the autumn of 1872 the residents of Modoc country were clamoring for Jack's arrest. His men made nuisances of themselves, barging into farmhouses, demanding food, and trying to extort "rent" from the farmers whom they regarded as interlopers; moreover, Jack had killed an Indian medicine man in cold blood for failing to save two sick members of his family. Although the latter act was a tribal affair, the whites thought Jack should be tried for murder. General E. R. S. Canby, a career officer and a veteran of the Civil War, ordered his subordinates to arrest Jack and some of his henchmen to quiet the complaints of the settlers. The Indians resisted and what became known as the Modic War ensued.

It now became the duty of Canby, who was sympathetic to the Indians and who had remarked that it would be "impolitic if not cruel" to make them return to the reservation, to round up the recalcitrants. It was a discouraging task, for the Modocs slipped into the lava beds of northern California and set up almost impregnable defenses. For example, in an assault made upon them in January 1873, the army lost forty men in a single day's fighting and made no headway against their enemy. A few days later army headquarters ordered a cessation of such frontal attacks and there ensued a long period of fruitless negotiation with the Indians. Finally, Captain Jack agreed to a parley to be held on April 11, halfway between the lava beds and the encampment of the troops.

Canby left behind his sidearms, and with several other white commissioners met with Jack and his followers. As the Modocs smoked the general's cigars and listened to him explain the federal government's Indian policy, they watched their leader for a prearranged signal. When it was given they drew revolvers and started firing. Canby was shot through the head; Reverend Elezar Thomas, a Methodist preacher acting as a commissioner, was also killed; Meacham was shot five times and left for dead; Commissioner L. S. Dyar escaped by outrunning the attackers. This affair, in which the first general officer of the United States Army to die at the hands of Indians was killed, thoroughly shocked the nation. The Modocs now were hunted down with a vengeance. Captain Jack and three accomplices were hanged, and the rest of the tribe was packed off to Indian Territory.

The rebellion of a small group of Indians, known as a "war," was typical of such disturbances in that it was costly in lives and money—considering the number of Indians involved—and was not a solution to the problem. When all the excitement had passed, some of the Indians were still off the reservation, the ghost-dancing had not stopped, and the manner in which Jack and a handful of his followers had stood off the troops made a deep impression upon other western Indians. Even more important, the government appeared to have learned nothing from the crisis. All during the decade of the 1870s it floundered with the Indian dilemma, applying alternate treatments of sweet reasonableness and force, a program that satisfied neither the Indians nor their white partisans.

TURMOIL IN THE SOUTHWEST

Making peace with the Indians was not so simple a matter as many churchmen believed. In the Southwest the Apache were cruel, cunning, elusive, and hard fighting. To Westerners there was one answer: Fight to the finish. An army officer reflected their sentiment in a remark he made to Kit Carson in 1862: "All Indian men of that tribe are to be killed whenever and wherever you can find them." Such notions were set aside as archaic by those who proposed to carry out the Quaker Policy. In 1870 Congress appropriated $70,000 to make peace with the Apache, and in the following year Vincent Colyer, secretary to the Board of Indian Commissioners, was sent to Arizona to negotiate with the Indians.

The Colyer mission was sparked by an atrocity against the Apache that rivaled the earlier Chivington affair in Colorado. A band of starving Indians had come to Camp Grant, Arizona, where they were fed by the commandant, who even encouraged them to send for their friends and relatives. A number of white and Mexican ranchers, annoyed by constant depredations against their herds, decided to administer punishment to any available Apache. At dawn, April 30, 1871, a group of these impromptu soldiers fell upon the Indian encampment near the fort, attacking sleeping men, women, and children. After a quick but bloody assault, they retreated to Tucson with about twenty-nine Indian children as prisoners, boasting that they had not lost a man in the battle. While western papers clucked mildly at the killing of women and children, Easterners were aghast. President Grant acted firmly, warning that if the perpetrators were not brought to justice immediately Arizona would be placed under martial law. To avoid such military control leaders of the group were persuaded to turn themselves in and after a brief trial were acquitted. The result of this farce was the coming of Colyer, and of General George Crook.

Although the administration acted firmly it also demonstrated, by what now took place in Arizona, that coordination in Indian affairs still remained only an ideal. Crook was ordered to cooperate with Colyer, who shortly laid off one reservation in New Mexico and three in Arizona. Many

Indians were assigned new homes, with such notable exceptions as the Chiricahua and some of the Mescalero and Pinal Apache who ranged the countryside as hostiles. Fearful that Crook would pursue too severe a course with his Indian charges, the Grant administration sent out Major General Oliver O. Howard as the ranking officer in the Southwest. The gentle, one-armed Howard, recently involved in the southern Reconstruction program, negotiated several treaties, including a surprising agreement from the tough-minded old Cochise of the Chiricahua Apache in the autumn of 1872. However, despite real progress, scattered and sporadic raids continued. Crook, who had been drilling his men while Howard talked peace, now was brought into action with orders to crush the unruly hostiles.

Crook, a tall, slender, and muscular man who used neither liquor, tobacco, nor profanity, was as tough-minded as he was industrious. After expressing sympathy for the Indians he ordered them back to their reservations and promised the severest punishment for those who did not obey. Crook's words could be trusted completely, and when the Indians flouted his commands he took the field. By dividing his forces into comparatively small parties he harried the minor hostile bands unceasingly until, by April 1873, they were at his mercy. For the first time in 300 years Arizona knew peace from Indian depredations.

In 1875 Crook was transferred north and his departure marked the renewal of trouble in Arizona. The Indians did not like reservation life, especially when they found themselves hungry. Denied the hunt, they were unable to subsist on inadequate and irregularly dispensed rations. Well-armed bands under such leaders as Victorio and Geronimo raided the countryside; when Arizona became too dangerous they crossed the boundary into Mexico, only to raid back across the border. Military expeditions found themselves hampered by the international boundary as well as by the conditions of Apache warfare. Ultimately, in 1880, Victorio was killed, but it was another six years before Geronimo was cornered and forced to surrender.

NORTHERN PLAINS WARFARE

The various southern Indian troubles were but side shows to the main performance that was taking place on the northern plains during the seventies. The Sioux was the one important tribe that had never experienced a major defeat by the whites and had even won several minor victories. The Sioux harbored a number of grievances. Bad conditions on their Dakota reservation had reinforced their desire to roam the plains farther west, where they came into collision with miners, stockmen, and a scattering of settlers. More important, white miners had invaded country reserved to the Indians, particularly the Black Hills region, where rumor had it there was "gold in the grass roots." Early prospectors were ejected, at Sherman's order, but a new group tagged along after the Custer expedition of 1874, and very soon the entire United States Army might have had trouble in freeing the country from white trespassers. Recalling earlier demands by volunteers to be allowed to retain all the loot they might capture from the Indians, the Sioux now made sarcastic inquiries about the possession of horses, wagons, and other equipment they might take from the white invaders. Grant's answer was an offer to buy off the Indians with $25,000 and hunting rights along the Platte River, an overture that was declined. The government now took the customary recourse of turning to force and peremptorily ordered all hostile Sioux back to the reservation by February 1, 1876, under the threat of punishment. This order was physically impossible to obey even if the Indians had so desired; consequently when the specified date arrived considerable bands of Indians were still roaming the country to the west. No less a figure than Phil Sheridan believed the Indians would regard the order as little more than a joke.

General Alfred Terry sent word to Sitting Bull, of the Hunkpapa Sioux, that after the specified date he would move against the roving bands. "You won't need any guides," Sitting Bull is reputed to have said, "You can find me easily; I won't run away." Perhaps the noted Sioux did not say these words—he denied having done so in later years—but his actions were far from friendly. When the dead line passed and there was no acquiescence from the Indians, both sides resolutely prepared for war. A punitive expedition made ready to enter the country of the hostiles in force to punish both Sioux and Cheyenne, but particularly the former.

The favorite strategy—a triple-headed strike—was decided on: one column under General Crook was to move north out of Wyoming into Montana; a second under Colonel John Gibbon was to move eastward from Fort Ellis, Montana; and a third under Terry was to march westward from Fort Abraham Lincoln (Bismarck), Dakota. Terry, who had won distinction in the Civil War but had had no experience in Indian fighting, did not relish the assignment and would have turned it over to the more experienced George A. Custer had Grant not prevented it. The President was angry at the flamboyant young Custer for having presented embarrassing evidence in the recent investigation of Secretary of War W. W. Belknap. It was bad enough that the Secretary was in trouble; even worse, the affair involved some of Grant's relatives. It was all that Phil Sheridan could do to get so much as permission for Custer to join the expedition.

Crook left Fort Fetterman, Wyoming, in March 1876. He marched his men slowly northward toward the rendezvous, penetrating hostile country cautiously, fully aware that a talented enemy lay somewhere ahead. In

The High Plains after the Civil War

March they came across the village of Crazy Horse, a camp of over 100
lodges of Sioux and some Cheyenne. Although the troops were victorious,
the affair was far from satisfactory to the military. General Joseph J.
Reynolds, in immediate command, pulled his troops out of the fight so precipitously that one of Crook's officers could write: "We practically abandoned the victory to the savages." The disgruntled Crook later preferred
charges against Reynolds and two other officers for misbehavior before the
enemy. The discordant group, tired and cold, returned to Fort Fetterman
to recuperate and prepare for further action. Late in May, Crook again
moved his forces northward and within two weeks he again engaged the
Sioux, this time along the South Fork of the Rosebud River; after a fight
that cost the general 9 of his 1325 men, both sides broke off the action.
In the latter days of June, Crook's little army went into camp, this time
along Goose Creek near the Big Horn Mountains in northern Wyoming,
where the men spent their time fishing and waiting for the next phase of
the campaign to commence. During these days, when one of Crook's officers
estimated that some 15,000 trout were caught and consumed by the troops,

events of a much more critical nature were taking place not far to the north on the Little Big Horn.

Terry did not leave Fort Abraham Lincoln until the middle of May. The main element of his force was the Seventh Cavalry commanded by Custer. Late in the month, Terry's troops met Gibbon's Montana column on the Yellowstone, at the mouth of the Powder River, where the officers conferred. Reports of an "Indian sign" on the Rosebud stirred the campaigners into action. Terry at once sent Custer ahead to follow the trail, with orders that gave him considerable freedom of action but that urged caution—largely to permit the deployment of the remainder of the army to cut off any Indian retreat. No one conceived of an Indian victory.

When Custer left on his fateful march he was only thirty-seven years old, but his strenuous life had made him in some respects older than his years. His chances of winning great fame seemed to be lessening and he was in the mood to wager everything on the single throw of the dice, for he was utterly confident that his Seventh Cavalry could beat all the Indians on the plains. Sherman recognized the nature of the gamble when he made the comment: "I suppose now the Indians will lead our troops a will-o'-the-wisp circle, until some lucky turn may give one of the columns a chance." As Custer pressed forward he revealed his anxiety that the "lucky turn" would fall to his command.

Although his scouts reported large bodies of hostiles in the region, Custer tended to underestimate the threat. Even had he known the exact number of the enemy it is doubtful that he would have altered his tactics: he was convinced that a hammer blow against almost any group of Indians would scatter them. He had struck such a blow with great success at Washita; he was sure he could do it again. On June 25, 1876, he came upon an encampment of Sioux and Cheyenne, their tepees spread out along the valley of the Little Big Horn; characteristically he ordered the charge. Without waiting for the remaining elements of the proposed three-pronged attack and apparently fearful that he might have to share some of the glory, he led his men into a fray in which they were outnumbered perhaps 8 to 1. Major Marcus Reno, leading some 134 officers and men (plus 16 scouts), was sent across the valley floor in a direct attack, while Custer took some of the men along the low-lying hills in a circling movement. Reno, a fine officer with a good Civil War record but with no Indian fighting experience, broke off the attack despite the consternation he caused among the Indians, and retreated instead of charging on through the camp. For whatever reason—irresolution, extreme caution, or a long background in more formal fighting—Reno failed to carry out his assignment and took refuge in the timber along the Little Big Horn River where he could better defend himself.

Meanwhile, Custer attempted to complete his movements along the bluffs overlooking the Indian village. There remains great speculation today with regard to the details of his movements after he left the others, but since none of those in the group survived the day there exists no proof of what happened. Presumably he tried to move down from higher ground, cross the river, and join the attack on the village, but was obliged to retreat to seek a better defensive position. It was on a knoll that terminates a series of ridges that Custer made his famous last stand as the warriors of Sitting Bull, Crazy Horse, Gall, and others swept up the grassy slopes to ride down the troopers. Reno's indecisiveness in the valley was fatal to the whole daring plan.

The annihilation of Custer's 225–man force turned out to be relatively unimportant in the general campaign. Terry had been delayed but not stopped by this single action, and in a relentless pursuit of the Sioux and Cheyenne that ensued the hostile bands were obliged to surrender while Sitting Bull and a few of his Sioux escaped into Canada. Even he later returned and was made into a reservation Indian.

THE NEZ PERCÉ WAR

During the remainder of 1876 and in early 1877, as the blue-clad troopers were running down scattered Sioux and Cheyenne bands, there were reverberations farther west that would erupt into another Indian war. The source of trouble surprised some Americans, for it came from the relatively peaceful Nez Percé Indians of Idaho, who had lived a quiet, pastoral life all during the years that Plains Indians had caused so much commotion. In 1875 President Grant approved the opening of part of their reservation to settlement, but this raised no eyebrows in a nation where such actions had become almost policy. What generated comment was the fact that the Indians registered objections to such an old and time-honored practice of encroachment and presented their complaints in the tangible form of rifles and raiding.

The gentle O. O. Howard was in Idaho at the time of the trouble—1877—and he at once ordered troops into the field to put down any uprising. Under the very capable direction of Chief Joseph, a young but wise leader, the Indians began a retreat toward Canada that is one of the classics in the annals of American Indian campaigns. With some 200 warriors, but hampered by almost twice that number of women, children, and aged, he moved eastward across the Bitterroot Mountains toward Montana. The frightened residents of Missoula sent for a hastily assembled group of some 200 volunteers, who erected a barricade in a nearby valley and prepared to stop the invasion. Joseph's advance scouts took one look, circled past what became known as "Fort Fizzle," and headed south toward Yellowstone

Park. By now Colonel John Gibbon and about 160 troopers were in hot pursuit, marching as much as 30 miles a day, or twice the rate made by the heavily encumbered Nez Percé warriors.

On the morning of August 9 Gibbon came across the sleeping camp of Chief Joseph and at once launched an attack. Despite the element of surprise, the soldiers found themselves in a sharp fight that cost them heavily. As their ammunition ran low they took up defensive positions and waited for reinforcements from Howard, who was in the Bitterroot Valley. The Indians, having lost 50 women and children and 30 warriors, according to Chief Joseph's account, took this opportunity to continue their flight. Once more they moved east, through Yellowstone Park, where they thoroughly frightened some of the tourists and narrowly missed encountering General Sherman, who was fishing there; they then headed north toward Canada.

The pursuing Howard covered 1321 miles in seventy days, but was outmaneuvered and outdistanced. Jeeringly the newspapers called his force the Indians' best supply line, and the general became so angered that Sherman was obliged to remind him that he was fighting Indians, not newspaper reporters. Nelson A. Miles, fresh from his pursuit of Sitting Bull's Sioux, was brought into the chase to cooperate with Gibbon, who was, in turn, trying to help Howard corner the elusive Joseph. Colonel Samuel D. Sturgis tried to make an interception along the Yellowstone River but was outfought and outmaneuvered. The chase went on, as frustrated army officers cursed their luck and the red race in general, and the nation's newspaper readers followed the curious pursuit with mounting fascination.

By the time Joseph and his band were in the Bear Paw Mountains of north central Montana the leader decided it was time to stop and care for the sick and wounded. There is some reason to believe he thought he was in Canada. It was here that General Miles caught up with the group and after a five-day siege in which the Indians, particularly the women and children, suffered from cold and hunger, Chief Joseph decided to surrender. It was October. Of the 700 Nez Percés who had left Idaho in June, nearly 100 had been killed, others had fled, and now there were only about 50 effective fighting men. "Hear me, my chiefs," Joseph told his warriors, "I am tired: my heart is sick and sad. From where the sun now stands, I will fight no more." Summarizing the affair General Sherman called it

> one of the most extraordinary Indian wars. . . . The Indians thoroughly displayed a courage and skill that elicited universal praise; they abstained from scalping, let captive women go free, did not commit indiscriminate murder of peaceful families which is unusual, and fought with almost scientific skill, using advance and rear guards, skirmish-lines and field-fortifications.

The wily Joseph and his followers were subdued at a cost of nearly $2 million, not including property destroyed. After receiving the due praise of Sherman, Miles, and others, the recreants were packed off to Indian Territory, in violation of a promise that they would be returned to Idaho. In a new, humid climate most of them died. It was an ironic end for those who had survived all kinds of weather, marches over unheard-of distances, and pursuit by several thousand federal troops.

The echoes of military-Indian strife in Montana had barely died out before a new struggle ensued in Colorado. The Ute Indians living on the White River Reservation were in a bad mood over the laxity of the government in providing them with supplies. In 1878 Nathan C. Meeker, once associated with Horace Greeley's newspaper, was appointed agent and he at once made the normal mistake of trying to reform the less fortunate natives. Not only did he push these nomadic hunters toward a new, agrarian life, but he tried to fit them into the white social structure as he envisioned it Grudgingly the Utes took to the plow, with occasional unauthorized flights from the reservation, and the agent began to have high hopes for their salvation. However, like the stern parent, he pushed his charges too hard, and when he plowed up their race track, he made a grave mistake.

In September 1879, Chief Douglass and a small group of his followers attacked the agency, killed a dozen white men (including Meeker), and captured the agent's wife, daughter, two other women, and a small baby boy. Meanwhile, other Utes ambushed an army relief party of 160 men, commanded by Major T. T. Thornburg, killing the major and 13 of his men. Only the prompt march of reinforcements from Fort Steele, Wyoming, saved the remnants. What became known as the "Thornburg massacre" and the other events at the agency caused a great deal of excitement and, of course, brought a large body of federal troops. The result was familiar: the subjection of the Indians, a "treaty," and the removal of the Utes from Colorado.

RESERVATION LIFE

During the post–Civil War years, in particular, it was the general policy of the United States government to segregate whites and Indians by placing the latter on their own reservations. As the policy developed, various Indians were placed on a number of reservations but in the early years after Appomattox a rather vague notion prevailed that the Plains Indians should be divided into two large groups, one north and one south of the main line of traffic up the Platte River, and that there should be no trespassing on them by the white population. As this idea took shape the northern

Indians were gathered along the west bank of the Missouri River in Dakota Territory and those of the southern plains were assigned lands in "Indian Territory," or, in essence, modern Oklahoma.

There were several difficulties with the reservation plan. Ever since they had acquired the horse the Plains Indians had pursued a nomadic existence, following the buffalo herds, and living off the shaggy humpbacks. They were more than a source of food: following them became a way of life. The "hunt" was something that ran in the Plains Indian's bloodstream from birth and to deny him that was to make him give up all he knew and loved. To abandon the chase was catastrophic enough, but to be forced to till the soil was to be reduced to woman's work: it was humiliation piled upon deprivation. In addition, the government tended to send some of the northern Indians into Indian Territory, where they literally pined away their lives. The climate was humid and unhealthy compared with that from which they came, and the Indian's sincere love of the land of his birth added to his anguish when he was, in effect, deported.

One of the most dramatic examples of rebellion against the strictures of reservation life is seen in the heart-rending efforts of the northern Cheyenne to get back to their homeland. This band had remained north when the southern Cheyenne moved down along the Arkansas River after the establishment of Bent's Fort. They lived in such a close relationship to the Sioux that the southern Cheyenne called them Sioux when they wanted to be insulting. After the violent campaign of 1876 General Miles had persuaded some of the northern Cheyenne to move south to Indian Territory, with the vague promise that if they did not like it there they could move back among the Sioux in Dakota.

One of the more important bands to accept the arrangement was one led by Chief Dull Knife. By 1878 his people were sick and dying; they were utterly unhappy with the amount of rations they received; there seemed to be little in common between them and the other Indians crowded onto the reservation. Interior Department officials were deaf to all pleas for a change of climate. Early one September morning Dull Knife and his people quietly slipped away from their encampment, left behind their tepees and all but the most necessary equipment, and commenced their flight home. After a running fight with pursuing soldiers, one that extended all the way across Nebraska, the fleeing Indians were overtaken and captured. The prisoners were held in log barracks at Fort Robinson, Nebraska, until early January, 1879, when orders came to remove them to Indian Territory. With new desperation the band again broke away, this time under the leadership of Wild Hog, a younger chief, and plunged northward through snow and bitter cold. In the confusion that followed, the Indians were scattered, old Dull Knife eluding his pursuers, and in a few days those who were not captured were ridden down and killed. Dull Knife died a natural death at the Tongue River Reservation in Montana years later, an embittered man to the end.

MESSIAH CRAZE

The Sioux War was the last important resistance of the Plains Indians against the United States government. As this realization came home to the tribesmen, restless in their new reservation homes, they began to turn increasingly to mysticism to recapture faded glories of their past history. The decade of the 1880s was particularly trying, for the imposition on the Indians of a new life not only shattered their old economy but caused a collapse of their traditional culture, which was based upon the earlier economy. Governmental attempts to break up the bands and to disperse the red plainsmen as ordinary farmers threatened to destroy the Indian as an Indian. Unable to combat the process openly, the northern reservation Indians, in particular, sought spiritual means of preserving what little remained to them.

Through all of Indian history certain individuals were thought to have peculiar and magical powers. Now, in their time of despair, rumor spread among the tribes that there was at hand the coming of an Indian Messiah who would eliminate the whites and unite the Indians, both living and dead, in an earthly paradise where there was no disease and where buffalo would be plentiful. The prophets of the Messiah were somewhat vague as to whether these idyllic conditions were to exist in actuality or only in the believer's mind, and whether on this earth or only in a future life after death. Most of the Indians who accepted the beliefs thought they would be fully realized in the near future.

The leading candidate for the role of Messiah was a Paiute Indian named Wovoka, sometimes referred to as Jack Wilson since he lived with the family of a white rancher named David Wilson. It was through his studies of the Bible, while living with the Wilsons, that Wovoka learned about the great white medicine man, Jesus, and his miraculous healing powers. His rise to power among Nevada Indians was assured when he successfully predicted that he could cause ice to flow down the Walker River in the summertime. He did not go into details about the nature of the miracle and the Wilson boys, who helped their adopted brother along in his profession by dumping a wagon load of ice blocks into the water upstream from the site of the performance, kept quiet about their part in the affair.

Word of Wovoka's fame spread, particularly the "Ghost Dance" feature of his religion that urged nonviolence as opposed to the customary emphasis upon war, and before long the Dakota Sioux and Cheyenne heard of this new spiritual power. In their time of doubt and distress it appeared to answer many needs. These people, so recently defeated on the field of battle, who now fared so badly at the hands of venal agents and who suffered continually from disease and hunger, grasped at Wovoka's religion as one last hope. Many of them acquired "ghost shirts," the symbol of the new cult. The shirt was a sacklike affair, usually made of cotton, and highly decorated with designs having special mystical significance. Of great interest was the medicine man's assurance that wearers would be invulnerable to bullets. Although the idea was not new, the Indians having long worn "medicine shirts" of various kinds for protection in battle, there was great stress among the Sioux over this particular virtue of the garment. The importance of this detail lies in the fact that the Sioux used it to transform Wovoka's doctrine of peace into one of war and violence against the whites.

The ghost-dance religion probably would have burned itself out had not the Indian agents become frightened and called for help. When troops, or Indian police, came on the scene the Indians usually fled. However, trouble developed when an effort was made to arrest Sitting Bull in 1890. In the struggle that ensued the old warrior was killed and excitement immediately erupted among the others. In the last days of that December some 500 soldiers surrounded a band of 300 Miniconjou Sioux, two thirds of whom were women and children, along a little Dakota creek called Wounded Knee. It was not a battle in the usual sense of the word, but a melee that occurred when the Indians refused to be disarmed, and in the shooting that followed 146 of them died in what amounted to an execution. A day or so later the frozen bodies were thrown into a mass grave. Commenting on this last great "battle" with the Plains Indians, a witness who watched the burial said: "It was a thing to melt the heart of a man, if it was a stone, to see those little children, with their bodies shot to pieces, thrown naked into the pit."

THE HUMANITARIAN VIEW

The crushing of hostile Indian tribes and their isolation on reservations were but the first steps in the solution of the Indian problem. To consider the Indians as wards of the nation, to be cared for and protected, was satisfactory only on the assumption that some day they would reach maturity and provide for themselves like other adult residents of the United States. Previous efforts to give the Indians the white type of education and to teach them the trades of the whites had been far from satisfactory. Because the natives did not always share their white neighbors' views on how the good life should be lived the attempts of both governmental and private philanthropic agencies to remodel Indian life had made an extremely small impression.

The desire to improve Indian conditions was demonstrated and reinforced about 1880 by the organization of several groups designed to study and assist the Indian: the Bureau of American Ethnology (1879), the Women's National Indian Association (1879), the Indian Rights Association (1882), the Lake Mohonk Conference (1883), and the National Indian Defense Association (1885). Not to be underestimated is the influence of Helen Hunt Jackson's books, *A Century of Dishonor* (1881) and *Ramona* (1884), which, overdrawn and romanticized as they were, had a powerful effect on the reading public. The end of any real danger from the Indians apparently inspired a more widespread tolerance and desire to help the vanquished.

To advance the Indians along the paths of white civilization two developments seemed at the time to be necessary: proper education, and the allocation of land to the Indians to be held individually rather than in a group. Such a plan offered the Indians the benefits of two highly prized American doctrines: improvement through formal learning, and an opportunity for economic betterment by participation in a program of private enterprise.

EDUCATION

Indian schooling on the reservation was financed largely by the federal government. Education of the adult Indian held little promise, but many hoped that influencing the children would produce a new kind of Indian within a generation. Unfortunately only one child in twelve was attending school as late as 1880. Moreover, the influence of the home often seemed more effective than that of the school for those children who attended day schools in the centers of Indian population. Parents tended to discount the importance of the school and this attitude was reflected in the classroom by students who were frequently hard to discipline. About the only weapon the teacher had was the threat of expulsion, and that was an end so fervently desired by all the pupils it was seldom invoked. The answer appeared to be the reservation boarding school, where the young could be removed from home influences during the educational process. Even here, however, there was a considerable amount of failure: the boy or girl went home for vacations, found his new ways of life not in accord with the opinion of the home community, and nearly always relapsed into tribal customs.

A novel and more effective method of education was introduced by an army officer, Captain Richard H. Pratt. While in charge of Indian prisoners consigned to St. Augustine in 1875, he experimented with the idea of allowing his prisoners a measure of self-government and of encouraging them to undertake various kinds of work in the neighborhood. The results were so encouraging that Pratt was convinced that if younger Indians could be taken from their homes and given good training at least for them the Indian problem could be solved. To realize this hope he persuaded some fifty children to go to the Negro school at Hampton, Virginia. Ultimately over a thousand Indian boys and girls attended Hampton, where they were quite successful in acquiring white customs.

But Pratt was not satisfied with anything short of an independent Indian school. Having obtained the aid of Congress, he toured the West and collected over a hundred children, with whom he started a school in an old army barracks at Carlisle, Pennsylvania, in 1879. The children divided their time between school and farm or shop; during vacations they worked in homes of the neighborhood. At first the school was handicapped by a lack of funds and by the homesickness of the children, but ultimately it was successful and led to the establishmeent of dozens of similar schools. Carlisle itself never went higher than junior high school, and was finally closed when the army needed the barracks during World War I.

Nonreservation schools were effective in educating the Indians, but their facilities were limited and the long-range results were not always encouraging. Youngsters educated in the ways of the white man found themselves social and economic misfits if they went home after graduation. Their manner, dress, and attitudes were un-Indian and they found themselves socially isolated among their own kind. If the boy or girl had learned a trade he often discovered that there was no place to employ it in the limited economy of the reservation. In this situation the young generally reverted to the old way of life despite a period of physical removal from home environment.

LAND ALLOTMENT

In addition to efforts to educate the Indian was the drive to make him a settled farmer. A nomadic, hunting Indian would never accept white ways —in fact he was bound to starve as the game disappeared. Most whites felt that the way to encourage the hunter to be a farmer was to divide the tribal domain and assign each individual a piece of land that would be his to cultivate and to improve. The idea of giving land in severalty was not new but it had never been applied on a large scale. It was generally accepted by the late 1870s as inevitable; the only real questions were when and how.

The great piece of land allotment legislation was the Dawes Act of 1887, which applied to almost all Indians except members of the Five Civilized Tribes, who were not forced into line until 1898. The President was allowed to allot land whenever he thought desirable. Provided that the supply of tribal land was sufficient, the head of each family was to receive 160 acres with lesser amounts going to others; the size of these allotments was later changed. The beneficiary was permitted to choose his own land so that he might include any improvements made on particular pieces prior to the passage of the act. The selections were to be held in trust for twenty-five years before they were turned over absolutely to the Indian or to his heirs; within this period the land could not be alienated. The Indian became a citizen as soon as his land designation was confirmed. If any surplus land remained after allotment it was to be opened for white purchase, with the proceeds going to the Indians.

From the standpoint of the Indian the Dawes Act did not work well. Often the wrong man received improved land, for Indian names were confusing to white clerks. Allottees were generally inefficient farmers living in poverty and filth and unprepared for complete ownership; as a result, when they received the final patents most of them either sold their land or lost it for debts—often fraudulent—and then became poverty-stricken dependents on charity.

Modifications of the Dawes Act brought little improvement. The permission to lease (1891) meant that allottees rented their land in order to live in idleness—and usually in comparative poverty. In 1902 the Secretary of the Interior was permitted to shorten the trust period if he thought such action was wise, which meant that in many cases the Indian lost his land in less than the twenty-five years of the Dawes Act. The Burke Act of 1906 deferred citizenship until after fee simple title had been granted, and further legislation of 1907 and 1908 allowed the Indian to dispose of his allotment before the end of the trust period. Presumably such laws were approved by the whites who were impatient to acquire Indian land.

The process of allotment fluctuated in speed, but it was particularly rapid after 1916. By 1920 something over half the Indians had received their allotments. In round numbers, 175,000 Indians had received 37,000,-000 acres; of these allottees, 117,000 had obtained their final patents, with about 90 percent of them in Oklahoma; 35,000,000 acres remained unallotted, the heritage of some 135,000 Indians. Presumably the end of the tribal system was in sight. In prospect of this conclusion all Indians were made citizens in 1924.

Although in theory the day was soon to come when the Indian would be a citizen and a landowner, according to white standards, conditions in the Indian country remained extremely bad. Division of the land was not producing economically independent farmers, for the Indian had not as yet achieved competence in farm management and was in consequence an ineffective competitor. The land soon went out of Indian hands and the former owner relapsed into poverty and squalor—the recipient of govern-

RETURN TO TRIBAL ORGANIZATION 509

ment charity. This increasing demoralization meant that the virtues of the old Indian culture were being replaced, not by a better white culture but by the worst traits of the whites. All friends of the Indian were distressed.

RETURN TO TRIBAL ORGANIZATION

In 1934, a decade after the citizenship law was enacted, the New Deal sponsored one of the most far-reaching pieces of Indian legislation ever passed by Congress. Under the Wheeler-Howard Act (or Indian Reorganization Act) of 1934, as expanded in 1936, a strong effort was made to turn back the clock and to utilize the better traits of Indian culture. Allotments were to cease and existing trust periods and other limits on alienation were to be continued indefinitely. So-called surplus land awaiting sale was to be restored to the reservations and new lands were to be acquired. The Indians were encouraged to continue their tribal organization—in fact, to incorporate and hold land as a corporation. The most important provisions of the act were those permitting the tribes self-government, for here the federal government explicitly recognized a principle followed by the courts since the days of John Marshall: that the Indians possessed the inherent right to rule themselves.

Although it may take several generations to assess fully the effects of the Indian Reorganization Act, several positive gains were apparent in the first three decades following its passage. During the first fifteen years after 1933 Indian-owned livestock increased from 171,000 to 361,000 head, and total agricultural income advanced from $1,850,000 to $49,000,000. Of equal interest is the fact that lands owned by Indians increased by almost 4 million acres, thus reversing a trend characterized by a steady relinquishment and diminution of holdings.

That the Indian "problem" was far from solved became apparent shortly after World War II, when the opponents of "big government" demanded that the period of federal trusteeship over the Indians come to an end at some foreseeable time. Legislation passed in 1953 provided that civil and criminal jurisdiction be transferred to specified states and, in general, allowed other states having Indian reservations to acquire such jurisdiction. In the same year a concurrent resolution made the sweeping declaration that the Indians should be released from federal supervision or control at the earliest possible time. Public reaction to such fundamental changes prevented a major uprooting of the course laid out by the New Deal and during the late 1850s pressures against federal control of the Indians relaxed.

By the 1960s administrative planners had adopted the less radical view that assistance to the Indians ought to continue until it was much more certain that special aid to this particular group of Americans was no longer an obvious necessity. All the Indians asked was sufficient help to find for themselves, in a space age, "some measure of adjustment they enjoyed as the original possessors of their native land."

READINGS

GENERAL STUDIES. William C. Macleod, *The American Indian Frontier* (1928); Jay P. Kinney, *A Continent Lost—A Civilization Won* (1937); and George E. Hyde, *Indians of the High Plains* (1959) provide a panoramic picture of the American Indians. For a discussion of policy see Loring B. Priest, *Uncle Sam's Stepchildren* (1942), perhaps the best of its kind; and Ralph H. Ogle, *Federal Control of the Western Apaches, 1848–1886* (1940). A fine contemporary account is D'Arcy McNickle, *The Indian Tribes of the United States: Ethnic and Cultural Survival* (1962). See also his volume, *They Came Here First* (1949). Also useful for the more recent period is Indian Commissioner John Collier's *From Every Zenith* (1963), a memoir.

THE TRIBES. John C. Ewers, *The Blackfeet: Raiders on the Northwestern Plains* (1958); Robert Lowie, *The Crow Indians* (1935); Michael S. Kennedy (ed.), *The Assiniboines* (1961); Verne Dusenberry, *The Montana Cree* (1962); and George E. Hyde, *Red Cloud's Folk* (1937), his *A Sioux Chronicle* (1956), and his *Spotted Tail's Folk (Brûlé Sioux)* (1961) all deal with the northern plains tribes. For the central Plains Indians see Don Berthrong, *The Southern Cheyennes* (1963); Wilbur S. Nye, *Bad Medicine and Good: Tales of the Kiowas* (1962); Mildred P. Mayhall, *The Kiowas* (1962); and John Mathews, *The Osages: Children of the Middle Waters* (1961). Indians of the Southwest are discussed in Frank C. Lockwood, *The Apache Indians* (1938); Rufus Kay Wyllys, *Arizona: The History of a Frontier State* (1950), Apaches, Chapter 9; Ruth M. Underhill, *The Navajos* (1956); Rupert N. Richardson, *The Comanche Barrier to South Plains Settlement* (1933); C. L. Sonnichsen, *The Mescalero Apaches* (1958); and Wilson Rockwell, *The Utes: A Forgotten People* (1956). For more information about the Oklahoma or Indian Territory tribes, see Grant Foreman, *The Five Civilized Tribes* (1934); Angie Debo, *Road to Disappearance* (1941), Creeks; and Grace S. Woodward, *The Cherokees* (1963). Brigham D. Madsen, *The Bannocks of Idaho* (1958) deals with mountain Indians.

INDIAN BIOGRAPHIES. Mari Sandoz, *Crazy Horse* (1942); Helen A. Howard and Dan L. McGrath, *War Chief Joseph* (1941); Lucullus V. McWhorter, *Hear Me, My Chiefs!* (1952), Nez Percé Joseph. See also his *Yellow Wolf,* (1948), Merrill D. Beal, *I Will Fight No More Forever* (1963), Nez Percé Joseph; Thomas B. Marquis, *A Warrior Who Fought Custer* (1931), story of the northern Cheyenne, Wooden Leg, reprinted (1962) as *Wooden Leg;* Stanley Vestal, *Sitting Bull* (1932, 1957), John G. Neihardt, *Black Elk Speaks* (1932, 1962), Oglala Sioux; Grace R. Hebard, *Washakie* (1930), the Shoshoni leader; Paul Bailey, *Wovoka: The Indian Messiah* (1957).

INDIAN WARS. No really good study of Plains Indian warfare exists. Paul I. Wellman's *The Indian Wars of the West* (1954) is exciting reading but not a penetrating study. Fairfax Downey, *Indian Fighting Army* (1941) is overly dramatic. Edgar I. Stewart's *Custer's Luck* (1955) and his *March of the Montana Column* (1961) are concerned with the events of 1876. J. W. Vaughn, *The Reynolds Campaign on Powder River* (1961) belongs to this period. William A. Graham, *The Custer Myth* (1953) is a documentary account. Robert M. Utley, *Custer and the Great Controversy* (1962) looks back at one of the great debates of the era of the Indian wars. Stan Hoig, *The Sand Creek Massacre* (1961) and Marshall Sprague, *Massacre: The Tragedy at White River* (1957) are set in Colorado. Keith A. Murray, *The Modocs and Their War* (1959) is well told. A dramatic account of the flight of the northern Cheyennes is Mari Sandoz, *Cheyenne Autumn* (1953). The same story is told from the viewpoint of a contemporary in Edgar Beecher Bronson, *Reminiscences of a Ranchman* (rev. ed., 1910, 1962). Sidney E. Whitman, *The Troopers: An Informal History of the Plains Cavalry, 1865–1890* (1962) and Don Rickey, *Forty Miles a Day on Beans and Hay* (1963) are descriptive of army problems in the Indian wars. George F. Brimlow, *The Bannock War of 1878* (1938) covers the brief intermountain campaign. See also Hiram M. Chittenden's *History of Early Steamboat Navigation on the Missouri River* (2 vols., 1903), Chaps. 30 and 31, Vol. II, for comments on the post-Civil War Indian problems. The best description of the Messiah craze among the Sioux is Robert M. Utley's *The Last Days of the Sioux Nation* (1963). Oliver Knight, *Following the Indian Wars* (1960) covers the campaigns from the standpoint of the newspaper reporters. Indian leadership is the theme of Alvin Josephy's *Patriot Chiefs* (1961).

PERSONAL REMINISCENCES OF THE INDIAN WARS. James H. Cook, *Fifty Years on the Old Frontier* (1923, 1957); George A. Forsyth, *The Story of a Soldier* (1916); Frazier and Robert Hunt, *I Fought with Custer* (1947); J. McLaughlin, *My Friend the Indian* (1926); Martin F. Schmidt (ed.), *General George Crook: His Autobiography* (1946); George A. Custer, *My Life on the Plains* (1874, 1962); Lucile Kane (ed.), *Military Life in Dakota* (1951), account of Philippe R. de Trobriand; Richard Irving Dodge, *Our Wild Indians* (1882, 1959); Nelson Lee, *Three Years among the Comanches* (1957 ed.); and John F. Finerty, *War-Path and Bivouac, or the Conquest of the Sioux* (1890, 1961).

CHAPTER 33

MINING ADVANCES

T hrough the pattern of Indian affairs always ran the thread of the mining boom as it appeared first here and then there, penetrating Indian country and drawing trade and settlement that otherwise might not have come for many years. On occasion the emergence of a mining region directly affected Indian life and economy, but as a rule the trouble with the tribes was caused by the establishment of travel routes to and from the camps. The multiplicity of new western roads that crisscrossed the plains spelled the end of the buffalo herds and, faced by this prospect, the native hunters were prepared to fight to the finish to protect their resources.

The wealth of the mining camps, the great populations they attracted, and the heavy demands they made on transportation facilities assured a growth of traffic over the plains that generated the last phase of the Indian wars. If the placer mining boom had not been succeeded by the longer-lived quartz mining frontier, the problems of western race relations might have emerged more slowly. It was the need for better transportation—the railroads—to haul in heavy machinery and to take out ore that led to permanent white settlement and demonstrated to the Indians that their last hope had died.

COLORADO

A good example of the transition from a placer mining frontier to one more permanent and more highly organized is shown in the mineral history of Colorado. Even before Californians heard about the Comstock Lode in Nevada, frontier towns along the Missouri River throbbed with the rumor of gold in what was then called the Pike's Peak region. The collapse of the placer boom and the resultant decline in population were followed by a steady upswing in quartz mining that began in the seventies. By then Californians had been mining for over twenty years and their annual output of gold far outstripped that of Colorado. However, the coming of the railroads in 1870 and the development of improved metallurgical methods provided the means necessary to probe deeper into mountains. Success meant that Colorado, too, would have a long and profitable period of mining.

The old placer mining camp of California Gulch, Colorado, in the upper reaches of the Arkansas Valley, was on the verge of becoming a ghost town until W. H. Stevens, a metallurgist, realized the richness of the locality's silver deposits. In 1877 a fellow mining engineer, August R. Meyer, representing a St. Louis smelting and refining company, built a successful smelter and the reborn town of Leadville made its appearance. Within three years Leadville, with nearly 15,000 residents, was the state's second most important city. Among the competitors who struggled for a share of the new silver boom were two railroads, the Denver & Rio Grande and the Atchison, Topeka & Santa Fe. Their dramatic contest over the Royal Gorge route to Leadville, often referred to as a "war," became a well-known chapter in Colorado's history. By 1880 the Rio Grande's trains were hauling ore over the newly won route. H. A. W. Tabor, who had struggled to make a living in his small grocery store, grubstaked the right prospectors and became one of Colorado's most famous "silver kings." Tabor and some of his fellow "kings" died bankrupt but many a solid fortune was established. Meyer Guggenheim, of Philadelphia, for example, sold his holdings in 1888 for $10 million. Another success was Charles Boettcher, who began as a Leadville merchant, later established the Colorado Portland Cement Company, and made his mark as one of the state's richest industrialists.

The Colorado boom was sustained by a major gold discovery at Cripple Creek in 1890–1891. Within three years the place was a thriving city of 10,000 people. Here a Colorado Springs carpenter named Winfield Scott Stratton demonstrated the rags-to-riches possibilities of the West by staking out claims that nine years later sold for $11 million. In 1901, when the mines were producing at their greatest, the annual value of gold production reached approximately $25 million. By that time the mining district had a population of about 50,000. The story of Cripple Creek is familiar in mining history for its fabulous wealth and its boom economy, but it stands apart from many another mining district because of its duration. As late as 1938 it was producing more than $5 million annually. At its height the district was composed of eleven differing mining cities or "camps," all connected by a system of electrically operated tramways. Its success at a time when silver slumped badly helped to stabilize the Colorado economy, not to mention the creation of a whole new crop of millionaires.

Another of Colorado's famed mining camps that became prominent in the 1890s was Creede, in the southwestern part of the state. Some of the frontier's well-known characters took up brief residence there before moving on. The fabled "Bat" Masterson ran a saloon while "Soapy" Smith, the bunco artist, plied his trade among the unsuspecting. Bob Ford, whose claim to fame was his shooting of Jesse James, died in one of Creede's saloons before the blast of a double-barreled shotgun. Cy Warman, editor of the Creede *Chronicle,* immortalized the place and characterized its around-the-clock existence with his oft-quoted lines:

> It's day all day, in the daytime
> And there is no night in Creede.

Before the declining price of silver ended the boom such mines as the Holy Moses, Last Chance, Amethyst, and Champion were names known all over America. By the end of 1892 the Amethyst had produced more than $2 million in silver ore, the Last Chance $1.6 million, and the others lesser amounts.

NEVADA SILVER

As was true in Colorado the Nevada miners were forced to find a firm base if their economy was to survive the first rush. The typical far western mining boom revolved around the finding of gold—at first the free gold of the placer mine and then the gold-bearing rock that stamp mills were required to crush. But with the profitable mining of silver in Nevada the number of desirable metals began to increase and the field of search to widen. Later rushes were to be concerned as frequently with silver or copper as with gold. Butte, Montana, for example, began its long and successful career of copper production with an initial period of gold mining.

As for Nevada itself, the original discoveries seemed to have been exhausted by the late 1860s. Adolph Sutro still had faith and was digging his famous tunnel to free the lower levels of the mines from water, but most people were pessimistic. Then came new finds, bigger and richer than anything that had preceded them—the "big bonanza." Within another twenty-two years two of the largest mines extracted some $150 million worth of metal, of which over half was returned as dividends to the lucky owners.

The history of the big bonanza is in large part the biography of a Scotsman and three Irishmen—James G. Fair, John W. Mackay, James C. Flood, and William S. O'Brien. The first two had been prospectors, which led them later to acknowledge that they were mining experts. The other two had run a saloon in San Francisco, with a little of the usual mining stock speculation on the side. Flood was later to be considered the financier of the group, while O'Brien is regarded as the silent partner. At the very nadir of Nevada production the four men showed their confidence in the future of the region by joining forces in an informal agreement for the purchase of mining properties as fast as funds were available.

The four partners rode the crest of the boom of the 1870s, with each man becoming many times a millionaire. Their two largest companies, the Consolidated Virginia and the California, were united in 1884 as the Consolidated California & Virginia Mining Company. Their spectacular rise to wealth may be followed in the great surge upward of the value of their companies. The Virginia, which had sold for $1 a share in 1870, reached $700 in 1875. The California made an almost unbelievable jump from $37 in September 1874 to $780 in January 1875.

The Nevada mines brought serious engineering problems for a young industry. Immense amounts of wood had to be hauled in to feed the necessary fires and to support the mine shafts. When haulage became impossibly expensive huge flumes were constructed down the mountainsides and across the ravines to wash the logs to the mines. Since the veins being worked often widened into large lodes, a new method had to be devised for supporting the roof and the walls. Best known of the engineering innovations, however, was the Sutro tunnel, completed in 1878. An impressive project constructed in the face of great obstacles, it permitted the draining of water even from the lower levels and at the same time provided for the transportation of the ore.

The glitter of the Comstock Lode tended to overshadow other mining ventures in Nevada. Aurora, in the Esmeralda district, was the site of a discovery made in 1860, one that drew some 10,000 people by 1864. A number of Virginia City miners were drawn toward central Nevada in 1862 when the Reese River mines were opened by William H. Talcott, a former pony express rider. The town of Austin, the best known in this district, had nearly 10,000 residents at one time. Before its decline in the late 1890s the Reese River district contributed some $50 million worth of precious metals. A little over a hundred miles distant lay the White Pine mining district. In its first winter that place claimed between 10,000 and 12,000 residents, although the census of 1870 suggested that the figure was somewhat exaggerated. By 1875 the boom days of White Pine were over and even the introduction of more capital, improved machinery, and scientific methods failed to revive it. There were others that failed as permanent mining centers. Eureka, Cherry Creek, and Pioche, heavy producers of gold, silver, and lead for a brief period, faded out around the turn of the century.

MONTANA

Early prospecting in Idaho and Montana, carried on principally during the 1860s, had been for deposits of free gold, of which many had been found. During the 1870s and 1880s interest turned first to silver and then to copper. The specific areas that loomed largest in the public mind were those near Butte, Montana, and near Coeur d'Alene, Idaho. Butte's origins as a mining camp began with the successful prospecting of two Virginia City miners who tried their luck along Silver Bow Creek in 1864. A small boom developed, but by 1870 it was fading rapidly as a placer mining site. As happened in Leadville, a miner—William L. Farlin—took another look in 1874 and decided that considerable amounts of silver were present. Before long a new rush of prospectors appeared, among whom was an Irishman named Marcus Daly. In his particular shaft lay copper, the discovery of which disappointed the young miner, but when it was found to be unusually pure his mood became one of unbounded optimism. From this small start, made in 1876, Daly built a copper empire and became a millionaire. William J. Parks, working his silver mine, the Parrot Lode, began to find copper so rich that, as "Uncle Billy" put it, the ore could be shipped "to hell and back" for smelting and still yield a profit. But he sold his property, which ultimately yielded $1 million in profit, for a mere $10,000. He did not become a "copper king." Another ambitious newcomer was William Andrews Clark, a precise, parsimonious, and ambitious little Scotsman who arrived in 1872. He was a merchant and a banker, but the great mineral prospects of Butte soon directed his attention to that source of wealth. Before long he and Daly became rivals and the "war of the copper kings" was under way.

The Clark-Daly feud was one of the epic struggles of the day. Clark was in control at Butte and advanced the fortunes of that young metropolis; his newspaper sneered at the pretensions of Daly. Daly was boss at his own new town of Anaconda, where his rival paper returned with interest all the jeers thrown in his direction. Ultimately both men spent money freely in a struggle for political control of the state.

Clark's great ambition was to become United States senator, and in 1899 he spent some half a million dollars persuading the state legislature of his merits. The ensuing scandal was so great that he resigned just before a Senate committee reported that he should not be seated. His place then being vacant, he was appointed to it by the Lieutenant Governor, an act that was later canceled by the Governor, who had been absent from the state at the time of the appointment. In 1900 Marcus Daly lay dying and a pro-Clark legislature voted to send their man to the Senate, where he served for six undistinguished years.

At about the close of the century Standard Oil money entered the copper industry and combined many of the firms, including the Anaconda, into the Amalgamated Copper Company, which later took the name of the Anaconda Mining Company. The Amalgamated made efforts to monopolize the copper business, but ultimately failed because of the power of Calumet and Hecla. It did manage, however, to play a dominant role in Montana affairs and for years was simply referred to as "the company." The cattle people were never able to compete effectively against the copper people. Much later, in the mid-twentieth century, "the company" sold its string of Montana newspapers and moderated the more obvious aspects of its political activities. By then the state's farm organizations were more powerful politically than either the cattle or the copper interests.

IDAHO

Typically, the "golden age" of Idaho mines was spectacular but brief. By the early 1870s the placer mining era of the Clearwater district (discussed in Chapter 28) had passed its peak and the promise of sudden riches was fading. Other places, such as Colorado, had staged a recovery after the decline of placer mining set in, but in Idaho prospects were less promising. In the seventies no railroads came, save one that crossed the territory's southeast corner en route from Ogden to Butte, and without them the transition from placer to quartz mining was much more difficult.

In 1880 Idaho's revival came in the form of a silver rush. The Wood River country, in the south-central section, proved to be rich in both silver and lead. By 1883 the Wood River district had a railroad and a flow of capital from at home and abroad. In 1883 northern Idaho witnessed a new gold rush in the Coeur d'Alene area when rumors of riches brought the usual motley crowd of miners, their suppliers, and their parasites. Dozens of new towns, such as Eagle, Delta, Murray, and Myrtle, had their evanescent moments of glory before free gold disappeared. The really big find (in 1885) was the Bunker Hill lode of silver and lead. In time the Bunker Hill and Sullivan mine paid some $50 million in dividends. This and other mines seemed to have inexhaustible supplies of silver, lead, and zinc.

The Coeur d'Alene mines attained something like national notoriety because of their labor troubles, particularly in the 1890s and later. Mining was a dangerous and arduous occupation. Both operators and laborers were rough and tough, with neither willing to make concessions. Labor troubles meant armed forces on each side, shafts and buildings dynamited, pitched battles, and sudden death. Here it was that both William Borah and "Big Bill" Haywood began their national careers. Here it was also that the Western Federation of Miners, with its Local Number 1 at Butte, had its baptism of fire and developed the ideology that a little later produced the International Workers of the World.

THE BLACK HILLS

The fluid characteristic of the placer mining frontier is well shown in the Black Hills rush. By the 1870s the Colorado miners, many of whom had moved on to Idaho and Montana, were looking for new mineral worlds to conquer. All three of those regions were beginning to "play out," as the prospectors used the phrase, and the time was ripe for another move.

Miners had followed on the heels of the Custer expedition of 1874 and their good luck had brought others by the thousands, with the peak of the boom coming in 1876. Try as it might the army could not keep the prospectors away from country allotted to the Sioux, and the harder it tried the more valuable the diggings appeared to be. The failure to ward off those who felt the Indians were sitting on a bonanza resulted in new treaties in 1876 that officially opened the Black Hills the following spring. Into the gold fields rushed miners who had made the trek from Georgia to California, into Nevada or Colorado, to the Blue Mountain region of eastern Oregon or Fort Colville, Washington, and on to Idaho, Montana and, briefly, Wyoming. Wide-open "boom towns" sprang up in the traditional fashion and were characterized by the presence of the newly rich and the absence of law.

The center of the excitement was Deadwood, which in its heyday served as a magnet for a very large share of the floating population of the West. Deadwood came into existence by the accident of gold discovery and grew haphazardly. The main street meandered along a gulch, to the sides of which houses clung precariously. The lower part of the town was sacred to the gambler and the prostitute, with no pretensions of even a little law and order that vaguely permeated the rest of the town.

The main street of Deadwood was jammed with the usual assortment of booted miners, teamsters, gamblers, storekeepers, and casual visitors. Long ox teams further increased the congestion, the usual equipage consisting of ten oxen and three wagons hitched together. The snap of the driver's long leather whip was hardly to be distinguished from the crack of the revolver that meant another addition to the long list of homicides. Twice a month the steel-lined treasure chest of Wells, Fargo and Company pulled out of town with as much as $350,000 in bullion. Altogether it carried some $60 million before it was replaced by the railroad.

The amusements of Deadwood were rough and rowdy, but a trifle more sophisticated than those of earlier camps. A theater, the Gem, presented an impressive variety of plays and vaudeville acts; "The Mikado" had a remarkable run of 130 nights. After the theatrical performance the floor was cleared, a bar was opened at one end of the theater, a band was installed at the other, and dancing begun. The ladies of the cast acted as hostesses. At the end of each dance the man was expected to order drinks, and from these the girl received a commission. Additional income might be derived from ventures in commercialized vice. The girls were encouraged in such activities by the presence of curtained boxes.

The most conspicuous members of the Deadwood community were its ministers and gamblers, two classes that unexpectedly had much in common. Both idled when other men worked, both wore good clothes, both were highly self-controlled, and both had better than average manners. Moreover, both had approximately the same clientele. The miner who lost his money at poker or roulette on Saturday night might well appear on Sunday morning to attend Methodist, Congregational, or Catholic services; all three were available by 1877.

Typical of many predecessors, the boom days of the Black Hills rush into Deadwood, Custer, Central City, Lead, and Rapid City were fleeting and were followed by the development of quartz mining carried out by corporations using expensive machinery. The most profitable single location was George Hearst's Homestake Mine, a venture that claimed a total production worth some $25 million by the early 1930s. Some cried out "monopoly" and "big money interests," but those who ventured their capital took long risks. It was their investment in technological improvements that made possible profitable extraction of minerals from low-grade ores through mass-production practices.

ARIZONA, NEW MEXICO, AND UTAH

It has been popular to say that the Black Hills rush represented the "last frontier" of western American mining, and in many respects it was the culmination of the era of placer rushes, but in point of time the mines of the Southwest have a better claim to the term "last."

Arizona's mineral richness had long been known; in fact various mines had been worked even in Spanish times. Wandering prospectors turned up new finds in the 1850s and 1860s, producing a series of small booms, most of the resulting business going to Tucson, Tubac, and Prescott, and to the towns on the Colorado River. The lack of large-scale exploitations was partly due to the fact that the early prospectors were looking only for gold and their discoveries were soon exhausted. More important deterrents, however, were the hostile Apaches and the great, arid distances. A lone prospector was looking for trouble as well as for gold in this forbidding country populated by natives who understood how to cope with its climatic vagaries. Even larger mining parties were in imminent danger of being cut off by roving bands of Indians.

The Southwest's Indian problem was only partially solved after the

Civil War. Kit Carson's campaign against the Navaho in 1863 resulted in the removal of these Indians first to a reservation in eastern New Mexico and later (1868) to a permanent location in the northwestern section of the territory. The Apache, who ranged both Arizona and New Mexico, were put under so much pressure by General George Crook during the 1870s that a great many of them were forced onto reservations. As was true in the North, all the Indians were not so corralled, and the Southwest was in a state of turmoil during most of the 1880s because of raids by these non-reservation Indians.

With the temporary quieting of the Apache by Crook the miners were able to ply their trade in greater safety, and the immediate result was more mineral discoveries. Outstanding were the numerous finds in the neighborhood of Globe, Arizona. The rich Silver King claim was discovered in 1875; rumor had it that some of the ore assayed as high as $1000 a ton.

Most famous of the Arizona boom towns of the late 1870s was Tombstone. Its original traced to a silver find by Edward Schieffelin in 1877, who had come to the territory determined to find a fortune or a tombstone for his lonely grave. From the prospector's discoveries in the southeastern part of Arizona grew one of the roughest and most wide-open towns in the West. Old yellowed files of the Tombstone *Epitaph* recall but faintly the turbulent days when the Earps, "Doc" Holladay, Billy the Kid, and other exponents of the Wild West tradition followed their violent careers. The story of the Earps' encounter with the Clantons at the O.K. Corral is one of the most oft-told stories of the frontier legend.

The Tombstone deposits were exhausted within a few years, and today one passes a country pock-marked with abandoned shafts to enter one of the most notable of the West's ghost towns. Rows of deserted houses and stores and saloons attest its once numerous population, while an imposing "boot hill" cemetery gives mute evidence of the frequent use of the "six-gun" in a long-departed past.

More important in the long run to Arizona than silver was copper, and, recently, rarer metals. The Cornelia mine in southwestern Arizona had been worked inefficiently but more or less continuously since the 1850s, but rich new finds were made in other parts of the territory during the 1870s. Work in the Morenci area of east-central Arizona began in 1871 and provided an inspiration and model for other copper districts, such as nearby Clifton. Copper mining had all the usual difficulties with transportation, water, and supplies, but in addition had imposing technical problems of extracting the copper. The Bisbee and Jerome regions were both opened in 1877, and in time the mines near Globe came to be concerned predominantly with copper; the first copper was extracted at Globe in 1878. Since copper mining required large amounts of capital it was particularly the domain of the large company. By the 1880s such organizations as the Calumet and Arizona Mining Company and Phelps, Dodge and Company were pre-eminent in copper production.

Mining in New Mexico dates back to 1828, when gold was discovered in the Ortiz Mountains south of Santa Fe. Although production was not large, amounting to around $70,000 a year, it grew to an annual figure of about $3 million by the time of American occupancy. After a lapse during the 1850s and early 1860s there were renewed mining efforts at the end of the Civil War. Taos, for example, witnessed a minor gold rush in 1867. Although New Mexico is not known as one of the "bonanza" states, especially with regard to gold, that mineral has been extracted in two thirds of its countries. So slow was the emergence of an important mineral production that it was 1937 before mining produced more revenue than agriculture. By 1958 the extraction of various minerals accounted for about a quarter of the state's gross product.

Utah's mineral history is also one of slow development. It is often said that the Mormon Church discouraged the search for subsurface treasure, but this is only partially true. Church fathers recognized the importance of all minerals and were anxious to incorporate them in the development of a balanced, self-subsistent economy. In the 1870s, silver mining in particular gained momentum in Utah, the church encouraged Mormon boys to work in the mines not only for the money their wages would bring into the community but to prevent the importation of large numbers of outside workers. What the church did not want was a rush that would bring in the usual human flotsam and jetsam to disrupt normal life. Here the farmer and stockman had preceded the miner, an inversion of the usual development, and mining was carried on in a somewhat different setting.

Utah mining is also associated with the day of corporate mining, of big investments, of outside financial participation. By the 1870s word of the West's mineral riches had reached around the globe and many were anxious to invest in the mines. Those such as the famed "Emma" were rich enough, but so much money was invested in them to find even more riches that many a stockholder was deeply disappointed in the result, and not a few were bilked. As was true in Montana and Arizona, copper became the leading mineral and provided the base for a more stable mining industry.

THE YUKON AND ALASKA

Alaska probably has a better claim to be the "last mineral frontier," even after that of Arizona or the Black Hills, unless a differentiation is made because of its remote location. By the late 1890s, as many a mining camp—placer or quartz—neared the end of a glamorous career, prospectors took part in the development of one last bonanza. With their usual disregard for international boundaries they moved north into western Canada and Alaska, lured by rumors that this was "the big one."

The existence of gold in western Canada had been known as early as the 1830s, and gold rushes had occurred from the 1850s. Now came the biggest of all rushes with the news in 1897 of rich finds near Dawson in the Yukon. Men came back to the States with tangible evidence in the form of nuggets and dust, and within a year the population of Dawson grew to 4,000, with other thousands spread over the claims of the surrounding region. Typically, the rush had widespread effects, Seattle being the principal beneficiary on the Pacific Coast. So well did the business interests of that city spread the word about a new gold rush to the north that by the spring of 1898 it is estimated some $25 million worth of business fell to it as compared with $5 million for all other ports on the Pacific Coast.

Alaskan mining presented new problems that were extraordinarily difficult for the flood of farmers and clerks who made up such a large part of the multitude seeking easy wealth. The early part of the trip to the new El Dorado was easy enough, with the inland passage providing a fairly comfortable trip past Juneau, where gold also had been found. The real troubles started at Skagway, for most men preferred the overland trip to the longer sea and river route. Six hundred miles of frozen waste, precipitous and ice-covered mountains, and boiling rivers had to be crossed before the newcomer attained his goal of Dawson. Not the least of his troubles were the clouds of man-eating mosquitoes that surpassed the most voracious in the States. Moreover, each man had to carry a year's supply of food, not only because of necessity but because otherwise the Canadian police would not let him enter the Yukon country. Aside from tents, tools, and other essentials, the police set a figure of 1150 pounds of food as the minimum amount. Another annoyance to the would-be prospectors was the Canadian customs duty assessed on them. One author estimates that during the spring and summer of 1898 the Canadians extracted in excess of $150,-000 in duties at Chilkoot Pass and White Pass.

Although the deposits near Dawson were rich enough to produce many fortunes, the hazards were very great. During the winter the men were forced to thaw out the gravel before it could be dug, and then pile it for later working since water was out of the question in winter. The common rule was that if the mercury froze, the weather was too cold to work outside. Until he worked this gravel in the summer the miner was not sure that he had any gold; thus he might have lost his entire winter's toil. During the short warm period the gravel was panned for gold, much of which went to the businesses of Dawson—not only for high-priced food and clothes, but for the saloons, gambling halls, and bawdy houses.

Dawson claimed the honor of being the most wide-open town of the

Alaska: Mineral Frontier

West; yet it had another distinction. The Northwest Mounted Police was effective in preventing the disorder and loss of life customary in other mining camps. Moreover, Dawson contained an unusual number of men who were later to use in their writings the material they had gathered in the Yukon. Among them were Robert W. Service, Rex Beach, who also went to Nome, Joaquin Miller, and Jack London.

The riffraff of the Yukon gold rush, such as the gang headed by the suave Jefferson R. ("Soapy") Smith—who had practiced his trade in Colorado—gathered mainly at the last American town of Skagway. One member of the Mounted Police called it the roughest place in the world at that time. One would like to believe that this concentration merely meant that the hoodlums were unwilling to make the long and severe trip to Dawson. But unfortunately the Skagway situation was repeated in later American boom towns farther north—Nome, Fairbanks, and others. The answer seems to be that the Northwest Mounted was a much more efficient organization than the marshal and his deputies on whom the United States depended.

The Klondike rush was in many ways similar to other and earlier rushes: bonanza fever, high prices, violence, and a tenuous existence. The coming of the Spanish-American War and discoveries at Nome stunted the Klondike's development and cooled the gold fever that burned there so brightly but so briefly. Such unusual circumstances as the extreme weather and the strictness of the Canadian government's officials merely modified the normal life of a boisterous, get-rich-quick mining community.

THE PASSING OF THE MINING FRONTIER

As the nineteenth century ended, the American West witnessed one final spasm of frantic prospecting as the "bonanza frontier" passed out of existence. The scene was Death Valley and to the north and east in Nevada, where rumors of gold had persisted since the days of the forty-niners. For years the rumors of discoveries in this region persisted, but no real boom developed until the 1870s. Then the town of Panamint had a brief but wild orgy during the middle of the decade, followed by a similar boom at Darwin. Neither lasted long, but the collapses were due not to a lack of good ore but to the high cost of transportation that made any but the richest ore unprofitable to mine. Senators J. P. Jones and W. M. Stewart, whose Panamint Mining Company was the dominant organization of the earlier boom, were rumored to have lost $2 million on the venture.

Sporadic later rushes hit Death Valley, numerous claims being staked and even worked for a time, but the costs of transportation continued to remain decisive. The real Death Valley fortune came from borax, which was discovered in 1880. F. M. Smith made a fortune and at the same time gave national fame to the twenty-mule teams that hauled the borax across a hundred and fifty miles of desert.

One other possible Death Valley fortune was that of Walter Scott, commonly known as Death Valley Scotty. Scotty lived in a two-million dollar house with electricity, paneled rooms, a pipe organ costing a quarter of a million, a glass-enclosed swimming pool, and other luxuries in proportion. From time to time he ostentatiously traveled to the East, where he was very successful in obtaining newspaper publicity: throwing money out of his hotel window was always good for a headline. Whether or not he really had a secret and rich gold mine is still argued.

A new center of excitement appeared at Tonopah, Nevada, in 1900, with millions of dollars' worth of metal being mined—mostly gold but also some silver. For a short time Tonopah could boast of plate-glass windows, the latest of French fashions, and dinners that included champagne, caviar, and oysters.

Tonopah was followed in 1903 by Goldfield, which originally bore the name of Grandpa. Here again millions were wrenched from the earth, with a single mine making the record extraction of $4.5 million in sixteen weeks. George Wingfield, a gambler who speculated in mining claims, was reputed to have attained a fortune of $2 million by the age of twenty-seven. Another gambler, Tex Rickard, who had earlier followed the Alaskan rush, ran a popular saloon and gambling hall where stakes at times exceeded $10,000. In 1906 he promoted a boxing match between Joe Gans and Battling Nelson, an adventure in ballyhoo that undoubtedly gave him much valuable experience for his later work as a nationally known sports promoter.

New booms followed one another in rapid succession—Amargosa City, Bonanza, Bullfrog, Beatty. The year 1905 saw the construction of a model town of Rhyolite with concrete buildings, modern schools, attractive stores, three-story office buildings, electric lights, and paved streets. At the time the town seemed permanent, for one mine alone had some $5 million of ore in sight. The permanence was an illusion, for the boom collapsed with great suddenness, and by the end of 1908 the town was dead—one of the most impressive of many such community corpses in the West.

INFLUENCE OF THE MINING FRONTIER

The long succession of western mining booms brought into sharp focus many picturesque persons and institutions as miners flocked from one rumored find to the next. The boom towns resembled each other in their congested living quarters, astronomic prices, and imposing "boot hill" cemeteries. Traders, gamblers, and prostitutes trailed after the horde of predominantly young and vigorous men. With each find a few men made their fortunes, others missed by an eyelash, and the majority soon moved to greener fields. The color, movement, boisterousness, and virility are obvious and spectacular.

In some respects the mining frontier made contributions of doubtful value. It was rapid, fluid, transitory, and wasteful. Many of its settlements were of only fleeting importance as the trail of ghost towns left behind demonstrates to the modern viewer. Some did not even become ghost towns; there are city sites today in the West where very little is left, the remains having disappeared almost completely. Where the buildings have fallen in decay or have been dismantled for use elsewhere are now pock-marked hillsides, a countryside stripped of trees (used to support mine shafts or to make charcoal used in ore reduction), and perhaps crumbling tombstones that mark the end of vain hopes of fame and wealth. From the most pessimistic view, mining is wasteful—it takes from the land and returns nothing. It does not reproduce.

Yet the mining booms made a contribution of a sort and meant a good deal more than material for picturesque episodes that later would furnish the framework for novels and scenarios. The men who were searching for wealth actually produced large quantities of real minerals and these had important effects on the industrial life of the United States. Certain obvious results come quickly to mind: the effects of vast new supplies of copper at a time when American streets were being transformed into mazes of telegraph and electric wires.

Most important was the effect of new supplies of precious metals on the total economy of the United States. American industrialization was expanding impressively during the late nineteenth century, which meant that the number of business transactions was increasing in proportion. The result was a vastly stimulated need for money—a need that the banking system of the day could not satisfy. The result would normally have been deflation—a fall in prices. This fall actually occurred, but it was tempered by the vast new flow of precious metals from the West. Without the addition of this gold and silver the depressions of 1873 and 1893 might have been longer and more severe.

This gigantic injection into the monetary system had some not altogether desirable side effects. The enormous increase in silver production destroyed the old ratio between the values of silver and gold that had been at least within hailing distance of the facts. The immediate consequence was that when the farmers wanted inflation they talked of the "crime of '73" and the remonetization of silver. Their demands precipitated the "money question" that plagued the political scene in the latter part of the nineteenth century. Continuing discoveries of gold in Alaska and in South Africa helped somewhat to redress the imbalance created by the "silver kings." During the late 1890s prices became more favorable and cries for the free and unlimited coinage of silver abated.

For the West itself, the mining rushes also had important implications. The movement of large numbers of miners into Indian country decidedly hastened the coming of white settlers and, as already mentioned, hastened the "solution" of the Indian problem. Each new boom meant new towns with commercial opportunities attractive to storekeepers, bankers, artisans, laborers, and railroad men, and these new residents in turn provided opportunities for still other people, including stockmen and farmers. When the "St. Paul" or the "Northwestern" went into the Black Hills or the Denver & Rio Grande followed the mining booms into central Colorado, transportation improved not only for the mine owners but for everyone else. There were, of course, loud outcries that rail rates were too high, but increased traffic ultimately brought these into a more reasonable scale. The farmer or the stockman was attracted to the area served by the railroad, and the result was more and faster western settlement than would have occurred otherwise, and often in more or less isolated spots. Although some of the western states waited much longer for statehood than their boosters thought reasonable, mining should be credited for the fact that their populations increased as fast as they did.

The chaotic conditions created by frontier mining have largely disappeared. Most mines have become stable enterprises, run much like factories, and surrounded by orderly towns that look and act much like other municipalities. But as an industry mining continues to be hazardous. A mine may be exhausted, but much more likely is a slight fall in the price of the metal, making operations temporarily or permanently unprofitable. There is always the possibility of new and financially rewarding discoveries. For example, in the 1950s occurred a brief uranium rush that faded when the quantity found quickly outstripped the market. A few became rich, a good many invested in stocks whose value fell drastically, and the boom was at least temporarily halted. Still, the West is a land of known mineral deposits and even though it has been thoroughly prospected, a new find, or a new metal, or a new market may appear and once more the hills will rock with excitement.

READINGS

GENERAL. One of the best works on the post-placer mining frontier is Rodman W. Paul, *Mining Frontiers of the Far West, 1848–1880* (1963). It stresses the technological side of mining. More general, and heavier in social history, is William S. Greever, *The Bonanza West: The Story of Western Mining Rushes, 1848–1900* (1963). Thomas A. Rickard, *A History of American Mining* (1932) is a compilation of a series of essays by a noted mining engineer. A more recent work of his is *The Romance of Mining* (1945). Older works such as C. H. Shinn's *Story of the Mine* (1906); W. J. Trimble's *Mining Advance into the Inland Empire* (1914); and Glenn C. Quiett's *Pay Dirt* (1936) are useful for an understanding of the later period. A general study of the copper industry is Angus Murdoch, *Boom Copper* (1943).

COLORADO. LeRoy R. Hafen (ed.), *Colorado and Its People* (4 vols., 1948), Vols. I and II. More recent and more entertainingly written is Marshall Sprague, *Money Mountain* (1953), the story of Cripple Creek. Mabel Barbee Lee, who grew up in the mining camp, has written a fine reminiscence, *Cripple Creek Days* (1958). George F. Willison's *Here They Dug the Gold* (1931) is a popular account of Colorado mining. For a detailed study of one of the mining towns see Don L. and Jean H. Griswold, *The Carbonate Camp Called Leadville* (1951).

NEVADA. A good history of Nevada mining is lacking. Effie M. Mack, *Nevada* (1936) contains some useful information. See also Carl B. Glasscock's *The Big Bonanza* (1931) and Richard G. Lillard, *Desert Challenge* (1942). The story of John W. Mackay is treated in Ethel Manter, *Rocket of the Comstock* (1950). Another biographical study is Robert E. Stewart, Jr., and Mary Frances Stewart, *Adolph Sutro* (1962). W. Turrentine Jackson, *Treasure Hill: Portrait of a Silver Mining Camp* (1963), is a study of a Nevada boom town.

MONTANA. Merrill G. Burlingame, *The Montana Frontier* (1942) has a chapter on the mineral frontier that deals largely with the original discoveries. *Copper Camp* (1943), a W.P.A. writers' program volume, is about Butte and is anecdotal and not always reliable but highly entertaining. Carl B. Glasscock's *The War of the Copper Kings* (1935) also centers its story at Butte. K. Ross Toole, *Montana: An Uncommon Land* (1959) is general but the author's special interest (mining) looms large in the volume. Joseph Kinsey Howard, *Montana: High, Wide and Handsome* (1943) is popular but interpretative with some discussion of later mining problems.

IDAHO. The history of Idaho is a much-neglected subject. John Hailey, *The History of Idaho* (1910), written by a pioneer, is by now almost a documentary source. It touches briefly upon mining. George W. Fuller, *The Inland Empire of the Pacific Northwest* (3 vols., 1928) discusses mining west of the Rockies. Stewart H. Holbrook's *The Rocky Mountain Revolution* (1956) is also concerned with the story of labor strife in the Idaho mines after 1900. Dorothy O. Johansen and Charles M. Gates, *Empire of the Columbia* (1957) touches briefly on mining in Washington, Idaho, and western Montana.

BLACK HILLS. Estelline Bennett, *Old Deadwood Days* (1929) is general. For transportation in the region see Jesse Brown and A. M. Willard, *The Black Hills Trails* (1924) and Agnes Wright Spring, *The Cheyenne and Black Hills Stage & Express Routes* (1949). Bruce Nelson, *Land of the Dacotahs* (1946) is a popular account.

ARIZONA, NEW MEXICO, AND UTAH. Rufus K. Wyllys, *Arizona: The History of a Frontier State* (1950) and Joseph Miller, *Arizona: The Last Frontier* (1956), both general histories, touch mining only lightly. Francis C. Lockwood, *Pioneer Days in Arizona* (1932) concerns an earlier era; see Chap. 9. Anne M. Peck, *The March of Arizona History* (1962) has several brief chapters pertaining to minerals. Boom-town mining is covered in Walter N. Burns, *Tombstone* (1929); Douglas D. Martin, *Tombstone's Epitaph* (1951) is concerned with the town's newspaper. Robert G. Cleland, *A History of Phelps Dodge* (1952) describes a great mining corporation; see Chaps. 5–8. Warren A. Beck, *New Mexico, A History of Four Centuries* (1962) discusses the state's mineral history; see Chap. 13. Erna Fergusson's *New Mexico* (1951) is a general treatment. Much of the writing about Utah is old. Orson F. Whitney, *History of Utah* (1916) touches on mining. Hubert H. Bancroft's *History of Utah*

(1889) also contains bits on the subject. Leonard J. Arrington's *Great Basin Kingdom* (1958), the best economic study of the area, contains information about mining.

ALASKA. William Ogilvie, *Early Days on the Yukon* (1913) is by a contemporary. More recent is Edward B. Lung, *Black Sand and Gold* (1956). See also Pierre Berton, *The Klondike Fever* (1958). Greever's *Bonanza West* (see above) has two chapters on the Klondike.

DEATH VALLEY. Lee Bourke, *Death Valley* (1930) is about Indians, emigrants, and miners. Neil C. Wilson, *Silver Stampede* (1937) covers Death Valley and Panamint.

CHAPTER 34

THE CATTLE COUNTRY

T he best-advertised feature of the post-Civil War West was the cattle business. A host of authors from Theodore Roosevelt to Zane Grey have given it a species of immortality. Painters such as Frederic Remington and Charles M. Russell have made it only slightly less vivid than did Buffalo Bill in his Wild West show of a previous generation. The movies and television have in their turn made the "horse opera" a staple of American entertainment. All this in spite of the secondary economic importance of the cattle industry, and in spite of the fact that the distinctive period of the long drive lasted less than two decades.

The raising of cattle was always characteristic of the frontier. Surplus grain fed to cattle and transformed into beef permitted it to be moved to market under its own power, which was highly desirable at a time when transportation facilities were poor. The big cattle areas of the early nineteenth century were Ohio and Kentucky, from where stock was driven east across the mountains to market. As land became more expensive the center of cattle raising moved to Indiana, to Illinois, to Iowa, and eventually to the Great Plains. The more sparsely settled areas bred the cattle, which were then fattened and marketed farther west.

Far western herds generally originated in California or Texas, where millions of cattle increased as much as 25 percent a year. Before the Civil War these western herds had been almost profitless because of the lack of available markets. The California rancher could sell a limited amount of hides and tallow to the New England trader. The Texas cattleman now and then pickled some of the meat for export, and occasionally drove a few animals as far as New Orleans or even St. Louis, but such incidents were rare.

Following the Civil War, conditions changed radically as the ex-

530

panding railroad network extended into the western plains and provided transportation to the growing cities farther east. Furthermore, the development during the 1870s of the tin can and of artificial refrigeration, both by railroad and by boat, sounded the death knell for the local butcher, who generally stopped doing butchering. The big packers began to dominate the national market, with locally raised and slaughtered cattle decreasing in importance. Cheap western herds, fattened on the grass of the public domain, could outcompete the better but more expensive animals grown farther east.

Texas cattlemen viewed the expanding railroads with hope, and in 1866 sent their first important herds over the long trail to the northern railroads. This first big drive was not very successful. Unfamiliarity with conditions of the trail led to the loss of an important fraction of the quarter million animals that started the trip. The resulting discouragement explains the slow development of the business.

ABILENE AND OTHER COW TOWNS

The man who saw most clearly the possibilities of the plains cattle business was a twenty-nine-year-old Illinois stockman, Joseph G. McCoy. The five dollars paid in Texas and the fifty dollars paid for a similar animal in the East suggested that profits existed for the taking. Carrying his idea to the railroads, McCoy persuaded them to give him special rates and then searched for a plains town that would meet his needs. The town he picked was Abilene, Kansas, which the Kansas Pacific was due to reach by 1867. Energetic advertising in Texas persuaded ranchers to overlook their failure of the previous year and again send cattle north. During 1867, the first year, McCoy received only 35,000 head, but the number grew steadily.

Abilene created the pattern that later cow towns followed. The economic heart of the town was the stock pens and railroad loading facilities, together with the three-story "Drovers' Cottage" and other hotels and boarding houses necessary to entertain visiting cattlemen. Almost equally vital were the amusements for the hundreds of cowboys who arrived from their long and tiring weeks in the saddle with a craving for bright lights and excitement, and with several months' pay in their pockets. For them the lights glittered in the saloons such as the Bull's Head and the Alamo, for them the balls of the roulette wheel clicked and the cards fell in the gambling parlors, for them the Novelty Theater offered its tawdry entertainment, and for them the "Devil's Half Acre" on the other side of the tracks offered its shopworn castoffs of the river traffic as a pathetic substitute for authentic romance. Drunkards and homicides were no news in Abilene in spite of sporadic and valiant efforts at law enforcement.

Although the lights of Abilene beckoned invitingly for the cowboy with money to spend, the prospect was not so pleasing for more permanent residents, who saw their surroundings in the cold light of day and during the bleak winters. Stock tenders, railroad employees, businessmen, farmers, artisans, schoolteachers, and ministers regretted the streets ankle deep in mud or dust, the rough wooden sidewalks, the shabby store fronts, the drunkenness, the personal violence, and the prostitution. In time their protests were effective; a better police force was installed, and a farmers' protective association limited the ranging of the herds. The result was that by 1872 Abilene was no longer important as a cow town.

Not least in importance among the supporters of the new order were the hard-working wives of Abilene citizens. Such a woman must have felt many pangs as the sun and wind of the plains dried her skin, and as hard work and excessive childbearing made her old. There must have been days when she could have cried bitterly as she saw the few obvious pleasures monopolized by the young and the immoral. Every fiber of her being called for a new and better social order where the usual social values were respected and where children could be reared without contamination from a crude and lawless society.

Abilene was but the first of a long succession of towns that utilized their railroad facilities to capture the cattle business of the plains. Although the gun-wielding Wes Hardin, who was an expert on the subject, has been quoted as saying of Abilene in 1871, "Have seen many fast towns, but I think Abilene beats them all," even Wes may have changed his mind when he saw Ellsworth, Newton, Julesburg, Wichita, Hays City, Ogallala, and other plains settlements take their turn at attracting the cows and the wickedness of the West.

Best known of all the cow towns was Dodge City on the Santa Fe, which ruled supreme as the "cowboy capital" in the decade from 1875 to 1885. During the height of its reign a quarter of a million cattle arrived each year; in 1884 alone it shipped 3648 carloads of beeves to Kansas City and Chicago. Along with the cattle came the usual horde of reckless cowboys who filled the tills of the saloons, supported the gamblers in ease, patronized the disreputable houses south of the tracks, and filled the well-populated Boot Hill Cemetery. In its moment of glory Dodge City was better known than Denver or St. Paul or Kansas City.

GUN WIELDERS

The cow towns of the plains provided a fine setting for men fast with their guns, and who later dominated fiction dealing with cattle. Both here and in the mining towns congregated many men who found more orderly communities undesirable. The West quite naturally had more than its fair share of violent action. Police authority did not keep pace with the expanding West; United States marshals and their deputies were limited both in numbers and by political boundaries. On the other hand, however, the days of the gun wielder were relatively short, his activities overadvertised, his abilities exaggerated. Frequently he has been remade into a sort of Robin Hood, with very curious results when applied to such a mentally inferior juvenile delinquent as Billy the Kid (William Bonney).

One peculiarity of the West was the faintness of the distinction between the lawful and the unlawful killer. Some of the most efficient gun wielders, such as Wyatt Earp, were generally law-enforcement officers. Others, such as Wes Hardin, were outside the law. But consider Wild Bill Hickok, for example, who by common knowledge was a professional gambler and a persistent murderer, and yet served at various times as an effective law-enforcement officer. Quite clearly he wandered from one side of the law to the other without the West's finding this mixture of good and bad particularly unusual or even deplorable.

The truth was that the western line between the law-abiding citizen and the criminal was not hard and fast. Many a cowboy lapsed now and again into cattle stealing, while not a few Westerners were involved in holdups as the men with the handkerchiefs in front of their faces. Perhaps here is part of the reason that holdup men, including particularly Frank and Jesse James, who originated the railroad holdup in 1873, were accorded a certain amount of sympathy. Even well-known killers were allowed to roam freely, since the western code of ethics did not always coincide with statute law. Generally speaking, if one killer beat another to the draw, the bystanders merely nodded approval. If nonprofessionals were included in the slaughter, the reaction might become one of decided disapproval that eventuated in an equally illegal lynching.

Any frontier town was an attractive rendezvous for men who depended on their guns for their livelihood, but the mining and the cattle town offered special opportunities. Each was a predominately male community filled with foot-loose and reckless men. Each was turbulent and unruly. Each emphasized the more boisterous amusements. Each had a plentiful supply of wealth that might be corralled without the usual legal niceties. Here congregated the riffraff of the West in a proper setting for the man highly skilled in the use of the six-shooter.

NATURE OF THE CATTLE BUSINESS

The cattle towns existed only because of the peculiar nature of the western cattle business as it was conducted from the late 1860s through the early 1880s. Each spring saw vast herds collected in Texas and driven north over the public domain, living on the free grass of the government. Most of the cattle, exclusive of those used to stock northern ranches, were shipped from such centers as Abilene and Dodge City. A few were fattened on midwestern farms before they were marketed. Others were wintered on the northern plains and then sent to market the following year. Conservative estimates hold that some 6 million animals were driven north during the twenty years following the Civil War.

These Texas cattle that flooded northern markets were long-horned and muscular. They were able to fight their own battles and to survive under bad conditions. No modern fat, stock-show prize cattle could have existed under plains conditions. The western beef of the generation after the Civil War was tough and stringy, and could be sold only because the price was low.

Sooner or later almost all Texas cattle ended at the large packing houses of Chicago, St. Louis, Kansas City, or Omaha. Of these centers Chicago was clearly the most important. Such men as Armour and Swift had begun their fortunes with lucrative war contracts, and by the 1870s were cooperating to dominate the market and hence to fix prices. The western cattlemen acting individually had no possible chance of fighting effectively against the packers operating in common.

THE COWBOY

The best-known figure of the western cattle business was the cowboy, who has sometimes been considered picturesque because of his unusual clothes. Actually his apparel was highly utilitarian. Loose, heavy, woolen trousers were covered with "chaps" for protection against brush. A woolen shirt was worn open at the throat; bright red or yellow sleeve garters ensured that the hands were free. A coat was seldom worn because it bound the arms and retained perspiration that might become dangerous with the sudden changes of temperature on the plains; in its place an unbuttoned vest was a receptable for watch, tobacco, cigaret papers, and matches. A large gray or brown Stetson hat, a leather thong keeping the brim straight, had a variety of uses beyond protection from sun, rain, snow, sleet, and wind; folded, it made a pillow, and in time of necessity it could be used to carry food or water. A bright handkerchief knotted around the neck also had its utility as a protection against cold and wind.

The cowboy took great pride in his gloves, boots, and saddle. Gloves were gauntlets of the best buckskin, usually embroidered. They were worn all year round, more as a protection against rope burns than against cold. Boots were black, tight, high-topped, and high-heeled. A cowboy was vain of his feet, even though he was shod in such a fashion that he hobbled awkwardly on foot. As for a gun, the usual cowboy found such hardware a nuisance, particularly since he was not a good shot. He would wear a gun only when one was really needed or when he dressed up to go to town.

Then when he called on his lady friend or attended a dance he was likely to remove his gun and retain his hat.

The cowboy's saddle was designed not for fast riding but for comfort on long rides and as a stable seat for roping. It was large, broad, and heavy, weighing some thirty pounds. The stirrups were so long that the rider almost stood upright. Each man owned his own saddle, which might be highly ornamented, and in which he had great pride. For a man to sell his saddle meant that he was dead broke and had lost a measure of his self-respect. A cowboy's whip (quirt) had lashes of twelve inches or more and was carried by a thong around the wrist. His lasso (or lariat or rope) was an eighteen-foot, loose-running coil with which he was adept. Seldom did a man practice fancy roping.

The cowboy's long solitary hours in the saddle may have been responsible for his quietness, which at times approached taciturnity. He seldom expressed his deeper emotions, and certainly never to strangers. Even in the bunkhouse among companions of long and tried friendship he was not likely to become loquacious. Typical is the story of the dude who turned to the cowboy Reddy to verify a long-winded tale of adventure. Reddy responded: "All that mought be so. But the true facts was. The bar [bear] there. The dude he stepped on a stick. Skiddoo."

The cowboy's limited conversation was couched in a vocabulary that was at once picturesque, profane, and obscene. After all, he was usually poorly educated. "Damn" was only an adjective and not an expletive. Language was rich in the metaphor of the plains. " 'Bring me a rib steak about an inch thick,' I says to the waiter, 'Don't cook it too much, but just cripple the critter and drag 'er in.' " Or a man might be described as the surest shot "since a horse pistol was raised from a Colt." Or, describing a spree, one man contended that "I was so drunk that I couldn't hit the ground with my hat in three throws."

The ordinary life of the cowboy was likely to be dull. Riding herd by himself was not an exciting occupation. The exclusively male companionship of the bunkhouse was not thrilling. Possibly here lies the explanation of the cowboy's exaggerated courtesy toward the women he so seldom saw. To him a woman was either all good or all bad, and toward the "good" woman he was almost unbelievably respectful. Even the most attractive of the opposite sex could travel the plains unescorted in much greater safety than she could walk the streets of New York, Philadelphia, or Chicago. Any mistreatment of a woman might bring vindictively cruel punishment to the perpetrator.

The typical cowboy was young and vigorous: a ranch was hardly a convalescent home for the old and sick. Being young and strong, the cowboy's ordinary ailments were fortunately seldom more than stomach-aches or sore throats. Doctors were rare. The ordinary medical treatment was a dose of some patent medicine—"cholera cure," "pain killer," "Universal Liver Remedy," or even diluted horse liniment. An aching tooth was removed by the blacksmith. Surgical treatment was available, if at all, only at the nearest settlement.

The amusements of the cowboy on the ranch were necessarily limited. Horse races, roping contests, and bulldogging combined business with pleasure. Athletic contests on foot were pretty well eliminated by the high-heeled boots and by the bowed legs that came from many hours of straddling a horse. The library of the ranch was confined to a few patent medicine almanacs, mail-order catalogues, saddle-makers' catalogues, and some old newspapers of various dates and places, with possibly a few novels or books of travel. The cowboy ordinarily did his only reading when he was extremely hard pressed for amusement or when he wanted to order a new suit or Stetson from Montgomery Ward and Company.

In the evening in the bunkhouse, when he got tired of slapping down greasy, dog-eared cards, the cowboy might be moved to express his soul in music. A banjo or a fiddle would be dug out of hiding and everyone would join enthusiastically in the singing. High notes were given lingering vibratos; "barber shop chords" were dwelt on lovingly. Included in the repertoire would always be such sentimental ballads as "Rosalie, the Prairie Flower" and "Annie Laurie." Ditties about home and death expressed sentiments impossible of ordinary statement: "I'm a poor, lonesome cowboy," "The dying cowboy," "The night my mother passed away."

Most interesting were the songs indigenous to the cattle business, and using local settings and vernacular:

> Whoopee, ti yi yo, git along, little dogies!
> It's your misfortune and none of my own.
> Whoopee, ti yi yo, git along, little dogies,
> For you know Wyoming will be your new home!

Many of the songs of unknown authorship were extremely sad and had to be rendered with long-drawn-out pathos:

> Oh, bury me not on the lone prairie,
> Where the wild coyotes will howl o'er me;
> Where the rattlesnakes hiss and the wind blows free,
> Oh, bury me not on the lone prairie!

Unfortunately the poor cowboy's prayer was not answered, at least in the song, and "his bones now rot on the lone prairie."

When the cowboy made his infrequent trip to town he tried to squeeze into a short time all the amusements he had missed most of the year. Poker, seven-up, faro, and keno brought the thrill of risking more money than he could afford to lose. Whiskey provided exhilaration up to the moment when the cowboy slid under the table. Prostitutes furnished a synthetic and commercialized romance. Such a spree, coming after payday or when cattle were being sold, afforded a much-needed relaxation from the usual humdrum life of the ranch. True, the cowboy drank to excess and lost his money at cards, but he was young and vigorous, and recuperated rapidly. A good night's sleep brought him back to work little the worse for his experience unless he had contracted venereal disease. The worst effects usually were on the towns he visited and on his own reputation.

Most of a cowboy's life was spent in such routine occupations as riding range, caring for animals in trouble, mending fences, and repairing harness, but certain outstanding events of the year broke the monotony. In the spring the horses had to be "broken" or "gentled" for the year's work. "Breaking" was a really descriptive word, since the refractory 20 percent of the horses actually had their spirits broken. The usual method of breaking was to snub, blindfold, saddle, and mount the horse. Then the blindfold was removed and the rider tried to keep his seat until the horse gave up the struggle. The occasion was something of a sporting event as the cowboys gathered around to see the fun. If the rider "grabbed leather" (the saddle horn) his reputation suffered; hence he held his hat in his hand to demonstrate mastery. To be thrown was unpleasant in several ways, but certainly was desirable in the rare event that the horse rolled over. Possibly one in a hundred horses was never broken to the saddle, and many remained so untamed that they bucked every time riders straddled their backs.

Controlling even the small horses of the plains was hard on the men and helps to explain why the average working life of a cowboy was estimated at seven years. Enough horses had to be broken to give each man a "string" of from six to ten, to be ridden successively and changed from time to time. Only rarely did a cowboy have a special affection for some particular horse. A good cow pony was trained to respond to the pressure of the knees rather than to the pull of the reins, to cut a steer out of the herd, and to brace itself on its haunches whenever its rider threw his rope.

THE ROUNDUP

Most important in the cattleman's year was the roundup. The spring roundup was common throughout the country as a means of identifying and marking calves while they were still with their mothers. At this time cattle in Texas were segregated for the drive north. A fall roundup was less frequent in the South than in the North, where cattle were selected for the market in the autumn. Because of the unfenced country of the early days the herds were badly mixed and a roundup was a cooperative venture, crews from the various ranches dividing the territory and driving the cattle to some central spot. If this happened to be in open country the cattle were held together by being made to mill (move in circles).

The real work of the roundup was the branding of the calves. Each calf had to be cut from the herd, roped, thrown, tied, and dragged to the fire. Cowboys sat on its head and feet while it was branded with a hot iron and sometimes had its ears notched. A tally man kept count for all ranches. When the calf was freed it ran back, bawling and frightened, to its mother. The whole operation seemed to be one of the utmost confusion. The calves bawled and their mothers bellowed; dust billowed and the herd milled; the horses ran and the struggling calves were dragged; the fire gave out a fierce heat, and the cowboys sweat and cursed. But beneath this confusing surface the work actually proceeded rapidly and methodically.

Cattle brands were at first simple markings developed at the pleasure of the owners, but with the vast increase of both herds and owners the system became complicated. To avoid confusion and duplication the stockmen formed associations which kept elaborate records. Certain markings were outlawed, as for example the so-called "frying pan" brand, which could be used to obliterate earlier markings. Common types of brands included the 4—28, called the four bar twenty-eight; the A2 or big A two; $\underline{\underline{M}}$ or lazy M bar; ⓖ or circle G; ⟨S⟩ or diamond S; ‑9‑ or flying 9. In addition some owners used various kinds of ear slits.

Many a western herd was marked by the bar sinister. On the plains there were always some unmarked "mavericks" that became the property of the finders. Since a maverick was ordinarily the progeny of a cow that had met an untimely end there was a tremendous temptation for the ambitious cowboy to help nature make orphans. Having started a herd this way he might later be among the most ardent supporters of law and order. If he entered cattle stealing as a profession he became an artist with a piece of hot wire. The ‑U‑ (flying U) was not hard to alter to ‑U⁰ (seven up); E (big E) was easy to convert to —E (pitchfork). The early defense against such depredations was a vigilance committee, a dark night, a tree, and a coil of rope. Later the stockmen's associations hired detectives and depended more upon the enforcement of regular processes of law.

THE LONG DRIVE

The other outstanding event in a cowboy's life in the 1870s and early 1880s was the "long drive" from Texas to the northern plains or to a shipping point in Kansas or Nebraska. The drive started in the early spring, immediately after the roundup. The most efficient size of the herd was some 2500 to 3000, accompanied by a dozen men and the necessary horses, mules, and chuck wagon. After a few days in which the herd was acclimated to the trail, the cattle moved at the rate of some 10 to 15 miles a day, which meant 300 to 500 miles a month. At this rate the cattle could gain flesh on the grass of the public domain.

A caravan on the long drive was headed by a trail boss, who was followed by the cook with the chuck wagon; the cook was usually an older man and the best-paid of the party. Then came the herd, with the more experienced hands on each side to keep the animals from straying and to avoid collision with other herds. Also on one side was the horse wrangler with the spare mounts. In the rear came the remainder of the cowboys, who had the unpleasant job of swallowing the billowing dust from the herd so that they could round up any stragglers. All in all the work was hard, dusty, and monotonous. It did bring, however, a splendid appetite for the bacon, flapjacks, and coffee that the "old lady" dished out at the end of the day. After supper the cowboy could not smoke his cigaret and roll into his blankets for a good night's sleep: he had to stand one of the three watches that prevented the herd from roaming during the night.

Numerous dangers confronted the men on the long drive. Cattle thieves and wild animals were possibilities. Swimming a river was dangerous because cattle are stupid and crowd enough to cause many deaths unless they are well handled. Worst of all was a stampede, which might be produced by any startling incident—the shot of a gun or a flash of lightning. Cattle are easily frightened, which was one of the reasons the cowboy so frequently sang as he was riding herd. Once a herd stampeded, the panic-stricken animals dashed wildly away from the object of their fears. If they came to a cliff they fell to their death, if to a river they drowned, if to a mountainside they trampled each other to death. The cowboy's only hope was to head them off by hard riding and then cause them to mill. With this object in mind he took desperate chances, and not infrequently was trampled to death for his pains.

PERMANENT RANCHES

The striking character of the long drive tended to obscure the development of a more permanent and more important type of western cattle business all the way from Texas to Montana, and as far west as California and Oregon. As much as three quarters of the drive from Texas has been estimated to have been used to stock the ranches of the northern plains, which in turn had large increases of their own. During the 1870s the cattle of Kansas and Nebraska increased from 500,000 to 2,500,000; of Montana from 36,000 to 430,000; of Wyoming from 11,000 to 520,000; of Colorado from 71,000 to 791,000. During these same years Henry Miller was building his cattle empire farther west in California and Oregon.

A cattle boom was evident on the western plains by the late 1870s, but even with the increasing herds the price of beef continued to rise. By 1882 the price of beef in Chicago had reached $9 a hundredweight, which meant that a steer on a Texas ranch, worth not over $5 or $6 in 1865, would bring around $35 dollars. Rumors were circulated of profits of 50 percent or more in a single year. The boom continued to grow in volume.

The boom of the late 1870s and early 1880s attracted large amounts of speculative capital, not only from the United States but also from abroad, primarily from England and Scotland. The stockman of the past was being replaced by the corporation that raised its initial capital from hundreds of small subscribers. Mammoth companies became frequent. The Prairie Land & Cattle Company, with ranches in Texas, Oklahoma, and New Mexico, could boast 7900 square miles of land and 140,000 head of stock. The Swan Land & Cattle Company of Wyoming, largely Scottish, held half a million acres of land and had an investment of some $3 million. The J A Ranch of Charles Goodnight in the Texas Panhandle comprised over a million acres. Like other American businesses, cattle raising had become big. The rapidly growing herds began to crowd the range, so that no longer was there an apparently limitless public domain where any man's cows might find sufficient grass. The result was a mad scramble to obtain control of the available land, particularly the part of it that contained water. Land without water was useless and there was always a lack of water. Many and bitter were the struggles to control springs and creeks.

Various stratagems were necessary to acquire large parcels of land, since most of it remained part of the public domain, and the American land system had been developed primarily with the object of providing small farms for settlers. Railroad land could sometimes be obtained, although the alternate-section pattern had disadvantages. Homesteaders could be bought out; in fact many men entered homestead claims in several names so that they could sell to the cattle companies. Cowboys were encouraged to acquire land by homesteading, pre-emption, or timber culture, and then assign it to their bosses. Of course such transactions were technically illegal, but punishment was most unlikely. Only in Texas, which controlled her own land, could a large quantity be obtained legally from the government. The most spectacular of such acquisitions was that of the Capitol Freehold Company, which in 1879 received a huge tract in the Panhandle in return for a promise to build the state capitol. The X I T brand soon appeared on some 160,000 cattle ranging 3,050,000 acres enclosed in 1500 miles of fence. Here was probably the world's largest ranch.

When all other methods failed, the cattleman merely fenced the needed land, regardless of ownership. The checkerboard of railroad sections might be so fenced that the alternate sections of public land were included.

Fences might be strung around land to which the cattleman had no possible claim, and even across roads so that the traveler had to cut the strands to continue his journey. This kind of illegal fencing amounted to a national scandal during the late 1870s and 1880s. President Cleveland made considerable efforts to enforce a law of 1885 that provided severe penalties, but was by no means entirely successful.

A permanent and fenced ranch, with its large capital investment, inspired efforts to produce better and hence more valuable beef. The low market value of small and scrawny Texas Longhorns was not satisfactory to the large operator; hence the breed was improved by adding such blooded stock as Shorthorn, Polled Angus, and Galloway. Better stock necessitated more care, since the better the beef the fatter and more helpless the animal, and the greater the loss if it died. Water supplies were husbanded carefully and natural running water was supplemented by dug wells. Hay was grown and the barns necessary for its protection were built, even though the cowboy was far from enthusiastic about spending his time digging postholes, watering stock, running a mowing machine, and pitching hay.

More competition for land and water brought a need for cooperative action by the owners. They subscribed to the cult of the self-made man and the superiority of rugged individualism, but like other contemporary businessmen were not hidebound in applying such principles. Cattlemen's associations were formed, of which the most important was probably the Wyoming Stock Growers' Association, founded in 1873; in time it operated in five states and controlled some 2 million head of cattle. Similar groups were soon created throughout the cattle country. They recorded the brands of their members, hired detectives to find cattle thieves, supervised roundups, settled conflicting claims, obtained railroad rebates, and did lobbying in both state and national legislatures. In time their various regulations were given legal authority by the several states.

The western cattle business underwent many changes during the middle 1880s. Most obvious to the casual observer was the end of the long drive. The railroads that had made the drive possible now made it impossible by bringing thousands of farmers to the plains. These farmers quite naturally objected to the passage of cattle that broke their fences and trampled their grain, while local ranchers opposed outside competition. Since these farmers and ranchers were permanent residents they could persuade the states by 1885 to pass a series of laws ostensibly designed to bar diseased cattle, which was entirely reasonable, but really aimed at the elimination of all cattle from the south. In consequence the long drive was at an end. The talk of a national cattle trail on the public domain never came to the point of action. In the future cattle were to be raised and shipped from their home ranches.

The omen of an even greater change came in 1883, when American beef exports dropped 50 percent. The next year saw a drop in domestic prices, which by 1887 descended to $2.50 a hundredweight. One drovers' magazine urged, "If you have steers to shed, prepare to shed them now." To make the stockmen even more unhappy, the year of 1885 was hard on the cattle and 1886 was even worse: a hot summer was followed by a very cold winter, and during 1886–1887 cattle died by the thousand. Some herds lost as much as 90 percent. The cattle boom was dead; the cattlemen, along with most of the West, tightened their belts to try to survive the bad times of the late 1880s and early 1890s.

The collapse of the fever for cattle meant that many investors lost their money. The mortality among the large companies was notable, but many smaller individual owners were able to recover. Expenditures could no longer be on the lavish scale of the past, and the ranchers had to find cheaper and more efficient methods of operation. The trend was to sell younger animals, since the lack of local grain made their fattening too expensive. Many of the animals were sent to the corn belt for feeding before they made their appearance in the Chicago stockyards.

SHEEP

The same land that was suitable for grazing cattle could also be used for sheep, and as eastern land became more expensive, there was a tendency for an increasing proportion of American sheep to be raised in the Far West. Even before the Civil War large flocks had grazed the land of California and New Mexico, and after the war there was great expansion to the north and east. These sheep frequently were driven east, mainly to Kansas and Nebraska, to be fattened for market. The drive was at its height between 1865 and 1885; estimates have been made that some 15 million animals were driven between 1870 and 1900. Mostly ewes were driven before 1880; later wethers predominated. The trip normally took over seven months, a day's travel being about eight to ten miles. Sheep were more docile than cattle; the main hazard was that they might wander away and get lost.

Sheep trails, like cattle trails, were gradually closed by state action. Starting with Kansas in the mid-1880s, all states acted by 1900, and in consequence sheep had to be raised without the aid of free public grass. The greatest concentration of the industry came to be in the mountain and coast states, the plains east of the mountains being dominated by cattle. By the end of the century such states as Wyoming, Montana, Colorado, Utah, California, New Mexico, and even Texas were raising more sheep than cattle. Wyoming, the traditional home of the little dogie, discovered that although it could boast in 1886 that cattle outnumbered sheep 3 to 1, in 1900 sheep outnumbered cattle by an impressive ratio of 8 to 1.

The main activities of the sheep business were driving the flocks to good pastures, protecting them from wild animals and other dangers, caring for newborn lambs, dipping, and shearing. Shearing was done once a year and hence was a seasonable occupation, much like threshing; shearing crews worked north from early spring until late June. Ordinarily the animal was dipped before and after shearing. The wool was the only important product, since until the twentieth century mutton was hardly worth shipping.

The sheepherder compared unfavorably in the popular mind with the cowboy. No one thought of the herder as a man of romance and excitement. He lived a life of solitude, except for his dog and his flock. If lucky he might have a permanent cabin, but more frequently he followed his woollies with a bedroll on his back, or possibly with a covered wagon if his employer were generous. Daily association with sheep was reported to make a man queer, although some held that the occupation attracted the odd personality. When in the cattle country you called a man a sheepherder, it was well to be prepared to reach fast for your gun.

Cattlemen and sheepmen never wasted love on each other, since they competed for the same range. The cattleman insisted that sheep cropped the grass too close and ruined the range with their sharp hooves, so that no self-respecting cow would graze on land formerly used by sheep; this statement was not true except in the sense that the close cropping by sheep possibly necessitated a considerable time before the grass was tall enough to be available for cattle. Moreover, the cowboy looked down with disgust and contempt on the lowly, unmounted, and usually unarmed sheepherder surrounded by his dirty, smelly woollies, and in return the sheepherder deeply resented the arrogance of the cowboy. Bitter feuds resulted, with the greater number and mobility of the cowboys ordinarily permitting them to take the offensive, although the sheepmen could hire professional gunmen to make the odds more even. Outstanding examples were the Tonti Basin war in Arizona in 1887, and the struggle in the Green River country of Wyoming in 1901. Thousands of sheep were clubbed, dynamited, driven over cliffs, fed poisoned grain, or given saltpeter, which was fatal to them but did not hurt the cattle; shooting was considered too expensive. At times the herders fought back by cutting fences and slaughtering cattle, and personal physical combat was far from unknown.

Vengeful clashes were not to last forever. By the 1900s the general place of cattle and sheep in the national economy had been fixed, and the days of violence were mostly past. In spite of the cattlemen's opposition to the introduction of sheep, many a rancher had actually changed from cattle to sheep. In the long run, economic forces had won over sentiment.

READINGS

REGIONAL. Practically every regional history treats both cattle and sheep; see particularly Chapter 36 under Athearn, Briggs, Dale and Wardell, Howard, Johnson, Nelson, Olson, Richardson, Rister, Shannon, and Toole. See also Maxwell S. Burt, *Powder River* (1938); Everett Dick, *Vanguards of the Frontier* (1941); Erna Fergusson, *New Mexico* (1951); W. Eugene Hollon, *The Southwest* (1961); Charles Lindsay, *The Big Horn Basin* (1932); and Rufus K. Wyllys, *Arizona* (1950).

THE CATTLE BUSINESS. Lewis Atherton, *The Cattle Kings* (1961), rather miscellaneous; Edward D. Branch, *The Cowboy* (1926), reads easily; Dee Brown, *Trail Driving Days* (1952); Edward E. Dale, *Cow Country* (1942) and *The Range Cattle Industry* (1930), very good; Joe B. Franz and Julian E. Choat, Jr., *The American Cowboy* (1955), literary image, with fine pictures; Robert G. Athearn, *Westward the Briton* (1953), comments of British visitors; John A. Lomax, *Cowboy Songs* (1922) and *Songs of the Cattle Trail* (1919); John L. McCarty, *Maverick Town* (1946), a synthetic Texas town; Joseph G. McCoy, *Historic Sketches of the Cattle Trade* (1940), reprint of a classic account; Ernest S. Osgood, *The Day of the Cattleman* (1929), informative; Louis Pelzer, *The Cattlemen's Frontier* (1936), an excellent study; William M. Raine and Will C. Barnes, *Cattle* (1930), interesting; Philip A. Rollins, *The Cowboy* (1922), has a literary flavor; Floyd B. Streeter, *Prairie Trails and Cow Towns* (1936), the long drive; and Clifford P. Westermeier, *Trailing the Cowboy* (1955).

INDIVIDUALS. Of the numerous accounts, frequently autobiographical, should be mentioned Andy Adams, *The Log of a Cowboy* (1903), good; Floyd C. Bard, *Horse Wrangler* (1960), reminiscences; John Clay, *My Life on the Range* (1924); James H. Cook, *Fifty Years on the Old Frontier* (1957), reminiscences; L. F. Crawford, *Rekindling Camp Fires* (1926); Angie Debo (ed.), *The Cowman's West* (1953); Chris Emmett, *Shanghai Pierce* (1953), Texas; Will Hale, *Twenty-Four Years a Cowboy and Ranchman in Southern Texas and Old Mexico* (1959); James E. Haley, *Charles Goodnight* (1936); Will James, *American Cowboy* (1942), *Cowboys North and South* (1924), *The Drifting Cowboy* (1925), *Lone Cowboy* (1930), all excellent; Frank M. King, *Wranglin' the Past* (1946), the Southwest; James E. McCauley, *A Stove-up Cowboy's Story* (1943); Bruce Siberts, *Nothing but Prairie and Sky* (1954), the Dakotas. The X I T ranch has extensive treatment in James E. Haley, *The X I T Ranch* (1953) and Cordia S. Duke and Joe B. Franz, *6,000 Miles of Fence* (1961). Wayne Gard, *The Chisholm Trail* (1954) is excellent.

SHEEP. Edward N. Wentworth, *America's Sheep Trails* (1948);
Charles W. Towne and Edward N. Wentworth, *Shepherd's Empire*
(1945); Winifred Kupper, *The Golden Hoof* (1945), centers in western Texas; Hughie Call, *The Golden Fleece* (1942), reminiscences; Harry
J. Brown (ed.), *Letters from a Texas Sheep Ranch* (1959), good.

BAD MEN. General accounts, to be read with caution, include Hoff-
man Birney, *Vigilantes* (1929); William M. Breakenridge, *Helldorado*
(1928); Eugene Cunningham, *Triggernometry* (1934); Wayne Gard,
Frontier Justice (1949), good; Fred H. Harrington, *Hanging Judge*
(1951), good on Oklahoma; Henry E. Hoyt, *A Frontier Doctor* (1929),
Texas and New Mexico; William M. Raine, *Famous Sheriffs and Western Outlaws* (1929), *45-Caliber Law* (1941), *Guns of the Frontier*
(1940); Glenn Shirley, *Six-Gun and Silver Star* (1955), Oklahoma. The
Texas Rangers can be followed in Walter P. Webb, *The Texas Rangers*
(1953). Individual biographies need even more caution. Typical are Dun-
can Aikman, *Calamity Jane* (1927); Walter N. Burns, *The Saga of Billy
the Kid* (1926); William E. Connelley, *Wild Bill and His Era* (1933),
Hickok; Emmett Dalton, *When the Daltons Rode* (1931), reminiscences;
Maurice G. Fulton (ed.), *Pat F. Garrett's Authentic Life of Billy the
Kid* (1927); Pat Jahns, *The Frontier World of Doc Holliday* (1957);
Stuart N. Lake, *Wyatt Earp* (1931); Robertus Love, *The Rise and Fall
of Jesse James* (1926); Miguel A. Otero, *The Real Billy the Kid* (1936);
Burton Rascoe, *Belle Starr* (1941); Lee Sage, *The Last Rustler* (1930),
an autobiography; Roberta B. Sollid, *Calamity Jane* (1958); Charles L.
Sonnichsen, *Roy Bean* (1943), better than most; Zoe A. Tilghman, *Mar-
shal of the Last Frontier* (1949), Bill Tilghman; Frank J. Wilstach,
Wild Bill Hickok (1926).

CHAPTER 35

TRANSCONTINENTAL
RAILROADS

The greatest single influence in the settlement of the trans-Mississippi West was the railroad. Without the railroad the settlement of the Great Plains would have been impossible. Steel streamers shot into the wilderness killed the traditional life of the Indian by eliminating his game, and replaced cattlemen with farmers in all areas where farming was even faintly possible. The wilderness that had seemed the permanent home of the coyote, the buffalo, and the Indian melted away to insignificance within a generation.

Railroads were necessarily the products of prosperity, when men controlling capital felt optimistic. The first small western boom of the 1850s collapsed with the panic of 1857 and did not revive until the end of the Civil War. The postwar expansion was relatively short-lived because of the depression in 1873, but the revival of the late 1870s brought the largest railroad boom in American history. The decade of 1878–1888 saw the peak of railroad construction, the bulk occurring west of the Mississippi.

EARLY TRANSCONTINENTAL PLANS
AND CHARTERS

The outstanding railroad accomplishment was the completion of a half-dozen transcontinental projects. The bridging of 2000 miles of plains, desert, and mountain overshadowed the more humdrum business of lacing steel fingers over the plains, even though both were vital. The long roads needed feeders if they were to be profitable; the short roads were valueless without connections to more distant points. The farmer needed his connections to remote markets to be within hauling distance. Once the railroad net was completed the frontier was a thing of the past.

The idea of a transcontinental railroad went back as far as the early 1830s, when it was entirely chimerical; its great enthusiast of the 1840s was Asa Whitney, a New York merchant engaged in the trade with China. Popular interest grew rapidly, and was intensified by a series of conventions in the late 1840s and early 1850s; notable were those convened at Chicago (1847), St. Louis (1849), Memphis (1849), Philadelphia (1850), Iowa City (1851), New Orleans (1852), and Little Rock (1853). There was general agreement that any railroad across the continent was so speculative that construction by private interests was extremely unlikely. On the other hand, construction by the government, although favored by a few, went contrary to the prevailing sentiment that business activities were run most efficiently by individuals, a sentiment reinforced by some unhappy experiences of states with toll roads and canals. The consequence was that the debate ranged around the amount and type of governmental assistance thought to be necessary.

During the 1850s the technical problems of building the transcontinental road were solved, but the chances of construction actually seemed to decline because of the increasing heat of sectional controversies over its route, with the assumption that only one road would be built, at least in the foreseeable future. Northern interests favored a road from Chicago by the northern route. Thomas Hart Benton dreamed of a "national road" from St. Louis in his home state of Missouri. Senator Gwin of California talked of the southern route, with branches from St. Louis, Memphis, and New Orleans. Douglas advanced the obvious political solution of building along all three routes, which in this case was suggesting the impossible.

The withdrawal of the South from the Union eliminated the southern route from competition, but at the same time the desire of Congress to please the West was at its height. As between the northern and central routes, the central route was shorter, had fewer physical obstacles, and possessed a larger population desirous of help on both local and national levels. Hence the first federal charter and assistance went to the central route in the act of July 1, 1862. Charters and subsidies for other routes soon followed. The Northern Pacific (1864) was given the northern route from Lake Superior to Puget Sound. The Atlantic & Pacific (1866) was to build along the 35th parallel from Springfield, Missouri, through Albuquerque to the Pacific. The Texas & Pacific (1871) was to run from Marshall, Texas, along the 32nd parallel to San Diego. Other roads, such as the Southern Pacific, Great Northern, and Chicago, Milwaukee & St. Paul were built without subsidies; the Atchison, Topeka & Santa Fe had subsidies for parts of its line.

THE UNION PACIFIC CHARTER

The first transcontinental charter of 1862 did not give the entire project to a single company. The western part of the main line went to the Central Pacific of California, which was already in existence, largely through the enthusiasm of Theodore D. Judah, a young engineer who had gone to California in 1854 as chief engineer for a railroad in the Sacramento Valley. Judah had become enthusiastic about railroad connections with the East, had made extensive surveys, and had interested the prosperous Sacramento businessmen Leland Stanford, Collis P. Huntington, Mark Hopkins, and Charles Crocker. These men chartered the Central Pacific, and Judah traveled to Washington, where he was successful in obtaining the inclusion of the Central Pacific in the railroad plans being considered by Congress.

The eastern part of the new line was given to a group called the Union Pacific Railroad. To compromise the pretensions of Chicago and St. Louis, the eastern terminus of the main line was placed between the two cities and west of both on the 100th meridian in central Nebraska. From that point to the west the road was to follow the old and well-known California trail. To the east, five branches were to radiate: to Kansas City, to Leavenworth, to St. Joseph, to Sioux City, and to some unnamed place on the western boundary of Iowa. This last place was ultimately fixed at Council Bluffs, although actually Omaha was the real terminus. This peculiar arrangement was evolved to compromise various local interests. The first four of the branches were given to companies already in existence, but none was built along the route specified in the charter; most important was the Kansas Pacific, which was completed from Kansas City through Denver to Cheyenne in 1871. The fifth branch was given to the Union Pacific itself; since this was the most direct route it became for practical purposes part of the main line.

Each of these roads was given five odd-numbered sections of land on each side and within ten miles of the road, and also the right to use necessary building materials from the public domain. In addition, a government loan was provided on the basis of mortgages on the roads. It was to be for $16,000 a mile over the greatest part of the route, but $48,000 in the Rockies and Sierras, and $32,000 in the region between the two ranges. Finally, the act made provision for organizing and financing the Union Pacific company and provided that all its property should revert to the government if the road were not completed by 1876.

The chartering of the Union Pacific was an occasion for great rejoicing. One orator proclaimed grandiloquently: "It was said of the Nile that it was a god. I think the Pacific railroad project comes nearer being the subject of deification than anything else I have ever heard in the Senate. Everyone is trying to show his zeal in worshiping the road." The whole country was realizing a long-deferred hope and looking forward eagerly to the opening of the new line.

Unfortunately for railroad hopes, enthusiasm did not lay tracks. Public meetings, glowing perorations, and enthusiastic newspaper publicity failed to drive a single spike. Potential investors looked dubiously at a wilderness railroad that might never pay dividends, and were not even tempted by the government loan and by land of doubtful value. Almost as soon as the company was organized, interested parties contributed $500,000 to a Washington "suspense account" to help persuade Congress to grant more aid. Their pleas were effective, and in 1864 Congress doubled the land grant and reduced the loan to a second mortgage.

BUILDING THE UNION PACIFIC

Actual construction of the Union Pacific was begun at Omaha in December 1863, but only 40 miles were completed in 1864 and 1865. The slowness was due primarily to the lack of enthusiasm on the part of investors, although there was also difficulty in obtaining the necessary supply of labor in wartime. The financial answer was finally found by T. C. Durant and his friends in the formation of a Pennsylvania corporation, the Crédit Mobilier of America, to handle construction contracts. Disregarding certain technical financial advantages of the new corporation, its main purpose was to profit by construction contracts, on the assumption that there would probably be no profit in running the completed railroad. The Crédit Mobilier was financed by advances from Durant and his friends and by short-term loans based on railroad bonds. Profits to the Crédit Mobilier on its construction contracts came, of course, from the railroad, and if they were too high the minority stockholders suffered but the insiders gained.

The amount of profit made by the insiders who controlled the Crédit Mobilier is still in dispute. The most recent estimate—one by Robert W. Fogel—is considered by the man who made it as probably only slightly more than a fair return in consideration of the risk. On the other hand, some of the financial and political manipulations of the men in the Crédit Mobilier were entirely deplorable. When Oakes Ames, a member of Congress interested in the Crédit Mobilier, distributed Crédit Mobilier stocks among his congressional friends with whom it would "do the most good" even the lax post-Civil War ethics were violated. When these transactions came to light, Ames was censured by the House for his conduct.

The first 40 miles of the Union Pacific were inspected and accepted by the government on January 24, 1866, and by July of the same year the road was completed 305 miles west of Omaha, forcing the overland stage

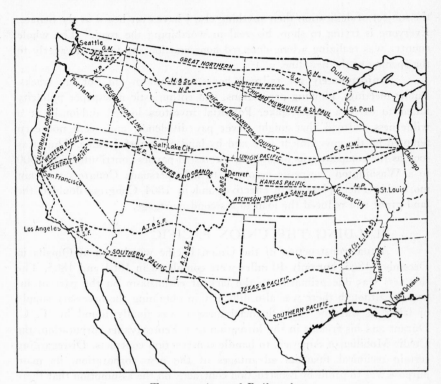

Transcontinental Railroads

to move its eastern terminus to Fort Kearney. The pace of construction increased during the summer of 1867, when a power struggle between Durant and Oliver and Oakes Ames for control of the project was settled, and when a railroad connection to the East was completed.

An adequate labor supply appeared in the years after the Civil War, when discharged soldiers were available in considerable numbers; the chief construction engineer was Colonel Grenville M. Dodge, a former army officer with extensive knowledge of western railroading and an unusual aptitude for handling men. The military training of these men was a real advantage, for there were many Indian depredations, and although there were troops on guard at times, the men usually had to fend for themselves. Each man was ordinarily armed, and the guns were stacked while work proceeded. Whenever an alarm was given the boss called on his men to "fall in," and the workmen became an army. Isolated workers and men wandering off alone were always in danger of being ambushed by hostile Indians.

Large fleets of wagons hauled materials and provisions. In the early days the Union Pacific had no rail connection with the East, and even after the completion of the Chicago & Northwestern to Omaha in 1867 all supplies had to be carried by wagons for crews working in advance of the track, a haul that might be as long as a hundred miles. A special problem was the lack of wood for railroad ties, but this difficulty was partially solved by developing a method to harden cottonwood.

The process of track laying was described this way by an eyewitness:

Track-laying on the Union Pacific is a science, and we pundits of the Far East stood upon that embankment, only about a thousand miles this side of sunset, and backed westward before that hurrying corps of sturdy operatives with mingled feelings of amusement, curiosity, and profound respect. On they came. A light car, drawn by a single horse, gallops up to the front with its load of rails. Two men seize the end of a rail and start forward, the rest of the gang taking hold by twos until it is clear of the car. They come forward at a run. At the word of command, the rail is dropped in its place, right side up, with care, while the same process goes on at the other side of the car. Less than thirty seconds to a rail for each gang, and so four rails go down to the minute! Quick work, you say, but the fellows on the U.P. are tremendously in earnest. The moment the car is empty it is tipped over on the side of the track to let the next loaded car pass it, and then it is tipped back again; and it is a sight to see it go flying back for another load, propelled by a horse at full gallop at the end of 60 or 80 feet of rope, ridden by a young Jehu, who drives furiously. Close behind the first gang come the gaugers, spikers, and bolters, and a lively time they make of it. It is a grand Anvil Chorus that these sturdy sledges are playing across the plains. It is in triple time, three strokes to a spike. There are ten spikes to a rail, four hundred rails to a mile, eighteen hundred miles to San Francisco. That's the sum, what is the quotient? Twenty-one million times are those sledges to be swung—twenty-one million times are they to come down with their sharp punctuations, before the great work of modern America is complete!

The men who built the Union Pacific lived in tent cities that moved west with the road. Whenever a stretch of track was completed all the equipment was moved to the next scene of operations. Rough streets were laid out, tents erected, and crude shacks built for the officers and the stores. To this hastily constructed town came the usual camp following of land speculators, petty merchants, saloon keepers, gamblers, and prostitutes. The bright lights of the saloons gleamed on streets that were ankle-deep in dust. The blare of cheap music and the allurements of the dancehall girls brought relief to the laborer after his toil. Drunkenness, immorality, and personal violence gave such towns the well-earned sobriquet of "hell on wheels." More permanent cities would rise where work ceased during the coldest part of the winter, as at Julesburg, Cheyenne, and Laramie. But each spring the railroad-built houses were torn down, the tents, supplies, and furniture packed, loaded on freight cars, and moved to the next camp.

THE CENTRAL PACIFIC

While the Union Pacific gathered increasing momentum westward the Central Pacific was building eastward with equal vigor. The Central Pacific had even greater difficulties with finances and labor supply than had its eastern counterpart; the labor situation was finally met by importing Chinese. Even geography worked against the Central Pacific; the snow-clad ranges of the Sierra Nevadas hindered the first construction, whereas two thirds of the Union Pacific road was built on a beautifully level plain. By 1867 the Central Pacific had conquered its worst obstacles; thereafter its building was rapid.

The Sacramento associates remained in control of the Central Pacific, although Judah had died in 1863. Huntington was the most important figure in his function of financial and purchasing agent; the thrifty Hopkins was treasurer and business manager; the optimistic and energetic Crocker was in charge of construction; Stanford, who had been wartime Governor of California, handled political problems within the state. This division of authority proved a happy one, and affairs were handled with complete mutual confidence.

The building of the Central Pacific was done by construction companies, first by Crocker & Company, and then by the Contract & Finance Company. Both were composed of the men who controlled the Central Pacific, and who hoped to garner the profits of construction since they had no idea the road could later be operated profitably. The methods of the Contract & Finance Company were similar to those of the Crédit Mobilier but the accounts were muddled even more thoroughly. Huntington, Stanford, Crocker, and Hopkins held the capital stock, for which they paid with their personal notes. Then, as controlling directors of the Central Pacific, they voted themselves lucrative construction contracts. The money for the construction was advanced by each man as he had the extra cash, and the only record of the transaction was his own memorandum. Profits were either put back into the business or divided equally. This scheme of bookkeeping had wonderful possibilities for preventing any close inquiry into the company's methods and accounts. The last dramatic bit of confusion was added with the "accidental" destruction of the company's books by fire in 1873, a date suspiciously close to the Crédit Mobilier scandal.

Both the Central Pacific and the Union Pacific were laying track furiously by 1868–1869, and by the spring of 1869 the two construction crews came in sight of each other. The surveys began to parallel each other, and as the track followed the surveys people ran to their copies of the *Statutes at Large* only to discover that although the legislation assumed that the tracks would join, there was no mandatory provision to this effect. What was to prevent each line from continuing to build and thus increase the subsidies it might receive from the federal government? Congress solved the difficulty by providing a meeting point at Promontory Summit, Utah, a little northwest of Ogden.

The final ceremony of connecting the rails took place on May 10, 1869. Governor Stanford of California represented the Central Pacific and Sidney Dillon, president of the Union Pacific, represented his road. Prayer was offered, congratulations were exchanged, and the last spike was driven home. All of the ceremony, including the blows of the sledge hammer, was carried to the rest of the country by telegraph. Then followed celebrations throughout the nation. Bells were rung, whistles tooted, guns fired, processions formed, banners hung, dinners held, toasts given. The great project was completed. The West was linked with the East, and the trade of the Orient lay ready for the taking. An epoch-making event had occurred.

Unfortunately for its reputation, the Union Pacific was involved immediately in all sorts of troubles. Much of it had been badly built and soon needed replacement. Financial troubles were omnipresent, including some caused by the manipulations of Jay Gould. The debt to the government was a source of seemingly unending trouble. Fraud, both public and private, emerged with distressing frequency. And yet the accomplishment had been great. Thanks to speculatively minded Americans, only approximately five years had been required to span the wilderness from the Missouri River to the Pacific Coast, and thus had been speeded tremendously the settlement of the trans-Mississippi West. The positive accomplishments should be given at least as much attention as the defects.

OTHER CONSTRUCTION BEFORE 1873

Several other railroads with transcontinental aspirations were able to start construction before 1873. The Atchison, Topeka & Santa Fe, chartered originally to connect Atchison and Topeka, had hopes of corralling at least the Santa Fe trade. Starting construction in the late 1860s it was completed by 1873 to Granada, Colorado, and threatened to draw all the business of southern Colorado away from Denver. Denver's answer turned out to be the narrow-gauge Denver & Rio Grande, chartered in 1870 to build south and collect the rich minerals from the mountain areas. The Rio Grande reached Pueblo in 1873, and planned to extend southward toward Santa Fe and westward to control the rich mining area near Leadville.

Farther to the south lay the Atlantic & Pacific on the 35th parallel route. The Atlantic & Pacific was chartered only from Springfield, Missouri, and thus depended on the state-aided railroads of Missouri for its eastern connections. This connection was made certain by the purchase of the Missouri Pacific. Construction was also started to the west, so that by 1873 the line had reached a junction with the Missouri, Kansas & Texas at Vinita in Indian Territory. Unfortunately the Atlantic & Pacific had expanded more rapidly than its financial resources permitted; consequently it suffered keenly from the panic of 1873. Its control of the Missouri Pacific was lost and its further expansion to the West postponed indefinitely.

The Texas & Pacific, which was the most southerly project to be aided by Congress, had been preceded by a number of local Texas roads that had already done some building. It was the pet idea of President Thomas Scott, who was also vice-president of the Pennsylvania Railroad. Scott succeeded in building as far as Dallas by 1873, and to Fort Worth three years later. He was particularly anxious to reach the western border of Texas, which marked the beginning of the congressional land grant.

The most northerly transcontinental project, the Northern Pacific, received particular attention because of its advantages in trade with the Orient. Its terminus in the East was on Lake Superior, so that it could draw on all the lake business, while its western outlet afforded a shorter route to the Far East than did the ports farther south. In consequence the Northern Pacific was unusually attractive to businessmen interested in Far Eastern trade and received more attention from the public at large than did any other road except the Union Pacific.

The Northern Pacific considered itself fortunate in having for its financial representative the famous Philadelphia firm of Jay Cooke & Company. Jay Cooke had had considerable experience in financing railroads and was also interested in western lands, notably in Minnesota. He had originally been skeptical of the prospects of the Northern Pacific, and had refused several offers, but he changed his mind, in part because of the favorable terms of the contract that he signed in 1870. Not only would he presumably receive a handsome profit; he would end with the controlling interest in Northern Pacific stock.

Once Cooke entered Northern Pacific affairs he read and talked extensively about all phases of western development, and apparently convinced himself completely that the Northern Pacific was a sound venture destined for a brilliant future. His enthusiasm for the land through which the road passed gave that area the name "Jay Cooke's Banana Belt," which accorded with the impression given by the Cooke advertising that Minnesota and the Dakotas were almost tropical in their luxuriant vegetation.

The construction of the Northern Pacific began in 1870 at Pacific Junction, so named because it was the prospective meeting point for lines from St. Paul and Duluth. Three years later the road reached Bismarck, North Dakota, a new town named for the German chancellor. Unfortunately this construction exhausted all available funds. American investors had proved unexpectedly timid about supporting the project, and foreign sales almost stopped during the Franco-Prussian War. Construction and management accounts had been padded lavishly, and advertising had been excessively costly. The result was that Jay Cooke was forced to accept the inevitable and admit that he was at the end of his resources. The doors of Jay Cooke & Company closed on September 18, 1873, although the company had sufficient securities to meet its obligations, and was merely hampered by a lack of ready cash.

The closing of the house of Jay Cooke & Company precipitated one of the worst financial panics in American history. Cooke had innumerable connections, and when he admitted his inability to pay his debts other businesses suffered. More important, other firms were also loaded with speculative paper, and Cooke's failure created a wave of suspicion and doubt. More banking houses closed, and commercial concerns all over the country had to follow suit. Business throughout the country was prostrated. Western railroads, being profitable only in times of great prosperity, collapsed almost simultaneously and all building stopped.

REVIVAL AND THE GOULD LINES

There was but little railroad construction in the West for the half-dozen years after the panic of 1873, but then came the revival. For the first time the plains were able to furnish enough traffic to make railroading profitable. The cattle business had continued to expand. Mining had become a stable year-round industry conducted mostly by large companies that extracted all the metals and not only gold and silver; by 1880 the single town of Leadville, Colorado, was shipping a million dollars' worth of minerals each month. Wheat growing was becoming a large-scale industry in the Northwest. Such towns as Minneapolis, St. Paul, Sioux City, Omaha, Council Bluffs, and Kansas City were becoming important shipping and distributing centers. Furthermore, the railroads were learning how to eliminate violent and disastrous fluctuations of rates by entering cooperative arrangements that started with the "Omaha pool" of 1870.

The vast railroad opportunities attracted capable and energetic men. Railroad building, which was done by the thousand miles, and railroad strategy, which involved half a continent, brought forth bold, striking personalities—men who could lead, who could fight, and who had vision. Sometimes they were conscientious men and sometimes they were unscrupulous, sometimes they benefited the nation and sometimes they injured it, but unquestionably they had capacity and genius.

Outstanding was the shrewd, capable, cruel Jay Gould. Primarily a Wall Street operator, Gould had little interest in railroads as operating organisms; rather, he looked on them as toys with which to play and as traps to catch the unwary. Never did he allow sentiment to interfere with the business of making money. Gould entered the western railroad field when he purchased the control of the Union Pacific in the early 1870s. He hoped to increase the price of the stock rapidly by establishing a sinking fund, but he was prevented by Grant's opposition and so sold the majority of his stock—of course at a profit.

Gould saw another and more splendid opportunity in the late 1870s. He reasoned that if he bought the Kansas Pacific he could hold the threat of competition over the Union Pacific and dictate his own terms. The project looked fine in theory, but the Union Pacific refused to be intimidated; whereupon Gould decided that his plan had not been sufficiently comprehensive. Making one of his infrequent trips west, he bought half a dozen roads, including most notably the Missouri Pacific, the Missouri, Kansas & Texas, the Texas & Pacific, and the Denver & Rio Grande. This larger and more intimidating gun, together with Gould's connections with Vanderbilt's New York Central in the East, caused the Union Pacific to surrender. It consolidated with the Kansas Pacific and its subsidiary the Denver Pacific on terms of equality (1880). Kansas Pacific stock, being smaller in value, rose in price; whereupon Gould sold out.

Gould's speculations brought a handsome profit but left him with a number of fairly useless western railroads. Further thought suggested the possibility of monopolizing the traffic of the Southwest, and so he disposed of the Colorado roads and consolidated his other holdings with the Missouri Pacific, a potentially strong road that could be held with a small investment because it had little outstanding stock. In addition to lines already in his possession, he added, by complicated leasing arrangements, several other lines including the St. Louis, Iron Mountain & Southern, the International & Great Northern, and the Wabash. With these additions, the Gould lines made connections as far east as Buffalo; in the West they entered Chicago, St. Louis, Omaha, Kansas City, Galveston, and most other important cities. A bitter struggle with the Chicago, Burlington & Quincy led that road to complete its extension to Denver in 1882.

Gould was not interested in good railroad service to the West, and came to be one of the most hated men of his time. He was disliked both by those who worked for him and by those whom he served. Labor troubles (notably in 1885 and 1886) were frequent and severe and, together with the financial manipulations in which Gould was adept, led to the bankruptcy of most of the Gould roads in the middle 1880s. Before the crash came, Gould quite typically had reduced his holdings to the vanishing point.

THE SOUTHERN PACIFIC

Gould's connection with transcontinental transportation came mostly in his holding of the Texas & Pacific. Earlier, under the leadership of Scott, that road had made tremendous building efforts to obtain the promised federal land grant. Meantime, on the Pacific Coast the Southern Pacific was trying to monopolize California traffic and so built south to Yuma, which was the prospective crossing of the Colorado River for the Texas & Pacific. The road to Yuma was of no value without eastern connections, so Huntington was sent East to see whether he could get congressional aid. Scott also went to Washington to ask for additional assistance: his funds were exhausted and his road was still on the plains of Texas.

The battle royal between Scott and Huntington for congressional support produced nothing for either man. Congress, loath to extend more aid to the Texas & Pacific, disliked helping a second line controlled by the California associates. At this point the Southern Pacific took matters in its own hands, crossed the Colorado and the Yuma Indian Reservation without authority, obtained charters in Arizona and New Mexico, and continued to build toward the east. It was at this point that Scott knew he was beaten, and was glad to dispose of his stock to Jay Gould.

Gould, no Don Quixote to tilt at windmills, immediately entered an agreement with Huntington by which the two lines were to be joined near El Paso, the traffic was to be prorated, and the Texas & Pacific land grant transferred to the Southern Pacific. The junction occurred in 1882, but Congress refused to permit the transfer of the land. The joint line was entirely satisfactory to Gould, but it did not realize the dreams of the Southern Pacific, which wanted its own complete road to New Orleans. Continuing work east of El Paso, and utilizing those Texas roads already constructed, the Southern Pacific was able to run its through trains over its own tracks from San Francisco to New Orleans late in 1882.

THE ATCHISON, TOPEKA & SANTA FE

The only other southern road to complete a line to the coast was the Atchison, Topeka & Santa Fe, since the Texas & Pacific was never completed west of El Paso. The Santa Fe had entered Colorado in 1873 on its way to Santa Fe, while the Denver & Rio Grande—a narrow-gauge road—was building south toward the same place. The critical point was Raton Pass, which the Santa Fe occupied first, thus forcing the Rio Grande to confine its attention to Colorado.

The two roads also found themselves in conflict in Colorado over the Grand Canyon of the Arkansas River (also known as the Royal Gorge), which was not wide enough for more than a single set of tracks beyond Canon City. The Leadville boom of 1878 inspired both roads to rush crews to the Royal Gorge, and again the Santa Fe crews arrived first; furthermore, they were supported by irate local citizens who resented what they felt to be former unnecessary delays by the Rio Grande. The Santa Fe consolidated its position by laying its track immediately, and by threatening to parallel the entire Rio Grande line to Denver with a standard-gauge road. The Rio Grande seemed completely defeated, and apparently threw up its hands in surrender when it leased its entire line to the Santa Fe.

The Rio Grande continued its hopeless fight in the courts, but suddenly, in 1879, won all along the line. The courts gave the Rio Grande prior rights to the Arkansas gorge, and enjoined a Kansas road from operating a Colorado road. Finally, a compromise was arranged. The lease of the Rio Grande was repudiated. The Rio Grande agreed to pay for the construction along the Arkansas and not to build competitively toward the south. The Santa Fe promised not to parallel any of the tracks of its rival, but in return received the right to run its trains directly into Denver, which meant the laying of a third rail. Half of the through business of the Rio Grande was to go east by way of the Kansas road.

The agreement between the Santa Fe and the Rio Grande made certain the direction of future expansion of both roads. The Rio Grande expanded in Colorado and built toward the west, being completed to Salt Lake City in 1883; it was then able to compete for the entire haul of the Union Pacific, although by a somewhat roundabout route, by using for its eastern connection the Santa Fe, the Burlington, or the Kansas Pacific. These connections became at least moderately practical when the Rio Grande changed most of its line to standard gauge by 1890. As for the Santa Fe, its exclusion from Colorado directed its attention entirely to the south and the west. In 1881 it joined its tracks with those of the Southern Pacific at Deming, New Mexico, thus completing the first transcontinental route to be opened after the construction of the Union Pacific. This junction was a landmark in western railroad construction but only incidental to the expansion of the Santa Fe, which wanted its own line to the coast rather than be dependent on the Southern Pacific.

When the Santa Fe considered building to the coast, its eye fell inevitably upon the Atlantic & Pacific, which had been chartered and given a land grant by Congress on the very route that was most desirable to the Santa Fe. It so happened that the Atlantic & Pacific was in bad financial circumstances, and that in consequence its construction had stopped, seemingly permanently, at Vinita in Indian Territory. During the latter 1880s it was owned by the St. Louis & San Francisco, popularly known as the "Frisco." But the Frisco was not rich, and listened eagerly to overtures by the Santa Fe. An agreement of 1880 provided that the two roads would build jointly the western part of the Atlantic & Pacific, which meant a continuation of the existing Santa Fe line. Furthermore, the eastern parts of the Santa Fe and the Frisco were to be joined by a short link from Pierce City to Wichita, thus furnishing through connections for the Frisco and an entrance to St. Louis for the Santa Fe.

While the Santa Fe moved west, the Southern Pacific evolved defensive measures to maintain its control of California. First it built to Needles in California, the only remaining crossing of the Colorado River. Then it joined Gould in buying control of the St. Louis & San Francisco, thereby giving the allies a half interest in the Atlantic & Pacific. Of course the Santa Fe retained the other half and the building contract, but it was obvious that the future of the western part of its line would be made miserable.

For the moment the Santa Fe seemed to abandon its dream of an independent line to the coast, for it built to a connection with the Southern Pacific at the Colorado. The line was completed in August 1883, although the bridge was not opened until the following year. But soon it was evident that the submission of the Santa Fe was more apparent than real, for it started to rush construction on a line that would pass through Mexico to an outlet on the Gulf of California. At this point the Southern Pacific felt compelled to compromise, and gave the Santa Fe a controlling interest in the Atlantic & Pacific, a half interest in and lease of the line from the Colorado River to Mojave, and trackage rights to San Francisco. The first big inroad had been made on the Southern Pacific's control of California. Subsequently the Santa Fe built other lines in southern California, and particularly to Los Angeles. It also made connections with Galveston (1887), Denver (its own line in 1887), and Chicago (1888), and thus by the end of the 1880s was one of the strongest roads in the West.

THE NORTHERN PACIFIC

Even before these southern lines completed their through connections the Northern Pacific had recovered from its prostration of the 1870s and showed new vitality under Frederick Billings, who became president in 1880. Its development came to be linked closely with that of the Oregon Steam Navigation Company, which had been chartered in the 1860s to improve the navigation of the Columbia River. The Oregon Steam Navigation Company introduced steamboats on the navigable portions of the river and short railroad lines on intervening gaps. It was obviously the best entry to Portland, and in consequence a controlling interest was purchased by Jay Cooke when he dominated Northern Pacific affairs. With the failure of Cooke, control reverted to the West.

The Oregon Steam Navigation Company was badly affected by the panic of 1873, and its numerous German bondholders thereupon sent Henry Villard to investigate the situation and to protect their interests. Villard was impressed by railroad possibilities in the Northwest, and began to acquire stock in those companies that he felt to be potentially important. Lacking sufficient funds of his own, he approached Jay Gould for assistance at the time that Gould controlled the Union Pacific. His plan was to join the tracks of the Oregon Steam Navigation Company and the Union Pacific along the general route of the old Oregon Trail, and thus give the Union Pacific an independent line to the coast. Gould agreed to the proposal, but he soon retired from Union Pacific affairs, and the plan was dropped.

After the Gould plans collapsed, Villard went ahead on his own initiative. Chartering the Oregon Railway and Navigation Company (1879) to combine the Oregon Steam Navigation Company and the Oregon Steamship Company, he started to build eastward. At the same time the Union Pacific started to build toward the Northwest, and the two roads joined their tracks at Huntington, Oregon, in 1884. A new transcontinental connection had been added.

Just as Villard began to feel that he had the situation well in hand he received the shocking information that the Northern Pacific had resumed construction. Its completion to the coast would create a new and shorter line that would offer bitter competition for much of the traffic hitherto handled by the Oregon Railway and Navigation Company. Villard's first reaction was to try to induce Billings to use the Portland road for his western connection, but Billings refused to make a definite promise. Then Villard conceived the boldest stroke of all. On the basis of no tangible security he advertised for subscriptions to a "blind pool" that he could spend as he pleased. The desired $8 million was oversubscribed at once.

Villard used the proceeds of this pool to charter the Oregon and Transcontinental Company, which took over his old roads and also bought control of the Northern Pacific. Work on the Northern Pacific was continued, with the last spike driven in September 1883 in central Montana. The completion of the main line to Seattle occurred in 1887.

OTHER LINES

North of the United States a Canadian road was completed during the same period, and one marvels at the persistence and energy required to cross the wide, uninhabited spaces of that country. The idea of the Canadian Pacific was conceived during the 1870s, and construction was started in 1880. Certain American bankers, such as Kuhn, Loeb & Company and

J. P. Morgan, had a hand in the undertaking. The last spike was driven on November 7, 1885.

These roads were all the transcontinental projects completed by the end of the 1880s. A few others were added later. The Great Northern was completed in 1893 under the guiding genius of James J. Hill. The Chicago & Northwestern attained a junction with the Northern Pacific in Montana in 1894. The San Pedro, Los Angeles & Salt Lake City was opened between Los Angeles and Salt Lake City in 1905, and later became part of the Union Pacific system. The Chicago, Milwaukee & St. Paul finished its road to Seattle in 1909, and was particularly notable for its long electrified section across the mountains. The Western Pacific connected Oakland with Ogden in 1911 as one of the links in the dream of George J. Gould for a railroad from ocean to ocean.

The transcontinental lines completed by the middle 1880s can be summarized briefly: first (1869), the Union Pacific–Central Pacific over the central route; second (1881), the Santa Fe–Southern Pacific combination; third (1882), the Texas & Pacific–Southern Pacific combination; fourth (1882), the through line of the Southern Pacific; fifth (1883), the complete Sante Fe line; sixth (1883), the Northern Pacific; seventh (1885), the Canadian Pacific. In addition were the important fragments of the Kansas Pacific (1871), the Denver & Rio Grande (1883), and the Oregon Railway & Navigation Company (1884), to say nothing of thousands of miles of connecting and contributory links. Forty thousand miles of western railroad had been built within a decade.

The immediate and inevitable result of the building of railroads was the annihilation of the frontier. Population was strewn broadcast over the prairies, actually going farther into the Dakotas, Kansas, and Nebraska than the average annual rainfall warranted, and forming islands of settlement wherever the land was available farther west. The frontier that had moved so steadily across the continent was no longer visible in the new population maps of the census of 1890.

READINGS

GENERAL. Accounts involving several railroads are Robert E. Riegel, *The Story of the Western Railroads* (1926); John F. Stover, *American Railroads* (1961), summary of railroad history; Stewart H. Holbrook, *The Story of American Railroads* (1947), popular; Glenn C. Quiett, *They Built the West* (1934); Ira G. Clark, *Then Came the Railroads* (1958), the Far Southwest; Julius Grodinsky, *Transcontinental Railway Strategy, 1869–1895* (1962), scholarly; practically every regional history includes some account of the railroads of the area. The land-grant situation is covered in detail in Lewis W. Haney, *Congressional History . . . to 1850* (1908) and *Congressional History . . . 1850–1887* (1910). Edward Gillette, *Locating the Iron Trail* (1925) is interesting on surveying.

FIRST TRANSCONTINENTAL RAILROAD. George T. Clark, *Leland Stanford* (1931), eulogistic; Stuart Daggett, *Chapters on the History of the Southern Pacific* (1922), analytical; Grenville M. Dodge, *How We Built the Union Pacific* (1910), by a builder; Robert W. Fogel, *The Union Pacific Railroad* (1960), a new interpretation by an economist; Wesley S. Griswold, *A Work of Giants* (1962), satisfactory; John D. Galloway, *The First Transcontinental Railroad* (1950), emphasizes engineering; Robert W. Howard, *The Great Iron Trail* (1962), a trifle fictionalized; George Kennan, *E. H. Harriman* (2 vols., 1922), detailed; Levi O. Leonard and Jack T. Johnson, *A Railroad to the Sea* (1939); Oscar Lewis, *The Big Four* (1938), Central Pacific associates; Neill C. Wilson and Frank J. Taylor, *Southern Pacific* (1952), eulogistic.

OTHER ROADS. Denver & Rio Grande: Robert G. Athearn, *Rebel of the Rockies* (1962), excellent. Atchison, Topeka & Santa Fe: Lawrence L. Waters, *Steel Rails to Santa Fe* (1950), popular; James L. Marshall, *Santa Fe: The Railroad That Built an Empire* (1945); William Greever, *Arid Domain* (1954), excellent on land grant. Canadian Pacific: Harold A. Innis, *A History of the Canadian Pacific Railway* (1923). Northern Pacific: James B. Hedges, *Henry Villard and the Railways of the Northwest* (1930), scholarly; Henry Villard, *Early History of Transportation in Oregon* (1944), contemporary; Henrietta M. Larson, *Jay Cooke* (1936), scholarly. Missouri, Kansas & Texas: Vincent V. Masterson, *The Katy Railroad and the Last Frontier* (1952). Great Northern: Joseph G. Pyle, *The Life of James J. Hill* (2 vols., 1917), best to date. Chicago, Burlington & Quincy: Richard C. Overton, *Burlington West* (1941) and *Gulf to Rockies* (1953), excellent. Gould lines: Julius Brodinsky, *Jay Gould* (1957); Richard O'Connor, *Gould's Millions* (1962).

CHAPTER 36

THE GREAT PLAINS

T he westward push of the agricultural frontier seemed to stop
during the generation after the panic of 1837. The population
map of 1840 had shown settlement as far west as the great bend
of the Missouri River, and but few restless farmers moved west of the
Missouri in the next thirty years; rather, they filled such thinly populated
areas as Wisconsin, Iowa, and Minnesota. A few made the long trek to the
Pacific Coast, but the Great Plains west of 98° continued the domain of
the buffalo and Indian. White intruders were travelers, soldiers, and
cattlemen.

CHARACTERISTICS OF THE PLAINS

American farmers were quite understandably skeptical of the Great
Plains that stretched impressively from Montana and the Dakotas south
into Texas. This region of flat or gently rolling plains, with little vegetation besides coarse grass, lacking water and harassed by perpetual winds
intimidated the farmer accustomed to conditions farther east. Even east of
the Mississippi he had long detoured open prairies to occupy wooded areas
along the streams, and now he was confronted with what the geography
books called the "Great American Desert."

The plains rivers ran in the wrong direction to carry pioneer
farmers to new homes, and with the exception of the Missouri there were
none suitable for carrying goods to market. The lack of trees was a sobering
condition, for although eastern forests had meant tremendous labor to clear,
they had provided material for homes and fences, furniture, utensils, railroad ties, and fires. Now the settler was at a loss for these basic essentials
of life. He might for a time burn buffalo chips or twisted hay, but what
would he do for a house and for protection against the herds of the long

drive? The more easterly pioneer had dependend on small game to eke out his food supply of the first few years, but similar resources were lacking on the plains. The buffalo was a truly magnificent animal and a fine source of food, but unfortunately his stupidity led to his rapid elimination. Other animals were largely coyotes and jack rabbits, neither a very useful source of food. The one apparent advantage of the plains was the possibility of planting a first crop without the backbreaking chopping of trees, but even this advantage was partially vitiated by the toughness of the prairie sod, which required a special plow drawn by eight or ten oxen to be broken for agriculture.

The settlement of the plains depended on solving these and other problems, and during the generation after the Civil War solutions were found, even though some of them were only partial; the lack of water, for example, always remained in spite of any ingenuity on the part of the settlers. These developments produced a new frontier process and a new frontiersman.

WATER

Undoubtedly the basic trouble of the plains was a lack of water. Rainfall was less than that of the East, and in the western part of the area it contracted to a pitiful 10 to 20 inches a year. Furthermore, the rivers varied from poor to bad. In the spring they were vast, raging torrents that carried away barns, houses, and livestock. By midsummer they had died away to thin trickles or less. Any utilization of their water was difficult.

The least onerous way of obtaining more water was to pray for rain, and many congregations adopted this method, although with disappointing results. Quite ingenious was the speculation that rain frequently fell during battles, and that hence large explosions might have the same results. Such speculations went back at least to the 1830s, and led to widespread experiments in the 1880s and later. Large dynamite explosions simulated battle noises, but although some successes were claimed, the general reaction was negative. As time passed, the efforts to overcome aridity concentrated on three general ideas.

A first plan was to try to get along with less water. Although all plants need moisture, special varieties of wheat, oats, barley, rye, and corn were discovered that could thrive on limited amounts. Moreover, new methods of cultivation were introduced. Deep plowing, sparse planting, frequent cultivation to keep down the weeds, allowing land to lie fallow part of the time—all helped to preserve the limited moisture. Such "dry farming" permitted the cultivation of land that otherwise would have remained only pasture for cattle, but even at the best farming was hazardous. Too little rainfall meant ruin to even the hardiest food crop.

A second possible solution was the utilization of subsurface water, the existence of which had long been known, and which could be brought to the surface with the necessary labor. The main trouble was that, although a man could dig a 20- or 30-foot well with a pick and shovel, he was entirely baffled when the water was five hundred feet below the surface. The solution was the use of drills, which became popular during the 1870s. Well-drilling crews toured the country, for the operation necessitated expensive equipment and specialized knowledge.

Once the well was drilled, the problem of raising the water still remained. At fifty feet or more a bucket was practically impossible, and a hand pump was so inefficient that immense effort was needed to produce even a thin trickle of water. Good pumping equipment was an unattainable luxury. The answer was to harness the indefatigable wind, thus giving it possibly its only desirable function. Again it was during the 1870s that windmills were put into large-scale production. Their first western use was by stockmen and railroads, but by the 1890s they dotted the entire countryside. A single mill was the mark of one farmhouse; a group indicated a town.

The windmill had limited functions. It could supply water for household uses and possibly for a vegetable garden. In time of drought it might help water the stock. But as a real solution for deficient rainfall it was far from adequate. Not even the most optimistic farmer ever considered cultivating 160 acres of farmland entirely on the basis of water from a windmill.

The third possibility was irrigation, but again the solution was of only limited applicability. Irrigation depends on river water, which has to come from rain or snow. Irrigation can hold that water and use it through the drier seasons, but it cannot supply the rainfall. Estimates have been made that possibly a sixteenth of the dry land of the West could be irrigated if every available drop of water were used. No such utilization is even now probable, and was certainly quite out of the picture in the 1870s and 1880s.

Irrigation had been practiced at certain Spanish missions and by the Indians of the Southwest and then not again until the Mormons used it in Utah. Others did not try it until after the Civil War, and then with no great success. Few farmers had money to invest in irrigation projects, while men with money were ordinarily skeptical of the possibilities of profits. In the few cases of irrigation furnished by private companies the price of water was so high that farming became unprofitable.

As in other times of trouble, the farmer looked to the government for relief, and the government, in accordance with nineteenth-century tradition, then searched for some persons or groups that could be persuaded by a subsidy to do the job. The first legislation was the Carey Act, passed in 1894, at a time when the well-watered part of the public domain was practically exhausted. Under this law the proceeds from the sales of arid lands in several western states were to go to those states to be used for irrigation projects. The results were negligible. The funds were not large and the states were dilatory, possibly in part because many of the better projects were interstate in character.

The most important irrigation law was the Newlands Act of 1902, by which the federal government itself was to build irrigation projects from money received from land in the arid states. The costs of such construction were to be met in time by the users of the water, the money then to be spent for other projects. By 1920 some 20 million acres had been irrigated under this program, and considerable tracts were added later. Few of the projects touched the Great Plains, however, and, all told, they served only a small part of the region deficient in rainfall.

A part of the whole water problem was the disposition of the water of western streams. Should neighboring cattlemen and farmers be permitted to use the water, and to what extent? Under the English common law, as commonly accepted throughout the United States, the riparian owner could use all the water he desired as long as he did not pollute the stream or perceptibly lessen its flow. With western watercourses, such a rule was folly. The water was small in amount, and anyone who used it reduced its flow perceptibly. The common-law rule, if applied literally, would mean that no one could use the water, and hence instead of being of limited benefit it would be of no use whatever.

Western reaction was to change the common law. The arid states ruled that anyone on a stream could use all the water he pleased, unless he had forfeited the right by a considerable period of nonuse. In some ways such a regulation was disastrous. Men down the stream could expect that for much of the year they would be without water. On the other hand, however, there seemed considerable virtue in allowing someone rather than no one to benefit. The immediate result was a rush to control the sources of the streams, and particularly when a stream rose from a spring.

TRANSPORTATION

Next to water, the greatest problem of the plains was transportation. Rivers were unusable most of the year, particularly in the fall, when produce was ready to be marketed. Dirt roads were such impossible bogs in wet weather that a horse might labor hard even to walk without a load. Improved roads seemed impossibly utopian unless a miracle could produce them without the use of rock. Canals were equally impossible because of the lack of water.

The solution of the transportation difficulty was the railroad, which could be built on a flat plain at the rate of 5 to 10 miles a day. Not that railroad construction was effortless. Funds were hard to raise in sparsely settled areas, and eastern capitalists were difficult to persuade of the potential profits of a line that was only a streak on a map that failed to show towns. Furthermore, the lack of wood and stone hampered the railroads. Stone had to be brought considerable distances. Wood also had to be hauled, with the alternate here and there of treating the native cottonwood to retard its rotting.

FENCES

A problem of less importance, but also necessary of solution, was the building of fences with inadequate supplies of wood. Unfenced land permitted the farmer's cattle to trample his corn unless perchance the Texas herds got there first. Building wooden fences, largely with wood from farther east, was estimated to cost about $500 a quarter section, which was altogether too large for the pocketbook of the homesteader, or even for that of the large farmer or cattleman with his thousands of acres. Various alternatives to wood proved generally impossible. In a few places, as in certain parts of Texas, stone could be used. Hedges were tried but cattle failed to show them proper respect. Wire was also unsatisfactory because cattle soon learned that it was harmless and that a hard push would topple over an entire fence.

The solution of the fencing problem came with the marketing of good barbed wire, starting in 1874. The rapidity of the introduction of barbed wire was little short of amazing. In 1874 only 10,000 pounds were sold at $20 a hundredweight. In 1884 sales passed the 80 million mark, while the price had been cut in half. This rapid introduction of barbed wire did not mean that every farmer accepted it immediately and enthusiastically. Some were naturally conservative, others had extremely unpleasant experiences in trying to untangle and string badly rolled wire, and many a farmer cursed feelingly as his valuable stock ran into the wire and cut itself unmercifully. Ultimately the enthusiasm for barbed wire passed all reasonable bounds and men strung it not only around their own land but around railroad and government land and even over the public highways.

REPLACING WOOD

One other great problem was the necessity for the pioneer to find something to replace wood in constructing, lighting, and heating his house. The lighting was the easiest part of the job, since the rise of the oil industry brought cheap kerosene in the generation after the Civil War. Heating was not so simple, and heat was essential for cooking as well as for warmth. Buffalo chips were soon exhausted, and the hauling of wood or coal was expensive. The most easily available fuels were sunflowers and straw, but straw burned out in one grand flare that hardly baked bread or cake satis-factorily.

As for houses, early settlers dug into the sides of hills or bought wood, but the first was definitely unpleasant and the second was expensive. Native ingenuity finally hit on the use of sod. Pieces of sod were cut and laid much like oversize bricks, with wood used only for door and window cases, and for rafters. The inside of the house might be whitewashed, and although the structure was not beautiful it kept out most of the weather and was at least moderately cool in the summer. Many a sod house backed into a hill, and it was not unknown to have the family cow wander onto the roof and come crashing into the house. A strong rain might drip through even the toughest prairie sod, and even a prolonged drought did not prevent some of the houses from being damp.

The frontier of the sod house was of comparatively short duration. Americans were never enthusiastic about dirt houses, and as soon as possible scraped together the money necessary for other materials. The sod house was outstanding for both its picturesqueness and its filth, but it had no permanent importance.

PROGRESS OF SETTLEMENT

The first prairie settlements had come in the 1850s, largely in Kansas, but any large-scale invasion of the plains waited until after the Civil War, when more migrants entered central Kansas and Nebraska. This particular boom stopped with the panic of 1873, but a new flood came in the late 1870s and early 1880s, occupying the country from the Dakotas south into Texas, where settlement before this time had stayed in the timbered areas. These plains pioneers owed their continued existence to the changes described earlier in this chapter. Many of them were lured by the comparatively good rainfall of the early 1880s to go too far west, and with the drier years of the late 1880s and early 1890s thousands were driven out of their new homes by the stark specter of hunger.

The first arrivals were often speculators looking for fertile land, for mill sites, for locations of future towns. These were the people who had produced the first Kansas boom, and who had then looked farther afield, south toward the Indian Territory and the plains of Texas, and north toward the Dakotas and Montana. As soon as the speculator saw what he considered a good location he tried to acquire the land—legally if possible, but otherwise by fraud. His favorite gamble was a potential town, and as soon as he acquired a thousand acres or more he had the land surveyed and laid out streets and building lots. By this time a name was necessary, and something impressive like Eureka or Garden City was preferred to a more prosaic title.

■ 45 AND OVER INHABITANTS PER SQUARE MILE

▨ 6-44 INHABITANTS PER SQUARE MILE

▧ 2-5 INHABITANTS PER SQUARE MILE

☐ LESS THAN 2 INHABITANTS PER SQUARE MILE

Population Density, 1870

Population Density, 1890

45 AND OVER INHABITANTS PER SQUARE MILE

6-44 INHABITANTS PER SQUARE MILE

2 - 5 INHABITANTS PER SQUARE MILE

LESS THAN 2 INHABITANTS PER SQUARE MILE

A speculative town desired publicity above all. Imaginative lithographed posters depicted impressive buildings, busy streets, and a river front crowded with boats, even though the actual stream was no greater than the Republican. A weekly newspaper would sound the clarion call for a new western metropolis, the natural center for transcontinental railroads. A few lots might be given away as bait, as to the first woman or the first child. If the idea caught hold, the promoter made his fortune, but more frequently he went broke; whereupon he tried to borrow money for a new try. Hope might wither, but it did not die. The speculator has often been called a parasite, but certainly he helped to produce the boom of the 1870s and 1880s.

Most of the new settlers on the plains came from nearby states and territories, as had been traditional on the frontier. Particularly in the north were many foreign-born, some coming from nearby regions and others from Europe. Practically every new state and every territory had a publicity agent or bureau to sing its attractions, the influence of these publicity men reaching as far as Europe. The railroads were even more active, since they wanted to sell their lands and at the same time create future traffic. Favorable installment terms helped the railroads sell their land, their agents carefully shepherding groups of foreign-born immigrants all the way to their destination lest some rival railroad divert them. Special rates were offered, sometimes free seeds were provided, and even temporary living quarters were arranged.

One unusual experiment in subsidized religious migration was made by the Catholic Bishop John Ireland, coadjutor bishop of St. Paul. Although the movement of small and distinctive groups to the frontier was not unusual, Bishop Ireland planned to transport some of the poorer of his coreligionists from the eastern United States and from Europe with the purpose of improving them economically as well as reinforcing their faith by isolating them from other religions. He bought his land from the railroads, and during the years 1876–1881 established ten rural villages and farming communities in western Minnesota. The results were disappointing but illuminating. Very few poor people were inspired to make the trip, and for those who did, the experience was generally bad; for example, poverty-stricken Irish proved shiftless and continued for many years to demand charity. The best results came from people with some capital and farming experience; in other words, not from people escaping from poverty but from people looking for better farms.

LAND LAWS

The prevalence of speculation on the western plains made difficulties for the man who really wanted to farm. In theory he might homestead 160 acres, but in cold fact he usually found all available land claimed in any section of the plains blessed by fair transportation, even though that transportation remained prospective. His option then was to buy either from the railroad or from an earlier arrival. In neither case was the land anything like the free homestead about which our legislators had talked in such glowing terms.

The sad truth was that the vast bulk of western land was never homesteaded; moreover, the part of it that was entered under the Homestead Act was seldom farmed by the original entrants. In fact, only about a third of the homestead entries between 1862 and 1882 were ever made final. Presumably many entries were made to sell relinquishments to later comers, or held only until the lumber could be removed, as in Wisconsin and Minnesota, and then the claims were abandoned. How many of the completed claims were fraudulent is anyone's guess, but no one doubts that the number was large.

The land laws of the 1870s and 1880s seemed designed to encourage fraud. The Homestead Act needed a close supervision that the undermanned land office could not afford. Men "settled" by placing four stones at the corners of a prospective house, and "cultivated" by running a short furrow. With even less conscience, a man might use a toy house on wheels or erect a stick with a piece of glass to represent a wall and a window, or he would not make even these gestures. If the man had money he could enter a pre-emption claim, which was still permitted; he could then take up unsurveyed land, whereas for a homestead claim he had to wait until after the surveys.

Various other laws were open invitations to fraud. The Timber Culture Act of 1873 gave 160 acres to the man who planted and kept healthy 40 acres of trees not over twelve feet apart. These modest requirements were reduced five years later to 10 acres of trees, with 2700 at the time of planting and 675 when the patent was granted; in actual fact many claims were purely fraudulent, with no trees planted. Also available was the ridiculous Desert Land Act of 1877, which provided up to 640 acres in various dry states (see Chapter 37) at $1.25 an acre if the claimant irrigated part of it; the amount of claimed land was considerable, but the amount of irrigation was negligible. Then, too, an ambitious man might buy directly from the states land that they had been granted for swamp reclamation or education.

Illegal entries were a public scandal, particularly during the 1880s. Secretaries of the Interior asked continuously and fruitlessly for a larger corps of inspectors, and pleaded for at least the proper classification of the public domain. Even the railroad land grants presented unexpected problems. Each had the provision that the land be returned if the road were not completed in a specified number of years, but the courts held in 1874 that

such forfeiture required additional and specific legislation. A general forfeiture act for all unearned land grants was passed in 1890, but again the
courts limited its application. The next year Congress passed a general
reform act, which included among its more important provisions the repeal
of the Timber Culture and Pre-emption Acts, the modification of the Desert Land Act and the commutation provision of the Homestead Act, and
the authorization of forest reserves. Unfortunately these long-needed reforms came too late to be of much value.

The government land available for homesteading was estimated in
1894 at 600 million acres, but because most of it was unfitted for general
farming, many people considered homesteading as largely a thing of the
past. But land-hungry Americans were not easily discouraged, particularly
when they were tempted by the attractive advertising of railroads with land
to sell. Montana alone saw 93 million acres filed between 1919 and 1922.
Much of this land was in regions of deficient rainfall, and settlers soon went
bankrupt. In the process, however, the public domain was further reduced
so that by 1929 less than 200 million acres were available for homesteading.
Practically all of this land needed irrigation.

The government recognized the difficulties of homesteading by the
acts of 1909 and 1912 that increased homestead claims to 320 acres and
decreased the time of cultivation to three years. The results were not good.
As one man put it: "The government bets title to 320 acres against your
filing fee that you'll starve before proving up—and the government usually wins." The truth was that the small farmer merely destroyed the good
range grass and encouraged dust storms, while the cattleman had no way
of obtaining adequate amounts of land from the government even by leasing. Very belatedly the Taylor Grazing Act (1934) improved the situation a trifle.

As long ago as 1878 John Wesley Powell, director of the United
States Geological Survey, had made suggestions that, if adopted, would
have avoided many later troubles. He insisted that general farming needed
rainfall of a yearly average of at least twenty inches, and that farmers
should not feel encouraged by short periods of exceptionally heavy rainfall;
in fact, he located the exact areas of inadequate rainfall. For dry land he
held that irrigation districts should be formed with grants of 80 acres per
person; otherwise the dry land should be used for ranches of not less than
2560 acres. Only by long and bitter experience did the nation discover that
Powell was right.

Powell was also interested in conserving the natural resources of the
West, but not until after 1890 did the conservation movement gain any
considerable acceptance. Even then the West was generally opposed, feeling
that conservation lessened economic growth and kept tax income low. Each

succeeding President added more and more land to the forest reserves and to the national parks. Various irrigation projects have redeemed much land that otherwise would have remained useless. One can hardly avoid regret at the haphazard gutting of a magnificent public domain, in spite of recent efforts to save a few odds and ends.

For the settler of the 1870s and 1880s the land problem was real and personal. He might join the jam at a land office and with luck get a free homestead. More likely he bought as best he could from an earlier arrival, and then faced his major problems of obtaining shelter, starting cultivation, and managing to exist until the first crop was harvested. These problems were essentially the same as those faced by his eastern predecessor, even though their exact solutions were frequently different.

FINANCES

In at least one respect the plainsman had the advantage over the earlier frontiersman. He found money much easier to borrow because post–Civil War prosperity in the Northeast produced more surplus funds for investment, and people raised on eastern farms looked favorably on farm mortgages as the soundest investment. Much of this money was handled by the mortgage companies, which had the double job of raising the funds in the East or in Europe and of discovering proper borrowers and supervising the investment. During the period immediately after the war, interest rates tended to be the maximum permitted by each state, which was usually 10 to 12 percent. In practice the rate tended to be nearer 15 percent because of commissions and other fees. As the century approached its end, interest rates dropped decidedly. These high rates seemed reasonable to the average western farmer, who was confident that prosperity was only a question of a short time.

Many farmers who contracted loans so eagerly were in time hard pressed to meet the payments, and their point of view reflected their difficulties: lenders became bloated capitalists who rolled in luxury by squeezing unmercifully poor and hard-working farmers. This point of view tended to obscure other factors. Many farmers made their first "improvement" by acquiring a mortgage, which they considered the first rung to success, as it often was. All too frequently they estimated unrealistically the prospects of the future. Sometimes the borrower had no real intention of farming, and decamped as soon as he got the mortgage money; many a New Englander saw the plains drink up his life savings as thirstily as they absorbed the inadequate rainfall. The lender was in trouble if payments were not made; usually he made every possible effort to avoid foreclosure, since he was in the business of lending money and not farming. In many cases the answer was tenancy. Although both mortgaging and tenancy might lead to a prosperous future, they might work the other way. Apparently most lending groups made reasonable profits, but they were by no means as large as their critics later contended.

HOMES

The first home of the pioneer might be a cave in a convenient hillside or a rough board shack covered with tar paper. Sometimes it was a sod house, utilizing half an acre of prairie sod. Wood was used for window frame, door frame, and roof, but the roof might also be covered by more sod, so that dandelions bloomed on it. At times the sod was used only as a facing for a frame shack. The inside of the house might be plastered roughly; it was always dark. Pieces of mud might drop on the dining table for weeks after a rain; sometimes the walls weakened, the roof timbers slid, and the roof collapsed. Any sod-house resident hoped to have a real frame house at least as soon as the mud one wore out in half a dozen years.

The furnishings of the plains house were much the same as the simple, rough articles customary for a century or more. Crude beds, tables, and chairs served until the family was more prosperous. A favorite rocking chair or a cherry table might be a reminder of a more comfortable life in the East. Even the old-fashioned fireplace was continued wherever possible, although the hauling of wood for twenty miles or more was quite a morning chore. Corn cobs or stalks would often be used, and quite frequently the cooking was done on a cook stove that burned corn cobs and that was the center of family life. An ingenious development was a stove that burned cylinders of pressed straw, a new cylinder replacing each old one as it was emptied.

The water supply of the earliest settlers was surface water, which not only was polluted by the cattle but tended to be entirely inadequate or completely absent at certain times of the year. Dug wells were the obvious solution, with rich rewards for the man who could sense the presence of water. Now and then it was possible to drive a pipe into the soil, and find water, but ultimately most wells were drilled, the pumping being done by a windmill. The cost of drilling was about a dollar a foot; the most important windmill makers were Fairbanks & Morse.

FARMING ON THE PLAINS

Plains agriculture in the early years was concerned primarily with the same grains that had followed the frontier west, but had several different problems to meet. The tough prairie sod required a special steel plow pulled by at least three yoke of oxen, which could break possibly one or two acres a day. Probably the total effort in starting a prairie farm was somewhat less than in starting a farm in the forests farther east, which required

Herculean chopping, clearing, and grubbing out roots. The first crop was probably limited to corn and vegetables. Fencing was done in time with barbed wire. The lack of rainfall in some years meant bankruptcy for thousands of farmers; the late 1880s and early 1890s were especially bad. Blizzards were very dangerous on the northern plains, and prairie fires were a hazard everywhere.

The particular pest of the plains was the grasshopper, notably bad after 1874. Grasshoppers filled the air like a dirty snowstorm and ate all the plants but native grass and a few trees. Still hungry, they consumed every available object, including the clothes on the line. Chickens became sick from gorging on them, and livestock were reluctant to drink the water the insects had polluted. Even trains were stalled by the carpet of grasshoppers that made tracks as slippery as if they had been greased.

The open plains country presented an excellent opportunity for the development of the large-scale farm, where operations were mechanized much as in a factory. The farm machinery invented by ingenious Americans before the Civil War was improved, supplemented, and put into use on a large scale. To the harvester was added a self-binder that first used wire, and then twine by the early 1880s; by then threshing was done with a straw-burning engine. The combine was the invention of a Michigan man, Hiram Moore, and the twine binder was the idea of a Wisconsin resident, J. F. Appleby. The early steel plow developed into a plow capable of turning four furrows at once and then into a disk gang plow. Planting came to be done by machine rather than by hand. A corn cultivator appeared before 1860 and a self-dump rake was in use during the 1880s.

The greatest concentration of large-scale farming was in the Red River Valley of the Dakotas. During the 1880s over two hundred highly mechanized farms in this district contained 1000 acres or more apiece. Such a farm might have an absentee owner or owners and a resident manager. It hired its labor just as a city factory did. Impressive pictures appeared of half a dozen huge harvesters in operation at one time on a single farm. Actually, the advantages of such large-scale production were not great, since most farmers could use approximately the same machinery if they worked cooperatively; moreover, there were certain inherent inefficiencies in absentee ownership. Many of these huge farms failed to weather the hard times of the late 1880s and early 1890s.

DAILY LIFE

The daily life of the average pioneer farmer on the prairies was not far different from that of his eastern predecessor. His clothing continued to be homemade, although more frequently from homespun (wool) than from linsey-woolsey. The cold of the northern plains led to the use of somewhat more bulky clothes. The frontier wife commonly wore calico, including a calico sunbonnet. Her dress was high-necked, long-skirted, and shapeless, with some ten yards or more of cloth draped over four or five petticoats. Her labors in making the family clothing were lightened somewhat, however, by the use of the sewing machine which became fairly common by the 1880s. Shoes continued to be made sometimes at home, and the family went barefooted whenever possible to save leather and labor. Food emphasized pork and corn, with the traditional surplus of grease in its cooking.

Poor food, bad cooking, improper sanitation, and hard work all produced an excessive amount of sickness, which included notably dysentery, ague, cholera, smallpox, and typhoid. In the more isolated districts a doctor was frequently unavailable, and dependence was of necessity placed on home remedies, patent medicine, and prayer. Such doctors as could be reached were too frequently badly trained and overworked. Dentists were rare and but little consulted.

Although the life of the pioneer farmer was difficult, special sympathy should go to his wife. Laboring to the limit of her strength from the time she rose until the time she went to bed, she was perpetually tired, and this fatigue was not lessened by a succession of children, born usually without the benefit of a doctor. Her entire life was spent in a bare shack, without a tree, a flower, or even a blade of grass, and the house was infested by fleas, gnats, flies, and various types of vermin. The work, the hard water, the heat, and the perpetual wind combined to make her look old by thirty. For months on end she might not see even her closest neighbor. Little wonder that many a pioneer wife sat down and cried bitterly at the memory of the lost life of her girlhood days in the East.

Religious observance tended to become less as population became more sparse, even though such churches as the Methodist, Christian, Presbyterian, Congregational, Catholic, and Episcopal followed the frontier quite closely. Communities were often rough and crude, with a high proportion of the ungodly. It was said commonly in Kansas that "there is no Sunday west of Junction City and no God west of Salina." The arrival of a church was important not only for bringing religious consolation to men confronted by a stern Nature but also for bringing a moderate amount of social contact in such forms as church suppers and "sociables" to people greatly in need of relaxation.

Education meant the typical one-room ungraded school, built and supported by private funds. Not until after the frontier period did the government find itself able to take over the function of education. Texas was the first of the states to give state aid to education, but actually the Texan educational system was of slow growth, largely because of the war experience. A sprinkling of secondary schools and colleges was evidence of a firm belief in the values of education, although the training they offered was anything but first-rate.

No one could work every waking hour, and the prairie farmer was no exception. Church suppers, dinners, bees, square dances, poker and other card games, spelling matches, visiting, reading, candy pulls, picnics, barbecues, and buggy rides were among the social diversions. Even such then current fads as croquet and bicycling struck the plains. Unfortunately some of the sports were not so innocent. On his visits to town the farmer's interests were not confined to the handful of poor stores, the tawdry traveling show, or the lyceum lecture. Saloons, gambling halls, and brothels, established mainly for the cowboy trade, proved to be not without attraction to the farmer.

NEW STATES

The settlement of the western plains made necessary further governmental changes. When Colorado became the centennial state in 1876, the greater share of the vast region beyond the Missouri remained in territorial status, and there was not sufficient population to merit any drastic change. Although mining rushes had brought pockets of settlement here and there, although the Union Pacific had inspired a few such towns as Cheyenne and Laramie, and although a few settlers had pushed elsewhere, as into southeastern Dakota, population in general remained sparse.

By 1880 conditions had changed. Washington, bristling with large hopes based in part on the approach of the Northern Pacific, had sufficient people for statehood, as had Dakota. But Congress failed to act. The new areas were supposed to favor the Republican faith, and for years the Republicans had not been able to control the presidency and both houses of Congress at the same time. The Democrats felt no glow of pleasure at the prospect of increasing their own handicaps. Furthermore, all conservative Easterners were alarmed at the repudiation sentiment in the West.

Early in 1889, when the complete Republican control of both houses was assured, Congress passed an omnibus bill to enable North and South Dakota, Montana, and Washington to form state constitutions preparatory to admission to the Union. All four states were admitted before the end of the same year. While these events were occurring, Wyoming and Idaho could see no good reason why they too should not become states, and so they followed their neighbors' example in adopting state constitutions, although of course without the blessing of Congress; Wyoming was unusual in providing woman suffrage. When these two new constitutions were presented to Congress, that body was not loath to acquire more Republican members, and so the two states were admitted in 1890.

After 1890 only four potential states remained in continental United

United States, 1880

States exclusive of Alaska—Utah, Indian Territory and Oklahoma, New Mexico, and Arizona. For some time Utah had had the necessary population, but had been held back by the polygamy controversy. This situation was solved in the early 1890s and the state was admitted in 1896.

Indian Territory presented a much more confused case. Presumably it was the exclusive domain of the Indians, but as other parts of the West were filled with white farmers, men began to look longingly at the sparsely settled Indian country. White cattlemen entered the country by leasing grazing land, which may have been illegal but was highly acceptable to the Indians. Other whites married Indian girls, apparently with some thought of the land they might thereby attain. Unauthorized traders slipped into the territory, and a few settlers edged past the army posts.

The prince of the Indian Territory "boomers" was David L. Payne, six-foot-four, handsome, jovial, and aggressive. Although Payne had had but little luck at farming in Kansas, his personal popularity had sent him to the state legislature and had then obtained for him the job of assistant doorkeeper for the federal House of Representatives. Forming a "colonization association" in 1879 he was undeterred by President Hayes' threat to eject any white trespassers, and planned to lead a body of settlers into the Indian country. Whether he really thought himself legally justified or whether he was only the paid agent of the railroads is still being argued. In any case, each year found him heading a body of settlers that would elude the soldiers for a time, only to be surrounded and ejected, after which Payne yelled persecution and planned a new party. After his death in 1884 W. L. Couch continued his work.

A new factor appeared in 1887 with the passage of the Dawes Act. Although this law was conceived by men who had the best interests of the Indians at heart, it was supported by more selfish individuals whose eyes were focused on the surplus land that would be available to whites after the allotments. The first offerings of such land came on April 22, 1889. At least 100,000 people lined up, ready for the gunshot that marked the opening. Then came the mad rush by carriage, horseback, train, and even on foot. Such towns as Guthrie and Oklahoma City came into existence overnight. Inevitably a few "sooners" had beaten the rush and picked out promising tracts, whereas many of the "boomers" never did get Oklahoma land. Oklahoma Territory was created in 1890.

The first land opening was followed by others, even though the Five Civilized Tribes opposed allotments with sufficient force to prevent the division of any of their land until the late 1890s. By 1910 the allotments had been practically completed, although no one could say that whites and Indians had been amalgamated into a unified and homogeneous society. As the territory of Oklahoma expanded, governmental process kept pace, mainly because of the wishes of the rapidly growing number of whites; actually the relations of the two races brought a multitude of difficulties. An enabling act of 1906 inspired a constitution, and the state of Oklahoma was admitted to the Union in 1907.

The last two states to be admitted at this time were New Mexico and Arizona. This entire area had been included (1850) in the territory of New Mexico, but this situation became increasingly obnoxious to the people of Arizona as their number grew. Arizonans were far distant from the towns on the Rio Grande and were vastly outnumbered. The movement for an independent territorial status was successful in 1863, and was followed in both Arizona and New Mexico by agitation for statehood. Both regions were supposedly Democratic, but the Democrats were practically never in control of all branches of the government; moreover, Arizona's population was insufficient. When the omnibus bill of 1889 was passed, the Democrats tried to include New Mexico but failed.

Matters dawdled along during the succeeding years, with seemingly an indefinite delay because the Republicans had control of Congress. In 1906 there was talk of joint statehood, but although this proposal was acceptable to New Mexico it was rejected by Arizona. Ultimately separate statehood was accepted by Congress, and the two were finally admitted in 1912, Arizona being the forty-eighth state.

READINGS

REGIONAL. The following accounts treat portions of the plains area, and include political developments for their particular regions. Robert G. Athearn, *High Country Empire* (1960), an excellent general treatment; Gilbert Fite, *The Agricultural Regions of the United States* (1955); Merrill D. Beal, *A History of Southwestern Idaho* (1942); Harold E. Briggs, *Frontiers of the Northwest* (1940), good on northern plains; Berlin B. Chapman, *The Founding of Stillwater* (1949), Oklahoma; Carroll D. Clark and Roy L. Roberts, *People of Kansas* (1936), detailed; Charles F. Coan, *A History of New Mexico* (3 vols., 1925); Edward E. Dale and Morris L. Wardell, *History of Oklahoma* (1948); Angie Debo, *Oklahoma* (1949), *Prairie City* (1940), composite picture, *Tulsa* (1943), all well done; Grant Foreman, *A History of Oklahoma* (1942); James M. Hamilton, *From Wilderness to Statehood* (1957), fair on Montana; William C. Holden, *Alkalai Trails* (1930), western Texas; Joseph K. Howard, *Montana* (1943), well written, and (ed.), *Montana Margins* (1946); Merrill Burlingame, *The Montana Frontier* (1942); Vance Johnson, *Heaven's Tableland* (1947), Texas and Oklahoma; Edwin C. Reynolds, *Oklahoma* (1954); Bruce O. Nelson, *Land of the Dacotahs* (1946), South Dakota; James C. Olson, *History of Nebraska* (1955), good; William S. Prettyman, *Indian Territory* (1957), good pictures; Rupert N. Richardson, *Texas* (1943); Rupert N. Richardson and Carl C. Rister, *The Greater Southwest* (1934); Carl C. Rister, *Land Hunger* (1942), *No Man's Land* (1948), Oklahoma, and *Southern Plainsmen* (1938), good essays; Howard P. Lamar, *Dakota Territory* (1956); Herbert S. Schell, *History of South Dakota* (1961), good; K. Ross Toole, *Montana* (1959), interpretive; Stanley Vestal, *Short Grass Country* (1945); Edith L. Waldo, *Dakota* (1936); William F. Zornow, *Kansas* (1957), clear, factual. Two excellent books on Canadian-American relations are Marcus L. Hansen and John B. Brebner, *The Mingling of the Canadian and American Peoples* (1940) and Paul F. Sharp, *Whoop-Up Country: The Canadian-American West 1865–1885* (1955).

PLAINS SETTLEMENT. Walter P. Webb, *The Great Plains* (1931) is the pioneering account; Everett Dick, *The Sod House Frontier* (1937) is also excellent; Edward E. Dale, *Frontier Ways* (1959), is fine on plains life; Carl F. Kraenzel, *The Great Plains in Transition* (1955); Fred A. Shannon, *The Farmer's Last Frontier* (1945) has a broader focus. Two useful special studies are Merrill E. Jarchow, *The Earth Brought Forth* (1949), Minnesota agriculture, and James C. Malin, *Winter Wheat* (1944). More limited accounts, usually firsthand, are Theodore L. Blegen and Philip D. Jordan, *With Various Voices* (1949), contemporary; Seth K. Humphrey, *Following the Prairie Frontier* (1931); John Ise, *Sod and Stubble* (1936), Kansas; Martha F. McKeown, *Them Was the Days* (1961), Nebraska homesteading; Aagot Raaen, *Grass of the Earth* (1950), the Dakotas; Mari Sandoz, *Old Jules* (1935), Nebraska; Charley O'Kieffe, *Western Story* (1960); Jack T. Sutley, *The Last Frontier* (1930), the Dakotas; Ernest V. Sutton, *A Life Worth Living* (1948), Minnesota and the Dakotas; Arthur E. Towne, *Old Prairie Days* (1941).

LAND DISPOSITION. Roy M. Robbins, *Our Landed Heritage* (1942) is the best general account; Harold H. Dunham, *Government Handout* (1941) is factual; E. Louise Peffer, *The Closing of the Public Domain* (1951) concerns 1900–1950. Vernon Carstensen (ed.), *The Public Lands* (1963) is an excellent collection of published articles. Margaret B. Bogue, *Patterns from the Sod* (1959) concerns Illinois but has parallels with conditions farther west. Two accounts of Powell are William C. Darrah, *Powell of the Colorado* (1951) and Wallace E. Stegner, *Beyond the Hundredth Meridian* (1954).

CHAPTER 37

THE FAR WEST

W est of the Great Plains lies practically a third of the continental
United States, with problems in some ways similar to those of
the plains, but in many ways different. With a few exceptions—
most notably western Washington and western Oregon—the Far West
suffers from deficient rainfall, and thus resembles the plains. On the other
hand during the frontier period it included a much larger area impossible
to cultivate, either because of its many mountainous regions or because of
the almost complete absence of constantly available water. In the coastal
area were such rapidly growing cities as Seattle, Tacoma, Portland, San
Francisco, and Los Angeles—all hoping to have the commercial importance
that would come with railroad connections with the eastern parts of the
United States and with steamship connections with the rest of the world.

LAND TITLES

The usual historic process of white expansion had been a rather
stereotyped series of events: white entrance into Indian country, racial
friction, war, Indian land cessions, and finally white acquisition of land
under the regular national land laws. This pattern held for the majority of
the transmontane West. Typical was the occupation of western Colorado
by the whites: conflict with the Utes, the Ute war of 1879, Indian cession
and removal, and the land opened to white entry. Here and there were
minor variations. Utah had been occupied for a good many years without
proper titles; consequently much rush and confusion attended the opening
of the first land office in 1869. In Washington and Oregon special provision was made for the early settlers in the Donation Law of 1850, a sort
of early Homestead Act, by which each adult could obtain a maximum of

320 acres if he were a citizen or if he had announced by December 1, 1851, his intention of becoming one.

The normal process of land disposition was impossible in much of the Far Southwest, where the Spanish and Mexican governments had made large grants that had been guaranteed by the United States in the Treaty of Guadalupe Hidalgo. Obviously there were problems: grants were sometimes vague, grantees or their heirs had often lost the necessary papers, Mexican revolutions had played havoc with the original records. From time to time large claims were asserted and the land was resold without proper title. Some of these may have been legitimate mistakes, but others were certainly deliberately fraudulent.

During the years immediately after the American acquisition of the Southwest, the only important problems concerned California. Texas managed its own land, and the country from Texas to California was of little importance because it contained millions of unoccupied acres of no use except to graze cattle, which went on regardless of landownership. California, and particularly the central part of the state, was a different matter. Into the area poured aggressive white farmers holding the then traditional attitude that unoccupied land should be available to anyone who wanted to use it. These men had considerable contempt for the Mexican grantees, and were not even impressed by such men as Frémont, Sutter, or Bidwell. They occupied any land that appealed to them, without regard for legal ownership, and sometimes, as happened with the holders of John Bidwell's land, they had to be bribed to leave. Even the city of San Francisco had difficulty in retaining enough of its grant to establish the present Golden Gate Park.

The California mess was placed in the hands of a committee of three, appointed under a law of 1851. The committee worked for five years (1852–1857), trying honestly to clarify the situation justly. It listened to over eight hundred cases, and decided in favor of the original claimant in three out of four of them, but in spite of this record many problems remained. The law placed the burden of proof on the claimant, who frequently had paid no attention to records, and had no funds to hire a lawyer or to make the necessary trip to San Francisco, where most of the hearings were held. An additional cost was involved for all but nineteen of the cases when the decisions were appealed to higher courts, either by the original claimant or by his defeated rival. The best estimate is that the average case took seventeen years to reach a final decision, and that during these protracted and expensive proceedings many a claimant went bankrupt or was forced to sell to speculators.

CATTLEMEN AND FARMERS

The mountain West first attracted whites with its supply of furs, but the fur trade involved few men and no permanent settlement except for a scattering of forts. Next came the miners, which meant larger numbers of men and some permanent towns, even though the average miner was foot-loose. In turn the miners opened the way for cattlemen and farmers. As was true of earlier frontiers, the raising of cattle was important while settlement was sparse. In the early days, cattle herds, as in California, had no value as meat, but this situation changed radically with the flood of miners after 1848. Cattle that had gone begging at $5 a head soared to an astronomical $500 in Sacramento in 1849, and although this highly inflated price was temporary, the demand still remained good. Not only were local cattle in demand, but new herds were attracted from Texas and the Mississipi Valley. All the way from Idaho to New Mexico the cattle business boomed, particularly after the expanding railroad network provided more adequate transportation.

As had occurred on the Great Plains, the cattleman was soon replaced by the regular farmer, since the growing of grains and vegetables was more lucrative per acre than the cattle business. In a few places, such as the Willamette Valley, rainfall was adequate for the kind of farming done in the East, but this was unusual. As was true of any frontier, and particularly a frontier with deficient rainfall, the main early crop was wheat, even though the lack of water produced obvious hazards. To the north, the future states of Idaho, Washington, and Oregon particularly emphasized wheat culture, with the business extending as far south as the Sacramento and San Joaquin valleys of California. Some areas, such as the Pendleton–Walla Walla region, are important for wheat production even today. Irrigation was not used; even the Sacramento Valley did not have it until after 1900.

IRRIGATION

Obtaining water in the Far West was almost entirely a matter of irrigation with supplies drawn from the streams; the digging of wells was tried, particularly in New Mexico in the 1870s and Oregon in the 1880s, but with very limited success and in many cases outright failure. The Mormons had been the first to use irrigation in the Far West, but non-Mormon farmers did not have the backing of a theocratic state and hence their first ventures were small, privately dug ditches during the 1850s. Such efforts had various limitations, depending on knowledge, money, and manpower. Hence the farmer was limited to the areas close to such rivers as the Rio Grande, San Joaquin, or South Platte, or their tributaries, provided they had adequate water. Some of the rivers were not useful, for example, much of the Colorado and Columbia, because of their deep gorges. Long ditches were economically impossible. It consequence the early results were only moderately satisfactory if it is agreed that some water is better than none.

Successful irrigation was necessarily a group effort, as the Mormons had demonstrated with their thousands of miles of communal ditches; in fact, every Mormon land transfer included water rights. Various kinds of group action were possible. A town might take such action; a famous example was the effort of the Greeley colony in Colorado in the 1870s; incidentally, the colony's efforts were entirely empirical, and there is no evidence that it obtained information from Utah even after the first failure. One object of any town was to obtain water for domestic use, but neither the Owen River project of Los Angeles nor the Hetch Hetchy project of San Francisco came until after 1900.

Another irrigation possibility was the incorporated company that sold water for profit, just as another company might sell steel or kerosene; a variant came when a railroad such as the Northern Pacific organized and financed irrigation companies—presumably in the hope of increasing railroad traffic. Still another possibility was the company organized by the farmers of an area to provide their own needs; in many cases, such as the important "76 Land & Water Company" of the 1880s in the San Joaquin Valley of California, the company might also sell water to nonmembers.

Almost inevitably, and in spite of the "individualism" of the American farmer, government was finally brought into the picture. California was the leader in this field. The legislature of 1875 authorized a West Side Irrigation District that could issue bonds for the construction of a canal in the lower San Joaquin Valley, but the courts threw out the law as unconstitutional. A dozen years later the Wright bill authorized the formation of water districts with elected officers and with the power to issue bonds and to levy taxes. The act was not immediately successful, even though the courts held it to be constitutional. There were continual fights between large and small owners and between old and new projects; of the fifty districts created under the law, only four were successful. In spite of these difficulties, however, other arid states soon copied the idea.

The federal government was also soon involved. Its first action was the Desert Land Act of 1877, which gave a man the right to occupy up to 640 acres of dry land if he made a down payment of 25¢ an acre; he could complete his claim within three years if he showed irrigation of part of the land and paid an additional $1.00 an acre. Why a bona fide settler would want to pay $1.25 an acre when he could get 160 acres free under the Homestead Act, and another 160 acres at $1.25 an acre and without improvement under the Pre-emption Act, is not clear. The later presumption has been that the Desert Land Act was essentially a gift to the cattlemen, who had their cowboys enter the land and do the smallest possible amount of irrigating, such as throwing a pail of water on the ground. Only slightly over a quarter of the land entered under the law was finally purchased, and the amount of irrigation was negligible.

The federal government entered the scene more directly with the Carey Act of 1894 but with disappointing results. Then came the Newland Act of 1902, under which very considerable progress was made. (See Chapter 36 for a discussion of the Carey and Newland Acts.) Although the federal projects have been profitable for the farmers who benefited directly and for the states in which farmers live, there have been increasing questions about the desirability of increasing farm production at the very time when farm surpluses were depressing prices.

Irrigation naturally was concentrated in the areas of the main rivers and their tributaries, including the basins of such rivers as the Colorado, Sacramento, San Joaquin, Rio Grande, and Columbia. The Colorado has been particularly interesting because of the long-drawn-out contest between California and Arizona over its control, and also because of the rather curious history of its harnessing. Observant men were impressed in the 1890s by the fact that the Colorado River was higher than the desert, and argued that merely scraping a ditch would permit its water to flow into what its promoters called rather grandiloquently the Imperial Valley. The first water arrived in 1901, along with a flood of opportunity-seeking farmers; the most optimistic hopes of the promoters were realized, and the Imperial Valley became one of the garden spots of the nation. Unfortunately the river did not cooperate with proper docility. First it threatened to cut off all water by filling the ditch with sand, and then in 1905–1906 it threatened to change its course and put the entire valley under water. A two-year fight, with E. H. Harriman of the Southern Pacific furnishing most of the financial ammunition, was necessary before the river was confined to its present channel. The newer, All-American Canal, was completed in 1941.

UTILIZING THE WARM WEATHER

The prevailing heat in the area from Texas through southern California was considered as nothing but a handicap by each early visitor as he plodded across the arid countryside. With the passing of time, the beginning of irrigation, and the improvement of transportation, men began to speculate that what grew in semitropical regions in other parts of the world might also be grown in the American Southwest. An olive boom of the mid-1880s soon collapsed but later revived. Figs and avocados were tried, but they were not important until after 1900. Cotton booms occurred periodically, particularly because of the efforts of the Mormons to approach self-sufficiency as they moved south into Arizona; cotton was grown in California as early as the 1840s but was not successful for many years. Several other experimental crops were less dependent on the warmth. Sugar beets were grown successfully by the Mormons, although they had trouble with the refining. Tobacco aroused much interest in the 1870s, but apparently the curing process proved a failure. One ever-recurring mania, both East and West, was silk culture. California went slightly mad on the subject during the 1860s, with the legislature in 1864 offering bounties, and with 10 million mulberry trees reported being grown in 1869; obviously, the industry failed of permanent success.

Outstanding among the warm weather crops are citrus fruits. Most important have been oranges, of which the real cultivation started with the work of William Wolfskill at Los Angeles in the 1840s. Early development was hampered by the lack of proper varieties of fruit, inadequate knowledge of methods of cultivation, and the absence of the necessary transportation; the number of producing orange trees in 1860 was only 4000, and by 1870 no more than 40,000. Expansion was rapid after that year. Railroad construction solved the transportation problem, the first carload lot being shipped in 1877. Also during the 1870s there was introduced the navel orange from Brazil by way of a missionary and the Department of Agriculture. The most serious insect pest was brought under control in the late 1880s by the introduction of the ladybird (or ladybug) from Australia, and oil heaters were in use to combat frost by the late 1890s. The Sunkist Fruit Growers' Exchange, organized to provide uniform sorting, packing, grading, and promoting, came into existence under a different name in the 1890s.

Although the center for citrus fruit was for a long time in southern California, other areas gradually became involved in citrus culture. The industry spread as far north as the Sacramento Valley in the 1870s. Moving east it gradually entered Arizona and New Mexico. Most important of the Arizona agricultural areas was the valley of the Salt River, a branch of the Gila. Irrigation began in the 1860s, with one of its products the city of Phoenix, which by 1871 could boast proudly of 300 residents. Phoenix in time became the largest city and the capital of the territory, taking the latter honor from Tucson, which was far from happy at being left with the second prize of the state university. The commercial growing of citrus fruit in the Phoenix area did not begin until the early 1890s.

A quite different value was attached to winter warmth by icebound Northerners, who viewed with enthusiasm the absence of cold weather. The focus of interest was the Los Angeles area, with such places as the desert communities of Palm Springs and Las Vegas and the "sun valley" of Arizona and New Mexico coming later. The added attractions of open gambling and easy divorce in Nevada did not make their appearances until the twentieth century. Although the delights of the climate of southern California had been extolled even before the gold rush, any considerable influx of visitors and permanent residents waited until the completion of railroads. Retired Iowa farmers could hardly be expected to visit southern California by stagecoach. Estimates have it that by 1900 the residents of southern California included at least a quarter who had come originally for their health.

The greatest southern California boom of the nineteenth century occurred in the Los Angeles area in the years 1886–1888. Hordes of people were lured by what was described as the nearest approach to the Garden of Eden since the beginning of the world. They inundated the streets of Los Angeles, trading enthusiastically in the city's many newly opened lots, and often boasting of large wealth—at least on paper. Suburban areas expanded rapidly, the enthusiasm for Pasadena rivaling that for Los Angeles; when Azusa was opened, eager buyers stood in line all the preceding night, and it was reported that the second in line refused a thousand dollars for his place. Burbank, San Bernardino, Santa Barbara, and dozens of other towns shared the general excitement, even though some of them, such as Sunset, Gladstone, Chicago Park, and La Ballina, failed to remain for posterity. This particular boom soon collapsed, but the total growth of the region continued, and in time with greater and greater acceleration.

FRONTIER WAYS

The newer frontier areas of the Far West were very small spots in a very large country. The population map of 1870 showed that west of a strip on the eastern slope of the Rockies from southern Wyoming south into the Rio Grande Valley, there was little population until one reached the San Joaquin and Sacramento valleys of California, the Willamette Valley of Oregon, and the Puget Sound area. The one exception was the Mormon settlements stretching north and south from the Great Salt Lake. Although settlement expanded during the next decade, the greatest impression conveyed by the population map of 1880 is the large white areas that indicate less than two inhabitants per square mile. Even the map of 1890 showed but little concentration of population, thus demonstrating the greater difficulties of settlement than was true, for example, of the Ohio Valley.

The frontier of the Far West in many ways repeated the developments farther east, but with some variations. The log cabin, crude homemade furniture, limited foods, candles, and horse transportation were just as typical of frontier Idaho as they had been of frontier Ohio. Health was precarious because of improper diet, lack of knowledge, and poor medical services; the usual family depended on home remedies, patent medicines, and superstition. Small children were in particular danger from the time they were ushered into the world by a midwife until they managed to survive the usual childhood diseases.

Like other frontier areas, the Far West had a great preponderance of men over women. One result was that women had a considerable scarcity value and were usually treated with exaggerated respect—that is, the "good" women were treated with adoration, for the West distinguished clearly between "good" and "bad." Good women were supposed to be as delicate and modest as their eastern sisters, and there is something humorous in the long discussions of how women could with modesty negotiate the mud holes that existed on every street, or in the fulminations of an early Oregon editor who protested the sight of a woman riding astride a horse, holding that it caused "the blush of shame to mantle even the cheek of manhood." The scarcity of women at least partly explains why women were given certain advantages, as in higher education and voting. The shortage led Asa S. Mercer to bring parties of New England girls to Oregon in 1864 and 1866. These "Mercer girls" came as teachers, but to no one's surprise proved in even greater demand as wives; unfortunately their number was not sufficient to supply even a perceptible part of the western demand.

The scarcity of women did not mean that the farm wife could sit back in luxurious ease, while her husband waited on her hand and foot. Husbands undoubtedly had as much affection for their wives as husbands have had at other times and places, but the division of functions at that time did not provide for feminine leisure. Although the man's farming duties were seasonal, the family ate its meals and wore its clothes every day of the year. Furthermore, the wife usually cared for the garden and the chickens, acted as family doctor and nurse, and arranged most social events. The fiction of women as the weaker sex had little evidence to support it.

The towns of the area exhibited many of the characteristics of the earlier plains towns, even though their origins were more likely to be based on mining than on the cattle business. In fact there were no sizable towns between Denver (4749 in 1860) and the Pacific Coast except Salt Lake City. Like its eastern predecessor, the early western town was characterized by unpaved streets, wooden sidewalks, hitching posts for the horses, inadequate and polluted water, and periodic epidemics, particularly smallpox. The streets of the mining town were lined with saloons, gambling halls, and brothels; every man went armed, life was held cheaply, and efforts at law enforcement were only the most cursory. Just as had happened in the East, the town changed with the arrival of the farmers. Sometimes the mining town disappeared and sometimes it was transformed into a more orderly community; in any case there appeared in time improved streets, less blatant vice, and ultimately better water systems, streetcars, telephones, and electric lights.

Naturally, the larger of the cities in the Far West were located on the coast. To the north, the most important was Portland, which benefited from its dominance of the Columbia Valley; theoretically it should have been an extremely important port, but actually it was greatly handicapped by the sand bars at the mouth of the river. On Puget Sound were Tacoma, which advertised itself as "The Second Greater New York," and Seattle, whose site was apparently something of an accident. All the northern cities grew rapidly after the completion of the Northern Pacific and the Great Northern and all had great hopes of trading with the Orient because they were closer to it than the cities farther south; these hopes were never realized completely.

Southern California had an excellent harbor at San Diego, but unfortunately San Diego had little useful back country and poor connections with the East; in consequence it failed to grow satisfactorily. Los Angeles had several disadvantages: it had no natural harbor, there were no early railroad connections to the East, and it was too far south for trade with the Orient; its population in 1880 was only 11,183. In time an artificial harbor was constructed at San Pedro and railroad connections were made; the Southern Pacific was finished from San Francisco in the 1870s, but, more important, both this road and the Santa Fe made connections from the East in the 1880s; a boom resulted, but still the Los Angeles population of 1890 was only 50,395. Farther north the old capital of Monterey, with its modest harbor, failed to grow.

San Francisco was supreme among the coastal cities. Located on one of the finest harbors of the world, it was the natural outlet for the large part of the state agricultural production that came from the San Joaquin and Sacramento valleys, and was the nearest point for eastern railroads; quite naturally the first transcontinental railroad had its western terminus at Oakland, across the bay. Then, too, San Francisco had the luck to be near the first gold discoveries and to be nearest the rich Nevada finds. It is not surprising that the city of the Golden Gate was the financial, industrial, transportational, and cultural center of the Pacific Coast. It was the largest manufacturing center of the Far West and had the most imposing labor troubles. The dynamic, rabble-rousing Dennis Kearney centered his activities at San Francisco during the 1860s and 1870s when he and his co-workers, shouting "the Chinese must go," inspired mob action all the way from Puget Sound to San Diego; the San Francisco riots involved the looting of the Chinese district. The Kearney groups, operating under the name of the Workingmen's Party of California, ultimately obtained such measures as changed taxation, a railroad commission, banking control, and restrictions on the Chinese, but the results were somewhat less utopian than had been hoped.

CULTURAL DEVELOPMENTS

The Far West in the generation after 1850 was very primitive in many ways, but no one desired that it remain that way. Most of the men and women had come from older communities farther east, and longed for the advantages of a more advanced civilization. Basic in everyone's mind was the advantage of education. Even the mining camps and the early farming communities established schools, and although emphasis is usually now placed on the poorness of such schools the real surpries should be the willingness of parents to part with some of their hard-earned money to provide education for their children. One of the first acts of each territorial legislature was to provide for a public school system, although New Mexico was somewhat delayed by the language difficulties. Free schools were developed rapidly and early; for example, Arizona authorized free schools in the early 1870s, when the total population of the territory was certainly less than 20,000.

Education above the elementary school was very largely private in the early days, as had been true in the East under similar circumstances, but the public high school appeared in San Francisco as early as 1856, and by the end of the century was replacing the private school everywhere in the Far West. Teachers colleges generally came into existence by the 1880s and 1890s. Schools that called themselves colleges were opened as early as the 1850s, but were usually in fact preparatory in character. Private colleges, frequently church-connected—Whitman and Gonzaga are examples —soon lost their precedence in favor of the state universities. The University of Utah (1850), begun early in the Mormon settlements, had many vicissitudes before it became prosperous. The University of Washington was opened at Seattle at the surprisingly early date of 1861. The University of California admitted its first students in 1869, and in a few years moved its campus from Oakland to Berkeley; its second president was the well-known Daniel Coit Gilman. The University of Nevada was established at Reno in 1874, when the territory had a population of not more than 50,000. The University of Oregon opened its doors at Eugene in 1876, being helped in its early years by gifts from Henry Villard. The University of New Mexico came into existence at Albuquerque in 1889. The University of Idaho was opened at Moscow in 1892, when the population of the state was no more than 90,000. The University of Arizona opened its agricultural school at Tucson in 1890 and the university proper a year later, at a time when the population of the territory was no greater than that of Idaho. Such developments, no matter how feeble in their early years, showed the very real concern of the West with education.

Religion was also a matter of vital concern to the early settlers. Everyone thought of religion as the basis for proper morality—the foundation upon which society rested. The Catholic Church had been dominant in the Southwest when the United States took possession, and had also done work in the Northwest, but Protestant faiths, such as the Methodist, Baptist, Presbyterian, Episcopalian, and Congregational, were carried along by the farming frontier. As had occurred on earlier frontiers, the very diversity of sects made the building of churches and the paying of regular ministers difficult; hence early meetings were often held in the local school-house or in private homes. The basic religious aspirations of the people received testimony in their willingness to deny themselves luxuries, even necessities, to be able to support a settled minister.

Among the first cultural institutions carried west of the mountains was the printing press. The first newspaper was *The Oregon Spectator,* a four-page, semimonthly publication that began its ephemeral existence at Oregon City in 1846. The famous *Alta California* was first published in San Francisco in 1849. The *Deseret News* appeared in 1850 in Salt Lake City; as early as 1859 *The Weekly Arizonian* started publication at Tubac but it soon moved to Tucson. The number of such early papers is surprisingly large; in addition there were pioneer magazines, such as the *Golden Era* (San Francisco) in 1852, and *The Utah Magazine* (Salt Lake City) in 1868. Best known was the *Overland Monthly* (1868), particularly when it was edited by Bret Harte. Among the western writers to obtain national recognition were Bret Harte himself, Mark Twain, Helen Hunt Jackson the novelist, and Joaquin Miller the poet; only the last of these was a native of the area—hardly surprising in view of the proportion of Far Westerners born elsewhere.

Leisure-time activities were numerous. Horse racing, candy pulls, barn dances, singing schools, church sociables, and baseball were among the dozens of amusements possible for even the poorest farm family. School exercises were attended regularly by parents who glowed with pride at the recitations of little John or Jane. The Fourth of July was celebrated with more enthusiasm than discretion. Although most of these amusements were certainly simple, there were numerous choirs and orchestras, serious lectures, and other more demanding cultural activities. A Philharmonic Society appeared in Portland in 1859, and a California Art Association made its bow at San Francisco in 1871. Preconceptions of western cultural aspirations should be severely jolted by the fact that a presentation of "The Messiah" at Salt Lake City in 1875 attracted an audience that paid $1200 for the concert.

Dramatic performances were also received with enthusiasm. In the earliest days all performers were amateurs, and the results had best be left to the imagination. Regular theaters were opened early, even during the gold rush in the larger towns, for example, at Sacramento in 1849 and at San Francisco in 1850. In spite of the rough audiences a considerable proportion of the plays came from the pens of such classic playwrights as Shakespeare, Knowles, Bulwer-Lytton, and Payne. The starring system then current permitted the Far West to see such well-known actors as Edwin Booth, James H. Hackett, Caroline Chapman, and Ellen Tree. Particularly identified with the West were the beautiful Adah Isaacs Menken, the notorious and fascinating Lola Montez, and Lotta Crabtree, who started her stage career as a child prodigy touring California. Since most of the Far West was sparsely settled, and the bigger towns were far apart, most theatrical productions in the early years were by third-rate touring companies playing in poor surroundings. Not until the 1880s and later did larger cities and improved transportation permit more adequate presentations. A little later Chautauqua and the motion picture made their contributions to filling the western demand for drama.

The Far West repeated in general the developments of more easterly frontiers, but a semifrontier status was often retained for a considerable number of years. Long after the frontier had theoretically "disappeared" large sections of the Far West had such few people that they showed on the population maps the white areas that indicated less than two to the square mile. In consequence many a farmer, stockman, or sheepman remained in fact a frontiersman long after most of the United States was absorbed by a high-speed, mechanical civilization.

READINGS

GENERAL. Accounts involving more than one state include Robert G. Athearn, *High Country Empire* (1960), the eastern part of region; W. Eugene Hollon, *The Southwest* (1961); Oscar O. Winther, *The Great Northwest* (1947); Sidney Warren, *Farthest Frontier* (1949), interesting on all phases of life of Pacific Northwest; John W. Caughey, *History of the Pacific Coast* (1933), good; George W. Fuller, *A History of the Pacific Northwest* (1931) and *The Inland Empire of the Pacific Northwest* (3 vols., 1928), clear if pedestrian.

INDIVIDUAL STATES. The material drawn upon for this chapter is widely spread. California: John W. Caughey, *California* (1953), good; Robert G. Cleland, *The Cattle on a Thousand Hills* (1951), southern California, *From Wilderness to Empire* (1944), and, with Osgood Hardy, *March of Industry* (1929), economic history; Wallace Smith, *Garden of the Sun* (1939), good on the San Joaquin Valley; Anne B. Fisher, *The*

Salinas (1945); William W. Robinson, *Land in California* (1948), scholarly; G. S. Dumbe, *The Boom of the Eighties in Southern California* (1944); Claude B. Hutchison (ed.), *California Agriculture* (1946), essays; George R. McMinn, *The Theater of the Golden Era in California* (1941), scholarly; Mary B. Ritter, *More Than Gold in California* (1933), reminiscences of a woman physician; Jackson A. Graves, *My Seventy Years in California, 1857–1927* (1927) and *California Memories, 1857–1930* (1930); Harris Newmark, *Sixty Years in Southern California 1853–1913* (1930). Oregon: Charles H. Carey, *History of Oregon* (1922); P. Maddox, *City of the Willamette* (1952), Portland; Alice H. Ernst, *Trouping in the Oregon Country* (1961), amusements of the 1850s and 1860s; Arthur L. Throckmorton, *Oregon's Argonauts: Merchant Adventurers on the Western Frontier* (1961), scholarly, centering in Portland; Nellie M. Young, *An Oregon Idyl* (1961), wife of Presbyterian minister, who made a trip to Oregon 1883–1884. Washington: Edmond S. Meany, *History of the State of Washington* (1924); Archie Binns, *Northwest Gateway* (1941), popular on Seattle. Idaho: Merrill D. Beal, *A History of Southwestern Idaho* (1942), detailed and somewhat antiquarian. Nevada: Effie Mack, *Nevada* (1936); Richard G. Lillard, *Desert Challenge* (1942), interpretation rather than history. Arizona: Rufus K. Wyllys, *Arizona* (1950); Francis C. Lockwood, *Pioneer Days in Arizona* (1932), to statehood, rather antiquarian. New Mexico: Warren A. Beck, *New Mexico* (1962), brief and clear; Erna Fergusson, *New Mexico* (1951), reads well. For Utah see the Readings for Chapter 26. For fringe states, see the Readings for Chapter 28 for Colorado and those for Chapter 36 for Montana.

WATER AND HEALTH. For accounts of irrigation see Remi A. Nadeau, *The Water Seekers* (1950) and Albert N. Williams, *The Water and the Power* (1951); both read well but both concern largely the years after 1900. Earl Pomerey, *In Search of the Golden West* (1957) is good on the tourist business. John E. Baur, *The Health Seekers of Southern California, 1870–1900* (1959), a good monograph.

CHAPTER 38

WESTERN PANACEAS

T he westward-moving farmer was a man of strong beliefs and
desires. Above all he was working to attain wealth, and although
he expected to advance as an individual on his own merits, he did
not allow any abstract theory of individualism to swerve him from his
course. When common efforts seemed desirable he was quite willing to work
with others, for example, building a house or creating a claims club. At
times he acted through the government as the only agency able to fulfill his
desires. In many states he was sufficiently numerous to be dominant, and
even in the federal government he had considerable power, and particularly
in the Senate. The West had played an important part in such movements
as the establishment of Jeffersonian democracy, the declaration of the War
of 1812, the development of Jacksonian democracy, the drive to realize
Manifest Destiny, the encouragement of internal improvements, and the
changing of land legislation. The West never had a legislative majority in
Congress but it could often obtain allies, sometimes by logrolling, to help
it realize its desires.

During the generation after the Civil War the West threw its support to several political movements that were based primarily on economic
aspirations. The Westerner had been working hard to make his fortune.
Sometimes he had succeeded, but more frequently he had failed more or less
decisively, and it was hard for him to believe that such failure was due to
personal inadequacies. A more palatable theory was that the rules of the
game had been developed by selfish and privileged Easterners, and needed
to be changed by law to open the way for a rosy future for the western
farmer. Quite naturally such political protest movements drew their
greatest strength in time of depression, when the number of the unsuccessful
was greatest, and declined in periods of prosperity.

Western reform movements were based fundamentally on the two factors that the West was an agricultural region and that it was in debt. The West had always been dominated by farmers, who were interested in farm production, marketing, and prices, but older areas had become at least partially industrialized with the passing of the years, whereas the process was much slower in the states west of the Mississippi. There the cities developed with their factories and stores, but the farmer continued to remain dominant, and legislative representatives continued to respond primarily to farming desires.

The West, of course, was not the only farming area of the United States. Every state had important agricultural interests, and whether the state was Maine, Pennsylvania, or Alabama, these interests might be supreme part of the time. As a consequence the West might expect considerable sympathy and support from other sections of the country. Stated in another way, the West had a high concentration of the very widespread industry of American agriculture.

The second basic factor was that the West, like any other agricultural region, was consistently a debtor area. Few rich people moved to the frontier, and the meager capital of the West was strained to the limit to buy new land, stock, and machinery. Additional funds were obtained from the East or from Europe through mortgages; state and municipal debts brought such improvements as railroads, while private mortgages provided individual funds. In consequence the West was interested in proposals that would benefit not only the farmer, but the farmer who was in debt.

GRANGERS

The first organization to arouse enthusiasm in the West after the Civil War was the Patrons of Husbandry, which was organized in 1867 by a clerk in the Department of Agriculture. The local unit of the organization was known as a grange; hence the members were called grangers and their agitation was labeled the granger movement. At its beginning it was secret in nature, with a ritual modeled along the lines of the Masons or the Odd Fellows. It emphasized social factors whose purpose was to lessen the isolation and loneliness of farm life by encouraging such activities as parties and picnics, lectures and concerts.

On the economic side the Grange placed its emphasis on cooperative enterprises in such fields as creameries, warehouses, insurance, purchasing, and manufacturing, for example, plows and threshers. The troubles of the farmer were presumed to be due not only to poor methods of production but to excessive costs of marketing. The feeling was that farmers, acting individually, had little control of the market as against manufacturers, elevator operators, packers, and railroad men, who tended to monopolize their products or services. The farmer cooperative enterprises were generally unsuccessful, partly because of inefficient management and partly because of the severe competition of larger business corporations intent on maintaining market control. The one positive result was the establishment in 1872 of the Montgomery Ward Company, endorsed by the Grange, to sell goods more cheaply by mail.

The Patrons of Husbandry made little progress in its first few years, for membership remained negligible. It benefited from the hard times of the early 1870s, for, like similar movements, it was more attractive in a period of depression when no other help seemed available. The membership figures leaped skyward during 1872 and 1873; shortly after the panic of 1873 the peak of over 1.5 million was reached. The center of the granger movement was the upper Mississippi Valley, principally in Illinois, Wisconsin, Minnesota, Iowa, and Missouri, but there were widespread repercussions, so that even today it is possible to find grange halls in as remote an area as rural New England.

Partly by accident the development of the granger movement coincided with the revulsion of feeling against the railroads. The farmers of the granges, like other farmers, were convinced that the main cause of the depression of the 1870s had been the high rates and the favoritism practiced by the railroads. Their solution was to have the government curb the railroads effectively, particularly by controlling rates and outlawing unfair railroad practices.

The grangers soon found that their original idea of keeping out of politics was impractical if immediate results were to be obtained. Their reaction was to form small political parties under such names as Independent, Reform, or Anti-Monopoly. These groups, depending mainly on the granges for their support, developed in eleven western states. Usually they cooperated with one of the older and larger parties, with the object of attaining their ends by supplying the margin of victory. United States senators with granger sympathies were elected in Illinois, Kansas, and California, while lesser victories occurred elsewhere.

The most important result of the granger activities was a series of state railroad regulation acts passed in the years 1871–1878 by Illinois, Missouri, Wisconsin, Minnesota, California, and Iowa; other states followed at later dates. Two general provisions were common. Included in each law except that of California was a schedule of maximum rates that the railroads of the state could charge. Every state provided for a commission to inspect the roads of the state, prosecute violators of the law, and report needed legislation to the government; only Missouri, however, gave the commission the power to adjust the rates specified by the original law. In addition to these main provisions there was ordinarily also a prohibition of specified forms of discrimination that had been practiced by the railroads.

The railroads naturally opposed this regulation, but not so much for its immediate effects as because it might open the way to later and more drastic measures. To show how foolish it was for the legislatures to meddle in the practical business of running a railroad, some of the larger roads made their rate structures as ridiculous and unjust as the law permitted. Incidentally, rigid laws were far from practical as conditions changed, and certain railroad commissioners were more interested in politics than in efficient railroading. Efforts were made to repeal the laws. Cases were taken to court on the pleas that private property was being taken in violation of the Constitution, and that only Congress had the right to regulate businesses that were primarily interstate in character. The Supreme Court of the United States, however, came to the conclusion in several cases in 1876, notably *Munn* v. *Illinois* and *Peik* v. *Chicago and Northwestern Railroad,* that the states had a regulatory power, even over rates on goods shipped across state lines.

No one realized better than the farmers that though the state laws were constitutional, they did not provide adequate regulation. The most important hauls were between East and West, and even at best they could be regulated only partially by individual western states. Furthermore, most of the railroad companies were foreign corporations (incorporated in some other state), and it was difficult to make them produce accounts and records that would have any meaning to local officials. Confusion also resulted from varying state regulations: a railroad, for example, might be required to change its type of headlight three or four times in a single run because it crossed state boundaries. It was therefore recognized as early as the 1870s that federal action was necessary to supplement and make effective local regulation.

Congress considered possible railroad regulation during the 1870s, but finally did nothing. The Windom report (1874), the Reagan report (1878), and the discussion of a multitude of bills presented the situation very fully, but the majority of the members of Congress felt that railroad regulation should be entirely a state matter. This attitude was made untenable in 1886, when the Supreme Court in the Wabash Case somewhat changed its former attitude and placed rather narrow limits on the powers of the states. In the following year Congress enacted the important Interstate Commerce Act, which, together with many later amendments, eventually resulted in making the Interstate Commerce Commission the most important regulatory body in the United States.

GREENBACKERS

The granger movement, which had played such an important part in the beginning of railroad control, declined during the late 1870s. Its decreasing importance was due in part to an increasing prosperity that made the people forget to some degree the sins of the railroads, and in part to the disastrous failure of the grange cooperative enterprises. During its latter years the grange shared the center of the stage with another reform movement that supported large issues of paper money as a way of helping the debtor portions of the community. Although the Greenback movement developed at the time that the granger movement declined, the only tangible connections between the two agitations were that large numbers of one group supported the program of the other, and that the leaders of one tended to move to the other as popular support veered.

The Greenback movement represented a demand for a managed currency. Greenbackers pointed accusingly at the decline of the per capita amount of money in circulation and to the corresponding decline in prices. They contended that an increase in paper money would help to restore prices to what they considered a proper level. They held that in the future prices might be stabilized by the proper manipulation of the nation's circulating medium, although the cynic suspects that they would have never desired to lower prices.

The average western Greenbacker was not a profound theorist on monetary matters, but he realized that large issues of paper money were good for debtors, and that the West was largely a debtor community. An increase of cheap currency tended, according to Gresham's law, to drive out the more expensive medium; no one would spend gold when the cheaper paper money did as well. The paper money tended to drop in value because of its very profusion; in practice, the visual evidence of such a drop was a rise in prices. With the rise in prices any given amount of money would be worth progressively less in purchasing power. This outcome would be unfortunate for bankers and other possessors of money, but would be good for farmer-debtors, whose dollar income would increase while their debts remained the same. An added factor was that farm prices tended to move more rapidly than other prices, thus giving the farmer another advantage in a period of rising prices.

A very considerable inflation of the American currency had come during the Civil War, when large quantities of unredeemable greenbacks were printed and put into circulation. The result was a rapid rise in prices, which was good for the debtor and a burden on the creditor. After the war the majority feeling was that paper money should once more be made redeemable in gold. Congress felt that this process should occur rather gradually; hence in 1866 it authorized the retirement of $4 million of existing greenbacks each month. Debtors throughout the country were distressed as they looked forward to a period of deflation, with falling prices, and ultimately to resumption of specie payments. Their mutterings rose to a crescendo that brought the repeal of the act of 1866 two years later, when there were still over $356 million of greenbacks in circulation.

The problem of the resumption of specie payments continued to agitate the public mind in the years after 1866. In the presidential campaign of 1868 the Republican party was generally understood to favor resumption and the Democratic party to oppose it, although the Democratic candidate, Horatio Seymour, did not agree with this principle of his party. In spite of the Republican victory no resumption act was passed until 1875, and then it was not to go into force for another four years. As the time for resumption approached, the price of greenbacks gradually rose; at the date set for the change they had attained par and consequently there was no rush to the Treasury to exchange them for gold.

As paper money rose in price the mutterings of the debtor class again became a loud roar. Monetary policy that added to the effects of the panic of 1873 brought prices down precipitously, with the result that the farmer was receiving less and less money to meet the debts he had contracted in a time of high prices. Protesting groups met all over the country, while larger conventions also gave expression to the existing dissatisfaction. Out of this rising wave of feeling came the call for a national convention to represent all who wanted more paper money. When it met in 1876 it took the name of the National Independent party, but by popular consent it was more usually called the Greenback (or Greenback Labor) party.

The convention held at Indianapolis in 1876 was composed of 240 delegates who represented eighteen states and the District of Columbia. After a long debate in which everyone had the opportunity to free his mind of his own pet grievances, a vigorous and oratorical platform was adopted. Then Peter Cooper of New York was nominated for the office of President of the United States. Cooper was a picturesque and appealing man who had made a fortune in iron, first at Baltimore and then at Trenton. More recently he had retired to New York to spend his money in philanthropy, his most notable achievement being the establishment of Cooper Union (to which he gave a total of $800,000) to aid workingmen by providing a free library and reading room, and by offering regular night classes. Mr. Cooper was an attractive figure, but in spite of his benevolences it still seemed inappropriate for this rich, elderly philanthropist to lead a movement composed primarily of farmers who wanted more paper money.

The Greenbackers were particularly fortunate in their choice of a man to organize their clubs throughout the country. Recognizing the power of advertising, they picked Marcus M. ("Brick") Pomeroy, a journalist by profession. According to Pomeroy's own claims he organized 4000 clubs; even allowing for a modest 50 percent of error, the figures are impressive. In addition he found time to write many propaganda tracts under such appealing titles as "Meat for Men" and "Hot Drops."

The election of 1876 was a disappointment to the new Greenback party, which received only 80,000 of 8 million votes. Its principal support in the West came from Illinois, Indiana, and Michigan, and in the East from Massachusetts. The Greenbackers consoled themselves over this failure by reminding themselves that they were a new party. Additional work brought many new recruits, and in the local elections of 1878 the party was able to cast 1 million votes. As later events showed, this election was the high point of the numerical strength of the movement, voting power ebbing with the return of prosperity. General James B. Weaver of Iowa was nominated for the presidency in 1880, but managed to gather only 308,000 votes. In 1884 the Greenbackers joined the Anti-Monopoly party in nominating General Benjamin F. Butler of Massachusetts, who, needless to say, did not win the election.

POPULISTS

The early 1880s proved to be a wonderful period of prosperity, with the consequence that the granger and Greenback movements disappeared. Labor found the unusual situation of rising wages and falling prices. The farmers had bumper crops and consequently profited in spite of a decline of prices; their income increased and the cost of articles they purchased declined. No considerable reform movement could live under such conditions because there was nothing that any considerable number of people wanted to reform. A party of protest was an anachronism.

Small and fairly isolated groups continued to struggle along the path of reform, for there is no conceivable situation in which everyone can be entirely satisfied. Labor groups, such as the Union Labor party and the United Labor party, maintained at least nominal existences. Socialists and anarchists talked loudly to generally hostile audiences. Farmer groups, many of them nonpolitical, struggled to keep their heads above water; among the more important were the National Farmers' Alliance and Industrial Union, the National Farmers' Alliance, the Agricultural Wheel, and the Farmers' Mutual Benefit Association. Although wielding little influence they at least had organizations in a position to take advantage of any period of depression that might occur.

Economic conditions became steadily worse during the late 1880s. Wages began to decline and unemployment to increase. Stockmen were hard pressed to survive. Crops failed in the West, especially in western

Kansas, Nebraska, and the Dakotas, while prices dropped. Once more the farmers were sure that they were being mistreated through a conspiracy of Easterners rolling in wealth and plotting to take the land away from hard-working, honest farmers. There was talk of interest rates of 50 percent and of widespread foreclosures. Although such charges were generally untrue, the farmers were certainly getting along badly, and in terms of potential action, beliefs are more important than facts.

Distressed farmers looking for relief turned toward political action, and many of the small protesting groups suddenly were deluged with a flood of new members. Here and there some of the smaller groups combined to obtain greater strength. The organizations receiving the greatest benefit, both from the attraction of new members and from the absorption of other groups, were the Farmers' Alliances, of which there were two, Northern and Southern. Their most radical proposal was that of the Southern Alliance: the government was to lend the farmers money at 1 percent on nonperishable products stored in government warehouses. Neither group constituted a political party, but each threw its strength toward whatever candidates were most favorable to its views, and this method of action brought a considerable number of local successes by 1891.

The development of many protest movements about 1890 suggested to various leaders the possibility of combining them all into one great political party that might have a chance of winning a national election. The main difficulty in this procedure was to formulate a program that was sufficiently broad to include all the reform elements without antagonizing anyone of importance. Obvious and huge difficulties faced anyone who undertook the Herculean task of reconciling such divergent elements as those favoring easy money, antimonopoly, protective legislation, woman suffrage, single tax, socialism, and temperance—to name only a few.

The most important and difficult problem in producing such a combination, then as later, was to reconcile the opposing viewpoints of the farmer and the industrial laborer. Labor desired high wages and low prices. The farmer, on the contrary, wanted high prices for what he sold and low prices for the goods he bought; but in a choice between prices that were all high and prices that were all low, he preferred the higher level. Furthermore, the farmer preferred a more modest wage scale, since he was an employer of labor. The fact was that the two groups had little in common except their objections to the existing economic system in a period of depression.

The Farmers' Alliance was at least willing to attempt to unite all protesting groups, and at a meeting at Ocala, Florida, in December 1890 issued a call for a meeting of all dissatisfied minorities at Cincinnati the following year. The convention met as scheduled, with its 1400 members representing so many varieties of reform that the meeting was nicknamed the "conglomerate conference." Its chances of success were greatly reduced, however, by the absence of various important farmer and labor groups, and particularly by the abstention of the Knights of Labor.

The platform adopted at Cincinnati showed the nature of the reform movements represented. It included a reduction of taxes, a perennial prayer that is almost never answered. It asked for government ownership of railroads, telegraphs, and telephones, which seemed a natural next step after the development of the granger movement. Landownership by aliens was to be prohibited and no land was to be held speculatively; these demands had a long history, and illustrated vividly the disappearance of the good land of the public domain. The circulating medium was to be plentiful, both paper and silver, and silver was to be coined freely at a ratio with gold of 16 to 1. The last plank was a logical continuation of the Greenback agitation, the only difference being in the increased emphasis on silver rather than on paper.

Other provisions of the platform of 1891 also demonstrated the state of mind of the reformers. The national currency of the United States was to be loaned liberally at an interest rate of 2 percent. A graduated income tax, postal savings banks, the Australian (secret) ballot, liberal pensions for veterans, the eight-hour day, and the initiative and referendum were to be introduced. The President of the United States was to be allowed only a single term. United States senators were to be elected by direct vote of the people.

The platform was obviously the combination of many proposals, including some designed to appeal to such groups as veterans and industrial labor. Read in the light of the present day, few of the demands seem unusual, and many of them have been put into practice. At the time the platform was adopted, however, it seemed very radical if not revolutionary. The more conservative elements of the population were so alarmed as to appear panic-stricken. They shook their heads dolefully and uttered loud lamentations over the degeneracy of the time. The principles of the Constitution were being undermined. Such a program, if adopted, would destroy the civilization that generations of patriotic Americans had constructed through their unremitting toil. Particularly dangerous were the proposals to put the government into business and thus reduce that individual competition that was "the life of trade," and dire calamities were predicted if even the least of the proposed reforms was put into practice.

By the time the new party held its most important convention at Omaha in 1892 it had acquired a name—the People's Party—and its members were called Populists. Thirteen hundred and sixty-six hopeful reformers attended this convention, and adopted a platform similar to the one

of the previous year. Its spirit was well expressed by the preamble written
by Ignatius Donnelly:

> We meet in the midst of a nation brought to the verge of moral, politi-
> cal, and material ruin. Corruption dominates the ballot box, the legisla-
> tures, the Congress, and even touches the ermine on the bench. The
> people are demoralized. The newspapers are largely subsidized or muz-
> zled, public opinion silenced, business prostrated, our homes covered
> with mortgages, labor impoverished, and the land concentrated in the
> hands of the capitalists. Urban workmen are denied the right of organ-
> izing; imported pauperized labor reduces their wages, while a hireling
> army shoots them down. The toils of the million are stolen to build
> up colossal fortunes. From the prolific womb of governmental injustice
> we breed the two great classes—tramps and millionaires. . . . Wealth
> belongs to him who creates it, and every dollar taken from industry is
> robbery.

The Populist candidate for President was General James B. Weaver
of Iowa, who was nominated among scenes of the wildest confusion.
Weaver illustrated very well the type of Westerner who was leading the
drive for reform. He came from a westward-moving family, and although
he had been born in Ohio he migrated as far as California before he settled
permanently in Iowa, where he practiced law. His first political affiliation
was Democratic, but he was attracted by the Free Soil party and then by
the new Republican party. During the Civil War he served in the army.
In 1877 he became a Greenbacker, and was elected to Congress on that
ticket. Nominated for the presidency by the Greenbackers, he waged a
magnificently energetic campaign, but obviously did not convince all of
the half million people who heard him speak, for his vote was 308,578.
During most of the 1880s he sat in Congress as a Greenbacker. With the
decline of the Greenbackers he followed his electorate into the Populist
party. Ultimately he supported Bryan, returning to the Democratic party,
where he stayed until his death in 1912. He therefore ended in the same
party in which he had started, but in the process his own views had remained fairly consistent, while those of the party had changed.

Weaver waged his usual vigorous campaign in 1892, traveling
widely and speaking continuously. When the votes were counted he had
attracted about 1 million as compared with the approximate 5 million each
for Cleveland and Harrison, most of Weaver's support coming, as expected,
from the South and the West. This result constituted an unqualified success.
Even the wildest optimist had no expectation of Populist victory, and a
million votes represented a splendid omen for the future of the new party.
Even a national victory four years later seemed possible.

CAMPAIGN OF 1896

The major political parties were also impressed by the million votes, and the minority Democratic party saw a splendid opportunity of winning the presidency if only these votes could be acquired. When the Democratic convention met in 1896 many of its members favored the Populist views, either through personal conviction or on grounds of political expediency, and many elements of the Populist program were inserted in the party platform. The greatest fight of the convention was over the Populist demand for the free coinage of silver, and here the Democrats seemed hopelessly split. The Westerners in general supported the idea and the Easterners opposed it. The debate was long and heated. Unity was desirable, and at the same time free silver was necessary to win Populist support.

At this dramatic moment the stage of national politics received a new actor in the person of William Jennings Bryan, a young lawyer from Nebraska. The "boy orator of the Platte" delivered the closing speech in the debate on the platform, and ended it with the most famous utterance of his long career:

> We care not upon what lines the battle is fought. If they say bimetallism is good, but that we cannot have it until other nations help us, we reply that, instead of having a gold standard because England has, we will restore bimetallism, and then let England have bimetallism because the United States has it. If they dare to come out in the open field and defend the gold standard as a good thing we will fight them to the uttermost. Having behind us the producing masses of this nation and the world, supported by the commercial interests, and the toilers everywhere, we will answer their demand for a gold standard by saying to them: You shall not press down upon the brow of labor this crown of thorns, you shall not crucify mankind upon a cross of gold.

At the conclusion of the "cross of gold" speech pandemonium broke loose. Everywhere there was wild enthusiasm. Men stood on chairs, stamped, waved, whistled, and shouted. The silver plank—in fact the entire platform—was adopted with a rush, and Bryan himself was nominated for the presidency. Incidentally, the Bryan speech killed the Populist party, for its chief appeal was gone. The only possible thing the Populists could do was to support Bryan.

The campaign of 1896 was a spirited contest, during which Bryan performed prodigious feats in miles traveled, the number of speeches made, and the hands shaken. William McKinley conducted a more dignified campaign from his own porch at Canton, Ohio. For some still unascertained reason "the producing masses of this nation," to say nothing of the world, failed to see that their hope of economic salvation rested with the Democratic party. Great numbers of them voted for the many minor parties in the field, or for McKinley, who won easily.

As prosperity returned, Populism disappeared and the demand for free coinage of silver passed into the realm of historical relics. Bryan ran for the presidency twice later, and although he still believed in free silver, he listened to councils of discretion and placed a continually decreasing emphasis on it, not even mentioning it in 1908.

WESTERN POLITICAL INFLUENCE

Western political influence did not stop with the Populist movement. Such democratic measures as woman suffrage, direct primary, direct election of senators, the initiative, referendum, and recall made better progress in the West than in the East. Theodore Roosevelt received much western support in 1912 from the West because of his support of such "progressive" measures. The Wilson nomination of 1912 depended in part on the influence of a Westerner, William Jennings Bryan, and the West was an influential factor in the elections of 1912 and 1916. The National Non-Partisan League (formed in 1915) was western, and the La Follette campaign of 1924 looked largely toward western support. Other illustrations merely reinforce the obvious statement of western influence in national elections.

More important in the long run to the West than its influence on national elections has been its importance in Congress. Because of the constitutional provision that each state shall have two senators, the less populated agricultural states have always had important voices in the Senate, and these voices have been loud in support of the desires of their farmer constituents. Even during the "businessman government" of the 1920s the farm bloc was able to obtain concessions, and with the coming of the New Deal its powers vastly increased. The various agricultural support acts passed since the days of the New Deal have reflected convincingly the political power of the farmers.

To speak of the political power of the farmers as a manifestation of the West is technically correct, but at the same time it is misleading because it implies a direct connection with the frontier. The result is to classify Illinois as a frontier state in the 1870s because it had an influential granger movement. In no reasonable sense were many of the granger states of the 1870s frontier states. The mere fact that they had many railroads would preclude that possibility. The Wisconsin of Robert La Follette was no more a frontier state than William Jennings Bryan was a later-day Daniel Boone.

The proper statement about western political sentiment seems to be that it has been and still is the sentiment of an area that is primarily agricultural. The important fact is that farmers are dominant and not that geographically the region is western; large areas in other parts of the United States are also farmer-oriented, and the western complexion exists only because so many states of the Mississippi Valley are agricultural. Possibly they remained agricultural later in our history because of the frontier background.

In only one sense can the western reform movements of the past century receive a frontier interpretation. The frontier was composed predominantly of farmers who believed in political democracy and in the governmental control of large aggregations of wealth; hence their point of view was similar to that of farmers of any place and at any time. Possibly the fairest attitude is to consider the frontier farmer as a special case of the universal farmer. But the caboose does not push the train. Any farmer confronted with certain conditions is likely to have predetermined responses, and the important fact is that farmers occupied the frontier and not that a few farmers were at one time frontiersmen.

READINGS

FARMER PROTEST MOVEMENTS. Among the better of the more general accounts are Russell B. Nye, *Midwestern Progressive Politics, 1870–1958* (1959); Theodore Saloutos and John D. Hicks, *Agricultural Discontent in the Middle West* (1950); Fred A. Shannon, *The Farmer's Last Frontier* (1945); Mary Wilma M. Hargreaves, *Dry Farming on the Northern Great Plains 1900–1925* (1957); Chester M. Destler, *American Radicalism, 1865–1901* (1946); Frederick E. Haynes, *Third Party Movements Since the Civil War* (1916); Walter Johnson, *William Allen White's America* (1947); Richard Hofstadter, *The Age of Reform* (1955); Solon J. Buck, *The Agrarian Crusade* (1920). The classic account of the granger movement is Solon J. Buck, *The Granger Movement* (1913). Railroad control is described in Robert E. Riegel, *The Story of the Western Railroads* (1926) and John Moody, *The Railroad Builders* (1919). Populism can be followed in John D. Hicks, *The Populist Revolt* (1931), excellent; Martin Ridge, *Ignatius Donnelly* (1962), very good; Norman Pollack, *The Populist Response to Industrial America* (1962); Frederick E. Haynes, *James Baird Weaver* (1919). Allan G. Bogue, *Money at Interest* (1955) is a careful study of the validity of some of the farmer protests. Money and the panic of 1893 may be followed in Charles J. Bullock, *Essays on the Monetary History of the United States* (1900); Alonzo B. Hepburn, *A History of the Currency* (rev. ed., 1924); William J. Lauck, *The Causes of the Panic of 1893* (1907). Bryan's activities can of course be followed in any life of Bryan, but see especially William J. Bryan, *The First Battle* (1896).

CHAPTER 39

THE WEST
ENTERS FICTION

The West has provided a tremendous store of material for the men and women who earn their bread and butter by writing. That western plots and incidents should have been used in novels, plays, and paintings is not remarkable. What is remarkable is that frontier themes appeared relatively late, and then in limited variety and presented with small imagination.

The one frontier theme that appealed to the writers of the early nineteenth century was the conflict between Indian and white. Here obviously was high adventure. For purposes of drama most authors saw the Indian as either a cruel and bloodthirsty savage who held back the progress of civilization, or a brave, noble, and virtuous primitive man who fought against overwhelming odds to protect his family and friends. Seldom was the Indian pictured as a credible human being. Here and there a novelist saw interesting material in other frontier topics such as banditry, but practically none saw opportunity in the ordinary struggle of the farmer to subdue the wilderness. Conflict between men seemed exciting, but conflict between man and nature seemed dull unless it involved great feats of exploration.

Early American novels were copied in both material and style from European models. Not until the frontier was well past the Appalachians did frontier stories make their appearance. A frontier at one's own back-door was visibly dirty, uncouth, vermin-ridden, and dominated by dull and backbreaking labor. A frontier became romantic and colorful only in the hazy distance where unsavory and often disgusting details softened or vanished. The difficulties and hardships changed from unpleasant experiences

609

to be forgotten to obstacles to be overcome by brave men and women. Day-by-day monotony was so telescoped that what was left was the picturesque incident, the heroic episode.

By the time the frontier reached the Great Plains there existed east of the Mississippi a large book-buying public to whom the West was remote, colorful, and exciting. To the average eastern factory worker or farmer, the West became a magic word, conjuring up alluring pictures of an open, wind-swept plain over which roamed bold and romantic riders to whom adventure was a daily experience. To someone tied to a daily round of farm chores or to a machine, the West appeared a land of freedom, where a man was his own master, bold and self-reliant, meeting human and physical challenges with heroic bravery and unvarying success.

And in truth the Far West of the late nineteenth century had certain elements of color that the more eastern frontier had possessed to a lesser degree. The 2000-mile trek of covered wagons inspired the imagination more than did the floating of flatboats down the Ohio river. The mad rush to gold fields hundreds of miles from civilization was more spectacular than the exploitation of the Georgia gold deposits or the lead outcroppings of Wisconsin and Illinois. Custer and Chief Joseph seemed more exciting than Harrison and Tecumseh had been. The cowboy had had no eastern rival. The pony express and the overland stage made the traffic on the National Road seem dull and plodding; the construction of the Union Pacific decisively outclassed the building of the Ohio Canal in its appeal to American imagination.

LOCAL COLOR FICTION

One outstanding literary trend in the generation after the Civil War was the exploitation of the peculiar and distinctive characteristics of various sections of the country. This "local color" writing was accurate about geography, language, and customs, but often highly romantic in its attitude toward life. Naturally certain authors saw opportunity in describing the West, even though they very possibly had had no personal experience with frontier conditions. One of the earliest of these writers was Edward Eggleston, who wrote of pioneer life in southern Indiana in *The Hoosier Schoolmaster* and other novels published in the early 1870s. Eggleston's continued reputation seems hard to understand: his characters are so badly overdrawn as to be almost caricatures, are sentimentalized into becoming heroes or villains, and are frequently mawkishly religious. He did, however, give a picture of the speech and customs of the area.

Standing head and shoulders above all other men who wrote about the West in the generation after the Civil War was Samuel L. Clemens, better known by his pen name Mark Twain. As a small boy Clemens lived in a Missouri River village that some romanticists have tried unsuccessfully to present as part of the frontier. He was steeped in the life and traditions of the river, and as a young man worked for some years as a steamboat pilot; his pen name was the call of the man who used the lead to plumb the depth of the river. Clemens' first experience with the Far West came in 1862, when he went to Nevada on the invitation of his brother, who had been made secretary of the territory by President Lincoln. Although Clemens tried a little unsuccessful mining, as did almost all Nevada residents, his major occupation was as a writer for the *Territorial Enterprise* of Virginia City.

Clemens' first national reputation came with a jumping frog story, which was not original with him. The tale described a jumping match between two frogs in which one outleaped the other because his owner had the foresight to feed lead to the frog of his opponent. Journalistic and literary success brought requests to lecture, at which Clemens was very effective, and soon he had acquired an international reputation. Clemens' angular body and eccentricities soon made him an American institution, and in time he became the most easily recognizable man in the United States with his luxuriant thatch of white hair and his preference for white suits. His thoroughgoing pessimism did him no harm, which was surprising in view of the childish optimism so characteristic of the American public.

Clemens' one book on the Far West was *Roughing It* (1872), concerned largely with life in Nevada. Its humor was typically American and typically western, heavily depending on exaggeration and unusual juxtapositions. Such incidents as the author's dinner with Brigham Young and his family and the effort of a rough miner to persuade a recent graduate of a theological school to preside at the obsequies of a pal are in the best Mark Twain tradition, and remain as funny today as when they were written. But in addition, *Roughing It* is a fine description of mining life in Nevada during the 1860s, provided only that allowance is made for exaggeration.

The major claim of Samuel Clemens to literary immortality rests on his charming descriptions of the life of a small boy along the Mississippi. The series started with *Tom Sawyer* (1876), and ended with *The Tragedy of Pudd'nhead Wilson* (1894). Here in Clemens' inimitable style the true flavor of the river is reflected in a delicate, understanding analysis of boyhood life. Charming when they were published, and equally vital today, these books have never been surpassed. Long after such a serious work as his *Gilded Age* is forgotten, Clemens' Tom Sawyer and Huckleberry Finn will remain vitally and lovably alive for all Americans.

Ranking well behind Mark Twain, but still with a considerable claim to fame, comes Bret Harte. Harte, an Easterner by birth and education, was something of an infant prodigy with a yearning to write. His father died when Bret was nine, and his mother took her family to California on the occasion of her remarriage. On the coast Harte tried various jobs, but gravitated toward journalism, where he attained something of a local reputation. In 1868 he became editor of the *Overland Monthly,* a West Coast effort to exploit western material and western writers. In this magazine appeared some of the best of his stories, including "The Luck of Roaring Camp" and "The Outcasts of Poker Flat."

Growing fame drew Harte to the East in 1871, where he was regarded with such great enthusiasm that the *Atlantic Monthly* offered him a magnificent $10,000 for anything he might produce in a year. Success had an unfortunate effect on Harte and his work declined both in quantity and in quality. Ultimately he moved to England, where in time he became little more than a hack writer, living in poverty. His death in 1902 came as a shock to most Americans because his productive period had been so far in the past that they thought him dead.

Harte's fame rests on his short stories of the West, masterpieces of artful craftsmanship and the results of years of painstaking literary experimentation. Typically they deal with such human paradoxes as the self-sacrificing gambler, the crude miner with the soul of a child, the prostitute filled with mother love. The climax of each story comes with some curious twist of fate. For some readers the Harte stories are exaggerated and artificial; for others they represent a peak in the art of the short story. Their permanent place in literature remains to be fixed.

DIME NOVELS

Artistic literary descriptions of the West found a good American market, but the real bonanza remained to be exploited by the western thriller. Increasing masses of people were now being taught to read, but the majority of them were not enthralled by the *Atlantic Monthly* nor could they afford a clothbound volume that might cost two day's pay. For them a cheaper and more sensational type of writing was desirable. The man first to exploit this profitable possibility as it related to the West was Edward Zane Carroll Judson, who wrote under the pen name of Ned Buntline.

Judson wrote from the background of varied and exciting personal experiences: he had served as a common sailor, he had been a soldier in the Seminole War, he had traveled up the Yellowstone for a fur company, he had fought and been imprisoned in the Civil War, and he had lectured extensively for the temperance movement about the delirium tremens he had known. Just prior to the Civil War he had written for the New York *Mercury,* a four-penny thriller, and had established his weekly, *Ned Bunt-*

line's Own. In both sheets he had exploited thrilling material, and particularly the kind related to the West. While in prison during the war he had used his spare moments to write three blood-and-thunder novels. All these activities had failed to make Judson wealthy, but they had demonstrated the existence of a wide market for rapid-action stories, and particularly those of the West.

The man who profited most from the Judson idea was Erastus Beadle, who published America's most famous series of "dime novels." Rather surprisingly the first of the series (1860) was from the pen of Mrs. Ann S. Stephens, a well-known editor and a novelist of considerable reputation. She called her book *Malaeska, the Indian Wife of the White Hunter.* The locale of the story was the Hudson in the early days of Dutch settlement. In this pathetic tale of the disastrous effects of an Indian-white marriage, the son of this union ultimately commits suicide, his bride-to-be remains in lifelong celibacy, and Malaeska herself fades away into a lonely grave. In spite of its sadness, the novel had a notable sale of some 65,000 copies, and opened the way for later books in the series.

During and immediately after the Civil War Beadle sold his dime, half-dime, and quarter series literally by the million. They were more truly a gold mine than most of the mineral discoveries in the West. The type of books they contained is indicated but feebly by such titles as *Carson the Guide, California Joe, Arizona Joe,* and *The Prairie Rover.* Many of them were written, or at least signed, by men who could claim competence in the subjects they handled. Among the presumed authors were such well-known Westerners as William F. Cody, Captain "Bruin" Adams, Major St. Vrain, and Captain Jack Crawford.

The Beadle novels were read by soldiers in the army, by small boys in the woodshed, and by anyone else seeking a vicarious thrill. In general they were considered somewhat immoral and reprehensible—at least for others to read. Parents used a hickory stick or the flat of the hand to persuade their progeny of the error of their ways. The fact of the matter was that they were far from immoral in the ordinary sense of the word. Rather, they were violently and blatantly self-righteous. No expressions were used that might shock even the most modest and prudish, and sex was almost entirely excluded. The hero was always everything that a hero should be, and the unbelievably bad villain was always confounded in the end. The sin committed by the small boy reading them was more that of wasting his time than being demoralized.

The vogue of the Beadle novels gradually declined during the 1890s, the last one being published in 1897. The later ones dealt less frequently with the West, and more often with detectives and train robbers. Their place was filled by the western story magazine, which included such titles as *Frontier Stories, West, Pioneer Tales, Western Story Magazine,* and *Cowboy Stories.* Hundreds of such magazines have since appeared to vie with the "art" and "movie" magazines for popular favor. Quite understandably they have sold well in such industrial areas as New England, but apparently they have also been read by ranch employees in the West; if their publishers are to be believed, a considerable proportion of their readers are not virile, red-blooded "he-men," but members of the opposite sex.

The western story magazine has been devoted exclusively to tales of rapid action, with a little sex interest to add spice to the story. Guns spit fire and redskins drop. Bloodstained fists strike yielding flesh. Wild rides through storm and danger bring rescue in the nick of time. Desperate bands of cattle thieves are defeated by the forces of right on the last page. The hero is brave, keen, farsighted, strong, and loyal. The villain is black-hearted, mean, cruel, and entirely despicable. The heroine is brave, beautiful, pure, and strong, but entirely feminine. Wickedness is always crushed at the last moment, right is triumphant, and the hero and heroine fall into each other's arms to live happily ever after. No wicked sex tangles or marital problems mar the pure and simple heroism of these tales.

WESTERN PLAYS

In addition to the literary expression given the West, it has also received dramatic interpretation. Here again the real story in relation to the present begins with the versatile E. Z. C. Judson, whose gifts included the ability to write drama. A play, "Buffalo Bill, the King of the Border Men," which was based on a Judson story, was produced successfully in New York in 1872. While it was playing it was visited by no less a person than Buffalo Bill himself. Cody, who had a large amount of childish naïveté, a love of admiration, and a keen sense of the dramatic, found the play immensely pleasing. He was persuaded to go on the stage and be introduced to the audience, which received him with a great ovation. As s result Buffalo Bill was at once violently attracted to the stage and wanted to become an actor.

Judson realized the financial advantages that would accrue from personal appearances of Buffalo Bill and other noted plains characters, and so he quickly utilized Cody's aspirations. It is said that he wrote the entire manuscript of "The Scout of the Plains" at Chicago in one evening—the story seems by no means unlikely considering the caliber of the play and Judson's facility with the pen. The cast of characters included Buffalo Bill, Texas Jack Omohundro, and a group of "Indians" gathered from the streets of Chicago. If the personnel was any criterion, the play was truly western in tone.

Within a year "The Scout of the Plains" was revised as "Scouts of the Plains," Buffalo Bill acquired a stage presence, Wild Bill Hickok was added to the cast, Judson was dropped, and New York crowds were receiving the presentation enthusiastically. Indians were killed wholesale, and the heroes and the beautiful heroine were rescued from all kinds of terrifying situations. Wild Bill's opening speech, as he galloped on the stage shooting a few Indians, ran: "Fear not, fair maid; by heavens, you are safe at last with Wild Bill, who is ever ready to risk his life and die if need be in defense of weak and helpless womanhood." In addition to certain rather obvious flaws in the realism of this form of address, particularly in view of Bill's reputation with women, it should be noted that the speech was given at the beginning of the play and was not the final dramatic incident.

Buffalo Bill, who liked the footlights, the posing, and the applause, thoroughly enjoyed his work on the stage. Wild Bill Hickok, on the other hand, longed for the real West. Many stories are told of how he failed to appear at various times and how he shot out the spotlight. Within a short time he left the show and drifted to Deadwood, where he met his death at the hands of a coward who shot him in the back.

This early effort to put the Far West before the public in dramatic form had at least two immediate and important results. The first was the opening of a real dramatic field, with high points in operatic presentations; particularly notable have been "The Girl of the Golden West" by Giacomo Puccini, which has become standard, and the more recent and excellent "Ballad of Baby Doe," by Douglas Moore, which is gaining increasing acceptance. The other development was the picturesque Wild West show with which the name of Buffalo Bill is linked so inextricably.

WILD WEST SHOW

The meteoric rise of Buffalo Bill to national prominence was due primarily to the work of his devoted friend and press agent Major John M. Burke, and secondarily to the wrtings of that dime novel expert Prentiss Ingraham. Thanks to these two boosters Buffalo Bill became one of the best-known men in the world. The idea of a Wild West show probably did not originate with Cody. P. T. Barnum had a similar idea as early as 1860. The immediate formation of the show was due in large part to the enthusiasm of the veteran actor Nate Salsbury, who later became Cody's partner. After the dramatic season of 1882–1883 Cody returned to the plains and gathered large numbers of cowboys, Indians, ponies, buffaloes, and other symbols of the West. With these he opened his first outdoor show at the Omaha Fair Grounds on May 17, 1883, calling it "The Wild West, Rocky Mountain and Prairie Exhibition." For a time the show was in perpetual danger of financial failure, largely because Cody was always a much better showman than business manager. Salsbury furnished most of the funds and financial judgment. Cody was frequently drunk, was generous to relatives and old friends, and embarked on many outside, and expensive, ventures; no matter how much the show brought in, he was always in debt.

By 1885 Buffalo Bill's Wild West Show was secure as a brilliant success. It played in England in 1887, which was the year of Queen Victoria's Jubilee, and made an instantaneous hit. At two command performances given for the Queen other members of royalty attended. The Prince of Wales rode in the Deadwood stage, and Buffalo Bill was presented to the Queen. For the moment the Wild West Show was the fashion in England. Two years later the show toured the Continent, and was again acclaimed. In 1893 Buffalo Bill set up his show opposite the main entrance of the Chicago Fair and rivaled the fair itself in drawing power.

A good part of the Wild West Show's attractiveness lay in the fact that it presented phases of American life that most people had never experienced except in fiction. At first it was purely western, with pony races, Indian dances and battles, bucking bronchos, steer roping, the pony express, and the attack on the Deadwood stage; the emphasis was on riding and shooting. By the early 1890s it had become a "Congress of Rough Riders of the World," and included Indians, cowboys, Mexicans, German uhlans, French chasseurs, British lancers, American cavalrymen, Cossacks, Gauchos, and Arabs. By the late 1890s it had added such regular circus side show attractions as snake charmers, midgets, giants, mind readers, magicians, fire-eaters, and jugglers. After it was combined with "Pawnee Bill's Far East" in 1908 it became less profitable; the last good season was 1910. Buffalo Bill lost everything in bad investments and was poverty-stricken when he died in 1917.

One of Buffalo Bill's chief attractions was the exhibition of wonderful shooting, both by himself and others. His own most admired shooting was done from horseback. His protégé, Johnny Baker, was a boy prodigy. Best known and most admired, however, was Annie Oakley. Annie was not herself a Westerner, having been born and raised in Ohio long after the frontier had passed that region, but dressed in a buckskin suit she was able to pass as the real article. By all reports she was a fine, modest woman, well liked by the other performers. Her death occurred as recently as 1926. The reputation of Annie Oakley was so widespread that a punched ticket became known popularly as an "Annie Oakley" because of its similarity to a card at which the lady herself had shot.

In spite of Buffalo Bill's excessive use of liquor, his lack of business judgment, and his exaggerated reputation based largely on press agent publicity, he remained an outstanding figure, and did much to impress a particular concept of the West on the American mind. For every child living in the years near 1900 one of the great thrills of life was to see Buffalo

Bill ride his white steed at the head of the procession; his movements were dramatic as was the great shock of snowy-white hair, which in his last years was replaced by a wig. Always somewhere in the program was the exciting Indian attack upon the Deadwood stage. As Buffalo Bill grew older his marksmanship declined, but even in the last of his "farewell tours" he was as impressive and picturesque as ever.

MOVING PICTURES

The year 1910 saw the arrival of a new dramatic possibility in the moving picture. It was in this year that Goldberg made his magic lantern slides of Buffalo Bill, that Powers took his moving pictures of Buffalo Bill, and that the Essanay Company started its weekly Saturday one-reel releases of "Bronco Billy." As the motion picture developed, one of its staples was the western story, which included such spectacles as "The Toll of the Desert," "The Taming of Texas Pete," "The Iron Horse," and "North of 36." Such names as Tom Mix, William S. Hart, Hoot Gibson, and Harry Carey were known to every small boy of the country and, for that matter, to his mother and father.

More recent moving pictures have included notable attempts at creating a realistic background, as in the building of the Union Pacific or the migration of the Mormons, but the usual production has been aimed at creating an imaginary and idyllic West. Every farmhouse seems to contain a beautiful and well-dressed daughter, with nails manicured, hair curled, and speech well chosen. For each lovely heroine there is a handsome hero who is an excellent horseman, a first-rate shot, careless of personal danger, clever with his fists, and with a cat's proverbial nine lives, for no western hero, as far as the record goes, has ever died. The idyllic peace of the beautiful West is marred only by the villain and his evil gang. The villain is an evil, ill-favored, sardonic chap who spends all his time concocting plans for stealing the old ranch or waylaying the hero. Luckily he is always outwitted and foiled by the hero before the play comes to an end.

The coming of television provided a new market for old westerns that otherwise would have passed to their well-merited deaths. Television also developed dozens of serials of its own under such provocative titles as "The Lone Ranger," "Gunsmoke," "Wagon Train," and "Rawhide." Now and then a picture is labeled "adult" for no very observable reason. They all have the general characteristics of earlier movies, with the addition of considerable efforts to make heroes out of such dubious characters as Billy the Kid and Wyatt Earp. The one point in their favor is that they give relaxation to children of all ages in much the same way as the adventures of Robin Hood do. Presumably their emphasis on violence and their disregard for the law, even by the "good" people, have no more deleterious effect on their audience than had older fairy tales such as Jack the Giant Killer.

The West of the movies and television is at least fascinating. Each cowboy has a bright and shining gun, which he carries continually and uses on the slightest provocation. Also, he always has a favorite horse to which he is passionately devoted. Indians are perpetually either saying "ugh" or giving war dances preparatory to attacking settlers. A continual series of overwhelming and seemingly inescapable dangers is matched by an equal series of hairbreadth escapes. Right always triumphs eventually, and villainy is crushed to earth. And so the younger generation is encouraged to build a beautiful and heroic myth of the West. Rather curiously, parents seem to object less strenuously to these vivid picturizations than they did to earlier and duller dime thrillers.

LITERATURE AFTER 1900

Books about the West sold more widely from about 1900. The literary trend of the period was toward the rather nostalgic type of novel about rural and small-town life, for example, *David Harum,* and the historical romance of the type of *When Knighthood Was In Flower.* The western novel combined the simple, unlearned virtues of the characters of the first type with the glittering romance of the second. Much of this new literature was concerned with the cowboy, who only recently had become an exciting and romantic figure; for most of the nineteenth century the stock tender had been on the whole a drab and pedestrian figure rather than the potential hero of a novel. One of the earliest to exploit the field was Emerson Hough, who in 1895 published his descriptive *Story of the Cowboy,* which was a reasonably interesting description of certain phases of the cattle business. Later he published such novels as *The Covered Wagon* (1922) and *North of 36* (1923), which at least did not possess the defects of dullness. Hough was exceedingly impressed with the heroic nature of the western experience, and viewed with nostalgic sadness the passing of the good old days.

Owen Wister was responsible for one of the better of the western novels of the early twentieth century with *The Virginian* (1902). Wister, born and reared in the East, graduated from Harvard in 1885. His interest in the West came from a trip to Wyoming for his health, and he became so enthusiastic about it that he returned several times and talked about it incessantly. Although his profession was the practice of law in Philadelphia, he affected loose-tied bow ties, short sleeves, and western stories. In fact he came to feel that he had a mission to bring the West into American literature. In *The Virginian* he described interestingly life in Wyoming during the late 1870s and 1880s. Although the Virginian himself is an unusual cowboy, the atmosphere and most of the incidents are admirable.

Other writers on western themes have been legion, but most of their work has been ephemeral. Jack London had great popularity for a time with such tales as *Call of the Wild*, which described the raw passions and the struggle for survival in the Far North. Harold Bell Wright depicted western scenes in such books as *When a Man's a Man*, and profited thereby. B. M. Bowers (Bertha M. Sinclair) contributed the enjoyable Flying U stories, such as *Chip of the Flying U*. C. E. Mulford created the unforgettable character Hopalong Cassidy. A little later the best-seller lists included Max Brand's *Destry Rides Again* (1930) and *Singing Guns* (1938), which were typical action stories. Most spectacular of the popular successes was Niven Busch's *Duel in the Sun* (1944), which concerned cattle raising in the Southwest during the 1880s. Early sales were poor, since, after all, the book was but one of a long series of action westerns; suddenly, however, sales boomed and when it was filmed, it was one of the most popular productions of its kind.

Two exceptional men, Andy Adams and Will James, both former cowboys, re-created the cattle country in a series of semiautobiographical descriptive books. Adams wrote vividly, and in his inimitable slang. His best work was probably the *Log of a Cowboy*, although other volumes were almost as good. Will James did similar work in his *Cowboys North and South* and *Cow Country*, and in addition illustrated his books with his excellent action drawings. Unfortunately the public taste in western literature had become quite standardized before Adams and James appeared on the scene, which meant that their sales were not as great as their works merited.

Adams and James belonged to the small group of westerners who grew up in the West of the frontier and who, with a minimum of formal training, managed to produce work that was acceptable in a literary sense. Possibly the California poet Joaquin Miller should be included in that group. In the field of painting, the Montana cowboy Charlie Russell deserves an important place. With only slight if any allowance for Russell's lack of formal training, his work compares favorably with that of his better-known contemporary, Frederic Remington.

Undoubtedly the best of all spinners of western yarns, presuming that popularity is the proper test, has been Zane Grey. Grey, a dentist, received his D.D.S. from Pennsylvania in 1896, and started his practice in New York City. His literary labor began in 1904 and found immediate popular favor. In time he became convinced that the public would always recognize and buy a good book with a strong appeal, by which he meant his own. His novels have been described by one commentator as grim stories of sadists who are supermen, and of strongly sexed but virginal women. The reading of Zane Grey is an experience that should not be missed. Any of his books will do, since it is hard to distinguish one from another. A copy should be easy to obtain: in his heydey Grey was producing about one a year and most of them ended on the best-seller lists.

LITERARY REALISM

The West has furnished material for hundreds of books of action and romance, but possibly more important to the literary historian have been efforts to create accurate pictures of the West, and particularly of the farming West. The great landmark of western realism was E. W. Howe's *The Story of a Country Town* (1883), which described the less pleasant aspects of a small and unlovely town in the wheat country of Kansas. Four years later Joseph Kirkland, the son of Caroline Kirkland, herself a writer, published his *Zury* (short for Usury), which did a similar job for frontier Illinois.

Howe and Kirkland were early practitioners of realism, but the popularizer was Hamlin Garland, who was born (1860) and reared in the upper Mississippi Valley at a time when that area was not far removed from frontier conditions. Garland worked long and hard as a farm boy, and managed to obtain an education only in the face of severe handicaps. Little wonder that he was critical of the world about him and became active in the Populist movement. As a radical young man with literary aspirations he naturally evolved a philosophy of life that he tried to apply to his writings. In his own words, he developed "two great literary concepts—that truth was a higher quality than beauty, and that to spread the reign of justice should everywhere be the design and intent of the artist."

Garland's first book was *Main Traveled Roads* (1891), but his best-known works were the various semiautobiographical *Middle Border* books, which tell of the pioneering of his own family. Garland told here of the dirt and vermin and fleas, of the monotonous and backbreaking drudgery, of the drabness and meanness of western life, but he also described hilarious parties, gorgeous sunrises, and the smell of sizzling sausages on a cold morning. Because of these latter and more pleasant incidents, certain literary highbrows profess to feel that he was really a romantic at heart.

Garland stated a point of view that was important and tried to exemplify it in some of his short stories, but his longer novels, such as *The Spirit of the Sweetwater* and *Her Mountain Lover,* tended to be nothing more than thin love stories. In spite of such failures to realize his literary goal he had tremendous influence by his recognition of the literary and dramatic values of a fight for existence by the frontier farmer pitting his brain and brawn and endurance against the forces of a reluctant nature.

Furthermore, he influenced and assisted important young writers, such as Stephen Crane and Frank Norris, who were both significant in American literary development. Crane was not concerned with western themes, but Norris was.

Frank Norris was more versatile than Hamlin Garland, but less intimately associated with the West, even though part of his education was obtained at the University of California. Among his varied works, *McTeague* (1899) was an attempt to treat the San Francisco area realistically; unfortunately for the western historian the background was contemporary, which made it remote from the frontier. Just before his early death, Norris was engaged in a trilogy to show the importance of wheat. *The Octopus* (1901) pictured the growing of wheat in southern California, *The Pit* (1903) described the Chicago grain exchange, and *The Wolf* (never written) was to treat the use of wheat to stop a European famine. *The Octopus* was an impressive story in which wheat dominated the canvas, with individual characters dwarfed by the immensity and power of the inanimate grain; the action was the struggle between the wheat growers and the railroad, which was the octopus.

Time brought an ever-increasing number of novelists who used western themes with attention not only to accuracy of detail but also to the larger truths. Among the better works may be mentioned Herbert Quick, *Vandemark's Folly;* Mari Sandoz, *Old Jules;* A. B. Guthrie, *The Big Sky;* H. L. Davis, *Honey on the Horn;* V. Fisher, *City of Illusion;* Walter V. Clark, *The Ox-Bow Incident;* Edna Ferber, *Cimarron.* Outstanding was the work of Willa Sibert Cather, born in Virginia but educated at the University of Nebraska. Her writings about the West included *O Pioneers!, My Ántonia,* and, above all, *Death Comes for the Archbishop,* which is considered her masterpiece. Miss Cather was not interested in plot in the usual fashion, but used the historical chronicle to describe the reaction of man to his environment.

High on any list of realistic novelists would be the Norwegian-born C. E. Rolvaag, who came to the United States as a young man. His best novel was *Giants in the Earth,* written first, as were his other books, in Norwegian, which recounted the experiences of Norwegian immigrants on the northern plains. The main character and the central theme of the book were the prairies, which dominated the lives of Per Hansa, his wife Beret, and their children. When the prairies smiled, life was happy and prodigal. When the locusts came or the snow descended, the prairies became malevolent, seeking whom they could destroy. The book ends as Per Hansa, traveling in the middle of the winter to get a minister for a dying man, loses his way in the snow and freezes to death. The last chapter is titled, "The Great Plains Drinks the Blood of Christian Men and Is Satisfied."

A slightly different type of work should be noted in passing. John G. Neihardt, often called the poet laureate of Nebraska, picked the 1820s as the inspiration of an epic of the plains and the Indian wars. A trilogy of three long poems—*The Song of Hugh Glass, The Song of Three Friends,* and *The Song of the Indian Wars*—was based on detailed and accurate research. Neihardt did not disdain prose, and his *The Splendid Wayfaring,* treating the travels of Jedediah Smith, had a lyric swing that made it not inferior to the poetry.

The increasing use of authentic western material by the novelists is a happy augury for the future, and yet the subject matter thus far unutilized is tremendous. Mining, land speculation, cattle raising, and other western occupations have been as yet little explored. Greatest enthusiasm has been shown for semifictionalized and heroic sagas of such heroes as Daniel Boone and Davy Crockett, whether in novels or on radio or television. Certainly there still remains an almost inexhaustible supply of the necessary raw material for whatever kind of tale the writer desires, from blood-and-thunder action stories to subtle analyses of human emotions. And just as certainly the most distinctive of American experiences deserve a greater number of honest and penetrating treatments than have as yet been accorded them.

READINGS

LITERATURE. General accounts include Robert E. Spiller and others, *Literary History of the United States* (1953), possibly the best general history; Percy H. Boynton, *The Rediscovery of the Frontier* (1931); Dorothy A. Dondore, *The Prairie and the Making of Middle America* (1926), very scholarly; Albert Keiser, *The Indian in American Literature* (1933); Lucy L. Hazard, *The Frontier in American Literature* (1927), scholarly; Ina H. Herron, *The Small Town in American Literature* (1939), good; Franklin D. Walker, *A Literary History of Southern California* (1950), and *San Francisco's Literary Frontier* (1939); Edwin W. Gaston, Jr., *The Early Novel of the Southwest* (1961), critical, based on forty major novels; Charles L. Sonnichsen, *The Southwest in Life and Literature* (1962), representative writings; dime novels are well covered in Edward L. Pearson, *Dime Novels* (1929); see also James Monaghan, *The Great Rascal* (1952), excellent on "Ned Buntline," and Frederick E. Pond, *Life & Adventures of "Ned Buntline"* (1919), less good. Cowboy literature is well covered in Edward D. Branch, *The Cowboy* (1926) and Joe B. Frantz and Julian E. Choate, Jr., *The American Cowboy: The Myth and the Reality* (1955), good. Humor is treated in Thomas D. Clark, *The Rampaging Frontier* (1939); Mody C. Boatright, *Folk Laughter on the American Frontier* (1949). Fanny K. Wister (ed.),

Owen Wister Out West (1958). George R. Stewart, *Bret Harte* (1931) is good. For Mark Twain see Bernard De Voto, *Mark Twain's America* (1935); Effie M. Mack, *Mark Twain in Nevada* (1947); Edward C. Wagenknecht, *Mark Twain* (1935).

BUFFALO BILL AND HIS WILD WEST SHOW. Don Russell, *The Lives and Legends of Buffalo Bill* (1960), concerned with sources of stories; Walter Havighurst, *Annie Oakley* (1954); Elizabeth J. Leonard and J. C. Goodman, *Buffalo Bill: King of the Old West* (1955); Henry B. Sell and Victor Weybright, *Buffalo Bill and the Old West* (1955); Raymond W. Thorp, *Spirit Gun of the Old West* (1957), the Wild West show; Richard J. Walsh, *The Making of Buffalo Bill* (1928).

OTHER TOPICS. Ramon F. Adams and Homer E. Britzman, *Charles M. Russell* (1948), an excellent treatment. Robert G. Athearn, *Westward the Briton* (1953), interesting on British travelers. Western stories and songs have been collected in Levette J. Davidson and Forrester Blake (eds.), *Rocky Mountain Tales* (1947); Charles J. Finger, *Frontier Ballads* (1927); John T. Flanagan (ed.), *America Is West* (1945); John A. Lomax, *Cowboy Songs* (1922) and *Songs of the Cattle Trail and Cow Camp* (1919). Two books concerning the theater are William S. Hart, *My Life East and West* (1929), western movies; Constance Rourke, *Trouper of the Gold Coast* (1928), Lotta Crabtree. Robert Taft, *Artists and Illustrators of the Old West, 1850–1900* (1953), largely biographies and pictures. See also the works of the authors mentioned in the chapter.

CHAPTER 40

THE HISTORIAN
DISCOVERS THE WEST

H istorians are a conservative species. Not until the frontier had disappeared did they accord it recognition as an important factor in American life. Quite typically, the epochal volumes of George Bancroft were concerned with the West only in connection with such notable legislation as the Northwest Ordinance. Francis Parkman wrote of the West primarily as the scene of the struggle between rival European empires. Our first important graduate school, the Johns Hopkins University, was overwhelmingly concerned with the Germanic origins of Anglo-Saxon political institutions.

The lack of interest in the West merely illustrates the obvious fact that historians are like other men, and influenced by their environment. Early historians were usually eastern by birth and training, with more contacts east of the Atlantic than west of the Appalachians. They were more conversant with Charlemagne than with Lewis and Clark. They praised a democratic government and a free people from the viewpoint of their own sections. Since most of them were New Englanders, New England appeared as the most important part of the country, and Boston the hub of American culture. Other parts of the nation were neglected.

EARLY INTEREST IN WESTERN HISTORY

New currents appeared in American history as more historians came to be drawn from the South and the West, and as these newcomers slowly translated their sectional pride into historical interpretations. The newcomers found oceans of material in the collections of local historical societies. Every city, county, or state has taken pride in its own past, and many have translated this pride into preserving and publishing material connected with their own histories. Such local historical societies increased so rapidly from about the mid-nineteenth century that some two hundred were in existence when the American Historical Association was formed in 1884. Of these the state societies were the most important, since they collected avidly the raw material for the historian, often provided mediums for publication, and always pushed enthusiastically the interest in local history. For each state the period of its frontier origins was of first interest, and for those of the western half of the United States the frontier period was so close that original material was comparatively easy to obtain.

The new historical trend became visible during the 1880s, and especially with the work of Hubert Howe Bancroft and of Theodore Roosevelt. H. H. Bancroft was one of America's most diligent collectors, scouring the Far West to acquire thousands of letters, diaries, and other documents that probably would otherwise have disappeared; in this work he was doing privately what Lyman Draper was doing at the same time for the Wisconsin Historical Society. Between 1874 and 1890 Bancroft signed his name to some forty volumes of history of the Far West, and his documentary collections provided in time a seemingly inexhaustible source for later publications. H. H. Bancroft, primarily a regional historian, made little effort to relate the West to the remainder of the nation or to find the basic significances of the western experience.

Of greater national popularity than Bancroft's writings were the volumes that Theodore Roosevelt published between 1889 and 1896 under the title of *The Winning of the West*. Roosevelt had gone west in 1884 to escape reminders of the death of his wife and of the nomination of Blaine, and had been so fascinated by western life that in time he wrote several books about it. *The Winning of the West* was concerned with the early trans-Appalachian frontier, and was confined largely to descriptions of such dramatic incidents as Indian fights and the American Revolution. Although Roosevelt contributed largely to an interest in western history, he was little concerned with the peculiar contributions of the West, if any, to national culture, and of course he described only a single frontier, limited in both time and place.

FREDERICK JACKSON TURNER

The real beginning of the modern history of the West came with the reading of a short paper by Frederick Jackson Turner in 1893 at a small meeting of historians convening at the World's Columbian Exposition in Chicago. The very descriptive title was "The Significance of the Frontier in American History." Turner was a Wisconsin product who had received his graduate training at Johns Hopkins, where he was somewhat dissatisfied with the lack of interest in his own part of the country. Teaching history at the University of Wisconsin, he had access to the files of the Wisconsin Historical Society, which, as collected by Lyman Draper and Reuben Gold Thwaites, were the best in the West. Naturally he became interested in the westward movement of population, and as a keen young college professor he was also aware of the current speculation concerning the importance of free land and of population distribution; for example, the important books of Josiah Strong and Henry George appeared during the 1880s. When the census of 1890 showed for the first time no clear population frontier Turner was ready to indicate what he thought had been the importance of the frontier in American history.

Turner's influence grew rapidly, and within a generation his ideas had become thoroughly embedded, not only in historical writing, but in other fields of research and even in general literature. And yet this effect came as the result of comparatively little writing. It was based much more on the enthusiastic championship of the Turner concepts by hundreds of students at Wisconsin, and later at Harvard. Above all, Turner was a teacher who had the gift of inspiring his students with a deep affection for himself and an abiding interest in the subject he taught. These students in turn carried the torch to all parts of the country and transmitted the Turner theses, even though at times exaggerated and overly dogmatic, and at other times diluted and modified, to their own students.

Turner's general theories were almost all advanced in his first paper. Later publications restated but did not change significantly these ideas. In fact, when the original essay was republished in 1920, Turner saw no reason for altering as much as a footnote in what he had written twenty-seven years earlier. Presumably the generalizations he had first expressed somewhat tentatively had turned out, in his judgment, to be accurate and sufficiently complete.

For Turner "the existence of an area of free land, its continuous recession, and the advance of American settlement westward, explain American development." The influence of the frontier had been the decisive factor in welding an American nation and in making it different from other nations. The seeds of American ideals may have existed in Europe and on the Atlantice seaboard, but without the environment of the frontier they could not have developed into full-blown plants.

The frontier of which Turner spoke began with the Atlantic coast and ended with the Pacific, but he noted that only "from the time the mountains rose between the pioneer and the seaboard, a new order of Americanism arose." Then for the first time were the pioneers thrown completely on their own resources to develop distinctively American traits. Of the vast area west of the Appalachians, Turner stressed the log cabin frontier of the Old Northwest even though he was aware of other regions.

The frontier meant to Turner a region of sparse settlement, "the meeting point between savagery and civilization," although now and then he spoke of the frontier as a line or as a process of change or even as a state of mind. The important attractive force was cheap land; freedom was a secondary objective. The great conditioning factor was the richness of that land. Comparatively little emphasis was placed on minerals, climate, rainfall, and other environmental factors.

The process of settlement was described by Turner in almost exclusively economic terms. Each new region recapitulated the general growth of society as well as the experiences of former frontiers. In succession came the hunter and trapper, the trader, the rancher, the pioneer farmer, the specialized farmer, and the manufacturer. The frontier stage ended with the pioneer farmer. Little attention was paid to artistic, educational, and intellectual factors, and Turner never spoke of such a concept as a literary or an educational frontier.

The traits that Turner saw as characteristic of the frontier were democracy, individualism, freedom, coarseness, strength, acuteness, inquisitiveness, ingeniousness, materialism, exuberance, laxness of business morals. The West was a region of great individualism ("society became atomic") even though Westerners cooperated effectively for the things they wanted. Westerners were impatient of restraint, even though they developed and were willing to follow strong leadership. They were ingenious innovators in material things and radicals in social and political thought. They were optimistic and nationalistic, believers in Manifest Destiny.

As to the importance of the West—or of the frontier, since Turner never distinguished the two words clearly—in the history of the United States, the West above all created and made firm American democracy. By democracy Turner meant not only certain political forms but also a consideration for the good of the common man, which implied programs of social amelioration. Westerners were fairly even in wealth and social status, and hence believed in political equality and in programs to assist the average citizen. Democracy came not from the "Mayflower" but "from the forest."

Along with democracy went individualism and freedom of opportunity. The frontier prevented the development of class lines by providing opportunity for the ambitious who felt circumscribed by European or eastern conditions. It was "a safety valve of abundant resources open to him who would take."

Moreover, the frontier was the region that effectively took various European stocks and welded them into one nation. The wilderness stripped the European of his customary clothes and habits, and forced him to adopt the garments and the usages of the frontier if he were to survive. In time he became entirely American, which meant not only that he adopted American habits but that he became an ardent patriot.

The frontier, held Turner, produced an aggressive nationalism as the pioneers dreamed of new frontiers and sought to attain them. It favored more lenient land legislation, internal improvements at federal expense, and a protective tariff, which all meant loose construction of the Constitution and a growth in the power of the federal government. The West was but little interested in European conditions, but it indicated its expansionist nationalism by backing the purchase of Louisiana and the War of 1812.

When Turner announced in 1893 that "the frontier is gone," he spoke partly in regret, for instead of the sectional struggles of the past, in which the West in general supported true Americanism, he envisaged an increasingly bitter class struggle. And yet he was basically optimistic, for he felt that the frontier ideals as they were retained in the Middle West would be the salvation of the nation. To accomplish this end the individualistic drive must be sacrificed at least in part to uphold the democratic tradition of the rights of the common man as against the power of the large corporation. The great task of the future, according to Turner, is to adjust democracy to an industrial nation, and here the Mississippi Valley will be decisive. "The social destiny of this Valley will be the social destiny, and will mark the place in history, of the United States."

Later historians have done but little systematic checking of the Turner theories, although many have accepted them as presumptions on which to work. The one really important and specific effort at testing has been Professor Merle Curti's study of Trempealeau County, Wisconsin (Merle Curti, *The Making of an American Community*, 1959). Curti and his co-workers covered exhaustively all phases of life, but emphasized particularly the situations that could be examined quantitatively and statistically. The general conclusions were that Turner had been correct in holding that the frontier increased economic equality, which in turn led toward political democracy. Some of the other conclusions, as the slowness of the Americanization of the foreign born, did not accord so well with Turner. As Curti cautiously observed, the study of one specific area for a limited number of years (mostly 1850–1880) can produce no universal generalizations, but only a method that, if applied more widely, might lead to important results. Unfortunately, the Curti methodology has not been followed by others.

One other piece of work based on the Turner ideas is worthy of special consideration. Professor Walter P. Webb, accepting the Turner generalizations, has described the American frontier as but one part of a European frontier that expanded magnificently between 1500 and 1900 (Walter P. Webb, *The Great Frontier*, 1952). According to him, such concepts as individualism and democracy were the products of the vast increase and the turmoil of ideas that accompanied Europen expansion. The end of the "great frontier" has meant a more socialized world, with emphasis on collective action to allocate known products. Webb resembled Turner in his imaginative approach to history, but his particular point of view has been received with much more reluctance than greeted the Turner ideas.

CRITICISMS OF TURNER'S IDEAS

Within the past generation the Turner ideas have been subjected to increasing criticism that has inspired vigorous defense, and at times the discussion has become vitriolic, with Turner admirers even contending that the ideas are beyond discussion. One enthusiast has asserted in respect to the Turner thesis that "its soundness . . . must in large measure be gauged by its effect on the men of its generation." This idea of estimating truth on the basis of contemporary agreement is at least novel.

Criticism of the Turner ideas starts frequently with questions as to Turner's use of the word "frontier." At various times he talks of a frontier as a line, an area, a process, and a state of mind. Somewhat more confusing is Turner's interchangeable use of "frontier" and "the West," especially when a reference to the West concerns an area that has long ceased to be a frontier. The serious investigator pleads for a more consistent and a clearer use of words; on the other hand the point is not tremendously important, for Turner's writings make reasonably clear in most cases the way in which he is using a specific word.

Turner's concept of the frontier has been challenged as being too limited in time and place to merit generalizations of presumably universal application. Did the frontier traits Turner describes appear in Russia or Brazil or South Africa, or even when the United States itself pushed overseas to Hawaii? Increasing studies of such places as Canada and Australia indicate important differences among the effects of various frontiers. Certainly one cannot properly assume that a given frontier will inevitably produce the same characteristics that another frontier produces.

Turner was preoccupied with the frontier of the pioneer farmer, which meant that he spoke little of the land speculator, the miner, the artisan, the mill owner, and other Westerners. Similarly, he devoted almost no attention to the rise of towns and cities. Even more important, he minimized such developments as of the arts, education, amusements. His critics insist that these segments of life are as important as the growing of hogs and corn, and that no analysis of the frontier that omits them can be valid.

Several modern writers have speculated that the physical is but one type of frontier for the ambitious and adventurous. An energetic man of

1830 might have migrated to Illinois, but also he might have entered a textile mill at Lawrence, or experimented with rubber, or become involved in the temperance movement. In more recent years he might find difficulty in obtaining good free land, but he could do mountain climbing or engage in the conquest of outer space. One of these critics (James C. Malin) labels the Turner reasoning as "unsound and vicious methodology and philosophy," and holds that all sorts of nonphysical frontiers remain, and that, instead of a vanishing frontier meaning the limitation of individualism to preserve democracy, even more important frontiers remain to be conquered if only the government permits private initiative and individualism to express itself.

Turner was also criticized for his analysis of the reasons why men went West. When he described the "westward marching army of individualistic liberty-loving democratic backwoodsmen" he has been accused of misemphasis on the ground that the desire for liberty, if it existed, was infinitesimal in comparison with the desire for wealth. Except for the sparse outer fringe of settlement, most migrants were merely taking new farms in less congested areas. Essentially they were doing the same kind of work they had left in the East, but under more difficult conditions, and their expected reward was greater wealth. The freedom to work harder with the object of later prosperity and freedom from labor was not the kind of liberty Turner had in mind.

Practically no critic has had the temerity to doubt that the frontier was crude, materialistic, unlettered, exuberant, and lacking in artistic development. But some doubts have been expressed that these and other traits were distinctive of the frontier. The West tended to emulate the East. Very possibly these western characteristics were only a slightly more primitive reflection of the culture prevailing in the East at any specific period.

The proposition that the West was a great innovator in both material things and in social ideals—a "region of revolt"—has met great opposition. The western farmer, for example the farmer on the open prairies, clung tenaciously to traditional methods of farming long after they were shown to be obviously inadequate. Comparatively few inventions came from the West, even though a list can be compiled that would include most notably certain types of farm machinery as well as the typewriter and the solar compass. But there were almost no novel political, economic, or social ideas from the West. The usual Westerner was basically conservative, striving to make his fortune so that he might obtain the good things of life as defined by eastern society. He had neither time, strength, nor desire for anything strange and new. Social conformity was as great in the West as in the East, with no remarkable differences between the sections in the

styles either of politics or of women's clothes. So-called radical proposals—
cheaper money is an example—have long been traditional with agricultural
groups and represented no distinctive frontier contributions.

Turner's great thesis—that democracy was a product of the forest—
has been discarded entirely by his critics, who point out that for Turner
democracy was a vague term, including at least such diverse elements as
the beliefs of Jefferson and those of Theodore Roosevelt. They insist that
the frontier was in many respects not highly democratic; for example, until
near its end it never gave the suffrage to women, to Negroes, or to Indians.
Turner himself held that southern expansion was the influence that fixed
the slave system securely in the South; certainly slavery and democracy
are not highly compatible bedfellows. His critics are insistent that democracy is an idea of long development, with roots deep in European history,
and that even specific devices, such as the secret ballot, were not American
in origin.

Democracy in the sense of helping the common man, state the
critics, was primarily eastern. Whether it was the antislavery movement,
missionary enterprise, railroad control, or prison reform, the West copied
the East, which in most cases had taken the idea from Europe. From this
point of view the West produced no new trends in social reform, in literary
endeavor, or in religious belief. The only way in which the West might be
considered radical is that it was enamored of certain politico-economic concepts, such as the free coinage of silver, that seemed desirable to an agricultural population.

Individualism, to the man who views Turner skeptically, was no
more western than steamboats. As one writer has said, the West contained
many individuals but very little individualism. The average Westerner
conformed to the general ideas of his time, and these ideas included a
minimum of social control over private enterprise, which was a product of
the Industrial Revolution. But in contradiction to this general theory, the
West, as in fact was the East, was quite ready to encourage government
interference whenever the government could be helpful, as in the building
of canals and railroads, the establishment of banks, and the control of railroads. Westerners were close to their governments and had no objection
to using them, although their ingenuity in this respect was to increase with
the years.

Regarding the Americanization of the foreign born by the frontier,
several criticisms have been raised. Comparatively few immigrants went to
the raw frontier, which was occupied mainly by American farmers. Turner
specifically and correctly repudiates the leapfrog process of settlement by
which each frontier was settled by a new group of frontiersmen from the
East or from Europe. When the immigrant did go to the frontier, he was

not usually Americanized rapidly. German, Scandinavian, and other customs were slow in being replaced. For example, the Anglo-Saxon and German frontiers were quite different in appearance. Some question is thus raised as to whether the more eastern states did not modify European customs more rapidly than did the West.

The critics have accepted the Turner statement that the frontier produced the most vigorous of American expansionism, but have added the corollary that such sentiment was almost entirely continental, stretching no farther than the West Indies. The forces favoring overseas expansion during the 1890s and later were very little western, not to mention frontier. The Middle West actually contributed notably to isolation sentiment during the twentieth century. In addition, nationalism did not necessarily imply a loose construction of the Constitution. True, Clay wanted his American system, but Jackson, at least as good a Westerner, opposed the Bank of the United States and vetoed the Maysville bill. And on what evidence is the West depicted as giving strong support to a protective tariff?

Possibly the most debated of Turner's points has been his suggestion that the frontier has been a "safety valve of discontent." Although he made a similar statement several times, he never elaborated on it, and apparently did not consider it of first importance. His exact meaning is therefore open to some doubts. Probably he was speculating that the opportunities afforded by cheap western land averted severe class conflicts in the United States because the discontented could find outlets for their dissatisfaction and their aspirations without trying to overthrow existing institutions. Unhappy Easterners became happy Westerners rather than bitter reformers.

As expanded by other men, this safety-valve concept came to mean that the most distressed eastern classes, particularly factory workers, provided a large share of western migration, and that they came in the periods of their greatest distress, that is, in periods of depression. In this form the idea is demonstrably false. No reasonable doubt exists that western migrants were predominantly eastern farmers. Detailed studies have been made of specific areas, both urban and rural, at different times. The conclusion is always the same: farmers and not industrial laborers moved to the frontier. Only a few artisans were attracted by the higher western wages, and factory workers were almost entirely absent. An unemployed factory worker on the frontier, even if he could have reached it, was a candidate for either charity or starvation.

Even less doubt exists that the westward movement was greater in prosperous than in depression times. Census figures, including special state enumerations, bear out this statement. New states tended to be admitted after their first big booms in population, and the dates of admission concentrate in the latter parts of periods of prosperity. Land sales reached their peaks just before the various panics, and again the evidence is suggestive, even after making allowance for the gap between settlement and land sales and the excess of speculation in prosperous times. Finally, all accounts by people who witnessed the migration agree that its peaks came in periods of prosperity: just before the panics of 1819, 1837, 1857, and 1873, and during the good times of the early 1880s.

The most drastic critics of the safety-valve theory insist that there never has been such a safety-valve in either short-run or long-run terms. They argue that the westward movement could have lessened eastern discontent only if it had created a real eastern labor scarcity, with resulting higher wages, but that in fact such an event did not occur; more migration merely produced a vacuum filled by immigrants and women workers. They agree that wages were higher in America than in Europe, but explain this situation as the consequence of American ingenuity and cheap raw materials rather than a scarcity of labor. Hence the so-called safety valve was no more than a suction pump to attract new labor, and produced no relative change of eastern classes. Professor Fred A. Shannon has suggested that the real American safety valve was the city because it furnished an outlet for rural discontent.

The Turner critics have been useful in raising doubts about generalizations that many people were accepting without adequate consideration. On the other hand, some of the criticism was ill-tempered, bad-intentioned, and irresponsible, shaking the foundations of perfectly valid ideas by innuendos and suggestions that had little if any merit. In some cases the criticisms were really designed to glorify their authors' own sections of the country as against Turner's West. The extent of the criticism led in some cases to throwing out all that Turner wrote, the good with the bad, the baby with the bath. This point of view apparently denied that the West had any specific influence, which was ridiculous. No one of intelligence can really believe that the conquering of three thousand miles of wilderness did not leave some stamp on American history and on the American character.

CHARACTERISTICS OF THE WEST

The frontier clearly attracted some people but not others. The economically successful Easterner seldom moved west. The migrant was presumably unhappy economically, socially, or emotionally, but possessed of sufficient energy and initiative to break home ties and start a new life in the wilderness. In intelligence he probably represented a cross section of American life, but in aggressiveness he was above average, which implies the inclusion of holdup men and claim jumpers as well as solid, substantial, law-abiding citizens. Basically these men and women were choosing between trying their fortunes in the West or in the factories and shops of the growing eastern cities.

The characteristics of the West varied somewhat with time and place. The outer fringes of the frontier—explorers, traders, trappers, miners, and the earliest speculators and farmers—were composed almost entirely of vigorous young men. Of necessity they were hardy and brave: no others could have survived. They made an important contribution by leading the way for the permanent occupiers, but they were relatively few, and their influence on the rest of the United States was slight. In consequence, the main significance of the frontier experience depended on the great body of migrants who occupied the more sparsely settled areas to the east of the outer fringe of the frontier.

For the average migrant to the West—and by the West is meant the sections of lesser population—life was above all a continuous round of hard work, with a minimum of conveniences. The average man was a farmer fighting against a reluctant nature, and suffering from inadequate and monotonous food, flood, drought, grasshoppers, and vermin of all kinds. Lice and bedbugs were more prevalent than feats of valor. The pioneer farmer seldom saw an Indian, although now and then the frontier was ravaged by Indian raids. He seldom performed any heroic exploit, unless washing in cold water could be put in that category. His health was not good, for he was scourged by ague, malaria, typhoid, and other ills.

The West cannot be considered primarily as a region in which guns flashed, redskins bit the dust, and fair maidens were rescued from a fate worse than death. Such incidents were rare, and seldom affected the average farmer-settler. But on the other hand, the courage to meet adverse conditions and monotonous routine as part of life should not be underestimated. Starting life anew in the West was a tremendous gamble that increased as the distance from home grew. The gamble might well fail, forcing the gambler either to try again or to return ignominiously to his friends and relatives—a failure. Virtue may inhere more in the ceaseless effort to overcome large hardships than in the dramatic willingness to sell life dearly on the Little Big Horn. Forty years of drudgery to provide increased comfort for one's family may be more admirable than forty days of heroic exploration.

Western life was endurable only to people who were basically optimistic. Men moved west because they were hopeful of the future, and that hope sustained them throughout life. The men who planned a New Buffalo as the metropolis of the Midwest were typical of the hopefulness of the frontier. And for each such optimist, exaggeration was as natural as breathing. Western stories were taller than eastern, partly because the West itself was a region of exaggerations, but some people unkindly call them lies. As they appeared in literary form, humorous tales of exaggeration probably originated in frontier Maine but they reached their highest point in the work of Mark Twain. Neither optimism nor exaggeration can be labeled as exclusively western, but the West certainly gave both a favorable environment.

Optimism had its corollary in aggressive nationalism. The emphasis should be on the aggressiveness even more than on the nationalism. Westerners gave little respect to Indians, Spaniards, or Mexicans when they desired new land—and they always desired new land, even when its necessity was very remote. Generally the Westerner was a patriot and linked his expansionist sentiment with his patriotism, but there were exceptions. Separatist sentiment all the way from Vermont to California was also a well-known point of view.

Western expansion sentiment was limited to the continent of North America and its adjacent islands, for the West was concerned primarily with agriculture, mining, and stock raising. Missionary opportunity in Hawaii or textile markets in the Orient were more an eastern than a western interest. Profits for eastern businessmen was never a major ambition of Westerners.

The very motives of western migration guaranteed that the West would be highly concerned with the material aspects of life. Men moved west to make their fortunes, not to obtain themes for novels or to educate their children. Success was measured in acres, in cattle, in buildings, in cash. This materialistic attitude toward life was common throughout the United States, and the West did no more than underline a trait that every foreign visitor observed as common to Americans.

The emphasis on materialism implied less attenttion to noneconomic activities. The West had neither time nor money for such inconsequential pursuits as landscape painting. And yet this frame of mind should not be overstated. A visitor to a log cabin might find its owner immersed in George Bancroft's *History of the United States* and anxious to discuss the latest European scientific discoveries. Parents wanted their children to be educated. A primitive St. Paul could boast a theater, and a cotillion party was not unknown in the cruder sections of the West. All that can be said is that the West was somewhat behind the East in the noneconomic interests of life, but not that the two sections were utterly different. Presumably the West exercised some sort of retarding influence on the cultural advance of the United States.

As an individualist, the Westerner was not perceptibly different from his eastern contemporary. Few Daniel Boones continued to search for elbowroom. Roads, canals, banks, steamboats, and stores were possible only as group activities, as also were theaters and Paris fashions. The Westerner, a sociable creature who wanted the good things of life, was no hermit. He gave a vague support to laissez faire, as did all Americans, and objected strongly when the government balked him in his desires. Who did not? But when the government could help him he was wholeheartedly enthusiastic about the assistance.

The frontier may be considered individualistic in its willingness to use personal force, whether in a gouging match or in a vigilance committee. Yet this trait has been visible throughout American history in all parts of the country. The American Revolution is possibly the most striking example, but the long-continued practice of dueling or the use of violence in labor disputes is equally typical. The West was somewhat more vigorous than the East, possibly because of the lack of policemen, but basically the sections were not vastly different.

Socially the Westerner was a conformist. Generally he lived in a farming community or in a small town where everyone knew and was interested in his neighbors, and where standards of acceptable conduct were fairly rigid. Western communities should not be considered as lacking class distinctions: the wife of the village banker seldom exchanged calls with the wife of the livery stable handyman, but the gulf was by no means impassable. The clerk of one day might be the proprietor of the next. A common code of conduct and a common test of success produced a general feeling of equality.

Politically and economically the Westerner was not radical. His criterion of individual wealth as the measure of success agreed with the ideals of the Easterner, and hence his political and economic thinking was not original. In general the West functioned inside the traditional two-party system. As a predominantly agricultural area it had certain desires that were sometimes labeled radical by their opponents, although by the time the West supported the Populist movement in such radical innovations as the direct election of senators, some question may be raised as to whether any important frontier influence was represented. The Wisconsin of Robert La Follette had little in common with the Kansas of Wild Bill Hickok.

Much more important than any specific political, economic, or social program was the basic desire of all Westerners to attain the values that were held in esteem farther east. The Ohio farmer who moved to Iowa had no idea of creating a new and glittering utopia. Rather, he desired heartily to attain as commodious a house as his richer Ohio neighbor, as smart a horse and carriage, as good clothes for his wife and children. Western culture was basically and almost inevitably imitative.

IMPORTANCE OF THE FRONTIER

The importance of the frontier in American history has been great. Most obviously, the frontier was the first step in the occupation of the continent. Without it we presumably today would all still be living in Europe and Africa and Asia. The energy and aggressiveness that carried Americans across the continent are living parts of the American tradition. Some have felt that they have made the nation unduly egocentric and self-righteous, but certainly they have been important.

Frontier expansion meant that until late in the nineteenth century the major part of American energy and wealth was devoted to internal development. Not until toward the end of that century did the United States have important amounts of capital or manufactured goods to export. The lateness of American interest in overseas expansion and in world politics must be credited largely to the frontier, and this point is emphasized by the long-continued isolationism of the Middle West as compared with the Atlantic Coast.

Not only did the existence of the frontier lessen American interest in world affairs; it slowed the industrial developments on which such interests are based. If the United States had been confined east of the Appalachians its magnificent birth rate, without considering the effects of immigration, would soon have produced a population density sufficient to bring a mechanical development similar to that of England. With slower industrialization such attending problems as those of labor were naturally delayed.

An expanding frontier meant a deficit of workers in terms of available resources. The existence of such a situation was indicated by the high American wage scale. High pay attracted immigrants, which meant a yearly crop of new citizens to be absorbed. Consequently the frontier may be credited with having slowed the production of a uniform American culture while attracting new stocks that have been a source of strength to the United States.

In so far as the frontier slowed industrialization it delayed the development of class warfare, particularly the struggle between capital and labor. American society was slow in solidifying, its fluidity being based on great opportunities of all kinds, notably agricultural and industrial. Although there was no safety valve in the sense of an outlet for the industrial unemployed in times of depression, a real safety valve was operating indirectly over a long period of time: migration to the West reduced eastern concentration of labor, which in turn kept wages high as compared with those in Europe, and lessened industrial discontent. Wages of the nineteenth century depended heavily on labor competition and but little on other factors.

A preoccupation with material goods slowed other developments. In this respect the West merely reinforced a trend existing throughout the nation. Americans have seldom been impressed with the virtues of starving in an attic for the love of art. A man's first job has been to make a comfortable home for his family. The body must be fed before the soul is free. The West clearly emphasized, although it did not create, this point of view.

The frontier did, however, produce at least a few effects on non-economic culture. No student of American literature can fail to note the varied use of frontier themes, and in particular the development of realistic writing concerned with western material. Exaggeration as a literary device has a definite western twang. In education, the introduction and increase of coeducation had western, and even frontier, implications. Singing schools, barn dances, quilting parties, and many other old American customs retained their popularity in part because of the influence of the frontier.

Politically, the frontier influence is linked inextricably with the economic. The frontier produced a large and lasting agricultural area that has entrenched itself through the American system of representation. Farmers have at one and the same time been capitalists and hand laborers. They have favored moderate wages, and at the same time high prices for farm products. They have believed in the control of large aggregations of capital, manufacturing, distribution, and transportation, and in low and easy terms on loans. Traditionally, the satisfaction of their desires was forwarded by giving more people the vote; hence their support for an expanded suffrage, direct elections, and similar democratic measures. With the increase in recent years of an urban laboring class, the appeal of the traditional type of democracy has become somewhat less.

The political influence of the frontier has in consequence of these factors been indirect. An expanding frontier meant a predominantly agricultural nation, which gave importance to the viewpoint of the farmer. The unique desires of the frontier, such as protection against the Indians, have had relatively little long-term significance.

Any generalizations as to the importance of the frontier should be considered as largely tentative. They are based on data that have been filtered through the minds of individuals who have their own personalities and points of view, regardless of how impartial they try to be. In general, the frontier seems to have had its greatest importance not in originating new trends, but in throwing its weight in one direction or another. From this point of view, however, the frontier has been of great importance in the development of the distinctive culture of the United States, and its influence is bound to continue into the remote future.

READINGS

FREDERICK JACKSON TURNER. Turner's books are *The Frontier in American History* (1920), *The Significance of Sections in American History* (1932), and *The United States 1830–1850* (1935), of which the first contains the famous essay. Fulmer Mood, *The Early Writings of Frederick Jackson Turner* (1938) includes a biography. Very perceptive is Merle E. Curti, *Frederick Jackson Turner* (1949) and "The Section and the Frontier in American History," in Stuart A. Rice (ed.), *Method in Social Science* (1931); his book *The Making of an American Community* (1959) supports the Turner ideas. John D. Barnhart, *Valley of Democracy* (1953) uses the Ohio Valley to illustrate the Turner ideas. O. Lawrence Burnette, *Wisconsin Witness to Frederick Jackson Turner* (1961) includes eleven essays. Avery Craven, "Frederick Jackson Turner," in William T. Hutchinson (ed.), *Marcus W. Jernegan Essays* (1937) is friendly. George R. Taylor (ed.), *The Turner Thesis* (1949) has both sides of the story. Walter P. Webb, *The Great Frontier* (1952) expands the Turner ideas. Generally critical are Dixon R. Fox (ed.), *Sources of Culture in the Middle West* (1934); James C. Malin, *The Grassland of North America* (1947), *Essays on Historiography* (1946), and *On The Nature of History* (1954). See also Jeanette P. Nichols and James G. Randall (eds.), *Democracy in the Middle West* (1941).

OTHER INTERPRETATIONS. Henry N. Smith, *Virgin Land* (1950) is stimulating. Louis B. Wright, *Culture on the Moving Frontier* (1955) emphasizes western culture. Somewhat varying interpretations are Laurence M. Larson, *The Changing West* (1937); John C. Parish, *The Persistence of the Westward Movement* (1943); Frederic L. Paxson, *When the West Is Gone* (1930). John W. Caughey, *Hubert Howe Bancroft* (1946) concerns the most prolific of western historians. Discussions of frontier theories appear largely in periodical articles, and have become very numerous.

INDEX